Springer Proceedings in Business and Economics

More information about this series at http://www.springer.com/series/11960

Waldemar Tarczyński · Kesra Nermend
Editors

Effective Investments on Capital Markets

10th Capital Market Effective Investments Conference (CMEI 2018)

Springer

Editors
Waldemar Tarczyński
Department of Insurance
and Capital Markets
University of Szczecin
Szczecin, Poland

Kesra Nermend
Institute of IT in Management
University of Szczecin
Szczecin, Poland

ISSN 2198-7246 ISSN 2198-7254 (electronic)
Springer Proceedings in Business and Economics
ISBN 978-3-030-21273-5 ISBN 978-3-030-21274-2 (eBook)
https://doi.org/10.1007/978-3-030-21274-2

This Springer imprint is published by the registered company Springer Nature Switzerland AG
The registered company address is: Gewerbestrasse 11, 6330 Cham, Switzerland

Preface

The capital market has become one of the most important components of the Polish economy, but unfortunately, little is known about this important sector and that needs to change. The duty of education and science development in this direction rests to a large extent on the scientific community and capital market institutions. It should be noted that research conducted about capital markets has a theoretical and practical dimension. Both of these areas are equally important in order to understand the market and the methods or processes, which are taking place on the market. It is also important to apply unpredictable methods in the investment process in order to minimize the risk of investing.

Research on the Polish capital market and its most important element—the Warsaw Stock Exchange—is advancing very fast. Following the publications in the recent years in this area, it is clear that apart from the popularity of known methods from developed markets, the Polish scientific knowledge starts to emerge. Scientists are still introducing new or modified classical approaches to the investment process. They also focus on researching the processes, which already exist on the capital market. It should be said that recently there is an increase of the importance of behavioral finance and experimental economics in these fields.

The book offers an opportunity to present experiences and innovative solutions and share a vision on the state of the capital market in Poland and where it is heading to, this all in comparison with countries where capital markets are more mature.

The book is divided into four parts

I. Theoretical aspects of investments on capital market
II. Quantitative methods on financial markets
III. Experimental economics and behavioral finance on capital markets
IV. Practical issues—case studies

Each of these parts begins with an introduction outlining its subject and summarizing each of its chapters. The purpose of the introduction is to help the reader navigate through the chapters contained in the given part. The authors of the introductions are their thematic editors.

According to the title, Part I of the book presents theoretical aspects of investments on capital market. It outlines some theoretical aspects of the capital market in Poland and selected countries in the world. Additionally, it provides a study on the interaction among various elements of stock as well as several other issues related to investments process. It also sheds the light on the financial integration between the markets and their hierarchical structure. From a theoretical point of view, there is an increasing significance of issues such as capital market models, market efficiency, and share liquidity. In addition, the chapter includes issues important for selected problems within finance. This applies, among others, to aspects of law and digital competence.

Part II of the book includes an application of quantitative methods on the capital market. It includes the usefulness of the quantitative methods in the investment process over the short-; medium- and long-term This part focuses on the incorporation of different approaches (usually classical and no classical) on making investment decisions or assessing investment efficiency on the capital market. Another important issue is defining factors (qualitative and/or quantitative) and their influence on rates of return, risk, or both on the capital market. Quantitative methods do not only help us measure phenomena occurring on the capital market, but also help us to understand the relationships between the financial instruments.

Part III of the book begins with an overview of the theoretical development of the first and the second generations of behavioral finance. Next we present the possibility of using quantitative methods to study various investors' behavior on the financial markets, such as uses the VEC DCC, M-GARCH models to estimate Sovereign Credit Default (CDS) for credit risk securities in selected EU countries. Furthermore, simulation experiments in the field of characteristics of dichotomous variable estimators were taken into account, beside the concentration of investor wealth as one of the most important factors shaping investment strategies. In this part, it shows how to use the methods for measuring psychophysiological data (in particular EEG) and microexpression in the context of the emotional states of financial market participants. The basic behavioral indicators (emotions, involvement, interests, and memory) are discussed based on the possibility of what determines the reactions of investors to various external stimuli.

Part IV the book includes selected issues of research conducted on capital market or financial market with the use of selected and various methods. Important are also different approaches introduced by researchers in relation to existing issues on the capital market. It also explains stock liquidity, abnormal rates of return, dividends of listed companies, and risks of shares or investment risk on the capital market. Case studies are very useful in this context. Case studies help us to show how to use many tools from different disciplines to investigate processes that take place on the financial or capital market. In this context, we shed the light on VAR models, econometric models, analysis of Granger causality, and analysis of HFT systems. The case studies underline particular problems that appear in the financial and capital markets.

Szczecin, Poland

Waldemar Tarczyński
Kesra Nermend

Contents

Contributors

Paweł Antonowicz Department of Business Economics, Faculty of Management, University of Gdansk, Sopot, Gdansk, Poland

Roman Asyngier Maria Curie-Sklodowska University, Lublin, Poland

Barbara Batóg University of Szczecin, Szczecin, Poland

Barbara Będowska-Sójka Poznań University of Economics and Business, Poznań, Poland

Konrad Biercewicz Department of Multimedia Systems, Faculty of Computer Science and Information Technology, West Pomeranian University of Technology Szczecin, Szczecin, Poland

Beata Bieszk-Stolorz University of Szczecin, Szczecin, Poland

Mariusz Borawski Department of Multimedia Systems, Faculty of Computer Science and Information Technology, West Pomeranian University of Technology Szczecin, Szczecin, Poland

Taylan Budur Department of Business and Management, Faculty of Economics and Administrative Sciences, Ishik University, Qirga, Sulaimani, Iraq

Manipadma Datta Department of Business and Sustainability, TERI School of Advanced Studies, New Delhi, India

Ahmet Demir Department of Business and Management, Faculty of Economics and Administrative Sciences, Ishik University, Qirga, Sulaimani, Iraq

Jarosław Duda Dean of Marine Engineering Faculty, Institute of Marine Electrical Engineering and Vessel Automation, Department of Automation and Robotics, Maritime University of Szczecin, Szczecin, Poland

Renata Dudzińska-Baryła University of Economics in Katowice, Katowice, Poland

Sokołowska Ewelina Faculty of Management, Department of Corporate Finance, University of Gdansk, Sopot, Poland

Kinga Flaga-Gieruszyńska Faculty of Law and Administration, University of Szczecin, Szczecin, Poland

Przemysław Garsztka Poznań University of Economics and Business, Poznań, Poland

Urszula Gierałtowska University of Szczecin, Szczecin, Poland

Wu Jinghua Sichuan Agricultural University, Sichuan Chengdu, China

Andrzej Karpio Warsaw University of Life Sciences—SGGW, Bialystok, Poland

Bogna Kaźmierska-Jóźwiak Department of Finance and Corporate Strategy, Faculty of Management, University of Lodz, Łódź, Poland

Donata Kopańska-Bródka University of Economics in Katowice, Katowice, Poland

Grażyna Krzyminiewska Department of Sociology and Business Ethics, Faculty of Economics, Poznań University of Economics and Business, Poznań, Poland

Bzhar Nasradeen Majeed Faculty of Economics and Administrative Sciences, Charmo University, Chamchamal, Sulaimani, Iraq

Agnieszka Majewska University of Szczecin, Szczecin, Poland

Elżbieta Majewska University of Bialystok, Białystok, Poland

Katarzyna Mamcarz Maria Curie-Sklodowska University, Lublin, Poland

Jerzy Marcinkowski Department of Operations Research, Faculty of Informatics and Electronic Economy, Poznan University of Economics and Business, Poznań, Poland

Iwona Markowicz University of Szczecin, Szczecin, Poland

Ewa Michalska University of Economics in Katowice, Katowice, Poland

Kamila Migdał-Najman Department of Statistics, Faculty of Management, University of Gdansk, Sopot, Gdansk, Poland

Danuta Miłaszewicz Department of Economics, Faculty of Economics and Management, Institute of Economy, University of Szczecin, Szczecin, Poland

Paweł Miłobędzki Department of Econometrics, Faculty of Management, University of Gdańsk, Sopot, Poland

Michał Mursztyn Bialystok University of Technology, Bialystok, Poland

Krzysztof Najman Department of Statistics, Faculty of Management, University of Gdansk, Sopot, Gdansk, Poland

Sabina Nowak Department of Econometrics, Faculty of Management, University of Gdańsk, Sopot, Poland

Joanna Olbryś Bialystok University of Technology, Bialystok, Poland

Krzysztof Piasecki Department of Investment and Real Estate, Poznan University of Economics, Poznań, Poland;
Poznan University of Economics, Poznań, Poland

Mateusz Piwowarski Department of Computational Methods in Experimental Economics, Faculty of Economics and Management, Institute of IT in Management, University of Szczecin, Szczecin, Poland

Jan Purczyński Faculty of Electrical Engineering, West Pomeranian University of Technology, Szczecin, Poland

Dominik Rozkrut University of Szczecin, Szczecin, Poland

Monika Rozkrut University of Szczecin, Szczecin, Poland

Sarkhel Shawkat Faculty of Economics and Administrative Sciences, Charmo University, Chamchamal, Sulaimani, Iraq

Ria Sinha Department of Business and Sustainability, TERI School of Advanced Studies, New Delhi, India

Joanna Siwek Department of Imprecise Information Processing Methods, Faculty of Mathematics and Computer Science, Adam Mickiewicz University, Poznań, Poland

Michał Dominik Stasiak Poznan University of Economics, Poznań, Poland

Żaneta Staszak Poznan University of Technology, Poznań, Poland

Szymon Stereńczak Poznań University of Economics and Business, Poznań, Poland

Adam Szyszka SGH Warsaw School of Economics, Warsaw, Poland

Małgorzata Tarczyńska-Łuniewska Faculty of Economics and Management, Institute of Econometrics and Statistics, University of Szczecin, Szczecin, Poland

Waldemar Tarczyński Faculty of Economics and Management, Institute of Finance, University of Szczecin, Szczecin, Poland

Grażyna Trzpiot University of Economics in Katowice, Katowice, Poland

Katarzyna Twarowska Maria Curie-Skłodowska University, Lublin, Poland

Małgorzata Twarowska-Ratajczak Maria Curie-Skłodowska University, Lublin, Poland

Katarzyna Wawrzyniak West Pomeranian University of Technology Szczecin, Szczecin, Poland

Dorota Witkowska University of Lodz, Łódź, Poland

Wiśniewski Jerzy Witold Faculty of Economic Sciences and Management, Department of Econometrics & Statistics, Nicholas Copernicus University, Toruń, Poland

Dorota Żebrowska-Suchodolska Warsaw University of Life Sciences—SGGW, Bialystok, Poland

Magdalena Ziolo Faculty of Economics and Management, University of Szczecin, Szczecin, Poland

Part I
Theoretical Aspects of Investment on Capital Market

Chapter 1
Analysis of Performance of the Warsaw Stock Exchange Companies from Finance Macrosector in Periods of Crisis

Beata Bieszk-Stolorz and Iwona Markowicz

Abstract The aim of the article is the assessment of response to a crisis situation for companies belonging to the macrosector of finance in comparison with other sectors on the Warsaw Stock Exchange. The survival analysis methods were applied. The authors analysed the periods of decrease and of the subsequent increase in share prices during the crisis of 2008–2009 and the bear market of 2011. The Kaplan–Meier estimator of the survival function made possible to assess the probability of decrease and of subsequent increase in the share prices. The similarity of the survival curves was investigated using the log-rank test. The Cox regression model was used to determine the intensity of the decrease and increase in share prices. The analysis made possible to assess and compare the performance of the financial sectors against the background of other sectors in both periods.

Keywords Warsaw stock exchange · Crisis · Survival analysis · Kaplan–meier estimator · Cox regression model

1.1 Introduction

The cyclical nature of the economy encompasses regular periods of recession. Nowadays, in the age of globalisation, the occurrence of crises and their international distribution are common and rather obvious. Discussions take place on how governments should react to minimise their impacts.

The years of 2008 and 2009 are recognised as a period of global financial crisis which affected the economies of many countries, including Poland. The effects of the crisis were also seen on the Warsaw Stock Exchange (WSE) [8]. Table 1.1 presents the Warsaw Stock Exchange Index (WIG) rates of return in the years 2005–2017.

B. Bieszk-Stolorz (✉) · I. Markowicz
University of Szczecin, ul. Mickiewicza 64, 71-101 Szczecin, Poland
e-mail: beata.bieszk-stolorz@usz.edu.pl

I. Markowicz
e-mail: iwona.markowicz@usz.edu.pl

W. Tarczyński and K. Nermend (eds.), *Effective Investments on Capital Markets*,
Springer Proceedings in Business and Economics,
https://doi.org/10.1007/978-3-030-21274-2_1

Table 1.1 WIG rates of return in the years 2005–2017 (%) [14]

Year	WIG rates of return
2005	33.66
2006	41.60
2007	10.39
2008	−51.07
2009	46.85
2010	18.77
2011	−20.83
2012	26.24
2013	8.06
2014	0.26
2015	−9.62
2016	11.38
2017	23.17

WIG, listing companies from the Warsaw Stock Exchange Main Market, hit a low in 2008. The next year, with a negative WIG rate of return, saw a record turnover in shares and derivatives, which reflected the increased activity of stock exchange investors. However, drops in the value of companies in the second half of the year consequently led to a decrease in the WIG index by 20.8% [7]. The 2011 decrease was not as spectacular as in the crisis of 2008–2009, but the WIG index plunged by at least 20%. According to Olbryś and Majewska [28], the increase or decrease by at least 20% in quotations is indicative of bull or bear market periods. In the paper, the Pagan–Sossounov procedure of determining the market phases was applied to identify the periods of crisis.

The aim of the article is to assess the reaction to crisis situations of companies in the following sectors: banks, developers and other financials in relation to other sectors listed on the Warsaw Stock Exchange. The study comprises four stages. The first one assesses the probability, intensity and duration of a decrease in share prices that occurred in the period from 1 January 2008 to 31 December 2009 (the crisis). The second step is to estimate the likelihood and intensity of recovery, i.e. the chance of share prices to increase within six months, as well as the time taken to catalyse losses. In the third stage, an assessment was made of the probability, intensity and duration of a decrease in the companies' share prices in 2011 (the decrease). The last stage of the study is focused on possible price increases by the end of 2013.

In the analysis, the multi-category explanatory variable (sector of companies' operation) was replaced with dichotomous explanatory variables and 0–1 coding was applied, which allowed to compare the intensity of events in the examined sectors with that in the other sectors [15, 23].

1.2 Financial Crisis

Financial crises disturb economies around the world from time to time. This is related to the economic cycles, i.e. the periods of economic expansion and economic slowdown. The increase in the incidence of crises was particularly evident in the twentieth century. During that time, the world economy experienced such phenomena as the liberalisation of trade flows and financial flows, the development of financial markets, deregulation of many areas of the economy and increasing globalisation. Each subsequent crisis had similar causes, and it occurred suddenly following a certain sequence of events and spread with increasing speed to other countries. The recent global economic crisis was triggered by the bursting of the property bubble in the USA in 2007. The mechanism of transformation of local disturbances in the financial system into a serious economic crisis of global scope was described, among others, by [20].

One of the sources of the global crisis indicated by European Commission [11] is the sharp growth of the financial sector's importance in the world's largest economies and the formation of bubbles on the assets market due to, among others, low inflation in developed countries as well as massive capital flows thanks to globalisation and integration of financial markets.

As highlighted in the NBP Report [27], the boom in the real estate and credit markets, the rapid growth in household consumption and a quest for high rates of return have led to serious imbalances and, consequently, macroeconomic and structural turbulences in many countries. One of the effects of the collapse in the real estate market in the USA and some European countries was a reduction in demand, further reinforced by restrictions on access to credit.

The five-stage Minsky model is increasingly being used to explain the crisis in today's global economy [22]. The first stage—displacement—is associated with high interest in a specific financial product (e.g. mortgage loans). The second stage, the boom, is related to the activity of speculators who are starting to collect income from investments while, at the same time, the prospect of further profits appears. The next, third stage is euphoria, which manifests itself in the appearance of more and more investors on the market (herd instinct). More and more people are eager to take out loans, and banks are expanding their lending activity by lowering their requirements. In the fourth stage (profit taking)—the bubble reaches its peak, prices are maximally exorbitant, small investors make large profits and they draw them out of the market. This triggers the final stage which is the panic in the market. Previous enthusiasm is being replaced by extreme pessimism. Investors are starting to dispose of their assets as soon as possible. Borrowers are stopping repaying their loans, and banks' assets are melting rapidly as prices fall. Minsky's hypothesis of the instability of the financial system states that the longer it has been since the recent crisis, the more risk-seeking the banks will be [26].

Economic and sentiment indicators are an important source of information on the economic situation of enterprises and, consequently, of the economy. They are among the first to provide information on the state of the economies. They are used

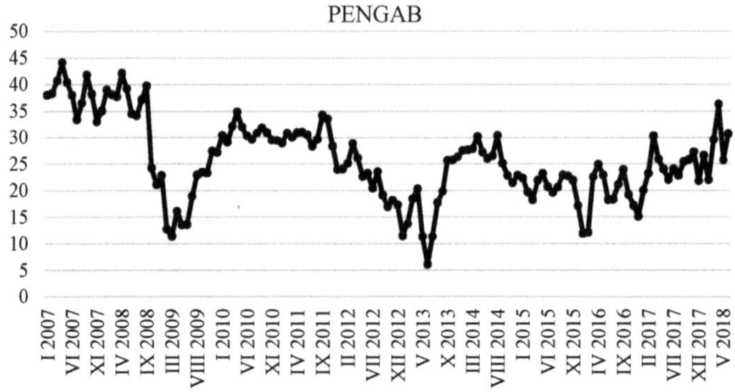

Fig. 1.1 PENGAB index, monthly data in the years 2007–2018 (points). *Source* Own calculation on the basis: [16]

by managers, economists, analysts, scientists, investors and governments. The leading economic and mood indicator is the Purchasing Managers' Index, published for several dozen countries, including Poland (it applies to the industrial, service, construction and retail sectors).

Every month in Poland, the Central Statistical Office examines the economic situation in industry, construction, trade and services, as well as consumer moods. The situation in the banking sector is reflected in the PENGAB index (the index measuring sentiment in the bank sector in Poland), published by the Association of Polish Banks. Practice has shown that economic and sentiment indicators are reliable barometers of the economic situation in the economy and have a forecast value, thus providing support in the analysis of the economic situation in individual countries and in the world. PENGAB index is a synthetic indicator of the economic situation in the banking sector, commissioned by the Polish Bank Association. Its values (in points) in the period from January 2007 to June 2018 are presented in Fig. 1.1, which shows two breakdowns in the trends at the turn of 2008/2009 and 2012/2013, clearly showing that a marked decrease in moods took place during the crisis periods covered by the study presented in this article.

1.3 Data Used in the Study

Four steps were considered in the study. They result from the situation on the Warsaw Stock Exchange and the share price movement. The first stage concerns the decrease in prices during the crisis, i.e. at the turn of 2008–2009. On 17 February 2009, the WIG index reached its minimum, and then, from January 2008 it decreased by ca. 60% to go up by about 80% in the following six months (24 August 2009). Therefore, the first two stages of the study included the observation of share prices fluctuations between 01 January 2008 and 31 December 2009 and the assessment

Table 1.2 Number of surveyed companies in 2008–2009 (stage I and II) by sectors

Sectors	Stage I—decrease in prices			Stage II—share prices		
	Complete	Censored	Total	Complete	Censored	Total
Banks	12	2	14	13	1	14
Developers	17	0	17	17	0	17
Other financials	18	3	21	11	10	21
Other	216	60	276	204	72	276
Total	263	65	328	245	83	328

Table 1.3 Number of surveyed companies in 2008–2009 (stage III and IV) by sectors

Sectors	Stage III—decrease of prices			Stage IV—share prices		
	Complete	Censored	Total	Censored	Complete	Total
Banks	10	2	12	10	2	12
Developers	26	1	27	24	3	27
Other financials	35	4	39	35	4	39
Other	257	42	299	249	50	299
Total	328	49	377	318	59	377

of the probability of achieving the specified 60% price decrease (stage I), followed by the examination of the possibility of making up for losses, i.e. the probability of share prices to rise by 80% from the lowest price (stage II). The next stages of the study concern the period of decrease, i.e. 2011 and two subsequent years. On the basis of the WIG observation, the threshold values were established again, that time at the level of 30% for the decrease in prices in 2011 (stage III) and 40% for the increase in prices in 2012–2013 (stage IV). The study was to result in an assessment of the situation of three sectors involved the financial market (banks, developers, other financials) as compared to other sectors.[1] Data used in the research come from [17].

In the first and second stages, 328 companies were investigated (Table 1.2), of which 263 achieved the above described 60% price decrease and 245 companies later saw an 80% price increase (complete observations).

In the third and fourth stages, 377 companies were surveyed (Table 1.3), of which 328 achieved the described 30% price decrease and the prices of 318 companies saw a 40% price increase in the months to follow (complete observations).

[1]A new classification of WSE sectors was introduced in 2017. However, due to the research period prior to that date, this article uses the earlier classification of listed companies.

1.4 Methodology

The study used models applied in the analysis of the history of events that took into account censored data [34]. This is a set of methods for studying the duration of phenomena occurring in various areas of human activity: in social, economic and political life. Methods of survival analysis have been increasingly popular in socio-economic research. The examples of their application are company survival analysis [13, 22, 29], credit risk analysis [25, 33], unemployment analysis [5], economic activity of the population [21] and poverty of households [31]. The methods of analysing the survival probability are also used in the analysis of financial phenomena [10, 24]. The subjects of such studies are often companies listed on the stock exchange. What is examined is the likelihood of companies form specific sectors to survive the crisis [2–4, 12]. The said methods can also be used to assess the impact of the crisis on national economies [30].

In this study, the following survival analysis methods were used: Kaplan–Meier estimator, log-rank test and Cox regression model.

The probability that a specific event would not occur (a trigger fall or increase in share prices) was estimated using a Kaplan–Meier estimator for the survival function [18]:

$$\hat{S}(t_i) = \prod_{j=1}^{i} \left(1 - \frac{d_j}{n_j}\right) \quad \text{for } i = 1, \ldots, k, \tag{1.1}$$

where t_i—a point in time when at least one event occurred, d_i—number of events in the time t_i and n_i—number of units under observation in the time t_i.

Basing on the survival function, the survival time quartiles can be determined. They will be determined at the points where the survival function is 0.25, 0.5 and 0.75, respectively [1].

The analysed populations may be divided into groups according to the characteristics under examination, the survival function may be estimated for each of them and the significance of differences between them may be investigated. Since the distribution of the survival time is not known, nonparametric tests based on the ranking of the survival times are used. Unfortunately, there are no commonly accepted methods of selecting a test in a given situation. Most of them give reliable results only with large samples, while the effectiveness of tests run on small samples is less known. A log-rank test is often used to compare the two survival curves [19]. It is used to verify the hypothesis H_0: $S_1(t) = S_2(t)$ of equal survival curves determined for both groups. At a given significance level, the test statistic is compared with the chi-distribution of a square with one degree of freedom. This test is most powerful when the difference between the hazard functions of individual subgroups is constant over time [21]. Preliminary analysis using the ln(–lnS(t)) function and some limitations resulting from assumptions for other tests have confirmed the validity of the use of the log-rank test in the study.

The relative intensity of the event was assessed by means of a Cox regression model [9], also known as the proportional hazards model [6, 18]:

$$h(t : x_1, x_2, \ldots, x_n) = h_o(t)\exp(a_1 x_1 + a_2 x_2 + \cdots + a_n x_n) \tag{1.2}$$

where $h_0(t)$—the reference hazard, $a_1, a_2, \ldots, a_n$—model coefficients and t—duration of observation.

1.5 Results

The study assessed the situation of three sectors related to the financial market (banks, developers and other financials) in comparison with other sectors during two periods of falling prices and during the following periods of making up for losses. As the study deals with the events that had occurred before 2017, this article uses the previous classification of listed companies. Due to the previous sector classification and because of small size of some sectors in the period under study (e.g. insurance), the authors decided to include a part of the WSE companies in the group of other financials.

In the first downward period (referred to as the 2008–2009 crisis) and the subsequent upward period until the end of 2009, the probability was assessed of achieving both a 60% price decrease (stage I) and the possibility of making up for losses, i.e. the probability of share prices rising by 80% from the lowest price (stage II). The Kaplan–Meier estimator was calculated for the three analysed sectors and for the companies from the other sectors (Fig. 1.2).

The first to reach the threshold price drop were developers. The log-rank test proved that the survival curve for this sector differed statistically significantly from

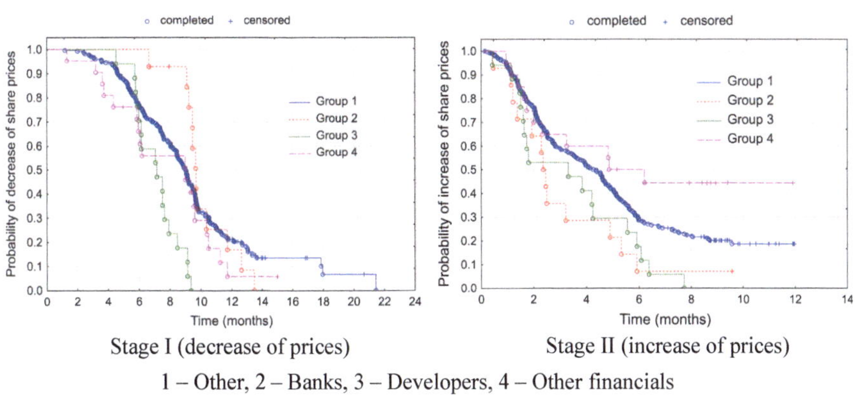

Fig. 1.2 Kaplan–Meier estimator for decrease in share prices (crisis 2008–2009) and increase in share prices. *Sources* Own calculation

Table 1.4 Results of log-rank tests for companies from examined sectors and for remaining WSE companies—the crisis of 2008–2009

Sectors	Developers	Other financials	Other
Decrease			
Banks	−3.8443 ($p = 0.0001$*)	−1.2545 ($p = 0.2097$)	−0.4701 ($p = 0.6383$)
Developers		1.9083 ($p = 0.0564$*)	2.7088 ($p = 0.0068$*)
Other financials			1.1084 ($p = 0.2677$)
Increase			
Banks	0.2694 ($p = 0.7876$)	2.1381 ($p = 0.0325$*)	1.6985 ($p = 0.0894$*)
Developers		2.5335 ($p = 0.0113$*)	1.8992 ($p = 0.0575$*)
Other financials			−1.7290 ($p = 0.0838$*)

*Significance of differences at the level of 0.1

Table 1.5 Survival quartiles for companies from examined sectors and for remaining WSE companies—crisis of 2008–2009

Sectors	First quartile	Median	Third quartile
Decrease			
Banks	9.26	9.67	10.41
Developers	5.91	7.12	7.86
Other financials	4.69	9.01	10.15
Other	6.21	9.02	11.10
Increase			
Banks	1.30	2.37	4.06
Developers	1.54	2.56	5.23
Other financials	1.74	4.87	–
Other	2.04	4.30	7.25

the other curves (at the level of 0.1). Other test results indicated that there were no significant differences between pairs of groups of companies in which there was no developer sector (Table 1.4). 75% of developers saw their prices fall by 60% in just eight months, while banks and other financials had not seen such a drop until over 10 months later (Table 1.5). The research conducted by [32] revealed that in the years 2006–2010, the other financials were the weakest sector in terms of their fundamental strength.

Banks and developers made up for their losses the fastest. Their survival curves are similar (Fig. 1.2, stage II). The log-rank test run only for banks and developers shows that their price growth curves did not differ significantly (Table 1.4). Three-quarters of banks reached a threshold 80% rise in share prices after just four months, while developers—after more than five months (Table 1.5). Out of 21 companies in the financial sector, only 11 managed to make up for previous losses, so that no third quartile could be determined for their survival.

Table 1.6 Results of Cox regression model estimation (stage I and II of the study)—crisis of 2008–2009

Variable—sector	Parameter	Standard error	Wald test	p	Relative hazard
Stage I (decrease in prices)					
Banks	−0.1290	0.2970	0.1886	0.6641	0.8790
Developers	0.9395	0.2580	13.2581	0.0003	2.5587
Other financials	0.2983	0.2458	1.4732	0.2249	1.3476
Stage II (increase in prices)					
Banks	0.5551	0.2869	3.7449	0.0530	1.7422
Developers	0.5138	0.2532	4.1188	0.0424	1.6716
Other financials	−0.4991	0.3097	2.5965	0.1071	0.6071

The Cox regression model was used to evaluate the relative intensity (relative hazard) of both the decrease and the subsequent increase in share prices (Table 1.6). The reference group in this case consists of companies from the other sectors. Among the sectors analysed, developers were characterised by a clearly greater relative hazard of a drop in prices (the intensity of the price drop was more than twice as high as in the other sectors). As regards making up for losses, companies from the banking and real estate development sectors had a similar high intensity. It should be noted that during the crisis period, banks saw the lowest relative intensity of price falls (0.8790) and the highest relative intensity of recovery (1.7422). These companies survived the crisis of 2008–2009 in the best condition.

In the second downward period (defined as a 2011 recession) and upward period until the end of 2013, the probability of experiencing a 30% price decrease (stage III) and the possibility of making up for losses (increase in share prices by 40%—stage IV) were examined. The curves of survival determined by the Kaplan–Meier estimator are shown in Fig. 1.3.

Similarly, developers and other financials were the fastest to see the threshold price drop. The course of survival functions for these sectors differs statistically significantly from those calculated for other companies (log-rank test, Table 1.7). 75% of developers and banks experienced price reductions by 30% in less than five months, while the remaining companies saw such a drop after more than six months. Developers and other financials responded to the crisis most quickly through share price reductions. But they also made up for their losses the fastest. They reached the third quartile of price rises after four and more than five months, respectively, while banks needed as much as 24 months to make up for losses (Table 1.8).

The results of the Cox regression model estimation are presented in Table 1.9. Once again, developers faced the highest relative hazard of a price drop (the intensity of the price reduction was higher by 75% than in other sectors). Also, when making up for losses, companies from this sector saw the highest intensity (by 57%).

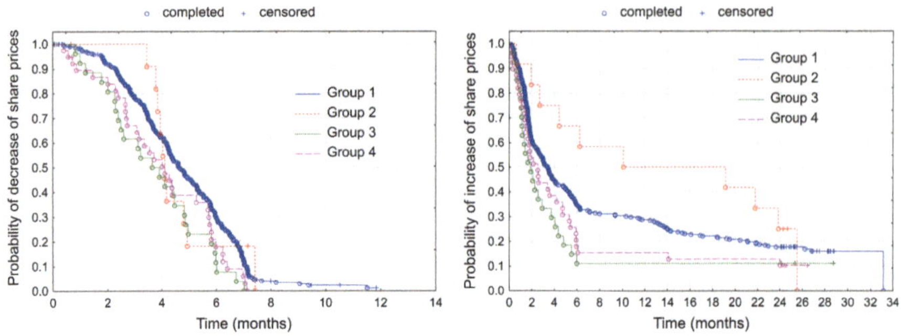

Stage III (decrease of prices) Stage IV (increase of prices)

1 – Other, 2 – Banks, 3 – Developers, 4 – Other financials

Fig. 1.3 Kaplan–Meier estimator for decrease in share prices (2011 recession) and increase in share prices. *Sources* Own calculation

Table 1.7 Results of log-rank tests for companies from examined sectors and for remaining WSE companies—2011 recession

Sectors	Developers	Other financials	Other
Decrease			
Banks	−1.2861 ($p = 0.1984$)	−1.1057 ($p = 0.2689$)	−0.0806 ($p = 0.9358$)
Developers		0.8614 ($p = 0.3890$)	2.28759 ($p = 0.0222$*)
Other financials			1.8114 ($p = 0.0701$*)
Increase			
Banks	−2.2649 ($p = 0.0235$*)	−2.2126 ($p = 0.0269$*)	−1.3330 ($p = 0.1825$)
Developers		0.5773 ($p = 0.5637$)	1.8074 ($p = 0.0707$*)
Other financials			1.5689 ($p = 0.1167$)

*Significance of differences at the level of 0.1

Table 1.8 Survival quartiles for companies from examined sectors and for remaining WSE companies—2011 recession

Sectors	First quartile	Median	Third quartile
Decrease			
Banks	3.83	4.08	4.83
Developers	2.28	3.65	4.92
Other financials	2.66	4.02	5.79
Other	3.35	4.63	6.31
Increase			
Banks	2.70	10.09	23.84
Developers	1.04	1.78	4.15
Other financials	1.09	2.33	5.55
Other	1.51	3.40	14.01

Table 1.9 Results of Cox regression model estimation (stages III and IV of the study)—2011 recession

Variable—sector	Parameter	Standard error	Wald test	*p*	Relative hazard
Stage III (decrease in prices)					
Banks	−0.0309	0.3233	0.0091	0.9240	0.9696
Developers	0.5573	0.2072	7.2324	0.0072	1.7460
Other financials	0.3665	0.1812	4.0936	0.0431	1.4427
Stage IV (increase in prices)					
Banks	−0.3570	0.3228	1.2228	0.2688	0.6998
Developers	0.4534	0.2144	4.4732	0.0344	1.5737
Other financials	0.3099	0.1809	2.9338	0.0868	1.3632

1.6 Conclusions

In order to summarise the results of the conducted research, the situation in three analysed sectors of listed companies in four periods was presented (two periods of decrease: the 2008–2009 crisis and the 2011 recession, as well as two subsequent periods of growth), as shown in Fig. 1.4. The relative intensities of decrease and rise of company prices in the analysed sectors are shown in axes which intersect in point 1, being the reference point (the intensity of decrease and increase in prices of companies from other sectors).

Figure 1.4 consists of four squares:

1. "low-low"—including banks (recession); in the time of recession companies in this sector experienced the low intensity of both the decrease and of the subsequent rise in the share prices (they were companies that had been least affected by the 2011 recession),
2. "high-high"—including developers (crisis), developers (recession) and other financials (recession) with highly intense price drops and rises (companies that strongly responded to crisis situations, but whose odds for subsequent price rebound were high),
3. "low-high"—including banks (crisis); in this sector companies saw low intensity of price drops followed by the high intensity of recovery (companies that barely responded to the crisis, but their subsequent odds for recovery were higher than in the remaining sectors),
4. "high-low"—including banks (crisis); this square indicates the worst position—intense price drop and difficulty in recovering.

All in all, it seems that the other listed financials were more affected by the 2008–2009 sector as the relatively high intensity of their price decrease was not accompanied by a similar intensity of subsequent price increases. Developer companies during the crisis and the recession, as well as other financials during the downturn, were strongly affected by the crisis periods in question, but only tem-

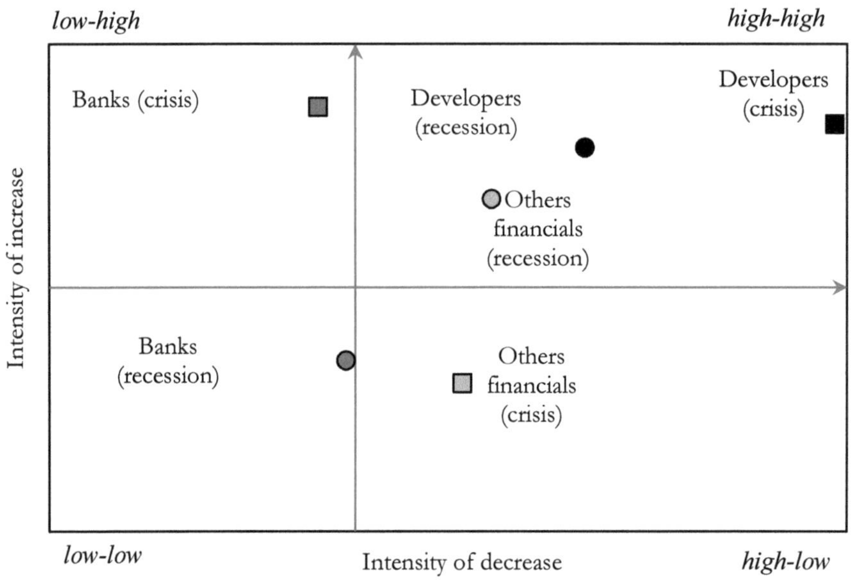

Fig. 1.4 Relative intensity of price decrease and increase by sectors during crisis (2008–2009) and recession (2011). *Sources* Own calculation

porarily and intensively making up for the losses. Therefore, in general, companies related to the financial market (except for other financial sectors) did not suffer the long-term effects of both the 2008–2009 crisis and the 2011 recession.

References

1. Aalen, O., Borgan, O., Gjessing, H.: Survival and Event History Analysis: A Process Point of View. Springer-Verlag, New York (2008)
2. Abbasian, E., Nemer, A.Y.: Investigating the recession sustainability of main industries in Tehran stock exchange: using Cox regression. Iran. J. Econ. Stud. **5**(1), 101–116 (2016). https://doi.org/10.22099/ijes.2017.26659.1354
3. Andersson, N.: Estimating companies' survival in financial crisis: using the Cox proportional hazards model. Dissertation. Retrieved from http://uu.diva-portal.org/smash/get/diva2:723216/FULLTEXT01.pdf (2014)
4. Balan, ChB, Robu, I.-B., Jaba, E.: The statistical assessment of financial distress risk in the case of metallurgical companies. Metalurgija **54**(3), 575–578 (2015)
5. Bieszk-Stolorz, B.: Analiza historii zdarzeń w badaniu bezrobocia. volumina.pl Daniel Krzanowski, Szczecin (2013)
6. Bieszk-Stolorz, B., Markowicz, I.: Modele regresji Coxa w analizie bezrobocia. CeDeWu, Warszawa (2012)
7. Bieszk-Stolorz B, Markowicz, I.: Analiza tendencji zmian cen akcji spółek na Giełdzie Papierów Wartościowych w Warszawie po bessie w 2011 roku. Finanse, rynki finansowe, ubezpieczenia 2(86):375–388. https://doi.org/10.18276/frfu.2017.86-31 (2017)

8. Bieszk-Stolorz B, Markowicz I.: The assessment of the situation of listed companies in macrosectors in a bear market—duration analysis models. In: Conference proceedings full text papers. Applications of Mathematics and Statistics in Economics, pp. 17–25 (2017). http://amse.ue.wroc.pl/proceedings2017.html. https://doi.org/10.15611/amse.2017.20.02
9. Cox, D.R., Oakes, D.: Analysis of Survival Data. Chapman and Hall, London (1984)
10. Deville, L., Riva, F.: Liquidity and arbitrage in options markets: a survival analysis approach. Rev. Finan. **11**(3), 497–525 (2007). https://doi.org/10.1093/rof/rfm021
11. European Commission: Economic crisis in Europe: causes, consequences and responses. European economy, 7/2009 (2009)
12. Evrensel, A.Y.: Banking crisis and financial structure: a survival-time analysis. Int. Rev. Econ. Finan. **17**(4), 589–602 (2008). https://doi.org/10.1016/j.iref.2007.07.002
13. Gepp, A., Kumar, K.: Predicting financial distress: a comparison of survival analysis and decision tree techniques. Proc. Comput. Sci. **54**, 396–404 (2015). https://doi.org/10.1016/j.procs.2015.06.046
14. GPW database. http://www.gpw.pl/analizy_i_statystyki. Accessed 15 June 2018
15. Hosmer, D.W., Lemeshow, S.: Applied Logistic Regression, 2nd edn. Wiley, New York (2005). https://doi.org/10.1002/0471722146
16. https://www.bankier.pl. Accessed 15 June 2018
17. http://bossa.pl/notowania/pliki/eod/omega/. Accessed 10 June 2018
18. Kaplan, E.L., Meier, P.: Nonparametric estimation from incomplete observations. J. Am. Stat. Assoc. **53**(282), 457–481 (1958). https://doi.org/10.2307/2281868
19. Kleinbaum,D., Klein, M.: Survival Analysis. A Self-Learning Text, 3rd edn. Springer, New York (2012). https://doi.org/10.1007/978-1-4419-6646-9
20. Konopczak, M., Sieradzki, R., Wiernicki, M.: Kryzys na światowych rynkach finansowych—wpływ na rynek finansowy w Polsce oraz implikacje dla sektora realnego. Bank i Kredyt **41**(6), 45–70 (2010)
21. Landmesser, J.: Wykorzystanie metod analizy czasu trwania do badania aktywności ekonomicznej ludności w Polsce. Wydawnictwo SGGW, Warszawa (2003)
22. Markowicz, I.: Statystyczna analiza żywotności firm. Rozprawy i Studia t. (CMIX) 835, Wydawnictwo Naukowe Uniwersytetu Szczecińskiego, Szczecin (2012)
23. Markowicz, I., Stolorz, B.: Model proporcjonalnego hazardu Coxa przy różnych sposobach kodowania zmiennych. Przegląd Statystyczny **2**(56), 106–115 (2009)
24. Markovitch, D.G., Golder, P.N.: Findings—using stock prices to predict market events: evidence on sales takeoff and long-term firm survival. Mark. Sci. **27**(4), 717–729 (2008). https://doi.org/10.1287/mksc.1070.0325
25. Matuszyk, A.: Zastosowanie analizy przetrwania w ocenie ryzyka kredytowego klientów indywidualnych. CeDeWu, Warszawa (2015)
26. Minsky, H.: Stabilizing an Unstable Economy. Yale University Press, London (1986)
27. NBP Raport: Polska wobec światowego kryzysu gospodarczego. http://www.nbp.pl/aktualnosci/wiadomosci_2009/polska_wobec_swiatowego_kryzysu_gospodarczego_2009.pdf (2009)
28. Olbryś, J., Majewska, E.: Bear market periods during the 2007–2009 financial crisis: direct evidence from the Visegrad countries. Acta Oeconomica **65**(4), 547–565 (2015). https://doi.org/10.1556/032.65.2015.4.3
29. Pereira, J.: Survival analysis employed in predicting corporate failure: a forecasting model proposal. Int. Bus. Res. **7**(5), 9–20 (2014). https://doi.org/10.5539/ibr.v7n5p9
30. Roszkowska, P., Prorokowski, Ł.: Model of Financial Crisis contagion: a survey-based simulation by means of the modified Kaplan-Meier survival plots. Folia Oeconomica Stetinensia **13**(21)/1, 22–55 (2013). https://doi.org/10.2478/foli-2013-0006
31. Sączewska-Piotrowska, A.: Dynamika ubóstwa w miejskich i wiejskich gospodarstwach domowych. Wiadomości Statystyczne **7**, 29–46 (2016)
32. Tarczyński, W., Tarczyńska-Łuniewska, M., Tarczyński, P.: Scoringowa metoda wyznaczania sektorowego wskaźnika siły fundamentalnej na przykładzie spółek notowanych na Giełdzie Papierów Wartościowych w Warszawie. Rynek Kapitałowy. Skuteczne Inwestowanie, Finanse, rynki finansowe, ubezpieczenia **2**(86), 21–31 (2017). https://doi.org/10.18276/frfu.2017.86-02

33. Wycinka, E.: Modelowanie czasu do zaprzestania spłat rat kredytu lub wcześniejszej spłaty kredytu jako zdarzeń konkurujących. Problemy Zarządzania **13**, 3(55)/2, 146–157 (2015). https://doi.org/10.7172/1644-9584.55.10
34. Yamaguchi, K.: Event History Analysis. SAGE Publications, Newbury Park CA (1991)

Chapter 2
Integration Level and the Hierarchical Structure of European Stock Markets in the Years 2004–2017

Elżbieta Majewska

Abstract The aim of this research is to conduct a dynamic analysis of the level of integration between the European stock markets including their hierarchical structure. The analysis of the structure of links between markets allows identifying those groups of markets that have a particularly strong impact on each other and those with weaker connections. That is an important issue from the point of view of investors as strong links between markets can significantly limit the benefits of internationally diversifying investment portfolios. The study has been carried out with the use of closing prices for 35 main European stock market indices for the time period from September 2014 to August 2017. In the first step, Ward's method was utilized to analyze the hierarchical structure of the entire set of markets. This allowed to identify groups of markets with the strongest levels of interconnectedness. Next, the level of financial integration was analyzed for the entire group of markets and for smaller subsets of the sample with the use of dynamic integration indicator—calculated as the share of variance explained by the first principal component in the overall variance of the original variables. The indicator was calculated over a moving window. This allowed not only to distinguish groups of markets with higher levels of financial integration but also to identify periods of rising and falling integration.

Keywords Financial integration · Index of integration · Hierarchical structure · Ward's method

2.1 Introduction

Integration is one of the key aspects of the development and growth of financial markets. It brings many benefits not only to markets but also to investors. By stimulating financial development, it contributes to economic growth and helps to weaken and eliminate barriers to international investment. However, strong integration also car-

E. Majewska (✉)
University of Bialystok, Świerkowa 20B, Białystok 15-328, Poland
e-mail: e.majewska@uwb.edu.pl

W. Tarczyński and K. Nermend (eds.), *Effective Investments on Capital Markets*, Springer Proceedings in Business and Economics,
https://doi.org/10.1007/978-3-030-21274-2_2

ries risks. According to many authors, it facilitates the transmission of disturbances and adverse changes including crisis contagion [14, 40, 56]. Strong integration can also limit the benefits of risk diversification, which are especially sought after during financial crises [4, 6].

Financial integration is a very broad issue; therefore, a single universal definition of it does not exist. Most commonly, financial integration is understood as a process in which the allocation of financial assets is not subjected to any significant limitations. Integrated markets are characterized by uninhibited flow of capital, which results in equalization of prices and returns on assets with the same levels of risk across multiple markets. According to Baele et al. [3], a given market of particular financial instruments or services is fully integrated if all of its participants: (1) are subject to same rules and regulations, (2) have equal access to these instruments (or services), (3) are treated equally while active in the market what follows from the definition is that the law of one price should hold on integrated markets. Law of one price states that assets with identical levels of risk and return should be traded at the same prices regardless of which market the transactions are being made [5]. Many authors point to another important aspect of integration—highly integrated markets will primarily price global risk factors. If markets are partially integrated, they will price both global and local risk factors [7, 9, 33].

The topic of financial integration and more broadly of the interconnectedness of markets became more widely discussed in recent years because of the 2007–2009 global financial crisis. Some authors analyze the influence of those disturbances on the structure of links between the markets on an international scale. Tools employed for such analyses include methods of hierarchical clustering of objects. Such methods result in subdividing the entire set of objects into subsets called clusters with objects within clusters being more similar to each other than to the objects from other clusters [48]. The subdivision is carried out based on the distances between the objects and between the clusters. In the case of financial markets hierarchical methods allow to analyze the structure of links between them, this, in turn, allows identifying markets that interact strongly with each other and markets that are less interconnected.

The structure of this paper is as follows. Section 2.2 consists of a short literature review on the topic of financial markets integration and their hierarchical structure. Hierarchical methods with a particular emphasis on agglomerative methods are described in Sect. 2.3. Principal components analysis and the integration indicator based on it are presented in Sect. 2.4. Section 2.5 consists of a description of the empirical analysis carried out with the use of methods described in Sects. 2.3 and 2.4, along with the obtained results. Section 2.6 contains a summary and conclusions from this study.

2.2 Hierarchical Methods and Financial Markets Integration—A Literature Review

A broad scope of the notion of financial integration implies the existence of many methods for measuring it. Most authors (e.g., Fung et al. [27]) specify two basic groups of methods: price-based measures and quantity-based measures. Price-based measures rely on the differences between the prices of assets listed on multiple markets. Significant discrepancies in those prices are a sign of lack of integration. Measures from this group allow verifying if the law of one price holds or not. Quantity-based measures focus on fundamental characteristics such as assets, liabilities, company stocks, bank loans, and financial flows from an international perspective. Those are quantitative tools for analyzing the consequences of frictions between markets.

One additional group of methods for analyzing the level of financial integration deserves attention, namely the news-based measures [3]. Those measures utilize the fact that new information with a regional scope should not significantly affect prices of assets whereas global news should have a much greater influence.

Among the price-based measures, the simplest tools utilize correlations. Rising integration can result in an increase in cross-correlations (e.g., Ang and Bekaert [2], Campbell et al. [16], Longin and Solnik [43]). Some authors study the interconnectedness of big groups of markets by analyzing the mean correlation coefficient for each pair (e.g., Goetzmann et al. [31], Mauro et al. [49], Quinn and Voth [60]). A rise in the value of cross-correlation can be interpreted as an increase in the level of integration between two markets (e.g., Chesnay and Jondeau [19], Longin and Solnik [42]). One more way to confirm this fact is to use the equality tests for the correlation matrices [31, 35, 39]. Results obtained with the use of this method can be found among others in articles by Chesnay and Jondeau [19], Briere et al. [13], Olbrys and Majewska [52–54].

However, measures based solely on correlations raise serious doubts. This is mostly due to unfavorable statistical and interpretative characteristics of the correlation coefficient (e.g., Carrieri et al. [17], Volosovych [65, 66]). Studies have shown [59] that even highly integrated markets can be only weakly correlated and vice versa—high correlation can exist with low levels of integration. Because of that, many different methods and tools for measuring integration are utilized. Those include among others: cointegration tests (e.g., Al Nasser and Hajilee [1], Bentes [8], Guidi and Ugur [32], Kizys and Pierdzioch [38], Oanea [51], Voronkova [67]) or GARCH-type models (np. Büttner and Hayo [14], Carrieri et al. [17], Fratzscher [26], Kenourgios [37]). Many authors utilize multivariate regression models. Most commonly those models are built by regressing rates of return on the stock market index on: macroeconomic variables (e.g., [58], rates of return on other indices (e.g., Al Nasser and Hajilee [1], Schotman and Zalewska [63]), or synthetic variables such as principal components (e.g., Lehkonen [40], Pukthuanthong and Roll [59]). One can also include in this group models that have investment portfolios of developed markets as regressors. Such models analyze the integration level measured as the percentage of variability in the rates of return that can be explained by the influence of global factors (e.g., Bekaert et al. [7], Boamah [9]). A comprehensive review of integration measures can be found in an article by Chen et al. [18].

Studies that analyze the hierarchical structure of financial markets usually utilize one of three methods: minimal spanning trees, asset graphs, and clustering analysis. Those methods are based on dissimilarity measures (distance) between the time series of market rates of return. Minimal spanning tree is a graph of n objects connected with $n - 1$ edges, with the sum of weights of all of the edges (distance between the objects) being subject to minimization [41, 55]. The structure obtained through such an algorithm does not contain cycles or isolated vertices. There are many studies that utilize minimal spanning trees to analyze financial markets. Mantegna [47] pioneered this approach by analyzing the structure of portfolios of DJIA and S&P 500 indices for the time period from July 1989 to October 1995. Other studies of the American market were carried out by Bonanno et al. [10] and Brida and Risso [12]. Studies of the structure of international markets were carried out by: Coehlo et al. [20], Gilmore et al. [29], Eryiğit and Eryiğit [22], Sandoval [61]. Asset graphs are structures in which both cycles and isolated vertices can occur [55]. The number of connections in the graph is dependent on the set threshold value of the distances between the objects. Examples of the application of graph methods can be found in the studies by Onnela et al. [55] and Sandoval [62].

Clustering methods are based on the analysis of similarities between the objects, and their results are presented as a binary tree [41]. This group of methods is not widely represented in the scientific literature on financial markets. One of the first studies on this topic was conducted by Panton et al. [57]—this work showed the results of grouping of 12 world markets for the time period 1963–1972. Hierarchical trees were utilized also among others by Sensoy et al. [64], Leon et al. [41], Majewska [44].

The author of this paper is not aware of any studies that would combine an analysis of the hierarchical structure of European financial markets with an analysis of their level of integration.

2.3 Agglomerative Clustering

Clustering methods are a known tool of multidimensional statistical analysis that allows investigating links between objects. They work by grouping objects into nonempty, disjoint, and homogeneous sets called clusters. Most similar objects should end up in the same cluster, whereas most dissimilar objects should end up in different clusters. Grouping can be either nonhierarchical or hierarchical. In the former case, it is necessary to determine the number of clusters in advance, whereas hierarchical methods allow to determine the clusters through agglomerative (merging) or divisive algorithms of the clusters established in the previous steps of the procedure. In the first step of the agglomerative algorithm, each object belongs to its own cluster. Most similar clusters are then merged together in the following steps up until all objects are gathered in a single cluster, whereas for the divisive algorithms in the first step, all of the objects are gathered in a single cluster that is then being divided into smaller ones up until each object is in a separate cluster. A dendrogram (binary tree) is used to graphically show the process of agglomeration or division with end nodes representing objects and other nodes representing clusters. Each vertex is placed at the level representing the value of the measure of similarity (distance) from its child/parent vertices.

A key aspect in clustering is the method of measuring the level of dissimilarity between two objects and two clusters. In the case of objects i and j, the Euclidean distance d_{ij} can be used to measure similarity:

$$d_{ij} = \sqrt{\sum_{p=1}^{n} \left(x_{ip} - x_{jp}\right)^2}, \quad i, j = 1, 2, \ldots, K \tag{2.1}$$

where

x_{ip} is the value of variable p for object i,
K is the number of grouped objects,
n is the number of observations for each variable.

The lower the value of d_{ij}, the more similar the objects.

Sometimes other measures of similarity are also used, e.g., Minkowski distance or Mahalanobis distance [23]. When it comes to financial time series, many authors utilize a distance measure based on the correlation coefficient [47]:

$$d_{ij} = \sqrt{2\left(1 - \varrho_{ij}\right)}, \quad i, j = 1, 2, \ldots, K. \tag{2.2}$$

Properties of the correlation coefficient require the assumption of normality of returns. Moreover, the correlation coefficient is biased due to the level of variability in rates of return [25]. Hence, a comparison of distances based on correlation coefficient during periods of changing variability (this applies to periods of financial crises) is not recommended.

The choice of a measure for comparing the similarity between two clusters is strictly related to the utilized method of grouping. In the case of agglomerative algorithms, most commonly used methods include [23]:

- single linkage method (nearest neighbor)—similarity between two clusters is measured as the minimal distance between two objects each belonging to one of the clusters in question.
- complete linkage method (furthest neighbor)—similarity between two clusters is measured as the furthest possible distance between two objects each belonging to one of the clusters.
- average linkage method—similarity between two clusters is measured as the average distance between the objects belonging to each of the clusters.

- Ward's method—similarity between two clusters is measured as the sum of squared deviations within those clusters.

There are no conclusive studies that would demonstrate which of those methods is most suited for applications with financial time series. However, many authors that utilize multiple methods, point to Ward's method as an advantageous one [15, 24, 34, 41]. Additionally, it is worth pointing out that Ward's method is the only one that is based on a kind of optimization, namely the minimization of the loss of information resulting from combining two clusters into one [68]. Moreover, dendrograms obtained with this method have a much clearer structure and thus are easier to interpret. For those reasons, Ward's method has been utilized in this study.

2.4 Index of Integration

One of the methods used in the research on the level of financial markets integration is the principal components analysis. It is a method of reduction of datasets that contain a big number of variables that are connected with each other. A new set of variables is constructed in a way that preserves the biggest possible amount of information contained in the initial set of variables. Observable input variables are transformed into new unobservable variables called the principal components, which are linear combinations of initial variables. Consecutive principal components are uncorrelated with each other and are constructed in a way that maximizes the variability that has not been explained by the first component [36]. Thanks to this approach; a few first principal components contain the vast majority of information from the initial dataset [21].

Let X be the vector of N variables with known variances, for which either the covariance or correlation matrix is known. Then, the kth principal component ($k = 1, 2, \ldots, N$) can be written as:

$$z_k = a_k^T x = \alpha_{k1}x_1 + \alpha_{k2}x_2 + \ldots + \alpha_{kN}x_N = \sum_{j=1}^{N} \alpha_{kj}x_j, \qquad (2.3)$$

where

$X = [x_1, x_2, \ldots, x_N]^{\mathrm{T}}$ is the vector of N initial variables,
$a_k = [\alpha_{k1}, \alpha_{k2}, \ldots, \alpha_{kN}]^{\mathrm{T}}$ is the vector of N coefficients.

Coefficients α_{kj} are selected in a way that maximizes the variance of the new variable z_k subject to constraint[1]: $a_k^T a_k = \sum_{j=1}^{N} a_{kj}^2 = 1$. Additionally, each following principal component is orthogonal to the one preceding it, that is, $a_k^T a_{k+1} = 0$.

This procedure boils down to calculating the eigenvectors a_k of the covariance matrix X corresponding to its eigenvalues λ_k. It is possible to demonstrate that

[1] This constraint ensures the normalization of the coefficients vector.

$var(z_k) = \lambda_k$; that is, the kth principal component corresponds to the kth highest eigenvalue. Additionally, due to the lack of correlation between the consecutive principal components, the overall variance of the new set of variables is equal to: $\sum_{i=1}^{N} \lambda_i$.

Principal components can be calculated with the use of covariance matrix when the input variables are expressed in the same units and do not differ significantly in terms of variability. Otherwise, one should standardize the variables (covariance matrix of standardized variables is equal to the correlation matrix of the variables before standardization). In practice, this approach is preferred.

Most commonly utilized standardization formula is given by the following equation:

$$z_{it} = \frac{r_{it} - \bar{r}_i}{s_i}, \tag{2.4}$$

where

z_{it} is the rate of return on index i at time t after standardization,
r_{it} is the rate of return on index i at time t before standardization,
$\bar{r}_i$ is the expected value of the rate of return on index i,
s_i is the standard deviation of the rate of return on index i.

Integration measures based on principal components have multiple advantages [65]. Principal components analysis is robust with respect to outliers and fat tails of distributions. It also allows diagnosing global disturbances that can be falsely interpreted as integration when using other methods. One of such measures, first introduced by Volosovych [65, 66], is the index of integration—calculated as the share of variance explained by the first principal component in the overall variance of the initial variables:

$$v_{\mathrm{PC1}} = \frac{\lambda_1}{\sum_{i=1}^{N} \lambda_i}, \tag{2.5}$$

where λ_i is the ith eigenvalue of the correlation (or covariance) matrix of the analyzed variables. When eigenvalues are calculated for a set of comparable variables such as prices or rates of return on instruments listed on studied markets, the first principal component has a natural interpretation. It can be considered as a multidimensional equivalent of the correlation coefficient. A substantial share of variance explained by the first principal component indicates a high level of interconnectedness between the markets. Conversely, when each of the principal components explains only a small (and roughly similar) share of the overall variance, it means that the markets are only loosely connected [30].

Analyses of the level of integration with methods based on principal components can be either static or dynamic. In the former case first principal component (or a number of first ones) is calculated for a given time period. Those types of analyses usually supplement studies are carried out with other methods and techniques [11,

28, 49, 50, 59]. A dynamic analysis investigates changes in the level of integration and consists in calculating principal components over a moving window. This allows for a graphical visualization of results which makes the dynamic analysis of the level of integration simpler [21, 46, 65, 66].

2.5 Data Description and Empirical Results

The analysis of the hierarchical structure of European markets and their levels of integration has been carried out with the use of monthly closing prices of 35 main European stock market indices (Table 2.1) from the time period from September 2004 to August 2017 (156 observations). This data was used to calculate monthly logarithmic rates of return which were the subject of further calculations.

Table 2.1 Stock market indices of 35 European markets included in the study

Country	Index	Market Cap. EUR billion Dec 2016	Country	Index	Market Cap. EUR billion Dec 2016
England	FTSE100	2889.39	Portugal	PSI 20	48.91
France	CAC40	2049.21	Greece	ATHEX	35.31
Germany	DAX	1630.41	Croatia	CROBEX	30.75
Switzerland	SMI	1331.21	Czech Republic	PX	22.19
Netherlands	AEX	811.72	Hungary	BUX	21.27
Spain	IBEX35	669.40	Romania	BET	16.81
Sweden	OMXS30	642.96	Iceland	OMXI	14.6
Russia	RTSI	588.15	Slovakia	SAX	5.28
Italy	FTSEMIB	525.05	Slovenia	SBITOP	5.00
Belgium	BEL20	358.91	Bulgaria	SOFIX	4.95
Denmark	OMXC20	319.19	Malta	MSE	4.21
Norway	OSEAX	219.48	Ukraine	UX	4.21
Finland	OMXH25	209.00	Lithuania	OMXV	3.50
Turkey	XU100	162.78	Montenegro	MONEX	2.88
Poland	WIG20	130.99	Cyprus	GENERAL	2.39
Ireland	ISEQ	113.85	Estonia	OMXT	2.29
Austria	ATX	95.20	Latvia	OMXR	0.80
Luxembourg	LuxX	57.87			

Source http://sdw.ecb.europa.eu, http://www.nasdaqomxnordic.com, http://fese.eu/

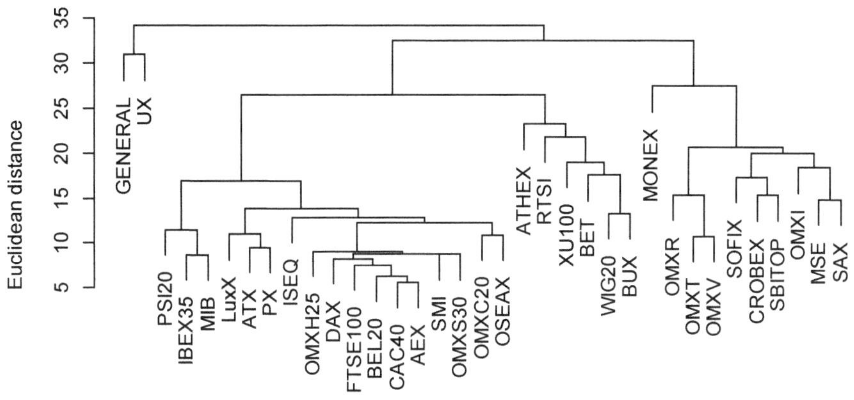

Fig. 2.1 Hierarchical tree of the investigated indexes

2.5.1 Hierarchical Structure of Investigated Markets

Logarithmic rates of return were standardized with the formula given in Eq. (2.4)—this allowed to avoid the scale and dispersion effects when investigating the hierarchical structure of the markets. Euclidean distances between the indices were calculated and their grouping was carried out with the use of Ward's method. Figure 2.1 presents the obtained dendrogram.[2]

There are four distinct clusters in the obtained structure. The smallest group consists of just two indices: GENERAL and UX. However, those two indices represent markets with very low levels of interconnectedness (distance between them is the highest in the entire group). Second cluster is significantly more numerous and consists of ten indices: MONEX, OMXR, OMXT, OMXV, SOFIX, CROBEX, SBITOP, OMXI, MSE, SAX. Strongest connections in this group exist between OMXT and OMXV; those two indices together with OMXR represent Baltic markets. Next, three-element cluster consists of indices: CROBEX, SBITOP, and SOFIX—and represents south European markets. Those two groups are examples of clusters consisting of markets which are in close geographical proximity. Not all clusters, however, share this characteristic. Next group consists of six indices: ATHEX, RTSI, XU100, BET, WIG20, and BUX. Within this group, Polish and Hungarian indices are most similar. The final cluster is the most numerous one and consists of 17 indices: PSI20, IBEX35, MIB, LuxX, ATX, PX, ISEQ, OMXH25, DAX, FTSE100, BEL20, CAC40, AEX, SMI, OMXS30, OMXC20, OSEAX. Two indices from this group proved most similar out of the entire group—the French CAC40 and Dutch AEX. Those along with the Belgian, English, and German markets constitute a cluster of indices that are least distant from each other in the entire group. This cluster contains the biggest European markets.

[2]Dendrogram was created with the use of *R* package.

2.5.2 Dynamics of the Integration Index

The indicator described by Eq. (2.5) was used to investigate the level of integration. Firstly principle components were calculated from the correlation matrix of the rates of return on all of the indices. Because the aim of the study is to analyze changes in the levels of integration, integration index was calculated over a 36-month moving window. Appropriate length for the window cannot be clearly specified. Previous studies show, however, that the length of the window does not significantly affect the shape of the integration curve. The longer the window, the smoother the curve with its shape remaining analogous [46]. Window with the length of 36 months used in this study allowed to obtain values of the integration index starting from September 2007 and thus to include the influence of the 2007–2009 financial crisis on the level of integration.

After considering the results of hierarchical clustering of the markets, the integration index has been calculated for three groups of indices:

Group A: PSI20, IBEX35, MIB, LuxX, ATX, PX, ISEQ, OMXH25, DAX, FTSE100, BEL20, CAC40, AEX, SMI, OMXS30, OMXC20, OSEAX, ATHEX, RTSI, XU100, BET, WIG20, BUX;

Group B: MONEX, OMXR, OMXT, OMXV, SOFIX, CROBEX, SBITOP, OMXI, MSE, SAX;

Group C: all indexes.

Integration curves obtained for all three groups are presented in Fig. 2.2.

The integration curve for group A markets is the highest at all time periods—indices that constitute group A had the highest level of integration during the entire studied period. The lowest values of integration index occurred for group B. This is confirmed by statistics presented in Table 2.2. It is worth noting that the first of those clusters comprises indices whose mutual distances were the smallest. Distances between indices in the second cluster were considerably bigger.

Differences between the mean values of the integration indicator for each group were statistically significant (Table 2.3).

The shapes of integration curves are analogous for each group. A significant increase in the value of the indicator can be observed from the end of 2007 until mid-2008 (phase I). A high level of the indicator persisted until the second half of 2011 (phase II), after which a visible decrease in its value occurs—this was, however, a less sudden change than the initial increase. Downward trends subsisted until the second half of 2015 (phase III) followed by a modest increase and stabilization of the integration index (phase IV) at a level similar to that of September 2007. Phases I and II correspond with declining European markets due to the global financial crisis and European debt crisis.

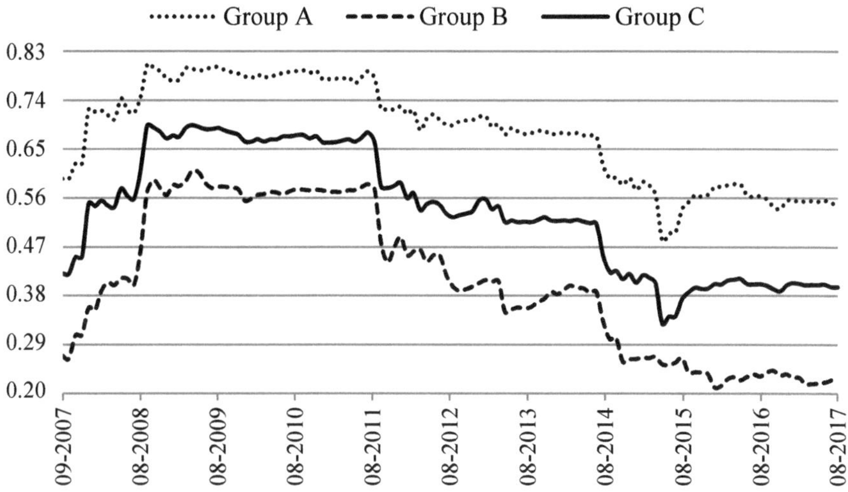

Fig. 2.2 Dynamics of the index of integration in the groups A, B, and C

Table 2.2 Descriptive statistics for the index of integration in each group

Group	Min	Max	Mean	Standard deviation
A	0.4816	0.8057	0.6813	0.0928
B	0.2120	0.6098	0.4034	0.1346
C	0.3290	0.6937	0.5338	0.1116

Source Own calculation

Table 2.3 Results of the equality test for mean values of the integration index in groups A, B, and C

Groups	*u*	*p*
A and B	18.6148	0.0000
A and C	11.1328	0.0000
B and C	−8.1651	0.0000

Source Own calculation

Because group A is a numerous one (23 indices), it was further subdivided into two following clusters:

Group A1: PSI20, IBEX35, MIB, LuxX, ATX, PX, ISEQ, OMXH25, DAX, FTSE100, BEL20, CAC40, AEX, SMI, OMXS30, OMXC20, OSEAX;

Group A2: ATHEX, RTSI, XU100, BET, WIG20, BUX.

Figure 2.3 shows the shapes of integration curves for the new groups.

The shape of those integration curves is analogous to those obtained in other groups. However, the levels of integration among the new groups are much closer than in the previously analyzed clusters (Table 2.4). Only in the final stabilization phase (beginning in the last months of 2015), the discrepancies become somewhat bigger.

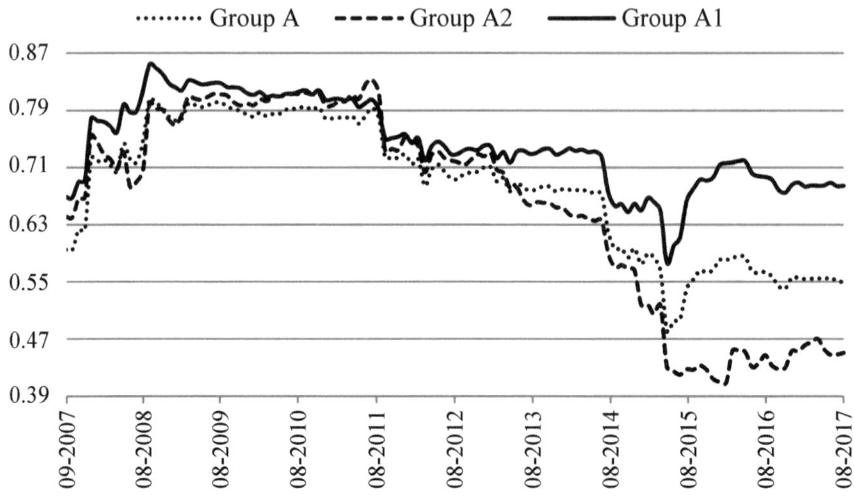

Fig. 2.3 Dynamics of the index of integration in groups A, A1, A2

Table 2.4 Variability of the index of integration in groups A, A1, and A2

Group	Min	Max	Mean	Standard deviation
A	0.4816	0.8057	0.6813	0.0928
A1	0.5764	0.8539	0.7436	0.0610
A2	0.4089	0.8328	0.6572	0.1414

Source Own calculation

Table 2.5 Results of the equality test for mean values of the integration index in groups A, A1, and A2

Groups	*u*	*p*
A and A1	−6.1379	0.0000
A and A2	1.5629	0.1181
A1 and A2	6.1433	0.0000

Source Own calculation

Results of the equality test for mean values of the integration index indicate that the difference between means of clusters A and A2 is not statistically significant (Table 2.5).

It is worth noting that obtained results reveal a certain regularity between the results of clustering and the level of integration. The lower the distance between clusters, the higher the integration level of markets that constitute those clusters.

2.6 Conclusions

The aim of this study was to analyze the hierarchical structure of European stock markets and to investigate the levels of integration among the entire studied group and selected smaller clusters. Prices of 35 main European stock market indices for the time period from September 2004 to August 2017 were the subject of the analysis.

Market grouping was carried out with the use of Ward's method on standardized monthly logarithmic rates of return. Obtained structure had four distinct clusters. Next, the integration indicator (share of variance explained by the first principal component in the overall variance of studied indices) was calculated for the entire group and for a couple of distinct clusters. The indicator was calculated over a 36-month moving window, which allowed to analyze the changes in integration level during the studied period.

Integration level varied among different groups of markets. Results show that higher levels of integration were present in clusters that contain markets with smaller mutual distances from each other and vice versa. One can hence deduce that the hierarchical tree is sufficient to identify groups of markets with the highest and lowest levels of integration.

The analysis of the dynamics of the integration indicator allowed to identify phases of increase, stabilization, and decline in the level of integration between the markets. Those phases were analogous for all studied groups of markets. One distinct feature was the sudden increase in the level of integration at the starting phase of the global financial crisis and a subsisting elevated level throughout the European debt crisis. In the final months of 2015, the integration indicator reverted to the level from before the financial crisis, after that the indicator remained stable until the end of the studied sample. This confirms the results of analogous research carried out for the other groups of markets (e.g., Majewska and Jamróz [45]).

A question of whether or not the outcome of the analysis in terms of consistency between the results of market grouping and integration levels would remain the same if another methodology of measuring distances between the indices was applied in the hierarchical analysis remains open (this study utilized the Euclidean distance). This issue can be investigated in further research.

Acknowledgements This publication has received financial support from the Polish Ministry of Science and Higher Education under subsidy for maintaining the research potential of the Faculty of Mathematics and Informatics, University of Bialystok.

References

1. Al Nasser, O.M., Hajilee, M.: Integration of emerging stock markets with global stock markets. Res. Int. Bus. Finan. **36**, 1–12 (2016)
2. Ang, A., Bekaert, G.: International asset allocation under regime switching. Rev. Finan. Stud **15**, 1137–1187 (2002)

3. Baele, L., Ferrado, A., Hördahl, P., Krylova, E., Monnet, C.: Measuring financial integration in the euro area. ECB Occasional Paper Series No. 14 (2004)
4. Beine, M., Cosma, A., Vermeulen, R.: The dark side of global integration: increasing tail dependence. J. Bank Finan. **34**, 184–192 (2010)
5. Bekaert, G., Harvey, C.R.: Time-varying market integration. J. Finan. **1**(2), 403–444 (1995)
6. Bekaert, G., Harvey, C.R., Lumsdaine, R.L.: Dating the integration of world equity markets. J. Financ. Econ. **65**, 203–247 (2002)
7. Bekaert, G., Harvey, C.R., Ng, A.: Market integration and contagion. J. Bus. **78**(1), 39–69 (2005)
8. Bentes, S.R.: On the integration of financial markets: How strong is the evidence from five international stock markets? Phys. A **429**, 205–214 (2015)
9. Boamah, N.A.: The dynamics of the relative global sector effects and contagion in emerging markets equity returns. Res. Int. Bus. Finan. **39**, 433–453 (2017)
10. Bonanno, G., Caldarelli, G., Lillo, F., Micciché, S., Vandewalle, N., Mantegna, R.N.: Networks of equities in financial markets. Eur. Phys. J. B **38**, 363–371 (2004)
11. Bordo, M.D., Murshid, A.P.: Globalization and changing patterns in the international transmission in financial markets. J. Int. Money Finan. **25**, 655–674 (2006)
12. Brida, J.G., Risso, W.A.: Multidimensional minimal spanning tree: the Dow Jones case. Phys. A **387**, 5205–5210 (2008)
13. Briere, M., Chapelle, A., Szafarz, A.: No contagion, only globalization and flight to quality. J. Int. Money Finan. **31**(6), 1729–1744 (2012)
14. Büttner, D., Hayo, B.: Determinants of European stock market integration. Econ. Sys. **35**, 574–585 (2011)
15. Calinski, T., Harabasz, J.: A dendrite method for cluster analysis. Commun. Stat. **3**(1), 1–27 (1974)
16. Campbell, J.Y., Koedijk, K., Kofman, P.: Increased correlation in bear markets. Finan. Anal. J. **58**(1), 87–94 (2002)
17. Carrieri, F., Errunza, V., Hogan, K.: Characterizing world market integration through time. J. Finan. Quant. Anal. **42**(4), 915–940 (2007)
18. Chen, M.-P., Chen, P.-F., Lee, C.-C.: Frontier stock market integration and the global financial crisis. N. Am. J. Econ. Finan. **29**, 84–103 (2014)
19. Chesnay, F., Jondeau, E.: Does correlation between stock returns really increase during turbulent periods? Econ. Notes **30**(1), 53–80 (2001)
20. Coelho, R., Gilmore, C.G., Lucey, B., Richmond, P., Hutzler, S.: The evolution of interdependence in world equity markets—evidence from minimum spanning trees. Phys. A **376**, 455–466 (2007)
21. Donadelli, M., Paradiso, A.: Is there heterogeneity in financial integration dynamics? Evidence from country and industry emerging market equity indexes. J. Int. Finan. Mark Inst. Money **32**, 184–218 (2014)
22. Eryiğit, M., Eryiğit, R.: Network structure of cross-correlations among the world market indices. Phys. A **388**, 3551–3562 (2009)
23. Everitt, B.S., Landau, S., Leese, M., Stahl, D.: Cluster analysis. Wiley, Chichester (2011)
24. Ferreira, L., Hitchcock, D.B.: A comparison of hierarchical methods for clustering functional data. Commun. Stat. Simul. C **38**(9), 1925–1949 (2009)
25. Forbes, K., Rigobon, R.: No contagion, only interdependence: measuring stock market comovements. J. Finan. **57**(5), 2223–2261 (2002)
26. Fratzscher, M.: Financial market integration in Europe: on the effects of EMU on stock markets. Int. J. Finan. Econ. **7**(3), 165–194 (2002)
27. Fung, L.K., Tam, C., Yu, I.: Assessing the integration of Asia's equity and bond markets. BIS Papers No. 42. (2008)
28. Gagnon, J.E., Unferth, M.D.: Is there a world interest rate? J. Int. Money Finan. **14**, 846–855 (1995)
29. Gilmore, C.G., Lucey, B.M., Boscia, M.: An ever-closer union? Examining the evolution of linkages of European equity markets via minimum spanning trees. Phys. A **387**, 6319–6329 (2008)

30. Gilmore, C.G., Lucey, B.M., McManus, G.M.: The dynamics of Central European equity market comovements. Q. Rev. Econ. Finan. **48**, 605–622 (2008)
31. Goetzmann, W.N., Li, L., Rouwenhorst, K.G.: Long–term global market correlations. J. Bus. **78**(1), 1–38 (2005)
32. Guidi, F., Ugur, M.: An analysis of South-Eastern European stock markets: evidence on cointegration and portfolio Diversification Benefits. J. Int. Finan. Mark I **30**, 119–136 (2014)
33. Hardouvelis, G.A., Malliaropulos, D., Priestley, R.: EMU and European stock market integration. J. Bus. **79**(1), 365–392 (2006)
34. Hossen, B., Siraj-Ud-Doulah, Hoque A.: Methods for evaluating agglomerative hierarchical clustering for gene expression data: a comparative study. Comput. Biol. Bioinform. **3**(6), 88–94 (2015)
35. Jennrich, R.I.: An asymptotic chi-square test for the equality of two correlation matrices. J. Am. Stat. Assoc. **65**(330), 904–912 (1970)
36. Jolliffe, I.T.: Principal component analysis. Springer series in statistics, 2nd edn. Springer, New York (2002)
37. Kenourgios, D., Samitas, A.: Equity market integration in emerging Balkan markets. Res. Int. Bus. Finan. **25**, 296–307 (2011)
38. Kizys, R., Pierdzioch, C.: The financial crisis and the stock markets of the CEE countries. Finan. Uver **61**(2), 153–172 (2011)
39. Larntz, K., Perlman, M.D.: A simple test for the equality of correlation matrices. Technical Report No. 63, Department of Statistics, University of Washington (1985)
40. Lehkonen, H.: Stock market integration and the global financial crisis. Rev. Finan. **19**(5), 2039–2094 (2015)
41. Leon, C., Kim, G.-Y., Martinez, C., Lee, D.: Equity markets' clustering and the global financial crises. Borradores de Economia 937 (2016)
42. Longin, F., Solnik, B.: Is the correlation in international equity returns constant: 1960–1990? J. Int. Money Finan. **14**(1), 3–26 (1995)
43. Longin, F., Solnik, B.: Extreme correlation of international equity markets. J. Finan. **56**(2), 649–676 (2001)
44. Majewska, E.: Impact of 2007–2009 financial crisis on hierarchical structure of European capital markets. Optimum. Econ. Stud. **3**(87), 61–76 (2017). (in polish)
45. Majewska, E., Jamróz, P.: Integration measures based on principal component analysis: Example of eurozone stock markets. In: Tsounis N, Vlachvei A (eds) Advances in time series data methods in applied economic research—Proceedings of the 2018 International Conference on Applied Economics (ICOAE). Springer Proceedings in Business and Economics (in press) (2018)
46. Majewska, E., Olbrys, J.: Measuring dynamics of financial integration on the euro area stock markets, 2000–2010. In: Tsounis N, Vlachvei A (eds) Advances in panel data analysis in applied economic research—Proceedings of the 2017 International Conference on Applied Economics (ICOAE). Springer Proceedings in Business and Economics, pp, 129–142 (2018)
47. Mantegna, R.N.: Hierarchical structure in financial markets. Eur. Phys. J. B **11**, 193–197 (1999)
48. Marti, G., Andler, S., Nielsen, F., Donnat, P.: Clustering financial time series: how long is enough? In: Proceedings of the Twenty-Fifth International Joint Conference on Artifical Intelligence, pp. 2583–2589 (2016)
49. Mauro, P., Sussman, N., Yafeh, Y.: Emerging market spreads: then versus now. Q. J. Econ **117**, 695–733 (2002)
50. Nellis, J.G.: A principal components analysis of international financial integration under fixed and floating exchange rate regimes. Appl. Econ. **14**, 339–354 (1982)
51. Oanea, D.-C.: Financial Markets Integration: a vector error-correction approach. J. Econ. Asymmetries **12**, 153–161 (2015)
52. Olbrys, J., Majewska, E.: The 2007–2009 financial crisis on emerging markets: quantitative identification of crisis in continent-based regions. Chinese Bus. Rev. **13**(7), 411–426 (2014)
53. Olbryś, J., Majewska, E.: Testing integration effects between the CEE and U.S. stock markets during the 2007–2009 Global Financial Crisis. Folia Oecon Stetin **14**(1), 101–113 (2015)

54. Olbryś, J., Majewska, E.: Increasing cross-market correlations during the 2007–2009 financial crisis: contagion or integration effects? Arg. Oecon. **39**(2), 263–278 (2017)
55. Onnela, J.-P., Chakraborti, A., Kaski, K., Kertész, J., Kanto, A.: Asset trees and asset graphs in financial markets. Phys. Scripta. **T106**, 48–54 (2003)
56. Oprea, O.R.: Financial Integration and Financial Contagion, a Problem for Financial Stability? J. Publ. ADM Financ. Law **11**, 121–136 (2017)
57. Panton, D.B., Lessing, P., Joy, O.M.: Comovement of international equity markets: a taxonomic approach. J. Financ. Quant. Anal. **11**(5), 415–432 (1976)
58. Peša, A.R., Wrońska-Bukalska, E., Bosna, J.: ARDL panel estimation of stock market indices and macroeconomic environment of CEE and SEE countries in the last decade of transition. Port. Econ. J. **16**, 205–221 (2017)
59. Pukthuanthong, K., Roll, R.: Global market integration: an alternative measure and its application. J. Financ. Econ. **94**, 214–232 (2009)
60. Quinn, D.P., Voth, H.-J.: A century of global equity market correlations. Am Econ Rev: Papers Proc. **98**(2), 535–540 (2008)
61. Sandoval, L.: Pruning a minimum spanning tree. Phys. A **391**, 2678–2711 (2012)
62. Sandoval, L.: Cluster formation and evolution in networks of financial market indices. Algorithmic Financ. **2**(1), 3–43 (2013)
63. Schotman, P.C., Zalewska, A.: Non-synchronous trading and testing for market integration in Central European emerging markets. J. Empir. Financ. **13**, 462–494 (2006)
64. Sensoy, A., Yuksel, S., Erturk, M.: Analysis of cross-correlations between financial markets after 2008 crisis. Phys. A **392**, 5027–5045 (2013)
65. Volosovych, V.: Measuring financial market integration over the long run: is there a U-shape? J. Int. Money Financ. **30**, 1535–1561 (2011)
66. Volosovych, V.: Learning about financial market integration from principal components analysis. CESifo Econ Stud **59**(2), 360–391 (2013)
67. Voronkova, S.: Equity market integration in Central European emerging markets: A cointegration analysis with shifting regimes. Int. Rev. Financ. Anal. **13**, 633–647 (2004)
68. Ward, J.H.: Hierarchical grouping to optimize an objective function. J. Am. Stat. Assoc. **58**(301), 236–444 (1963)

Chapter 3
In Search of the Best Proxy for Liquidity in Asset Pricing Studies on the Warsaw Stock Exchange

Szymon Stereńczak

Abstract Stock liquidity is unobservable, and thus, its level needs to be approximated. There is a large body of liquidity measures recorded in the existing literature. The main goal of this paper is to investigate which measure is the most appropriate one to measure stock liquidity for the purposes of asset pricing studies on the Warsaw Stock Exchange. To indicate the most appropriate proxy for liquidity, a series of correlation analysis between different liquidity measures and estimation error measures have been applied. Four high-frequency liquidity measures were used as a benchmark for liquidity, and fourteen low-frequency liquidity proxies were examined. The study was conducted on a group of 100 companies listed on the Warsaw Stock Exchange between 2006 and 2016. The ranking of low-frequency proxies for liquidity has been created based on eleven performance dimensions. It shows that the most appropriate liquidity measure on the Warsaw Stock Exchange is that developed by Fong et al. [12], which is a simplification of the zero-return-days measure developed by Lesmond et al. [20]. In addition, two modifications of Amihud's [2] illiquidity are presented as the second and third best-performing ones. To the best of the author's knowledge, this is the first such extensive study of the performance of liquidity measures on the Warsaw Stock Exchange. It examines both existing liquidity measures and some modifications proposed on the basis of the literature overview.

Keywords Stock liquidity · Liquidity measures · Liquidity proxies

3.1 Introduction

Liquidity is viewed as the investor's ability to buy or sell large quantities of an asset quickly, at low cost and without causing adverse price impact [24]. This is an extremely important issue on the stock market, from both practitioners' and academics' perspective. Its relevance comes from its effects on asset pricing (see, e.g.,

S. Stereńczak (✉)
Poznań University of Economics and Business, Poznań, Poland
e-mail: szymon.sterenczak@ue.poznan.pl

W. Tarczyński and K. Nermend (eds.), *Effective Investments on Capital Markets*, Springer Proceedings in Business and Economics,
https://doi.org/10.1007/978-3-030-21274-2_3

[4]; Amihud [1–3, 24], on portfolio allocation (see, e.g., [14–17, 21, 25] as well as on risk management. Undoubtedly therefore, stock liquidity is of great interest for investors on the capital market. For investors, its measurement is equally important as the stock liquidity itself. For several reasons, accurate measurement of the level of asset liquidity on the market is difficult. This difficulty is mainly due to the elusiveness and multidimensionality of the concept of liquidity. Predominantly, the bid-ask or effective spread is used as a measure of liquidity, as it reflects the cost of immediate trade execution.

To compute some of the liquidity measures, ultra-high-frequency data on order flows is needed. As pointed out in the literature, these are the most appropriate measures to analyse the effect of liquidity on stock returns [13]. It results from the nature of liquidity, which depends on the equilibrium of buy and sell orders that flow into the market. Applying these measures allows us to measure the level of liquidity costs more accurately and thus indirectly infer the level of stock or market liquidity. However, access to ultra-high-frequency data is barely available or even impossible to obtain in some markets, especially emerging ones. Acquiring this type of data is usually expensive [20], and, in addition, it is not available for longer periods of time [1]. It is worth noting the fact that for NYSE and NYSE MKT (formerly AMEX) exact data on order flow is available only for the period after 1983 [8]. In turn, for many other, smaller, less developed and less liquid markets, data on order flow is unavailable or availability is limited (for example in the Polish market).

Due to the difficulties in obtaining data for the calculation of ultra-high-frequency measures, many authors use measures that are less data-demanding, i.e. low-frequency proxies that require data only on a daily frequency. They are an alternative for high-frequency measures or are simply the only option if ultra-high or high-frequency data is not available. Moreover, the use of daily data is far less costly and time-consuming. The use of low-frequency measures also allows us to obtain much longer time series than in measures based on order flow data and intra-daily data [19, 22, 30]. As noted by Goyenko et al. [18], low-frequency measures are just as effective as the measures using higher-frequency data. Fong et al. [12] come to a similar proposition from their research. The popularity and usefulness of low-frequency measures is evidenced by the fact that they have even become commonplace in studies focusing on the US markets for which ultra-high-frequency data is available [5].

The main goal of the paper is to investigate which measure is the most appropriate one to measure stock liquidity for the purposes of asset pricing studies on the Warsaw Stock Exchange. It is considered that liquidity should be measured using the so-called high-frequency measures whose application requires often costly and scarcely available data on order flows. For this reason; for time, computational and cost savings, a number of proxies are used instead, which require more affordable low-frequency data, in particular daily data on prices and volumes. These proxies measure liquidity with varying degrees of accuracy, and the studies carried out so far do not provide clear indications as to which of them is the best one, in particular with regard to emerging markets. Research conducted in this paper includes data from the Warsaw Stock Exchange in the period from 2006 to 2016. In this period, WSE was the biggest and fastest growing emerging market in the region of Central and Eastern

Europe. It can be therefore assumed that the results obtained for the WSE could be widened to the other stock exchanges in the CEE region.

This paper contributes mainly to the literature on the measurement of liquidity in stock markets. Similar studies done so far were carried out for several reasons including the search for the best liquidity measure for international research or testing the usefulness of newly developed liquidity measures. Fong et al. [12] tried to find the best liquidity proxy for global research. They utilised data on 42 securities exchanges from 38 countries around the world in the period from 1996 to 2014. Porcenaluk [26] investigated estimation errors of six different bid-ask spread estimators, namely Roll's [27], Thompson and Waller's [29], Choi et al.'s [9], Chu et al. [10] and two versions of CS estimators. He indicated that the above-mentioned estimators are characterised by large estimation errors on the Polish capital market and also noted that, due to the positive autocorrelation of stock returns, it is reasonable to use estimators based on the price range. In addition to the aforementioned research, one should also recall the paper of Będowska-Sójka [6]. Using the data of 52 companies listed on the WSE in the years 2009–2016, she indicated that the best liquidity proxies on the WSE are Amihud's [2] illiquidity measure, daily price range and CS estimator.

So far, research done in search of the best proxy for liquidity on the Warsaw Stock Exchange was carried out only to a limited extent. With the aim of indicating the most useful liquidity measure on the Polish stock market, an empirical study on the sample of companies listed on the WSE was carried out. The results of the study indicate that the best proxy for liquidity in asset pricing studies is the measure developed by Fong et al. [12], which is a simplification of the zero-return-days measure developed by Lesmond et al. [20]. In addition, two modifications of Amihud's [2] illiquidity measure are presented as the second and third best-performing ones in asset pricing studies on the WSE.

The rest of this paper is organised as follows. The following section describes the methodological design of the study carried out. Section 3.3 is devoted to the presentation of the empirical results of the study. The final section contains the summary and concluding remarks.

3.2 Design of the Empirical Study

When assessing the usefulness of a measure for measuring the liquidity in a given market, one should pay attention to several important issues. Primarily, it should be assessed if a given measure can be applied for measuring liquidity in this market (applicability); so whether it fits to the organisation of the trade in this market (i.e. whether the assumptions made while constructing the measure are fulfilled), whether the required data is available and how complicated and time-consuming the calculations are. The two latter issues are important mainly from the investors' point of view; in academic research, they have much less importance. The assessment of selected liquidity measures in terms of their applicability on the Warsaw Stock Exchange is presented in the paper of Stereńczak [28].

Next, one should decide whether each given indicator reflects the level of liquidity accurately (the veracity of the measurement), i.e. that it orders the stocks according to their liquidity in line with the reality, and also has minimal error in estimating the real liquidity cost. The former criterion is important mainly in asset pricing research, as in these studies it is important to order stock according to the decreasing or increasing level of liquidity. In turn, the measures characterised by low estimation errors are more useful in research on market efficiency, as in this type of analysis, one should obtain properly calibrated measures of transaction costs [18].

The accuracy of the measurement was assessed using several criteria, which were commonly used in other studies in this field. For the measure to be considered the best measure of liquidity, it had to be characterised by:

(1) the highest average cross-sectional correlation with the benchmark of liquidity,
(2) the highest average Spearman rank cross-sectional correlation with the benchmark of liquidity,
(3) the highest average time-series correlation with the benchmark of liquidity (at single stock level),
(4) the highest time-series correlation with the benchmark of liquidity (at the level of a portfolio containing all stocks),
(5) the highest time-series correlation of first differences with the benchmark of liquidity (at the level of a portfolio containing all stocks),
(6) the highest pooled cross-sectional time-series correlation with the benchmark of liquidity,
(7) the lowest average value of the root-mean-squared error (RMSE hereafter),
(8) the lowest value of the average mean error.

In this paper, to compare low-frequency liquidity measures in terms of the accuracy of measurement, 14 liquidity proxies were chosen and four ultra-high-frequency measures constitute liquidity benchmarks. The selection of liquidity measures was based primarily on the frequency of their use in the research on liquidity in other stock markets. In addition, some of the measures were chosen because of their good applicability on the Polish stock market [28]. A few proxies used in the study are modifications of existing ones, aiming to fit better to the organisation of trading on the Polish stock exchange. In turn, high-frequency measures, serving as a benchmarks of liquidity, were selected based on other studies on the accuracy of liquidity level measurement by various liquidity proxies (among others [6, 12, 18]).

3.2.1 High-Frequency Liquidity Benchmarks

High-frequency liquidity measures are considered as benchmarks of liquidity due to the fact that they measure liquidity *ex ante* and liquidity measured in such a way is useful in investors' decision-making. The first of such measures used in the study is the relative bid-ask spread computed using the following formula:

$$s_t = \frac{p_t^A - p_t^B}{p_t^M} \tag{3.1}$$

where p^A, p^B and p^M reflect, respectively, the best ask price, the best bid price and the midquote, which is the average of the best bid and the best ask prices.

The values of the bid-ask spread were computed for each transaction. If the value of the spread was nonpositive (equal to zero or negative), it was set as missing. A nonpositive value of the spread indicates that the best ask price is lower than or equal to the best bid price, which indicates that the transaction should occur. The monthly bid-ask spread was calculated as the average of the spread for each transaction in a given month. On the Warsaw Stock Exchange, bid-ask spread calculated in this way reflects the level of price concession that the investor should make in order to execute a trade of a volume not exceeding the volume of the best bid or ask order.

In the study, as a liquidity benchmark, the effective spread was also used. It is computed using the following formula:

$$s_t^{\text{eff}} = \frac{\left|p_t - p_t^M\right|}{p_t^M} \tag{3.2}$$

where p is the transaction price.

The values of the effective spread were computed for each transaction and then averaged monthly. Two different averages were used: simple average and the volume-weighted average. The former version will be marked as s^{eff}, and the latter one as $s^{\text{eff,V}}$.

The aforementioned high-frequency liquidity measures allow us to measure the level of price concession that the investor willing to trade has to accept. The values of the bid-ask spread or effective spread, computed using Formulae (3.1) and (3.2), inform us of the costs incurred by the investor, regardless of the transaction volume. The transaction volume has an effect on the liquidity cost; therefore, a measure taking into account the transaction volume was proposed. This measure is given by the following formula:

$$PI_t = \frac{s_t^{\text{eff}}}{Vol_t} \tag{3.3}$$

The measure described by Eq. (3.3) was calculated for each transaction, while its monthly value was calculated as an arithmetic average.

3.2.2 Low-Frequency Liquidity Proxies

The first of low-frequency liquidity measures analysed is the Amihud's [2] illiquidity measure, which seems to be the most frequently applied liquidity measure in studies on the relationship between liquidity and stock returns. This measure is given by the following formula [2]:

$$\text{ILLIQ}_{im} = \frac{1}{D_{im}} \sum_{t=1}^{D_{im}} \frac{|r_{imt}|}{\text{Vol}_{imt}} \tag{3.4}$$

where D_{im} denotes the number of days with available data for stock i in month m, r is the stock return, and *Vol* denotes the respective dollar volume denominated in thousands of PLN. To include the stock in the sample, it was required that the data needed to compute the Amihud measure would be available for at least 15 days of each month of the study period.

Due to various weaknesses of the above measure, pointed out among others by Tobek [30], some modifications were introduced. These modifications consist of changing the numerator and/or the denominator, or changing the frequency of its calculation. The first proposed modification subtracts the market return from the stock return in the numerator of the measure:

$$\text{ILLIQ}^{E}_{im} = \frac{1}{D_{im}} \sum_{t=1}^{D_{im}} \frac{|r_{imt} - r_{Mmt}|}{\text{Vol}_{imt}} \tag{3.5}$$

where r_M denotes the market return, approximated by the daily percentage change in the value of the Warsaw Stock Index WIG. Such treatment allows us to eliminate stock price changes resulting from general market movements and eliminates zero estimates for less liquid stocks. It is expected that values of ILLIQ^{E} will be higher than values of ILLIQ for less liquid stocks and lower than values of ILLIQ for more liquid ones.

Another modification is aimed at eliminating the underestimation of the short-term pressure of demand or supply on stock prices, which disappears before the end of trading day and is not reflected in the daily rate of return. Such modification consists in replacing the rate of return in Eq. (3.4) with the log of a daily price range:

$$\text{ILLIQ}^{R}_{im} = \frac{1}{D_{im}} \sum_{t=1}^{D_{im}} \frac{\left|\ln\left(p^{H}_{imt} / p^{L}_{imt}\right)\right|}{Vol_{imt}} \tag{3.6}$$

where p^H and p^L denote, respectively, the highest and the lowest stock price observed in day t.

The next two modifications were made in order to take into account the specifics of the schedule and the organisation of the trading session. On the WSE, after closing call, there is additional phase of trading, namely “trading at last”, during which transactions are executed at a fixed price, regardless of the volume of these transactions. So that the measure should consist of adequate components, the trading volume in the denominator should be lowered by the trading volume from the “trading at last” phase of a session. Next, the rate of return in the numerator was decreased by the market return. These two modifications are given by the following formulae:

$$\mathrm{ILLIQ}_{im}^{D} = \frac{1}{D_{im}} \sum_{t=1}^{D_{im}} \frac{|r_{imt}|}{\mathrm{Vol}_{imt} - \mathrm{Vol}_{imt}^{D}} \tag{3.7}$$

$$\mathrm{ILLIQ}_{im}^{ED} = \frac{1}{D_{im}} \sum_{t=1}^{D_{im}} \frac{|r_{imt} - r_{Mmt}|}{\mathrm{Vol}_{imt} - \mathrm{Vol}_{imt}^{D}} \tag{3.8}$$

where Vol^D denotes the trading volume from the "trading at last" phase of a session.

The last proposed modification of Amihud's illiquidity measure concerns the frequency of measurement. Instead of a daily basis, the measurement was made at one-minute intervals. This measure was averaged for the whole month and does not include the "trading at last" phase. Hereafter, it will be marked as $\mathrm{ILLIQ}^{\mathrm{I}}$.

Pástor and Stambaugh [24] developed another liquidity measure—γ. It is supposed to measure the price impact of trading volume, similarly as Amihud's [2] illiquidity measure. However, it is estimated using the following OLS regression [24]:

$$r_{i,d+1,m}^{e} = \theta_{im} + \phi_{im} r_{idm} + \gamma_{im} sign\left(r_{idm}^{e}\right) \mathrm{Vol}_{idm} + \varepsilon_{i,d+1,m} \tag{3.9}$$

Apart from the price impact measures, the study also analysed measures of transaction costs belonging to the group of measures based on the rates of return, price range or zero-return days. Roll's estimator is given by the formula [27]:

$$s_{\mathrm{Roll}} = 2\sqrt{-\mathrm{cov}(\Delta p_t; \Delta p_{t-1})} \tag{3.10}$$

Computing Roll's estimator for each of the 132 months of the study period for each of the companies included in the sample was not possible due to the existing positive values of the autocovariance of the rates of return. Existence of the positive autocovariances makes it impossible to compute the square root in Eq. (3.10), because its value does not belong to a set of real numbers, but to a set of complex numbers. Therefore, in order to eliminate this inconvenience, one author's modification and two modifications existing in the literature were applied. Each of these modifications is a departure from the original Roll's model; therefore, each will be examined in terms of accuracy of measurement on the Warsaw Stock Exchange.

First of the modifications, introduced by Goyenko et al. [18], is about replacing the positive autocovariances of returns with zeros. In such a situation, if a positive autocovariance of returns exists, it is assumed that transaction costs are equal to zero. Formally, this modification is calculated as follows [18]:

$$\mathrm{Roll}^{0} = \left\{ \begin{array}{ll} 2\sqrt{-\mathrm{cov}(\Delta p_t; \Delta p_{t-1})}, & \text{if } \mathrm{cov}(\Delta p_t; \Delta p_{t-1}) < 0 \\ 0, & \text{if } \mathrm{cov}(\Delta p_t; \Delta p_{t-1}) \geq 0 \end{array} \right\} \tag{3.11}$$

Another modification aimed to eliminate the inconveniences related to positive autocovariances of returns and omitting the necessity of extracting the square root from a negative number consists of replacing the value opposite to the autocovariance with its absolute value, i.e.

$$\mathrm{Roll}^{\mathrm{Abs}} = 2\sqrt{|\mathrm{cov}(\Delta p_t; \Delta p_{t-1})|} \tag{3.12}$$

A similar solution was introduced by Olbryś [23]. It consists in multiplying the expression on the right side of Eq. (3.12) by the inverse of the sign of the autocovariance of returns. Such a solution has quite a serious disadvantage; namely, if positive autocovariances of returns appear in some periods, it is assumed that the effective spread was negative in these periods. As a rule, spread should not take values less than zero. A modification introduced by Olbryś can therefore be used to approximate the level of liquidity, but not to estimate the transaction costs as a part of liquidity costs. This modification is given by the formula [23]:

$$\mathrm{Roll}^{\mathrm{Olb}} = -2\,\mathrm{sgn}\left[\mathrm{cov}(\Delta p_t; \Delta p_{t-1})\right]\sqrt{|\mathrm{cov}(\Delta p_t; \Delta p_{t-1})|} \tag{3.13}$$

As the only measure based on the price range, the spread estimator of Corwin and Schultz [11] was analysed. It is given by the formula:

$$HL = \frac{2(\mathrm{e}^{\alpha} - 1)}{1 + \mathrm{e}^{\alpha}} \tag{3.14}$$

where

$$\alpha = \frac{\sqrt{2\beta} - \sqrt{\beta}}{3 - 2\sqrt{2}} - \sqrt{\frac{\gamma}{3 - 2\sqrt{2}}}$$
$$\beta = \sum_{j=0}^{1}\left[\ln\left(\frac{p^H_{t+j}}{p^L_{t+j}}\right)\right]^2$$
$$\gamma = \left[\ln\left(\frac{p^H_{t,t+1}}{p^L_{t,t+1}}\right)\right]^2 \tag{3.15}$$

For each day in a given month, the values of α, β, γ and the expression HL in line with Eqs. (3.14) and (3.15) were calculated. Next, regarding the authors' guidelines, negative values of the expression HL were replaced with zeros [11]. It allows us to eliminate the possibility of obtaining negative values of the effective spread, which is calculated as the average value of HLs in a given month.

Another analysed measure is included in the group of measures based on zero-return days. It is based on the limited dependent variable (LDV) model of the relationship between the observed (r) and "true" (r^*) rate of return. The parameters of the model are estimated with the maximum likelihood method, and the log of likelihood function has the following form [20]:

$$\sum_{t\in U_1}\left\{-\frac{1}{2}\ln(2\pi\sigma^2)-\frac{1}{2\sigma^2}(r_t+\alpha_1-\beta r_{mt})^2\right\}+$$
$$+\sum_{t\in U_2}\left\{-\frac{1}{2}\ln(2\pi\sigma^2)-\frac{1}{2\sigma^2}(r_t+\alpha_2-\beta r_{mt})^2\right\}+$$
$$+\sum_{t\in U_0}\ln\left(\phi\left(\frac{\alpha_2-\beta r_{mt}}{\sigma}\right)-\phi\left(\frac{\alpha_1-\beta r_{mt}}{\sigma}\right)\right)\to \max \quad (3.17)$$

where α_{1j} and α_{2j} denote the thresholds for transactions on negative and positive information, respectively.

Spread is then calculated in the following way [20]:

$$\text{LOT}=\alpha_2-\alpha_1 \quad (3.18)$$

In their paper, Lesmond et al. [20] assumed that U_0 are the days in which the stock return was equal to zero ($r_t=0$); the first region (U_1) are days with negative market return and nonzero stock return ($r_t\neq 0$, $r_{mt}<0$); the last region (U_2) are days with a positive market return and nonzero stock return ($r_t\neq 0$, $r_{mt}>0$). Goyenko et al. [18] proposed a slightly different division: region U_0 are days with the stock return equal to zero ($r_t=0$); region U_1 are days with negative ($r_t<0$), and region U_2— with positive ($r_t>0$) stock return. According to Zhao and Wang [31], the method proposed by Lesmond et al. generates large biases that cannot be eliminated even by enlarging the research sample, which indicates the inconsistency of this estimator. In turn, the Goyenko et al. method is more effective and econometrically correct [31]. In order to indicate the best low-frequency liquidity proxy for the Polish stock exchange, both versions of LOT estimator were analysed in the study. The original one will be hereafter denoted as LOT-M, and the version of Goyenko et al. [18] will be denoted as LOT-Y.

Based on the same assumptions as the LOT estimator, but less computationally demanding is the measure introduced by Fong et al. [12]. It does not require the maximisation of the likelihood function, but it uses the cumulative distribution of a standardised normal distribution. This measure is given by the formula [12]:

$$\text{FHT}_m=2\sigma_m\phi^{-1}\left[\frac{1+\text{Zero}_m}{2}\right] \quad (3.19)$$

where $Zero_m$ denotes the proportion of zero-return days in the month m, σ is the standard deviation of daily stock returns, and $\Phi(\cdot)$ is the cumulative distribution of standardised normal distribution.

3.2.3 Data

To calculate all liquidity measures, both data on order flow and daily and intra-daily data on transactions were needed. Data on order flow was delivered by the Warsaw Stock Exchange and covered the period from 1 January 2006 to 31 December 2016. The database contains information on five best bid and five best ask orders before each transaction. In addition, it contains data on transaction volume, price and time. Data on order flow was used to compute ultra-high-frequency liquidity benchmarks. Data on transactions with a one-minute frequency is from the bossa.pl service. They were used to obtain trading volume from the "trading at last" phase and the intra-daily version of Amihud's illiquidity measure. Thus, intra-daily quotations were useful to compute $ILLIQ^D$, $ILLIQ^{ED}$ and $ILLIQ^I$, which are the modifications of Amihud's measure.

Daily quotations, needed to calculate the remaining part of low-frequency liquidity proxies, originate from the GPWInfoStrefa service. Quotations were corrected by corporate actions, i.e. dividend payouts, subscription rights issuances, splits and reverse splits. This required the creation of a database of these actions, which was created by the author on the basis of the information contained in companies' card, WSE annals, the WSE session archives, Official Quotations of Warsaw Stock Exchange (Cedula GPW) and GPWInfoStrefa service. The calculations were mainly carried out with the use of a spreadsheet together with the use of Visual Basic for Applications, while R programming was used to compute LOT measures. Operationalisation of the data on order flow required the use of the filtrating programme.

3.3 Empirical Results

3.3.1 Coherence of Liquidity Proxies with Liquidity Benchmarks

The coherence of liquidity proxies with liquidity benchmarks is assessed based on the six measures of correlation. Tables 3.1, 3.2, 3.3, 3.4, 3.5 and 3.6 show the values of the correlations of low-frequency liquidity proxies with high-frequency liquidity benchmarks. The highest correlations are highlighted in bold. The presented values are averaged for the whole period. The highest average cross-sectional correlation with bid-ask spread, effective spread and volume-weighted effective spread has the FHT measure. The LOT measures are characterised by slightly lower correlation, both in the original version (LOT-M) and in the modified one (LOT-Y). Aforementioned measures are also well correlated with the PI measure, which reflects the cost-per-dollar-volume. However, the intra-daily version of Amihud measure ($ILLIQ^I$) is best correlated with the PI measure.

It is worth noting that the correlations of ILLIQ and HL measures with volume-weighted effective spread are similar to those presented by Będowska-Sójka [6]. In

Table 3.1 Average cross-sectional correlation of liquidity proxies with liquidity benchmarks

Measure	s	s^{eff}	$s^{\text{eff,V}}$	PI
ILLIQ	0.4397	0.4047	0.3757	0.2782
ILLIQ^{E}	0.4311	0.3946	0.3637	0.2711
ILLIQ^{R}	0.5374	0.4984	0.4582	0.4092
ILLIQ^{D}	0.4021	0.3668	0.3383	0.2373
ILLIQ^{ED}	0.3607	0.3290	0.3010	0.2121
ILLIQ^{I}	0.4547	0.4405	0.4121	**0.7227**
P-S	0.4840	0.4625	0.4334	0.3605
Roll^{0}	0.4451	0.4426	0.4289	0.3708
Roll^{Abs}	0.3902	0.3878	0.3848	0.3324
Roll^{Olb}	0.3803	0.3618	0.3487	0.3013
HL	0.3198	0.3228	0.3100	0.3928
LOT-M	0.5720	0.5505	0.5369	0.4496
LOT-Y	0.5812	0.5526	0.5344	0.4697
FHT	**0.6102**	**0.5823**	**0.5639**	0.4838

Table 3.2 Average cross-sectional Spearman rank correlation of liquidity proxies with liquidity benchmarks

Measure	s	s^{eff}	$s^{\text{eff,V}}$	PI
ILLIQ	0.8806	0.8706	0.8153	0.7296
ILLIQ^{E}	0.8797	0.8674	0.8119	0.7198
ILLIQ^{R}	**0.8937**	**0.8858**	**0.8303**	0.7788
ILLIQ^{D}	0.8758	0.8642	0.8084	0.7169
ILLIQ^{ED}	0.8727	0.8593	0.8031	0.7053
ILLIQ^{I}	0.7509	0.7574	0.7203	**0.9430**
P-S	0.6928	0.7014	0.6865	0.7099
Roll^{0}	−0.0300	−0.0163	−0.0093	0.0103
Roll^{Abs}	0.2140	0.2290	0.2307	0.2467
Roll^{Olb}	0.2343	0.2305	0.2140	0.2001
HL	0.1872	0.2118	0.2149	0.3520
LOT-M	0.5132	0.5163	0.5072	0.5188
LOT-Y	0.5077	0.5010	0.4860	0.4911
FHT	0.5318	0.5256	0.5076	0.5219

Table 3.3 Average time-series correlation of liquidity proxies with liquidity benchmarks (single stock level)

Measure	s	s^{eff}	$s^{eff,V}$	PI
ILLIQ	0.4073	0.3486	0.2943	0.3802
ILLIQ^E	0.4121	0.3519	0.3068	0.3969
ILLIQ^R	0.4695	0.3984	0.3539	0.4581
ILLIQ^D	0.3457	0.2911	0.2563	0.3139
ILLIQ^{ED}	0.2946	0.2497	0.2330	0.2539
ILLIQ^I	**0.5606**	**0.4692**	**0.3749**	**0.6370**
P-S	0.3353	0.2940	0.2659	0.3297
Roll^0	0.2545	0.2411	0.1977	0.1479
Roll^{Abs}	0.2109	0.1989	0.1773	0.1006
Roll^{Olb}	0.1470	0.1367	0.1147	0.1280
HL	0.2202	0.2046	0.1766	0.1151
LOT-M	0.3294	0.2906	0.2791	0.1903
L1OT-Y	0.3657	0.3090	0.2883	0.2365
FHT	0.4087	0.3471	0.3264	0.2609

Table 3.4 Time-series correlation of liquidity proxies with liquidity benchmarks (portfolio level)

Measure	s	s^{eff}	$s^{eff,V}$	PI
ILLIQ	0.6948	0.4948	0.6725	0.4484
ILLIQ^E	0.7083	0.4989	0.6847	0.3931
ILLIQ^R	0.7013	0.4882	0.6726	0.4501
ILLIQ^D	0.7197	0.5211	0.7087	0.3424
ILLIQ^{ED}	0.4020	0.2836	0.4017	0.1108
ILLIQ^I	0.8434	0.6216	0.8090	0.2943
P-S	0.6228	0.4761	0.6202	0.4569
Roll^0	0.6562	0.4725	0.6143	0.3994
Roll^{Abs}	0.4114	0.3119	0.3912	0.1813
Roll^{Olb}	0.4754	0.3511	0.4449	0.3630
HL	0.1822	0.1345	0.1689	−0.1281
LOT-M	0.3838	0.2812	0.3617	0.1815
LOT-Y	0.8279	0.5696	0.8051	**0.6353**
FHT	**0.9373**	**0.6348**	**0.9016**	0.6121

Table 3.5 Time-series correlation of first differences liquidity proxies with liquidity benchmarks (portfolio level)

Measure	s	s^{eff}	$s^{\text{eff,V}}$	PI
ILLIQ	0.1971	0.0098	0.1215	0.2468
ILLIQ^{E}	0.2174	0.0085	0.1060	**0.2780**
ILLIQ^{R}	0.2143	0.0438	0.1297	0.2036
ILLIQ^{D}	0.2699	0.0295	0.1815	0.2142
ILLIQ^{ED}	0.1849	0.0114	0.1094	0.0937
ILLIQ^{I}	0.4525	0.0445	0.3269	0.1659
P-S	0.1578	0.1014	0.1758	0.2371
Roll^{0}	0.4444	0.1623	0.4133	0.1500
Roll^{Abs}	**0.5283**	**0.1951**	**0.5273**	0.0824
Roll^{Olb}	−0.0887	0.0181	−0.1279	0.0886
HL	0.4678	0.0653	0.4685	−0.0404
LOT-M	−0.0602	0.0018	−0.0376	−0.0980
LOT-Y	0.1265	−0.0230	0.0699	0.1180
FHT	0.4798	−0.0042	0.3508	0.2225

Table 3.6 Pooled cross-sectional time-series correlation of liquidity proxies with liquidity benchmarks

Measure	s	s^{eff}	$s^{\text{eff,V}}$	PI
ILLIQ	0.4474	0.2345	0.3928	0.3699
ILLIQ^{E}	0.4435	0.2325	0.3906	0.3518
ILLIQ^{R}	0.4430	0.2287	0.3886	0.4882
ILLIQ^{D}	0.3563	0.1865	0.3161	0.2306
ILLIQ^{ED}	0.1078	0.0577	0.0955	0.0670
ILLIQ^{I}	0.4510	0.2388	0.4111	0.2729
P-S	0.4301	0.2264	0.3903	0.3108
Roll^{0}	0.8248	0.4357	0.7835	0.4736
Roll^{Abs}	0.7498	0.4034	0.7019	0.4225
Roll^{Olb}	0.6222	0.3378	0.5775	0.3197
HL	0.4392	0.2394	0.4311	0.1772
LOT-M	0.3909	0.2134	0.3632	0.1568
LOT-Y	0.8174	0.4410	0.7501	0.5260
FHT	**0.9367**	**0.5058**	**0.8717**	**0.5711**

her sample, Amihud's ILLIQ was correlated with spread at 0.3523 (0.3757 in this study), and the Corwin and Schultz estimator (HL) was correlated with spread at 0.3378 (0.3100 in the present study). However, the correlations for the two other measures differ quite significantly from each other. Roll's estimator (marked here as $Roll^0$) in Będowska-Sójka's [6] study was correlated with volume-weighted effective spread at 0.1279, and the LOT measure (the original version, i.e. LOT-M) was correlated at 0.2739. Corresponding correlations in the present study are equal to 0.4289 and 0.5369. Discrepancies are probably the result of differences in the research sample.

The analysis of cross-sectional correlation of liquidity measures is complemented by the cross-sectional Spearman rank correlation. The highest rank correlation with the measures of spread in the whole study period has $ILLIQ^R$ measure. Slightly lower values of the coefficients have the other versions of Amihud's measure, except for $ILLIQ^I$. The latter one is in turn best correlated with the PI measure, similar to the case of Pearson correlation.

Taking into account correlation over time, the $ILLIQ^I$ measure is most strongly linked with the high-frequency liquidity measures at the level of a single stock. Subsequently, these measures are $ILLIQ^R$, $ILLIQ^E$, FHT, ILLIQ and LOT-Y. Also the remaining versions of Amihud's measure are characterised by high time-series correlation with liquidity benchmarks.

At the portfolio level, in which liquidity was calculated as a simple average of liquidity of all stock; the best correlated with spread measures turns out to be the FHT measure. The correlations of $ILLIQ^I$ and LOT-Y, as well as the other versions of Amihud's measure, are slightly weaker.

Changes in the liquidity of the portfolio are best reflected by $Roll^{Abs}$ and $ILLIQ^E$ measures. The former one reflects the changes in the spread measures well, while the latter one shows the changes in the level of the PI measure. The FHT measure also has the highest coefficients of pooled cross-sectional time-series correlation with three measures of the spread and the PI measure. Slightly lower values of these coefficients can be observed in the case of $Roll^0$ and LOT-Y measures.

3.3.2 Estimation Errors

Two measures of estimation errors are utilised in the study: namely, the root-mean-squared error of estimation and mean error of estimation. Estimation errors of liquidity measures are presented in Tables 3.7 and 3.8. The lowest values of the error are highlighted in bold. The root-mean-squared errors of estimation (RMSE) of a given measure should be analysed jointly with the values of mean errors of estimation. Working solely on the basis of the value of RMSE, one cannot discern if this is a result of a different order of magnitude than the benchmark, or if it is an effect of the inaccurate reflection of the level of liquidity. The lower the value of RMSE and the lower the absolute value of mean error, the better the liquidity proxy reflects the liquidity costs measured with high-frequency measures.

Table 3.7 Root-mean-squared errors of estimations

Measure	s	s^{eff}	$s^{eff,V}$	PI
ILLIQ	1.3027	2.1941	2.526	139.215
ILLIQ^E	1.4845	2.6643	2.8012	179.908
ILLIQ^R	1.1197	1.5563	1.6204	54.202
ILLIQ^D	1.7268	3.1990	3.3936	944.037
ILLIQ^{ED}	8.1118	16.6453	18.4906	6074.38
ILLIQ^I	13.0104	26.8263	29.0302	1008.02
P-S	0.9972	**0.9945**	**0.9944**	**2.4536**
Roll^0	2.7818	4.8853	5.0162	7849.58
Roll^{Abs}	3.9266	6.9200	7.0432	11,646.5
Roll^{Olb}	4.5317	7.5442	7.6663	11,646.9
HL	1.3237	2.3958	2.4281	4947.61
LOT-M	3.4049	6.6718	6.9283	8594.85
LOT-Y	1.4923	2.9064	3.1636	2514.15
FHT	**0.7773**	1.2854	1.3795	1822.95

Table 3.8 Mean errors of estimations

Measure	s	s^{eff}	$s^{eff,V}$	PI
ILLIQ	−0.7627	−0.4955	−0.4572	42.389
ILLIQ^E	−0.6645	0.2932	−0.2342	58.226
ILLIQ^R	−0.8613	−0.7082	−0.6854	25.246
ILLIQ^D	−0.6067	**−0.1741**	**−0.1084**	156.434
ILLIQ^{ED}	0.3830	1.8806	2.1583	802.12
ILLIQ^I	4.5892	10.2146	10.8545	850.37
P-S	−0.9972	−0.9943	−0.9941	**−0.0676**
Roll^0	0.5425	1.8041	1.8915	2443.7
Roll^{Abs}	1.8185	4.0733	4.1814	4515.8
Roll^{Olb}	−0.73334	−0.4650	−0.3984	371.52
HL	0.1942	1.1491	1.1905	1929.3
LOT-M	1.7578	4.1401	4.2955	3584.4
LOT-Y	**−0.0507**	0.8096	0.8901	985.04
FHT	−0.3429	0.2490	0.2998	739.31

According to both RMSE and the mean error of estimation, the best proxy for the PI measure is Pástor–Stambaugh's γ. The mean error of estimation is −0.0676, which means that the values of P-S measure are on average 6.76% lower than the corresponding values of PI measure. Pástor–Stambaugh's measure is also characterised by relatively low values of RMSE when reflecting the measures of a spread. However, taking into account the mean error of estimation, such value is due to the fact that it has a much smaller order of magnitude and gives estimates on average 99.5% lower than the values of the spread. Therefore, despite being characterised by the lowest RMSEs in the estimation of the effective spread and the volume-weighted effective spread, the P-S measure cannot be considered as a good reflection of the level of liquidity costs. In this case, when considering the RMSE, the best proxy for the spread measures (also the bid-ask spread) is the FHT measure.

Summarising the results of the study of the accuracy of the measurement of liquidity by low-frequency liquidity proxies, one may indicate a few proxies that are characterised by good correlation with benchmarks and low estimation errors. As the best ones, one should indicate the following measures: FHT, ILLIQ^{I}, ILLIQ^{R}, LOT-Y and P-S. The two latter proxies measure liquidity well mainly due to the low estimation errors.

3.3.3 Ranking of Liquidity Measures

When summarising the considerations regarding the usefulness of individual measures to proxy for liquidity on the Polish stock market, one should compare its applicability with the accuracy with which they measure liquidity. As mentioned, the applicability of selected liquidity measures is presented and assessed in the paper of Stereńczak [28]. Table 3.9 contains the comparison of low-frequency liquidity measures, which is basically a ranking of liquidity proxies. Similar ranking is done (among others) by Bleaney and Li [7]. Each measure was evaluated in terms of its applicability and accuracy of measurement. Within each criterion, 0–4 points were awarded. Points within the scope of the applicability of the measure have been granted to take care that the number of points awarded reflects the most objective assessment as possible. Measures correlated with the benchmark at less than 0.2 received 0 points; a correlation between 0.2 and 0.4 was awarded with 1 point; between 0.4 and 0.6—2 points; between 0.6 and 0.8—3 points; above 0.8—4 points. The measure which was the best in terms of estimation errors received 4 points, two more measures—3 points, measures in places 4 to 7—2 points, measures in places 8 to 12—1 point, and the rest—0 points.

Each criterion has an assigned weight, which reflects its importance in studies on asset pricing. According to Goyenko et al. [18], the most important ones are criteria related to the coherence with high-frequency benchmarks. Therefore, to each correlation criterion, a 10% weight was assigned. Thus, the criteria related to the correlation with liquidity benchmarks are jointly assigned with 60% weight. Both of the criteria referring to estimation errors were assigned weights of 5%, due to

Table 3.9 Comparison of the usefulness of low-frequency liquidity measures

Measure	Fitting to market	Data requirements	Computational efforts	Cross-sectional correlation	Cross-sectional rank correlation	Time-series correlation (single stock level)	Time-series correlation (portfolio level)	Time-series correlation of first differences	Pooled cross-sectional time-series correlation	RMSE	Mean error of estimation	SUM
ILLIQ	2	4	4	1.5	3.8	1.3	2.5	0.3	1.3	2.3	2	2.16
$ILLIQ^E$	3	3.5	3.5	1.3	3.8	1.3	2.3	0.5	1.3	2	2.5	2.23
$ILLIQ^R$	2.5	3.5	3.5	2	3.8	1.5	2.5	0.5	1.5	2.3	2	**2.29**
$ILLIQ^D$	2.5	2	3	1.3	3.8	1	2.3	0.5	0.75	1.3	3	1.89
$ILLIQ^{ED}$	3.5	2	3	1	3.8	1	1.3	0.5	0	0.3	1.3	1.70
$ILLIQ^I$	4	2	3	2.3	3.3	2	3	0.8	1.5	0.5	0.3	**2.26**
P-S	3	3	2	1.8	3	1	2.5	0.3	1.3	3.3	1.8	2.08
$Roll^0$	1	4	3.5	1.8	0	0.5	2.3	1	2.8	1	1	1.65
$Roll^{Abs}$	1	4	3.5	1	1	0.3	1	1	2.5	0	0	1.40
$Roll^{Olb}$	1	4	3	1	1	0	1.5	0	1.8	0	1.8	1.31
HL	4	3	3	1	0.8	0.5	0	1	1.3	1.8	1.5	1.66
LOT-M	3	3	1	2	2	0.8	0.8	0	0.8	0.8	0	1.46
LOT-Y	3	3	1	2	2	1	3.3	0	2.8	1	2.3	2.06
FHT	3	3	2.5	2.3	2	1.3	3.5	1	3	2.8	2.5	**2.44**

the fact that in the studies on the relationship between the level of liquidity and rates of return, the accuracy of estimating liquidity costs is of secondary importance. Another important criterion is also the fulfilment of the assumptions adopted in the construction of the measure, and hence the conformity to market organisation—this criterion is assigned a weight of 15%. The criterion related to the data requirements is assigned with a weight of 10%. This is not a very important criterion, but when constructing a set of weights, the liquidity measures for the needs of investors were also taken into account, albeit to a lesser extent. The smallest weight has been assigned to the criterion of computational efforts, due to the fact that this criterion is important primarily for investors and is less important in scientific research. The table shows the average number of points obtained when comparing each of the four benchmarks. In the last column, the average number of points awarded under all criteria is given, with specific weights. In the presented ranking, the largest number of points was granted to the FHT measure. The $ILLIQ^R$ measure was ranked second. The third place in the ranking taking into account the estimation errors was the intra-day version of Amihud's measure ($ILLIQ^I$).

3.4 Summary and Conclusions

This paper was aimed at indicating the most appropriate proxy for liquidity for the purposes of asset pricing studies on the Warsaw Stock Exchange. The measurement of liquidity is extremely important from the investors' point of view, as well as from the scientific researchers' perspective. Equally as important, measurement of liquidity is difficult, what results from its multidimensional and elusive nature. Using a set of eleven assessment criteria, fourteen liquidity proxies were assessed in terms of their usefulness in measuring liquidity on the Warsaw Stock Exchange. Each criterion was assigned with a specific weight, which was justified by the significance of this criterion in measuring liquidity for the purposes of asset pricing studies. The weights may seem arbitrary, as all interested parties (e.g. investors, researchers) are able to freely modify the presented set of weights such that it will correspond to the assessment of liquidity proxies for other purposes, e.g. studies on market efficiency.

In the presented empirical study, the measure developed by Fong et al. [12]—FHT—was indicated as the most useful in asset pricing studies on the Warsaw Stock Exchange. FHT measure reflects the average price concession that has to be made by an investor in order to trade immediately, regardless of the volume of the transaction. The next two best-performing measures are two modifications of Amihud's [2] illiquidity measure. These modifications are intended to improve the fit of the measure to the market and include: replacing the absolute value of return in the numerator of the measure with the absolute value of the log of the price range ($ILLIQ^R$), and computing the measure with intra-daily frequency ($ILLIQ^I$). The study has its own limitations, the largest of which is the arbitrariness of the weights. Nevertheless, 70% of the final assessment of each proxy for liquidity is a result of objective criteria, i.e. the accuracy of measurement.

Acknowledgements I am grateful for helpful comments from Jarosław Kubiak and Paweł Miłobędzki. The study was financed by the National Science Centre, Poland, as a research project (2017/27/N/HS4/00751).

References

1. Acharya, V.V., Pedersen, L.H.: Asset pricing with liquidity risk. J. Financ. Econ. **77**(2), 375–410 (2005). https://doi.org/10.1016/j.jfineco.2004.06.007
2. Amihud, Y.: Illiquidity and stock returns: cross-section and time-series effects. J. Financ. Markets **5**(1), 31–56 (2002). https://doi.org/10.1016/S1386-4181(01)00024-6
3. Amihud, Y., Hameed, A., Kang, W., et al.: The illiquidity premium: International evidence. J. Financ. Econ. **117**(2), 350–368 (2015). https://doi.org/10.1016/j.jfineco.2015.04.005
4. Amihud, Y., Mendelson, H.: Asset pricing and the bid-ask spread. J. Financ. Econ. **17**(2), 223–249 (1986). https://doi.org/10.1016/0304-405X(86)90065-6
5. Bekaert, G., Harvey, C.R., Lundblad, C.: Liquidity and stock returns: lessons from emerging markets. Rev. Financ. Stud. **20**(6), 1783–1831 (2007). https://doi.org/10.1093/rfs/hhm030
6. Będowska-Sójka B (2018) The coherence of liquidity measures: the evidence from the emerging market. Finance Research Letters, Article in press. https://doi.org/10.1016/j.frl.2018.02.014
7. Bleaney, M., Li, Z.: The performance of bid-ask spread estimators under less than ideal conditions. Stud. Econ. Financ. **32**(1), 98–127 (2015). https://doi.org/10.1108/SEF-04-2014-0075
8. Brennan, M.J., Chordia, T., Subrahmanyam, A.: Alternative factor specifications, security characteristics, and the cross-section of expected stock returns. J. Financ. Econ. **49**(3), 345–373 (1998). https://doi.org/10.1016/S0304-405X(98)00028-2
9. Choi, J.Y., Salandro, D., Shastri, K.: On the estimation of bid ask spreads: theory and evidence. J. Financ. Quant. Anal. **23**(2), 219–230 (1988). https://doi.org/10.2307/2330882
10. Chu, Q.C., Ding, D.K., Pyun, C.S.: Bid ask bounce and spreads in the foreign exchange futures market. Rev. Quant. Financ. Acc. **6**(1), 19–37 (1996). https://doi.org/10.1007/BF00290794
11. Corwin, S.A., Schultz, P.: A simple way to estimate bid-ask spread from daily high and low prices. J. Financ. **67**(2), 719–759 (2012). https://doi.org/10.1111/j.1540-6261.2012.01729.x
12. Fong, K.Y.L., Holden, C.W., Trzcinka, C.A.: What are the best liquidity proxies for global research? Rev. Financ. **21**(4), 1355–1401 (2017). https://doi.org/10.1093/rof/rfx003
13. Gao, Y., Wang, M.: A new effective spread estimator based on price range. Available at SSRN https://ssrn.com/abstract=2895360 (2017). Accessed 13 Feb 2017
14. Gârleanu, N.: Portfolio choice and pricing in illiquid markets. J. Econ. Theory **144**(2), 532–564 (2009). https://doi.org/10.1016/j.jet.2008.07.006
15. Gârleanu, N., Pedersen, L.H.: Dynamic trading with predictable returns and transaction costs. J. Financ. **68**(6), 2309–2340 (2013). https://doi.org/10.1111/jofi.12080
16. Garsztka, P.: Konstrukcja portfela papierów wartościowych z uwzględnieniem płynności walorów. Zesz. Nauk. Uniw. Ekonomicznego w Poznaniu **242**, 56–68 (2012)
17. Gonzalez, A., Rubio, G.: Portfolio choice and the effects of illiquidity. SERIEs **2**(1), 53–74 (2007). https://doi.org/10.1007/s13209-010-0025-4
18. Goyenko, R.Y., Holden, C.W., Trzcinka, C.A.: Do liquidity measures measure liquidity? J. Financ. Econ. **92**(2), 153–181 (2009). https://doi.org/10.1016/j.jfineco.2008.06.002
19. Hasbrouck, J.: Trading costs and returns for US equities: estimating effective costs from daily data. J. Financ. **64**(3), 1445–1477 (2009). https://doi.org/10.1111/j.1540-6261.2009.01469.x
20. Lesmond, D.A., Ogden, J.P., Trzcinka, C.A.: A new estimate of transaction costs. Rev. Financ. Stud. **12**(5), 1113–1141 (1999). https://doi.org/10.1093/rfs/12.5.1113
21. Longstaff, F.A.: Optimal portfolio choice and the valuation of illiquid securities. Rev. Financ. Stud. **14**(2), 407–431 (2001). https://doi.org/10.1093/rfs/14.2.407
22. Nyborg, K.G., Östberg, P.: Money and liquidity in financial markets. J. Financ. Markets **112**(1), 30–52 (2014). https://doi.org/10.1016/j.jfineco.2013.12.003

23. Olbryś, J.: Wycena aktywów kapitałowych na rynku z zakłóceniami w procesach transakcyjnych. Difin, Warsaw (2014)
24. Pástor, L., Stambaugh, R.F.: Liquidity risk and expected stock returns. J. Polit. Econ. **111**(3), 642–685 (2003). https://doi.org/10.1086/374184
25. Pereira, J.P., Zhang, H.H.: Stock returns and the volatility of liquidity. J. Financ. Quant. Anal. **45**(4), 1077–1110 (2010). https://doi.org/10.1017/S0022109010000323
26. Porcenaluk, P.: Zastosowanie kowariancji do szacowania spreadu bid-ask dla akcji notowanych na GPW w Warszawie. Zeszyty Naukowe Uniwersytetu Szczecińskiego. Finanse Rynki Finansowe Ubezpieczenia **75**, 403–410 (2015). https://doi.org/10.18276/frfu.2015.75-33
27. Roll, R.: A simple implicit measure of the effective bid-ask spread in an efficient market. J. Financ. **39**(4), 1127–1139 (1984). https://doi.org/10.1111/j.1540-6261.1984.tb03897.x
28. Stereńczak, S.: Przydatność wybranych miar płynności akcji na Giełdzie Papierów Wartościowych w Warszawie. Finanse Rynki Finansowe Ubezpieczenia **89**(2), 207–218 (2017). https://doi.org/10.18276/frfu.2017.89/2-15
29. Thompson, S.R., Waller, M.L.: The execution cost of trading in commodity futures markets. Food Res. Inst. Stud. **20**(2), 141–163 (1987)
30. Tobek, O.: Liquidity proxies based on trading volume. Available at SSRN https://ssrn.com/abstract=2736584 (2016). Accessed 28 Jan 2017
31. Zhao, W., Wang, M.: On the computation of LOT liquidity measure. Econ. Lett. **136**, 76–80 (2015). https://doi.org/10.1016/j.econlet.2015.08.030

Chapter 4
International Capital Markets and the Global Real Economy

Adam Szyszka

Abstract This text focuses on two aspects of the relations between the financial sector and the global real economy. First, it discusses the impact of quantitative easing programs (QE) on the situation on global capital markets. The efficiency of such programs as tools to stimulate economic growth is analyzed and compared across different countries. The author puts forward a hypothesis that the efficiency of QE depends on the capital market model in a given country and the different channels of transferring capital between the financial sector and the real economy. The second aspect of the relations between capital markets and the economy discussed in this article is the problem of market efficiency. The thesis advanced here is that capital market inefficiency not only leads to wrong asset pricing and wealth transfer between investors, but also contributes to the wrong allocation of resources and underinvestment or overinvestment in given real sectors, bringing about significant losses for the entire economy.

Keywords Quantitative easing (QE) · Capital market models · Capital market efficiency · Asset pricing

4.1 Introduction

There are different opinions in the literature about the relationship between financial markets and the real economy. The former are considered as both ancillary and superior to the real sphere. Some researchers also admit that there are mutual relations between the two. Moreover, it is often mentioned that the mutual influence of both spheres is changing and, specifically, that the financial sector tends to become more and more autonomous of the real economy.

This text focuses on two aspects of the relations between the real economy and the financial sector. First, it shows the impact of quantitative easing programs on

A. Szyszka (✉)
SGH Warsaw School of Economics, Warsaw, Poland
e-mail: aszysz1@sgh.waw.pl

W. Tarczyński and K. Nermend (eds.), *Effective Investments on Capital Markets*, Springer Proceedings in Business and Economics,
https://doi.org/10.1007/978-3-030-21274-2_4

the situation on global capital markets and analyzes the efficiency of such programs as tools to stimulate economic growth in different countries. The author claims that quantitative easing programs implemented by central banks by means of asset purchasing contributed to a significant drop in bond profitability and a spectacular boom on global stock exchanges over the last decade. However, how efficient such programs are in achieving economic objectives differs across countries, which may be related, among others, to the differences in financial market models and the different channels of transferring capital between the financial sector and the real economy.

The other aspect of the relations between capital markets and the economy discussed in this article is the problem of market efficiency. The thesis advanced here is that inefficiency of financial markets not only leads to wrong asset pricing and wealth transfer between investors, but also contributes to the wrong allocation of resources as well as underinvestment or overinvestment in individual sectors, bringing about significant losses for the entire economy. The debate over the importance of capital market efficiency broke out with a particular force in the context of the 2008 turmoil and the ensuing problems in the real sphere of the global economy.

The structure of this article reflects its planned scope and advanced theses. The text is divided into two basic parts. The first comprises three sections discussing, first, the separate nature of the financial sector and the real economy, second, the impact of financial sector support schemes and quantitative easing programs on the market situation as well as the consequences of these programs for economic growth, and finally, the differences in the way quantitative easing programs impact the economy depending on the capital market model prevailing in a given country. These reflections expand on the first of the advanced theses.

The other part contains two sections that focus on the different aspects of market efficiency and the relationship between the efficiency of capital markets and of the economy. The main conclusion of this part is that capital market inefficiency leads to a waste of resources in the real sphere. This confirms the second thesis.

The text ends with a conclusion that summarizes all its main findings and identifies the importance of the reflections for potential further studies as well as political and economic practice.

4.2 Separate Nature of the Financial and the Real Spheres of the Economy

It is commonly acknowledged that the economy operates in two fundamental dimensions. The first of these is the real sphere which encompasses everything that relates to material and physical processes of goods production or service provision. The other dimension is the financial (monetary) sphere. Initially, its role was to assist the real economy and was supposed to be limited primarily to financial matters and settlements: money is used to enter into contracts between good producers and their customers, entrepreneurs need sources of financing, households need consumer loans or mortgages, exporters and importers have to exchange currencies, and many entities must make savings. While the real economy produces physical goods or provides services, the only result generated by the financial sphere is cash flows.

The traditional view is that the source of wealth for societies is the real sphere as it is there that goods are produced and services provided as the genuinely new value. Inventing more and more sophisticated instruments as well as repacking and reselling financial assets only create the appearance of wealth and can at most enrich individual financial market players at the expense of others. The financial sphere is not the place where new value is created in the economy. The only outcome of financial transfers is to reallocate the value created in the real sphere. These fundamental truths are often forgotten by the financial markets.

Over at least two last decades, there have been important changes in the mutual relations between the real and the financial (monetary) spheres. The financial sphere stopped playing a role that was only ancillary to the real economy, becoming more and more independent and detached from it. Traditional transactions involving money and goods were dominated by money–money transactions. Not only did the value of trade in financial instruments skyrocket, but there were also new categories of financial assets that were being created on an unprecedented scale. These became more and more complicated and disconnected from the original sources of cash flow creation so that it was increasingly difficult to identify the true risk factors that determined their value. All these issues came dramatically to the fore during the financial crisis of 2008, a painful lesson of how transient and illusory the value of created financial instruments can get.

For the first time in history, the 2008 turbulences in financial markets were caused directly by the financial factors. Previous financial crises have always taken place in the wake of different shocks that originated in the real economy. This time, it was the monetary–financial sphere that experienced problems first, the entire global economy suffering the consequences as a result.

The chaos in the financial sphere forced state governments and watchdogs of international economic order to take action. Contrary to what some populist critics claim, the aid provided to financial institutions was not motivated by any particular preferences or strong lobbying from financial actors. It was primarily driven by concerns that, once it becomes impossible to use transfers uninterruptedly and capital is no longer available, the real economy will go into a long-term and deep tailspin.

4.3 Support for the Financial Sector and Quantitative Easing Programs

The cost of keeping the global financial system stable through a recapitalization of financial institutions and offering state guarantees proved to be huge—the International Monetary Fund estimated that, at the turn of 2009, such costs in the G20 countries amounted to the equivalent of 5.3% of their GDP figures from 2008. This average is made up of over 6% of the GDP in the USA and about 20% of the GDP in the UK. State expenditure in Ireland intended for bank recapitalization corresponded to the G20 average, but the Irish government also provided guarantees to banks amounting to 257% of the Irish GDP [14].

In addition to the direct recapitalization of financial institutions in danger of bankruptcy, actions were taken at an almost global scale to increase the supply of money. Having brought interest rates down to unusually low levels, central banks (Federal Reserve System in the USA, Bank of England, Bank of Japan and European Central Bank) launched policies of quantitative easing on an unprecedented scale by purchasing assets on financial markets. Over the three phases of the quantitative easing program implemented in the years 2009–2014, the Fed pumped over $3 trillion into the American financial market. This gigantic operation was accompanied by a campaign of purchasing risky assets: the Fed purchased not only governmental securities, but also cooperate stocks and bonds, and even huge amounts of the notorious subprime bonds, helping commercial banks to get rid of assets that could compromise their financial stability. Undoubtedly, the Fed's actions did much to alleviate the consequences of the crisis for the American economy and helped it to recover relatively quickly.

The European Central Bank (ECB) started purchasing assets from commercial banks only in March 2015, which is at the moment when the Fed was already at the end of the process of decelerating its own quantitative easing program. At the beginning, the ECB purchased assets worth €60 bn per month, and then the figure was increased temporarily to €80 bn. From 2018, however, the program was reduced by half to €30 bn per month and it was announced that it will continue at least to September 2018. There are many reasons to believe that the efficiency of quantitative easing in stimulating inflation and economic growth in Europe is much lower than in the case of the programs implemented in the USA by the Fed and that the European process of transmission from the financial sector to the real economy is much more complex and resistant. With the exception of the German economy, which does spectacularly well, practically all the other economies in the eurozone are still struggling to get back on the path to sustainable growth and ward off the spectra of stagflation.

The Bank of Japan (BoJ) was the first to apply quantitative easing. BoJ maintained short-term interest rates close to zero since 1999. The country was mired in a crisis caused by accumulated debts of large corporations, lack of investment, and deflation. Unable to decrease interest rates any further, BoJ started handing out cash to commercial banks as early as March 2001, promoting loans and hoping that the economy will recover. This was done by purchasing treasury bonds and stocks. In 2010, the Bank of Japan announced that it will consider another asset purchase program. It was an attempt to decrease the value of the yen to the dollar in order to stimulate the domestic economy by making Japanese exports cheaper. In 2013, the central bank increased the asset purchasing program to JPY70 trillion annually with the aim of bringing inflation to 2%. This policy was named Abenomics. In 2014, BoJ announced that the program will be expanded, purchasing bonds worth JPY80 bn annually. Despite these efforts, the situation has not improved significantly so far, even though asset purchasing in Japan has grown to monstrous proportions. It is enough to say that, as a consequence of the ongoing purchase of assets (including stocks), the Bank of Japan has become the largest shareholder in Nikkei 225.

The impact of the policy of quantitative easing on the real economy is difficult to assess clearly at this stage as we do not know how the global economy would look like had the financial sector not been pumped with unimaginable funds. There are a lot of signals that quantitative easing proved to be more effective in boosting the real economy in the Anglo-Saxon economies (USA and the UK) compared to the economies of the eurozone (except for Germany) or in Japan.

As for capital markets, the policies of quantitative easing resulted in a huge supply of capital. Besides provoking a drop in bond yields (in the case of both governmental bonds—as a result of enabling cheaper deficit financing—and corporate bonds—by facilitating investment), but it also caused a long-term and spectacular boom on stock markets, which took stock market indexes to levels that much exceeded the values from before the crisis of 2008.

4.4 Capital Market Models and Channels for Capital Transfers Between the Financial Sector and the Real Economy

There are two opposed institutional models of capital markets: Anglo-Saxon (also referred to as Anglo-American) and European-Japanese (sometimes called the German-Japanese or continental model). The Anglo-Saxon model prioritizes capital markets and institutional investors. It is dominated by direct financing carried out through securities issue. The main functions of commercial banks in this model have to do with settlements, payments, and, possibly, short-term financing. On the other hand, the basic channel of supplying the capital to companies is the capital market where companies issue stocks, bonds, or other financial instruments. Stock exchanges play a key role in the pricing and allocation of capital. Also, important are institutional investors, i.e., investment funds (including pension funds), insurance companies, and investment banks. The Anglo-Saxon model is characterized by advanced capital markets, high liquidity (i.e., easy trading in large packages of securities), active market for corporate control (understood as a large volume of merger and acquisition transactions), and a great share of public capital market in the total economy (measured as a ratio of overall market capitalization to GDP). Suppliers of capital are often anonymous, the relations between companies and suppliers of capital are frequently short-term and opportunistic, and investors allocate their funds being motivated primarily by the risk-return relationship.

In the European-Japanese model, capital allocation in the economy is done mainly through the banking sector and, to a lesser extent, through the capital market. The financial system is dominated by universal banks responding to short- and long-term needs of customers, whether depositors or borrowers. A lot depends on capital links between banks and companies reflected by a large share of banks in the financing of companies. Here, capital suppliers are not anonymous, and relationships between entrepreneurs are often long-term and multilayered. In the European-Japanese model, it is not the capital market but banks that control companies (e.g., through special provisions in loan contracts—the so-called covenants). In this model, strong universal banks also play an important role in public-sector financing as they are one of the chief buyers of government bonds issued to finance budget deficits. It is also worth mentioning the links between the banking sector and politics.

Globalization of financial markets and regulatory changes (such as making it legally possible for universal banks to operate in the United States) should contribute, at least theoretically, to the convergence of the two capital market models mentioned above. Even so, historical differences between the Anglo-Saxon and the European-Japanese models seem to be persistent and have far-reaching consequences. The fact that the two models have different channels of transferring capital from the financial sector to the real economy may explain the differences in the efficiency of the quantitative easing programs launched by the major global central banks.

In the Anglo-Saxon model, the key channel for the allocation of capital is the capital market, and in particular the public market. The growth of capital supply caused by asset purchases as part of quantitative easing programs increases asset prices, lowering the cost of capital for companies. Noticing positive developments on the capital market, companies issue stocks or corporate bonds, placing them on the market at comparatively high prices to raise relatively cheap capital. Among other things, the lower cost of corporate financing means that more investment projects become profitable [low-weighted average capital costs (WACC) increase the net present value (NPV)]. This is how the economy stimulates investment and, consequently, consumption to boost economic growth.

In the European-Japanese model, the main channel for distributing extra capital from quantitative easing is the banking sector. Theoretically, a higher supply of funds in banks should bring down loan prices and foster lending. On the other hand, access to cheap credit should generate more investment from companies, as well as higher private consumption figures. It turns out, however, that the banking channel of transferring capital from the financial sector to the real economy is less efficient in this case than a well-developed and active capital market. Despite access to cheap financing sources, banks are risk averse and do not increase lending sufficiently. Instead of engaging in risky investment projects, banks used the funds from the asset purchase program primarily to rebuild their own capital base weakened as it was by the crisis. Furthermore, banks often prefer to invest funds in new issues of government bonds as the market is never short of them given the fact that most governments experience never-ending problems with budget deficits. As a result, in the European-Japanese model, only some funds from the quantitative easing program reach companies. This is done either through lending, which has been partially increased after all or by means of the capital market which does account for some of the transfers into the real economy in the European-Japanese model in spite of the domination of the banking sector.

4.5 Efficiency of Capital Markets and Efficiency of the Real Economy

The concept of market efficiency is not clear-cut, although its individual meanings are more or less related. Nonetheless, even specific interpretations of the term contain detailed definitions that may be so different as to produce serious theoretical and practical consequences. On the most general level, we may differentiate between operational efficiency, informational efficiency, and allocational efficiency of capital markets.

4.5.1 Operational Efficiency

Operationally speaking, a market is efficient when it ensures attractive conditions for making transactions. Among other factors, this concerns primarily asset liquidity, price continuity, no investor discrimination, rational transaction costs, and access to information. In other words, the operational efficiency of the market is technical and should be understood as a situation where investors enjoy equal rights and are able to make transactions cheaply and quickly. The closer the market gets to the idealistic conditions of the perfect market, the higher the level of its operational efficiency. Overestimated or excessively diverse transaction costs, unequal access to information, investment restrictions for some categories of investors, segmentation, poor liquidity, or other market inefficiencies may lead to an imbalance in the relationship between return rates and investment risk. This means that high operational efficiency is a necessary (but inefficient) condition to obtain market efficiency in the areas of information and allocation.

4.5.2 Informational Efficiency

Informational efficiency is understood as the ability of the market to reflect information correctly in the quotes of financial instruments. When people talk about capital market efficiency in general, what they mean most often is precisely informational efficiency. It was difficult to arrive at a formal and precise definition of the concept right from the outset and, with the passage of time, its understanding became more and more intuitive or common sense which led to misunderstandings and interpretations that were frequently wrong.

Arguably, the most well-known definition of informational efficiency was offered by Fama [7]: "A market in which prices always "fully reflect" available information is called "efficient."" (p. 383). However, Fama [7] himself noticed that this definition is too general and, as such, cannot be verified empirically. Hence, in the same article, he put forward the concepts of potentially testable predictions i.e., the so-called fair game, submartingale and random walk models. The models are different in several aspects—for example, the martingale and submartingale models are less restrictive compared to the random walk model—but they all claim that neither future no current information can be used to predict the future situation on the market in the way that would guarantee extraordinary return rates, i.e., rates higher than justified for a given level of risk (see Samuelson [21], Mandelbrot [17, 18]).

In response to that, LeRoy [16] made the objection that the formal account based on the fair game model Fama advanced to enable verification of the efficient market hypothesis is, in fact, a tautology. Moreover, one could not equate the martingale, submartingale, and random walk models with the efficient market hypothesis.

Answering LeRoy's objection, Fama [8] suggested a new formal account of informational efficiency whereby "in an efficient market the true expected return on any security is equal to its equilibrium expected value, which is, of course, also the market's assessment of its expected value" (p. 144). Put differently, the balance price set by an efficient market is such that the expected market return rate on investment reflects the "real" return rate for a given level of risk. The account implies that long-term return rates should always offer an adequate reward for the amount of risk involved in an investment.

This, however, presents us with the fundamental problem of the so-called joint hypothesis. The problem is that we are actually testing two hypotheses: one concerns the validity of the risk-reward pricing model itself; the other concerns informational efficiency of the market. If it turns out that the empirical results are much different from those that were predicted on the basis of the tested formula, we cannot say whether there was an error in the theoretical structure of the model or whether the market is inefficient. This was the line of argument adopted by the proponents of the informational efficiency hypothesis in response, for example, to the observed empirical anomalies related to the so-called company size effect [3] or the possibility to predict return rates based on the price/book value index [10]. For instance, the literature does not generally challenge the empirical results of parameter estimates in the Fama and French [9, 11] three-factor model. The debate focuses only on the interpretations of the observed bonuses for company size and bonuses for high price/book value ratios. Representatives of behavioral finance provide convincing arguments to demonstrate psychological errors and irrational investor behavior. Still, the point of departure for the proponents of market efficiency is that, if a given category of companies experiences higher return rates, it must be because the rates are a rational reward for the extra risk. Consequently, instead of rejecting the market efficiency hypothesis, we should change the model of risk estimation. Thus, in this account, the market efficiency hypothesis becomes unfalsifiable.

Depending on the type of information that is to be reflected by asset prices, informational efficiency is usually divided into three forms: weak form (current prices reflect all important information contained in historical instrument quotes), semi-strong (current prices reflect all publicly available information), and strong form (current prices reflect all important information, including private and confidential) [3]. It is easy to notice that progressively stronger forms of efficiency contain weaker forms. For example, if market efficiency is semi-strong, the market should also display weak-form efficiency. In other words, the entire set of publicly available information contains a subset comprised of potential signals coming from the series of historical quotes.

Jensen [15] suggested the following definition of informational efficiency that is valid for any information set: “A market is efficient with respect to information set θt if it is impossible to make economic profits by trading on the basis of information set θt. ‘By economic profits’, we mean the risk adjusted returns net of all costs.” (p. 95). The problem of the costs of obtaining and using information was also raised by Grossman and Stiglitz [12] and Cornell and Roll [4] who demonstrated that, when information is not entirely free, the market cannot be perfectly efficient in the strict sense and may at most move toward the conditions of quasi-efficiency under which marginal costs of obtaining new information is equal to the marginal benefit an investor can earn thanks to this information. In time, informational efficiency started to be equated with an inability to predict future price changes and obtain long-term net return rates (cost adjusted) that would be higher than suggested by the level of risk.

Even though Fama made the reservation that, in the world of uncertainty, intrinsic values cannot be known precisely, he also argued that, at any time, prices of securities take account of the effects of information about both the events that have already taken place, as well as those that the market expects to take place in the future based on the current situation. In other words, in an efficient market, “actual prices at every point in time represent very good estimates of intrinsic values” (Fama [6], p. 54). In the literature that has been written over several decades, whether popular, textbook, or scientific, there are many examples where the fundamental value of an instrument is directly equated with its market pricing (see the critical review presented by Guerrien and Gun [13].

In fact, Shiller et al. [22] already warned against making the error of linking the unpredictability of price changes with the conclusion that they offer a good approximation of intrinsic values, calling this one of the biggest mistakes in the history of economic thought. It is actually a classical fallacy of inverse induction in logical reasoning. Granted, if market quotes are to reflect all available information, prices should change only in response to new information, which is unpredictable by definition, which means that price changes themselves should also be random. Nonetheless, the unpredictability of price changes does not prove that the market is able to price assets correctly. Prices may change at random and still be incorrect. After all, it is also difficult to predict human action and, by the same token, behaviorally motivated errors. Among others, this is illustrated by the General Behavioral Asset Pricing Model (GBM), which illustrates the scale of incorrect pricing resulting from irrational, psychologically motivated investor behavior, is a random variable that generates stochastic price changes and leads to unpredictable return rates as a result [25].

Referring to the fair game hypothesis that he himself suggested, [21] warned against its misunderstanding or overinterpretation: “It does not prove that actual competitive markets work well. It does not say that speculation is a good thing or that randomness of price changes would be a good thing. It does not prove that anyone who makes money in speculation is ipso facto deserving of the gain or even that he has accomplished something good for society or for anyone but himself" (p. 48). In spite of the author's warning, the fair game hypothesis was used by Fama [7] rather uncritically to construct theoretical arguments in support of the efficiency hypothesis.

Discussing the events of the last financial crisis, DeLong [5] wrote that many wrong economic decisions have been made over the last decades as a result of the failure to differentiate between two fundamental implications of market efficiency, i.e., "there is no free lunch" (related to the concept of fair game and the unpredictability of return rates) and "market price is always right" (which is supposed to be related to the market's ability to reflect information in prices quickly and correctly). While the former element has consequences primarily in the area of investment strategies and the results obtained by individual investors, the ability to price assets correctly has a direct impact on the allocational efficiency of the market and can potentially bring about more serious repercussions for the general economy.

4.5.3 Allocational Efficiency

In the microeconomic sense, one may define the allocational efficiency of the market as the ability to allocate capital among different available investment options in a way that offers the investor the highest expected return rate at a particular level of risk or makes him accept the lowest risk given the expected return rate. In this account, allocational efficiency is equivalent to efficiency as understood by Markowitz [19].

Macroeconomically speaking, allocational efficiency of capital markets is understood as the ability to allocate capital to such individual sectors of the real economy where it will be used in the most efficient way. Hence, allocational efficiency of capital markets is an element of the broadly understood economic efficiency where all assets are allocated optimally in the sense of Pareto, i.e., in such a way that there is no alternative method of allocation that could make any player earn profit without worsening the situation of another player.

The first fundamental tenet of welfare economics says that perfect competition always leads to the Pareto optimum. This is because, under conditions of perfect competition, the market mechanism forces allocation of resources where the marginal rates of transformation are equal for all resources, whereas the structure of consumption ensures the equal marginal rate of substitution for all goods. Given that the competition on capital markets is very intense, it was claimed that such markets ensure efficient allocation of the basic resource traded there, i.e., capital, contributing in this way to the efficiency of the entire economy. Unfortunately, the restrictive requirements on which this first fundamental hypothesis of welfare economics was based were all too often forgotten. Besides perfect market conditions, another requirement is the rationality of decision-makers who are able to process all available information correctly and it is on this basis that they make the right choices focused on maximizing individual usefulness of each of them (the *homo oeconomicus* concept).

4.6 Efficiency of Capital Markets and Efficiency of the Economy

Stiglitz [24] provided a number of arguments of both formal and practical importance to demonstrate that informational efficiency of capital markets is neither necessary nor sufficient as a condition to achieve the allocational efficiency of the economy in the sense of Pareto. Among other things, he identified such inefficiencies of the economy as the costs of obtaining information, agency costs, market incompleteness, or divergent motives of suppliers and receivers of capital. For example, wherever information is obtained at a cost, the prices on the market will not reflect "all available information" but only such information that was obtained and used at a cost that does not exceed the economic benefits it may bring. Therefore, formally speaking, the market will not display informational efficiency as it will not take account of the information for which the cost of obtaining and application is too high (see Grossman and Stiglitz [12]; Cornell and Roll [4]. Still, this does not preclude allocational efficiency in the sense of Pareto, provided that the potential methods of allocating resources factor in the costs of obtaining information. The same goes the other way round—even supposing that capital markets are characterized by perfect informational efficiency and are able to price each company adequately, it does not automatically mean that the entire economy is allocationally efficient in the sense of Pareto. Even if the market pricing of a company is correct, the obtained value is not necessarily the maximal possible value resulting from the optimal use of resources by this company. In fact, there are many reasons for which management boards, whether consciously or not, make decisions that are not optimal and do not try to maximize the market value of the company using the available resources. Thus, inefficient management on the microscale may lead to the cumulative effect of wasting and non-optimal use of resources in the economy as a whole.

In spite of the above reservations, the relationship between informational efficiency and allocational efficiency of the market is commonly considered to be quite obvious. The inability of the market to reflect the available information correctly in asset prices leads, on the one hand, to an imbalance in the relations between return rates and risk (potential surplus return rates and the lack of efficiency in the sense of Markowitz), and on the other, to a situation where market equilibrium prices cannot be used as reliable indicators for the assessment of the true value of specific assets (there are no grounds for a correct allocation of resources).

With no informational efficiency, allocational efficiency becomes defective on the micro- and macrolevels. Capital markets characterized by informational inefficiency offer no guarantee that using a well-diversified investment portfolio as part of the so-called passive strategy will be an optimal kind of investor behavior in the long term. It cannot be excluded that a combination of investments that are potentially inefficient in the sense of Markowitz will provide investors with higher return rates than should be expected for a given level of systemic risk. If we reject the hypothesis about the informational efficiency of the market, it makes sense to allocate capital actively by looking for specific rules of investment or analytical tools that are based on, for example, repeatable patterns of behavior displayed by market players. We should always remember, however, that it is not easy to predict return rates, even on inefficient markets, as it is difficult to predict human behavior, including the one triggering market anomalies [26].

Incorrect asset pricing also means that the costs of capital are priced incorrectly. Changing investor fads or moods may lead to periodical overpricing of stocks from one sector or underpricing of companies from another. This disturbs the optimal allocation of capital among particular sectors of the real economy. Due to mispricing, part of resources may be used in a non-optimal way.

Let us try to trace the mechanisms whereby mispricing of financial instruments may lead to losses in the general economy. First, let us imagine that some companies or even the entire sectors are incorrectly priced on the market for a long time because of growing investor irrationality. If an investment fad, excessive expectations related to new technologies, pure speculation, or other factors result in a situation where stocks of a specific group of companies are overpriced (e.g., the dotcom bubble at the turn of the twentieth century), the cost of equity is automatically underpriced for these entities. Being an incentive for a given type of issuers to step up their activities, this generates the supply of new stocks purchased by the capital flowing into the sector. With the low cost of equity, the weighted average cost of capital also drops, which increases the net present value (NPV) of potential new projects. In this situation, the management boards of such companies will be inclined to engage in more expansive investment policy. Unfortunately, at least some of their projects should not have been implemented if the market cost of capital had been priced correctly. The capital they engage could be used alternatively in more efficient way in other companies or sectors of the economy that offer a better relation between the expected return rate and the actual, correctly priced, risk.

The same is true for the situation where incorrect asset pricing affects not only individual companies or sectors but the entire capital market. At times of irrational booms, the overestimation of most securities is accompanied by underestimated risk. Financing that is too cheap and incorrectly priced in relation to risk induces management boards to launch investment initiatives that should not be implemented under normal circumstances. When the risk materializes later according to the true, rather than overly optimistic, distribution of probability, part of the launched projects turn into real losses that, accumulated, can spread onto the general economy.

On the other hand, when the market is bearish and the cost of equity is too high, attractive investment projects are in danger of being put off for later. Available capital resources will not be properly used, and the economy will develop slower than it could have if assets on the capital market had been priced correctly.

Of course, the problems with incorrect estimation of the cost of capital do not only apply to the stock market, but may also have equally serious consequences for the debt market. Too low a cost of foreign capital impacts real investment policy in two ways. First, it boosts the appetite for investment due to the lower average cost of financing projects. Second, it increases the tendency to leverage, i.e., finance projects with foreign capital to a greater extent, which burdens investment activities with extra risk related to financial leverage. The terrible consequences of excessive leverage could be observed, for example, during the last period of turbulence on global financial markets caused by the US subprime mortgage crash.

Finally, capital market inefficiency also has a direct impact on the economy by influencing the mood among small investors who are not only suppliers of capital but also consumers. At times of "irrational exuberance" (a term popularized by Shiller [23]), when company pricing is on the rise and investment portfolios of small players have more and more value, the propensity to consume is often also on the rise, driving specific sectors of the economy. For example, the luxury goods market in California experienced a significant upturn during the time of the dotcom boom. The rental market for luxury summerhouses in The Hamptons on Long Island—the favorite destination of Wall Street bankers—is also rather well correlated with the situation on the stock exchange and the amount of paid out bonuses.

In conclusion, it should be observed that, even if a capital market displaying informational efficiency made it possible to allocate capital optimally in the sense of Pareto, this allocation would not necessarily be desirable in the social sense. Capital that is priced adequately in the sense of the relation of return rate to risk may be supplied to sectors that are socially harmful (such as armaments, gambling, or the production of substances with an adverse impact on health), which would not really contribute to general prosperity.

4.7 Summary

The relationship between financial markets and the real economy becomes most evident during times of destabilization and extraordinary interventions. This calls for a deeper reflection on the actual links between the two structures.

The present article focuses on two important aspects of the relations between the real economy and the financial sector. First, it analyzes the impact of quantitative easing programs on the situation of global capital markets and the efficiency of such programs as tools to stimulate economic growth in different countries. On the one hand, quantitative easing programs implemented by central banks through asset purchasing contributed to a significant drop in bond profitability and a spectacular boom on global stock exchanges over the last decade. On the other, the efficiency of such programs in achieving economic objectives differs across countries. It may be assumed that this is due, at lest partially, to the differences between the Anglo-Saxon and the European-Japanese models of capital markets. The reason is that these models use different channels for capital transfers between the financial sector and the real economy. The channel that is based on capital markets seems to be more efficient in transferring funds to the economy than the one based on the banking sector.

The second part of the article focuses on the problem of capital market efficiency versus the efficiency of the economy. The lack of efficiency on capital markets has serious consequences not only on the microlevel (for investors), but also the macrolevel of the real economy. On the microscale, it leads to a situation where wealth is transferred from the investors who make mistakes in asset pricing to the investors who take advantage of them. Additionally, incorrect asset pricing also results in incorrect allocation of resources as well as underinvestment or overinvestment in individual sectors, which generate substantial losses in the entire economy.

The reflections presented in this article may have a considerable impact on future macroeconomic policies and the issue of supervising financial markets. They may provide inspiration for further studies in this field, especially those involving empirical research.

References

1. The text was written as part of Statutory Research carried out in the Collegium of World Economy at the Warsaw School of Economics, Poland
2. Although the identification of the three forms of informational efficiency mentioned above is often attributed to E. Fama (1970), it should be noted that the classification was suggested a little earlier by H. Roberts (1967) who was the supervisor of E. Fama's Ph.D. thesis

Literature

3. Banz, R.: The relationship between return and market value of common stocks. J. Financ. Econ. **9**(1), 3–18 (1981)
4. Cornell, B., Roll, R.: Strategies for pairwise competitions in markets and organizations. Bell J. Econ. 201–213 (1981)
5. DeLong, B.: Two "efficient market hypothesis" (2009). http://delong.typepad.com/sdj/2009/07/two-efficient-market-hypotheses.html
6. Fama, E.: The behavior of stock-market prices. J. Bus. **38**(1), 34–105 (1965)
7. Fama, E.: Efficient capital markets: A review of theory and empirical work. J. Financ. **25**(2), 383–417 (1970)
8. Fama, E.: Reply. J. Financ. **31**(1), 143–145 (1976)
9. Fama, E., French, K.: Common risk factors in the returns of stocks and bonds. J. Financ. Econ. **33**, 3–56 (1993)
10. Fama, E., French, K.: Size and book-to-market factors in earnings and returns. J. Financ. **50**(1), 131–155 (1995)
11. Fama, E., French, K.: Multifactor explanations of asset pricing anomalies. J. Financ. **51**(1), 55–84 (1996)
12. Grossman, J., Stiglitz, J.: On the impossibility of informationally efficient markets. Am. Econ. Rev. **70**(3), 393–408 (1980)
13. Guerrien, B., Gun, O.: Efficient market hypothesis: what are we talking about? Real-World Econ. Rev. **56**, 19–30 (2011)
14. IMF.: World Economic Outlook. Washington, DC (2010)
15. Jensen, M.: Some anomalous evidence regarding market efficiency. J. Financ. Econ. **6**, 95–101 (1978)
16. LeRoy, S.: Efficient capital markets: comment. J. Financ. **31**(1), 139–141 (1976)
17. Mandelbrot, B.: Forecasts of future prices, unbiased markets, and 'martingale' models. J. Bus. **39**(1), 242–255 (1966)
18. Mandelbrot, B.: Some aspects of the random walk model of stock market prices. Int. Econ. Rev. **9**(2), 43–68 (1968)

19. Markowitz, H.: Portfolio selection. J. Financ. **7**(1), 77–91 (1952)
20. Roberts, H.: Statistical versus clinical prediction of the stock market. Working paper, Centre for Research in Security Prices. University of Chicago (1967)
21. Samuelson, P.: Proof that properly anticipated prices fluctuate randomly. Ind. Manag. Rev. **6**, 41–50 (1965)
22. Shiller, R.: Stock prices and social dynamics. Brookings Pap. Econ. Act. 457–498 (1984)
23. Shiller, R.: Irrational Exuberance. Princeton University Press, Princeton (2000)
24. Stiglitz, J.: The allocation role of the stock market. J. Financ. **36**(2), 235–251 (1981)
25. Szyszka, A.: Belief and preference based models. In: Baker, H.K., Nofsinger, J. (eds.) Behavioral Finance. Investors, Corporations, and Markets, pp. 351–372. Wiley, Hoboken, NJ (2010)
26. Szyszka, A.: Behavioral Finance and Capital Markets. How Psychology Influences Investors and Corporations. Palgrave Macmillan, New York (2013)

Chapter 5
Tax Planning in Bank Tax—Analysis of the Use of Treasury Bonds

Małgorzata Twarowska-Ratajczak

Abstract Purpose: The issue of taxation of the financial sector has long been widely discussed both in the European Union and in other countries of the world. It is extremely important to construct a proper tax, which would ensure the objectives set for it, and at the same time would generate as little negative effects as possible and would be as little burdensome for taxpayers as possible. The aim of the study is to verify the hypothesis that banks in Poland use the possibility of purchasing treasury bonds in order to lower the tax base. Methods: The paper analyses the use of treasury securities as an instrument of tax optimisation. The study includes theoretical and empirical research. A descriptive comparative analysis has been used to assess if after the introduction of the tax on some financial institutions there was an increase in treasury bond purchases in the last days of the month and an increase in sales at the beginning of the following month. Results and conclusions: The author confirmed the research hypothesis that banks in Poland use the possibility of buying treasury bonds in order to lower the tax base.

Keywords Bank levy · Bank tax · Tax optimisation · Treasury bonds

5.1 Introduction

The issue of taxation of the financial sector has long been widely discussed both in the European Union and in other countries of the world. The main functions of taxation of the financial sector include the fiscal function providing public revenues, as well as the anti-crisis function, which is expressed in increasing the stability of financial markets and reducing risk in these markets. Among EU member states, 17 have introduced a bank levy: Austria (2011), Belgium (2012), Cyprus (2011), Finland (2013), France (2011), Germany (2011), Hungary (2010), Latvia (2011), the Netherlands (2012), Portugal (2011), Poland (2016), Romania (2011), Slovakia (2012), Slovenia (2011),

M. Twarowska-Ratajczak (✉)
Maria Curie-Skłodowska University, Lublin, Poland
e-mail: m.twarowska@umcs.pl

W. Tarczyński and K. Nermend (eds.), *Effective Investments on Capital Markets*,
Springer Proceedings in Business and Economics,
https://doi.org/10.1007/978-3-030-21274-2_5

Spain (2013), Sweden (2009) and the UK (2011), while 3 have introduced a financial transaction tax: France (2012), Italy (2013) and Hungary (2013). The implemented tax models differ between countries. Liabilities or their selected items are tax bases in 12 EU countries, while 5 have chosen to tax assets (Hungary, Poland, Slovenia) or risk-weighted assets (Finland, France). In addition, the UK has introduced an additional tax on banks' profits since 2016. It is extremely important to construct a proper tax, which would ensure the objectives set for it, and at the same time would generate as little negative effects as possible and would be as little burdensome for taxpayers as possible. The aim of the study is to verify the hypothesis that banks in Poland use the possibility of purchasing treasury bonds in order to lower the tax base. The paper will analyse the use of treasury securities as an instrument of tax optimisation. The importance of the discussed topic results from the important role played by the financial sector in the modern economy. The case of the Polish bank levy was chosen because of its specific construction, where treasury bonds are excluded from the tax base. The paper analyses the use of treasury securities as an instrument of tax optimisation. The study includes theoretical and empirical research based on Polish Financial Supervision Authority, Central Securities Depository of Poland and Supreme Audit Office data. A descriptive comparative analysis has been used to assess if after the introduction of the tax on some financial institutions there was an increase in treasury bond purchases in the last days of the month and an increase in sales at the beginning of the following month.

5.2 Theoretical Background

Applying tax optimisation allows the company to reduce its tax burden and thus improve its financial results. Entrepreneurs may pay lower taxes and remain in compliance with tax regulations [1]. The specialist literature defines tax optimisation as tax planning aimed at creating the most beneficial structures and solutions in respect of tax burdens and quasi-fiscal charges related to specific economic actions taken by taxpayers [2]. The concept of tax optimisation (also referred to as tax planning) means such a choice of the structure of a planned legal act so that the total tax burden can be reduced to a minimum. Tax optimisation should, however, be distinguished from tax evasion. That means that tax planning takes place within the limits of the applicable legal regulations. The term tax savings is not tantamount to tax optimisation as the former consists in refraining from actions that result in creating a tax liability. On the other hand, tax planning is aimed at creating optimal structures and solutions related to specific economic actions taken by the taxpayer [1]. The literature distinguishes between two forms of tax resistance: tax avoidance and tax evasion [3]. Tax avoidance consists in reducing the tax burden using the methods permitted by tax law and aimed at exploiting the possibilities arising from them, within the limits and within the limits of the regulations in force, tax relief. On the other hand, tax evasion involves actions that lead to their minimisation or complete elimination, but are prohibited by tax law [1].

Banks, despite their specific function in the economy, are also enterprises whose aim is to generate profits. Therefore, the issue of minimising the fiscal burden also concerns this group of entities. Especially due to the universal banking system dominating in Poland, banks are an interesting subject of legal and financial analyses due to the various tax consequences of their operational activities [4].

One of the recently popular problems of tax policy is the new model of taxation of financial institutions, especially in the context of postulates of wider tax interventions in this area of economic activity. The introduction of additional public levies on the financial sector has been considered for many years in various forms. The first proposals for such instruments were formulated by Keynes [5] and Tobin [6]. The recent financial crisis has intensified the discussion at both the EU and national level on the possibility and consequences of an additional tax on financial institutions [7–26]. Different countries have decided to introduce various forms of additional taxation of the financial sector. Additional taxation of the financial sector includes bank levies, financial transaction tax and financial activity tax [27]. The design of bank levies may also vary, particularly with regard to the taxable entities, the tax base and the exemptions and exclusions applied. Marcinkowska carried out an assessment of the bank tax base variants, indicating the advantages and disadvantages of particular solutions [28].

5.3 Tax on Certain Financial Institutions in Poland

The objective of bank levy in Poland is to mobilise an additional source of financing for budgetary expenditure and to increase the financial sector's share of budgetary expenditure. Therefore, it can be assumed that the banking tax in Poland has mainly a fiscal function. Moreover, bank levy in Poland is a tax on the scale of business activity of banks, but it does not refer to the level of risk undertaken by banks [29]. The aim of introducing in Poland an additional levy on banks, insurers and loan institutions was to obtain an additional source of financing of budgetary expenditure, in particular social expenditure. The project proponents justified the new contribution by the need to increase the share of the financial sector in the financing of budgetary expenditure. The Act of 15 January 2016 on Tax on Certain Financial Institutions entered into force on 1 February 2016. The tax is levied on banks with a tax base higher than PLN 4 billion, insurance companies with a tax base higher than PLN 2 billion and loan institutions with assets exceeding PLN 0.2 billion. The subject of taxation is the excess of the total value of taxpayers' assets, resulting from the statement of turnover and balances established on the last day of the month, over the tax-free amount. The tax rate is 0.0366% of the tax base per month (0.44% per year). The amount of tax paid is not deductible for corporate income tax purposes. State banks, entities in relation to which the Polish Financial Supervision Authority issued a decision on suspension of operations, entities subject to reorganisation proceedings are exempt from the obligation to calculate and pay the tax [30] (Table 5.1).

Table 5.1 Tax on certain financial institutions in Poland—the tax base thresholds

Taxpayers	Tax-free amount (billion PLN)	Tax base
Banks, branches of banks, credit institutions and cooperative banks	4	Assets decreased by equity and certain financial assets, e.g. treasury bonds, funds of cooperative banks on accounts in affiliating banks, securities purchased from the National Bank of Poland as collateral for NBP refinancing loan
Insurers, reinsurers and their branches	2	Tax base is calculated jointly for all taxpayers related or co-related directly or indirectly to one entity or a group of related entities
Loan institutions	0, 2	

Source [30]

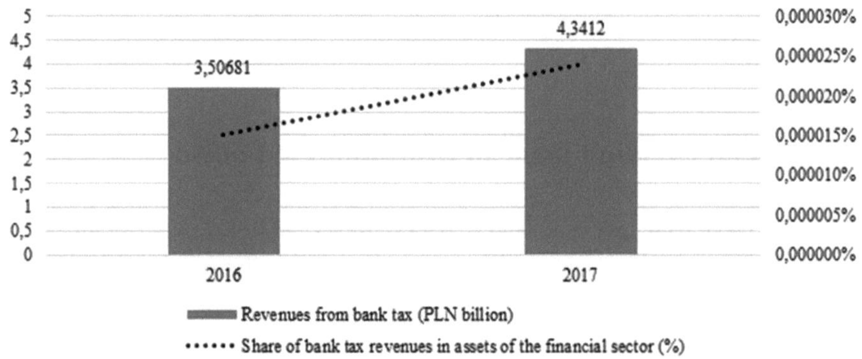

Fig. 5.1 Revenues from the tax on certain financial institutions in Poland (PLN billion). *Source* [31]

Revenues from bank tax in Poland in 2016 were lower than assumed, while in 2017, they exceeded the amount assumed in the Budget Act. The revenue forecast for 2016 was overestimated. Tax revenues from some financial institutions realised in the period from March to December 2016 amounted to PLN 3506.8 million, i.e. 63.8% of the forecast assumed in the Budget Act for 2016, including PLN 2935.4 million from the banking sector and PLN 550.4 million from insurance and reinsurance companies. Revenues in 2017 amounted to PLN 4341.2 million (110.3% of the plan) [31; Fig. 5.1).

The number of entities which at least once submitted a FIN-1 declaration varied from 79 to 82 per month in 2016 and from 75 to 81 in 2017. In total, between March 2016 and September 2017, 90 financial institutions submitted their FIN-1 declarations at least once. Among the entities which submitted FIN-1 declarations, the largest number was domestic insurance companies (from 34 to 37 in particular months) and domestic banks (from 24 to 26). The number of loan institutions submitting declarations ranged from 9 to 10. Domestic banks and domestic insurance companies had the dominant share in the realised income. Their share in 2016 was 83.6 and 15.6%, respectively. Other entities realised a total of 0.8% of revenues (including loan institutions 0.6%). In 2017 (until September), this share slightly changed and amounted to 83.3, 16.0 and 0.7%, respectively (including 0.5% loan institutions) [32].

In Poland, the tax base is assets decreased by equity capital. Equity capital is excluded from the tax base (the government is interested in banks having as much of it as possible in relation to the scale of their operations, because then they are safer). Banks pay tax when they borrow money from outside to finance credit activities (e.g. take deposits from customers, borrow money from another bank or issue bonds).

Among the consequences of the introduction of a bank levy in Poland are: a reduction in the availability of loans and an increase in their cost, transfer of tax costs to bank customers, a decrease in liquidity on the interbank market and an increase in demand for treasury securities, which are excluded from the bank levy base. Banks may purchase treasury bonds in order to aggressive tax avoidance. Particularly noteworthy should be the situation when a bank decides to purchase treasury bonds of an appropriate value on the last day of the month, which will lower the bank's tax base. At the same time, it will sell the same bonds on the second day, thus freeing the assets that have not been covered by the tax obligation.

5.4 Assessment of the Use of Treasury Bonds to Reduce the Tax Base by Banks

Figure 5.2 shows the shifted positions in the balance sheet of the bank's balance sheet which influenced the shifted tax base. From January 2016, the interest of banks in treasury bonds increased. Banks also increased the equity capital, which are also exempted from tax. As a result, at almost constant level of assets, the tax base decreased. Banks have taken steps to tax optimisation, because they try to reduce tax base. The largest change can be observed in treasury bonds, which since December 2015 (month before tax introduction) has increased by 48%. In the quantitative use, it is a change in the portfolio by PLN 76.1 billion. In the same period, assets increased by 6% (PLN 76.6 billion) and total tax base decreased by 2% (PLN 20.2 billion) [33].

From the point of view of servicing the government debt, the increased demand for treasury bonds is positive. However, it should be remembered that this tendency will be very unfavourable for the country from the point of view of falling tax revenues.

The construction of a bank tax may have an impact on the long-term bank's strategy. Treasury bonds (exempted from taxation) and loans (non-exempted) are the bank's assets. Banks may face a dilemma of whether to invest in treasury bonds or

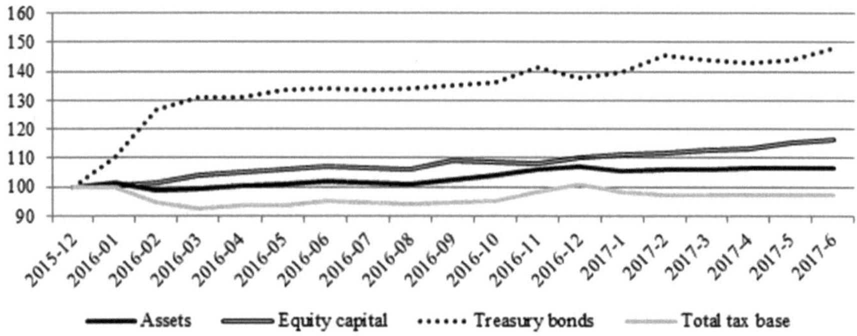

Fig. 5.2 Dynamics of tax base components (banks that have paid tax, 2015–12 = 100). *Source* [33]

whether to lend loans, which on the one hand are subject to bank tax and on the other hand are exposed to economic risk (Fig. 5.3).

On the basis of data from the system of the Central Securities Depository of Poland (banks' own accounts), the Ministry of Finance estimated daily debt balances of the

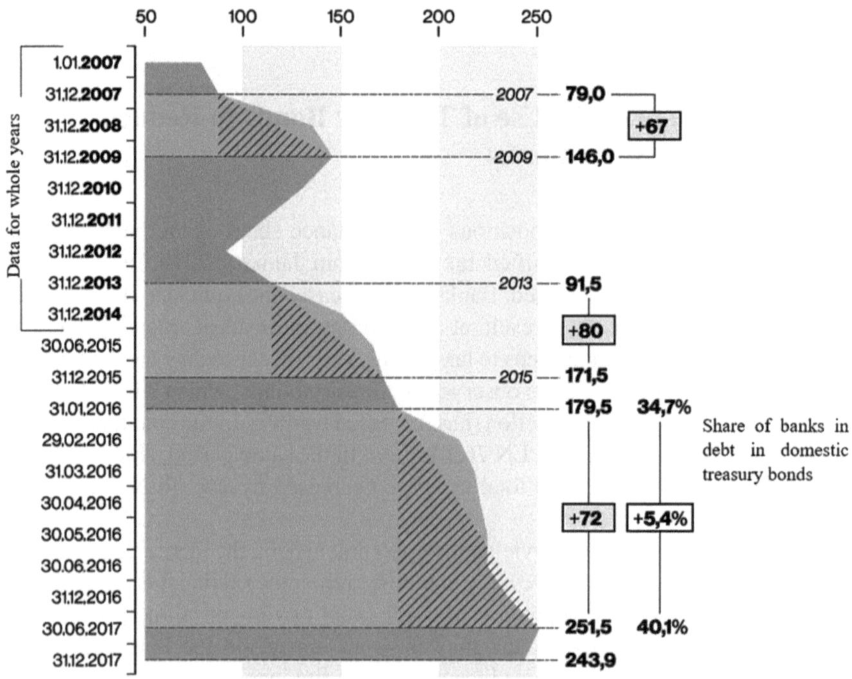

Fig. 5.3 Value of domestic treasury bonds portfolio in the banking sector (billion PLN). *Source* [32]

banking sector in treasury bonds issued on the domestic market. These data covered the period from the end of 2015 to the end of August 2017. The amounts reported at the end of the month were based on financial institutions' reporting data.

In the case of banks in the analysed periods of 2015 (i.e. before the introduction of the tax on certain financial institutions), there were increased purchases of treasury bonds (above average) in the last days of the month and increased sales at the beginning of the following month. In 2016 and 2017, this trend was no longer so unambiguous. Increased purchases at the end of the month (above the average) took place only in some of the analysed periods (in majority, they were lower than the average). On the other hand, sales of treasury bonds at the beginning of the month were clearly higher in most of the analysed periods. Increased purchases of treasury bonds in the last days of the month and sales in the first days of the following month were more frequently used for tax optimisation by branches of credit institutions, but their value was not significant in terms of the total value of treasury bonds held by branches of credit institutions in relation to the value of treasury bonds held by banks, purchase and sale transactions and their impact on tax. Banks held approximately 98% of treasury bonds and branches of credit institutions approximately 2% [32].

According to the data of the Supreme Audit Office in Poland, from the end of January 2016 to the end of June 2017, the value of the portfolio of domestic treasury bonds in the banking sector increased by PLN 72.0 billion (from PLN 179.5 billion to PLN 251.5 billion), and the share of banks in debt in treasury bonds issued on the domestic market increased from 34.7 to 40.1%. More than half of the increase in bank exposure took place in the first two months since the introduction of the tax—an increase by PLN 31.0 billion in February and by PLN 7.8 billion in March 2016, although the increase in purchases could already be observed at the end of 2015. In the period from the end of December 2015 to the end of May 2016, the value of bonds held by banks increased by PLN 54 billion, i.e. by over 33%.

Increased demand from the domestic banking sector for Polish treasury bonds was a factor reducing their yields and, as a result, the cost of public debt. This resulted in an additional effect on the state budget in the form of lower costs of financing public debt. It is not possible to quantify the effect of the introduction of the tax on certain financial institutions due to the influence of many other factors, which influenced in different directions during the period under consideration. According to the Tax Collection Department of the Ministry of Finance in Poland in the first half of 2016, when the largest increase in bank involvement in treasury bonds took place, the factors affecting the treasury bonds market included in particular [32]:

- downgrade of Poland's rating by Standard & Poor's in January 2016, resulting in an increase in the profitability of domestic bonds and a decrease in the formal possibilities of investing in Polish treasury bonds by some institutions requiring an appropriate rating level for the instruments they purchase,
- outflow of foreign investors from the domestic treasury securities market (in the first half of 2016—PLN 10.2 billion, and in 2016—PLN 14.2 billion), which in practice means additional supply on the domestic market and pressure to increase profitability.

5.5 Conclusions

Many countries are considering the possibility or have introduced additional taxation of banks as an alternative to prudential regulation or income taxation. Theoretical analyses of the impact of individual tax measures are carried out on a large scale. Also, the practice and experience of many countries that have introduced bank taxes allow lessons to be learned and tax structures that will increasingly meet the objectives of taxation with the least harmful effects. Poland has also introduced a tax on some financial institutions since 2016. Even such a short period after the implementation of the tax allows for initial assessment and drawing conclusions for the future.

Among the consequences of the introduction of a bank levy in Poland are: a reduction in the availability of loans and an increase in their cost, transfer of tax costs to bank customers, a decrease in liquidity on the interbank market and an increase in demand for treasury securities, which are excluded from the bank levy base. As a result, banks may purchase treasury bonds in order to avoid tax liabilities. The conducted research allowed for a positive verification of the hypothesis that banks in Poland use the possibility of purchasing treasury bonds in order to lower the tax base.

Based on Polish Financial Supervision Authority, Central Securities Depository of Poland and Supreme Audit Office data, it can be concluded that after the introduction of the tax on some financial institutions in the last days of the month, there was an increase in treasury bond purchases and an increase in sales at the beginning of the following month. However, it is not possible to quantify unambiguously the impact of the introduction of a tax on certain financial institutions due to the influence of many other factors which influenced in different directions during the period under consideration.

From the point of view of servicing the government debt, the increased demand for treasury bonds is positive. However, it should be remembered that this tendency will be very unfavourable for the country from the point of view of falling tax revenues. The construction of a bank tax may have an impact on the long-term bank's strategy. Treasury bonds (exempted from taxation) and loans (non-exempted) are the bank's assets. Banks may face a dilemma of whether to invest in treasury bonds or whether to lend loans, which on the one hand are subject to bank tax and on the other hand are exposed to economic risk.

References

1. Nyk, M.: Tax planning for small and medium enterprises (SMEs), Ann. Mark. Mgmt. Econ. **2**(1) (2016)
2. Wyciślok, J.: Optymalizacja podatkowa. Legalne zmniejszenie obciążeń podatkowych, CH Beck, Warszawa (2013)
3. Filip, P.: Planowanie finansowe a optymalizacja obciążeń fiskalnych działalności gospodarczej. Zeszyty Naukowe Uniwersytetu Rzeszowskiego **15** (2009)

4. Pomorski, P.: Celowość i efektywność preferencji podatkowych dla instytucji finansowych. In: Kucia-Guściora, B., Munnich, M., Zdunek, A., Zieliński, R. (eds.) Stanowienie i stosowanie prawa podatkowego w Polsce. Ocena i kierunki zmian, Lublin (2016)
5. Keynes, J.M.: The General Theory of Employment, Interest Rates and Money. Harcourt Brace & World, New York (1936)
6. Tobin, J.: A proposal for international monetary reform. Eastern Econ. J. **4** (1978)
7. Buch, C.M., Hilberg, B., Tonzer, L.: Taxing banks: an evaluation of the German Bank Levy. J. Bank. Finance **72** (2016)
8. Cannas, G., Cariboni J., Marchesi, M., Nicodème, G., Giudici M., Zedda, S.: Financial activities taxes, Bank Levies and Systemic Risk. Working Paper No. 43, European Commission (2014)
9. Capelle-Blancard, G., Havrylchyk, O.: The Impact of the French securities transaction tax on market liquidity and Volatility. Working Paper **33** (2015)
10. Devereux, M., Johannesen, M., Vella, J.: Can taxes tame the banks? Evidence from the European Bank Levies, Oxford University Centre for Business Taxation (2015)
11. Dvořáková, V., Nerudováa, D.: Financial transaction tax: can it be sufficient resource of eu budget when introduced through enhanced cooperation ? Procedia Econ. Finance **12** (2014)
12. European Commission.: Tax reforms in EU member states, Vol. 8014. N.p., 2015. Web (2015)
13. Grahl, J., Lysandrou, P.: The European Commission's proposal for a financial transactions tax: a critical assessment. **52**(2) (2014)
14. Hemmelgarn, T., Nicodème, Tasnadi, B., Vermote P.: Financial transaction taxes in The European Union. National Tax J. **69**(1) (2016)
15. Huizinga, H., Voget, J., Wagner. W.: International taxation and cross-border banking, NBER working paper series. National Bureau of Economic Research (2012)
16. Hvozdyk, L., Rustanov, S.: The Effect of financial transaction tax on market liquidity and volatility: an Italian perspective. Int. Rev. Financial Anal. **45** (2016)
17. Jurgen, H., Kleinlercher, D., Kirchler, M.: The impact of a financial transaction tax on stylized facts of price returns—evidence from the Lab. J. Econ. Dynamics Control **36** (2012)
18. Kil, K., Ślusarczyk, R.: Podatek Bankowy w Krajach Unii Europejskiej—Ocena Implementacji. Prace Naukowe Uniwersytetu Ekonomicznego we Wrocławiu **348** (2014)
19. Koļesņika, M., Dovladbekova I.: Financial transaction tax as an instrument for banking sector regulation in the EU. Econ. Business **25** (2014)
20. Masiukiewicz, P, Dec, P.: Growth. Finance Regul. **11**(2) (2012)
21. Rabatinová, M., Kušnírová, J.: The Bank Levies in Slovakia and in Other EU Countries. Bankov é odvody v SR a v EÚ 4(1) (2015)
22. Ramona, M.: Taxation of financial sector after the crisis in the European Union. J. Faculty Econ.Econ. **1**(2) (2012)
23. Schweikhard, F., Wahrenburg, M.: The internalization of systemic risk: an analysis of Bank Levy Schemes. SSRN Electron. J. (2013)
24. Sun, E. Kruse, T., Min-Teh Yu.: Financial transaction tax: policy analytics based on optima trading. Compu. Econ. **46**(1) (2015)
25. Szołno-Koguc, J., Twarowska, M.: Taxation of the financial—an attempt to find the best solution. J. Econ. Mgmt. **18** (2014)
26. Szołno-Koguc, J., Twarowska, M.: Dodatkowe Daniny Publiczne Sektora Finansowego (Banków)—Przegląd Międzynarodowy. ALTERUM Ośrodek Badań i Analiz Systemu Finansowego (2015)
27. Claessens, S., Keen, M., Pazarbasioglu, C.: Financial sector taxation. The IMF's Report to the G-20 and Background Material, IMF (2010)
28. Marcinkowska, M.: Dodatkowe podatki i opłaty od banków—potrzeby praktyki i dylematy teorii finansów, "Prace Naukowe UE we Wrocławiu" Nr 170, K. Jajuga (red.), Finanse—nowe wyzwania teorii i praktyki. Problemy wiodące, Wrocław (2011)
29. Twarowska, M., Skorulska, K.: The consequences of banking sector taxation in Poland and Germany in terms of different tax models. In: Proceedings of the 5th International Multidisciplinary Scientific Conference on Social Sciences & Arts SGEM 2018, vol. 5, Modern Science Issue 1.1, Vienna (2018)

30. Act on Tax on Certain Financial Institutions. https://mf-arch2.mf.gov.pl/documents/764034/6401579/20180601_Omowienie+sprawozdania+za+2017+r.pdf, 15 January (2016)
31. Ministry of Finance.: Sprawozdanie z wykonania budżetu państwa za okres od 1 stycznia do 31 grudnia 2017 r., Warszawa https://www.mf.gov.pl (2017)
32. Najwyższa Izba Kontroli (Supreme Audit Office).: Pobór podatku od instytucji finansowych. Informacja o wynikach kontroli, Warszawa (2018)
33. KNF (Polish Financial Supervision Authority).: Syntetyczna informacja na temat wpływu podatku od niektórych instytucji finansowych na sytuację banków komercyjnych. Warsaw (2017, August)

Chapter 6
The Role of a Court Expert in Determining the Sale Price of an Enterprise or Individual Assets in the Polish Bankruptcy Law—Selected Legal Aspects

Kinga Flaga-Gieruszyńska

Abstract The study refers to cases in which an investor decides to purchase an enterprise, its organized part or individual assets constituting the bankruptcy estate. In this situation, apart from economic aspects, the legal conditions referring to the role of the court expert in determining the sale price of an enterprise or assets are of particular importance, both as part of the pre-pack solution and in the case of bankruptcy proceedings conducted on general terms. Resolutions of the bankruptcy proceedings issued on the basis of the expert opinion regarding this price are decisive in determining the conditions of purchase of the above-mentioned components of the bankruptcy estate.

Keywords Investing in a company in bankruptcy · Court expert · Bankruptcy proceedings

6.1 Introduction

The essence of bankruptcy proceedings is the liquidation of the debtor's assets, including the enterprise, in order to satisfy the creditors. However, this rule is not absolute, because according to Art. 2 paragraph 1 of the Act of 28 February 2003—Bankruptcy law (i.e. Journal of Laws of 2017, item 2344), proceedings regulated by an Act should be carried out in a way to satisfy the creditors as much as possible and if rational considerations allow it—to preserve the debtor's current enterprise. Thus, despite the parallel existence of restructuring law in Poland, the purpose of which is to restructure the debtors' obligations and keep them on the market; in the course of bankruptcy proceedings, it is also possible to enter into an arrangement with creditors. In the context of the below considerations, the modes of

K. Flaga-Gieruszyńska (✉)
Faculty of Law and Administration, University of Szczecin, Szczecin, Poland
e-mail: kingaflaga@gmail.com

W. Tarczyński and K. Nermend (eds.), *Effective Investments on Capital Markets*, Springer Proceedings in Business and Economics,
https://doi.org/10.1007/978-3-030-21274-2_6

proceedings, in which the assets of the debtor, being a part of the bankruptcy estate, are liquidated, are of fundamental importance.

Liquidation of assets depending on the circumstances may have a different course, which is particularly important from the point of view of the investor who is a potential buyer of a part of the bankruptcy estate. According to Art. 316 paragraph 1 of the Bankruptcy law, the enterprise of the debtor should be sold as a whole, unless it is not possible. This provision applies to the enterprise in the material aspect, which is an organized set of intangible and physical components intended for conducting business operations and includes in particular: (1) designation individualizing an enterprise or its organized parts (company name)—with this restriction that the purchaser may use the designation of the enterprise which contains the bankrupt's name, only with his or her consent; (2) ownership of real estate and movable property, including devices, materials, goods and products, and other property rights referring to real estate or movable property; (3) rights arising from lease or tenancy agreements for real estate or movable property and rights to use real estate or movable property resulting from other legal relationships; (4) claims, rights from securities and cash (these components do not refer to enterprises in bankruptcy); (5) concessions, licences, and permits; (6) patents and other industrial property rights; (7) property copyright and related rights; (8) company secrets; (9) books and other documents related to running a business. Consequently, when talking about an enterprise in this aspect, both the value of tangible and intangible assets, which, however, have a material value that is significant for the purchase price of the enterprise, should be taken into account.

The lack of possibility to sale the enterprise as a whole indicated in the said regulation may result from: (1) its character, when the debtor's assets are not an organized whole serving the achievement of an economic goal but an accidental collection of objects and rights; (2) presence in the assets of objects and rights which are related to expensive obligations (binding employment contracts connected with overstaffing, unorganized archive of several decades of operation, landfill of post-production waste, etc.)—causing individual assets to achieve a much higher price when sold separately; (3) lack of demand for the production of the enterprise, or other circumstances that make reaching the economic goal for which the enterprise was created is no longer attractive [1]. In such a situation, the bankruptcy proceedings authorities should strive for alternative solutions, i.e. the sale of an organized part of the enterprise (this term generates problems of interpretation, as will be discussed below) or individual assets included in the bankruptcy estate. However, such a solution not only reduces the amount obtained from the sale of a company in a fragmented formula but also affects the need to multiply actions performed by the authorities carrying out the bankruptcy proceedings.

This does not mean that the sale of the company as a whole in the course of the bankruptcy proceedings is an ideal solution. In relation to this mode of liquidation of debtor's assets, in practice also negative aspects are raised, mainly concerning such factors as costs and time of proceedings. The mode of liquidation sales of an enterprise requires firstly the assessment of the company and then the organization of the tender. Therefore, financial resources are needed to order an expert valuation and to organize a tender. Conducting the tender procedure is naturally related to the extension of the bankruptcy proceedings, generating further costs associated with its continuation [2]. For this reason—in accordance with the intention of the legislator—if the debtor manages to acquire an investor interested in acquiring the company at the stage preceding the submission and recognition of the application for bankruptcy, this fact should be used to apply the so-called prepared liquidation (pre-pack), due to the possibility of accelerating actions aimed at changing the owner of the enterprise or its organized part or assets constituting a significant part of the enterprise.

In each of these cases, regardless of the adopted sales mode, the purchase price is only partially determined by economic conditions (expressed in parameters used in the expert opinion regarding the description and estimation of the company or its part), and not without significance are legal and organizational solutions relating to the scope of application of the expert opinion, the admissibility of specific actions of the authorities conducting the proceedings, assessment of the expert opinion by these authorities, etc., which will be the subject of the analysis in this study.

6.2 Status of a Court Expert in Bankruptcy Proceedings—General Issues

In bankruptcy proceedings, which are a type of civil proceedings, the status of court expert is the same as in the case of other categories of civil cases. The difference of this procedure is that the judicial body does not have such freedom as in ordinary civil proceedings and cannot decide whether in a specific case it is necessary to use special information. The legislator decides about the necessity of using an expert opinion, indicating precisely the situations in which it is to be prepared and constitutes one of the elements relevant to the decision of the body of the proceedings. Proof from an expert opinion due to an ingredient in the form of special information is evidence of the kind that cannot be replaced by another Act of proof, such as hearing a witness. In fact, the expert opinion is intended to help the judicial authority to assess the material collected when special information is needed. However, it cannot be treated as a source of factual material in the case or the basis for determining the circumstances that are the subject of the expert's assessment. Therefore, the general principles indicated in the opinion must be referred by the court to the specific circumstances of the case examined, taking into account the final factual findings [3]. It is worth emphasizing that in the Polish legal system, the role of an expert and a witness is treated as two separate procedural roles, which are not combinable. Therefore, the construction of an expert witness as a witness with special information known from the common law system is unacceptable.

At the same time, there is no doubt that in bankruptcy proceedings, like in general civil proceedings, there is a clear departure from the obsolete concept of the court as "the highest court expert", putting on people who have appropriate in-depth knowledge and high professional qualifications. This results in the fact that the knowledge of the authority is not evidence in the case; it only allows and facilitates the assessment of the expert opinion. Even if the body of the proceedings had special knowledge (e.g. completed post-graduate studies in the field of business valuation), it is still obliged to use the evidence in the form of an expert opinion. The judicial body cannot resign from an expert opinion if the determination of the fact requires special knowledge. Nor can it reject all specialist opinions and adopt its own alternative position in a given case [4]. Proof of this kind, due to its specificity, is subject to the assessment of the body of the proceedings only in terms of compliance with the principles of logical thinking, life experience, and general knowledge. The criteria for assessing this proof are also: the level of expert knowledge, the theoretical basis of the opinion, the manner of motivating the position expressed in it, and the degree of firmness of the assessments expressed in it. This means that the body of the proceedings cannot adjudicate contrary to the expert opinion, if it is coherent, categorical and properly justified, and if in the course of proceedings the participant in the proceedings will not effectively deny the assessment made by a specialist (e.g. by effectively questioning the methods or calculations made in order to estimate the value of the subject of sale) [5]. Thus, expert evidence is subject to the assessment of the body of the proceedings, according to the measures appropriate for the subject of a particular opinion, and therefore from the point of view of compliance with the principles of logical reasoning, general knowledge, theoretical basis of opinions indicating expert knowledge, the way of formulating opinions and its conclusions, also due to their unambiguity and compliance with the questions asked, but without going into the scope of the matter, which results from expert knowledge [6]. If such an obligation results from the provisions of the Bankruptcy law, the proceedings authority must use the services of an expert and take into account the conclusions of the opinion, provided that it will meet the standards discussed later in the considerations.

At the same time, in the practice of Polish bankruptcy proceedings, another problem arises, which is often the uncritical approach of the proceedings authorities to the expert opinion, which results in its recognition as almost "infallible". This is a too far-reaching approach to special messages, on the basis of which the authority (bankruptcy court, judge-commissioner, etc.) issues the decision, in particular as to the sale price of an enterprise, its organized part or individual asset. Thus, in many cases, it is de facto a court expert, not a judicial authority that decides about the price to be paid by the investor intending to acquire part of the bankruptcy estate. Such situations should be considered as inadmissible, because the evidence of an expert opinion differs from other evidence in a way that its purpose in principle is not to determine facts relevant to the case but to provide the judicial authority with clarifications on matters requiring special knowledge. It is the body of the proceedings which is appointed to make all findings in the proceedings, not an expert. In other words, the body of the proceedings can and should use the help of an expert in the area requiring special information, but the expert cannot replace the court in making findings, and in particular, make legal assessments for which he or she is not appointed or authorized [7]. As a consequence, the terms of sale of a part of the bankruptcy estate must be determined by a body of the proceedings—based on the expert opinion as one of the elements of the decision-making process.

As a consequence, in the scope of determining the purchase price of the indicated components of the bankruptcy estate, the expert only supports the authority of the proceedings in the obligation to comprehensively and reliably shape the beliefs about circumstances essential for the correct estimation of their value [8]. Moreover, the court expert—as an assistant to the judicial authorities—must carry out his or her task in accordance with the guidelines contained in the order issued in the ordinance of the body of the proceedings. By admitting evidence from an expert opinion, the authority should mark an evidential thesis that sets the subject scope of the opinion. The evidential thesis is binding for the expert in the sense that, on the one hand, the expert is obliged to comprehensively explain all matters that have been covered by the evidential thesis, and on the other, he or she cannot go beyond this scope. However, it is impossible to accept an understanding of binding the expert with the thesis, according to which the expert would not have the opportunity to express the views on the matters, from the examination of which the correctness of preparing an opinion depends as such [9]. With regard to bankruptcy proceedings, the scope of the court expert opinion is clearly defined in the provisions of the Act, and it includes a description and estimation of the subject of the transaction with an investor purchasing part of the bankruptcy estate, drawn up in accordance with the standards expressed in Art. 319 of the Bankruptcy law, which will be discussed below. This does not mean, however, that this provision also exhaustively outlines the manner and scope of the opinion, and this causes a number of practical problems related to the different approach of court experts to similar assets. An example is the method of preparing an opinion, which is an element of the special knowledge, and therefore only in obvious situations of error in the methodology, the court may question such opinion. For the same reasons, there are no grounds to consider that it is necessary to order a court expert to perform another supplementary opinion or a new opinion of another expert if the methodology used by the expert is admissible [10]. However, in a situation where this method, due to the purpose of the opinion (in this case the valuation of certain assets), in the assessment of the body of the proceedings is inappropriate, the body should use the opportunity to modify the opinion or order another one.

It is worth noting here, referring to the detailed provisions of the Bankruptcy law, that in the Polish legal system bankruptcy proceedings are divided into two stages—proceedings on the application for bankruptcy, which ends with a declaration of bankruptcy or dismissal or rejection of the bankruptcy application; and the so-called proper bankruptcy proceedings, the essence of which is to quickly and effectively carry out the liquidation of the debtor's assets included in the bankruptcy estate. For this reason, further considerations will refer to each of these stages of the proceedings separately, because the legislator has differently defined the scope of using evidence from the court expert opinion, having in perspective the different nature and course of actions performed in each of them, aimed at determining the value of the component parts of the bankruptcy estate. However, regardless of the stage of the proceedings, the subsidiary role of the expert, both towards the body and the participants in the proceedings, should be emphasized. The opinion presented by the expert does not have a compulsory meaning for both participants and authorities, as on the one hand—participants in the proceedings may criticize and attempt to refute it with proof to the contrary, and on the other hand—the body should evaluate it together with all collected evidence [11]. Certainly, in the bankruptcy proceedings, the evidence to be taken into account when determining the final terms for the sale of an enterprise, its organized part or individual parts is the hearing of the debtor (bankrupt) or creditors, as they may indicate additional circumstances relating, for example, to the choice of the most effective mode of sale of the components of the bankruptcy estate, because the liquidation of the bankruptcy estate is carried out by single-source sales, tender or auction of a bankrupt enterprise in its entirety, its organized parts or real estate and movable property.

6.3 The Role of an Expert in the Implementation of the Prepared Liquidation (Pre-pack)

As indicated above, the first stage of bankruptcy proceedings is the procedure before the bankruptcy application is resolved. At this stage, no expert opinion is carried out, with the exception specified in Art. 56b paragraph 1 of the Bankruptcy law. This last case will be discussed later. This quite radical and doubtful solution is justified mainly by the separation of bankruptcy proceedings and restructuring proceedings, which allows deciding whether there is any indication of bankruptcy or restructuring obligations without any need to reach for special information, as well as remove other doubts relating to the premises of bankruptcy (e.g. disputability of claims). Practice will show whether this exclusion does not adversely affect the quality of decisions regarding bankruptcy.

The said provision of Art. 56b paragraph 1 of the Bankruptcy law refers to the so-called prepared liquidation as a procedure initiated yet at the stage of the proceedings before the announcement of bankruptcy. The prepared liquidation is a new solution under the Polish Bankruptcy law. Its structural assumptions derive directly from Anglo-Saxon law (*pre-packaged administration*), where this mechanism is popular in practice [12]. This procedure was conceived by the Polish legislator as a way of supporting those entrepreneurs who rely on the reputation and trust of customers, and thus the chance for their further functioning on the market in new hands is high but conditioned by the right speed of proceeding in the field of change of ownership. In practice, it is pointed out that the process of the ongoing liquidation of the bankruptcy estate may result in a decrease in the value of the bankrupt enterprise as a whole. The main reason for this will be the loss of contractors' trust, lowering the reputation, and reducing the presence on the market. These reasons will have a particularly negative impact on the intangible assets of a company with trademarks and a good name at the forefront [13]. For this reason, the legislator decided that the introduction of such a solution may have a positive impact on the effectiveness of disposal of assets included in the bankruptcy estate, also from the perspective of the debtor, who by independent search for an investor intending to acquire an enterprise or individual assets, has a direct impact on who will take over a significant part of the assets, as well as such important components of the company's future as the reputation on the market or continuation of employment of the debtor's existing staff.

The purpose of introducing a pre-pack solution is to optimize the process of liquidation by selling the bankrupt enterprise, its organized part or even just specific assets included in it, which are of high value and economic significance. In this respect, the key role is played by shifting the buyer search phase and negotiation of the terms of sale to the period preceding the initiation of the bankruptcy proceedings. Thus, an entrepreneur with the prospect of bankruptcy can search for an investor who decides to buy an enterprise or part of it, which will also allow the issue of time-consuming bankruptcy proceedings to be resolved. Model bankruptcy proceedings with prepared liquidation are carried out in such a way that an entrepreneur experiencing financial problems (recognizing a threat of insolvency or insolvency at a very early stage), while continuing his or her activity and avoiding public information about his or her problems, seeks a buyer for the company. The entrepreneur sets the terms of the sale transaction with the buyer and then submits to the court an application to declare bankruptcy [1]. In this case, the debtor adds to the application for bankruptcy an additional application, the content of which is a request for approval of the terms of sale of the debtor's company, its organized part, or assets which constitute a significant part of the company (Art. 56a paragraph 1 of the Bankruptcy Law). In addition, the application for approval of the terms of sale must contain the terms of sale by indicating at least the price and the buyer. The terms of sale may be specified in the submitted draft of an agreement to be concluded by the trustee. What is more, the application for approval of the terms of sale may provide for the release of the company to the buyer from the date of declaration of the bankruptcy of the debtor. In this case, the application is accompanied by proof of payment of the full price to the court's deposit account.

However, from the perspective of these considerations, the most important is that the application for approval of the terms of sale is accompanied by a description and estimation of the component covered by the application prepared by a person entered on the list of court experts. It should be clearly indicated that the above-mentioned description and estimation have the character of a private expert opinion, which raises a number of doubts as to its reliability. Although there is no definitive test for determining the reliability of expert testimony, the Supreme Court U.S. has identified a number of factors bearing on reliability, including (1) whether a theory or technique "can be (and has been) tested", (2) "whether the theory or technique has been subjected to peer review and publication", (3) a technique's "known or potential rate of error", and "the existence and maintenance of standards controlling the technique's operation", and (4) whether a particular technique or theory has gained "general acceptance" in the relevant scientific community [14].

These dilemmas refer not only to the situation of intentional ill will of the ordering party and expert (deliberate falsification or distortion of conclusions in the opinion), but also to the terms of the accuracy of the selection of the expert as to his or her knowledge and qualifications, especially if the valued set of components includes unusual types of structures, installations, etc., requiring a special substantive preparation of the valuer. In any case, the extrajudicial expert opinion prepared at the request of the party is not subject to review by the court as evidence from an expert opinion [15]. This is due to the fact that private expert opinions prepared at the request of the parties, whether during the proceedings or before their initiation, should be treated in the event of their acceptance by the adjudicating court as an explanation supporting the position of the parties, taking into account special information [16]. For this reason, the body of the proceedings must approach the attached description and estimation with particular caution, as it may lead to intentional or unintentional irregularities in the formulation of conclusions in this expertise. The attitude presented by the expert, which raises doubts as to his or her impartiality, may result in attributing a low evidential value to the presented opinion [17] and in some cases also in expert's liability for damages. For this reason, literature claims that the application should be accompanied not only by the description and estimation of the components covered by the application prepared by a person entered on the list of court experts, but also by evidence of the expert's civil liability insurance contract, where the guarantee sum is not less than the difference between the sum of the debtor's liabilities and the sum resulting from the estimation [18]. The American doctrine of Bankruptcy law indicates that the trial court judge serves as "gatekeeper" and excludes expert witnesses who are deemed not qualified, reliable, or able to provide relevant testimony. The gatekeeper's duty, in essence, is to ensure that the fact finder is not tainted by evidence that does not meet "the same level of intellectual rigour that characterizes the practice of an expert in the relevant field [19]".

The discussed provision of the Bankruptcy law considering the description and estimation also does not specify the method of valuation of an enterprise, its organized part or individual assets. The economics of enterprises have developed various valuation methods, but attention is drawn to the fact that the *in concreto* analysis of the company's assets is conditional upon the purpose for which this valuation is to be used. Most commonly, the valuation of an enterprise is made in the following cases: (1) sale of the enterprise, (2) contribution to the company, in particular a capital company, (3) buyer's responsibly for the liabilities related to this enterprise. In the face of the dispute existing in the field of economics of enterprises in the adoption of the most favourable method reflecting the value of a specific enterprise, the judicial authorities face the problem of choosing the method of valuation and determining whether it is possible to clearly determine a reliable method in all situations in which the element of the facts covered by the hypothesis of the legal norm is the value of the enterprise as a whole or a value of its organized part [20]. This ambiguity causes many practical problems both with regard to the suitability of both private expertise and opinions prepared at the request of the court, an example of which will be the description and estimation for the purposes of bankruptcy proceedings in the discussed scope. As indicated in the doctrine, a well-prepared valuation analyst can be an important asset for a party in a bankruptcy dispute. Such a valuation expert can also be a real benefit for the judicial finder of fact. However, before the valuation analyst can help anyone, the analyst's expert testimony must be admissible. If the valuation analyst considers the factors that a court will consider, then the valuation analyst should be able to tailor his or her report and testimony to ensure that the expert testimony admissibility thresholds are met [20].

However, referring to the price indicated in the estimate made to sell the company, it should be noted that this price, determined on the basis of the adopted valuation method, is only a possible, never effective price. The potential price of an enterprise can be transformed into an effective price, meaning a specific sum of money that is transferred from the buyer's assets to the seller's assets. However, the actual occurrence of such an effect depends on many circumstances, including among others the two basic factors shaping the prices of goods in the course of trade, namely supply and demand. However, in the case of the valuation of the enterprise, the methods of determining the potential price are different, which in turn is related to the principles that this price has to meet [21]. It should be remembered that from the point of view of different parties (debtor and creditors), this price has different functions: it can be the maximum, minimum, and sometimes the only acceptable price, hence it is important to determine it correctly, which on one hand will not discourage the investor from acquisition of the components of the bankruptcy estate, and on the other—will not jeopardize creditors who will not be satisfied in an optimal manner due to their undervaluation.

In order to prevent detriment to creditors, of particular importance are the provisions of Art. 56b paragraph 1 of the Bankruptcy law, which states that the sale to the entities indicated in Art. 128, this Act is permissible only at the sale price not lower than the price of the estimate. The estimated price is determined by the court based on the evidence from the expert opinion. In this case, these are entities that for emotional or property reasons will not keep the rules of economics in terms of investment in the bankruptcy estate, due to their close relationship with the debtor (bankrupt). These are: (1) his or her spouse, relative by blood or relative by affinity in direct line, relative by blood or relative by affinity in secondary line up to the second degree, including the person remaining with the bankrupt in the actual relationship, who is jointly managing the household or the adopted or adopter; (2) a company in which the bankrupt is a board member, the sole partner or shareholder, and companies in which the persons mentioned in point 1 are members of the board of directors or only partners or shareholders; (3) partners of the bankrupt being a commercial company or a person, their representatives or their spouses, as well as related companies, their associates, representatives or spouses of such persons; (4) another company, if the bankrupt is a company, and one of them was the parent company. The applicant and the possible buyer submit a declaration as to whether there are any relations between them and the debtor referred to in Art. 128 of the Bankruptcy law. However, this mechanism also raises doubts as to its real effectiveness, because in practice entities that have such connections build complex constructions of indirect links, which allow them to bypass the requirement of an obligatory construction of the description and estimation, which is often related to the actual detriment to the creditors.

The solution from the so-called prepared liquidation clearly raises many practical problems, but it is certainly one of the basic regulations that allow the investor to effectively finalize the transaction with the debtor (bankrupt), which is of economic importance not only for the investor but also for creditors seeking satisfaction in bankruptcy proceedings and in many cases also for the social and economic environment (debtor's employees, contractors, etc.).

6.4 Determination of the Sale Price of an Enterprise or Assets After the Declaration of Bankruptcy—General Principles

While referring to the so-called proper bankruptcy proceedings in the scope of an expert opinion, essential for shaping the terms of acquisition of an enterprise, its organized part or individual assets, attention should also be paid to the scope of participation of a court expert in this proceeding. The taking of evidence from an expert opinion cannot be limited to the expert's submission of a written opinion to the case files, and the expert should be summoned to a court session in order to allow the authorities and the parties to the proceedings to ask questions. Similar regulation is present in the German code of civil procedure, where on the basis of § 411 of *Zivilprozessordnung* the court calls for the preparation of an expert opinion in writing and its presentation in a given period. The court may also summon an expert to appear in court in person in order to clarify the written opinion [22]. This matters when the party raises new allegations to the content of the opinion if the case is resolved in the next instance. The demand for oral explanation of the opinion is a court's right, not an obligation, but it becomes its obligation not only when such explanations are clearly demanded by the participants in the proceedings but also when they raise objections requiring clarification, or when the authority notices lacks or illogicality in the written opinion [23]. However, in the case of bankruptcy proceedings, in which efficiency and effectiveness are of paramount importance, the legislator has also introduced other organizational possibilities as to how to receive additional explanations from a court expert. The Act provides for the following acceptable forms of hearing: (1) hearing by a court or by a judge-commissioner in the presence of interested persons or without their presence; (2) making a statement in writing; (3) making a statement in writing with a signature certified by a notary public. The choice of the form of the hearing is made by the court or judge-commissioner by way of order—it is its exclusive competence, and the decision in this matter is not subject to appeal. This gives the opportunity to speed up the proceedings by departing from the need to conduct a court session to discuss the content of the court expert opinion on the description and estimation of the company in its entirety, its organized part or individual assets.

As already indicated, the Bankruptcy law petrifies the rules for the execution of an expert opinion on the description and estimation to a greater extent than it results from the general provisions of civil procedural law. This applies to a situation in which the so-called prepared liquidation has not been applied, which is associated with the conduct of a full proceeding aimed at liquidating the assets of the debtor which are parts of the bankruptcy estate. If the sale of the bankrupt company is planned as a whole, when preparing the inventory and estimating the bankruptcy estate, or in parts, if the possibility of such sale is revealed at a later stage, the expert selected by the trustee makes a description and estimation of the bankrupt enterprise.

Therefore, the basis for taking actions by a court expert is the direction of opinion indicated by the body of the proceedings, thanks to which the expert has the opportunity to explicitly refer to the indicated scope in the prepared and presented opinion. Thus, the emphasis on the literature on the subject of the need to cooperate with the court expert is important [24]. At the same time, however, according to the will of the legislator, the description of an enterprise should specify in particular the subject of the enterprise's activity, real estate included in it, its area and the number of land register or a set of documents, other fixed assets, established rights, and burdens. If the company's components are encumbered with mortgage, pledge, registered pledge, fiscal pledge, sea mortgage, or other rights and effects of disclosure of rights and personal claims, the estimate should specify separately which of these rights remain in force after the sale, as well as their value and the value of the components burdened with them and the ratio of the value of individual encumbered components with the value of the enterprise (Art. 319 paragraph 4 of the Bankruptcy Law). The elements of the company description define the minimum content of this description; in addition, it must always include a valuation of the entire company, and if the "organized part of the enterprise" is suitable for sale—also the valuation of this part. An essential element of the description of the company is the data indicated in Art. 319 paragraph 4 of the Bankruptcy law, with the proviso that it considers the ratio of the value of the encumbered enterprise component to the value of the entire enterprise, and not the ratio of the value of the encumbering right to the value of the enterprise [25]. At the same time, the justification of the opinion should be formulated in a way to allow the court expert to confirm the comprehensiveness of his or her specialist knowledge in the most credible way. It must be adapted to the specific circumstances of the case, and it should also express a specific reasoning of the expert in an understandable way, taking into account the analysis of the material provided by the body of the proceedings. At the same time, it is important that the justification of the opinion is drawn up in a diligent manner, omitting unnecessary divagations, which go beyond the opinion-making process [26].

Objections to the description and estimation are submitted within a week of the date of the announcement of their transfer to the judge-commissioner. Objections are recognized by the judge-commissioner. In case of doubts as to the reliability or correctness of the description and estimation, the judge-commissioner appoints an expert to prepare a new description and estimation. It is assumed that an expert opinion is incomplete if it does not answer all the questions asked to the expert, which according to the scope of special information and materials available to him or her should be answered, or if it does not take into account all the circumstances relevant to the resolution of the examined issue, or it does not contain justification of expressed assessments and views. On the other hand, the expert's opinion is unclear if its wording does not allow to understand the assessments and opinions expressed in it, as well as the way of reaching them, or if it contains internal contradictions or uses illogical arguments. The jurisprudence established position is that if evidence from an expert opinion is convincing and understandable to the authority of the proceedings, and the opinion is properly justified the fact that the evidence is not convincing for the participant in the proceedings cannot create a basis for the re-appointment of experts or seeking the opinion of new experts [27]. In this case, it is crucial to precisely determine the terms of sale of the enterprise, its organized part or individual assets. The supervisory actions of the authorities of the proceedings are intended to protect the interests of creditors and other entities affected by the bankruptcy. All the more, the judge-commissioner should not let his or her actions or omissions to act to the detriment of the bankrupt's creditors. If the terms of sale of the company were possible to establish in an enigmatic way, the necessity of obtaining permission for single-source sales would not make sense [28]. Thus, in this case, a properly prepared expert opinion in relation to the valuation of the enterprise, its organized part or individual assets must be precise, and prepared with the use of an appropriate method, taking into account the specific subject of valuation, which is part of the bankruptcy estate subject to actions aimed at its liquidation.

6.5 Conclusions

As it appears from previous considerations, the expert opinion is used in those areas in which the court as a layman is not able to assess certain facts and determine proper values on their basis [29]. American literature indicates that the valuation standards may be vague, but the tools of valuation are well established. Though there are many names and variants, methods for valuing a company as a going concern are typically classified into three groups: discounted cash flow (DCF), comparable company multiples (CCM), and comparable transaction multiples (TM). A fourth method that is often used in bankruptcy cases is what we will call direct market evidence, such as a stock price, or an offer to buy securities or assets on a given date. Finally, if liquidation is being considered, book value or some other estimate of liquidation value may be used. However, a detailed discussion of these methods goes beyond the scope of the study [30].

The certificate submitted by an expert is only an expression of his or her personal opinions, established on the basis of the factual material provided by the procedural body and after a thorough analysis of similar situations [31]. However, this does not mean that he or she enjoys full discretion, as he or she must apply both general standards for the preparation of court expert opinions in civil matters, and the rules for enterprise valuation arising from economic sciences, but also the detailed rules discussed above regarding the description and estimation of an enterprise or its organized part in bankruptcy proceedings.

However, from the perspective of an authority of the bankruptcy proceedings, two types of problems can be discussed—quality and time. In the first scope, violation of the provisions of procedural law occurs when from the very beginning a person appointed in this capacity did not have expert knowledge and did not meet the criteria of being appointed as an expert or failed to meet such criteria in the scope of the research subject entrusted to him or her, but not in a situation when the expert was formally appointed correctly, but his or her knowledge and skills proved to be insufficient for a particular subject of research [32]. Thus, the body of the proceedings should exercise due diligence in selecting a court expert adequately to the needs of a specific opinion. The evidence from the expert opinion is properly carried out when the opinion contains justification of the final conclusions, formulated in an accessible and understandable way for people without special knowledge. Not the number of opinions testifies to their value, but the explanations contained in them that require special knowledge. The expert opinion is the whole position and as such is subject to the assessment of the body of the proceedings, and any deficiencies in the written form may be supplemented by the expert's position presented in an oral form [33]. Therefore, the body of the proceedings is responsible for the proper selection of an expert and enforcement of the opinion, which may be a basis for a correct decision.

The second problem important for bankruptcy proceedings, which is largely dependent on the efficiency of action of the bodies of the proceedings, is the criterion of the time of actions carried out during the proceedings. Actions taken by a court in connection with the admission of evidence from an expert opinion may contribute to the length of the proceedings. Firstly, such a situation is incorrect formulation of the decision on the admission of this evidence; secondly, refraining from determining in advance whether a person indicated as an expert is a specialist in a particular scope; thirdly, the excessive duration of the proceedings is caused by the lack of supervision over the timeliness of an expert's opinion [34]. These circumstances should be taken into account, in particular, when the investor is interested in acquiring the enterprise, its organized part and individual assets, especially if the prepared liquidation is not applied and time-consuming bankruptcy proceedings take place.

References

1. Zimmerman, P.: Prawo upadłościowe. Prawo restrukturyzacyjne. Komentarz. C.H. Beck, Warsaw (2018)
2. Judgment of the Court Appeal in Łódź of 29 March 2017, I ACa 1260/16, Legalis (2017)
3. Judgment of the Court of Appeal in Łódź of 30 June 2017, I ACa 1698/16, Legalis (2017)
4. Judgment of the Supreme Court of 2 March 2017, II KK 358/16, Legalis (2017)
5. Judgment of the Court of Appeal in Szczecin of 20 June 2017, III AUa 645/16, Legalis (2017)
6. Decision of the Supreme Court of 10 August 2017, I CSK 328/17, Legalis (2017)
7. Judgment of the Supreme Court of 20 January 2015, V CSK 254/14, Legalis (2015)
8. Judgment of the Court of Appeal in Cracow of 5 December 2014, I ACa 1090/14, LEX (2014)
9. Judgment of the Court of Appeal in Katowice of 7 July 2017, V ACa 640/16, Legalis (2017)
10. Judgment of the Court of Appeal in Warsaw of 10 January 2018, VII AGa 39/18, Legalis (2018)
11. Klich, A.: Dowód z opinii biegłego w postępowaniu cywilnym. C.H. Beck, Warsaw, Biegły lekarz (2016)
12. McCormack, G.: National report for England. In: Faber, D., Vermunt, N., Kilborn, J., Richter, T. (eds.) Commencement of insolvency proceedings, oxford international and comparative law series, pp. 234–283. Oxford University Press, Oxford (2012)

13. Witosz, A.J.: Przygotowana likwidacja w postępowaniu upadłościowym—wybrane uwagi. In: Studia Ekonomiczne. Zeszyty Naukowe Uniwersytetu Ekonomicznego w Katowicach, No 329 (2017)
14. Daubert v. Merrell Dow Pharmaceuticals, Inc., 509 U.S. 579, 509 U.S., pp. 593–94 (1993)
15. Judgment of the Supreme Court of 8 June 2001, I PKN 468/00, OSNAPiUS No 8, item 197 (2003)
16. Judgment of the Supreme Court of 11 June 1974, II CR 260/74, Legalis (2015)
17. Nicklisch, F.: Der Teshnische Sachverständige im Prozess. In: Habscheid W.J. (ed.), Effektiver Rechtsschutz und verfassungsmässige Ordnung. Generalberichtezum VII. International Kongress für Prozessrecht, Gieseking Verlag, Würzburg (1983)
18. Hrycaj A.: Komentarz do art. 56a Prawa upadłościowego. In: Hrycaj A., Jakubecki A., Witosz A. (eds.), Prawo restrukturyzacyjne i upadłościowe, System Prawa Handlowego, vol. 6, C.H. Beck, Warsaw (2016)
19. Harris, Ch. R., Baker, H.G.: Practice pointers for working with expert witnesses in bankruptcy Court. New York Law Journal, 16 April 2012, p. 3 (2012)
20. Litwińska-Werner, M.: Wartość przedsiębiorstwa. In: Włodyka, S. (ed.), Prawo handlowe—część ogólna. System Prawa Handlowego. Tom 1, C.H. Beck, Warsaw (2009)
21. Reilly, R.F.: Valuation analyst guidelines related to bankruptcy expert reports and expert testimony. Dispute Resolut. Insights J. **7**, 48 (2010)
22. Gottwald, P.: The culture and science of gathering information and proof-taking. In: Gilles P., Pfeiffer Th. (eds.), Prozeßrecht und Rechtskulturen, Baden-Baden (2004)
23. Judgment of the Supreme Court of 17 Match 2017, III CSK 84/16, LEX (2017)
24. Daub, S.: Die Tatsachenerhebungdurch den Sachverständigen. Peter Lang Frankfurt/M, Berlin, Bern, New York, Paris, Wien (1997)
25. Gurgul, S.: Prawo upadłościowe. Prawo restrukturyzacyjne. Komentarz. C.H. Beck, Warsaw (2018)
26. Mayr, D.: In: Bayerlein, W. (ed.) Praxishandbuch Sachverständigenrecht, München (2008)
27. Judgment of the Court of Appeal in Cracow of 7 May 2015, II AKa 64/15, Legalis (2015)
28. Judgment of the Supreme Court of 29 June 2007, SNO 39/07, Legalis (2007)
29. Trilsch, J.: Die Stellung des Sachverständigen gegenüber dem Gericht im deutschen und englischen Zivilprozessrecht. Shaker Verlag GmbH, Aachen (1994)
30. Ayotte, K., Morrison, E.R.: Valuation Disputes in Corporate Bankruptcy (January 19, 2018). University of Pennsylvania Law Review (2018)
31. Stewart, A.: The Value of Expert Evidence. In: The American Law Register and Review vol. 41, no 6 (1893)
32. Decision of the Supreme Court of 5 June 2007, IV KK 53/07, Legalis (2007)
33. Judgment of the Court of Appeal in Warsaw of 28 June 2017, 28.06.2017, I ACa 561/16, Legalis (2017)
34. Decision of the Supreme Court of 10 January 2017, III SPP 66/16, Legalis (2017)

Chapter 7
Inclusion of ESG Factors in Investments and Value Addition: A Meta-Analysis of the Relationship

Ria Sinha, Manipadma Datta and Magdalena Ziolo

Abstract The research explores the impact of ESG factors on investments by conducting a global study considering 100 academic papers dealing with the interlinkage between ESG factors and financial performance. The papers are selected using Cochrane methodology across different geographical domains over a time period of 1990–2015 and analyzed using a meta-analytic approach. The idea was not only to assess the relationship between sustainability and financial performance but also to decipher the impact of different control variables on the relationship. The results emphasize the positive impact of ESG factors on financial performance.

Keywords Sustainability · ESG · Responsible investment · Finance

7.1 Introduction

Over the past decade, there has been an increased growth of responsible investments around the world, resulting in a multitrillion dollar market in the developed countries [1]. A slow transition has been witnessed from the emergence and growth of ethical investments to socially responsible or responsible investments (SRI or RI) and still further to environmental, social and governance (ESG) investing. The fundamental motivation behind these investments has changed from being philanthropic to material, keeping in mind the financial profitability of such investments. Unlike the conventional investments, SRI funds apply a set of screening norms, involving both positive and negative screens based on certain indicators such as environmen-

R. Sinha (✉) · M. Datta
Department of Business and Sustainability, TERI School of Advanced Studies, New Delhi, India
e-mail: rias.echo@gmail.com

M. Datta
e-mail: manipadma.datta@terisas.ac.in

M. Ziolo
Faculty of Economics and Management, University of Szczecin, Szczecin, Poland
e-mail: magdalena.ziolo@usz.edu.pl

W. Tarczyński and K. Nermend (eds.), *Effective Investments on Capital Markets*, Springer Proceedings in Business and Economics,
https://doi.org/10.1007/978-3-030-21274-2_7

tal, social and governance factors. The study intends to find an answer to the vital question, i.e., whether it is possible to perform good by doing good. Simply put whether SRI or ESG investments lead to financial and market value addition of business portfolios. Hence, in this paper we have attempted to decipher the financial impact of the inclusion of ESG factors in investments. Several academicians have resorted to empirical studies both at the company and at the portfolio levels to assess the impacts. The authors from several studies have adhered to fund analysis, firm-level analysis and analysis of the sustainable indices, to test the performance of the sustainable funds vis-à-vis their conventional counterparts using several financial models such as capital asset pricing model (CAPM), Carhart's alpha, matched pair, multifactor and multivariate regression models. For establishing the relationship, corporate social performance (CSP) has been majorly used as a proxy for sustainability measurement to assess the firm- or company-level impacts. Meta-analysis has also been used as a statistical tool to meaningfully assimilate the existing literature. There are certain advantages of this particular approach. First, incorporation of a large number of studies helps to improve the statistical power of small or inconclusive studies to answer questions and the ability to identify sources of diversity across various types of studies. Second, meta-analysis also helps to summarize the results from various studies conducted at different points of time and at varied geographical locations. Third, meta-analysis can be used to detect cases of publication bias as well as deficiencies in the design, conduct, analysis and interpretation of research. Fourth, the application of this approach helps to reveal cases of heterogeneity among studies which may otherwise affect the overall findings of the studies. Hence at first, a detailed review of these studies has been conducted to understand its historical roots and methodologies. Secondly, a meta-analytic review is conducted to comprehend the global findings have been presented by incorporating 100 academic studies conducted at different points of time from 1990 to 2015. Studies conducted prior to 1990 have not been considered due to the concern raised by Buerden and Gössling [2]. According to them, the Brundtland Commission Report was published in 1987, which is believed to be one of the pioneering reports on the sustainable development and can be viewed as a turning point in the attention toward CSR. In this context, the role of business was discussed from an alternative perspective. The organizational consequences of the report and the stakeholder responses are highly unlikely to be reflected in academic studies conducted prior to 1990. The present study is in strong concurrence with the concerns pointed out by previous researchers and hence does not incorporate studies conducted before 1990. The present paper is organized as follows: Sect. 2 includes a review of the literature, Sect. 3 presents the methodology, Sect. 4 presents the research results, and this is followed by conclusions.

7.2 Literature Review

There have been several meta-studies and primary surveys conducted in the developed markets to assess the importance and potentiality of ESG integration in investment portfolios. The crucial question addressed here is whether ESG investing leads to increased financial returns in the form of profits and shareholder value, i.e., whether ESG factors are material. Materiality of ESG factors in investment portfolios will encourage investors to focus more on the sustainable value of investments, thereby leading to achieve the larger goals of sustainability. Positive relationship between ESG factors and portfolio performance based on research carried reported: [3–7]. At the same time, other researchers pointed out neutral [8, 9] or negative relationship [10] between ESG factors and portfolio performance. RobecoSAM [11] refers to a study conducted by the US-based Governance & Accountability Institute, Inc. (G & A). It has found that, in 2011, approximately 53% of S & P 500 companies reported on ESG topics compared to 19–20% in 2010. According to the report, these numbers are even higher in other parts of the world and are partially reflected in the 66.6% increase in RobecoSAM's Corporate Sustainability Assessment (CSA) response rate since 2003. The increased numbers are fueled by increasing stakeholder pressure in the environment and social domains. Companies are strengthening the accountability of ESG metrics to meet investors' needs to provide more comparable and meaningful information. A recent study by the Association of Chartered Certified Accountants (ACCA) and Eurosif suggests that 66% of investors agree to the European Commission's proposal to cover a minimum number of environmental, social, employee, human rights and anticorruption issues. Accordingly, governments, national stock exchanges, local communities and employees demand more reporting transparency and accountability. Innovest [12] had carried out a meta-analysis of 60 studies to assess the relationship between environmental governance and financial performance. Environmental governance has been defined as the state of governance that describes a company's management of its environmental impacts, risks, performance and opportunities. The fundamental financial performance parameters used in this report are shareholder value, share price, market cap, market share, BMV, EBIT, EBITDA and operating costs. According to the report, 72% of the studies reported a positive relation between environmental governance and financial performance, 17% highlighted negative correlation, and 11% confirmed a neutral relationship. Sector-specific studies reflected 79% positive correlation between environmental and financial performance, 14% reflected negative correlation, and 7% reported a neutral relationship. Lastly, fund studies highlighted 70% positive correlation, 24% showed negative correlation, and 6% witnessed neutral relation between environmental and financial performances. The market studied in the report pertained to developed markets. Although the definition of corporate financial performance (CFP) is not debated in the literature, there exists incongruity with respect to the best way to quantify CFP [13]. According to Orlitzky et al. [5], the wide gamut of the academic literature available to capture CFP highlights basically three forms: market, accounting and survey measurements. The approach based on market emphasizes the degree of shareholder satisfaction; the second approach captures the internal efficiency of a firm, and the third provides a qualitative and subjective estimation of financial performance. The accounting and market measures of CFP, viz. ROA, ROE, ROS, cost of capital, turnover, Tobin's Q, operating expenses, P/E ratio and ratio of profits to assets, have been used in several studies [4, 10, 14–30]. Studies have also resorted to fund analysis mechanisms, and the financial indicators mostly used in such studies are Jensen's alpha, Carhart's alpha, Sharpe ratio and Treynor ratio [31–48]. In this context, the study intends to emphasize that the financial variables employed to measure CFP are supported in the literature by precise forms. On the other hand, there is no universally accepted variable to measure CSP that is unanimously acknowledged by every stakeholder. Weber et al. [10] have conducted a study by comparing 151 SRI funds against the MSCI conventional fund using Jensen's alpha and Sharpe ratio. The study which covers Europe, Asia-Pacific, North America, South Africa and Latin America has clearly shown the outperformance of the SRI fund over its conventional peers. On the other hand, Kreander [33] had performed a study by considering 80 funds, out of which 40 belonged to the ethical group and other 40 belonged to the non-ethical group. The study covered the European countries of UK, Sweden, Germany, the Netherlands, Norway, Switzerland and Belgium. With the help of CAPM, Fama French 3-factor and Carhart 4-factor models, the risk-adjusted returns were measured by Jensen's alpha and Sharpe and Treynor ratios. The study surprisingly found the under-performance of the ethical funds over the non-ethical ones. However, most of the studies mentioned have used negative screens in selecting companies and funds. There is another set of studies (through limited) which assess the impact of both the positive and negative screens on financial performance. Such a study by Stenstrom and Thorell [48] conducted in Sweden measured the performance of SRI funds over its conventional peers. The study has used CAPM and Carhart 4-factor models to estimate Jensen's alpha and Sharpe ratio and found an inverse U-shaped relationship between CSR and financial performance. Moreover, the results of the study have also emphasized on the fact that investors should carefully estimate the screening method and fund management of SRI fund investments as they seem to have an effect on the fund performance. Fund management of regular funds has been found to perform better than that of the SRI funds. Stock exchanges in both developed and developing economies across the globe have launched sustainability indices to comprehend the market mood of the sustainable investments. Examples of this include the stock exchanges in several developed economies of UK, USA, Australia, France and South Africa. This proliferation is based on the fact that market is evolving from largely value-oriented investors and now involves a great segment with a growing emphasis on investors seeking long-term value. However, the role of the stock exchanges has not been limited to launching of sustainability indices but has also been instrumental in providing sustainability guidance to listed companies and assists in the development of carbon markets in developing countries as well. The growing awareness has also led some stock exchanges such as the stock exchanges of South Africa and Istanbul to become signatories to the UNPRI. Sustainability reports are also published by the Spanish and Hong Kong stock exchanges.

The existing studies in this domain lack comprehensiveness in approach. There have been a plethora of studies to establish the relationship between sustainable performance and financial performance of companies. However, corporate entities such as investors and companies are still not convinced about the value-adding potential of ESG investments. This is because most of the studies have been sector-specific and concentrated in the USA. Some studies have focused on company performance, while several studies have focused on fund performance. More to this, the time period considered for such studies has also been constricted to a narrow time period. The meta-studies existing in this domain are also subjected to the mentioned shortcomings along with accommodating a small sample of studies. Moreover, these studies also do not address the influence of other intervening or control variables which may impact the relationship. The present study attempts to address these limitations by incorporating a larger sample and time period of study, a wider gamut of sectoral classification of portfolios, types of analysis, control variables and domiciles to accentuate comprehensiveness and clarity in approach.

7.3 Methodology

The use of meta-analytic approach in determining whether the inclusion of ESG factors results in increased financial value has been one of the very innovative approaches in the academic literature. Screening of relevant studies based on the authors' objective has indeed produced desired results. Usually, two types of statistical methods have been applied to summarize the results. First, use of descriptive statistics and synthesis of the academic studies have been used to integrate the findings [49]. Secondly, explanatory variables have been used to synthesize the different indicators of sustainability performance [5, 51–53]. Most of the studies mentioned here have been domiciled in USA and have established a positive relationship. As a matter of fact, meta-analysis has proven to be a very useful technique in several substantive areas where findings from several studies have yielded inconclusive and conflicting results [5]. Corporations and academicians have used this statistical technique to establish the relationship between sustainable factors and financial performance of companies. Phillips, Hager and North Investment Management [51] had performed a meta-analysis with 17 studies on SRI funds, considering the time period 1993–2007, and established a neutral to positive relationship between CSR and investment returns. In another study, Rathner [52] had applied a logit model to meta-analytic data extracted from 25 key studies to understand the performance of SRI funds. The study had embarked on a positive relationship. Large sample studies have also been conducted with the help of meta-analysis. In a recent report by Allianz GI Solutions [50], meta-analysis was performed with the help of 190 studies to check the materiality of ESG factors on equity portfolios. Vishwanathan and Heugens [53] had assimilated results from 280 core studies, collected over a period of 40 years to establish a positive relationship between CSR and financial performance. There are at least two approaches which may be used to analyze secondary data accrued through meta-analysis of the relevant literature. First, according to Buerden and Gössling [2], a meta-analytic approach can be used to evaluate studies using descriptive analysis, in which each evaluated study constitutes a unit of analysis. Secondly, a meta-analysis can be used for a particular number of studies to extract information relating to data sets and correct for sampling and measurement errors [5].

The present study is classified according to the first definition of meta-analysis due to the following reasons. First, the primary aim of this chapter has been to gauge the direction of relationship between CSP and CFP (positive, negative or neutral) and uncover the key factors which influence the relationship in an inductive way, such as the moderating and control variables. Secondly, the data accrued from the selected studies is qualitative in nature. Hence, descriptive statistics seem to be the most relevant and appropriate technique to summarize the data. Additionally, this method has also been applied by Boaventura et al. [49] to establish the causal relationship between CSP and CFP.

7.3.1 Sampling Technique

The Cochrane methodology for systematic reviews[1] has been followed for searching and selecting the studies. First, we conduct an extensive search with keywords in JSTOR, Google Scholar, SSRN and ResearchGate. The terms used for searching are "ESG investing and financial performance", "the relationship between corporate social performance and financial performance", and "sustainable business adds value". Secondly, the researcher has communicated over emails with other researchers working in similar areas for getting access to unpublished studies. Thirdly, references and cross-references have been used to collect papers for the purpose. This has resulted in assembling 100 relevant studies over the time period 1990–2015.

7.3.2 Statistical Analysis

Every article extracted has been analyzed at depth to understand whether the sustainable factors add value to business and business investments in particular. All the studies have been critically and carefully reviewed according to the following specifics: (1) year of publication, (2) type of document, (3) time period of study, (4) domain or geographical location studied, (4) mode of data collection and databases used, (5) financial instrument applied, (6) approach used for selection of stocks (wherever applicable), (7) statistical models considered, (8) financial performance indicators taken into consideration, (9) sustainable performance measures taken into account, (10) control variables and (11) the direction of relationship established between sustainable factors and CFP.

[1] It is by far the most comprehensive document which provides guidance to the authors for conducting systematic reviews in accordance with Cochrane Collaboration Group Controls. The handbook provides eight steps for the reviews: (1) defining the review question(s) and developing criteria for including studies; (2) searching for studies; (3) selecting studies and collecting data; (4) assessing risk of bias in included studies; (5) analyzing data and undertaking meta-analyses; (6) addressing reporting biases; (7) presenting results and "summary of findings" tables; and (8) interpreting results and drawing conclusions.

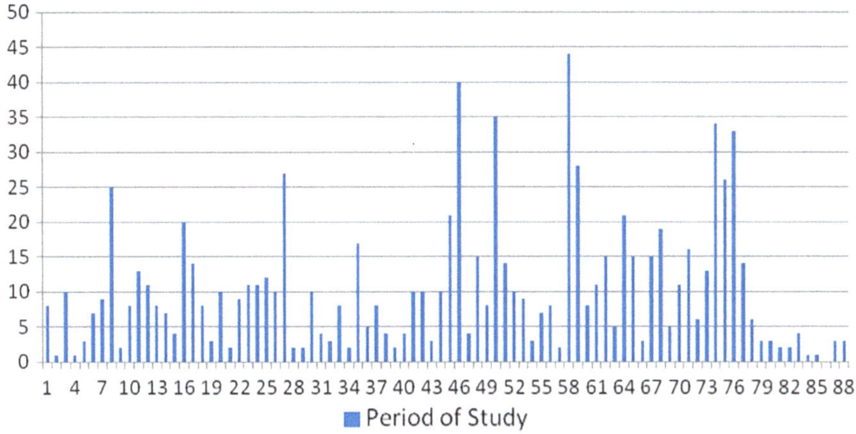

Fig. 7.1 Depth of studies considered for meta-analysis

Table 7.1 Descriptive statistics of empirical analysis

Type of Document	Percent
Secondary	81.0
Primary	1.0
Meta-analysis	13.0
Behavioral study	1.0
Content analysis	1.0
Theoretical model	1.0
Event analysis	1.0
Literature review	1.0
Total	100.0

The sample considered for our analysis constitutes of 100 studies of varied time periods under study. The lowest time period of the sample has been one year, and the highest has been 44 years. This variability has been illustrated in Fig. 7.1.

The compendium of studies consider several types of analysis for the purpose, namely secondary analysis, primary analysis, meta-analysis, content analysis, behavioral study, theoretical modeling, literature review and event analysis, as illustrated in Table 7.1. For the sample covered under our study, there has been a predominance of the use of secondary sources. The second most important type of analysis has been meta-analysis with the help of relevant academic studies.

The different studies considered under our period of study take into account several sustainability factors concerning environmental, social, CSR, corporate governance and ethical concerns. Very few studies have actually mentioned the key ESG factors considered. However, the plethora of key factors is stated in Table 7.2. As is evident from the table, the environmental factors considered mostly include the production of harmful substances which directly or indirectly can affect the ecological system. The

Table 7.2 ESG factors considered

Environment	Social	Corporate governance
No. of inspections by the environmental agency	Communication to employees	Shareholder advocacy
Eco-efficiency in products and processes	Health-related benefits to employees	Community investing
Energy efficiency of buildings	Compensation to employees	Shareholder rights
Effective emission reductions	Teamwork and philanthropy	CG disclosures and transparency
Variability of air pollutants	Dimensions of charitable contributions	Board composition; board and CEO compensation
Quantity of hazardous waste	Revealed misdeeds	Litigation fees
Ozone-depleting chemicals	Employer–employee relations	Range of takeover Defense
Agricultural emissions	Gender ratio at workplace	Rights and duties of shareholders
Carbon intensity (calculated)	Human rights	
Gross production of fossil energy	Product quality	
Operation of energy plants based on fossil energy or nuclear energy	Policies on health and safety	
Production of harmful substances according to the Stockholm agreement	Working hours and wages	
Sustainable fishery or forestry	Child/forced labor issues	
Production of nuclear reactors	Community involvement policy and programs	
Operations related to genetically modified organisms	Supplier information	
Production of weapons or military machines		
Production of tobacco and cigarettes		

social factors deal mostly with the well being of employees, and governance domain includes several indicators starting from transparency to shareholder proposals.

Analytical review of the sample indicates that majority of studies relating to materiality or value addition of ESG or socially responsible investments have been carried out in developed economies, especially USA and UK, with an extremely insignificant fraction conducted in developing economies. Table 7.3 illustrates the same. Table 7.3 is reflective of the wide range of developed and developing economies which have been covered in this paper. As is also consistent with the findings of Orlitzky et al. [5], most of the academic studies undertaken have focused on USA.

Different studies have adhered to different types of databases for obtaining data for both financial and sustainability factors. The most commonly used databases considered for the studies are Thomson Reuters, Datastream, Bloomberg, Compustat, Morningstar and CRSP. Different types of documents have been considered for the study, namely academic papers, PhD thesis/M.Sc. dissertations and reports by some of the ESG research consulting houses. Information on this has been highlighted

Table 7.3 Descriptive statistics on geographical domain of study

Country N	Responses		Percent of cases	Country N	Responses		Percent of cases
Global	12	7.5	12.0	Switzerland	3	1.9	3.0
Europe	12	7.5	12.0	Belgium	4	2.5	4.0
Australia	5	3.1	5.0	Austria	2	1.3	2.0
Sweden	7	4.4	7.0	France	4	2.5	4.0
UK	11	6.9	11.0	Italy	2	1.3	2.0
USA	55	34.6	55.0	Luxembourg	2	1.3	2.0
Asia-Pacific	2	1.3	2.0	Denmark	2	1.3	2.0
North America	2	1.3	2.0	Canada	4	2.5	4.0
South Africa	2	1.3	2.0	Taiwan	1	0.6	1.0
Latin America	1	0.6	1.0	Czech Republic	1	0.6	1.0
Vietnam	1	0.6	1.0	Japan	1	0.6	1.0
Greece	2	1.3	2.0	Spain	2	1.3	2.0
Korea	1	0.6	1.0	Portugal	1	0.6	1.0
Germany	7	4.4	7.0	Ireland	2	1.3	2.0
The Netherlands	5	3.1	5.0	India	1	0.6	1.0
Norway	2	1.3	2.0	Total	159	100	159

Table 7.4 Descriptive statistics of document type

Type Frequency	Percent	
Academic papers	86	86.0
Thesis/dissertation	8	8.0
Report	6	6.0
Total	100	100.0

Table 7.5 Descriptive statistics of relationship established

Relationship	Percent
Negative	14.0
Positive	66.0
Neutral	20.0
Total	100.0

in Table 7.4. Academic papers have been mostly considered for the purpose of the study.

As we have previously mentioned, the studies considered for our analysis entail different kinds of analysis, namely mutual fund performance over the benchmark asset, comparison of SRI funds vis-a-vis its conventional counterpart, portfolio studies and firm-level analysis. Taking all these studies together, we have found that the overall influence of ESG or sustainability factors on financial performance is positive. Table 7.5 provides the frequency distribution.

7.4 Results and Discussion

For the purpose of the analysis, 100 academic studies, reports and thesis/dissertations have been considered which vary according to the financial variables of performance evaluation, control variables, methodology employed, statistical model considered, databases and depth of study. We will decipher these variabilities one by one. The variables considered for the study have been provided in Table 7.6. The financial performance indicators take account of company or firm's financial performance measures including accounting and market measures. Return on assets (ROA) measures the short-term performance and does not reflect the long-term performance. Table 7.6 illustrates in detail both the percentages of studies which have considered the indicators (Column B) and also the relative performance of the indicators with respect to the whole (Column A).

As we observe from Table 7.6, the measures such as ROA, ROE, ratio of profits to assets, EBIT, ROI, leverage, Tobin's Q, cash flow and total shareholder returns (TSRs) measure the financial position of the firm. Other indicators which have been used to measure mutual fund performance include Jensen alpha, Fama French alpha, Carhart alpha, Sharpe ratio and Treynor ratio. These measures have been used to compare

Table 7.6 Descriptive statistics of financial performance indicators

Financial variable	N	Column A	Column B	Financial variable	N	Column A	Column B
Jensen's alpha	28	13.3	28.6	EPS	2	0.9	2.0
Sharpe ratio	17	8.1	17.3	Total shareholder returns (TSRs)	1	0.5	1.0
Treynor ratio	4	1.9	4.1	ROCE	2	0.9	2.0
ROA	24	11.4	24.5	M2 ratio	1	0.5	1.0
ROE	16	7.6	16.3	Appraisal ratio	1	0.5	1.0
Ratio of profits to assets	4	1.9	4.1	Leverage	1	0.5	1.0
Stock returns	12	5.7	12.2	Sales growth	1	0.5	1.0
Tobin's Q	15	7.1	15.3	Market value	6	2.8	6.1
Operating performance	3	1.4	3.1	Net profit margin (NPM)	1	0.5	1.0
ROS	7	3.3	7.1	Other	18	8.5	18.4
NAV	2	0.9	2.0	Carhart alpha	18	8.5	18.4
ROI	1	0.5	1.0	Treynor measure	3	1.4	3.1
Asset turnover	1	0.5	1.0	Fama French alpha	14	6.6	14.3
Cost of capital	3	1.4	3.1	Cash flow	2	0.9	2.0
Volatility	2	0.9	2.0	EBIT	1	0.5	1.0
Total		211		100		215.3	

with the benchmark index as a part of the fund analysis. This apart, portfolio analysis has also been conducted, where stock returns and net asset value are considered for evaluation purpose. The most important part of the study is this one where the authors have used more than one regression model for the purpose. Table 7.7 presents a synopsis of the models used. In reality, CAPM has been commonly used to estimate expected returns from an asset or portfolio and compare the returns from a sustainable asset vis-à-vis the traditional counterpart. Different types of regression analysis have been resorted to by the authors depending on the type of data estimated. The table is also reflective of the not-so-common financial models such as O-bucket adjusted model, and Ohlson and GARCH models for the purpose.

The analyzed studies considered a broad range of variables that influence the concerned relationship. These are control variables or intervening variables, depending on the statistical model used. The list of variables and the frequency distribution is illustrated in Table 7.8. So, the other important and intervening variables which might have a significant influence on the estimated relationship include firm size, book-to-market ratio, investment patterns and operating risk. Time fixed effects have also been considered in certain types of analysis to eliminate the time-invariant fixed effects.

The current study presents a meta-analytical approach to the role of sustainability factors on financial value addition. Taking into account the financial model considered for evaluation, financial and control variables, nature of data analysis, databases and time period of the study, the statistical evaluation of the studies pooled together highlights the significant positive value addition by ESG or sustainability factors. However, there is a significant opportunity to expand this research. First, studies can be screened further to include only those which provide numerical data on the level of correlation between sustainability factors and value addition. Second, the impact of the explanatory financial variables could be further analyzed through the help of studies which include numerical data. This requires access to a large number of relevant databases. Third, there is also a possibility of analyzing the causal relationship between sustainability factors and financial variables. Nevertheless, we expect that the present study will provide the necessary impetus and assurance to business entities, policy makers and institutional investors to take up strategic actions related to ESG investments.

7.5 Conclusions

At present, developed economies are going through their phases of fiscal consolidation. Not only that, even developing and emerging economies are facing their fair share through resource scarcity in light of increased population and ever-increasing environmental problems. Yet, they are converging toward the helm of global economic activity. As a result, traditional models of analysis that investors use to identify investment opportunities may fall short of covering the range of variables that are important for analyzing emerging economies. Local and global companies operating

Table 7.7 Descriptive statistics of financial models

Model	Responses			Model	Responses		
	N	Column A	Column B		N	Column A	Column B
CAPM	26	19.4	26.0	GARCH model	1	0.7	1.0
Fama French 3 factor model	13	9.7	13.0	Ohlson model	1	0.7	1.0
Carhart 4-factor model	23	17.2	23.0	Life cycle assessment (LCA)	1	0.7	1.0
Multivariate panel regression	23	17.2	23.0	Data envelopment analysis (DEA)	1	0.7	1.0
O-bucket adjusted model	1	0.7	1.0	Other	22	16.4	22.0
Markov switching model	2	1.5	2.0	Fama–MacBeth regression	1	0.7	1.0
Multifactor model	6	4.5	6.0	Nonparametric regression	1	0.7	1.0
Logistic regression	3	2.2	3.0	Moderated regression analysis	1	0.7	1.0
Probit regression	3	2.2	3.0	Markowitz model	1	0.7	1.0
Tobit regression	1	0.7	1.0	Treynor–Mazuy (TM) and the Henriksson–Merton (HM) models	3	2.2	3.0
Total	134	100	134				

Table 7.8 Descriptive statistics of control variables

Variable	Responses				Variable	Responses	
N		Percent of Cases		N		Percent of Cases	
Sales growth	4	3.5	11.1	Media exposure	2	1.8	5.6
Research and development intensity	5	4.4	13.9	Strategic holdings	1	0.9	2.8
Firm/fund size	27	23.9	75.0	Slack	1	0.9	2.8
Age of firm assets/fund	6	5.3	16.7	Financial activities	1	0.9	2.8
Capital intensity	2	1.8	5.6	Advertising intensity	3	2.7	8.3
Firm financial leverage	4	3.5	11.1	Multinationality	1	0.9	2.8
Operating risk	6	5.3	16.7	Volatility of fund returns	1	0.9	2.8
Industry specification	9	8.	25.0	Macro-economic factors	1	0.9	2.8
Debt level	1	0.9	2.8	Time fixed effects	6	5.3	16.7
Book-to-market ratio	10	8.8	27.8	Survivorship bias	1	0.9	2.8
Momentum	7	6.2	19.4	Global customers	1	0.9	2.8
Time variation in betas	2	1.8	5.6	Business type	1	0.9	2.8
Price-to-earnings ratio	1	0.9	2.8	Profit of the firm	1	0.9	2.8
Investment style	4	3.5	11.1	Liquidity	1	0.9	2.8
Management company traits	1	0.9	2.8	Dividend	1	0.9	2.8
Geographic area 1 of investment		0.9	2.8				
Total		113		100		313.9	

in these countries face unique social, economic and environmental risks related to the efficient extracting and exploiting of commodities. As a result, a growing number of investors are asking about corporate responsibility and sustainability in the emerging markets. As a matter of fact, emerging market companies that effectively address sustainability risks and opportunities are becoming global leaders in their field and in the creation of long-term shareholder value. The materiality of ESG investments has been debated a number of times at various academic gatherings. Although there are certain evidences of negative to neutral impact of ESG factors in business investments, majority of the studies have established beyond doubt the value-adding potential of such type of investments. If the market recognizes and acknowledges this value, it is highly likely that the sustainable company shares fetch a price premium in the market. This will lead to increase of the market capitalization, a reduction in the cost of equity capital and a subsequent increase in the value of the firm. Additionally, if the information perceived by the market participants about value addition potential of the sustainable firms is correct, this will enhance the intrinsic value of the company which is reflected in the financial ratios ROA, ROE and ROS. Hence, if the company decides to keep its dividend policy intact, then a rise in ROE will accentuate the sustainable growth rate of the firm. Now, if the company increases the dividend rate, the amount of earnings retained will fall. However, if the rate of increase of ROE overpowers the decrease of the retention rate of the firm, the growth rate of the firm is expected to rise. In case, the rate of increase in ROE just offsets the decrease in retention rate, the sustainable growth rate of the firm remains unchanged.

Acknowledgements Research results presented in this paper are an element of a research project implemented by the National Science Centre, Poland, under the Grant OPUS13 no UMO-2017/25/B/HS4/02172.

References

1. Renneboog, L., Horst, J, Zhang, C.: Socially responsible investments: methodology, risk exposure and performance. ECGI Working paper, 1–51 (2007)
2. Buerden, P.V., Gossling, T.: The worth of values: a literature review on the relation between corporate social and financial performance. J. Bus. Ethics **82**, 407–424 (2008)
3. Derwall, J., Guenster, N., Koedijk, K.: The eco-efficiency premium puzzle. Finan. Anal. J. **61**(2), 51–62 (2005)
4. Gompers, P.A., Ishii, J.L, Metrick, A.: Corporate governance and equity prices. Wharton Working paper series, 1–68. Retrieved from www.fic.wharton.upenn.edu (2003)
5. Orlitzky, M., Schmidt, M.L., Rynes, S.L.: Corporate social and financial performance: a meta-analysis. Organ. Studies **24**(3), 403–441 (2003)
6. Smit, T.J., Trigeorgis, L.: Strategic Investment. Real Options and Games. Princeton University Press, Princeton and Oxford (2004)
7. Statman, M.: Socially responsible mutual funds. Association for Investment Management and Research, 30–39 (2000)

8. Core, J.E., Guay, W.R., Rusticus, T.O.: Does weak governance cause weak stock returns? An examination of firm operating performance and investors' expectations. J. Finan. **61**(2), 655–687 (2006)
9. Bauer, R., Otten, R., Rad, A.T.: Ethical investing in Australia: is there a financial penalty? Pacific-Basin Finan. J. **14**, 33–48 (2006)
10. Hong, H., Kacperczyk, M.: The price of sin: the effects of social norms on markets. J. Finan. Econ. **93**, 15–36 (2008)
11. RobecoSAM What are the financially material ESG factors in the pharma sector? Insight, 3. Retrieved from www.robecosam.com (2015)
12. Innovest Corporate Environmental Performance: environmental governance has been defined as the state of governance that describes a company's management of its environmental impacts, risks, performance and opportunities. Retrieved from www.kellogg.northwestern.edu (2004)
13. Cochran, P.L., Wood, R.A.: Corporate social responsibility and financial performance. Acad. Mgm. J. (27), 42–56 (1984)
14. Nham, P.T., Tran, H.C., Nguyen, T.H.: Impact of firms environmental performance on its financial performance: empirical evidence from Vietnam's Small and medium manufacturing firms. JSPS Asian CORE Program, Nagoya University and VNU University of Economics and Business, 1–17. (2012)
15. Ganzi, J.T., Steedman, E., Quenneville, S.: Linking environmental performance to business value: A North American perspective. Background paper was prepared for the Secretariat of the Commission for Environmental Cooperation (CEC) and Environment Canada, 1–80. Retrieved from www.cec.org (2004)
16. Core, J.E., Guay, W.R., Rusticus, T.O.: Does weak governance cause weak stock returns? An examination of firm operating performance and investors' expectations. J. Finan. **61**(2), 655–687 (2006)
17. Yang, F.J., Lin, C.W., Chang, Y.N.: The linkage between corporate social responsibility and corporate social performance. Afr. J. Bus. Manage. **4**(4), 406–413 (2010)
18. Hart, S.L., Ahuja, G.: Does it pay to be green? An empirical examination of the relationship between emission reduction and firm performance. Bus. Strategy Environ. **3**, 30–37 (1996)
19. Earnhart, D., Lizal, L.: Does better environmental performance affect revenues, costs or both? Evidence from a transitional economy. 1–42 (2008)
20. Guenster, N., Bauer, R., Derwall, J., Koedijk, K.: The economic value of corporate efficiency. European Financial Management, 1–26 (2010)
21. Tsoutsoura, M.: Corporate social responsibility and financial performance. Working paper Series, Centre for Responsible Business, UC Berkeley, 1–22. Retrieved from www.responsiblebusiness-new.haas.berkeley.edu (2004)
22. Dowel, G., Hart, S., Yeung, B.: Do Corporate Global Environmental standards create or destroy market value? 1–32. Retrieved from www.people.stern.nyu.edu (2000)
23. Mans-Kemp, N.: Corporate governance and the financial performance of selected Johannesberg Stock Exchange Industries. Ph.D. Thesis, Stellenbosch University, 1–332 (2014)
24. Hillman, A.J., Keim, G.D.: Shareholder management, stakeholder management and social issues: what's the bottom line? Strateg. Manag. J. **22**(2), 125–139 (2001)
25. Evans, J., Peiris, D.: The relationship between environmental social governance factors and stock returns. Australian School of Business Research Paper, 1–18 (2010)
26. Trunow, N.A., Linder, J.: Perspectives on ESG integration in equity investing. Calvert Investments, 1–24. Retrieved from www.calvert.com (2015)
27. Semenova, N., Hassel, L.G.: Industry risk moderates the relation between environmental and financial performance. Sustainable Investment Research Platform Working Papers, 1–28 (2008)
28. Balatbat, M.: ESG scores and its influence on firm performance. 1–32. Retrieved from www.business.unsw.edu.au (2012)
29. Klein, A., Zur, E.: Entrepreneurship activism: Hedge funds and other private investors. 1–68. Retrieved from www.hedgerelations.com (2007)
30. Ghosh, A.: Corporate sustainability and corporate financial performance: The Indian Context. IIM Working paper Series. 1–37. Retrieved from www.financelab.iimcal.ac.in (2013)

31. Weber, O., Mansfeld, M., Schirrmann, E.: The financial performance of an SRI Fund portfolio in Times of Turmoil. 1–24. Retrieved from www.accounting.uwaterloo.ca (2010)
32. Edmans, A.: Does the stock market fully value intangibles? Employee satisfaction and equity prices. J. Finan. Econ. **101**, 621–640 (2011)
33. Kreander, N., Gray, R.H., Power, D.M., Sinclair, C.D.: The financial performance of European Ethical funds. 1–14. Retrieved from www.st-andrews.ac.uk (1999)
34. Cortez, M.C., Silva, F., Areal, N.: The performance of European socially responsible investment funds. 1–35. Retrieved from www.ifk-cfs.de (2008)
35. Cheung, V.K.A., Li, H., Roca, E.: The performance of socially responsible investments across different market regimes. Griffith University Discussion papers. 1–22. Retrieved from www.griffith.edu.au (2010)
36. Mollet, J.C., Ziegler, A.: Is SRI really beneficial? New Empirical evidence from the US (2012)
37. Rathner, S.: The relative performance of SRI funds: new evidence from Austria. Working Papers in Economics and Finance, University of Salzburg, 1–28. Retrieved from www.uni-salzburg.at (2013)
38. Bazo, J.G., Verdu, P.R., Santos, A.A.P.: The performance of SRI Funds: the role of fees and management companies. J. Bus. Ethics **94**(2), 243–263 (2010)
39. Bauer, R., Koedijk, K., Otten, R.: International evidence on ethical mutual fund performance and investment style. J. Bank. Finan. **29**, 1751–1767 (2004)
40. Bauer, R., Otten, R., Rad, A.T.: Ethical Investing in Australia: Is there a financial penalty? Pacific-Basin Finan. J. **14**, 33–48 (2006)
41. Schroder, M.: The performance of socially responsible investments: investment funds and indices. Swiss Society for Financial Market Research, 122–142, (2004)
42. Liang, J.: Canadian ethical mutual funds: risk adjusted performance of specialty funds versus general mutual funds. M.Sc. Dissertation, Concordia University, 1–64. Retrieved from www.spectrum.library.concordia.ca (2012)
43. Ito, Y., Managi, S., Matsuda, A.: Performances of socially responsible investment and environmentally friendly funds. MPRA Archive, 1–33. Retrieved from www.mpra.ub.uni-muenchen.de (2012)
44. Utz, S., Wimmer, M.: Are they any good at all? A financial and ethical analysis of socially responsible mutual funds. 1–17. Retrieved from www.epub.uni-regensburg.de (2014)
45. Vincent, L.: Financial performance of SRI: does the visibility of firms in the portfolio matter? 1–34 (2015)
46. Taiana, L.: Extra-financial performance in socially responsible investment. Center for Microfinance Thesis Series, 1–69. Retrieved from www.cmf.uzh.ch (2012)
47. Blancard, G.C., Monjon, S.: The performance of socially responsible funds: does the screening process matter? CEPII, 1–51. Retrieved from www.cepii.fr (2012)
48. Stenstrom, H.C., Thorell, J.J.: Evaluating the performance of socially responsible investment funds: a holding data analysis. 1–49. Retrieved from www.responsible-investor.com; Suchman, M.C.: Managing legitimacy: strategic and institutional approaches. Academy of Management Review, **20**(3), 571–610 (2007)
49. Boaventura, J.M.G., Silva, R.S., Bandeira-de-Mello, R.: Corporate financial performance and corporate social performance: methodological development and the theoretical contribution of empirical studies. Revista Contabilidade & Financas **23**(60), 232–245 (2012)
50. AllianzGI Global Solutions ESG in Equities. Retrieved from www.allianzgi.com, (2015)
51. Phillips, Hager and north investment management does socially responsible investing hurt investment returns? 1–16. Retrieved from www.phn.com (2007)
52. Rathner, S.: The Performance of SRI Funds: A Meta-analysis. 1–13. Retrieved from www.uni-salzburg.at (2011)
53. Vishwanathan, P., Heugens, P.: Assessing the 'mechanisms turn' in corporate social and financial performance studies: a meta analysis. 1–57. Retrieved from www.portal.uc3m.es (2008)
54. Vromen, J.J.: Evolution and efficiency: an inquiry into the foundations of new institutional economics. Eburon Publishers, Delft (2008)

Chapter 8
Financial Services Market in an Ageing Society. Challenges for the Development of Silver Economy

Grażyna Krzyminiewska

Abstract The article addresses the issue of the ageing of societies and the need to adopt a new strategy for financial services aimed at the elderly people. Attention is drawn to the specifics of behaviour of senior citizens as financial services customers, resulting from historical experiences, income opportunities, competencies and their cognitive abilities. It is emphasised that financial services constitute a significant part of the silver economy development, necessary due to the need for protecting capital, preserving assets and preventing loss of savings of senior citizens. The article also points to the need to use the achievements of experimental economics, economic psychology and socioeconomics to study the causes of financial behaviours. The article fits into the trend of economic and social analyses and uses the achievements of social research. It was based on existing sources and own research. Desk research and descriptive analysis were used in the presentation of the issues addressed.

Keywords Financial services · Silver economy · Financial behaviours of elderly people

8.1 Introduction

In the modern world, accompanied by the society ageing process, there is a chance of developing silver economy if there is a clear change in attitude to the older generation. The first step towards the success of senior economy is to combat the phenomenon of ageism, which marginalises or even directly excludes senior citizens from mainstream social and economic life. Undoubtedly, cultural change related to the necessary changes in the mentality of all generations is crucial for the success of senior economy. This regards the elevation of the so-called III age as active and valuable both among the senior citizens, who withdraw from mainstream society due

---

G. Krzyminiewska (✉)
Department of Sociology and Business Ethics, Faculty of Economics, Poznań University of Economics and Business, al. Niepodległości 10, 61-875 Poznań, Poland
e-mail: grazyna.krzyminiewska@ue.poznan.pl

W. Tarczyński and K. Nermend (eds.), *Effective Investments on Capital Markets*, Springer Proceedings in Business and Economics,
https://doi.org/10.1007/978-3-030-21274-2_8

to age (and not necessarily medical condition), and younger generations, reluctant or hostile towards the growing population of elderly people. Older people, as a social category, much more often than in previous decades refuse to 'stay in the shadows', so it becomes necessary to use the potential of older people and their growing activity, develop intergenerational communication, change the image of the elderly as poor, clumsy, unnecessary and actively use their knowledge, experience and skills. This means overcoming intergenerational prejudices and stereotypes and creating social order friendly for all generations. The economy of the ageing population is both a challenge and chance for development, and its nature, concepts and assumptions may be beneficial for economy due to economic reasons and be a sign of concern for older people and their needs.

8.2 Silver Economy and Megatrends in the Global Economy

The dynamic social and economic phenomena occurring in the modern world encourage forecasting the development of the globalised world. Therefore, researchers take up the challenge of identifying megatrends which will affect the future economy. Experts from Deloitte, an international consulting company, determined which factors will be the most important on a global scale based on extensive analyses. Six megatrends were identified, including:

1. Industry 4.0—which blurs the boundaries between the physical, manufacturing and biological spheres in manufacturing processes, and its most significant solutions include the Internet of things, machine learning, artificial intelligence as well as augmented and virtual reality.
2. Circular economy enabling better allocation of resources. The existing linear resource use model 'manufacture-use-throw away' will be supported by the 'closed-loop' model in which any potential waste becomes a raw material.
3. Sustainable finance and investment with a view to environmental impact, where while measuring their income and return on investments, investors and entrepreneurs take into account not only costs and financial gains but also social and environmental benefits.
4. Electric vehicles as the answer to the interest of consumers and the increasing cost-effectiveness of such vehicles, which are crucial in the development of 'sustainable cities'.
5. The growing importance of the talent labour market—the spread of flexible forms of employment and the coexistence of different generations in the labour market.
6. Silver economy related to longer professional activity, combined with the projected low pensions from the public system, influencing the tendencies regarding saving money and investing, searching for assets that will constitute a safe capital deposit and 'old-age policy' [5].

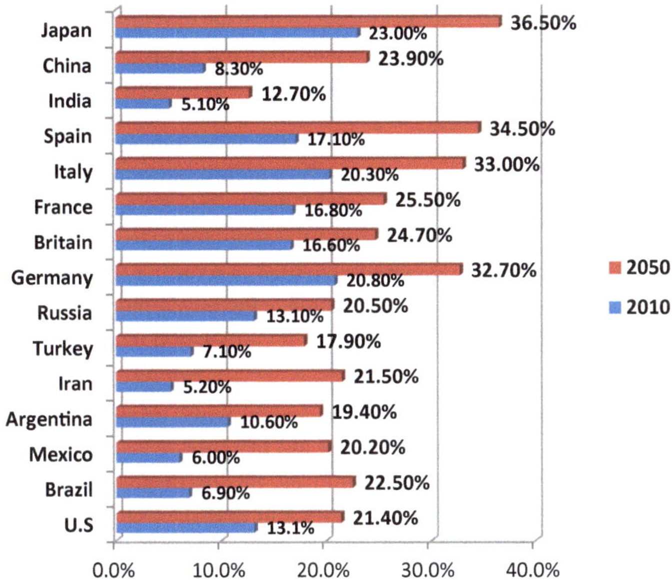

Fig. 8.1 Proportion of people 65 and older in a country's population, estimates for 2010 and 2050 in %. *Source* United Nations, Department of Economic and Social Affairs, World Population Prospects: 2012, Revision, June 2013, http://esa.un.org/unpd/wpp/index.htm, Pew Research Centre

The last megatrend mentioned here is the subject of multiple economic and social analyses due to the dynamics of population ageing, particularly characteristic of some regions of the world. Referring to the research by the Pew Research Center [14], it can be stated that 'The global population is on the brink of a remarkable transformation. Thanks to the ageing of today's middle-aged demographic bulge and ongoing improvements in life expectancy, the population of seniors is projected to surge, increasing from 530.5 million in 2010 to 1.5 billion in 2050. The result will be a much older world, a future in which roughly one-in-six people is expected to be 65 and older by 2050, double the proportion today'. The proportion of people aged 65 and more in the population of selected countries is presented in Fig. 8.1.

Also in Poland, according to the forecasts of the Central Statistical Office (GUS), the share of people aged 65 and older in the total population in 2050 will amount to 30.2% and people aged 80 and older will constitute 10.4% of the total population (in 2013—3.9%) [17].

In view of the above, there is no doubt that societies which use ageing processes as soon as possible and make them an advantage for the economy, and at the same time eliminate (weaken) the existing threats, will prove to be the most competitive.

The definition of silver economy used by the OECD points to the need of developing economy through the implementation of silver production, that is, one that produces and supplies products and services targeted at older people, creating an environment in which people over 60 years old cooperate and achieve successes in the workplace, engage in innovative projects, help in the development of the market as customers and lead healthy, active and productive lives [12]. The assumptions of the silver economy are the answer to the advanced ageing processes; therefore, the implementation of the silver economy should enable the transformation of demographic problems into development opportunities, and the development strategy which takes into account the needs of the ageing population should contribute to the improvement of life quality not only with regard to the elderly but also the remaining population.

Silver economy is not only the production of goods and services dedicated to senior citizens but also a wide range of activities. According to Enste et al. [6], the areas in which the silver economy may stimulate the development of market sectors directly or indirectly related to the ageing of the population are, among others:

- information technologies (IT) in health care;
- flat adaptation and services that make life easier, based primarily on IT;
- independent life based on of the growing use of IT;
- areas which are gerontologically significant for the health economy, including medical technologies and e-health, vision and hearing technologies, prosthetics and orthopaedics;
- education and culture as the answer to the desire for development and leisure time management;
- IT and media combined with medicine, promoting independence and safety;
- service robotics and the promotion of independent life in the case of elderly people with severe diseases;
- mobility and promotion of its constituents, e.g. road traffic safety;
- leisure, travel, culture, communication and entertainment;
- fitness and wellness as the response to raising awareness of healthy lifestyle;
- clothing and fashion as a manifestation of the desire for social integration;
- services facilitating the day-to-day functioning and other housework;
- insurance primarily related to the forms of risk specific to older people;
- financial services, particularly with regard to protecting capital, preserving assets and preventing loss of savings.

The last of the mentioned areas is the subject matter of this discussion. The organisation and management of this area become the key to securing the financial future of elderly people and reducing the impact of the demographic burden. Here, we are faced with the need for a long-term project consisting of several activities: readiness of financial institutions to provide services in an ageing society, preparing society members of all generations for conscious financial management—rational attitude to money, savings and investment strategies as well as preventing the financial exclusion of senior citizens. Undoubtedly, the implementation of these ideas requires the development of an integrated educational and organisational system which takes into account the knowledge of experimental economics, economic psychology and socioeconomics as well as the internal differences between senior citizens.

8.3 Theoretical Explanations of Financial Behaviours

Both economy and other fields of science undertake to discover the reasons behind decision-making and financial behaviours. By conducting laboratory experiments in this area, experimental economics is intended to minimise the impact of uncontrollable external factors and at the same time, arrange the optimal test conditions and values of relevant parameters. This allows, first and foremost, to learn the preferences of an individual and determine the economic decision-making process, although the experimental economics researchers are less interested in individual decisions of the participants and more in their effects on the entire market [9]. The use of methods of experimental economics in other sciences enabled a more comprehensive definition of decision-making mechanisms by taking into account the social, psychological and cultural impacts. Such analyses attempt to explore the economic behaviours of individuals and households, decision-makers in business and in the public sector.

In the studies on attitudes towards money, the *Money Attitudes Scale* (MAS) by Yamauchi and Templer [22], *Money Ethic Scale* (MES) Tanga [19] and *Money Beliefs and Behaviour Scale* (MBBS) Furnham [7] are effectively used. These are characterised in Table 8.1.

In turn, sociological research (referring to experimental economics and economic psychology) draws attention to the fact that attitudes towards money largely depend on cultural conditions in which an economic culture characteristic of a given society [11], constituting an integrated system of economic behaviours of an individual, is created. An important issue here is economic socialisation as well as the economic knowledge of the individual and the community. People acquire economic culture through their own life experience, upbringing and the influence of the social environment; therefore, the mechanisms and channels of learning play an important role here. On the basis of the process of primary and secondary socialisation, a value system is created which influences the assessment of social reality, decisions regarding consumption, attitude to work and entrepreneurship as well as towards money and money saving [10].

Four approaches were distinguished with regard to the studies on money saving. These are:

1. Surveys on habits, attitudes and motives related to saving.
2. Segmentation studies (on groups of people saving money), mainly with the use of surveys.
3. Controlled laboratory experiments.
4. Qualitative research on money saving as a process [21].

An important economic saving theory is the Life-Cycle Hypothesis (LCH) based on the assumption that people are forward-looking and limit their consumption in certain periods in order to maintain a similar consumption level in the future, when their income is smaller. This hypothesis has been repeatedly supplemented and changed, pointing (with regard to the issues addressed) to the issues of time horizon and changes in attitudes resulting from changes in the circulation of information, learning processes and the consequences of social impact. The significant factors here are

Table 8.1 Attitudes towards money in classic studies of economic psychology

Name of the scale	Author	Characteristics
Money Attitudes Scale (MAS)	Yamauchi and Templer	Psychological aspects of money include: a sense of security and a sense of danger, self-control and refraining from spending money, recognising money as a symbol of power and social status Attitudes towards money: power and prestige as a symbol of success; refraining from spending money through the planning of financial future and control over the current financial situation; distrust indicating a tendency to perceive issues related to money as suspicious and prompting dishonesty; quality—factor related to the need of spending money in the most reasonable way; unrest, when money is the cause of anxiety and negative emotions
Money Ethic Scale (MES)	Tang	Attitudes towards money: money is perceived by people as something that is either good or bad (emotional element), people see the relationship between money and success, respect and freedom (cognitive aspect), people pay attention to expenditure planning (behavioural aspect)
Money Beliefs and Behaviour Scale (MBBS)	Furnham	Attitudes towards money: obsession with money, money as a symbol of power, refraining from spending money, saving, constant feeling of scarcity of money, making efforts to get money

Source Tyszka and Zaleśkiewicz [20]

psychological aspects such as: the role of providence (personality and upbringing), self-control (willpower), income uncertainty in the future (or certainty that the income will decrease upon retirement), selective perception and limited cognitive abilities (significant with age), attitude towards the future (e.g. related to the desire to leave a legacy to the loved ones or allocating it for specific purposes), change of objectives and preferences. The Life-Cycle Hypothesis drew attention to the importance of future orientation and the long-term objective of preparing for lower incomes in old age and maintaining the same level of consumption throughout life [ibid., p. 558.].

8.4 Attitudes of Poles Towards Finances and the Challenges for Financial Institutions

The mentality of Polish society with regard to finance was shaped by various factors. These are the objective capabilities of individuals resulting from the social structure, but also the developed patterns of behaviour, values and ways of thinking. They were formed throughout the course of historical changes, overall social conditions in which the individual and the community function. Furthermore, it largely depends on the level of trust vested in the institutions and in Polish society, trust (the so-called culture of trust) is low. There is no doubt that there are many reasons for this state of affairs and that they are rooted both in the past of Poland and in the current experiences (this regards i.a. perceiving the social environment as a sequence of reforms, modifications and changes), and the Amber Gold affair further reinforces this mistrust. However, the importance of the older group of financial consumers is increasing and this will be an ongoing trend. Nonetheless, the issue of low financial competence of elderly people, particularly negative for Polish senior citizens, still remains.

According to the Adult Financial Literacy Competencies report [1], based on the thirty countries and economies study, 17 OECD countries participated in an international survey of financial literacy, using the OECD/INFE toolkit to collect cross-comparable data. In total, 51,650 adults aged 18–79 were interviewed using the same core questions. This report provides high-level highlights of the survey's findings focusing on relevant aspects of financial knowledge, behaviour, attitudes and inclusion. The highest possible score was 21 points (7 points for knowledge, 9 points for behaviour and 5 for attitude). The average score for the countries surveyed was 13.2 and for OECD countries 13.7. Among the populations surveyed, Poland was in the last place with the score of 11.6 points (where the highest score was obtained by France—14.9). What is particularly alarming is the fact that only three in ten Poles think about the financial future in a long-term perspective.

In the *Postawy Polaków wobec finansów* report (Polish attitudes towards finance) (Kronenberg Foundation [16]), 28% of the Poles surveyed (based on a representative sample) declare that they save money to secure their future or the future of their loved ones, while 21% explicitly indicate that they save money with a view to retirement. Unfortunately, 50% of the people who are not currently retired are unaware of the amount of their pension in the future.

Biuro Informacji Gospodarczej InfoMonitor [3] indicates that Polish senior citizens (345 thousand people over 64) have as much as PLN 7.3 billion of debt and one in eighteen senior citizens does not make payments on time. The average debt of people over 64 is PLN 21-23 thousand, while the major part of pensioners' debts are liabilities to banks and loan companies, and the remaining are unpaid phone, utility or rent bills.

Naturally, these studies do not exhaust the knowledge about the attitudes of Pole to money and saving, the real issues with income; however, they point out some alarming phenomena.

These also include the issue of demand for financial services which are limited due to the financial and digital exclusion. Studies on financially excluded consumers show that in the vast majority of cases, these are people who are subject to the so-called self-exclusion. In their case, the main reason is the declared absence of the need to use financial services. The group of self-excluded people declaring that their situation is a result of a conscious decision, arising from a profitability calculation, lack of trust in banks or preference for cash, is significantly smaller [8, 15, 18].

The different behaviours of older people in the financial products market show that it is not only Poles who are most focused on bank services—depositing money (mainly deposits) or running up a debt and much less frequently investing money in bonds, shares or investment funds.

Studies by Czerwiński [4] show that the use of financial services by elderly people mostly includes the simplest offers—personal account, general insurance and life insurance. The oldest people (over 70) used these services to a lesser extent than younger people (over 50). This is primarily influenced by age, education and income. As the author of the study concludes, financial institutions should verify the service offer and adapt it to the needs of senior citizens with different socio-demographic characteristics. Treating senior citizens as a homogeneous category is a clear loss for financial institutions and senior citizens themselves, especially since it is those to whom the world of finance is not unknown anymore that will become senior citizens in the long run.

It should also be taken into account that the demand for broadly understood financial services is gradually growing along with the growth of the overall wealth of Poles. According to the report on wealth forecast for Poles [2], the reason for the enrichment of Poles in the coming years will be i.a. an increase in income, higher return on investment in assets, an increase in the value of inheritances and the establishment of new companies and savings. It is assumed that by 2040 their net wealth will triple from PLN 6.5 to PLN 18 billion. This means that it will be 70% higher than at present (even after adjustment for inflation) (ibid). In the face of these (and other) forecasts, strategic plans concerning this issue should already be developed under the financial sector. If—as the authors claim—there is a wealth revolution in the next few years and the generation of older Poles, who got richer during the economic transformation, will bequest their wealth to their children, it means that the younger generations will become richer by several hundred thousand zlotys on average. In this case, the demand for wealth management and protection services will be growing gradually.

However, at the moment, elderly people in the financial services market constitute unused capital. First of all, the market offer should be aimed both at people who are still professionally active and, functioning at the so-called dawn of old age, may still be interested in investments, depositing money for the future retirement, but cannot always find themselves in this market and need professional advice, and at those who are already retired but managed to accumulate certain funds. Even if people over the age of 70 have relatively low incomes, they often own properties which they have already paid off while still professionally active (asset rich and cash poor). This right here is the most important area of activities for financial institutions which, in accordance with social responsibility, should expand services aimed directly at senior citizens. This regards financial services related to protecting capital, preserving assets and preventing loss of savings. Senior citizens as potential customers of financial institutions constitute a very sensitive, difficult segment when it comes to making financial decisions. This results from two issues: people of the oldest age groups with the least experience in markets and financial instruments, and at the same time with low level of trust, may not be interested even in the most favourable offers for them, but also, due to the decrease in cognitive skills with age, they will not be able to make conscious decisions. Unfortunately, there were cases of abuse against older persons in financial institutions where the weaker analytical capacity of older persons was taken advantage of in order to persuade them to purchase products more beneficial for the institution than the senior citizen. However, the aim is for a customer entering a bank to know that they are coming to an institution of public trust and be sure that the funds they entrusts it with are safe.

> At this point, it is worth to refer to the recommendations developed in 2013 on the initiative of the Commissioner for Human Rights in the field of facilitating the financial decisions of senior citizens. This refers to legislative measures that increase the legal protection of elderly people by extending the period for withdrawal, improving control and introducing sanctions for fraudulent sales activities. It is also the development of training for sellers and financial intermediaries in the field of services for elderly people, as well as including it in the code of good market practice. Another important area of activities defined was the establishment of financial institutions friendly for senior citizens, where it is possible to, e.g., borrow glasses, use the toilet, print out documents in bigger letters and increase the transparency of agreements so that older customers are aware of the monthly or total price associated with a given service. (Osoby starsze….[13])

8.5 Summary

The above considerations are headed towards the conclusion that meeting the needs of older customers, taking into account the skilful adaptation of financial services, may constitute an enhancing factor and development potential for the financial sector and the silver economy as a whole. On the other hand, the increased activity of elderly people in the financial services market may improve their quality of life, which ultimately positively affects the society as a whole. If the tendency to save money and preferences regarding the directions of allocation of savings are shaped by multiple factors, such as financial, fiscal, economic, legal, technological, demographic, psychological and cultural factors, then the adaptation of the financial services sector to those factors should be more dynamic. This also applies to increasing educational activity which develops the knowledge and skills in the field of finance. Educating senior citizens is necessary in accordance with the life-long learning concept, by placing high value on learning and improving universal access to information and advice on educational opportunities.

References

1. Adult Financial Literacy Competencies: OECD/INFE International Survey, OECD, http://www.oecd.org/daf/fin/financial-education/OECD-INFE-International-Survey-of-Adult-Financial-Literacy-Competencies.pdf (2016)
2. Arak, P., Czerniak, A.: Prognoza majątku - jak demografia zmieni aktywa Polaków, BZ WBK, http://www.politykainsight.pl/gospodarka/ryzykaitrendy2016/_resource/multimedium/20102540 (2016)
3. Biuro Informacji Gospodarczej InfoMonitor, https://www.infomonitor.pl/ (2018)
4. Czerwiński, B.: Zachowania seniorów z Polski Północnej na rynku usług finansowych w świetle wyników badań Handel Wewnętrzny. **3**(362), 76–87 (2016)
5. Deloitte: 6 megatrendów będzie miało największy wpływ na kształt globalnej gospodarki, (https://www2.deloitte.com/pl/pl/pages/press-releases/articles/megatrendy-ekonomiczne-2018.html (2018)
6. Enste, P., Naegele, G., Leve, V.: The discovery and development of the silver market in Germany. In: Kohlbacher, F., Herstatt, C. (eds) The Silver Market Phenomenon. Business Opportunities in an Era of Demographic Change, pp. 330–331. Springer, Heidelberg (2008)
7. Furnham, A.: Inflation and the estimated size of notes. J. Econ. Psychol. **4**, 349–352 (1983)
8. Kieżel E., Smyczek S.: Analfabetyzm finansowy jako bariera w akceptacji innowacji na rynku usług finansowych, Marketing i Rynek, no. 2 (2015)
9. Kopczewski, T., Malawski, M.: Ekonomia eksperymentalna. Decisions **8**, 79–100 (2007)
10. Krzyminiewska, G.: Kultura ekonomiczna młodzieży wiejskiej i jej znaczenie w rozwoju społeczno-gospodarczym obszarów wiejskich. Wydawnictwo Naukowe Uniwersytetu Ekonomicznego w Poznaniu, Poznań (2010)
11. Krzyminiewska, G.: Kultura ekonomiczna mieszkańców obszarów wiejskich. Problemy – Przekształcenia – Wyzwania, Wydawnictwo Adam Marszałek, Toruń (2013)
12. OECD: University of Oxford, Global Coalition for Ageing, The Silver Economy as a Pathway for Growth. Insights from the OECD-GCOA Expert Consultation. https://www.oecd.org/sti/the-silver-economy-as-a-pathway-to-growth.pdf (2014)
13. Osoby starsze na rynku usług finansowych. Analiza i zalecenia (2013), Biuletyn RPO. Sources no. 4
14. Pew Research Center: Attitudes about aging: a global perspective, http://www.pewglobal.org/2014/01/30/attitudes-about-aging-a-global-perspective/ (2014)
15. Polasik, M., Piotrowska, A.: Transakcyjne wykluczenie finansowe w Polsce w świetle badań empirycznych., Prace Naukowe Uniwersytetu Ekonomicznego We Wrocławiu. Research Papers of Wrocław University of Economics no. 330 (2014)
16. Postawy Polaków wobec finansów (2015) Kronenberg Foundation Citi Handlowy, http://www.citibank.pl/poland/kronenberg/polish/files/postawy_polakow_wobec_finansow_(2015).pdf
17. Population forecast for 2014–2050, (2014) GUS, Departament Badań Demograficznych i Rynku Pracy. Warszawa
18. Smyczek, S., Matysiewicz, J.: Financial exclusion as barrier to socio-economic development of the Baltic Sea region. J. Econ. Manag. **15** (2014)
19. Tang, T.: The meaning of money revisited. J. Organ. Behav., 14 (1992)
20. Tyszka, T., Zaleśkiewicz, T.: Psychologia pieniądza, Psychologia ekonomiczna. In: Tyszka, T. (ed), Gdańskie, pp. 161–191. Wydawnictwo Psychologiczne, Gdańsk (2004) (2012)
21. Wärneryd, K.-E.: Oszczędzanie, in: Psychologia ekonomiczna. Tyszka, T. (ed) Gdańskie, p. 558. Wydawnictwo Psychologiczne, Gdańsk (2004)
22. Yamauchi, K., Templer, D.: The development of a money attitude scale. J. Pers. Assess., 46 (1982)

Chapter 9
Towards Measurement Framework of Digital Skills in Finance

Monika Rozkrut and Dominik Rozkrut

Abstract The ongoing technological transformation and increasing the areas of application of digital tools are naturally also observed in finance. The development of new e-finance solutions increasingly requires the digital competence of customers of the financial sector. This article aims to propose and discuss digital financial competence framework that together with a prospective statistical measurement system may help to identify problems posed by emerging digitalisation of society and economy. It attempts to systemise the measurement through the proposed framework, also dealing with conceptual and practical issues related to digital competences and skills. The article attempts to define critical competences of individuals, for the financial sector. There have been many propositions so far of generic digital skills frameworks and digital literacy assessment tools. However, there has been no proposition of digital skills framework for financial services. This paper adds to the existing works by proposing the relevant scheme of digital competences for digital financial services that subsequently may be used as a reference framework for statistical measurement.

9.1 Digital Society and Economy

The development and dissemination of information and communication technologies give rise to the digital economy and information society [1]. The economy and society become increasingly dominated by technology and automation. Big data, artificial intelligence, machine earning, digital privacy, digital government, remote sensing, one might continue to enumerate all the similar terms that were never before used in the public discourse, yet are ubiquitous now.

Recent trends shaping the development of modern states are the digital economy and the information society. Along with the widening uptake of IT tools and the

M. Rozkrut · D. Rozkrut (✉)
University of Szczecin, Szczecin, Poland
e-mail: dominik.rozkrut@usz.edu.pl

M. Rozkrut
e-mail: monika.rozkrut@usz.edu.pl

W. Tarczyński and K. Nermend (eds.), *Effective Investments on Capital Markets*, Springer Proceedings in Business and Economics,
https://doi.org/10.1007/978-3-030-21274-2_9

increase in the number of users, a new type of society has evolved, whose functioning to the greatest extent determines the broad application of IT achievements. Progress in the development of advanced computer technologies has led to a revolution in the field of collecting, processing, storing and transmitting information. Undoubtedly, new technologies are currently one of the fastest growing sectors of the economy in developed countries, characterised by an increasing share in generating GDP. The process of digitisation in the entire economy fundamentally changes the way consumers, businesses and public and private institutions operate, including education and administration. Digital technologies are more and more integrated into the economy.

The development of modern enterprises is related to the use of IT achievements. Modern digital technologies are revolutionising the way of running a business. ICTs allow companies to expand the scope of their operations, speed up and facilitate access to information, data processing and help to use resources more efficiently. The use of the potential of digital technologies requires, on the one hand, the creation of an appropriate supply offer (i.e. access to broadband infrastructure and an attractive offer of e-services and e-content), on the other, creating demand for them through dissemination of knowledge about the benefits and practical ways of applying new technologies and also building user competence. Companies that see the impact of technological solutions on the efficiency of their operations build strong foundations of digital business. They commit to it more often and willingly than other companies. They decide to test new digital solutions. They are active in social media. They develop and implement new products and services based on the potential of digital technologies, which allow them to sustain a competitive advantage. There is a dynamic growth in the use of the Internet in business, in the exchange of information, making purchases and sales, financial settlements, promotions and searching for suppliers. Some studies predict that a business based on digital technologies will account for 25% for the whole world economy in 2020.

The use of new technologies creates more significant opportunities, brings positive effects and is ubiquitous and necessary for everyday life, in communication, learning, work, access to information and knowledge. We observe the growing importance of computers and the Internet in all spheres of life. ICTs diffuse into many areas of life, resulting in all new areas of e-learning, e-services, e-shopping, e-banking, e-government. Intensive development of the Internet and digital networks has resulted in minimising the time needed for information flow, increased opportunities in business contacts and improved the quality of life of the society. The full use of the potential of digital technologies is one of Poland's development priorities for the coming years. The dissemination of information and communication technologies is the subject of observation of academic research and statistical surveys. There is a wide range of studies at national and international levels regarding the measurement of the development of the information society, prepared by national statistical institutes and international organisations [5]. These publications regularly show continuous progress in the use of newer and more advanced information and communication technologies in the economy and society. The statistics on the information society are presented by National Statistical Institutes. These studies are carried out following methodological recommendations used in OECD and Eurostat. They concern aspects of the development of the digital economy and development of the ICT sector and its use in the economy and households.

9.2 Digitalisation and Finance

Information processing and management systems and activities related to digital technology have been developing intensively since the 1980s. Today, the digital revolution radically changes almost every business environment, and the financial service industry is no exception. The development of modern computer technology and telecommunications is an essential force in the transformation of the finance sector. Innovative solutions in the field of financial services appear, and the accelerating pace of changes makes it necessary to keep up to date with the latest achievements. Keeping up with the pace of change is a great challenge for people. There is a vast need to quickly adapt to changing conditions and challenges, as well as show high flexibility. Innovative applications of digital technologies for financial services alter communication between financial consumers and service providers and at the same time require an appropriate level of experience to use them.

The technological advances have significantly improved the quality and speed of data processing. To a large extent, it helped to reduce information costs and other transaction costs. These changes have undoubtedly affected both suppliers and users of financial products and services. The new financial technologies include distributed accounting technology, big data, Internet of things, cloud computing, artificial intelligence, biometrics and an extended/virtual reality. These technologies are associated with applications such as payments, planning, saving, lending and financing, trade and investment, insurance, security, operations and communication. Emerging new technologies can affect many aspects of the financial landscape, including new business models and product designs, competition, operational efficiency, brokering, accessibility, consumer engagement, speed, automation, analytics, privacy and transparency, digital security.

The notion of digital financial services is fundamental in this context. This very general term covers the broad range of financial services accessed and delivered through digital channels, like payments, transfers, savings, credits and insurance, but also bookkeeping, analytics and financial management. Digital channels include new solutions such as smartphones and other NFC-enabled devices, electronically enabled cards, biometric sensors and devices, tablets, phablets and all other relevant digital systems. It also comprises “old-fashioned” channels like the Internet, ATMs or POS terminals (which anyway become more and more advanced).

Modern solutions for the provision of financial services are adapted to the changing needs of clients. They provide a different standard, a higher level of service and customer relations. Other sources of changes come from specific needs and new expectations of digital customers who become immersed in the world of the Internet and mobile applications. These customers know how to search the network to find the best-suited product and service. Modern technologies boldly enter the financial sector. The financial sector's digitisation is done through digital sharing solutions and products, thus changing the standards of services offered, among others regarding payments.

9.2.1 User Experiences, Innovations and FinTech

Consumers want financial institutions that can respond quickly to their needs with products tailor-made to them. Large technology players, for example, have a very successful experience in taking the friction out of business processes. Consumers require then the same level of commitment, quality and ease of use from financial intermediaries. In an era where retail products can be ordered and delivered on the same day, people want their financial transactions to also occur in real time. The same expectation applies to other financial products. Consumers want services that make sense within their day-to-day lives. The expectations and needs of digitally savvy individual clients have changed radically.

Enhancing the customer experience is the most important objective of financial institutions that are aware of the importance of FinTech strategies. Systematic push for innovation is also triggered by the need to transform current operations, safeguard against threats and broaden existing and entering new markets. New technologies change the functioning of the financial system, bringing further benefits to the users, like providing services that are tailored to individual needs or offering faster and secure transactions. They allow for more effective communication channels, improve access to the services and broaden the range of providers.

Naturally, digital technology is not magic enough to increase financial inclusion by itself. It is important that also people with low skills use digital financial services. The services must be well adjusted to their needs and capabilities. The digitalisation of financial products and services results in the need to strengthen digital financial literacy.

One of the strong trends observed recently is the formation of FinTechs [6]. FinTech, or financial technology, is an innovative financial service based on information technology. They may not necessarily be strictly financial institutions but also entities that want to operate in the financial sector. Actually, by providing disruptive financial services, FinTech can boost financial inclusion. They aim at using the latest technology achievements in providing financial services to the user. Products and business models that have worked for decades are no longer relevant to the digital economy. The pressure from customers and the proliferation of technology have moved FinTech to the top of the growth agenda. Actually, recent years have been an impressive march of companies from this sector through the markets of Asia, Europe and the USA. Innovative companies from the FinTech sector are doing better and better on the market.

With a proliferation of mobile Internet, FinTech has exploded, introducing a wide variety of technological innovations into personal and commercial finance, as well as business models. Emerging technologies like artificial intelligence and machine learning, the blockchain and the Internet of things combined with quickly changing customer needs are transforming how financial institutions deliver services. The scope of FinTech activities is extensive: from tools supporting investors in searching the market or making decisions, through algorithms verifying creditworthiness, to various facilitations in the payment process, and from innovations in financial literacy an financial education to redefined retail banking and crypto-currencies. Most often, the focus is on developing a single product, which makes the services they provide highly specialised and user-friendly at the same time. What is important, these companies usually have access to a vast amount of data about their clients, extending the potential of extensive data analytics. FinTech companies generally offer better customer service than the traditional financial sector.

9.2.2 The Need for Digital Skills for the Financial Sector

Living in the digital, however, creates the need to acquire new digital competences and skills. Only mastering the ability to use the potential of digitalisation appropriately gives full opportunities for the development of both society and individual citizens [2]. Digital competences are increasingly necessary for everyday life, but also more and more desirable in the labour market [3]. Lack of these skills, skill gaps or mismatch may constitute a significant barrier to the development.

It should be emphasised that the full potential of modern technology requires not only infrastructure and services but also the competence of the digital society. The competences are necessary to be able to participate in an increasingly digitalised society. It is, therefore, necessary to examine the digital competences of society and their impact on the ability to use emerging new e-government services.

More and more individuals across EU use the Internet every day. Most of them have smartphones. Many of them use it to for banking operations, conducting daily payments, including contactless. The number of active users of online banking is systematically growing, of which many use mobile banking. We may observe the rise of a digitised consumer. However, there are limits. The critical problem may be the relatively low level of digital competence of still many people. This poses a serious obstacle to the digitisation of the economy. Following this, it is relatively easy to identify other related risks, like a lack of trust in digital financial services, the digital financial system or technological innovation in general. This leads to new types of exclusion for certain groups of the population, as in the general case of digital skills, mainly the elderly and those on with low education. They might not be able to afford the use of digital devices to access financial services. The interesting part of the problem is the so-called self-exclusion. The most frequent answer among individual to the question on the reasons for not using the Internet is the lack of need. The true reasons, however, may include low levels of digital literacy or income or worries related to privacy and security.

The notion of digital literacy is one of many terms used to describe the area of competence related to the ability to use information, media and ICTs. The fundamental concepts of this area are digital competences, digital literacy, digital skills, e-skills. These terms are vastly used in policy-related documents, programmes, strategies, scientific literature, international organisations and institutions. Digital competences relate not only to digital skills but also to the attitudes and social aspects of skilful use and comprehension of digital devices. For example, the application of digital technologies to personal finance management may provide new tools to support consumers in improving their well-being. However, it is important to note that new challenges and risks are created by the digitalisation.

The ongoing technological transformation and increasing the areas of application of digital tools are naturally also observed in finance. Increasing the availability of new technologies translates into the development of new services. The development of new e-finance solutions increasingly requires the digital competence of customers of the financial sector. Employees are also faced with increasing demands. Working on large data sets, using sophisticated software and practical usage of communication tools are now desirable or even necessary skills in the financial sector. The appropriate level of these skills can also positively contribute to the efficient implementation of modern financial services. On the other hand, customers, users of modern solutions and services in the financial market will need to have appropriate competences as well.

Many proposals for general digital qualifications, competences and skills frameworks have been developed in recent years, to support socio-economic policy making, including policies tackling the problem of digital and social exclusion. It seems, however, that there is a strong need to develop more focused and detailed frameworks for selected specialised areas of social and professional activity, crucial for sustainable development. Adoption and dissemination of modern digital solutions in finance, bearing so many different names, like FinTech or emerging PropTech, but still sharing the same technological backgrounds, depend heavily on the digital readiness and skills of the society. Therefore, it seems that there is a need to develop an appropriate framework for assessing the competences of individuals regarding the potential to the uptake of the digital financial services.

9.3 Proposition of the Competence Framework

9.3.1 Measurement, Monitoring and Competence Frameworks

The role of financial innovation should not be underestimated. Many of the international organisations and individual governments are committed to assessing the effects of technological change in the financial landscape. Evidence-based policies need, however, robust statistical data to properly design the policy responses to the problems. Data collection to produce statistics may be organised by the national statistical institute. In this case, the data would have the value of official statistics. The measurement system may be based on different data sources including traditional questionnaire-based survey. In order to design the whole process correctly, there is a need for a conceptual framework that may be the basis for identification of the most relevant issues and problems, and tackle them with appropriate questions. In the case of the measurement of digital skills, the conceptual framework might be guided by relevant competence framework for digital finance. The paper aims to address this issue by proposing the relevant competence framework, tailor-designed for the need to analyse the issue of skills necessary to increase the uptake of digital financial services.

The discussion about digital competences is not easy, the first impediment being the very notion of competence, to which several meanings are assigned. The same applies to digital competences. It is not easy to define their semantic scope, since they are interdisciplinary in nature, referring rather to the practical ability to use the richness of tools and methods offered by modern technologies. The explanations regarding the terminology used in terms of digital competences can be found in many national and international strategic documents and scientific literature. These terms are widely used by research institutes, public organisations and international institutions. The variety of definitions and approaches to digital literacy is undoubtedly related to the dynamic development of information and communication technologies and the increase in their use in society and the economy.

Usually, the competence frameworks are presented in terms of three layers of a specification, i.e. competences, including awareness, knowledge and understanding, then skills and behaviour and finally attitudes. Some define competences as a "harmonious set of knowledge, skills and attitudes that allow effective use of digital technologies in various areas of life" (…). Similarly, other authors refer to defining digital competences as a set of skills conditioning the effective use of electronic media and therefore both IT skills (hardware, software and application support) and information (searching for information in various sources to process them and use them in accordance with need). The digital literacy, therefore, covers a very wide set of skills determining the efficient and conscious use of new technologies and active participation in the life of the information society.

The directions of the development of digital competences in the broadly understood financial sector should be analysed on the side of both employees of the financial sector and its recipients. In this paper, however, competence framework for users of services is considered and proposed. The development of digital competence of employees in the sector is enforced by technological changes as well as customer expectations. For employees of the broadly defined financial sector, there is a need to develop new digital skills related to working on large data sets, modern software, business processes in the big data model and cybersecurity. They should be able to use e-tools in finance, sell online financial products and participate in the development of electronic banking, which results in a change in the nature of existing work. What's more, automation is used for back office tasks, risk management, big data analytics. The emergence of artificial intelligence provides the opportunity to create support and chatbots, but it is also used for automatic trading and advice. Technology is changing the employment structure, leading to the digitisation of routine tasks and enabling the creation of new, different types of jobs.

As innovation and modern technologies change the financial sector, the need for human skills also changes. Service beneficiaries should have appropriate competences to be able to use emerging modern solutions and capabilities. Broad digital competences will provide users of the financial system with an active use of electronic channels of access to financial services (provided electronically by finance and insurance), e-banking solutions, opportunities offered by e-investment.

9.3.2 Digital Competence Framework for Financial Services

Digital financial competence framework proposed is presented below. The framework has been developed based on a thorough critical analysis of similar frameworks with related scope, as well as stocktaking exercise and profound examination of available digital financial services. In particular, the existing frameworks of digital and financial competences were analysed. It is the DigComp, the Digital Competence Framework for Citizens [7] developed by the Joint Research Centre, Core Competencies Framework on Financial Literacy for Adults [4] developed under the auspices of the OECD. It consists of six thematic areas and thirty-five competences. The proposed competence areas consist of information and communication, the financial landscape, service uptake, managing finances, safety and risk management, problem-solving. The competences were defined in terms of title indicating a rather but well-established scope, then followed by identification of knowledge elements and accompanied by awareness and understanding. In this form, the competence framework will be supplemented in future with two more layers, refining the semantic scope, i.e. concerning skills and attitudes corresponding to the knowledge layer.

1. **Information and communication**

   1.1 **Browsing, searching and filtering information**. Understands how information is produced, processed, managed and made available. Aware of different search engines and how and why they operate, especially how they index and classify information. Understands which digital tools, like search engines or databases, best answer to own information needs. Understands how information can be found in different sources.

   1.2 **Evaluating information**. Aware of the varying quality of available data and information. Aware of the risks of misinformation and the concepts of post-truth and fake news. Understands the varying reliability of information sources, regardless of the communication channels. Understands the need to evaluate digital media content. Knows hot to gather, process, evaluate, cross-check and interpret information, including the information acquired through digital platforms.

1.3 **Interacting through technologies**. Aware of different digital communication channels (e.g. email, chat, VoIP, video conference, SMS). Aware of the benefits and limits of different means of communications. Knows how digital communication means work. Knows the functionality of communication apps (on mobile devices) and (desktop) applications. Knows how to choose the most appropriate means of communication for the context. Knows how to interact through a variety of digital devices, apps and applications.

2. **Financial landscape**

2.1 **Understanding digital environment**. Answers that money and financial assets may take digital forms, and related transactions may be conveyed digitally.
2.2 **Understanding consumer protection system**. Aware of digital financial services consumer protection regulations. Knows where to find relevant information regarding the extent of the protection for various digital financial products and contexts. Aware of redress mechanisms for unsatisfactory service or products. Knows how to complain about financial products and services to a relevant body.
2.3 **Understanding rights and responsibilities**. Knows and understands the rights and responsibilities of digital financial services consumers.
2.4 **Gathering information and advice on digital financial services**. Knows where to find information and advice on digital financial services. Aware of existing sources of information on digital financial services and the availability of independent financial advice.
2.5 **Staying up to date with digital financial services offerings**. Aware of the variety of available digital financial services. Aware of available digital financial services providers offering relevant products. Knows that the right choice of the digital financial product depends on many factors.
2.6 **Understanding digital financial services landscape**. Aware that digital financial products may be offered by non-financial organisations including big tech companies and small FinTech start-ups. Understands the mechanisms of services used and knows organisations involved.
2.7 **Keeping up with innovations and changes**. Aware that digital financial services evolve over time and sometimes can change rapidly and radically.

3. **Services uptake**

3.1 **Making digital payments**. Aware of various digital payment methods. Knows how to assess the potential benefits and risks of various payment methods. Understands the advantages and limitations of different methods of making digital transactions.
3.2 **Making money transfers**. Understands different digital payments and money transfer methods; knows how to make a payment or transfer money using digital platforms (including mobile).

3.3 **Doing currency exchange**. Aware of various exchange practices on digital platforms; knows how to convert currencies using digital services; understands the differences between digital services of currency exchange used in different contexts.
3.4 **Managing financial records**. Understands the importance of systematic reviewing of digital financial records and assuring access to them if necessary, also through making copies or backups.
3.5 **Using digital financial management services**. Aware of integrated digital personal financial management services. Understands the differences between functionalities offered.

4. **Managing finances**

4.1 **Managing the budget**. Aware of the need to create budgets, taking into account incomes and expenses. Knows how to monitor them. Understands the importance of planning for expenses.
4.2 **Managing savings**. Aware of different savings options available on digital platforms, that may differ in terms of interest rates, fees, and taxes. Knows about savings options available through digital finance services.
4.3 **Managing an investment portfolio**. Aware of digital financial investment services. Knows how to invest using digital services. Aware of the difference between different investment instruments available digitally when making long-term investments, especially for retirement.
4.4 **Managing liabilities and contracts**. Aware that in some cases it may be possible to renegotiate the terms for digital financial services. Knows when and how the terms can be renegotiated.
4.5 **Managing debt**. Aware that digital financial products can affect personal debt. Understands why it is essential to manage the ratio of the individual or household debt to income. Knows that digital financial services may be used for debt management.
4.6 **Managing credit score**. Aware that financial decisions on digital platforms as on traditional channels may be assessed and taken into account in future, for example by the third-party credit provider for assessment of a borrower's ability to repay the credit purposes. Knows which digital transactions and related factors are taken into account in a credit score, and how it is assessed.

5. **Safety and risk management**

5.1 **Identifying risk of information deficiencies**. Aware of the risks linked to making uninformed financial decisions, especially on digital platforms.
5.2 **Identifying risks associated with excessive advertising**. Aware that in the digital environment, advertising and similar activities targeted at engaging clients may be even more effective than in the real world. Understands the consequences of compulsive or excessive buying.
5.3 **Identifying emotional risks**. Aware that emotions can have an impact on financial decisions, primarily related to investments.

5.4 **Identifying risks related to ease of use of the platform**. Aware that simplified lending processes on digital platforms make it easy to access credit without considering consequences or to spend more than initially planned or necessary, especially that all forms of deferred payment are also a form of credit.
5.5 **Identifying mistakes**. Aware that when using digital financial services, mistakes can be made. Knows how to reveal them.
5.6 **Identifying market risks**. Aware of the risks related to digital financial products, related to, among other things, making inappropriate product choices including excessive exposure to market interest rates or currency exchange risks. Aware of how internal or external shocks may impact financial markets and possible consequences for digital financial services users and providers.
5.7 **Safeguarding against scams and frauds**. Aware of the risk of scams and frauds. Understands why it is important to report them to the relevant bodies even if not personally a victim. Knows whom to report suspected scams and frauds. Knows how to report scams and frauds.
5.8 **Protecting personal data**. Aware of personal data protection importance and existing regulations. Aware that digital service providers may use the personal data of users. Aware of online fraud, cyberbullying and threats in the digital world. Understands basic concepts like confidentiality, privacy, data security and data protection. Understands the risk of identity theft and related credentials' thefts. Understands the importance of keeping all the personal data and financial information secure (including security-related information like passwords and PINs). Understands how others can see user's digital footprint. Knows that most of the digital services collect and use information about users, also for commercial reasons. Knows about appropriate behaviour in the digital domain.
5.9 **Managing digital identity**. Aware of the connections between the online and the offline worlds. Understands the benefits of having one or more digital identities to be able to secure against risks and threats, to protect reputation.
5.10 **Protecting devices**. Aware of the risks and threats associated with the use of digital technologies. Knows about current and up-to-date strategies to avoid risks and deal with threats.

6. **Problem-solving**

6.1 **Solving technical problems**. Knows how digital devices are built and the way they function. Knows how to solve possible technical problems or where to look to solve a problem.
6.2 **Identifying needs and technological responses**. Understands the potential and limitations of digital technologies and tools. Knows available technologies, their strengths and weaknesses and how to use them to achieve per-

sonal goals and increase productivity. Knows the most relevant applications of digital technologies.

6.3 **Identifying digital competence gaps**. Aware of the broader context of the information society, digitalisation and globalisation. Understands where own digital skills and competences need to be improved or updated, also to keep up to date with new developments. Knows about the important digital technologies used.

6.4 **Identifying digital financial competence gaps**. Knows that it is possible to improve an individual's digital and financial literacy.

It seems significant that the most competences were distinguished for the area of security (ten). This confirms the importance of the problem in the context of the degree of use of digital financial services. The issues related to ensuring privacy and security are certainly the greatest concern of users who refrain from using digital channels. These fears are additionally intensified by the lack of appropriate competences and skills in the field of individual protection against threats occurring in this sphere. It is probably even more important, and perhaps even above all, in the case of attitudes. The shaping of attitudes should be at the beginning of all considerations regarding the development of upcoming policies aimed at promoting the use of modern digital financial services.

9.4 Conclusions

Digitalisation is affecting individuals and businesses, and strengthening the digital economy and information society. Mobile devices and the Internet have given rise to a new generation of financial services. The digitalisation of financial products leads to a need to increase digital financial literacy. Following this, appropriate policies should be developed to address the issues of digital and financial exclusion. This requires substantial empirical evidence based on a robust measurement framework in the form of data collection systems for statistical production processes. Policy-makers need timely and relevant statistics to better understand this crucial area of digital economy development.

competence, skills and attitude frameworks are an essential prerequisite facilitating the production of meaningful statistics. This paper proposes the competence framework for digital financial services. The proposed competences, grouped into six major areas, have been identified and defined in terms of the first layer of usual description, i.e. awareness, understanding and knowledge. The work presented here should be continued in the form of making the framework more granular by adding skills and attitudes corresponding to identified competences. It may, however, already be used as a guide in design of set of indicators necessary to monitor and evaluate policies targeting digital financial exclusion. The framework proposed identifies critical core competences that should be developed to ensure the everyday and safe use of digital financial services by consumers.

References

1. Bell, B.: The Coming of Post-Industrial Society. Basic Books, New York (1973)
2. Erstad, O.: Educating the digital generation. Nord. J. Digital Literacy 1 (2010)
3. OECD: Skills Matter: Further Results from the Survey of Adult Skills. OECD Publishing, Paris. http://dx.doi.org/10.1787/9789264258051-en (2016a)
4. OECD: G20/OECD INFE Core Competencies Framework on Financial Literacy for Adults, OECD, http://www.oecd.org/daf/fin/financial-education/Core-Competencies-Framework-Adults.pdf (2016b)
5. OECD: OECD Digital Economy Outlook 2017. OECD Publishing, Paris, http://dx.doi.org/10.1787/9789264276284-en (2017)
6. OECD: Financial Markets, Insurance and Private Pensions: Digitalisation and Finance (2018)
7. Vuorikari, R., Punie, Y., Carretero Gomez S., Van den Brande, G.: DigComp 2.0: The Digital Competence Framework for Citizens. Update Phase 1: The Conceptual Reference Model. Luxembourg Publication Office of the European Union. EUR 27948 EN. https://doi.org/10.2791/11517 (2016)

Part II
Quantitative Methods on Financial Markets

Chapter 10
The Motives of Name Changes and Share Quotations on the Warsaw Stock Exchange

Roman Asyngier

Abstract The aim of this article is to analyse the motives of name changes made by public companies listed on the Warsaw Stock Exchange and to identify abnormal returns before and after this event depending on the motives given by issuers. The research methodology using cumulated abnormal return (CAR) was to determine the relative strength of quoted shares in relation to the WIG index before and after changes in companies' names. The results of the research done indicated abnormal returns before the name change as well as unambiguously negative trends afterwards. The article is a continuation of the author's previous research into the problem of name changes, which has not yet been carried out on the Polish market.

Keywords Name change · Abnormal return · Warsaw Stock Exchange · Event study · Market performance

10.1 Introduction

Every year, a lot of companies in the world change their names. The motives for such operations may be mergers and acquisitions, a change of the business profile, creating a new capital group or marketing activities. In the last 20 years, companies listed on the Warsaw Stock Exchange have changed their names exactly 200 times. The investigation of the relationship between the motives of name changes and stock quotations may provide some important information for managers and investors. The results of the research on the impact of name changes on quotations of the listed companies do not bring, however, sufficiently clear indicators.

The purpose of the article is to analyse the motives behind name changes undertaken by public companies on the Warsaw Stock Exchange and to identify the occurrence of abnormal returns before and after this event, depending on the motives given by the issuers. The research methodology which uses cumulated abnormal returns

R. Asyngier (✉)
Maria Curie-Sklodowska University, Lublin, Poland
e-mail: roman.asyngier@poczta.umcs.lublin.pl

W. Tarczyński and K. Nermend (eds.), *Effective Investments on Capital Markets*, Springer Proceedings in Business and Economics,
https://doi.org/10.1007/978-3-030-21274-2_10

(CARs) is to determine the relative strength of listed shares in relation to the WIG index, before and after the change of the company's name. The article continues the previous research on the problem of name changes, which has an aspect of novelty on the Polish stock market.

The structure of the article goes as follows: literature review, description of a research methodology, research findings and conclusions. The already existing research carried out on various capital markets highlighted differences in the obtained results. The methodological part presents the description of the stages of creating a research sample along with the division into subgroups and the applied research method. The research findings show CARs dependent on the motives of name changes before and after this operation in the established subgroups. The last part of the article includes the research conclusions compared with the results achieved by other authors together with the discussion on these results.

10.2 The Motives of Name Changes

The brand is usually defined as a notion, symbol, design or combination meant to help identify goods or services of one seller or a group of sellers and to distinguish them from an offer of competition [27]. The name of the brand is discussed as a main means or a signal thanks to which a company may communicate publicly with market participants [36]. Competition enhances the strength of brands because they allow for non-price differentiation [1]. According to Turley and Moore [39], the importance of a name and a brand is more significant when a given product is of intangible nature (service), because it is a fairly good source of information about a company provided by customers' opinions.

A change of the name of a company is often referred to as rebranding. Yet, rebranding is defined broader not only as renaming but also as makeover, reinvention or reposition [32]. It may be connected with a change in the strategy of the company's activity, launching new products, entering new areas of operational activity or a total change of a business profile. The rebranding model proposed by Muzellec and Lambkin [35] covers four factors: a change in the ownership, a change in the company's external environment and a change in its competitive position. According to Rooney [37], rebranding may refer to corporate industrial and service rebranding.

Renaming sensu stricto is a name strategy lying in the exchange of a name for a new one. More often, it is connected with changes in the companies' names than names of products. It is due to the fact that it is much easier to introduce changes in the company's name than in its product. Clients are emotionally attached to the name of a given product; thus, it is more difficult for them to accept these changes. Renaming often results from the need to change the image following the change in the strategy. Researchers suggest that a change of the name should be a measure of the last resort and it should be undertaken only when there is no other option of resolving such a problem [25].

Renaming aims at bringing market benefits and as a consequence also financial ones. This may stem from two mechanisms due to which a change of the name not only helps companies but also influences the manner investors perceive their shares—these are inherent value and signalling value (see also [24, 34]). Inherent value covers the name itself, increasing the company's cash flows, raising customers' awareness or perception of the company. A change of the name may also signal a promise to make value-generating changes in its business operations. The likely improvement of the perception of the company's brand will bring about higher incomes of the company and, thus, profits for shareholders (expected higher share prices and dividends).

A change of the name itself does not always have to result in long-term benefits that might exceed the cost of the operation. The complexity of the process may be connected with considerable legal costs, advertising costs and the need to inform market participants of the change made [18]. Quite often, such costs are variable and difficult to estimate (see other examples [23]). Badly prepared and poorly managed, such a change might have disastrous effects, worse than merely losing the existing customers.

One of the key factors determining changes of brands and companies' names is mergers and acquisitions [19, 35, 43]. A merger may result in creating a new brand or a company name, adopting a stronger brand or the joint use of both brands. A choice of a solution should in the best possible way communicate the potential synergies arising from M&A transactions [5, 29].

A change of the name most often has got a strategic background, but it may also be caused by fashion or vice versa, by some reluctance to identify the company's business activity with a particular industry. It was proved that during the dot-com boom on the NASDAQ Stock Market a lot of companies were undertaking changes of their names by adding 'dot' or 'com' [10]. Such a move had a positive effect on share prices (cf. [6, 28]). The research done after the bursting of the speculative bubble revealed that a lot of companies decided to remove these elements from their names due to the wrong perception of the company by investors [11].

10.3 Literature Review

The subject literature referring to the research into the issue of the influence of name changes on share prices, although quite extensive, does not give unambiguous results. More often, positive CARs were indicated; however, the strength of this effect and the influence of the event time on quotations were identified differently.

A clearly positive reaction to a change of the issuer's name was proved by, inter alia, DeFanti and Busch [12] and Karim [22]. Their results were confirmed by Biktimirov and Durrani [7] on the Canadian market who recorded a close relation between a type of the change in the name and share prices as well as trading volume. Essential changes connected with core business activity, such as M&As or product launch, are of much greater importance than pure name changes. Also, Agnihotri and

Bhattacharya [2], basing on quotations of Indian companies, noted a positive effect of name changes. Greater abnormal returns occurred when companies' names were not referring to their geographical location and were fluent, specific and related to the owner's family. Positive return rates on the Indian stock markets were also observed by Gupta and Aggarwal [16], but in the group of small cap stocks exclusively.

Horsky and Swyngedouw [17] on the basis of a narrow research sample covering only 58 American companies showed a strong positive effect of the change of the name in a group of industrial firms and firm of investment risk. In the case of financial entities, there was a negative response to the prices. The research by Mayo [31] run on the basis of a 30-day observation of quotations on the NYSE after the change of the name confirmed a positive effect of this event. However, the impact of this was not significant enough. Kot [26], basing on his observations of the Hong Kong market, noted a short-term impact of a change of the name on share prices. He proved, however, that the reactions of investors vary depending on the motives of such a change. The market reactions were positive when the change of the name followed an M&A transaction, undertaken restructuring or a change in the business profile of the company. Changes meant to improve the company's reputation did not bring about any price reactions. In this context, the conclusions drawn from the analysis by Kashmiri and Mahajan [24] are worth noting as the authors showed that American companies while making significant marketing investments in the change of the name are viewed much better by investors. The research on the British market confirmed the importance of information on the change of the name for stockholders because they brought significant CARs after the announcement [30]. It was found out that there are various dependencies between shortening or lengthening of the name and a direction of price changes. A removal of an element of the name met a negative reaction, contrary to an addition an element to the company's name which gave positive price effects.

In contrast to the research indicating positive abnormal rates, there are research findings showing no relation between name changes and a value for stockholders of the US companies (e.g. [8, 18, 23]). Even though Bosch and Hirschey [8] confirmed slightly positive abnormal returns before publishing the information, this effect was temporary as it was entirely eliminated by the price changes within the subsequent three weeks. Similar results were recorded in the research on the Malaysian market [21]. They concluded that the changes of names not accompanied by formal, national regulations on restructuring, have no significant impact on share prices.

Few studies demonstrated unequivocally negative price effects for companies which were changing names. A negative long-run effect of a name change was pointed by Andrikopoulos et al. [3], while investigating 800 cases of companies based in the UK after a considerable change in the name within the next 36 months. The authors claimed markets respond slowly to the contents of the information on the change in the name and a downward trend spread in time occurs regardless of the results obtained by companies before the change of their names. Short-run negative effects of changes were, in turn, indicated by the analysis of quotations on Australian companies [20]. Significantly, negative results within 21 days after announcing the change were particularly limited to enterprises undertaking major name changes while being restructured and to small companies.

Part of publications, besides examination of abnormal returns, referred to the influence of name changes on the volume of trading. The analyses of several thousand name changes of companies of the US markets allowed to state that changes in names generally increase the average liquidity of shares [15]. A linguistic aspect of the changes made was highlighted there. More fluent names and easier to pronounce extended shareholding and increased the company's value. Similar results for liquidity were recorded by Wu [42]. While analysing changes of nearly 200 tickers of listed companies in the USA, he proved a positive reaction of prices for companies which take the name of one of the well-recognized brands, which may be associated with good activity. However, names meant to cut off from the company's bad reputation, on giving the information, were even negative. Biktimirov and Durrani [7] claimed that the changes on the Toronto Stock Exchange are accompanied by an increase in the trading volume for a few days from the date of approval.

The only research dealing with the impact of a change of the name on share prices of the companies on the Polish market was published in 2018 [4]. The research was of a pilot nature, and it was limited to essential name changes of the companies listed on the WSE's main market in 2006–2015. On the basis of a selected research group (70 name changes), positive abnormal returns from shares were confirmed before the change and clearly negative ones after this operation in a long-term perspective. The present study continues the above-mentioned analyses with the extension of a research group, taking into account motives for these changes and applying more advanced research tools.

10.4 Research Sample and Research Methodology

Initially, the analysis of dependencies between name changes of public companies and their return rates covered the period of 1998–2017, i.e. 20 years of the WSE's functioning. During this time, the number of name changes amounted to 200, and all the changes resulted in a change of the company's ticker, its name given in the listing or both of them. Split operations and share issuances with the rights issue carried out by issuers at the time of the analysis were also included into the research. Share prices in these cases were adjusted for theoretical values of the rights issue and split coefficients.

Having considered the information available in the WSE's annual reports and the Internet content, the period of 1998–2000 was excluded from the analysis. The data accessible from this period did not allow to establish the accurate dates of name changes. With the assumption of conducting the analysis of share price movements within two years, the cases from occurring after 30 September 2016 were also excluded. Eventually, subject to the analysis were 162 events of name changes which took place on the WSE between January 2001 and the end of September 2016.

In order to receive possibly the most representative research sample, it underwent a two-stage selection. At the first stage, two time criteria of a name change were established, which due to the adopted research methodology could distort the achieved results. It was assumed that those events will be excluded from the analysis if they take place in companies performing renaming within three calendar years, if companies are de-listed from the market within two years after the event or companies which changed their names within a year from their debut on the stock exchange. As a result, 54 such cases were identified (33, 13 and 7, respectively) and the research sample was reduced to 108 events. At the second selection stage, the analysis aimed at detecting all the name changes in terms of specific operations which might disrupt the research. At this stage, the following companies were excluded: OPTIMUS and GRUPA ONET (created due to the transfer of part of the publicly listed OPTIMUS's assets), ASSECO POLAND (in 2005, it performed rebranding, and in 2007 it merged with SOFTBANK—another public company), GETINOBLE (there were two mergers in 2010-2012), ABADONRE, ALPRAS, DZPOLSKA (following the name change, their quotations were suspended for over a year) and BICK (following the name change, its quotations were suspended for over a half a year). Taking into account the above nine cases, the research sample further investigated comprised 99 changes of the name.

At this point, two bizarre cases of name changes made on the WSE by the issuer might be worth mentioning (both of them would not have been subject to the analysis anyway due to the time criteria). The first one refers to WDMCP, the company which debuted on the stock market on 26 November 2014. The listings showed WDM's ticker and its abbreviated name WDMCP. According to the information given by the company, on the debut day the stock exchange changed the abbreviated name because of a spelling mistake in the application for the admission to trading (the company made a mistake giving this abbreviated name WMDCP). The company was listed in quoting under the corrected name for less than three months, as already in February 2015, it changed its name to 'EVEREST'. The other case refers to a company which debuted on the WSE as early as 2008 under the name 'HARDEX', and in 2012 it changed its brand to Libra. In May 2013, the same company changed the name twice within only 8 days—at first to GLOBAL NGR and then to GLOBAL NRG. Also in this case, a highly probable reason for a fast change was a spelling mistake. Eventually, after the change made in 2014, the company took the name 'STARHEDGE'.

The next stage of the analysis was to determine the motive of a change of the name. First, name changes were attributed to the research sample by four motives: mergers and acquisitions, rebranding, a new operational strategy and a change of the business profile of an issuer. The motives were identified on the basis of the information published by companies in their current reports (referring to the very name change) or interim reports (most often annual with the description of the most significant events from the issuer's activity).

Apart from M&A transactions defined clearly as such, also adverse acquisitions and ownership transformations were included. A change of a strategy in a business activity may be related to, e.g., a new business strategy, sales of products and cooperation with other entities, and at the same time, it may be connected with a new holding strategy, creating a capital group, reorganization of the group, restructuring or wide co-operation with an strategic investor. All marketing activities that aim at enhancing or changing the brand were qualified to rebranding. Consequently, a change of the profile means core changes in the area of the company's operational activity (a total change of operational activity after discontinuing current activity or entering new areas of activity, which were to be core activities in giving revenues and generating profits).

In cases of multifaceted name changes in public companies (e.g. the issuer performed an acquisition, which changed the strategy of their activity and justified rebranding), the importance of a given motive in the operation was subject to subjective evaluation. The most decisive motive was that one which in the course of publishing current information (occasionally with financial results obtained later) exerted the highest impact of the functioning of a public company.

The research carried out allowed to determine unambiguously a leading motive of the change of the name in 91 cases:

- Mergers and acquisitions—30,
- Rebranding—39,
- New strategy of activity—11,
- Change of the issuer's activity.

Out of eight cases, a sample of five name changes made by National Investment Funds (NIFs) [1] was distinguished. Each time, when a name change took place after a merger with other entities (including NIF funds), the companies strongly accentuated rebranding. Full homogeneity of this sample as well as the lack of possibility of evaluating of the key factor for the name change contributed to the identification of the fifth research sample. The remaining three cases were excluded from the study as it was not possible to relate the operations to the adopted motives of the issuers' activity (NEW WORLD—relocation, ORION—a change of the share quotation market, INVISTA—officially given motive was 'to beautify ticker').

Commonly used in the world, the calendar-time portfolio method was applied based on the cumulative abnormal returns (CARs) and recommended for long-term event studies [9, 14, 33]. To calculate surplus returns, the model based on the market index was engaged. Therefore, the analysis took into account a relative strength of quotations related to a general market index to eliminate impacts of existing trends on the listing of the companies. The index at issue was the index of a wide share market in Poland—WIG.

The date of the name change of the company (t_0) was assumed to be the actual day of the change in the name or the ticker. The quotations of selected shares were taken as single time point (t_0), giving CAR value 100 to the whole research sample. For a given day t, above-average return rate from the share wallet was calculated as

[1] An investment fund of the close-ended type, a public company set up by the Polish State Treasury in 1995; within the Mass Privatisation Programme, 15 funds were created whose shares were admitted to trading at the WSE. The appropriate abbreviation for the Polish language is NIF (also officially used in WSE listing).

the average from abnormal returns which were subject to the analysis. The research was run within 250 sessions before and 500 sessions after that day. Considering the fact that on average there are 250 market sessions, it corresponds approximately to one year before and two years after the change of the companies' names.

The source of information on the dates of the name changes was annual reports of the WSE [40] as well as current information on shares published by the issuers [41]. The data on share quotations and the WIG index used for this research came from the services EMIS [13] and Stooq [38].

10.5 Research Findings

The research carried out proved that in the period of one year before the name change, the quotations of the analysed companies showed a clear upward trend (Fig. 10.1). Positive abnormal returns of the whole sample were 20%. This clear upward trend was over 38 sessions before the name change. For the remaining two months, the companies' quotations before the change were in a side trend of a limited liquidity. Reinforcement of the quotations from the last 15 sessions before the name change accounted for nearly 4%.

The least liquidity of quotations and fluctuations of CARs were characteristics of the companies' name changes motivated by marketing activities. In the case of this research group, the effect was zero. The companies motivated by a new strategy to change their names strengthened their quotations against the benchmark by about 20% and in the case of entities performing M&As by nearly 30%. In both cases, upward trends lasted almost till the end of the period before the name change. High liquidity and high positive CARs were recorded for the quotations of NIFs, and the companies performing renaming die to the change in their activity profiles. It is worth

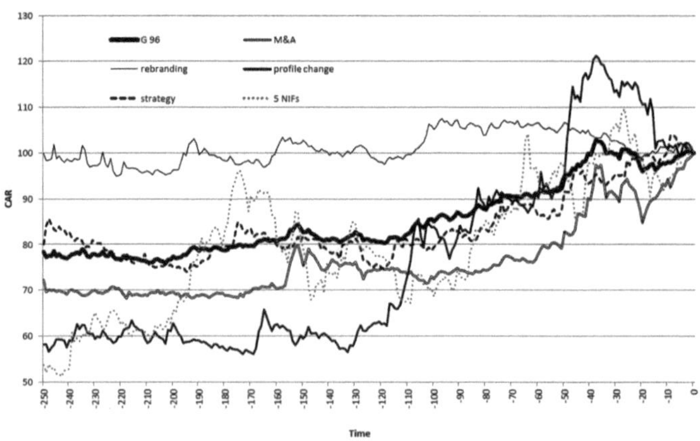

Fig. 10.1 CAR before the name change (*source* The author's own study)

noting, however, that in the case of these entities, the name change was preceded by clear falls of the relative strength of share listing.

The analysis of abnormal returns after the change of the name of a company shows a downward trend (Fig. 10.2). In the first 46 sessions after the event, each of the companies was relatively cheaper by 8.3%. This declining tendency remained until the 168th session after the change, adjusting the relative values of the companies by 17.0% on average. The growth which followed for the subsequent weeks was finished after a year of the change. The falls observed at the end of the analysis did not bring quotations below the earlier established minimum (−13.5%).

Apart from NIF funds, all the research samples distinguished because of a motive for name changes in the first weeks after these operations recorded negative CARs. Definitely the weakest were return rates of those companies where a change of their activity profile was the decisive factor while changing their names. As early as after 23 session days, relative losses in this group exceeded 10%, while in the remaining groups they were similar and fluctuated from −1.9 to −2.6%. In the following weeks, the quotations of these companies were the weakest and after 136 sessions of the date of the change, the falls in prices accounted as many as 38.4%. Since then, the trend in this subgroup was noticeably changed and the losses were quickly mitigated.

A quite interesting observation can be made regarding 182 sessions after the change of the name. With the average change for the whole sample −13.0%, CARs for particular subgroups differ from this value by maximum ±2%. Since that point, the average CARs for particular research samples evidently ‘go apart’. The quotations continue to weaken in the companies, which while changing their names are motivated by a change in their strategy and performing M&As. An upward trend starts in the companies performing rebranding, and it is still continued by issuers who change the profile of their activity. In the NIF subgroups, a short increase appears preceding a strong downfall trend.

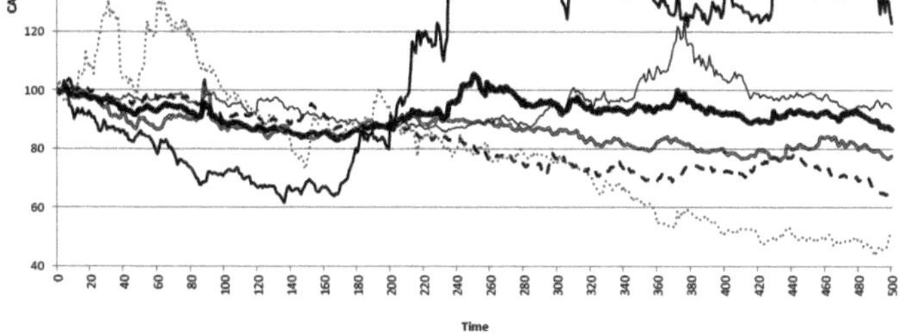

Fig. 10.2 CAR after the name change (*source* The author’s own study)

Eventually, after the change of the name, only the companies motivated by the change in their profile of activity end up with a clearly positive CAR (over 22.7%). Slightly negative CARs were recorded for quotations of the companies undertaking rebranding (−5.8%). The rest had declines in the relative strength in relation to the benchmark, in the case of M&As exceeding −22.3% and for those changing their strategy by 34.9%. In the selected subgroup of NIF funds, falls of CARs were almost 50%.

10.6 Conclusions

The results obtained clearly indicate that investors respond positively to the announcement of a change of the name by issuers. A long-term effect of the name change just before the operation was positive regardless of its motives. The only exception is entities undertaking rebranding. The lack of a distinct reaction of the share prices before the name change proves a neutral reception of this relevant information by investors. These results are in contrast to the observations made on the American market [24]. Yet, they are in line with the essence of the research findings suggesting a higher positive effect of the name change on the quotations in the case of significant motives (M&A, new strategy) decisive for renaming [7]. The highest positive CARs in subgroups of NIFs and companies changing their activity profile in general may be justified by high expectations of improvement in the financial situations of issuers. In the majority of cases, these companies (including NIFs) before the change were in a poor financial state. Investors were likely to treat the name change and its motives as 'a new opening' and an opportunity for the future.

The change reverses the positive trends evident before this event in the company's quotations. After the operation, the quotations are considerably weakened and the company's listing regardless of the motives of the name change showed negative CARs for at least a few months. The effect can be observed in a short-term perspective—a few weeks, a few months or even years. It confirms some observations made in the course of the research run on the world financial markets (e.g. for short-run observations: [8, 20, 21]; for long-run: [3]). Nonetheless, the results do not correspond with the majority of the findings which indicated a positive effect after the name change (e.g. [2, 7, 12, 22]). Neither do they confirm the observations by Kot [26], relying positive returns on the motives of the change, although at the same time they show that the most significant for investors are actual M&As transactions and the changes in the company's business profile.

When related to the benchmark, the highest losses are for shares of companies undertaking renaming as a consequence of a merger/acquisition and the change of the profile. The same companies enhanced their quotations before the name change. It may be proved by the well-known rule of buying shares before some event and selling them afterwards. The quotations of the companies changing as a follow-up of the change of the profile of activity in the long-run much differ from the rest of the subgroups. After about 8 months of the change, their quotations mark a strong uptrend. It is difficult to point at reasons for such movements of share prices. On the one hand, it may be a pure speculation quite often appearing on the companies with weak foundations. Any positive aspect connected with starting activity in a new industry may be met by enthusiastic reactions of the market. On the other hand, one should note a not very big research sample made up by only 11 companies. In this case, strong rises of 2–3 companies may distort the results of the whole subgroup. The same refers to CAR observations in NIF quotations. But in this case in the long term, all the five funds recorded significantly negative CARs.

The research results are evident and unambiguous as for general trends which accompany quotations of companies before and after the name change. Therefore, their findings may be valuable for investors and managers of share wallets while taking proper investment decisions. The discrepancies between the results obtained on the Polish market when compared with the results of scientific studies on other world capital markets are a valuable contribution to the existing subject literature. They also provide grounds for further analyses to verify the achieved results. It appears that the research problem of the impact of the name changes on quotations is interesting enough to be continued in future.

References

1. Aaker, D.A.: Managing Brand Equity—Capitalizing on the Value of a Brand Name. Free Press, New York (1991)
2. Agnihotri, A., Bhattacharya, S.: Corporate name change and the market valuation of firms: evidence from an emerging market. Int. J. Econ. Bus. **24**(1), 73–90 (2017). https://doi.org/10.1080/13571516.2016.1253186
3. Andrikopoulos, P., Daynes, A., Pagas, P.: The long-term market performance of UK companies following corporate name changes. Retrieved from http://papers.ssrn.com/sol3/papers.cfm?abstract_id=1002188 (2007)
4. Asyngier, R.: Does the change in the company's name affect the share price? The case study of the Polish capital market. J. Econ. Manage. **32**, 18–29 (2018). https://doi.org/10.22367/jem.2018.32.02
5. Bahadir, S.C., Bharadwaj, S.G., Srivastava, R.K.: Financial value of brands in mergers and acquisitions: is value in the eye of the beholder? J. Mark. **72**(6), 49–64 (2008). https://doi.org/10.1509/jmkg.72.6.49
6. Berkman, H., Nguyen, N., Zou, L.: The value impact of name changes evidence from Chinese firms during the technology boom. J. Chin. Econ. Bus. Stud. **9**(1), 85–96 (2011). https://doi.org/10.1080/14765284.2011.545590
7. Biktimirov, E.N., Durrani, F.: Market reactions to corporate name changes: evidence from the Toronto Stock Exchange. Int. J. Manage. Financ. **40**(1), 50–69 (2017). https://doi.org/10.1108/ijmf-08-2015-0154
8. Bosch, J.C., Hirschey, M.: The valuation effects of corporate name changes. Financ. Manage. **18**(4), 64–73 (1989). https://doi.org/10.2307/3665798
9. Brown, S.J., Warner, J.B.: Using daily stock returns: the case of event studies. J. Financ. Econ. **14**(1), 3–31 (1985). https://doi.org/10.1016/0304-405X(85)90042-X
10. Cooper, M.J., Dimitrov, O., Rau, P.R.: A Rose.com by any other name. J. Financ. **56**(6), 2371–2388 (2001). https://doi.org/10.1111/0022-1082.00408

11. Cooper, M.J., Khorana, A., Osobov, I., Patel, A., Rau, P.R.: Managerial actions in response to a market downturn: valuation effects of name changes in the dot.com decline. J. Corp. Financ. **11**, 319–335 (2005). https://doi.org/10.1016/j.jcorpfin.2004.02.005
12. DeFanti, M., Busch, P.: Image-related corporate name changes: their effects on firms' stock prices. J. Brand Manage. **19**(3), 241–253 (2011). https://doi.org/10.1057/bm.2011.34
13. EMIS Emerging Markets Information Service. https://www-1emis-1com-1000945ry00fb.han.bg.umcs.edu.pl/php/companies/overview/index. Accessed 30 Aug 2018
14. Fama, E.F.: Market efficiency, long-term returns, and behavioral finance. J. Financ. Econ. **49**, 283–306 (1998). https://doi.org/10.1016/S0304-405X(98)00026-9
15. Green, T.C., Jame, R.: Company name fluency, investor recognition, and firm value. J. Financ. Econ. **109**, 813–834 (2013). https://doi.org/10.1016/j.jfineco.2013.04.007
16. Gupta, M., Aggarwal, N.: The impact of stock name change on shareholder wealth: evidence from Indian stock markets. J. Manage. Res. **14**(1), 15–24 (2014)
17. Horsky, D., Swyngedouw, P.: Does it pay to change your company's name? A stock market perspective. Mark. Sci. **6**(4), 320–335 (1987). https://doi.org/10.1287/mksc.6.4.320
18. Howe, J.S.: A rose by any other name? A note on corporate name changes. Financ. Rev. **17**, 271–278 (1982). https://doi.org/10.1111/j.1540-6288.1982.tb00510.x
19. Jaju, A., Joinier, C., Reddy, S.K.: Consumer evaluations of corporate brand redeployments. J. Acad. Mark. Sci. **34**(2), 206–215 (2006). https://doi.org/10.1177/0092070305284989
20. Josev, T., Chan, H., Faff, R.: What's in a name? Evidence on corporate name changes from the Australian capital market. Pac. Acc. Rev. **16**(1), 57–75 (2004). https://doi.org/10.1108/01140580410818469
21. Karbhari, Y., Sori, Z.M., Mohamad, S.: Shareholder wealth effects and corporate name change: evidence from Malaysia. Corp. Ownership Control **2**(1), 38–49 (2004). https://doi.org/10.2139/ssrn.596184
22. Karim, B.: Corporate name change and shareholder wealth effect: empirical evidence in the French stock market. J. Asset Manage. **12**(3), 203–213 (2011). https://doi.org/10.1057/jam.2011.9
23. Karpoff, J.M., Rankine, G.: In search of a signaling effect: the wealth effects of corporate name changes. J. Bank. Financ. **18**(6), 1027–1045 (1994). https://doi.org/10.1016/0378-4266(94)00058-1
24. Kashmiri, S., Mahajan, V.: The name's the game: does marketing impact the value of corporate name changes? J. Bus. Res. **68**, 281–290 (2015). https://doi.org/10.1016/j.jbusres.2014.07.007
25. Kilic, C., Dursun, T.: The effect of corporate identity changes on firm value: an empirical investigation. J. Am. Acad. Bus. **10**(1), 234–240 (2006)
26. Kot, H.W.: Corporate name changes: price reactions and long-run performance. Pac.-Basin Financ. J. **19**(2), 230–244 (2011). https://doi.org/10.1016/j.pacfin.2010.10.003
27. Kotler, P.T., Keller, K.L.: Marketing Management, 14th edn. Prentice-Hall, Upper Saddle River (2012)
28. Lee, P.M.: What's in a name.com?: the effects of '.com' name changes on stock prices and trading activity. Strateg. Manag. J. **22**(8), 793–804 (2001). https://doi.org/10.1002/smj.177
29. Loukianova, A., Nikulin, E., Vedernikov, A.: Valuing synergies in strategic mergers and acquisitions using the real options approach. Investment Manage. Financ. Innov. **14**(1–1), 236–247 (2017). https://doi.org/10.21511/imfi.14(1-1).2017.10
30. Mase, B.: The impact of name changes on company value. Manage. Financ. **35**(4), 316–324 (2009). https://doi.org/10.1108/03074350910935812
31. Mayo, R.L.: Do corporate name changes affect share price? An event studies analysis of corporate rebranding on the NYSE. Retrieved from https://robertmayo.files.wordpress.com/2014/03/do-corporate-name-changes-affect-share-price-an-event-studies-analysis-of-corporate-rebranding-on-the-nyse.pdf (2013)
32. Merrilees, B., Miller, D.: Principles of corporate rebranding. Eur. J. Mark. **42**(5/6), 537–552 (2008). https://doi.org/10.1108/03090560810862499
33. Mitchell, M.L., Stafford, E.: Managerial decisions and long-term stock price performance. J. Bus. **73**(3), 287–329 (2000). https://doi.org/10.1086/209645

34. Morris, L.J., Reyes, M.G.C.: Corporate name changes: the association between functional name characteristics and stock performance. J. Appl. Bus. Res. **8**(1), 110–117 (1992). https://doi.org/10.19030/jabr.v8i1.6190
35. Muzellec, L., Lambkin, M.: Corporate rebranding destroying, transferring or creating brand equity? Eur. J. Mark. **40**(7/8), 803–824 (2006). https://doi.org/10.1108/03090560610670007
36. Ponsonby-Mccabe, S., Boyle, E.: Understanding Brands as experiential spaces: axiological implications for marketing strategists. J. Strateg. Mark. **14**(2), 175–189 (2006). https://doi.org/10.1080/10427710600662983
37. Rooney, J.A.: Branding: a trend for today and tomorrow. J. Prod. Brand Manage. **4**(4), 48–55 (1995). https://doi.org/10.1108/10610429510097690
38. Stooq information service, https://stooq.pl/. Accessed 4 Sept 2018
39. Turley, L.W., Moore, P.A.: Brand name strategies in the service sectors. J. Consum. Mark. **12**(4), 42–50 (1995). https://doi.org/10.1108/07363769510095298
40. WSE annual reports, https://www.gpw.pl/biblioteka-gpw-lista?gpwlc_id=10. Accessed 6 Sept 2018
41. WSE information service, http://infostrefa.com/infostrefa/pl/index/. Accessed 30 Aug 2018
42. Wu, Y.: What's in a name? What leads a firm to change its name and what the new name foreshadows. J. Bank. Financ. **34**(6), 1344–1359 (2010). https://doi.org/10.1016/j.jbankfin.2009.11.029
43. Zhang, M.C., Luo, X.: An affair not to remember? It might help to change your name. Research Collection Lee Kong Chian School of Business. https://ink.library.smu.edu.sg/lkcsb_research/3773 (2013)

Chapter 11
The Investor's Preferences in the Portfolio Selection Problem Based on the Goal Programming Approach

Donata Kopańska-Bródka, Renata Dudzińska-Baryła and Ewa Michalska

Abstract Goal programming is the approach used for multicriteria decision making when the decision maker aims to minimize deviations between the achievement of goals and their aspiration levels. In the presence of skewness in the portfolio selection problems, the goal programming technique is an excellent and powerful quantitative tool in which the investor's preferences among objectives are incorporated. In this study, in the mean–variance–skewness framework, the utilization of the goal programming model allows to determine the trade-off frontier or efficient frontier for a given level of decision maker's preferences in relation to the selected parameters. Each change in the strength of preference for the expected value in relation to the third moment is a trade-off frontier in the appropriate two-dimensional space or on the surface of efficient portfolios in three-dimensional space.

Keywords Mean–variance–skewness portfolios · Efficient frontier · Trade-off frontier · Goal programming

11.1 Introduction

The analysts basing on the Markowitz portfolio selection model have focused on the expected return and variance and have stated that an investor should always choose an efficient portfolio. They have assumed that the return rates of stocks have a normal (symmetrical) probability distribution or the utility function is quadratic. The assumption regarding a symmetrical distribution of the rate of return is unrealistic and has no empirical evidence [12, 15, 23]. Many researchers argue that higher order

D. Kopańska-Bródka · R. Dudzińska-Baryła (✉) · E. Michalska
University of Economics in Katowice, 1 Maja 50, 40-287 Katowice, Poland
e-mail: renata.dudzinska-baryla@ue.katowice.pl

D. Kopańska-Bródka
e-mail: donata.kopanska-brodka@ue.katowice.pl

E. Michalska
e-mail: ewa.michalska@ue.katowice.pl

W. Tarczyński and K. Nermend (eds.), *Effective Investments on Capital Markets*, Springer Proceedings in Business and Economics,
https://doi.org/10.1007/978-3-030-21274-2_11

moments of the portfolio's return are relevant to investors' decisions and cannot be ignored. Scott and Horvath [25] have shown that if the distribution of random rates of return is asymmetric or the investor's utility function is a function of a higher degree than the quadratic function, the assessment of the investment should be based on at least the third and fourth order moments. As a result of the evidence against the assumption of the normality of the rate of return distribution, the multiobjective portfolio selection model incorporates the higher moments. In general, investors prefer high values for odd moments and low ones for even moments. Increasing the positive value of an odd moment can be interpreted as decreasing extreme values on the side of losses and increasing them on the gains' side.

The importance of skewness in the rate of return distribution is introduced by Arditti in the stocks' pricing [1, 2]. He claims that investors prefer positive skewness as a result of decreasing absolute risk aversion. The preference for positive skewness is also related to the concept of prudence introduced by Kimball [16]. A prudent investor is characterized by a special behavior in a situation of risk i.e. a precautionary saving or limiting consumption. In the context of the theory of expected utility, prudence means the convexity of marginal utility [5, 18, 19].

The first publications in which portfolio selection models incorporating skewness measures were proposed, appeared in the 1970s [26, 27]. Maximizing skewness expresses the basic preferences of the decision maker and leads to an increase in the chances of achieving above-average rates of return. Currently, different approaches to the multicriteria portfolio selection are proposed, such as the use of goal programming or the use of the utility functions of distribution moments [13, 20, 21].

The literature also explores efficient portfolios in terms of the first three moments of the rate of return distribution [3, 10]. In addition, the problem of diversification of optimal portfolios depending on the investor's preferences regarding the skewness of the rate of return is discussed. Independent research confirms that the greater the strength of preference for skewness, the lower the degree of portfolio diversification [11, 14, 26].

To sum up, the main purpose of this study is to propose a mean–variance–skewness goal programming model for portfolio selection based on the investor's preferences.

The paper is organized as follows: Sect. 11.2 provides discussion on the portfolio selection problem with third-order moments. The theoretical framework of the goal programming model is discussed in Sect. 11.3. The numerical results are illustrated in Sect. 11.4. Conclusion of the study and some computational details are presented in the final section.

11.2 Skewness in Portfolio Selection

In the presence of skewness, the portfolio selection problem turns into a nonconvex optimization problem which can be characterized by a number of conflicting and competing objective functions. To solve this complicated task, various approaches have been proposed in the literature. Konno et al. [17], Boyle and Ding [4] applied the method of linear approximation of quadratic and cubic expressions in the optimization model and in this way brought the issue to the convex programming problem.

The goal programming (GP) has been the most widely used approach in decision-making problems with several conflicting and competing objectives. An important feature of GP is the existence of optimal solution. Generally, the GP models vary in the form of the achievement function, which minimizes the unwanted deviations (absolute or relative) of the model's goals [20].

The polynomial goal programming (PGP) approach to the portfolio selection with skewness was proposed by Lai [21]. This article initiated the intensive development of literature, in which portfolio optimization is conceived as a multiple goal programming problem. Lai [21] and authors of the other papers [8, 9, 24] assumed that the portfolio decision depends on the percentage invested in each asset and constructed a PGP model that the portfolio choice can be rescaled and restricted on the unit variance space. This PGP methodology has become popular for empirical research looking at skewness persistence in a variety of international markets [7, 22]. Canela and Collazo [6] pointed that under certain conditions, the PGP method can produce mathematically feasible solutions, which would be unfeasible from a financial point of view.

Chen and Shia [7] stressed that assets and portfolio returns tend to be asymmetrically distributed and using variance as the measure of investment risk is inappropriate and unreasonable. They proposed a new portfolio selection model which uses downside risk in the form of "lower partial moments" instead of variance as the risk measurement in the goal programming portfolio model.

Yaghoobi and Tamiz [28] considered the GP portfolio selection model in which aspiration levels were not known precisely. They used the fuzzy approach where imprecise level was treated as a fuzzy goal.

In our approach, the goal programming model with the weighted linear function of relative deviations from the model's goals is considered. We utilize the GP to determine the trade-off frontiers of portfolios of selected stocks which constitute WIG20 index on the Warsaw Stock Exchange.

11.3 Goal Programming Models

In this study, the investor's preferences for skewness and expected value of the distribution of the rate of return are incorporated in portfolio selection problem.

Let us introduce some symbols. Shares of stocks in portfolio form a vector $\mathbf{x} = [x_1, x_2, \ldots, x_N]$, where $x_1 + x_2 + \cdots + x_N = 1$ and $x_i \geq 0$ for $i = 1, \ldots, N$. The condition for nonnegativity of shares means that short sale is forbidden. Random rates of return of stocks in portfolio make up a vector $\mathbf{R} = [R_1, R_2, \ldots, R_N]$. Rate of return of portfolio is a random variable which distribution is generated by the random rates of return of shares $R_P = R_1x_1 + R_2x_2 + \cdots + R_Nx_N$. Our optimization models make use of three moments of a portfolio random rate of return R_P: the expected value of the portfolio (E_P) which is the first-order moment, the variance of the portfolio (V_P) which is the second central moment and the skewness of the portfolio (S_P) measured by the third central moment and written as

$$S_P = \mathbb{E}[R_P - E_P]^3 = \mathbf{x} \cdot \mathbf{M}_3 \cdot (\mathbf{x}^{\mathrm{T}} \otimes \mathbf{x}^{\mathrm{T}}) \tag{11.1}$$

where the symbol $\otimes$ denotes the Kronecker product. The matrix $\mathbf{M}_3$ consist of the third central moments and co-moments of the random rate of return of stocks

$$\mathbf{M}_3 = \mathbb{E}[(\mathbf{R} - \mathbb{E}(\mathbf{R})) \cdot (\mathbf{R} - \mathbb{E}(\mathbf{R}))^{\mathrm{T}} \otimes (\mathbf{R} - \mathbb{E}(\mathbf{R}))^{\mathrm{T}}] \tag{11.2}$$

Our method of research (optimization) has three stages. In the first stage for a given value of portfolio variance (V_0), the expected value of optimal portfolio (E_P^*) is determined. Next, in the second stage for a given value of portfolio variance (V_0), the skewness of optimal portfolio (S_P^*) is determined. And in the last stage, optimal values E_P^* and S_P^* are used as goal values (aspiration levels) and for given values V_0, E_P^* and S_P^* the optimal portfolio with the minimal deviation from the goal values is determined. In our procedure (method), the meaningful values of variance has to be higher than the variance of the global minimum variance portfolio and lower than the minimum of the variances of stock with the highest expected rate of return and stock with the highest skewness.

In the first stage for selected values of variance V_0, we optimized a well-known Markowitz portfolio selection model of the form

$$\begin{aligned} &\max E_P \\ &V_P = V_0 \\ &\sum_{i=1}^{N} x_i = 1 \\ &x_i \geq 0, \quad i = 1, \ldots, N \end{aligned} \tag{11.3}$$

The expected rate of return of optimal portfolio based on model (11.3) is noted as E_P^*. The optimal portfolio which maximizes the skewness for a given variance is the following:

$$\begin{aligned} &\max S_P \\ &V_P = V_0 \\ &\sum_{i=1}^{N} x_i = 1 \\ &x_i \geq 0, \quad i = 1, \ldots, N \end{aligned} \tag{11.4}$$

The desirable value of skewness is noted as S_P^*. To determine an optimal portfolio which for a given variance is closest to the desirable values of expected rate of return and skewness, we propose the following goal programming model

$$\begin{aligned}
&\min \alpha\left|\frac{de}{E_P^*}\right| + (1-\alpha)\left|\frac{ds}{S_P^*}\right| \\
&E_P + de = E_P^* \\
&S_P + ds = S_P^* \\
&V_P = V_0 \\
&\sum_{i=1}^{N} x_i = 1 \\
&x_i \geq 0, \quad i = 1, \ldots, N
\end{aligned} \tag{11.5}$$

where *de* is a deviation of the expected portfolio rate of return from a desired value E_P^*, *ds* is a deviation of portfolio skewness from a desired value S_P^*, $\alpha \in \langle 0, 1\rangle$ is a weight (weighting coefficient). The objective function minimizes the relative deviations from desired values. The strength of preference toward a desired expected return is reflected by a weight α, and the strength of preference toward a desired skewness is reflected by a weight $(1-\alpha)$. If $\alpha = 1$, the portfolio preferred by an investor is that whose expected rate of return is as close as possible to the maximum rate of return for a given risk level and the optimal portfolio of (11.5) is the same as a solution of model (11.3). Similarly if $\alpha = 0$, the investor prefers a portfolio that guarantees the achievement of extreme values of a positive rate of return for a given level of risk and the optimal portfolio of (11.5) is the same as a solution of model (11.4). For the assumed values of V_0 and α, the solution of model (11.5) is the optimal portfolio $\mathbf{x} = [x_1, x_2, \ldots, x_N]$; however, in our research the parameters of the distribution of the return rate of the portfolio $\mathbf{x}$ will be analyzed, not its structure.

Moreover, for different values of variance the optimal values of objective function of (11.3) and (11.4) are used to determine the boundary lines of the expected rate of return and skewness of the optimal portfolios of (11.5). In the mean–variance space, an area between the efficient frontier based on the solutions of model (11.3) and the line of the expected returns of the optimal portfolios of (11.4) is a set of feasible portfolios when the strength of preference toward the desired expected rate of return is considered. Likewise, in the skewness–variance space, there is the set of portfolios when the strength of preference toward a desired skewness of rate of return is considered.

11.4 Data and Tools

Our major interest is to determine the set of efficient portfolios consisting of solutions of goal programming approach to portfolio selection problem. The purpose of our analysis is to illustrate how selected parameters of the return rate distribution of the optimal portfolio vary for investors with different preferences for the expected value and skewness. These preferences are expressed by means of the α parameter.

The data set contains daily logarithmic rates of return for the year 2017 for all 20 shares being components of the WIG20 index on the Warsaw Stock Exchange. Calculations were made in the SAS software using the NLP solver and self-prepared programs.

In this paper, we analyze the expected values and skewness of logarithmic rates of return of optimal portfolios for various values of variance. Values of variance have to be from the interval $V_0 \in \left\langle V_{\text{GMVP}}, \min_i \left\{ V_{\max E_i}, V_{\max S_i} \right\} \right\rangle$ where V_{GMVP} is a variance of the global minimum variance portfolio, $V_{\max E_i}$ is a variance of a stock with the highest expected value, $V_{\max S_i}$ is a variance of a stock with the highest skewness. In other words, the assumed variance V_0 has to be not lower than the minimal variance of all portfolios and not higher than the lower from variances of the maximum expected value share and the maximum skewness share. Table 11.1 shows the first three moments of logarithmic returns for all 20 shares and the global minimal variance portfolio (GMVP) in the analyzed period.

Based on the values in Table 11.1, the interval of the assumed variance V_0 is $\langle 0.592, 2.908 \rangle$. In the optimization models (11.3)–(11.5), we considered values rounded to 0.1.

11.5 Results

By changing the values of variance in models (11.3) and (11.4), we obtain optimal portfolios and we can construct efficient frontiers in mean–variance and skewness—variance spaces. In addition, for each efficient frontier, a sequence of values of the considered parameter: the third moment (as a measure of skewness) and the expected value (mean), can be calculated for optimal solutions of the other model. Precisely, in the mean–variance space, we determine the line of expected values for the optimal portfolios of the model with the skewness maximization (11.4), and in the skewness—variance space the line of the values of third moments for the optimal portfolios of the model with the maximization of the expected value (11.3). Area between the efficient frontier and the obtained line represents a set of trade-offs between the expected return and skewness.

The optimal solution of the goal programming model (11.5) for a fixed level of α and variance V_0 is the portfolio with the following parameters: the expected value of the portfolio's rate of return $E_P(\alpha, V_0)$, variance V_0, and skewness of the portfolio's

Table 11.1 Expected values (E), variances (V), and skewnesses (S) of shares and GMVP

Share	E	V	S
ALIOR	0.153	3.363	2.887
ASSECOPOL	−0.082	2.116	−0.011
BZWBK	0.091	**3.225**	**2.985**
CCC	0.135	3.627	0.971
CYFRPLSAT	0.004	2.350	−0.982
ENERGA	0.134	3.809	2.924
EUROCASH	−0.158	4.101	−11.802
JSW	0.146	6.110	2.573
KGHM	0.074	3.960	2.780
LOTOS	0.164	5.005	1.669
LPP	0.181	3.628	−0.138
MBANK	0.131	4.399	1.343
ORANGEPL	0.020	3.591	−0.634
PEKAO	0.012	1.923	−0.846
PGE	0.057	3.500	−0.132
PGNIG	0.044	3.012	−0.097
PKNORLEN	0.087	4.376	−5.085
PKOBP	**0.182**	**2.908**	2.105
PZU	0.095	2.221	0.178
TAURONPE	0.027	3.086	2.655
GMVP	0.047	**0.592**	0.093

rate of return $S_P(\alpha, V_0)$. Generally, by solving the model (11.5) for a fixed α and any value of variance $V_0 \in \left\langle V_{\text{GMVP}}, \min_i\left\{V\max_{E_i}, V\max_{S_i}\right\}\right\rangle$, we obtain optimal portfolios whose expected values of the portfolio's rate of return $E_P(\alpha, V_0)$ and skewness of the portfolio's rate of return $S_P(\alpha, V_0)$ create trade-off frontier in a corresponding two-dimensional space (mean–variance space in Fig. 11.1a, skewness–variance space in Fig. 11.1b).

Let $P1$ be the portfolio with the maximum expected value for a given variance, and $P2$, the portfolio with the maximum skewness for a given variance. Both portfolios can be presented in two spaces: mean–variance (Fig. 11.1a) and skewness–variance (Fig. 11.1b). Any portfolio P belonging to the $P1P2$ segment has higher expected value than $P2$ (Fig. 11.1a) at the expense of lower skewness than $P2$ (Fig. 11.1b), and at the same time, portfolio P has higher skewness than $P1$ (Fig. 11.1b) at the expense of lower expected value than $P1$ (Fig. 11.1a).

Applying the proposed goal programming model (11.5) for any level of preference α for the expected value in relation to the skewness allows to picture the corresponding trade-off frontier in two-dimensional space (mean–variance or skewness–variance).

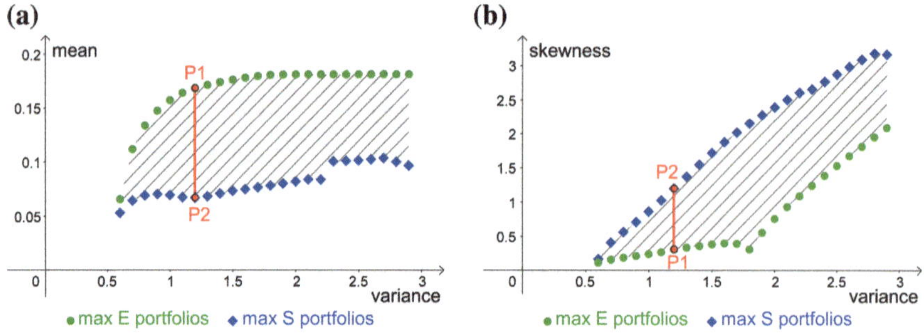

Fig. 11.1 Set of trade-offs for expected value (**a**) and skewness (**b**)

Changing the value of parameter α allows us to analyze various alternatives in which a different emphasis is placed on the expected value and skewness.

The trade-off frontiers are situated between the efficient frontier and the lower restrictive line. For α close to 1, in the mean–variance plane the trade-off frontiers are close to the efficient frontier, and in the skewness–variance plane to the lower restrictive line. Figure 11.2a–d shows the trade-off frontiers for four levels of the preference strength α (0.3, 0.4, 0.6 and 0.7, respectively), in the mean–variance plane based on the quotations of 20 stocks listed on the Warsaw Stock Exchange in 2017. The value 0.5 of the preference strength means that for an investor, the high expected value of the portfolio is just as important as the high skewness. We have analyzed the trade-off frontiers for many values of α and noted that when decreasing the value of α initially the trade-off frontiers move away from the efficient frontier relatively slower than for lower values of α. Similar behavior was observed for data from other periods we have analyzed. This means that if the investors prefer higher values of expected rates of return of optimal portfolios at the expense of lower skewness, a gradual weakening of the preference strength causes a slow decrease in the expected value, while further lowering a value of α (which is equivalent to stronger preference for skewness) causes a radical reduction in the expected value.

Opposite patterns are observed in the skewness–variance plane. Figure 11.3a–d illustrates the trade-off frontiers for four levels of the preference strength α (0.3, 0.4, 0.6 and 0.7, respectively), in the skewness–variance plane. Analyzing the trade-off frontiers for different values of α, we stated that when decreasing the value of α initially the trade-off frontiers move closer to the efficient frontier (in skewness—variance plane) relatively faster than for lower values of α. We noted that the small changes in the investor's preferences for the expected rate of return of a portfolio are related to the relatively large changes in the portfolio skewness. Thus, the sensitivity to changes in the investor's preferences is greater for the skewness of the portfolio rate of return than for the expected value. Analogous behavior was observed for data from the other periods.

Such behaviors for arithmetic means of expected values and skewnesses of the portfolio rates of return for various values of α are illustrated in Fig. 11.4a, b, respectively.

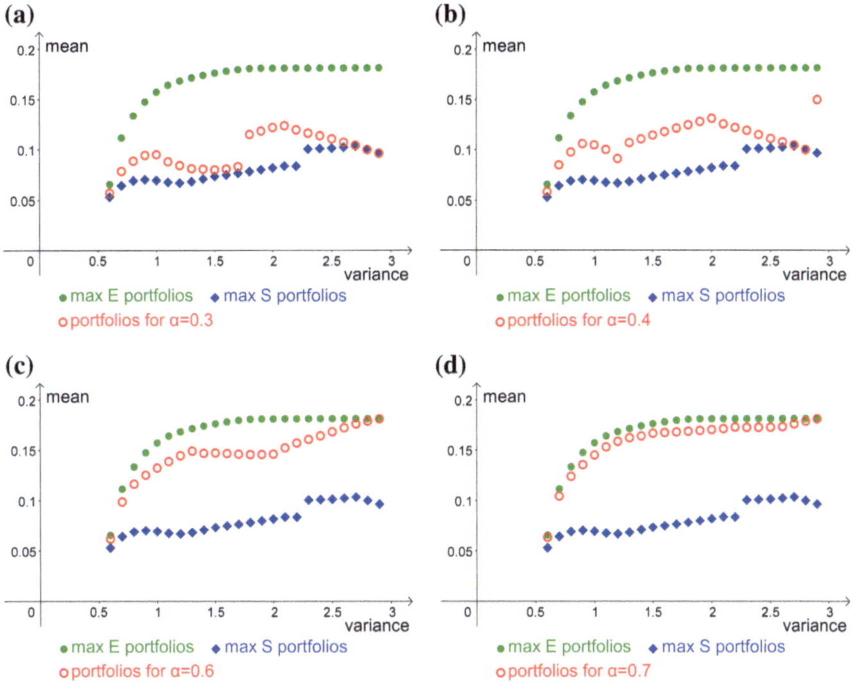

Fig. 11.2 Trade-off frontiers for selected values of α in mean–variance plane

As we consider the first three moments of the distribution of the portfolio rate of return, the trade-off frontier can be presented in three-dimensional space mean—variance–skewness. Figure 11.5 shows the parameters of optimal portfolios being the solutions of the model (11.5) for selected α (1, 0.4 and 0). For continuous values of α, the trade-off frontiers would create an irregular surface of efficient portfolios, which results from nonlinear conditions in the model (11.5).

The nonlinear optimization models (11.4) and (11.5) are nonconvex. Due to the fact that there is no algorithm for solving such optimization problems and often they have many local optima, the solution reported by a computer solving tool sometimes may not be a global optimum. Furthermore, if a solver is run multiple times, different solutions can be obtained. The SAS optimization NLP solver can be run in multistart mode in which a number of starting points are randomly generated and can converge to different local optima. The solution reported as optimal is in fact one of the local optima with the best objective value. Therefore, the obtained solution is not guaranteed to be global optimum.

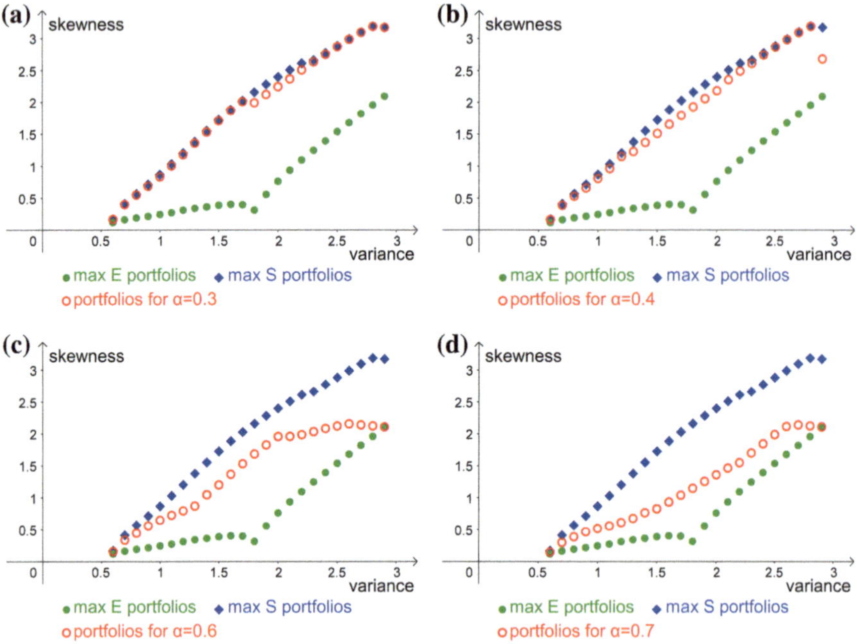

Fig. 11.3 Trade-off frontiers for selected values of α in skewness–variance plane

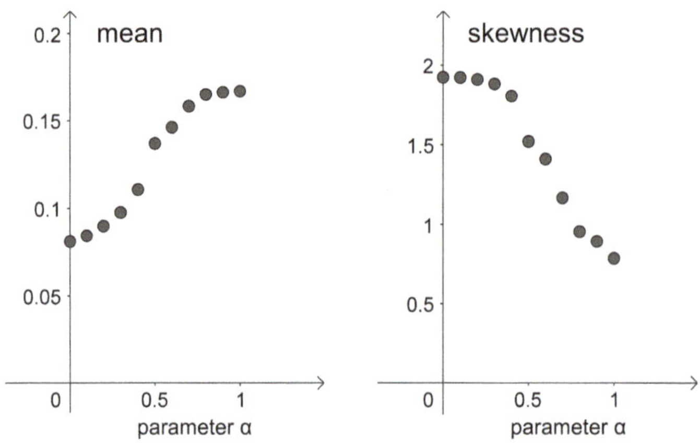

Fig. 11.4 Arithmetic means of expected values and skewnesses of the portfolio rates of return for $\alpha \in \langle 0, 1\rangle$ with step 0.1

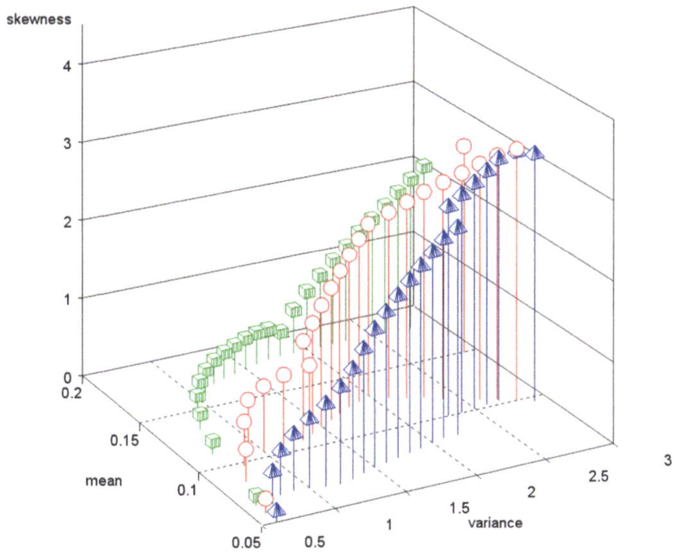

Fig. 11.5 Optimal portfolios in mean–variance–skewness space

11.6 Conclusion

Our results clearly show a strong trade-off between expected value and skewness which was traditionally assumed to be present only between expected value and variance. The investors aware of additional criteria would have to accept a lower rate of return if they chose to optimize the skewness of the portfolio rate of return. This means that the observed efficient frontier based only on mean–variance optimization is not an adequate efficient frontier and could lead investors toward sub-optimal decisions when the skewness is considered. The incorporation of skewness into an investor's portfolio decision provokes a great change in the resultant optimal portfolio allocation.

Our study adopts the GP approach to include third moment of rate of return distribution in portfolio optimization process. The investors' aim is to provide portfolios with the highest expected rate of return and the highest third central moment. Because these criteria are mutually competitive, investor expresses his own preferences for one criterion relative to the other one by the subjective value of the parameter measuring the preference strength. This parameter appears in the objective function in a properly constructed GP model. We have proposed to use optimal solutions of the GP model to determine trade-off frontiers which show how individual preferences trade expected rate of return for skewness. Moreover, trade-off frontiers allow us to examine the intensity of changes in the value of the rate of return distribution parameters of optimal portfolios depending on the subjective measure of the strength of preferences.

References

1. Arditti, F.D.: Risk and the required return on equity. J. Financ. **22**, 19–36 (1967)
2. Arditti, F.D.: Skewness and investor's decisions: a reply. J. Financ. Quant. Anal. **10**, 173–176 (1975)
3. Arditti, F.D., Levy, H.: Portfolio efficiency analysis in three moments: the multiperiod case. J. Financ. **30**(3), 797–809 (1975)
4. Boyle, P., Ding, B.: Portfolio selection with skewness. In: Breton, M., Ben-Ameur, H. (eds.) Numerical Methods in Finance, pp. 227–240. Springer (2005)
5. Briec, W., Kerstens, K., Jokung, O.: Mean-variance-skewness portfolio performance gauging: a general shortage function and dual approach. Manage. Sci. **53**(1), 135–149 (2007)
6. Canela, M.A., Collazo, E.P.: Portfolio selection with skewness in emerging market industries. Emerg. Mark. Rev. **8**(3), 230–250 (2007)
7. Chen, H.H., Shia, B.C.: Multinational portfolio construction using polynomial goal programming and lower partial moments. J. Chin. Stat. Assoc. **45**, 130–143 (2007)
8. Chunhachinda, P., Dandapani, K., Hamid, S., Prakash, A.J.: Portfolio selection and skewness: evidence from international stock markets. J. Bank. Finance **21**, 143–167 (1997)
9. Davies, R.J., Kat, H.M., Lu, S.: Fund of hedge funds portfolio selection: a multiple-objective approach. J. Deriv. Hedge Funds **15**(2), 91–115 (2009)
10. Dudzińska-Baryła, R., Kopańska-Bródka, D., Michalska, E.: Analiza portfeli narożnych z uwzględnieniem skośności. Finanse, Rynki Finansowe, Ubezpieczenia **75**, 123–133 (in Polish) (2015). https://doi.org/10.18276/frfu.2015.75-10
11. Dudzińska-Baryła, R., Kopańska-Bródka, D., Michalska, E.: Diversification problem in mean-variance-skewness portfolio models. In: Pražák, P. (ed.) Conference Proceedings, 35rd International Conference Mathematical Methods in Economics, University of Hradec Králové, Czech Republic, pp. 137–142 (2017)
12. Fama, E.F.: The behavior of stock market prices. J. Bus. **38**(1), 34–105 (1965)
13. Harvey, C.R., Liechty, J.C., Liechty, M.W., Müller, P.: Portfolio selection with higher moments. Quant. Financ. **10**(5), 469–485 (2010)
14. Kane, A.: Skewness preference and portfolio choice. J. Financ. Quant. Anal. **17**, 15–25 (1982)
15. Kendall, M.G., Hill, A.B.: The analysis of economic time-series—Part I: Prices. J. R. Stat. Soc., Ser. A **116**(1), 11–34 (1953)
16. Kimball, M.S.: Precautionary saving in the small and in the large. Econometrica **58**(1), 53–73 (1990)
17. Konno, H., Shirakawa, H., Yamazaki, H.: A mean-absolute deviation-skewness portfolio optimization model. Ann. Oper. Res. **45**, 205–220 (1993)
18. Kopańska-Bródka, D.: Miary intensywności zachowań rozważnych. Studia Ekonomiczne. Zeszyty Naukowe Uniwersytetu Ekonomicznego w Katowicach **135**, 79–87 (in Polish) (2013)
19. Kopańska-Bródka, D.: Związki miar awersji do ryzyka z funkcjami zależnymi od parametrów rozkładu. Studia Ekonomiczne. Zeszyty Naukowe Uniwersytetu Ekonomicznego w Katowicach **163**, 253–266 (in Polish) (2013)
20. Kopańska-Bródka, D.: Optymalny portfel inwestycyjny z kryterium maksymalnej skośności. Studia Ekonomiczne. Zeszyty Naukowe Uniwersytetu Ekonomicznego w Katowicach **208**, 46–58 (in Polish) (2014)
21. Lai, T.Y.: Portfolio selection with skewness: a multiple-objective approach. Rev. Quant. Financ. Acc. **1**, 293–305 (1991)
22. Naqvi, B., Mirza, N., Naqvi, W.A., Rizvi, S.K.A.: Portfolio optimisation with higher moments of risk at the Pakistan Stock Exchange. Econ. Res.-Ekonomska Istraživanja **30**(1), 1594–1610 (2017)
23. Piasecki, K., Tomasik, E.: Rozkład stóp zwrotu z instrumentów polskiego rynku kapitałowego. Edu-Libri, Kraków-Warszawa (in Polish) (2013)
24. Prakash, A.J., Chang, C.H., Pactwa, T.E.: Selecting a portfolio with skewness: recent evidence from US, European, and Latin American equity markets. J. Bank. Finance **27**, 1375–1390 (2003)

25. Scott, R., Horvath, P.: On the direction of preference for moments of higher order than the variance. J. Finance **35**, 915–919 (1980)
26. Simkowitz, M.A., Beedles, W.L.: Diversification in a three-moment world. J. Financ. Quant. Anal. **13**(5), 927–941 (1978)
27. Simonson, D.: The speculative behavior of mutual funds. J. Finance **27**, 381–391 (1972)
28. Yaghoobi, M.A., Tamiz, M.: On improving a weighted additive model for fuzzy goal programming problems. Int. Rev. Fuzzy Math. **1**, 115–129 (2006)

Chapter 12
Early Warning Against Insolvency of Enterprises Based on a Self-learning Artificial Neural Network of the SOM Type

Kamila Migdał-Najman, Krzysztof Najman and Paweł Antonowicz

Abstract The article describes the use of a self-learning neural network of the SOM type to forecast insolvency of enterprises in construction industry. The research was carried out on the basis of information regarding 578 enterprises that went into bankruptcy in the years 2007–2013. These entities constituted a sample singled out from a population of 4750 enterprises that went bankrupt in Poland during that time, for which it was possible to obtain financial statements in the form of balance sheets and profit-and-loss accounts for the period of 5 years prior to the bankruptcy. Twelve (12) variables in the form of financial analysis indicators have been assessed, which are most commonly used in the systems of early warning about insolvency. The network constructed allowed effective classification of nearly all entities as insolvent a year before the announcement of their bankruptcy.

Keywords Bankruptcy · Insolvency · Artificial neural network · Forecasting

12.1 Introduction

Current analytical and controlling practice uses, among others, information from the financial statements of enterprises. The value of this information is as much useful as it allows diagnosing not only the events from the past, but also inferring about the future of an enterprise. Along with the increase in the multiplicity and the level

K. Migdał-Najman (✉) · K. Najman
Department of Statistics, Faculty of Management, University of Gdansk, Armii Krajowej 101, 81-824 Sopot, Gdansk, Poland
e-mail: kamila.migdal-najman@ug.edu.pl

K. Najman
e-mail: krzysztof.najman@ug.edu.pl

P. Antonowicz
Department of Business Economics, Faculty of Management, University of Gdansk, Armii Krajowej 101, 81-824 Sopot, Gdansk, Poland
e-mail: pawel.antonowicz@ug.edu.pl

W. Tarczyński and K. Nermend (eds.), *Effective Investments on Capital Markets*, Springer Proceedings in Business and Economics,
https://doi.org/10.1007/978-3-030-21274-2_12

of the complexity of the relationships occurring between business entities, the risk of cooperation with entities that become financially ineffective in business trading increases. In accordance with the bankruptcy law applicable, not only in Poland [1, 2], but in other legislations (e.g., EU [3]), insolvency of these entities may, in an extreme scenario, lead to their bankruptcy. This, in turn, means very serious problems [4] involving collection of the claims due on the part of the cooperators, who become unsatisfied creditors.[1]

Explicitly for the needs of economic practice, a stream of research on improvement of the systems of early warning about insolvency (bankruptcy) of enterprises has been developed within the theory of economic sciences, particularly in the discipline of finance and management [5]. Most often, these systems are mainly based on the integrated indicators of financial analysis in the form of a discriminant function [6]. A well-executed financial analysis supports the decision-making processes of managers in many aspects (areas) of an enterprise's operations.

Numerous empirical studies exhibit the need to analyze the changes occurring over time in a large number of various entities, the state of which is described by many parameters. Such needs also exist in the financial analysis of enterprises, particularly in that oriented not so much on traditional (*ex post*) assessment of the economic and financial condition of business entities, but rather on the so-called prospective (*ex ante*) assessment, i.e., an analysis preceding the assessment of their ability to function on the market. Conduction of a study on these entities, using a traditional index analysis referring to separate areas of entity functioning (such as assessment of financial liquidity, debt service capacity, profitability and productivity or the turnover) does not allow drawing objective general conclusions, but only a fragmentary evaluation of the examined entity.

In order to determine the scoring, particularly that focused on a future assessment of an enterprise's survivability on the market, the theory of economic sciences has developed various methods and techniques of business research. In the field of research on improvement of the systems of early warning about insolvency, advanced computational techniques are used, among others, including self-learning artificial neural networks.

The main objective of this study was to construct a neural network of the SOM (*self-organizing map*) type, enabling diagnosis and early capture of the quantitative symptoms of an insolvency threat (de facto a bankruptcy threat) in enterprises. In the process of creating an SOM neural network, 12 variables were used, constituting selected indicators of financial analysis, calculated for 578 enterprises in the construction industry, which went into bankruptcy in Poland during the years 2007–2013.

The main goal of the study formulated as such allowed assumption of the following research hypothesis: The use of an artificial neural network of the SOM type

[1] International-wise, a synthetic description of the functionality of bankruptcy registers of EU member states, which in the future is to become a centralized database system, is available on the European Justice Web site: https://beta.e-justice.europa.eu/110/PL/bankruptcy_and_insolvency_registers; (accessed on: September 11, 2018).

enables a diagnosis of an enterprise's financial condition and its observation in a time perspective.

As the authors' previous research experience and the literature studies in this area indicate that a classification analysis aimed at detecting the risk of enterprise bankruptcy (with a minimum 1-year forecasting horizon) is difficult, due to the existence of many factors, the first involves the selection of the variables, in the form of the financial indicators that should be taken under consideration. The indicators that seem to be most appropriate, from the perspective of their construction and interpretation, often insufficiently differentiate the entities under examination. Namely, due to their statistical properties, they are not suitable for distinction of the enterprises that are threatened with bankruptcy. Another problem is the construction of a synthetic index that would be able to jointly take into account the variables expressed on different measurement scales. Typical aggregate indicators are of no use here. It seems that the above problems can be solved by basing the analysis on self-learning artificial neural networks. Such a network allows to detect the variables significantly differentiating the set of objects, while the neuron's structure ensures construction of an aggregate of the objects being described by the variables of almost any measuring scale.

12.2 Research Methodology, Description of the Research Sample and Justification for the Selection of the Research Problem

Research on the assessment of the effectiveness of using a self-learning neural network of the SOM type for the purpose of early warning about bankruptcy of enterprises has been based on the results of ratio analyses of a population of enterprises that went bankrupt in Poland in the years 2007–2013. In total, statistical data for all 4750 companies that filed for bankruptcy were collected during the 7-year research period, i.e., starting from 2007: 446 business entities and successively 422, 694, 679, 726, 893 and 890 business units in 2013 [7].

The population structure of these bankruptcies includes enterprises with diversified profiles of their business operations. Nevertheless, the most significant (most numerous) group of the entities, homogenous in terms of the industry, were the bankruptcies of construction companies (20.69% without considering industrial processing), whose business activity, in particular, involved:

- construction works related to erection of buildings;
- construction works related to the construction of civil engineering structures;
- specialized construction works.

During the 7-year research period, the share of the bankruptcy of construction companies increased significantly, on average, by 33.14% each year. Generalizing the conclusions on the structure of bankruptcy during this period, it should be emphasized that in Poland, in recent years, almost every second bankruptcy concerned enterprises from the construction industry (taking into account not only the strictly service activity, but also the production for this sector). Therefore, it seems reasonable to attempt the development of a diagnostic tool that would enable assessment of the economic and financial condition, aimed at early warning about the bankruptcy of enterprises from the construction sector. A review of the literature in this area clearly indicates the dominance of models without their sector-specific distinction and dedication to the enterprises of specific sectors.

From the population of the enterprises that went bankrupt during the research period, we managed to obtain financial statements of 2739 business entities by analyzing court files (from the National Court Register) containing financial statements for at least 4 years preceding the court declaration of bankruptcy. At the same time, it should be emphasized that the process of obtaining these data is extremely difficult, since it covers the business entities whose functioning was affected by the escalation of the economic crisis and resulted in a court ruling on the debtor's insolvency, that is bankruptcy. The files of these entities are often incomplete and are kept in the prosecutor's office, by the judges who deal with the case or the syndicates (currently replaced by restructuring advisors). This largely hinders the development of early warning models, since the financial data precedent to the bankruptcy, quite difficult to obtain, constitutes the basis for estimation of such models. Ultimately, 578 construction companies constituted the sample analyzed in this study, for which 12 financial analysis indicators were calculated for the period of 4 years prior to the announcement of bankruptcy:

1. The Current Ratio—a quotient of the current assets and the short-term liabilities of an enterprise, calculated at the end of a given reporting period.
2. The Debt Ratio (of external financing)—a quotient of the sum of long- and short-term liabilities, in relation to the balance sheet total, calculated at the end of a given reporting period.
3. The Productivity Ratio of Assets—a quotient of the sales revenue generated, in relation to the average annual value of the balance sheet total.
4. The Return on Total Assets (ROA)—a quotient of the net financial result, in relation to the average annual value of the balance sheet total.
5. The Return on Investment Ratio (ROI)—a quotient of the operating result, in relation to the average annual value of the balance sheet total.
6. The Net Cash Flow to Total Liabilities Ratio—being the ratio of the value of the net financial result adjusted (*in plus*) by amortization, in relation to the average annual value of long- and short-term liabilities.
7. The Self-financing Ratio of Assets—the share of equity (own capital) in the total financing of business operations, calculated at the end of a given reporting period.
8. The Short-term Receivables Turnover Ratio (in days)—a quotient of the average annual value of short-term receivables and the contractual number of days in a year (365), in relation to the sales revenues achieved in a given reporting period.

9. The Inventory Turnover Ratio (in days)—a quotient of the average annual value of the inventories and the contractual number of days in a year (365), in relation to the sales revenues achieved in a given reporting period.
10. The Gross Margin Ratio—a quotient of the gross financial result, in relation to the value of the sales revenues achieved in a given reporting period.
11. The Quick Ratio—a ratio of the difference between the current assets and the inventories (tangible current assets), in relation to the value of short-term liabilities;
12. The Working Capital to Total Assets Ratio—a quotient of the difference between the current assets and the current liabilities, in relation to the balance sheet total, calculated at the end of a given reporting period.

Selection of the above-listed 12 variables for construction of the artificial neural network was carried out based on the analysis of the frequency of the occurrence of the financial analysis indicators in 29 discriminant functions developed (by Polish scientific and research units) using a sample of enterprises located in Poland, which was aimed at early detection of the quantitative symptoms of enterprise bankruptcy [8].

12.3 Neural Networks of the SOM Type in Forecasting Enterprise Bankruptcy—Methodological Aspects

One of the types of artificial neural networks that are widely used in socioeconomic research is the self-learning networks. The self-learning neural networks is a non-model process of mapping the objects' space of entrance into the low-dimensional space of a small number of functional units, neurons, maintaining the topographical similarity of the objects. The group of self-learning networks includes, among others, neural networks of: the SOM (*self-organizing map*) type [9], the GSOM (*growing self-organizing map*) type [10], the HSOM (*hierarchical SOM*) type [11], the NG (*neural gas*) type [12], the GNG (*growing neural gas*) type [13], the GSOM+GNG type [14]. Self-learning networks are used in various disciplines and fields of science [15]. They are used, for example, to analyze shopping habits and preferences [16–19], to forecast the threat of bankruptcy of enterprises [20–22] and to diagnose the financial condition of enterprises [23].

One of the self-learning networks used quite frequently is the SOM network, also referred to as the Kohonen network or map, proposed and developed around 1982 by a Finnish professor Teuvo Kohonen. It is now one of the most well-known unsupervised models of artificial neural networks. The SOM network is modeled on a biological phenomenon called a *retinotopy*. It is one of the best-known and effective data mining applications, mainly used for classification, grouping, dimensionality reduction, searching for anomalies and deviations from typical values, visualization of multidimensional data sets and studies on the dynamics of phenomena [24–28].

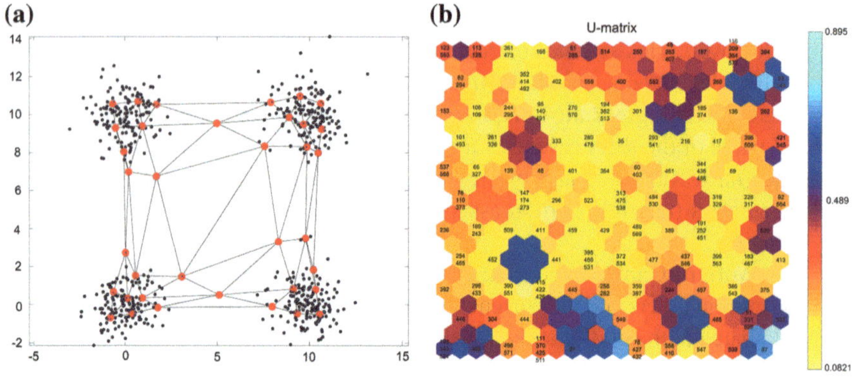

Fig. 12.1 **a** Neural network of the SOM type in the feature space; **b** Matrix of unified feature distances (*Source* Own elaboration)

The algorithm for building an SOM network is well established in the literature on the subject [14, 29]. In the first stage of building of the network, neurons are placed in the initial feature space, which then become the local approximators of the analyzed objects. The neurons are ordered in a certain structure called a network, where they are in certain relationships with each other. The network is "pre-scattered" in the space of objects (see Fig. 12.1a).

Following that, alternate objects are shown in the network. The neuron that is closest to the given object is the "winner" neuron, and it is subject to learning (change of weight, coordinates in space, approaching the object presented). That neuron's neighbors also learn, proportionally to the distance in which they are from the winner neuron. Some neurons never become a winner and act as "middlemen," allowing the network's fuller expansion in space. They are the so-called dead neurons. An SOM network can have the structure of a chain, a rectangle or a square. Each network structure adopted has different properties, while selection of an appropriate structure for a given research problem is crucial. The most commonly used network structure is the square network, which allows recognition of clusters in any geometric configuration, being a great tool for visualizing multidimensional data. At the same time, the square structure is the least economical and learns the longest. Table 12.1 shows the basic properties of an SOM network.

12.4 Neural Networks of the SOM Type in Forecasting Enterprise Bankruptcy—Results of Empirical Research

The empirical analysis took into account 578 enterprises described by 12 financial indicators, as of 4 years prior to their bankruptcy. After elimination of the enterprises for which there were numerous data gaps in the values of the indicators and the

Table 12.1 Properties of the SOM network

Properties	SOM network
Network structure	Constant
Number of critical control parameters	4
Grouping quality at optimal parameters	High
Learning speed	Average
Memory capacity requirements	Large
Any configuration of clusters	Yes
Dead neurons	Yes
Twisting of the network	Yes
Fuzzy of the clusters	Acceptable (small classification errors)
Non-separable clusters	Acceptable (small classification errors)
Visualization of multidimensional data	Yes
Network visualization	Yes
Data mining tool	Yes

Source Own elaboration

enterprises whose indicator values were below the 1st percentile of or above the 99th, 177 enterprises were used to build the network.[2] Considering the number of these objects, as well as the number and the statistical properties of the financial indicators, an SOM network was built with a hexagonal structure of neuronal connections, a Gaussian neighborhood function and a size of 11 × 11 neurons. The network is characterized by a small average quantization error (0.0662), topographical error (0.2542) and distortion error (0.0078). Its graphical representation, in the form of a map of unified distances, is shown in Fig. 12.1b. The color at the bottom of the scale signifies the minimum existing distances, at the top—the maximum ones.

Based on the analysis of the map of unified distances, four clusters of enterprises that are characterized by a similar financial situation, as part of the class, have been identified (see Fig. 12.2a, b). Clusters 1 and 2 include enterprises whose financial situation is definitely unfavorable. These are the companies that were at the highest

[2]In accordance with the adopted research methodology, described in the first part of the study, the construction enterprises that went bankrupt in the years 2007–2013 have been described by financial analysis indicators and subjected to the indicator analysis. The indicators that required averaging of the balance sheet values, which directly results from the calculation procedure used in the financial analysis, should contain data for the reporting periods even 5 years prior to the year in which the bankruptcy took place. This often caused numerous data gaps, because despite the obligatory submission of such documents to the commercial courts, the entities subjected to restructuring transformations, particularly those at risk of bankruptcy, did not meet this obligation. The lack of sanctioning of the law in this aspect poses a big problem for the development of research on the models of early warning about bankruptcy, because it prevents acquisition of financial data regarding these entities, see e.g., [30].

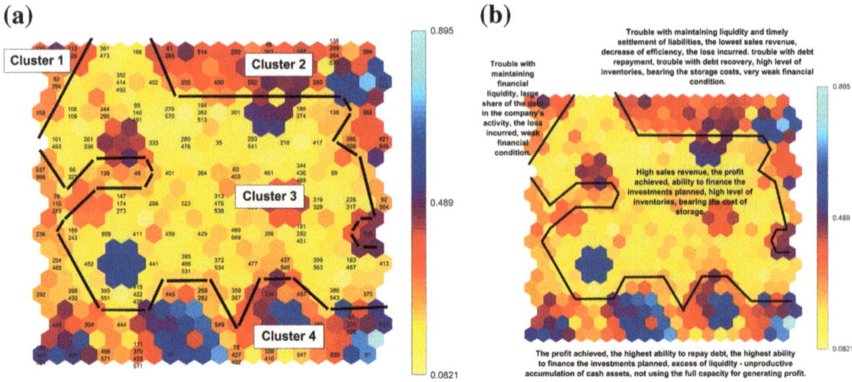

Fig. 12.2 **a** Division of enterprises into homogenous clusters; **b** Description of the clusters distinguished based on the financial analysis indicators (*Source* Own elaboration)

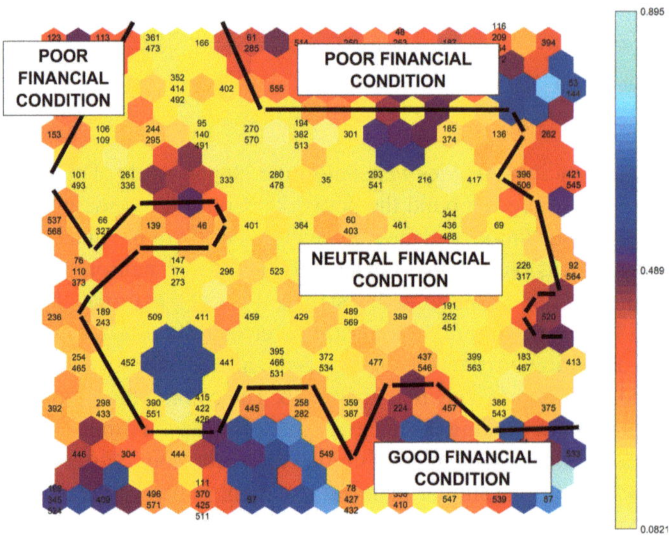

Fig. 12.3 Map of the enterprises' financial condition (*Source* Own elaboration)

risk of bankruptcy.[3] Appearance of an enterprise in this area of the SOM network should be considered as a serious warning sign. In cluster 3, there are enterprises that are characterized by a neutral financial condition. The values of the analyzed indicators for the entities in this group are at the level considered to be average, while in cluster 4, there are companies whose financial ratios suggest that they are in good financial condition (see Fig. 12.3).

[3]This risk was materialized in the form of a court ruling on the bankruptcy of these entities in the ($t0$) period.

The SOM shown in Fig. 12.3 presents, in a static manner, the enterprises' situation 4 years prior to the bankruptcy. In the further part of the study, the values of the indicators for the examined enterprises, from the following three reporting years, were plotted on the map. This allowed observation of the changes in the financial condition of the researched enterprises.

Figure 12.4 shows the changes in the position of four sample companies on the map of uniform distances. These points correspond to subsequent reporting periods in which financial results were announced, from (*t*-4), that is 4 years prior to the company's declaration of bankruptcy, to (*t*-1), that is the year of publication of the last financial report before its bankruptcy.

The charts (see Fig. 12.4) show that in the (*t*-4) period, the enterprises were in the area of those with good or neutral financial condition. They remained in this area for 1, 2 or 3 years, and in the (*t*-1) period, they always moved to the area of units with poor financial condition. Regardless of the starting point on the SOM, after 4 years all the enterprises moved to the clusters of the companies with the lowest values of the financial indicators. Very interesting conclusions were also made while analyzing the clustering path in the period of 4 years prior the bankruptcy announcement, on which the companies that went bankrupt in the year (t0) moved. It turned out that

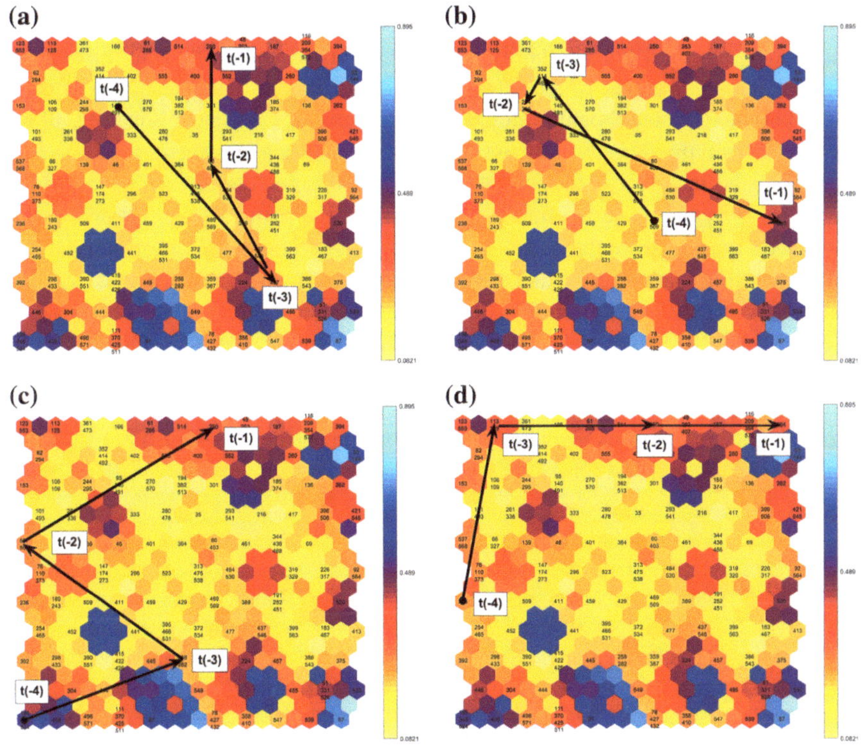

Fig. 12.4 Trajectories of four sample companies (*Source* Own elaboration)

52.5% (93 entities) of the analyzed bankruptcies in the periods (*t*-4) to (*t*-2) were in cluster 3 (thus having a neutral economic and financial condition). Their ability to stay on the market has dropped dramatically only 1 year before bankruptcy, which is why they moved to cluster 1 or 2.

In the set of the examined bankruptcies, there were also such entities (20 cases), which 4 years prior to the bankruptcy were in cluster 1 or 2, then, within subsequent 2 years, moved to cluster 3—i.e., the units with a neutral economic and financial condition, and a year before the final court declaration of bankruptcy—again they were classified within cluster 1 or 2. The results of these partial studies confirm the hypothesis put forward in the literature on the subject about a possible, earlier than the usually assumed 1 year, forecasting of solvency (market survival capability) of business entities.

Out of the 177 companies that were analyzed in the study, 176 were correctly classified in the area of the enterprises with poor financial standing. Only one exception was observed in the study—the enterprise which even in the (*t*-1) period did not move to cluster 4.

12.5 Conclusion

The study presented here certainly is not exhaustive. Only 177 enterprises were taken into consideration, which after the announcement of the financial results for the *t*(-1) period declared bankruptcy. The SOM network presented, however, allows the information that is extremely useful for the company's management to be easily read from the map. Identification of the "safe" and the "dangerous" areas allows to control the changes in the financial standing of the entities being observed. The company's moving from the "safe" area to the "dangerous" one is a serious warning sign, indicating that the company should be closely watched. At the same time, the enterprises located in the area of risk may come out of it, which can be interpreted as effective remedial actions taken by the companies' managements and improvement of their overall situation.

SOM networks surely are worth to be included in the set of the tools used by decision makers. It seems that networks of this type perfectly complement and often replace other analytical tools.

References

1. Ustawa z dnia 28 lutego 2003 r. Prawo upadłościowe, Dz.U. 2003 nr 60 poz. 535
2. Ustawa z dnia 15 maja 2015 r. Prawo restrukturyzacyjne, Dz.U. 2015 poz. 978
3. Regulation (EU) 2015/848 of the European Parliament and of the Council of 20 May 2015 on insolvency proceedings OJ L 141, 5.6.2015, 19–72; (http://data.europa.eu/eli/reg/2015/848/oj; dostęp z dnia: 10.09.2018)

4. Czapracka, A., Babiarz-Mikulska, K., Morawska, S.: Ocena efektywności procedur upadłościowych wobec przedsiębiorców. Difin, Warszawa (2012)
5. Kitowski, J.: Metody dyskryminacyjne jako instrument oceny zagrożenia upadłością przedsiębiorstwa, Rzeszów, Wydawnictwo Uniwersytetu Rzeszowskiego, 12–23 (2015)
6. Balicki, A.: Statystyczna analiza wielowymiarowa i jej zastosowania społeczno-ekonomiczne, Gdańsk 2009, Wydawnictwo Uniwersytetu Gdańskiego, 20–23 (2009)
7. Antonowicz, P.: Bankructwa i upadłości przedsiębiorstw. Teoria – praktyka gospodarcza – studia regionalne. Wydawnictwo Uniwersytetu Gdańskiego, Gdańsk (2015)
8. Antonowicz, P.: Zmienne egzogeniczne funkcji dyskryminacyjnych w polskich modelach prognozowania upadłości przedsiębiorstw. In: Balcerzak, A.P., Rogalska, E. (eds.) Stymulowanie innowacyjności i konkurencyjności przedsiębiorstwa w otoczeniu globalnej gospodarki wiedzy. Wydawnictwo Naukowe Uniwersytetu Mikołaja Kopernika, Toruń (2010)
9. Kohonen, T.: Self-organizing formation of topologically correct feature maps. Biol. Cybern. **43**(1), 59–69 (1982)
10. Alahakoon, D., Halgamuge, S.K., Sirinivasan, B.: Dynamic self organizing maps with controlled growth for knowledge discovery. IEEE Trans. Neural Networks, Spec. Issue Knowl. Disc. Data Min. **11**, 601–614 (2000)
11. Rauber, A., Merkl, D., Dittenbach, M.: The growing hierarchical self-organizing map: exploratory analysis of high-dimensional data. IEEE Trans. Neural Networks **13**(6), 1331–1341 (2002)
12. Martinetz, T., Schulten, K.: A neural gas network learns topologies. In: Artificial Neural Network, pp. 397–402. Elsevier (1991)
13. Fritzke, B.: A growing neural gas network learns topologies. In: Tesauro, G., Touretzky, D.S., Leen, T.K. (eds.) Advances in Neural Information Processing Systems, vol. 7, pp. 625–632. MIT Press, Cambridge (1995)
14. Migdał-Najman, K., Najman, K.: Samouczące się sztuczne sieci neuronowe w grupowaniu i klasyfikacji danych, Teoria i zastosowania w ekonomii. Wydawnictwo Uniwersytetu Gdańskiego, Gdańsk (2013)
15. Kaski, S., Kangas, J., Kohonen, T.: Bibliography of self-organizing map (SOM) papers: 1981–1997. Neural Comput. Surv. **1**, 102–350 (1998)
16. Decker, R.: Market basket analysis by means of a growing neural network. Int. Rev. Retail Distrib. Consum. Res. **15**(2), 151–169 (2005)
17. Decker, R., Monien, K.: Market basket analysis with neural gas networks and self-organising maps. J. Target. Meas. Anal. Mark. **11**(4), 373–386 (2003)
18. Migdał-Najman, K.: Analiza porównawcza samouczących się sieci neuronowych typu SOM i GNG w poszukiwaniu reguł asocjacyjnych, Prace Naukowe Uniwersytetu Ekonomicznego we Wrocławiu. Taksonomia 18. Klasyfikacja i analiza danych - teoria i zastosowania, 176, 272–281 (2011)
19. Migdał-Najman, K.: Badowska S. Wykorzystanie samouczących się sieci neuronowych w analizie zachowań zakupowych i identyfikacji ich wzorców wśród konsumentów w wieku 60 lat i więcej. Zarządzanie i Finanse **3**, 295–307 (2017)
20. Serrano-Cinca, C.: Self organizing neural networks for financial diagnosis. Decis. Support Syst. **17**(3), 227–238 (1996)
21. Séverin, E.: Self organizing maps in corporate finance: quantitative and qualitative analysis of debt and leasing. Neurocomputing **73**(10–12), 2061–2967 (2010)
22. Chen, N., Ribeiro, B., Vieira, A., Chen, A.: Clustering and visualization of bankruptcy trajectory using self-organizing map. Expert Syst. Appl. **40**(1), 385–393 (2013)
23. Migdał Najman, K., Najman, K.: Diagnozowanie kondycji finansowej spółek notowanych na GPW w Warszawie w oparciu o sieć SOM, Zeszyty Naukowe nr 389, Rynek Kapitałowy, Skuteczne Inwestowanie, część I, Wydawnictwo Naukowe Uniwersytetu Szczecińskiego, Szczecin, 507–519 (2004)
24. Corridoni, J.M., Bimbo, A., Landi, L.: 3D object classification using multi-object Kohonen networks. Pattern Recogn., Pergamon **29**(6), 919–935 (1996)

25. Ye, H., Lo, B.W.N.: A visualised software library: nested self-organizing maps for retrieving and browsing reusable software assets. Neural Comput. Appl. **9**(4), 266–279 (2000)
26. Deboeck, G.J.: Value maps: finding value in markets that are expensive. In: Oja, E., Kaski, S. (eds.) Kohonen Maps, pp. 15–32. Elsevier Science B.V. (1999)
27. Vesanto, J., Alhoniemi, E.: Clustering of the self-organizing map. IEEE Trans. Neural Networks **11**(3), 586–600 (2000)
28. Migdał-Najman, K., Najman, K.: Applying the Kohonen self-organizing map networks to select variables. In: Preisach, C., Burkhardt, H., Schmidt-Thieme, L., Decker, R. (eds.) Data Analysis, Machine Learning and Applications, Studies in Classification, Data Analysis and Knowledge Organization, pp. 45–54. Springer (2008)
29. Kohonen, T.: Self-Organizing Maps. Springer, Berlin (1995)
30. Antonowicz, P., Szarmach, Ł.: Teoria i praktyka funkcjonowania piramidy finansowej versus studium przypadku upadłości Amber Gold Sp. z o.o., "Zarządzanie i Finanse. J. Manage. Finance" 11, 1/2 (2013)

Chapter 13
Alternative Estimators for the Effective Spread Derived from High-Frequency Data

Joanna Olbryś and Michał Mursztyn

Abstract According to the literature, various proxies for the effective bid/ask spread are utilized by researchers. They can be estimated from low- or high-frequency data. In this study, three alternative estimators for the effective spread derived from high-frequency data are investigated. We analyse the basic version of percentage effective spread and two modified versions of the Roll's estimator for the effective spread. Data set contains intraday data rounded to the nearest second for 86 Warsaw Stock Exchange (WSE) traded companies, in the period from January 2005 to December 2016. We test distributional properties, linear and nonlinear dependences, as well as stationarity of the analysed daily time series. Moreover, the research hypothesis concerning the statistical significance of correlations between daily values of various effective spread estimates is tested. Furthermore, the study provides robustness analyses of the obtained results with respect to the whole sample and three consecutive subsamples, covering the pre-crisis, crisis and post-crisis periods. The empirical findings confirm significant relationships between alternative proxies for the effective spread and turn out to be robust to the choice of the period.

Keywords Effective bid/ask spread · Roll's estimator · Intraday data · Warsaw Stock Exchange

13.1 Introduction

Liquidity/illiquidity research has rapidly expanded over the last years influencing conclusions regarding asset pricing, corporate finance and market microstructure. The related literature indicates that various versions of the bid/ask spread are proper measures for stock illiquidity because they approximate the cost of immediate exe-

J. Olbryś (✉) · M. Mursztyn
Bialystok University of Technology, Wiejska 45A, 15-351 Bialystok, Poland
e-mail: j.olbrys@pb.edu.pl

M. Mursztyn
e-mail: m.mursztyn@student.pb.edu.pl

W. Tarczyński and K. Nermend (eds.), *Effective Investments on Capital Markets*, Springer Proceedings in Business and Economics,
https://doi.org/10.1007/978-3-030-21274-2_13

cution of a trade. Specifically, the effective spread is employed as a proxy for the bid/ask spread.

It is worthwhile to mention that the nomenclature concerning the effective bid/ask spread measure is not unambiguous. For example, in his seminal work, Roll [36] introduces the estimator of the effective bid/ask spread in an efficient market, but he does not utilize intraday data. Hasbrouck [18] proposes a Gibbs sampler Bayesian estimation of the Roll's effective spread by setting a non-negative prior density for the spreads. However, this measure is very intensive numerically. Lesmond et al. [24] introduce an estimator of the effective spread (the so-called LOT model) based on the assumption of informed trading on non-zero-return days and the absence of informed trading on zero-return days. Fong et al. [12] create a new per cent-cost proxy (the so-called FHT measure) by simplifying the LOT model. Holden [20] and Goyenko et al. [15] jointly develop a proxy of the effective spread called the effective tick measure and based on observable price clustering. Holden [20] modifies the Roll's estimator of the effective spread and proposes the Extended Roll proxy. Corwin and Schultz [8] define high–low impact (the so-called HL measure) that is calculated based on high and low prices. Chung and Zhang [6] introduce the closing per cent quoted spread as a new per cent-cost proxy. More recently, Abdi and Ranaldo [1] propose a new method to estimate the bid/ask spread when quote data are not available—the so-called CHL estimator.

In the literature, various measures of the effective spread are usually calculated by using low-frequency daily data, e.g. Lesmond [23], Holden [20], Goyenko et al. [15], Corwin and Schultz [8], Chung and Zhang [6], Fong et al. [12], Abdi and Ranaldo [1] and Będowska-Sójka [3]. However, estimators for the effective spread based on high-frequency data are nowadays more frequently utilized due to the increasing availability of intraday data.

In this research, we assess basic versions of percentage effective spread and two modified versions of the Roll's estimator for the effective spread. All measures are estimated from high-frequency data. The data set contains intraday data for 86 WSE-traded companies, in the period from 3 January 2005 to 30 December 2016. We test distributional properties, linear and nonlinear dependences, as well as stationarity of the analysed daily time series. In order to carry out a study of interaction between three alternative proxies for the effective spread, the research hypothesis concerning the statistical significance of correlation coefficients is tested.

Furthermore, the study provides robustness analyses of the empirical results with respect to the whole sample and three consecutive subsamples, each of equal size, covering the pre-crisis, crisis and post-crisis periods. The crisis period on the WSE is formally defined based on the papers by Olbrys and Majewska [29, 30]. In these papers the Pagan and Sossounov [35] method for the statistical identification of market states is utilized. The empirical findings of correlations between the alternative estimators for the effective spread turn out to be robust to the choice of the sub-period.

To the best of the author's knowledge, the empirical findings for the WSE presented here are novel and have not been previously reported in the literature.

The remainder of the study is organized as follows. Section 13.2 describes the methodological background concerning the measurement of the effective bid/ask spread from high-frequency data. Section 13.3 discusses the empirical results for the WSE. Section 13.4 covers the main findings and presents the conclusions.

Nomenclature	
WSE	Warsaw Stock Exchange
%ES	Percentage effective spread
MRoll1	First modified version of the Roll's estimator for the effective spread
MRoll2	Second modified version of the Roll's estimator for the effective spread

13.2 Measuring the Effective Spread from High-Frequency Data

According to the literature, high-frequency financial data are crucial in studying a variety of issues related to the microstructure of markets and trading processes. In this research, a database containing intraday data rounded to the nearest second is utilized. The data set contains opening, high, low and closing prices for security over one unit of time.

The mid-point price P_t^{mid} at time t is calculated as the arithmetic mean of the best ask price $P_t(a)$ and the best bid price $P_t(b)$ at time t. Considering that the bid and ask prices are not made public on the WSE, the mid-point price at time t is rounded by the arithmetic mean of the lowest price P_t^L and the highest price P_t^H at time t, which approximate the best ask price and the best bid price, respectively [31]:

$$P_t^{\text{mid}} = \frac{P_t^H + P_t^L}{2}. \tag{13.1}$$

The transaction price P_t at time t is approximated by the closing price.

13.2.1 Percentage Effective Bid/Ask Spread

The literature proposes at least three basic versions of the effective bid/ask spread estimator derived from intraday data. One of them is calculated using a quote mid-point in the denominator, e.g. Korajczyk and Sadka [22], while the second is computed using a transaction price in the denominator, e.g. Chordia et al. [5]. The third version uses the natural logarithm of prices, e.g. Goyenko et al. [15], Fong et al. [12]. However, the empirical results obtained by using all alternative versions are very similar.

In this paper, the effective spread value is estimated by relating the transaction price to the mid-point of the bid and ask quote.

The percentage effective bid/ask spread value is given by Eq. (13.2):

$$\%\mathrm{ES}_t = \frac{200 \cdot \left|P_t - P_t^{\mathrm{mid}}\right|}{P_t^{\mathrm{mid}}}, \tag{13.2}$$

where the mid-point price P_t^{mid} at the moment t is given by Eq. (13.1). Percentage effective spread is in fact a measure of illiquidity. Small value of percentage effective spread denotes high liquidity, while the high value of this estimator denotes low liquidity. %ES at moment t is equal to zero when $P_t = P_t^{\mathrm{mid}}$. The estimator (13.2) is calculated as a volume-weighted average of percentage effective spreads computed over all the trades within a day. The value of percentage effective spread is non-negative.

13.2.2 The Roll's Estimator for the Effective Spread

Roll [36] develops a simple model to estimate the effective bid/ask spread from daily data. A market is assumed to be efficient in gross terms, and the bid/ask spread is the only source of cost. Therefore, serial covariance in returns is due to the bid/ask bounce caused by the shifting of the price from the bid to the ask prices.

It is a well-known fact that the original version of the Roll's estimator for the effective spread is well defined only for negative first-order serial covariance of price changes, which is not guaranteed in practice. Roll has shown that the presence of a bid/ask bounce induces negative serial covariance in price changes. Roll interprets his estimator as a measure of the effective spread at which transactions actually occur. The Roll's estimator is a prospective measure as it depends on price changes after the trade [21]. Stoll [37] stresses that the friction measured by the Roll's estimator reflects primarily non-informational factors. According to Stoll, friction in financial markets measures the difficulty with which an asset is traded.

However, the related literature contains some critical remarks concerning the statistical properties of the Roll's estimator. For example, Glosten [14] points out that the Roll's measure may provide upwardly biased estimates of the effective spread. Harris [17] emphasizes that the serial covariance estimator is very noisy in daily data and is biased downward in small samples. Hasbrouck [19] finds that daily positive serial covariance occurs for roughly one-third of the firm years in the sample. To avoid this problem, the Roll's proxy has to be set to zero when the serial covariance is positive. Corwin and Schultz [8] note that even with a long time series of daily data, the serial covariance of price changes is frequently positive. In such cases, researchers usually do one of three things: (1) treat the observation as missing, (2) set the Roll's estimator to zero or (3) multiply the serial covariance by negative one, estimate the spread and multiply the spread by negative one to obtain a negative spread estimate.

In the literature, the Roll's estimator is usually calculated for stock i for each month, e.g. Huang and Stoll [21], Goyenko et al. [15], Holden [20], Corwin and Schultz [8], Lischewski and Voronkova [25], Foran et al. [13] and Będowska-Sójka [3]. In this paper, we compute the daily values of the Roll's estimator. Therefore, daily serial covariance on day d is estimated using trade-to-trade price changes within a day, e.g. Stoll [37, p. 1493].

In our study, two modified versions of the Roll's estimator for the effective spread are utilized and compared to each other. First of them, MRoll1, is given by Eq. (13.3):

$$\text{MRoll1}_{i,d} = \begin{cases} 200 \cdot \sqrt{-\text{cov}\left(R_{i,t}, R_{i,t-1}\right)}, & \text{when}\, \text{cov}\left(R_{i,t}, R_{i,t-1}\right) < 0 \\ 0, & \text{when}\, \text{cov}\left(R_{i,t}, R_{i,t-1}\right) \geq 0 \end{cases} \tag{13.3}$$

where $R_{i,t}$ is a logarithmic ultra-short rate of return of stock i at moment t on day d. The constant 200 instead of 2.0 converts the units to percent.

The second modified version of the Roll's estimator,MRoll2, is defined by the following Eq. (13.4):

$$\text{MRoll2}_{i,d} = \begin{cases} 200 \cdot \sqrt{-\text{cov}\left(R_{i,t}, R_{i,t-1}\right)}, & \text{when}\, \text{cov}\left(R_{i,t}, R_{i,t-1}\right) \leq 0 \\ -200 \cdot \sqrt{\text{cov}\left(R_{i,t}, R_{i,t-1}\right)}, & \text{when}\, \text{cov}\left(R_{i,t}, R_{i,t-1}\right) > 0 \end{cases} \tag{13.4}$$

where $R_{i,t}$ is a logarithmic ultra-short rate of return of stock i at moment t on day d. The spread proxy (13.4) is analogous to the spread estimator proposed by Harris [17, p. 585] or Campbell et al. [4, p. 134].

13.3 Intraday Data Description and Empirical Results on the WSE

The data sample consists of high-frequency data rounded to the nearest second for the group of the 86 WSE-listed equities (available at www.bossa.pl). The raw data contains the opening, high, low and closing prices, and volume for a company over one unit of time. The whole sample period spans data from 2 January 2005 to 30 December 2016. The database includes only these equities which were traded on the WSE during the sample period since 31 December 2004, and were not suspended. The 138 WSE companies met these basic conditions, and they were initially selected. Nevertheless, a large number of the WSE-listed equities unveil a substantial non-trading effect [28]. To mitigate this problem, we excluded the stocks that exhibited extraordinarily many non-trading days during the whole sample period, precisely, above 300 zeros in daily volume, which constituted about 10% of all 2994 trading days. In this way, 104 companies were gathered into the database. In the next step, we excluded stocks that were suspended or removed from the WSE in 2017. Furthermore, we identified various gaps in data for some companies and therefore we decided to exclude them from our database. Finally, 86 firms have been comprised in the database. In the last step, we removed the period between 16 January 2014 and 30 January 2014 (11 trading days) from intraday data set as the common (technical) gap in data for all companies [32].

13.3.1 Statistical Properties of the Effective Spread Estimators

In the first step, we analyse daily time series of the effective spread estimators %ES (13.2), MRoll1 (13.3) and MRoll2 (13.4) in the context of their distributional properties. Table 13.1 presents the overall cross-sectional results of descriptive statistics and tests for asymmetry, tail thickness, normality and both linear and nonlinear dependences. In total, 258 daily time series of alternative effective spread estimates are tested for the whole group of 86 WSE-listed companies. Table 13.1 is based on all observations within the whole sample from 2 January 2005 to 30 December 2016. The test statistic for skewness and excess kurtosis is the conventional t-statistic. The Doornik and Hansen [9] test has a χ^2 distribution if the null hypothesis of normality is true. LB(q) and LB^2(q) are the Ljung and Box [26] statistics for returns and squared returns, respectively, distributed as $\chi^2(q)$, $q \approx \ln T$, where T is the number of data points [38]. In all cases, $q \approx 8$. The McLeod and Li [27] method is utilized to test the null hypothesis that there is no ARCH effect in the series.

Empirical findings reported in Table 13.1 need some comments. We observe right skewness in the cross section of the daily time series, as the sample means exceed medians. The estimates of skewness reveal that all daily series are positively and significantly skewed. This observation is similar to the evidence regarding the return series. Campbell et al. [4] point out that the skewness proxies are generally positive for the individual stock return daily time series. Testing for excess kurtosis shows that all series are leptokurtic with respect to the normal distribution. Campbell et al. [4] indicate that daily data series often have high sample excess kurtosis, which is a sign of fat tails, i.e. the series are leptokurtic. To test for normality, the Doornik and Hansen [9] test is used, and it rejects normality for each of the series at the 5% level of significance. This phenomenon is typical and consistent with the literature. The Ljung and Box [26] test confirms the presence of significant linear dependencies in the case of 254 out of 258 series. It is rather consistent with the literature, because time series of an asset daily data could be significantly autocorrelated. The McLeod and Li [27] test indicates the presence of significant ARCH effects in the case of 213 out of 258 series, which is a quite typical feature, e.g. Tsay [38], Campbell et al. [4].

Table 13.1 Overall cross-sectional results of descriptive statistics and tests for skewness, excess kurtosis, normality, and interdependence for daily time series of alternative effective spread proxies (for the whole group of 86 WSE-listed equities)

	%ES	MRoll1	MRoll2
Mean	0.128	0.675	0.613
Median	0.035	0.361	0.361
Standard deviation	0.266	1.004	1.086
The null hypothesis that skewness = 0 can be rejected at 5% significance level. The series is positively and significantly skewed	All series	All series	All series
The null hypothesis that skewness = 0 can be rejected at 5% significance level. The series is negatively and significantly skewed	–	–	–
The null hypothesis that excess kurtosis = 0 can be rejected at 5% significance level. The series is leptokurtic	All series	All series	All series
The null hypothesis that excess kurtosis = 0 can be rejected at 5% significance level. The series is platykurtic	–	–	–
The null hypothesis of normality can be rejected at 5% significance level (the Doornik-Hansen test)	All series	All series	All series
The null hypothesis that there is no linear dependence in the series can be rejected at 5% significance level (the LB(8) test)	82/86 series	All series	All series
The null hypothesis that there is no ARCH effect in the series can be rejected at 5% significance level (the $LB^2(8)$ test)	41/86 series	All series	All series

Notes Description of the results was proposed by Olbrys and Mursztyn [32, Table 13.1]

13.3.2 Testing for Stationarity

In the next step, we detect with the ADF-GLS test [10] whether the analysed daily time series of the effective spread proxies are stationary. Daily data are used, and hence, we utilize a maximum lag equal to five and then remove lags until the last one is statistically significant [2]. The critical value of the ADF-GLS τ-statistics for the rejection of the null hypothesis of a unit root at the 5% significance level is equal to -1.94 (for $T = 2500$ and the intercept model) or -2.86 (for $T = 2500$ and the trend model) [7, pp. 271–272]. Table 13.2 reports the overall cross-sectional results of testing for stationarity of 258 daily time series of alternative effective spread proxies, for the whole group of 86 WSE-listed equities. The table is based on all observations in the whole sample on 2 January 2005–30 December 2016. We confirmed that the unit-root hypothesis can be rejected for all series at 5% significance level.

Table 13.2 Overall results of testing for stationarity of daily time series of alternative effective spread proxies (for the whole group of 86 WSE-listed equities)

	%ES	MRoll1	MRoll2
Unit-root hypothesis can be rejected at 5% significance level (ADF-GLS test). The series is stationary	All series	All series	All series

Notes Description of the results was proposed by Olbrys and Mursztyn [32, Table 13.2]

13.3.3 Correlation Analyses

To carry out a study of the interaction between three alternative proxies for the effective spread, research hypotheses concerning the statistical significance of correlation coefficients are tested. The basic idea is to apply Fisher's [11] z-transformations of sample correlation coefficients to avoid the problem of a time series distribution being non-normal. Therefore, the %ES/MRoll1 and %ES/MRoll2 correlations are represented by Fisher's z-transformation of the corresponding Pearson's sample correlation coefficient.

Table 13.3 reports the overall results of the z-transformed correlation coefficients between the values of daily percentage effective spread and two modified versions of the Roll's estimator for the effective spread, for the study group of 86 WSE-listed companies over the whole sample period from 2 January 2005 to 30 December 2016. The correlation critical value is equal to 0.036 at the 5% significance level (2994 daily observations). One can observe that mean and median values are greater in the case of the %ES/MRoll1 correlations. Therefore, it seems that the relationship between the %ES and MRoll1 estimators is stronger in the whole sample period.

Table 13.3 Summarized results of the coefficients of correlation between the values of daily percentage effective spread and two modified versions of the Roll's estimator, for the study group of 86 WSE-listed equities over the whole sample period

	%ES/MRoll1	%ES/MRoll2
Mean	0.196	0.162
Median	0.192	0.160
Min	−0.073	−0.073
Max	0.411	0.356
Positive and statistically significant correlation coefficients	83/86	83/86
Negative and statistically significant correlation coefficients	2/86	2/86
Statistically insignificant correlation coefficients	1/86	1/86

13.3.4 Robustness Analyses

To verify the robustness of the results, empirical analyses are applied to the whole sample (2994 trading days) and three consecutive periods, each of equal length (436 trading days): (1) the pre-crisis period, 6 September 2005–31 May 2007, (2) the crisis period, 1 June 2007–27 February 2009, and (3) the post-crisis period 2 March 2009–19 November 2010, e.g. Olbryś [33, 34]. The crisis period on the WSE is formally defined based on the papers by Olbrys and Majewska [29, 30], in which the Pagan and Sossounov [35] procedure for the statistical identification of market states is utilized. Precise detection of market states is crucial, due to many practical implications. Among other things, the issue regarding the existence of the interaction between stock market declines and market liquidity is very important, e.g. Hameed et al. [16].

Table 13.4 presents overall results of the *z*-transformed correlation coefficients between the values of daily percentage effective spread and two modified versions of the Roll's estimator for the effective spread, for the whole group of 86 companies, during the pre-crisis (P_1), crisis (P_2) and post-crisis (P_3) periods. The correlation critical value is equal to 0.094 at the 5% significance level (436 daily observations).

As expected, correlation analyses are robust to the choice of the period. Positive and statistically significant relations among daily values of the percentage effective spread and two modified versions of the Roll's estimator are denoted. However, the robustness tests confirm that the %ES/MRoll1 relationships (marked in bold in Table 13.4) are more pervasive compared to the %ES/MRoll2 relations. Therefore, we recommend the MRoll1 proxy (13.3) as a better alternative estimator for the effective spread on the WSE.

Table 13.4 Summarized results of the coefficients of correlation between the values of daily percentage effective spread and two modified versions of the Roll's estimator for the effective spread, for the study group of 86 WSE-traded companies over the pre-crisis, crisis and post-crisis periods

	%ES/MRoll1			%ES/MRoll2		
	P_1	P_2	P_3	P_1	P_2	P_3
Mean	0.229	0.222	0.243	0.199	0.201	0.218
Median	0.231	0.197	0.210	0.188	0.170	0.179
Min	−0.180	−0.046	0.008	−0.205	−0.049	−0.005
Max	0.916	0.554	0.719	0.888	0.554	0.719
Positive and statistically significant correlation coefficients	**78/86**	**73/86**	**78/86**	73/86	68/86	71/86
Negative and statistically significant correlation coefficients	2/86	0/86	0/86	2/86	0/86	0/86
Statistically insignificant correlation coefficients	6/86	13/86	8/86	11/86	18/86	15/86

13.4 Conclusion

The core goal of this study was to assess three estimators for the effective spread that are approximated from high-frequency data: percentage effective spread and two modified versions of the Roll's estimator. Major statistical characteristics of daily time series of these liquidity estimates were tested. The empirical findings unveiled some stylized facts and typical features of the analysed time series. Furthermore, we proved that all analysed daily time series of liquidity measures are stationary.

Moreover, correlation analyses were provided and they confirmed positive and statistically significant relations among daily values of the alternative measures of the effective spread. Moreover, the robustness tests indicated that the empirical results turned out to be robust to the choice of the period. Nevertheless, it is important to mention that various correlation analyses for liquidity proxies on the WSE might be biased by the substantial non-trading effect. A consequence of non-trading is a problem with extraordinarily many zeros appearing simultaneously in daily time series of liquidity estimates for some WSE-listed equities [28].

Eventually, we recommend the first modified version of the Roll's estimator (MRoll1) as a suitable alternative proxy for the effective bid/ask spread on the WSE. This evidence is important for further study regarding commonality in liquidity on the WSE, because we need various alternative liquidity/illiquidity estimators in our planned research.

Acknowledgements This study was supported by the grant 'Comparative research on commonality in liquidity on the Central and Eastern European stock markets' from the National Science Centre in Poland, No. 2016/21/B/HS4/02004.

References

1. Abdi, F., Ranaldo, A.: A simple estimation of bid-ask spreads from daily close, high, and low prices. Rev. Financ. Stud. **30**(12), 4437–4480 (2017)
2. Adkins, L.C.: Using Gretl for Principles of Econometrics, 4th edn. Version 1.041
3. Będowska-Sójka, B.: The coherence of liquidity measures. The evidence from the emerging market. Financ. Res. Lett. **27**, 118–123 (2018)
4. Campbell, J.Y., Lo, A.W., MacKinlay, A.C.: The Econometrics of Financial Markets. Princeton University Press, New Jersey (1997)
5. Chordia, T., Roll, R., Subrahmanyam, A.: Commonality in liquidity. J. Financ. Econ. **56**, 3–28 (2000)
6. Chung, K.H., Zhang, H.: A simple approximation of intraday spreads using daily data. J. Financ. Mark. **17**, 94–120 (2014)
7. Cook, S., Manning, N.: Lag optimization and finite-sample size distortion of unit root tests. Econ. Lett. **84**(2), 267–274 (2004)
8. Corwin, S.A., Schultz, P.: A simple way to estimate bid-ask spreads from daily high and low prices. J. Financ. **67**(2), 719–759 (2012)
9. Doornik, J.A., Hansen, H.: An omnibus test for univariate and multivariate normality. Oxf. Bull. Econ. Stat. **70**(Suppl 1), 927–939 (2008)

10. Elliott, G., Rothenberg, T.J., Stock, J.H.: Efficient tests for an autoregressive unit root. Econometrica **64**(4), 813–836 (1996)
11. Fisher, R.A.: On the probable error of a coefficient of correlation deduced from a small sample. Metron **1**, 3–32 (1921)
12. Fong, K.Y.L., Holden, C.W., Trzcinka, C.: What are the best liquidity proxies for global research? Rev. Financ. **21**, 1355–1401 (2017)
13. Foran, J., Hutchinson, M.C., O'Sullivan, N.: Liquidity commonality and pricing in UK. Res. Int. Bus. Financ. **34**, 281–293 (2015)
14. Glosten, L.R.: Components of the bid-ask spread and the statistical properties of transaction prices. J. Financ. **42**(4), 1293–1307 (1987)
15. Goyenko, R.Y., Holden, C.W., Trzcinka, C.A.: Do liquidity measures measure liquidity? J. Financ. Econ. **92**, 153–181 (2009)
16. Hameed, A., Kang, W., Viswanathan, S.: Stock market decline and liquidity. J. Financ. **65**(1), 257–293 (2010)
17. Harris, L.: Statistical properties of the Roll serial covariance bid/ask spread estimator. J. Financ. **45**(2), 579–590 (1990)
18. Hasbrouck, J.: Liquidity in the futures pits: inferring market dynamics from incomplete data. J. Financ. Quant. Anal. **39**, 305–326 (2004)
19. Hasbrouck, J: Trading costs and returns for U.S. equities: estimating effective costs from daily data. J. Financ. **64**(3), 1445–1477 (2009)
20. Holden, C.: New low-frequency liquidity measures. J. Financ. Mark. **12**, 778–813 (2009)
21. Huang, R.D., Stoll, H.R.: Dealer versus auction markets: A paired comparison of execution costs on NASDAQ and the NYSE. J. Financ. Econ. **41**, 313–357 (1996)
22. Korajczyk, R., Sadka, R.: Pricing the commonality across alternative measures of liquidity. J. Financ. Econ. **87**(1), 45–72 (2008)
23. Lesmond, D.A.: Liquidity of emerging markets. J. Financ. Econ. **77**(2), 411–452 (2005)
24. Lesmond, D.A., Ogden, J.P., Trzcinka, C.A.: A new estimate of transaction costs. Rev. Financ. Stud. **12**(5), 1113–1141 (1999)
25. Lischewski, J., Voronkova, S.: Size, value, and liquidity. Do they really matter on an emerging stock market? Emerg. Mark. Rev. **13**(1), 8–25 (2012)
26. Ljung, G., Box, G.E.P.: On a measure of lack of fit in time series models. Biometrika **66**, 67–72 (1978)
27. McLeod, A.I., Li, W.K.: Diagnostic checking ARMA time series model using squared residual autocorrelations. J. Time Ser. Anal. **4**, 269–273 (1983)
28. Nowak, S., Olbryś, J.: Direct evidence of non-trading on the Warsaw Stock Exchange. Research Papers of Wroclaw University of Economics. Wroclaw Conference in Finance: Contemporary Trends and Challenges, vol. 428, pp. 184–194 (2016)
29. Olbrys, J., Majewska, E.: Direct identification of crisis periods on the CEE stock markets: the influence of the 2007 U.S. subprime crisis. Proc. Econ. Financ. **14**, 461–470 (2014)
30. Olbrys, J., Majewska, E.: Bear market periods during the 2007–2009 financial crisis: direct evidence from the Visegrad countries. Acta Oecon **65**(4), 547–565 (2015)
31. Olbrys, J., Mursztyn, M.: Liquidity proxies based on intraday data: the case of the Polish order driven stock market. In: Tsounis, N., Vlachvei, A. (eds.) Advances in Panel Data Analysis in Applied Economic Research. Springer Proceedings in Business and Economics, pp. 113–128. Springer, Cham (2018)
32. Olbrys, J., Mursztyn, M.: On some characteristics of liquidity proxy time series. Evidence from the Polish stock market. In: Tsounis N., Vlachvei A. (eds) Advances in Time Series Data Methods in Applied Economic Research. Springer Proceedings in Business and Economics, pp. 177–189. Springer, Cham, (2018)
33. Olbryś, J.: Components of the effective spread: evidence from the Warsaw Stock Exchange. In: Bem, A., Daszyńska-Żygadło, K., Hajdiková, T., Juhász, P. (eds.) Finance and Sustainability. Proceedings from the Finance and Sustainability Conference Wroclaw 2017. Springer Proceedings in Business and Economics, pp. 149–163. Springer, Cham (2018)

34. Olbryś, J.: Testing stability of correlations between liquidity proxies derived from intraday data on the Warsaw Stock Exchange. In: Jajuga, K., Locarek-Junge, H., Orlowski, L. (eds.) Contemporary Trends and Challenges in Finance. Proceedings from the 3rd Wroclaw International Conference in Finance. Springer Proceedings in Business and Economics, pp. 67–79. Springer, Cham (2018)
35. Pagan, A.R., Sossounov, K.A.: A simple framework for analysing bull and bear markets. J. Appl. Econ. **18**(1), 23–46 (2003)
36. Roll, R.: A simple implicit measure of the effective bid-ask spread in an efficient market. J. Financ. **39**(4), 1127–1140 (1984)
37. Stoll, H.S.: Friction. J. Financ. **55**(4), 1479–1514 (2000)
38. Tsay, R.S.: Analysis of financial time series. Wiley, New York (2010)

Chapter 14
Investment Strategies Determined by Present Value Given as Trapezoidal Fuzzy Numbers

Krzysztof Piasecki and Joanna Siwek

Abstract In the article, the present value is considered as a trapezoidal fuzzy number, same as obtained expected discount factor. The imprecise value of this factor may be used as a decision premise in creating new investment strategies. Considered strategies are built based on a comparison of a fuzzy profit index and the value limit. In this way, we obtain imprecise investment recommendation. Financial equilibrium criteria result from a special case of this comparison. Further in the paper, the following criteria are generalized: Sharpe's ratio, Jensen's alpha and Treynor's ratio. Moreover, the safety-first criteria are generalized into the fuzzy case, along with Roy's criterion, Kataoka's criterion and Telser's criterion. The obtained results show that the proposed theory can be used in investment applications.

Keywords Fuzzy imprecision · Probabilistic uncertainty · Return rate · Expected discount factor · Portfolio

14.1 Introduction

The imprecision results from our lack of a clear recommendation for one alternative among various others, as well as from a lack of explicit distinction between recommended and not recommended alternatives. Zadeh [1] proposed modelling imprecision with fuzzy set membership function, which is widely accepted.

The uncertainty, on the other hand, is a result of a lack of knowledge about future state of affairs [2]. Kolmogorov [3, 4] postulated that uncertainty may be modelled

K. Piasecki (✉)
Department of Investment and Real Estate, Poznan University of Economics, Poznań, Poland
e-mail: krzysztof.piasecki@ue.poznan.pl

J. Siwek
Department of Imprecise Information Processing Methods, Faculty of Mathematics and Computer Science, Adam Mickiewicz University, Poznań, Poland
e-mail: joanna.siwek@amu.edu.pl

W. Tarczyński and K. Nermend (eds.), *Effective Investments on Capital Markets*, Springer Proceedings in Business and Economics,
https://doi.org/10.1007/978-3-030-21274-2_14

by a probability distribution, if and only if we can point out a particular time in future in which the considered state of affairs will be already known.

Both financial theorists and practitioners noticed a problem of imprecise return rate assessment and imposed imprecise limitations. At the same time, rapid development of fuzzy mathematics led to creation of a fuzzy portfolio analysis and various fuzzy portfolio models. The idea behind the most popular approach was to apply the existing portfolio theory and fuzzify some of its parameters, such as return rate or present value [5–7] or probability distribution parameters [8].

Fuzzy mathematics is also used in portfolio analysis when considering uncertainty. In most of the papers regarding this notion, it is assumed in advance that the return rate is a fuzzy set [9–14]. Yet, this assumption is connected, in most of the cases, with uncertainty of the return rate and unclear or incomplete information used by the investor. In order to model such a portfolio, the authors apply mostly the possibility theory [15–17] or the credibility theory [18]. Recent years resulted in fuzzy return portfolio research which allows for a modification of the portfolio content before the end of the investment [5, 19–26]. In the works of [27–29], the authors suggest creating financial portfolios which are able to model the imprecision risk burdening the return rate.

Kahraman et al. [30] introduced research in which both cash flows and their return rates are given as trapezoidal fuzzy numbers. This kind of approach was aimed to show that market experts, while appointing a net present value, operate only on some imprecise values. Monographies [31, 32] describe the above-mentioned approach in detail. A common feature connecting all these models is using fuzzy set membership function as a substitute for probability distribution. This means that the uncertainty researched in these models is, in fact, replaced by imprecision. This kind of research postulate was first formulated by Kosko [33].

The most significant disadvantage of all fuzzy portfolio theory publications stated above is defining the fuzzy return rate of a portfolio ex cathedra as a linear function in the multidimensional space of return rates from the portfolio components. The only justification for this is the mechanical generalization of Markowitz's model [34] to the fuzzy case. The proposed forms of linear functions, appointing a portfolio return rate to each component's return rate, are not justified by means of mathematical deduction. This highly undermines the reliability of performed analyses.

In most models satisfying Kosko's postulate, inclusion of imprecision is shown in the assumption about a priori given fuzzy return rates. In the works of [28, 35–43], the membership function does not replace the probability distribution, but only interacts with it as a distinct entity, and thus, Kosko's postulate does not apply. This kind of model extension significantly enhances the possibilities of a reliable return rate description. Despite encompassing the imprecise information in the return rate assessment, the proposed fuzzy model can use all existing empirical knowledge about the return rate probability distribution without any further amendments. This feature is highly beneficial, especially by allowing realistic applications. Moreover, in these models uncertainty interacts with imprecision, which stands in agreement with research paradigm formulated by Hiroto [44]. Sadly, the number of models analysing these interactions is significantly smaller. It is highly probable that this situation stems from the mathematical complexity of the models.

In [6], the imprecise return rate is determined by combining a trapezoidal fuzzy present value and the random future value. In [45], imprecise investment recommendations are determined as pieces of advice given based on generally defined fuzzy return rate. Moreover, in [6, 42, 43] it is shown that the expected fuzzy discount factor is a better tool for appraising considered securities than the fuzzy expected return rate. This implies new possibilities for financial assets' analysis.

Therefore, the main goal of this article is to research investment recommendations for securities with the use of fuzzy trapezoidal present values and random future value. During the analysis, the authors research fuzzy financial equilibrium criteria and the safety-first criteria. To clarify, the main idea is to allow an investor to take imprecision risk into consideration when appointing their investment strategies.

The paper is organized as follows. Section 14.2 stands as a theoretical background and outlines fuzzy numbers and their basic properties. It includes the description of the term "imprecision" and its measures. Some of the methods for ordering fuzzy numbers are presented in Sect. 14.3. In Sect. 14.4, the present value is imprecisely evaluated by trapezoidal fuzzy numbers. The fuzzy expected discount factor is then determined in Sect. 14.5. The next five sections contain authors' original contribution. Section 14.6 shows the fuzzy expected discount factor as a primary premise for investment recommendation. It is used to determine the fuzzy expected return rate, which is a secondary premise for investment decision-making. An upgraded model for investment recommendations dependent on expected return system is described in Sect. 14.7. Section 14.8 considers investment recommendations dependent on fuzzy expected return. The financial equilibrium criterions are discussed in Sect. 14.9 and the safety-first criterions in Sect. 14.10. Section 14.11 concludes the article, summarizes the main findings and proposes some future research directions.

14.2 Elements of Fuzzy Number Theory

By $\mathcal{F}(\mathbb{X})$, we denote the family of all fuzzy subsets of an arbitrary space $\mathbb{X}$. An imprecise number is a family of values in which each considered value belongs to it in a varying degree. A commonly accepted model of an imprecise number is the fuzzy number (FN), defined as a fuzzy subset of the real line $\mathbb{R}$. The most general definition of FN was given by Dubois and Prade [46]. Goetschel and Voxman [47] proved that any FN may be equivalently defined in the following way.

Definition 1 Let us suppose that for any nondecreasing sequence $(a, b, c, d) \subset \mathbb{R}$ the left reference function $L_{\mathcal{L}} \in [0; 1]^{[a,b]}$ and the right reference function $R_{\mathcal{L}} \in [0; 1]^{[c,d]}$ are upper semi-continuous monotonic functions satisfying the condition

$$L_{\mathcal{L}}(b) = R_{\mathcal{L}}(c) = 1. \tag{14.1}$$

Then, the identity

$$\mu_{\mathcal{L}}(x) = \mu_{\mathcal{FN}}(x|a, b, c, d, L_{\mathcal{L}}, R_{\mathcal{L}}) = \begin{cases} 0, & x \notin [a, d], \\ L_{\mathcal{L}}(x), & x \in [a, b], \\ 1, & x \in [b, c], \\ R_{\mathcal{L}}(x), & x \in [c, d] \end{cases} \tag{14.2}$$

describes the membership function $\mu_{\mathcal{L}} \in [0, 1]^{\mathbb{R}}$ of the FN $\mathcal{L} = \mathcal{L}(a, b, c, d, L_{\mathcal{L}}, R_{\mathcal{L}})$. □

The space of all fuzzy numbers is denoted by $\mathbb{F}$. We have $\mathbb{R} \subset \mathbb{F}$. Therefore, any real number $a \in \mathbb{R}$ may be considered as FN $a = \mathcal{L}(a, a, a, a, L_{\mathcal{L}}, R_{\mathcal{L}})$.

Algebraic operations on fuzzy numbers were defined in [46] as extension of arithmetic operations on real numbers. These algebraic operations are coherent with Zadeh's extension principle [48–50]. In a special case, for FN $\mathcal{L} \in \mathbb{F}$ represented by its membership function $\mu_{\mathcal{L}} \in [0, 1]^{\mathbb{R}}$ and for any monotonic function $h : \mathbb{R} \supset \mathbb{A} \to \mathbb{R}$ the value

$$\mathcal{Z} = h(\mathcal{L}), \tag{14.3}$$

is described by its membership function $\mu_{\mathcal{Z}} \in [0; 1]^{\mathbb{R}}$ given by the formula:

$$\mu_{\mathcal{Z}}(z) = \sup\{\mu_{\mathcal{L}}(x) : z = h(x), x \in \mathbb{A}\}. \tag{14.4}$$

Finally, let us note that if membership function $\mu_{\mathcal{L}} \in [0, 1]^{\mathbb{R}}$ is given by (14.2), then we have:

– for the case of increasing function $h : \mathbb{R} \supset \mathbb{A} \to \mathbb{R}$

$$\mu_{\mathcal{Z}}(x) = \mu_{\mathcal{L}}\big(h^{-1}(x)\big) = \mu_{FN}\big(x|h(a), h(b), h(c), h(d), L_{\mathcal{L}} \circ h^{-1}, R_{\mathcal{L}} \circ h^{-1}\big), \tag{14.5}$$

– for the case of decreasing function $h : \mathbb{R} \supset \mathbb{A} \to \mathbb{R}$

$$\mu_{\mathcal{Z}}(x) = \mu_{\mathcal{L}}\big(h^{-1}(x)\big) = \mu_{FN}\big(x|h(d), h(c), h(b), h(a), R_{\mathcal{L}} \circ h^{-1}, L_{\mathcal{L}} \circ h^{-1}\big). \tag{14.6}$$

FNs are widely used for modelling assessments or estimations with imprecisely given parameters.

After [51], we understand imprecision as a superposition of ambiguity and indistinctness of information. Ambiguity can be interpreted as a lack of clear recommendation between one alternative among various others. Indistinctness is understood as a lack of explicit distinction between recommended and not recommended alternatives. An increase in information imprecision makes it less useful, and therefore it is sensible to research the problem of imprecision assessment.

Let us take into account an arbitrary FN $\mathcal{L} \in \mathbb{F}$, represented by its membership function $\mu_{\mathcal{L}} \in [0, 1]^{\mathbb{R}}$. The proper tool for measuring the ambiguity of a fuzzy subset $\mathcal{A} \in \mathcal{F}(\mathbb{R})$ is an energy measure $d : \mathcal{F}(\mathbb{R}) \to \mathbb{R}_0^+$, proposed by de Luca and Termini [52]. For given FN $\mathcal{L} \in \mathbb{F}$, we can apply the following formula

$$d(\mathcal{L}) = m(\mathcal{L}) = \int_{-\infty}^{+\infty} \mu_{\mathcal{L}}(x)\mathrm{d}x. \tag{14.7}$$

The right tool for measuring indistinctness is the entropy measure, proposed also by de Luca and Termini [53] and modified by Piasecki [54]. In this article, the entropy measure $e : \mathcal{F}(\mathbb{R}) \to \mathbb{R}_0^+$ will be described as in [55]. For given FN $\mathcal{L} \in \mathbb{F}$ with support

$$\mathbb{S}(\mathcal{L}) = \{x \in \mathbb{R} : \mu_{\mathcal{L}}(x) > 0\}, \tag{14.8}$$

we have

$$e(\mathcal{L}) = \frac{m\left(\mathcal{L} \cap \mathcal{L}^C\right)}{m\left(\left(\mathcal{L} \cup \mathcal{L}^C\right) \cap \mathbb{S}(\mathcal{L})\right)}, \tag{14.9}$$

where $\mathcal{L}^C$ denotes the complement of the fuzzy subset representing FN $\mathcal{L} \in \mathbb{F}$. In our study, we distinguish the following kind of FNs.

Definition 2 Let us suppose that for any nondecreasing sequence $(a, b, c, d) \subset \mathbb{R}$ the left reference function $L_{\mathcal{T}} \in [0; 1]^{[a,b]}$ and the right reference function $R_{\mathcal{T}} \in [0; 1]^{[c,d]}$ are given by the identities

$$L_{\mathcal{T}}(x) = \begin{cases} \frac{x-a}{b-a} & x \in [a, b[, \\ 1 & x = b, \end{cases} \tag{14.10}$$

$$R_{\mathcal{T}}(x) = \begin{cases} \frac{x-d}{c-d} & x \in]c, d], \\ 1 & x = c. \end{cases} \tag{14.11}$$

Then, the trapezoidal FN (TrFN) $\mathcal{T} = \mathcal{T}r(a, b, c, d)$ is determined by its membership function $\mu_{\mathcal{T}} \in [0, 1]^{\mathbb{R}}$ given by the identity

$$\mu_{\mathcal{T}}(x) = \mu_{\mathcal{T}r}(x|a, b, c, d) = \mu_{\mathcal{FN}}(x|a, b, c, d, L_{\mathcal{T}}, R_{\mathcal{T}}). \tag{14.12}$$

For any arbitrary TrFN, $\mathcal{T}r(a, b, c, d)$, we have

$$d(\mathcal{T}r(a, b, c, d)) = \frac{1}{2} \cdot (d + c - b - a), \tag{14.13}$$

$$e(\mathcal{T}r(a,b,c,d)) = \frac{d-c+b-a}{3\cdot d+c-b-3\cdot a}. \tag{14.14}$$

14.3 Ordering of Ordered Fuzzy Numbers

Let us consider the pair $(\mathcal{K},\mathcal{L}) \in \mathbb{F}\times\mathbb{F}$ of FN represented, respectively, by their membership functions $\mu_{\mathcal{K}}, \mu_{\mathcal{L}} \in [0,1]^{\mathbb{R}}$. In space $\mathbb{F}$, we define a relation $\mathcal{K} \succcurlyeq \mathcal{L}$, which reads:

$$FN\mathcal{K}\text{ is greater or equal to }FN\mathcal{L}. \tag{14.15}$$

This relation is, in fact, a fuzzy pre-order $\mathcal{Q} \in \mathcal{F}(\mathbb{F}\times\mathbb{F})$, determined by such membership function $\nu_{\mathcal{Q}} \in [0,1]^{\mathbb{F}\times\mathbb{F}}$ that fulfils the condition [56]

$$\nu_{\mathcal{Q}}(\mathcal{K},\mathcal{L}) = \sup\{\min\{\mu_{\mathcal{K}}(x),\mu_{\mathcal{L}}(z)\} : x \geq z\}. \tag{14.16}$$

From the point view of multivalued logic, the value $\nu_{\mathcal{Q}}(\mathcal{K},\mathcal{L})$ may be interpreted as a truth value of the sentence (14.15). For any $\mathcal{K} = \mathcal{K}(a,b,c,d,L_{\mathcal{K}},R_{\mathcal{K}})$, we have:

$$\nu_{\mathcal{Q}}(\mathcal{K},[\![g]\!]) = \sup\{\mu_{\mathcal{K}}(x) : x \geq g\} = \begin{cases} 0, & g > a, \\ L_{\mathcal{K}}(g), & a \geq g > b, \\ 1, & b \geq g, \end{cases} \tag{14.17}$$

$$\nu_{\mathcal{Q}}([\![g]\!],\mathcal{K}) = \sup\{\mu_{\mathcal{K}}(x) : x \leq g\} = \begin{cases} 1, & c \leq g, \\ R_{\mathcal{K}}(g), & c > g \geq d, \\ 0, & d > g. \end{cases} \tag{14.18}$$

In the next step, we define a relation $\mathcal{K} \succ \mathcal{L}$ in the space $\mathbb{F}$, which reads:

$$FN\mathcal{K}\text{ is greater or equal to }FN\mathcal{L}. \tag{14.19}$$

This relation is a fuzzy strict order $\mathcal{S} \in \mathcal{F}(\mathbb{F}\times\mathbb{F})$ determined by its membership function

$\nu_{\mathcal{S}} \in [0,1]^{\mathbb{F}\times\mathbb{F}}$ given by identity

$$\nu_{\mathcal{S}}(\mathcal{K},\mathcal{L}) = 1 - \nu_{\mathcal{Q}}(\mathcal{L},\mathcal{K}). \tag{14.20}$$

From the point view of multivalued logic, value $\nu_{\mathcal{S}}(\mathcal{K},\mathcal{L})$ may be interpreted as the truth value of the sentence (14.19). For any $\mathcal{K} = \mathcal{K}(a,b,c,d,L_{\mathcal{K}},R_{\mathcal{K}})$, we have

$$\nu_{\mathcal{S}}(\mathcal{K}, [\![g]\!]) = \begin{cases} 0, & c \leq g, \\ 1 - R_{\mathcal{K}}(g), & c > g \geq d, \\ 1, & d > g. \end{cases} \tag{14.21}$$

$$\nu_{\mathcal{S}}([\![g]\!], \mathcal{K}) = \begin{cases} 1, & g > a, \\ 1 - L_{\mathcal{K}}(g), & a \geq g > b, \\ 0, & b \geq g. \end{cases} \tag{14.22}$$

In the last step, we define a relation $\mathcal{K} \approx \mathcal{L}$ in the space $\mathbb{F}$, which reads:

$$FN\mathcal{K} \text{ is greater or equal to } FN\mathcal{L}. \tag{14.23}$$

This relation is a fuzzy equivalence $\mathcal{E} \in \mathcal{F}(\mathbb{F} \times \mathbb{F})$ determined by its membership function
$\nu_{\mathcal{E}} \in [0, 1]^{\mathbb{F}\times\mathbb{F}}$ given by identity

$$\nu_{\mathcal{E}}(\mathcal{K}, \mathcal{L}) = \min\{\nu_{\mathcal{Q}}(\mathcal{K}, \mathcal{L}), \nu_{\mathcal{Q}}(\mathcal{L}, \mathcal{K})\}. \tag{14.24}$$

From the point view of multivalued logic, value $\nu_{\mathcal{E}}(\mathcal{K}, \mathcal{L})$ may be interpreted as the truth value of sentence (14.23).

For any $\mathcal{K} = \mathcal{K}(a, b, c, d, L_{\mathcal{K}}, R_{\mathcal{K}})$, we have:

$$\nu_{\mathcal{S}}(\mathcal{K}, [\![g]\!]) = \nu_{\mathcal{S}}([\![g]\!], \mathcal{K}) = \begin{cases} 0 & g > a, \\ L_{\mathcal{K}}(g) & a \geq g > b, \\ 1 & b \geq g \geq c, \\ R_{\mathcal{K}}(g) & c > g \geq d, \\ 0 & d > g. \end{cases} \tag{14.25}$$

14.4 Imprecise Present Value

In the interest theory, present value (PV) is defined as discounted cash flow. Generally, PV is defined as in [57], that is, as a present equivalent of a payment available in a particular time in future or at the moment. It is determined as the utility of a cash flow [57], which has a subjective nature due to behavioural influences [58]. Imprecise estimation of PV is a result of the subjective approach to security valuation [59]. Therefore, PV is widely accepted as an approximate value, with FNs being one of the main tools of its modelling. In 1985, Ward [60] defined fuzzy PV as a discounted fuzzy forecast of a future cash flow's value. FNs were introduced into financial arithmetic by Buckley [61]. As a result, Ward's definition was then further generalized by [62, 63] and [37] who expand Ward's definition to the case of a future cash flow given as a fuzzy variable. More general definition of the fuzzy PV was proposed by Tsao [64] who assumes that future cash flow can be considered as a fuzzy probabilistic set. All mentioned authors depict PV as a discounted, imprecisely estimated future cash flow. A different approach was proposed by Piasecki [39, 65], where fuzzy PV is estimated by an FN dependent only on the market price and the behavioural premises. On the other hand, security quotes are discreet. Therefore, in [42] and [66], PV is modelled by a discrete FN [67]. Additionally, some applications of fuzzy PV are discussed in [38, 68–71]. Works of Buckley [61], Gutierrez [72], Kuchta [73] and Lesage [74] had previously proved the sensibility of using triangular FN or TrFN as a fuzzy financial arithmetic tool. Regretfully, entropy measure of an arbitrary triangular fuzzy number is constant, which makes it difficult to analyse the impact of the indistinctness on the imprecision of a PV. On the other hand, trapezoidal fuzzy numbers do not have this disadvantage. Therefore, we will imprecisely evaluate PVs by TrFN.

Let us consider a fixed security, for which we observe its market price $\check{C} > 0$. Then, in agreement with assumptions introduced above, we can imprecisely determine PV as TrFN

$$\mathcal{PV} = \mathcal{T}r\left(V_{\min}, V_{\sqsubseteq}, V_{\sqsupseteq}, V_{\max}\right) \tag{14.26}$$

where the nondecreasing sequence $\left(V_{\min}, V_{\sqsubseteq}, \check{C}, V_{\sqsupseteq}, V_{\max}\right) \subset \mathbb{R}^+$ is given as follows:

- $V_{\min}$ is the infimum of values perceptible as equal to PV.
- $V_{\max}$ is the supremum of values perceptible as equal to PV.
- $V_{\sqsubseteq}$ is the supremum of values perceptible as smaller than PV.
- $V_{\sqsupseteq}$ is the infimum of values perceptible as greater than PV.

Then, the PV membership function $\mu_{\mathcal{PV}} = \mu_{\mathcal{T}r}\left(\cdot|V_{\min}, V_{\sqsubseteq}, V_{\sqsupseteq}, V_{\max}\right) \in [0,1]^{\mathbb{R}}$ is described by (14.12).

14.5 Discount Factor of a Security

According to the uncertainty theory, as viewed by Mises [2] and Kaplan [75], any unknown future state of affairs is uncertain. This kind of Mises–Kaplan uncertainty will be further referred to as "uncertainty". The uncertainty results from our lack of knowledge about the future state of affairs. After [3, 4, 76–80], we say that uncertainty may be modelled with probability if and only if we can point out a particular time in future in which the considered state of affairs will be already known. This postulate is referred to as "Kolmogorov's postulate".

By a security, we understand an authorization to receive a future financial revenue, payable to a certain maturity. The value of this revenue is interpreted as an anticipated future value (FV) of the asset. Yet, in the researched case, we can point out this particular time in future in which the considered income value will be already known to the observer. This, together with Kolmogorov's postulate, leads to a conclusion that FV is a random variable. It is worth noting that FV is not burdened by Knight's uncertainty [81].

Let us assume a fixed time horizon $t > 0$ of an investment. Then, a security is determined by two values: anticipated FV V_t and assessed PV V_0. The basic benefit connected with this security is usually characterized by simple return rate r_t given as follows

$$r_t = \frac{V_t - V_0}{V_0}. \tag{14.27}$$

where:

- V_t is a FV described by random variable $\tilde{V}_t : \Omega \to \mathbb{R}^+$.
- V_0 is a PV assessed precisely or approximately.

The set Ω is a set of elementary states ω of the financial market. In a classical approach to the problem of return rate estimation, PV of a security is identified with observed market price $\check{C}$. Thus, the return rate is a random variable determined by identity

$$r_t(\omega) = \frac{\tilde{V}_t(\omega) - \check{C}}{\check{C}}. \tag{14.28}$$

In practice of financial market analysis, the uncertainty risk is usually described by probability distribution of return rate determined by (14.28). Nowadays, we have an extensive knowledge about this subject. Let us assume that mentioned probability distribution is given by cumulative distribution function $F_r(\cdot|\bar{r}) : \mathbb{R} \to [0; 1]$. We assume that the expected value $\bar{r}$ of this distribution exists. Moreover, let us note that we have

$$\tilde{V}_t(\omega) = \check{C} \cdot (1 + r_t(\omega)). \tag{14.29}$$

Let us now consider the case when PV is imprecisely estimated by TrFN $\mathcal{P}v$ represented by its membership function $\mu_{Pv} = \mu_{Pv}(\cdot|V_{\min}, V_{\sqsubseteq}, V_{\sqsupseteq}, V_{\max}) \in [0, 1]^{\mathbb{R}}$ given by identity (14.12).

According to (14.6), (14.27) and (14.29), a return rate is a fuzzy probabilistic set [44] represented by its membership function $\tilde{\rho} \in [0; 1]^{\mathbb{R}\times\Omega}$ as

$$\tilde{\rho}(r, \omega) = \mu_{\mathcal{PV}}\left(\frac{V_t(\omega)}{1+r}\right) = \mu_{\mathcal{PV}}\left(\frac{\check{C} \cdot (1 + r_t(\omega))}{1+r}\right). \tag{14.30}$$

The membership function $\rho \in [0; 1]^{\mathbb{R}}$ of an expected return rate (ERR)$\mathcal{R} \in \mathbb{F}$ is calculated as

$$\rho(r) = \int_{-\infty}^{+\infty} \mu_{\mathcal{PV}}\left(\frac{\check{C}\cdot(1+y)}{1+r}\right)\mathrm{d}F_r(y|\bar{r}) = \mu_{\mathcal{PV}}\left(\frac{\check{C}\cdot(1+\bar{r})}{1+r}\right). \tag{14.31}$$

The ERR $\mathcal{R} \in \mathbb{F}$ is not a TrFN [42, 43]. In [42, 43], it is shown by examples that the expected fuzzy discount factor (EDF) $\mathcal{D} \in \mathbb{F}$ is a better tool for appraising considered securities than the ERR $\mathcal{R} \in \mathbb{F}$. Therefore, we aim to determine the EDF for the considered case. The EDF $\bar{v}$ is calculated using the return rate $\bar{r}$ by the formula

$$\bar{v} = \frac{1}{1+\bar{r}}. \tag{14.32}$$

Therefore, the function $\delta \in [0; 1]^{\mathbb{R}}$, described by

$$\delta(v) = \delta\left(\frac{1}{1+r}\right) = \rho(r), \tag{14.33}$$

is a membership function of the EDF $\mathcal{D} \in \mathbb{F}$ calculated using ERR $\mathcal{R} \in \mathbb{F}$. Combining (14.31) (14.32) and (14.33), we get

$$\begin{aligned}\delta(v) &= \delta\left(\frac{1}{1+r}\right) = \rho\left(\frac{1}{v} - 1\right) = \mu_{PV}\left(\frac{\check{C}\cdot v}{\bar{v}}\right)\\ &= \mu_{\mathcal{PV}}\left(v|V_{\min}\cdot\frac{\bar{v}}{\check{C}}, V_{\sqsubseteq}\cdot\frac{\bar{v}}{\check{C}}, V_{\sqsupseteq}\cdot\frac{\bar{v}}{\check{C}}, V_{\max}\cdot\frac{\bar{v}}{\check{C}}\right).\end{aligned} \tag{14.34}$$

The formal simplicity of obtained EDF description encourages its further application as a portfolio analysis tool. It is proved that for any portfolio, its EDF is a simple function of the component EDFs. Therefore, in the next section we will assume that the basic benefit from a financial instrument is characterized by a fuzzy EDF.

14.6 Premises of Recommendations

Let us consider an arbitrary financial instrument Φ consisting of a single security. Then, in agreement with assumptions introduced in the previous section, the basic benefit from this financial instrument is characterized by a fuzzy EDF

$$\mathcal{D} = \mathcal{T}r\left(D_{\min}, D_{\sqsubseteq}, D_{\sqsupseteq}, D_{\max}\right), \tag{14.35}$$

where the nondecreasing sequence $\left(D_{\min}, D_{\sqsubseteq}, D_{\sqsupseteq}, D_{\max}\right) \subset \mathbb{R}^+$ is given as follows:

- $D_{\min}$ is the infimum of values perceptible as equal to EDF.
- $D_{\max}$ is the supremum of values perceptible as equal to EDF.
- $D_{\sqsubseteq}$ is the supremum of values perceptible as smaller than EDF.

– $D_{\sqsupseteq}$ is the infimum of values perceptible as greater than EDF.

Then, the EDF membership function $\mu_{\mathcal{D}} = \mu_{Tr}(\cdot|D_{\min}, D_{\sqsubseteq}, D_{\sqsupseteq}, D_{\max}) \in [0, 1]^{\mathbb{R}}$ is described by (14.12). EDF $\mathcal{D} \in \mathbb{F}$ will be considered as a primary premise for investment recommendations.

An increase in ambiguity of the EDF $\mathcal{D} \in \mathbb{F}$ suggests a higher number of alternative recommendations to choose from. This may result in making a decision which will be ex post associated with a profit lower than maximal, that is, with a loss of chance. This kind of risk is called an ambiguity risk. The ambiguity risk of fuzzy EDF $\mathcal{D}$ is measured by energy measure.

An increase in the indistinctness of the EDF $\mathcal{D} \in \mathbb{F}$ suggests, on the other hand, that the differences between recommended and not recommended decision alternatives are harder to differentiate. This leads to an increase in the indistinctness risk, which is in a risk of choosing a not recommended option. The indistinctness risk of an fuzzy EDF $\mathcal{D}$ is measured by entropy measure $e(\mathcal{D})$.

The usefulness of a primary investment premise increases in inverse proportion to the value of energy measure $d(\mathcal{D})$ and the entropy measure $e(\mathcal{D})$. The usefulness of primary investment premise is equal to the usefulness of an investment premise which is a monotonic function of the first one.

On the other hand, most well-known models of financial mathematics are described using the concept of ERR. Therefore, using (14.1) and (14.2), the secondary investment premise will be designated as fuzzy ERR

$$\mathcal{R} = \mathcal{R}(R_{\min}, R_{\sqsubseteq}, R_{\sqsupseteq}, R_{\max}, L_{\mathcal{R}}, R_{\mathcal{R}}), \tag{14.36}$$

where the nondecreasing sequence $(D_{\min}, D_{\sqsubseteq}, D_{\sqsupseteq}, D_{\max}) \subset \mathbb{R}^{+}$ is given as follows:

– $R_{\min}$ is the infimum of values perceptible as equal to ERR given as follows

$$R_{\min} = \frac{1}{D_{\max}} - 1, \tag{14.37}$$

– $R_{\max}$ is the supremum of values perceptible as equal to ERR given as follows

$$R_{\max} = \frac{1}{D_{\min}} - 1, \tag{14.38}$$

– $R_{\sqsubseteq}$ is the supremum of values perceptible as smaller than ERR given as follows

$$R_{\sqsubseteq} = \frac{1}{D_{\sqsupseteq}} - 1, \tag{14.39}$$

– $R_{\sqsupseteq}$ is the infimum of values perceptible as greater than ERR given as follows

$$R_{\sqsupseteq} = \frac{1}{D_{\sqsubseteq}} - 1, \tag{14.40}$$

- $L_{\mathcal{R}}$ is left reference function given for $x \in \left[R_{\min}, R_{\sqsubseteq}\right[$ by the identity

$$L_{\mathcal{R}}(x) = R_{\mathcal{D}}\left(\frac{1}{1+x}\right) = \frac{\frac{1}{1+x} - D_{\max}}{D_{\sqsupseteq} - D_{\max}} = \frac{\frac{1}{1+x} - R_{\min}}{R_{\sqsubseteq} - R_{\min}}, \tag{14.41}$$

- $R_{\mathcal{R}}$ is right reference function given for $x \in \left[R_{\min}, R_{\sqsubseteq}\right[$ by the identity

$$R_{\mathcal{R}}(x) = L_{\mathcal{D}}\left(\frac{1}{1+x}\right) = \frac{\frac{1}{1+x} - D_{\min}}{D_{\sqsubseteq} - D_{\min}} = \frac{\frac{1}{1+x} - R_{\max}}{R_{\sqsupseteq} - R_{\max}}. \tag{14.42}$$

Then, the ERR membership function $\mu_{\mathcal{R}} = \mu_{\mathcal{FN}}\left(\cdot|R_{\min}, R_{\sqsubseteq}, R_{\sqsupseteq}, R_{\max}, L_{\mathcal{R}}, R_{\mathcal{R}}\right) \in [0,1]^{\mathbb{R}}$ is described by (14.2).

14.7 Investment Recommendations Dependent on Expected Return

An investment recommendation is counsel given by an advisor to an investor. For convenience, these recommendations may be expressed by means of standardized advices. In this article, we will consider the following vocabulary:

- **Buy** suggests that evaluated security is significantly undervalued.
- **Accumulate** suggests that evaluated security is undervalued.
- **Hold** suggests that evaluated security is fairly valued.
- **Reduce** suggests that evaluated security is overvalued.
- **Sell** suggests that evaluated security is significantly overvalued.

Many advisors use a different terminology and vocabulary when forming advice. Yet, we will concentrate on the five-element advisor's vocabulary considered in [45]. The pieces of advice mentioned above form a set

$$\mathbb{A} = \left\{A^{++}, A^{+}, A^{0}, A^{-}, A^{--}\right\}, \tag{14.43}$$

which is called the advisor's vocabulary, where

- A^{++} denotes the advice **Buy**.
- A^{+} denotes the advice **Accumulate**.
- A^{0} denotes the advice **Hold**.
- A^{-} denotes the advice **Reduce**.

– A^{--} denotes the advice **Sell**.

Let us take into account a fixed financial instrument Φ represented by ERR $\bar{r}$. For such a case, the advisor's counsel depends on the ERR. The quality criterion for the advice can be given as a comparison of values $g(\bar{r})$ and $\hat{G}$ defined as follows:

– $g : \mathbb{R} \to \mathbb{R}$ is an increasing function of substantially justified form.
– $\hat{G}$ denotes the substantially justified limit value.

The function $g : \mathbb{R} \to \mathbb{R}$ serves as a profit index. By denoting the power set of the set $\mathbb{A}$ as $\mathcal{P}(\mathbb{A})$, we define advice choice function $\Lambda : \mathbb{R}^2 \to \mathcal{P}(\mathbb{A})$ as follows

$$\begin{cases} A^{++} \in \Lambda\left(\bar{r}, \check{G}\right) \Leftrightarrow g(\bar{r}) > \hat{G} \Leftrightarrow \neg g(\bar{r}) \leq \hat{G}, \\ A^{+} \in \Lambda\left(\bar{r}, \check{G}\right) \Leftrightarrow g(\bar{r}) \geq \hat{G}, \\ A^{0} \in \Lambda\left(\bar{r}, \check{G}\right) \Leftrightarrow g(\bar{r}) = \hat{G} \Leftrightarrow g(\bar{r}) \geq \hat{G} \wedge g(\bar{r}) \leq \hat{G}, \\ A^{-} \in \Lambda\left(\bar{r}, \check{G}\right) \Leftrightarrow g(\bar{r}) \leq \hat{G}, \\ A^{--} \in \Lambda\left(\bar{r}, \check{G}\right) \Leftrightarrow g(\bar{r}) < \hat{G} \Leftrightarrow \neg g(\bar{r}) \geq \hat{G}. \end{cases} \tag{14.44}$$

This way, we assign the advice subset to a security $\breve{S}$. Value $\Lambda\left(\bar{r}, \check{G}\right)$ is called an investment recommendation. This recommendation may be used as a good starting point for the equity portfolio strategies. On the other hand, the weak point of the proposed choice function is the omission of the fundamental analysis results and the impact of behavioural factors. When analysing the above-stated choice function, it is easy to spot the lack of visible boundaries between the advice **Buy** and **Accumulate** as well as **Reduce** and **Sell**. The justification for this distinction lies in the fundamental analysis and behavioural aspects of the investment process.

14.8 Investment Recommendations Dependent on Fuzzy Expected Return

Let us assume that the basic benefit from a financial instrument Φ is characterized by a given fuzzy ERR $\mathcal{R}$, which may be dependent on some fundamental or behavioural factors.[1] Therefore, advisor's counsel should be dependent on the ERR $\mathcal{R}$, which is determined by its membership function $\mu_{\mathcal{R}} = \mu_{\mathcal{FN}}\left(\cdot | R_{\min}, R_{\sqsubseteq}, R_{\sqsupseteq}, R_{\max}, L_{\mathcal{R}}, R_{\mathcal{R}}\right) \in [0, 1]^{\mathbb{R}}$.

In the first step, we extend the profit index domain $\mathbb{R}$ to the space $\mathbb{F}$. According to (14.5), the profit index $g(\mathcal{R})$ is described by its membership function $\gamma \in [0, 1]^{\mathbb{R}}$

[1] For example, [39, 65].

$$\gamma(x) = \mu_{\mathcal{R}}\left(g^{-1}(x)\right). \tag{14.45}$$

In the second step, we extend the advice choice function's domain $\mathbb{R}^2$ to the set $\mathbb{F} \times \mathbb{R}$. The value of the advice choice function $\Lambda\left(\mathcal{R}, \check{G}\right)$ is described by its membership function $\lambda \in [0, 1]^{\mathbb{A}}$, which is determined [due to (14.17), (14.18), (14.20) and (14.21)] by:

$$\lambda\left(A^{++}\right) = 1 - \sup\left\{\gamma(x) : x \leq \check{G}\right\}, \tag{14.46}$$

$$\lambda\left(A^{+}\right) = \sup\left\{\gamma(x) : x \geq \check{G}\right\}, \tag{14.47}$$

$$\lambda\left(A^{0}\right) = \min\left\{\sup\left\{\gamma(x) : x \geq \check{G}\right\}, \sup\left\{\gamma(x) : x \leq \check{G}\right\}\right\}, \tag{14.48}$$

$$\lambda\left(A^{-}\right) = \sup\left\{\gamma(x) : x \leq \check{G}\right\}, \tag{14.49}$$

$$\lambda\left(A^{--}\right) = 1 - \sup\left\{\gamma(x) : x \geq \check{G}\right\}. \tag{14.50}$$

This way, we define a fuzzy advice choice function $\Lambda : \mathbb{F} \times \mathbb{R} \rightarrow \mathcal{F}(\mathbb{A})$. The value $\Lambda\left(\mathcal{R}, \check{G}\right)$ is called an imprecise investment recommendation. Moreover, the value $\lambda(A)$ may be interpreted as a degree in which the advice $A \in \mathbb{A}$ was chosen.

Above, the ERR is replaced by a fuzzy ERR, which also takes into account fundamental behavioural aspects of decision-making in finance. However, such an increase in cognitive value has its price, that is, the imprecise formulation of investment recommendations. By taking into account the imprecision of information about a security, we cannot precisely indicate the recommended action out of a set of pieces of advice. Each advice is thus recommended to some extent. The investor shifts some of the responsibility to the advisors. For this reason, the investor restricts their choice of investment decisions to advices recommended to the greatest degree. This way, the investor minimizes their individual responsibility for making a financial decision. However, a final investment decision will, in the end, be made by the investor themselves. Guided by their own knowledge and intuition, an investor can choose an advice which is recommended in a lower degree.

However, let us note that:

$$\lambda\left(A^{++}\right) = 1 - \lambda\left(A^{-}\right), \tag{14.51}$$

$$\lambda\left(A^{0}\right) = \min\left\{\lambda\left(A^{+}\right), \lambda\left(A^{-}\right)\right\}, \tag{14.52}$$

$$\lambda\left(A^{--}\right) = 1 - \lambda\left(A^{+}\right). \tag{14.53}$$

This shows that function values $\lambda\left(A^{+}\right)$ and $\lambda\left(A^{-}\right)$ are sufficient to determine an imprecise investment recommendation. For this reason, we will use them when creating a specific method of choosing advice. Let us note that using an imprecisely estimated return allows for determining differences between advice **Buy** and **Accumulate** and between **Reduce** and **Sell**.

In the next two sections, examples of imprecise recommendation methodologies are presented. We limit our discussion to the case when the security return is described by means of a simple return rate given by (14.28). All methodologies presented below are generalizations of well-know classical methodologies to the fuzzy case.

14.9 Financial Equilibrium Criteria

Each financial equilibrium model is given as the comparison of expected return on a considered security and an expected return of the market portfolio. We will consider fixed financial instrument Φ.

14.9.1 Sharpe's Ratio

It is a well-known fact that any financial instrument may be represented by the pair $\left(\varrho, \varsigma^2\right)$ where the symbol ϱ denotes ERR and the symbol ς^2 denotes the return rate variations. We assume that there exists a risk-free bond represented by a pair $(r_0, 0)$ and a market portfolio represented by $\left(r_M, \sigma_M^2\right)$. If the financial instrument Φ is represented by a pair $\left(\bar{r}, \sigma^2\right)$, then Sharpe [82] defines a profit index $g : \mathbb{R} \to \mathbb{R}$ and a limit value $\hat{G}$ as follows

$$g(\bar{r}) = \frac{\bar{r} - r_0}{\sigma}, \tag{14.54}$$

$$\hat{G} = \frac{r_M - r_0}{\sigma_M}. \tag{14.55}$$

Sharpe's profit index estimates the amount of premium per overall risk unit. Sharpe's limit value is equal to the premium of the market portfolio risk.

If the financial instrument Φ is represented by the pair $\left(\mathcal{R}, \sigma^2\right)$, then profit index $g(\mathcal{R})$ is described by its membership function $\gamma \in [0, 1]^{\mathbb{R}}$ determined as follows

$$\gamma(x) = \mu_{\mathcal{R}}(\sigma \cdot x + r_0). \tag{14.56}$$

Then, in accordance with (14.47) and (14.49) we have

$$\lambda\left(A^+\right) = \sup\left\{\gamma(x) : x \geq \frac{r_M - r_0}{\sigma_M}\right\} = \sup\left\{\mu_{\mathcal{R}}(r) : \frac{r - r_0}{\sigma} \geq \frac{r_M - r_0}{\sigma_M}\right\}, \tag{14.57}$$

$$\lambda\left(A^{-}\right)=\sup\left\{\gamma(x): x \leq \frac{r_M-r_0}{\sigma_M}\right\}=\sup\left\{\mu_{\mathcal{R}}(r): \frac{r-r_0}{\sigma} \leq \frac{r_M-r_0}{\sigma_M}\right\}. \tag{14.58}$$

Values $\lambda\left(A^{++}\right)$, $\lambda\left(A^{0}\right)$ and $\lambda\left(A^{--}\right)$ are determined by relations (14.51), (14.52) and (14.53), respectively.

14.9.2 Jensen's Alpha

On the capital market, we can observe a risk-free return r_0 and the expected market return r_M. Financial instrument Φ is represented by a pair $(\bar{r}, \beta)$ where β is the beta coefficient of the CAPM model assigned to this instrument. Jensen [83] defines the profit index $g : \mathbb{R} \to \mathbb{R}$ and the limit value $\hat{G}$ as follows

$$g(\bar{r})=\bar{r}-\beta\cdot(r_M-r_0), \tag{14.59}$$

$$\hat{G}=r_0. \tag{14.60}$$

Jensen's profit index estimates the amount of premium for the market portfolio risk. Jensen's limit value is equal to the risk-free return.

If a the financial instrument Φ is represented by a pair $(\mathcal{R}, \beta)$, then profit index $g(\mathcal{R})$ is described by its membership function $\gamma \in [0,1]^{\mathbb{R}}$ and determined as follows

$$\gamma(x)=\mu_{\mathcal{R}}(x+\beta\cdot(r_M-r_0)). \tag{14.61}$$

In accordance with (14.47) and (14.49), we have

$$\lambda\left(A^{+}\right)=\sup\{\gamma(x): x \geq r_0\}=\sup\{\mu_{\mathcal{R}}(r): r-\beta\cdot(r_M-r_0) \geq r_0\}, \tag{14.62}$$

$$\lambda\left(A^{-}\right)=\sup\{\gamma(x): x \leq r_0\}=\sup\{\mu_{\mathcal{R}}(r): r-\beta\cdot(r_M-r_0) \leq r_0\}. \tag{14.63}$$

The values $\lambda\left(A^{++}\right)$, $\lambda\left(A^{0}\right)$ and $\lambda\left(A^{--}\right)$ are determined by relations (14.51), (14.52) and (14.53), respectively.

14.9.3 Treynor's Ratio

Let us make the same assumptions as those used in subsection 14.9.2. Additionally, we assume that the security return is positively correlated with the market portfolio return. Treynor [84] defines the profit index $g : \mathbb{R} \to \mathbb{R}$ and the limit value $\hat{G}$ as follows

$$g(\bar{r}) = \frac{\bar{r} - r_0}{\beta}, \tag{14.64}$$

$$\hat{G} = r_M - r_0. \tag{14.65}$$

Treynor's profit index estimates the amount of premium per market risk unit. Treynor's limit value is equal to the premium of the market risk.

If a financial instrument Φ is represented by a pair $(\mathcal{R}, \beta)$, then the profit index $g(\mathcal{R})$ is described by its membership function $\gamma \in [0, 1]^{\mathbb{R}}$ and determined as follows

$$\gamma(x) = \mu_{\mathcal{R}}(\beta \cdot x + r_0). \tag{14.66}$$

In accordance with (14.47) and (14.49), we have

$$\lambda\left(A^+\right) = \sup\{\gamma(x) : x \geq r_M - r_0\} = \sup\left\{\mu_{\mathcal{R}}(r) : \frac{r - r_0}{\beta_s} \geq r_M - r_0\right\}, \tag{14.67}$$

$$\lambda\left(A^-\right) = \sup\{\gamma(x) : x \leq r_M - r_0\} = \sup\left\{\mu_{\mathcal{R}}(r) : \frac{r - r_0}{\beta_s} \leq r_M - r_0\right\}. \tag{14.68}$$

The values $\lambda\left(A^{++}\right)$, $\lambda\left(A^0\right)$ and $\lambda\left(A^{--}\right)$ are determined by relations (14.51), (14.52) and (14.53), respectively. Investment recommendation made by means of Treynor's ratio is identical with investment recommendation made by Jensen's alpha.

14.10 The Safety-First Criteria

We consider the simple return rate $\tilde{r}(\omega)$ of a fixed security. For each assumed $\bar{r} \in \mathbb{R}$ of an expected simple return rate, the probability distribution is given by a cumulative distribution function $F(\cdot|r) : \mathbb{R} \to [0; 1]$, which is strictly increasing and continuous. Then, the safety condition [23] is given in the following way

$$F(L|r) = \varepsilon, \tag{14.69}$$

- L denotes minimum acceptable return rate.
- ε is equal to probability realization of a return below the minimum acceptable rate.

The realization of a return below the minimum acceptable rate is identified with loss. Therefore, the variable ε denotes the loss probability.

Additionally, let us note that the function $G_l : \mathbb{R} \to [0; 1]$ is defined for fixed $l \in R$ as follows

$$G_l(r) = F(l|r). \tag{14.70}$$

Let us take into account a fixed financial instrument Φ with expected return $\bar{r}$. The distribution of this return is described by its cumulative distribution function $F(\cdot|\bar{r}) : \mathbb{R} \to [0; 1]$.

14.10.1 Roy's Criterion

Roy's criterion [23] says that for a fixed acceptable minimum return rate L, the investor minimizes the loss probability. Additionally, in order to ensure the financial security, the investor assumes a maximum level ε^* of a loss probability. Then, the profit index $g : \mathbb{R} \to [-1; 0]$ and the limit value $\hat{G}$ are defined as follows

$$g(\bar{r}) = -G_L(\bar{r}), \tag{14.71}$$

$$\hat{G} = -\varepsilon^*. \tag{14.72}$$

If a financial instrument Φ is represented by the fuzzy ERR $\mathcal{R}$, then profit index $g(\mathcal{R})$ is described by its membership function $\gamma \in [0, 1]^{[-1,0]}$ and determined as follows

$$\gamma(x) = \mu_{\mathcal{R}}\big(G_L^{-1}(-x)\big). \tag{14.73}$$

In accordance with (14.47) and (14.49), we have

$$\lambda\big(A^+\big) = \sup\big\{\gamma(x) : x \geq -\varepsilon^*\big\} = \sup\big\{\mu_{\mathcal{R}}(r) : F(L|r) \leq \varepsilon^*\big\}, \tag{14.74}$$

$$\lambda\big(A^-\big) = \sup\big\{\gamma(x) : x \leq -\varepsilon^*\big\} = \sup\big\{\mu_{\mathcal{R}}(r) : F(L|r) \geq \varepsilon^*\big\}. \tag{14.75}$$

The values $\lambda\big(A^{++}\big)$, $\lambda\big(A^0\big)$ and $\lambda\big(A^{--}\big)$ are determined by relations (14.51), (14.52) and (14.53), respectively.

14.10.2 Kataoka's Criterion

Kataoka's criterion [85] says that for a fixed loss probability ε, investor maximizes the acceptable minimum return rate. In addition, in order to ensure the interest yield, the investor assumes a minimum level L^* of a return. Then, the profit index g : $[0; 1] \to \mathbb{R}$ and the limit value $\hat{G}$ are defined in the following way

$$g(\bar{r}) = F^{-1}(\varepsilon|r), \tag{14.76}$$

$$\hat{G} = L^*. \tag{14.77}$$

If the financial instrument Φ is represented by a fuzzy ERR $\mathcal{R}$, then the profit index $g(\mathcal{R})$ is described by its membership function $\gamma \in [0, 1]^{\mathbb{R}}$ and determined as follows

$$\gamma(x) = \mu_{\mathcal{R}}(G_{\varepsilon}(x)). \tag{14.78}$$

In accordance with (14.47) and (14.49), we have

$$\lambda\left(A^{+}\right) = \sup\left\{\gamma(x) : x \geq L^{*}\right\} = \sup\left\{\mu_{\mathcal{R}}(r) : (\varepsilon|r) \geq L^{*}\right\}, \tag{14.79}$$

$$\lambda\left(A^{-}\right) = \sup\left\{\gamma(x) : x \leq L^{*}\right\} = \sup\left\{\mu_{\mathcal{R}}(r) : F_{s}^{-1}(\varepsilon|r) \leq L^{*}\right\} \tag{14.80}$$

The values $\lambda\left(A^{++}\right)$, $\lambda\left(A^{0}\right)$ and $\lambda\left(A^{--}\right)$ are determined by relations (14.51), (14.52) and (14.53), respectively.

14.10.3 Telser's Criterion

Based on the safety and profitability of an investment, investor assumes a minimum level L^{*} of acceptable return and a maximum level ε^{*} of loss probability. If the probability that return on a financial instrument Φ is not acceptable is lower than the acceptable loss probability, then Φ is called safe haven security.

Let the return on financial instrument Φ be given as a fuzzy probabilistic set outlined in (14.30) by its membership function $\rho : \mathbb{R} \times \Omega \to [0; 1]$. Then, for any acceptable minimum return $L \in \mathbb{R}$, the loss is a fuzzy probabilistic set described by a membership function $\eta(\cdot|L) : \Omega \to [0; 1]$ and determined as follows

$$\eta(\omega|L) = \sup\{\rho(r, \omega) : r < L\} = \sup\left\{\mu_{\mathcal{P}v}\left(\tilde{V}_t(\omega) \cdot (1 + r)^{-1}\right) : r < L\right\}. \tag{14.81}$$

In accordance with (14.3), for expected return $\bar{r}$, the probability distribution of FV $\tilde{V}_t : \Omega \to \mathbb{R}^{+}$ is described by conditional cumulative distribution function $F_V(\cdot|\bar{r}) : \mathbb{R}^{+} \to [0; 1]$ determined in the following way

$$F_V(x|\bar{r}) = F_s\left(\frac{x - \check{C}}{\check{C}}|\bar{r}\right). \tag{14.82}$$

The loss probability $P_s(L)$ may be calculated as follows [86]

$$P_s(L) = \int_{-\infty}^{+\infty} \sup\left\{\mu_{\mathcal{P}v}\left(x \cdot (1 + r)^{-1}\right) : r < L\right\} \mathrm{d}F_V(x|\bar{r})$$

$$= \int_{-\infty}^{+\infty} \sup\{\mu_{\mathcal{P}v}\left(x \cdot (1+t)(1+r)^{-1}\right) : r < L\} \mathrm{d}F(t|\bar{r})$$

$$= \int_{-\infty}^{L} \mathrm{d}F(t|\bar{r}) + \int_{L}^{+\infty} \mu\left(\check{C} \cdot (1+t) \cdot (1+L)^{-1} | \check{C}\right) \mathrm{d}F(t|\bar{r}). \quad (14.83)$$

The security $\check{S}$ is safe haven iff it fulfils the condition

$$P_s\left(L^*\right) \leq \varepsilon^*. \quad (14.84)$$

Telsers's criterion [87] says that the investor maximizes the return on safe haven securities. In addition, due to the profitability investment, the investor takes into account the equilibrium rate $r^* > L^*$. Then, the profit index $g : \mathbb{R} \to \mathbb{R}$ and the limit value $\hat{G}$ are defined in following way

$$g(\bar{r}) = \bar{r}, \quad (14.85)$$

$$\hat{G} = r^*. \quad (14.86)$$

If financial instrument Φ is represented by a fuzzy ERR $\mathcal{R}$, then profit index $g(\mathcal{R})$ is described by its membership function $\gamma \in [0, 1]^{\mathbb{R}}$ determined as follows

$$\gamma(x) = \mu_{\mathcal{R}}(x). \quad (14.87)$$

In accordance with (14.47) and (14.49), we have

$$\lambda\left(A^+\right) = \sup\{\mu_{\mathcal{R}}(r) : r \geq r^*\}, \quad (14.88)$$

$$\lambda\left(A^-\right) = \sup\{\mu_{\mathcal{R}}(r) : r \leq r^*\}. \quad (14.89)$$

The values $\lambda\left(A^{++}\right)$, $\lambda\left(A^{0}\right)$ and $\lambda\left(A^{--}\right)$ are determined by relations (14.51), (14.52) and (14.53), respectively.

14.11 Summary

Imprecision is relevant to the investment decision-making process. It is proved above that imprecise present value and random future value may be considered as a sufficient basis for an investment recommendation. Due to evaluating the present value by a trapezoidal fuzzy number, the obtained model has a computational complexity that is lower than computational complexity of the model presented in [45, 88, 89]. The low computational complexity of introduced models has its price—the detailed assumptions about the present value. On the other hand, the accepted restrictions are in line with practical applications of fuzzy arithmetic.

Obtained results may be applied in behavioural finance theory as a normative model for investment decisions. The results may also provide theoretical foundations for constructing an investment decision support system.

On the other hand, imprecise estimation of an expected return could be a consequence of taking into account the behavioural aspects of an investment process. Thus, we showed that the behavioural premises can influence investment recommendations in a controlled manner.

In this paper, the main achievement lies in proposing a useful methodology for imprecise investment recommendations. Moreover, the paper also offers original generalization of the financial equilibrium criteria and of the safety-first criteria to the fuzzy case.

Obtained results may well be a starting point for a future investigation of the impact of the present value's imprecision on imprecision of investment recommendations.

Acknowledgements The article is financed by the National Science Centre, Poland, Grant No. 2015/17/N/HS4/00206.

References

1. Zadeh, L.: Fuzzy sets. Inf. Control **8**, 338–353 (1965). https://doi.org/10.1016/S0019-9958(65)90241-X
2. von Mises, L.: The Ultimate Foundation of Economic Science an Essay on Method. D. Van Nostrand Company Inc, Princeton (1962)
3. Kolmogorov, A.N.: Grundbegriffe der Wahrscheinlichkeitsrechnung. Julius Springer, Berlin (1933). https://doi.org/10.1007/978-3-642-49888-6
4. Kolmogorov, A.N.: Foundations of the Theory of Probability. Chelsea Publishing Company, New York (1956)
5. Li, X., Quin, Z., Kar, S.: Mean-variance-skewness model for portfolio selections with fuzzy returns. Eur. J. Oper. Res. **202**(1), 239 (2010). https://doi.org/10.1016/j.ejor.2009.05.003
6. Quin, Z., Wen, M., Gu, C.: Mean-absolute deviation portfolio selection model with fuzzy returns. Iran. J. Fuzzy Syst. **8**(4), 61 (2011)
7. Tsaur, R.: Fuzzy portfolio model with different investor risk attitudes. Eur. J. Oper. Res. **227**, 385 (2013). https://doi.org/10.1016/j.ejor.2012.10.036
8. Tanaka, H., Guo, P., Turksen, B.: Portfolio selection based on fuzzy probabilities and possibility distributions. Fuzzy sets Syst. **111**, 387 (2000). https://doi.org/10.1016/S0165-0114(98)00041-4
9. Duan, L., Stahlecker, P.: A portfolio selection model using fuzzy returns. Fuzzy Optim. Decis. Mak. **10**(2), 167–191 (2011). https://doi.org/10.1007/s10700-011-9101-x
10. Guo, H., Sun, B., Karimi, H.R., Ge, Y., Jin, W.: Fuzzy investment portfolio selection models based on interval analysis approach. Math. Probl. Eng. (2012). https://doi.org/10.1155/2012/628295
11. Gupta, P., Mittal, G., Mehlawat, M.K.: Multiobjective expected value model for portfolio selection in fuzzy environment. Optim. Lett. **7**, 1765 (2013). https://doi.org/10.1007/s11590-012-0521-5
12. Gupta, P., Mittal, G., Saxena, A.: Asset portfolio optimization using fuzzy mathematical programming. Inf. Sci. **178**, 1734 (2013). https://doi.org/10.1016/j.ins.2007.10.025

13. Huang, X., Shen, W.: Multi-period mean-variance model with transaction cost for fuzzy portfolio selection. In: Seventh International Conference on Fuzzy Systems and Knowledge Discovery, Yantai, Shandong, pp. 894–898 (2010). https://doi.org/10.1109/FSKD.2010.5569108
14. Liu, Y., Sun, L.: Comparative research of portfolio model using fuzzy theory. In: Fourth International Conference on Fuzzy Systems and Knowledge Discovery, Haikou, pp. 106–110 (2007). https://doi.org/10.1109/FSKD.2007.223
15. Liu, Y.-J., Zhang, W.-G.: Fuzzy portfolio optimization model under real constraints. Insur. Math. Econ. **53**(3), 704–711 (2013). https://doi.org/10.1016/j.insmatheco.2013.09.005
16. Wang, S., Zhu, S.: On fuzzy portfolio selection problems. Fuzzy Optim. Decis Mak **1**, 361 (2002). https://doi.org/10.1023/A:1020907229361
17. Wu, X.-L., Liu, Y.K.: Optimizing fuzzy portfolio selection problems by parametric quadratic programming. Fuzzy Optim. Decis. Mak. **11**(4), 411–449 (2012). https://doi.org/10.1023/A:1015731117218
18. Mehlawat, M.K.: Credibilistic mean-entropy models for multi-period portfolio selection with multi-choice aspiration levels. Inf. Sci. **345**, 9–26 (2016). https://doi.org/10.1016/j.ins.2016.01.042
19. Guo, S., Yu, L., Li, X., Kar, S.: Fuzzy multi-period portfolio selection with different investment horizons. Eur. J. Oper. Res. **254**(3), 1026–1035 (2016). https://doi.org/10.1016/j.ejor.2016.04.055
20. Peng, J., Mok, H.M.K., Tse, W.-M.: Credibility programming approach to fuzzy portfolio selection problems. Int. Conf. Mach. Learn. Cybern. Guangzhou, China **4**, 2523–2528 (2005). https://doi.org/10.1109/ICMLC.2005.1527368
21. Li, Ch., Jin, J.: Fuzzy portfolio optimization model with fuzzy numbers. In: Li, S., Wang, X., Okazaki, Y., Kawabe, J., Murofushi, T., Guan, L. (eds.) Nonlinear Mathematics for Uncertainty and its Applications, Advances in Intelligent and Soft Computing, vol. 100, pp. 557–565 (2011). https://doi.org/10.1007/978-3-642-22833-9_68
22. Li, J., Xu, J.: Multi-objective portfolio selection model with fuzzy random returns and a compromise approach-based genetic algorithm. Inf. Sci. **220**, 507 (2013). https://doi.org/10.1016/j.ins.2012.07.005
23. Roy, A.D.: Safety-first and the holding of assets. Econometrics **20**, 431–449 (1952)
24. Yan, L.: Optimal portfolio selection models with uncertain returns. Modern applied science **3**(8), 76 (2009)
25. Zhang, Y., Li, X., Wong, H.S., Tan, L.: Fuzzy multi-objective portfolio selection model with transaction costs. In: IEEE International Conference on Fuzzy Systems, Jeju Island, pp. 273–278 (2009). https://doi.org/10.1109/FUZZY.2009.5277135
26. Zhang, X., Zhang, W.-G., Xiao, W.: Multi-period portfolio optimization under possibility measures. Econ. Modell. **35**, 401–408 (2013). https://doi.org/10.1016/j.econmod.2013.07.023
27. Haifeng, G., Bai Qing, S., Hamid, R.K., Yuanjing, Ge, Weiquan, J.: Fuzzy investment portfolio selection models based on interval analysis approach. Math. Probl. Eng. (2012). https://doi.org/10.1155/2012/628295
28. Huang, X.: Two new models for portfolio selection with stochastic returns taking fuzzy information. Eur. J. Oper. Res. **180**(1), 396–405 (2007)
29. Huang, X.: Portfolio selection with fuzzy return. J. Intell. Fuzzy Syst. **18**(4), 383–390 (2007)
30. Kahraman, C., Ruan, D., Tolga, E.: Capital budgeting techniques using discounted fuzzy versus probabilistic cash flows. Inf. Sci. 142 (2002). https://doi.org/10.1016/S0020-0255(02)00157-3
31. Fang, Y., Lai, K.K., Wang, S.: Fuzzy portfolio optimization. Theory and methods Lecture Notes in Economics and Mathematical Systems 609, Springer, Berlin (2008)
32. Gupta, P., Mehlawat, M.K., Inuiguchi, M., Chandra, S.: Fuzzy portfolio optimization. Advances in Hybrid Multi-criteria Methodologies, Studies in Fuzziness and Soft Computing 316, Springer, Berlin (2014). https://doi.org/10.1007/978-3-642-54652-5
33. Kosko, B.: Fuzziness vs probability. Int. J. General Syst. **17**(2/3), 211–240 (1990). https://doi.org/10.1080/03081079008935108
34. Markowitz, H.S.M.: Portfolio selection. J. Finan. **7**(1), 77–91 (1952). https://doi.org/10.1111/j.1540-6261.1952.tb01525.x

35. Hao, F.F., Liu, Y.K.: Portfolio selection problem in fuzzy random decision systems. In: 3rd International Conference on Innovative Computing Information and Control, Dalian, Liaoning, pp. 271–271 (2008). https://doi.org/10.1109/ICICIC.2008.423
36. Hasuike, T., Katagiri, H., Ishii, H.: Portfolio selection problems with random fuzzy variable returns. In: 2007 IEEE International Fuzzy Systems Conference, London, pp. 1–6 (2007). https://doi.org/10.1109/FUZZY.2007.4295402
37. Huang, X.: Risk curve and fuzzy portfolio selection, International Journal Production. Economics **106**, 1102–1112 (2007)
38. Piasecki, K.: Effectiveness of securities with fuzzy probabilistic return. Oper. Res. Decisions **21**(2), 65–78 (2011)
39. Piasecki, K., Siwek, J.: Behavioural present value defined as fuzzy number—a new approach. Folia Oeconomica Stetinensia **15**(2), 27–41 (2015). https://doi.org/10.1515/foli-2015-0033
40. Piasecki, K., Siwek, J.: Two-asset portfolio with triangular discrete fuzzy present value. In: Szkutnik W et al (eds.) 8th International Scientific Conference, Analysis of International Relations 2017. Methods and Models of Regional Development, Conference Proceedings, Wyd. UE, Katowice, pp. 39–46 (2017)
41. Piasecki, K., Siwek, J.: Two-Assets Portfolio with Triangular Fuzzy Present Values. Springer, Berlin (2018)
42. Piasecki, K., Siwek, J.: Two-assets portfolio with trapezoidal fuzzy present values. In Szkutnik, W. et al. (eds.) 9th International Scientific Conference Analysis of International Relations 2018. Methods and Models of Regional Development. Winter Edition, Conference Proceedings, Wyd. UE, Katowice, pp. 76–82 (2018)
43. Piasecki, K., Siwek, J.: Multi-assets portfolio with trapezoidal fuzzy present values, Statistical Review (in print) (2018)
44. Hiroto, K.: Concepts of probabilistic sets. Fuzzy Sets Syst. **5**, 31–46 (1981)
45. Piasecki, K.: On imprecise investment recommendations. Stud. Logic, Gramm. Rhetoric **37**(50), 179 (2014). https://doi.org/10.2478/slrg-2014-0024
46. Dubois, D., Prade, H.: Operations on fuzzy numbers. Int. J. Syst. Sci. **9**, 613–626 (1978). https://doi.org/10.1080/00207727808941724
47. Goetschel, R., Voxman, W.: Elementary fuzzy calculus. Fuzzy Sets Syst. **18**, 31–43 (1986). https://doi.org/10.1016/0165-0114(86)90026-6
48. Zadeh, L.: The concept of a linguistic variable and its application to approximate reasoning-I. Inf. Sci. **8**, 199 (1975). https://doi.org/10.1016/0020-0255(75)90036-5
49. Zadeh, L.: The concept of a linguistic variable and its application to approximate reasoning-II. Inf. Sci. **8**, 301 (1975). https://doi.org/10.1016/0020-0255(75)90046-8
50. Zadeh, L.: The concept of a linguistic variable and its application to approximate reasoning-III. Inf. Sci. **8**, 43 (1975). https://doi.org/10.1016/0020-0255(75)90017-1
51. Klir, G.J.: Developments in uncertainty-based information. Adv. Comput. **36**, 255–332 (1993)
52. de Luca, A., Termini, S.: A definition of a non-probabilistic entropy in the settings of fuzzy set theory. Inform. Contr. **20**, 301–313 (1972)
53. de Luca, A., Termini, S.: Entropy and energy measures of fuzzy sets. In: Gupta, M.M., Ragade, R.K., Yager, R.R. (eds.) Advances in Fuzzy Set Theory and Applications, pp. 321–338 (1979)
54. Piasecki, K.: Some remarks on axiomatic definition of entropy measure. J. Intell. Fuzzy Syst. **33**(3), 1945–1952 (2017). https://doi.org/10.3233/JIFS-15364
55. Kosko, B.: Fuzzy entropy and conditioning. Inf. Sci. **40**, 165–174 (1993). https://doi.org/10.1016/0020-0255(86)90006-x
56. Orlovsky, S.A.: Decision making with a fuzzy preference relation. Fuzzy Sets Syst. **1**(3), 155–167 (1978). https://doi.org/10.1016/0165-0114(78)90001-5
57. Piasecki, K.: Basis of financial arithmetic from the viewpoint of the utility theory. Oper. Res. Decisions **03**, 37–53 (2012)
58. Dacey, R., Zielonka, P.: A detailed prospect theory explanation of the disposition effect. J. Behav. Finan **2**(4), 43–50 (2005)
59. Barberis, N., Shleifer, A., Vishny, R.: A model of investor sentiment. J. Financ. Econ. **49**, 307–343 (1998)

60. Ward, T.L. Discounted fuzzy cash flow analysis. In; 1985 Fall Industrial Engineering Conference Proceedings, pp. 476–481 (1985)
61. Buckley, I.J.: The fuzzy mathematics of finance. Fuzzy Sets and Systems. **21**, 257–273 (1987). https://doi.org/10.1016/0165-0114(87)90128-X
62. Greenhut, J.G., Norman, G., Temponi, C.T.: Towards a fuzzy theory of oligopolistic competition, IEEE Proceedings of ISUMA-NAFIPS, pp. 286–291 (1995)
63. Sheen, J.N.: Fuzzy economical analysis of cogeneration project, TENCON 2004. In: 2004 IEEE Region 10 Conference, vol. 3, pp. 311–314 (2004). https://doi.org/10.1109/TENCON.2004.1414769
64. Tsao, C.-T.: Assessing the probabilistic fuzzy Net Present Value for a capital, Investment choice using fuzzy arithmetic. J Chin. Ins. Industr. Eng. **22**(2), 106–118 (2005)
65. Piasecki, K.: Behavioural present value. SSRN Electron. Jo. nr 01/2011 (2011). https://doi.org/10.2139/ssrn.1729351
66. Siwek, J.: Multiple asset portfolio with present value given as a discrete fuzzy number. In: Prazak P. (ed.) 35th International Conference Mathematical Methods in Economics MME 2017. Conference Proceedings. Gaudeamus, University of Hradec Kralove (2017)
67. Voxman, W.: Canonical representations of discrete fuzzy numbers. Fuzzy Sets Syst **54**, 457–466 (2001). https://doi.org/10.1016/S0165-0114(99)00053-6
68. Baerecke, T., Bouchon-Meunier, B., Detyniecki, M.: Fuzzy present value. In: Computational Intelligence for Financial Engineering and Economics, 2011 IEEE Symposium, Paris, pp. 1–6 (2011)
69. Biswas, P., Pramanik, S.: Fuzzy approach to replacement problem with value of money changes with time. Int. J. Comput. Appl. **30**(10), 28 (2011). https://doi.org/10.5120/3676-5151
70. Chiu, C.Y., Park, C.S.: Fuzzy cash flow analysis using present worth criterion. Eng. Econ. **39**(2), 113–138 (1994). https://doi.org/10.1080/00137919408903117
71. Nosrstpour, M., Nazeri, A., Meftahi, H.: Fuzzy net present value for engineering analysis. Manag. Sci. Lett. **2**, 2153 (2012)
72. Gutierrez, I.: Fuzzy numbers and Net Present Value. Scand. J. Mgmt. **5**(2), 149–159 (1989)
73. Kuchta, D.: Fuzzy capital budgeting. Fuzzy Sets Syst. **111**, 367–385 (2000). https://doi.org/10.1016/S0165-0114(98)00088-8
74. Lesage, C.: Discounted cash-flows analysis, an interactive fuzzy arithmetic approach. Eur. J. Econ. Soc. Syst. **15**(2), 49–68 (2001)
75. Kaplan, S., Barish, N.N.: Decision-making allowing uncertainty of future investment opportunities. Manage. Sci. **13**(10), B569–B577 (1967). https://doi.org/10.1287/mnsc.13.10.B569
76. Caplan, B.: Probability, common sense, and realism: a reply to Hulsmann and Block. The Quarterly Journal of Austrian Economics **4**(2), 69–86 (2001)
77. Czerwiński, Z.: Enumerative induction and the theory of games. Studialogica **10**, 24–36 (1960). https://doi.org/10.1007/BF02120396
78. von Lambalgen, M.: Randomness and foundations of probability: von Mises' axiomatization of random sequences. Inst. Math. Stat. Lect. Notes—Monogr. Ser. **30**, 347–367 (1996)
79. von Mises, R.: Probability, Statistics and Truth. The Macmillan Company, New York (1957)
80. Sadowski, W.: Forecasting and decisionmaking, Quantitative Wirtschafts- und Unternehmensforschung, Springer-Verlag, Berlin Heidelberg (1980)
81. Knight, F.H.: Risk, Uncertainty, and Profit. Hart, Schaffner & Marx; Houghton Mifflin Company, Boston, MA (1921)
82. Sharpe, W.F.: Mutual fund performance. J. Bus. **19**, 119–138 (1966)
83. Jensen, M.C.: Risk and pricing of capital assets, and the evaluation of investments portfolios. J. Bus. **42**(2), 167–247 (1969)
84. Treynor, J.L.: How to rate management of investment fund. Harvard Bus. Rev. **43**, 63–75 (1965)
85. Kataoka, S.: A stochastic programming model. Econometrica **31**(1/2), 181–196 (1963)
86. Zadeh, L.A.: Probability measures of fuzzy events. J. Math. Anal. Appl. **23**, 421–427 (1968)
87. Telser, L.G.: Safety first and hedging. Rev. Econ. Stud. **23**(2), 1–16 (1955)

88. Lin, P., Watada, J., Wu, B.: Portfolio selection model with interval values based on fuzzy probability distribution functions. Int. J. Innov. Comput. Inf. Contr. **8**(8), 5935 (2012)
89. Saborido, R., Ruiz, A.B., Bermúdez, J.D., Vercher, E., Luque, M.: Evolutionary multi-objective optimization algorithms for fuzzy portfolio selection. Appl. Soft Comput. **39**, 48–63 (2016). https://doi.org/10.1016/j.asoc.2015.11.005

Chapter 15
Application Quantile-Based Risk Measures in Sector Portfolio Analysis—Warsaw Stock Exchange Approach

Grażyna Trzpiot

Abstract The measurement of financial risk has been one of the main goals of the investors as well as actuaries and insurance practitioners. Measuring the risk of a financial portfolio involves firstly estimating the loss distribution of the portfolio, next computing chosen risk measure. In the resent study, the robustness of risk measurement procedures and their sensitivity into point out for the dataset in present. The results show a gap between the subadditivity and robustness of risk measurement procedures. We apply into analyses alternative risk measurement procedures that possess the robustness property. The quantile-based risk measures have been applied in sector portfolio analysis for the dataset from Warsaw Stock Exchange.

Keywords Risk measurement · Value-at-risk · Expected shortfall · Robustness

JEL Classification G11 · C19

15.1 Introduction

The main aim of quantitative modeling in finance is to quantify the risk, especially the risk of financial portfolios. The Basel Committee guidelines for risk-based requirements for regulatory capital, and frequent use of Value-at-Risk, had created related risk measurement methodologies and methodologies for measuring of the risk of financial portfolios [1–3, 8]. Generally, in theoretical approach to risk measurement, a risk measure is represented as an assignment to each random payoff a number (a measure of risk). The goal in most of theoretical approach has been on the properties of defined maps and requirements for the risk measurement procedure to be coherent, in a static or dynamic setting. Usually, in real applications, the probability distribution is unknown and should be estimated from (historical) data, which means as part of the risk measurement procedure. Thus, in practice, measuring the risk of

G. Trzpiot (✉)
University of Economics in Katowice, Katowice, Poland
e-mail: grazyna.trzpiot@ue.katowice.pl

W. Tarczyński and K. Nermend (eds.), *Effective Investments on Capital Markets*, Springer Proceedings in Business and Economics,
https://doi.org/10.1007/978-3-030-21274-2_15

a financial portfolio involves two steps: estimating the loss distribution of the portfolio from available observations and computing a risk measure that we chosen for measures the risk of this loss distribution. Estimation method connected with these procedure errors on the portfolio loss distribution can have an important impact on the final results on risk measures [9, 10].

The main goal of this paper is an application of the two-parameter quantile-based risk measure to sector portfolio analysis for data from Warsaw Stock Exchange. Next, the evaluation of the empirical results points out the existing gap between the subadditivity and robustness of risk measurement procedures.

15.2 Estimation of Risk Measures

The payoff of a portfolio over a specified horizon may be represented as a random variable $X \in L \subset L^1(\Omega, F, P)$, where negative values are assumed to be a convex cone containing all constants. A risk measure on L is a map $\rho : L \to R$ assigning to each $X \in L$, a number representing measure of risk. Artzner et al. [3] defined the axioms of coherent risk measures.

Below we list some properties for risk measures: for X; $Y \in L$,

(a) Monotonicity: $\rho(X) \leq \rho(Y)$ if $X \leq Y$;
(b) Cash invariance: $\rho(X + c) = \rho(X) + c$ for any $c \in R$;
(c) Positive homogeneity: $\rho(\lambda X) = \lambda\rho(X)$ for any $\lambda > 0$;
(d) Subadditivity: $\rho(X + Y) \leq \rho(X) + \rho(Y)$;
(e) Law determination: $\rho(X) = \rho(Y)$ if X and Y have the same distribution.

Definition 1 A monetary risk measure satisfying conditions (a) and (b), and a coherent risk measure is a risk measure satisfying (a)–(d).

For a set $C \subset D \subset L^1$ representing the set of admissible (robust) return distributions, we can notice according to the literature [4] the condition of qualitative robustness of a risk estimator and use it to examine the robustness of the chosen for application risk estimators.

Definition 2 A risk estimator $\hat{\rho}$ is C-robust at F (the empirical return distributions) if, for any $\varepsilon > 0$, there exist $\delta > 0$ and $n_0 \geq 1$ such that, for all $G \in C$, $d(G, F) \leq \delta$ where d is the Lévy distance.[2]

When $C = D$, then we have situation not interesting in econometric or financial applications[3] since requiring robustness against all perturbations of the distributions F that means it is restrictive and excludes estimators with the lower break point such as the sample mean. In application, first we have to estimate the return distribution F of the portfolio from available data and then apply the risk measure ρ to this

[1] $D \subset L$ is the convex set of cumulative distribution functions (cdf) on R.

[2] Huber [12].

[3] If $C = D$, we have qualitative robustness called asymptotic robustness as outlined [12].

Table 15.1 Behavior of sensitivity functions for some risk estimators

Risk estimator	Dependence in z of S(t)
Historical VaR	Bounded
Gaussian ML for VaR	Quadratic
Laplace ML for VaR	Linear
Historical expected shortfall	Linear
Gaussian ML for expected shortfall	Quadratic
Laplace ML for expected shortfall	Linear

Source Cont et al. [4]

distribution. As the estimation of the loss distribution $F(X)$, we can use an empirical distribution from a historical or simulated sample (e.g., Monte Carlo) or a parametric form whose parameters are estimated from available data. Coherent measures as ES_α has a non-robust historical estimator [4]. In this paper, authors proposed a robust family of risk estimators by modifying its definition.

Definition 3 Consider $0 < \alpha_1 < \alpha_2 < 1$; we can notice the robust risk measure

$$\frac{1}{\alpha_2 - \alpha_1} \int_{\alpha_1}^{\alpha_2} \mathrm{VaR}_u(F)\mathrm{d}u \tag{15.1}$$

and, respectively, a discrete version of the above risk measure:

$$\frac{1}{k} \sum_{j=1}^{k} \mathrm{VaR}_{u_j}(F), 0 < u_1 < \cdots < u_k < 1 \tag{15.2}$$

We will call ρ_{eff} the effective risk measure[4] associated with the risk estimator $\hat{\rho}$. In order to quantify the degree of robustness of a risk estimator, we can notice the concept of the sensitivity function [4]. The function $S(t; F)$ measures the sensitivity of the risk estimator to the addition of a new data point in a large sample.

Definition 4 (*sensitivity function of a risk estimator*) The sensitivity function of a risk estimator defined as a function of distribution F belongs to set of all effective risk measure distribution (D_{eff}) is the function defined by

$$S(t) - S(t; F) = \lim_{\varepsilon \to 0^+} \frac{\rho_{\mathrm{eff}}(\varepsilon\delta_t + (1-\varepsilon)F) - \rho_{\mathrm{eff}}(F)}{\varepsilon} \tag{15.3}$$

for any $t \in R$ such that the limit exists. See Table 15.1.

[4]In other words, while ρ is the risk measure, we are interested in computing.

15.3 Two-Parameter Quantile-Based Risk Measures

The one-parameter families of risk measures, VaR and ES, can be noticed as a more general two-parameter family of risk measures, called the Range-Value-at-Risk (RVaR). The family of RVaR was introduced in Cont et al. [4].[5] This transformation into RVaR was used by Embrechts et al. [6] to understand properties and comparative advantages of risk measures. It helps on application RVaR as the underlying risk measures in the real problem. Measures as VaR, ES, and RVaR can be represented as average quantiles of a random variable.

Definition 5 For $X \in L$, the RVaR at level $(\alpha;\beta) \in R^2_+$ is defined as

$$\mathrm{RVaR}_{\alpha,\beta} = \begin{cases} \frac{1}{\beta}\int\limits_{\alpha}^{\alpha+\beta} \mathrm{VaR}_u(F)\mathrm{d}u & \text{if } \beta > 0 \\ \mathrm{VaR}_\alpha(F) & \text{if } \beta = 0 \end{cases} \tag{15.4}$$

The family of risk measures Range-Value-at-Risk (RVaR) is the family of the truncated average quantiles of a random variable. $\mathrm{RVaR}_{\alpha;\beta}$ is continuous with respect to convergence in distribution (weak convergence). RVaR belongs to the large family of distortion risk measures.[6]

Definition 6 For α, β; $\in [0; 1)$ and $\alpha + \beta < 1$, $\mathrm{RVaR}_{\alpha;\beta}$ belongs to the class of distortion risk measures, that is, risk measures ρ_h of the Stieltjes integral form

$$\rho_h(X) = \int\limits_0^1 \mathrm{VaR}_\alpha(X)\mathrm{d}h(\alpha) \tag{15.5}$$

for some non-decreasing and left-continuous function h: $[0; 1] \to [0; 1]$ satisfying $h(0) = 0$ and $h(1) = 1$, such that the above integral is properly defined. Here h is called a distortion function.

For α, β; $\in [0; 1)$ and $\alpha + \beta < 1$, the distortion function of $\mathrm{RVaR}_{\alpha;\beta}$ (X) is given by

$$h^{(\alpha,\beta)}(t) = \begin{cases} \min\left\{ I_{\{t>\alpha\}}\frac{t-\alpha}{\beta}, 1 \right\} & \text{if } \beta > 0 \\ I_{\{t>\alpha\}} & \text{if } \beta = 0 \end{cases} \quad t \in [0, 1] \tag{15.6}$$

For application on real data, especially in portfolio analysis, the important are some of the relationship between the individual RVaR and the aggregate RVaR.

---

[5]For any $0 < \alpha_1 < \alpha_2 < 1$, we can notice as $\beta = \alpha_2 - \alpha_1$.

[6]Kusuoka [15], Song and Yan [17], Dhaene et al. [5], Grigorova [11], Wang et al. [18].

Theorem 1 [6]
For any $X_1, \ldots, X_n \in L$ and any $\alpha_1, \ldots, \alpha_n; \beta_1, \ldots, \beta_n > 0$, we have

$$\text{RVaR}_{\sum_{i=1}^{n} \alpha_i, \vee_{i=1}^{n} \beta_i}\left(\sum_{i=1}^{n} X_i\right) \leq \sum_{i=1}^{n} \text{RVaR}_{\alpha_i \beta_i}(X_i) \tag{15.7}$$

By setting $\alpha_1 = \cdots = \alpha_n = 0$ and $\beta_1 = \cdots = \beta_n$, Theorem 15.1 reduces to the classic subadditivity of ES. By setting $\beta_1 = \cdots = \beta_n = 0$, we obtain the following inequality for VaR.

For any $X_1, \ldots, X_n \in L$ and any $\alpha_1, \ldots,\alpha_n > 0$, we have

$$\text{VaR}_{\sum_{i=1}^{n} \alpha_i}\left(\sum_{i=1}^{n} X_i\right) \leq \sum_{i=1}^{n} \text{VaR}_{\alpha_i}(X_i) \tag{15.8}$$

For $n = 2$, we can notice

$$\text{RVaR}_{\alpha_1+\alpha_2,\beta_1 \vee \beta_2}(X_1 + X_2) \leq \text{RVaR}_{\alpha_1,\beta_1}(X_1) + \text{RVaR}_{\alpha_2 \beta_2}(X_2) \tag{15.9}$$

for all $X_1; X_2 \in L; \alpha_1; \alpha_2; \beta_1; \beta_2 \in R_+$. This subadditivity involves a combination of the summation of the random variables $X_1, \ldots, X_n \in L$ and the summation of the parameters $(\alpha_1; \beta_1), \ldots, (\alpha_n; \beta_n) \in R_+^2$ with respect to the two-dimensional additive operation $(+; v)$. Note that v-operation is known as the tropical addition in the max-plus algebra [16].

In portfolio analysis, we had to find the optimal allocations for the corresponding aggregate risk value for the RVaR family of risk measures. The following result proved by Embrechts et al. [6] can solve this problem.

Definition 7 The inf-convolution of n risk measures $\rho_1, \ldots, \rho_n$ is a risk measure noticed as

$$\square_{i=1}^{n} \rho_i(X) := \inf\left\{\sum_{i=1}^{n} \rho_i(X_i) : (X_1, \ldots, X_n) \in A_n(X)\right\} \tag{15.10}$$

That is, the inf-convolution of n risk measures is the infimum over *aggregate risk* values for all possible allocations.

Definition 8 For risk measures $\rho_1, \ldots, \rho_n$ and $X \in L$:

(i) An n-tuple $(X_1, \ldots, X_n) \in A_n(X)$ is called an optimal allocation of X if

$$\square_{i=1}^{n} \rho_i(X_i) = \sum_{i=1}^{n} \rho_i(X_i) \tag{15.11}$$

(ii) An n-tuple $(X_1, \ldots, X_n) \in A_n(X)$ is called a *Pareto-optimal allocation* of X if for any $(Y_1, \ldots, Y_n) \in A_n(X)$ satisfying $\rho_i(Y_i) \le \rho_i(X_i)$ for all $i = 1; \ldots, n$, we have $\rho_i(Y_i) = \rho_i(X_i)$ for all $i = 1; \ldots, n$.

Now we can notice the theorem that has been used in portfolio optimization.

Theorem 2 [6]
For any $X_1, \ldots, X_n \in L$ and any $\alpha_1, \ldots, \alpha_n; \beta_1, \ldots, \beta_n > 0$, we have

$$\square_{i=1}^{n} \mathrm{RVaR}_{\alpha_i \beta_i}(X) = \mathrm{RVaR}_{\sum_{i=1}^{n} \alpha_i, \forall_{i=1}^{n} \beta_i}(X) \tag{15.12}$$

Now we can notice portfolio risk in the presence of uncertainty of distribution F by using the resulting aggregate risk value. The assumption is that the distribution of the total risk $X \in L$ is misspecified. That in general implies problems for estimation using VaR as a risk measures but not for RVaR or ES. This relates to the issue of the robustness of VaR and RVaR, for a relevant discussion on robustness properties for risk measures.[7] Instead of the robustness of the risk measures themselves, we can write the robustness of the optimal allocation.

Theorem 3 [6]
For risk measures $\mathrm{RVaR}_{\alpha_1 \beta_1}, \ldots, \mathrm{RVaR}_{\alpha_n \beta_n}$, $(\alpha_i; \beta_i) \in [0; 1)$, $\alpha_i + \beta_i > 0$, $i = 1, \ldots, n$, $\sum_{i=1}^{n} \alpha_i + \forall_{i=1}^{n} \beta_i < 1$ and a doubly continuous random variable $X \in L$:

(i) There exists an L^1-robust optimal allocation of X if and only if $\beta_1, \ldots, \beta_n > 0$.
(ii) If X is bounded, then there exists an L^∞-robust optimal allocation of X if and only if $\beta_1, \ldots, \beta_n > 0$.

Assuming $\sum_{i=1}^{n} \alpha_i + \forall_{i=1}^{n} \beta_i < 1$, a Pareto-optimal allocation for any $X_1, \ldots, X_n \in L$ can be constructed explicitly as in Theorem 15.2, with the aggregate risk value

$$\sum_{i=1}^{n} \mathrm{RVaR}_{\alpha_i \beta_i}(X) = \mathrm{RVaR}_{\sum_{i=1}^{n} \alpha_i, \forall_{i=1}^{n} \beta_i}(X) \tag{15.13}$$

15.4 Application RVaR in Sector Portfolio Analysis

Sector portfolio analysis was dedicated to food sector. WIG food is a sector index listed on the Warsaw Stock Exchange, containing companies that participate in the

[7] Cont et al. [4], Kou et al. [13], Krätschmer et al. [14], and Embrechts et al. [7].

Table 15.2 Parameters of rate-of-return distribution

	ASTARTA	COLIAN	GOBARTO	HELIO	IMCOMPA
R	0.001	0.000	0.001	0.003	0.002
V	0.000	0.000	0.000	0.001	0.000
S	0.019	0.013	0.022	0.032	0.016
Skewness	0.512	0.571	−1.838	1.966	0.362
Kurtosis	1.892	4.344	46.205	10.51	3.385
	INDYKPOL	KANIA	OTMU	MILKILAND	MBWS
R	0.000	0.000	−0.001	0.001	−0.001
V	0.000	0.000	0.001	0.001	0.001
S	0.022	0.019	0.025	0.034	0.023
Skewness	0.931	0.327	0.819	1.200	−1.407
Kurtosis	6.676	1.406	6.553	6.158	10.87
	MILKILAND	MBWS	OTMU	PEPEES	WAWEL
R	0.001	−0.001	−0.001	0.003	0.000
V	0.001	0.001	0.001	0.001	0.000
S	0.034	0.023	0.025	0.028	0.017
Skewness	1.200	−1.407	0.819	2.243	0.159
Kurtosis	6.158	10.87	6.553	10.941	7.036

Source Main calculation

WIG index. The base date for the WIG food index was set as December 31, 1998. The subindex is characterized by the same methodology with the main WIG index. This means that it is an income index, and when calculating it, you should take into account both the prices of the shares it contains, as well as the right to collect and the income from dividends. The WIG food index consists of 23 companies, of which 15 were selected for analysis, which brings together 86.37% of the total shares in the portfolio and almost total shares in the market, as their sum amounts to 97.80%. The surveyed period from February 18, 1 to February 19, 2018, consisted of 503 observations of closing prices for each of the companies.

The use of risk measures requires examining the types of rates of return distributions. The consistency of the distribution of rates of return with the hypothetical distribution was checked, which is necessary when using quantile risk measures. For this purpose, the Kolmogorov–Smirnov test was used, with the help of which the hypothesis on the compatibility of the distributions of rates of return with both normal and lognormal distribution was verified. In each case, the significance of the test is less than the assumed level of significance of 0.05. This means that distributions of the rates of return are consistent with the normal or lognormal distribution. Next, the parameters of rate-of-return distribution for each of the companies were calculated (Table 15.2), especially the third central moment, which is a measure of the asymmetry of the observed rates of return.

Table 15.3 ES values for selected quantiles

ES	ASTARTA	HELIO	IMCOMPANY	KSGAGRO	PEPEES	Portfolio
0.95	0.0454	0.0821	0.0354	0.0813	0.0704	0.0498
0.96	0.0477	0.0897	0.0370	0.0860	0.0774	0.0531
0.97	0.0511	0.0969	0.0394	0.0920	0.0870	0.0574
0.98	0.0537	0.1077	0.0428	0.0984	0.1005	0.0628
0.99	0.0570	0.1334	0.0486	0.1089	0.1259	0.0727

Source Main calculation

Table 15.4 RVaR measurement values for selected value values (α, β)

RVaR	ASTARTA	HELIO	IMCOMPANY	KSGAGRO	PEPEES	Portfolio
(0.95, 0)	0.0368	0.0599	0.0293	0.0652	0.0457	0.0384
(0.96, 0.01)	0.0417	0.0717	0.0312	0.0736	0.0542	0.0433
(0.97, 0.01)	0.0482	0.0786	0.0348	0.0835	0.0675	0.0498
(0.98, 0.01)	0.0537	0.1077	0.0428	0.0984	0.1005	0.0628
(0.99, 0.01)	0.0610	0.1467	0.0511	0.1488	0.1325	0.0793

Source Main calculation

Next the optimal portfolio was built; it has been assumed that the expected rate of return on the portfolio had to be greater than or equal to 0.001. In addition, it was assumed that the number of companies in the portfolio should be in the range from 5 to 7, and therefore, simulations were carried out to finally choose the optimal solution. Wallet received the optimal parameters. The following companies were included in the portfolio companies: IMCOMPANY (43,3%), ASTARTA (28%), PEPEES (14,8%), HELIO (0,77%), and KSGAGRO (0,61%). Portfolio parameters $E(Rp) = 0.001860$, $V(Rp) = 0.000115$, $S(Rp) = 0.010713$.

Following to final step, an assessment of the risk of the designated portfolios with the use of quantitative ES and RVaR risk measures has been made. Consideration of all possible combinations of values (α, β) is a demanding task. In order to secure the capital of the designated portfolio, we save selected results of the application of the downside risk measures presented in the previous points.

Analyzing the obtained results, it can be concluded that the highest levels of capital collateral are determined by the ES measure, followed by RVaR with a fixed value of $\beta = 0.01$. By changing the value of β and a fixed value of α, the lowest levels of capital collateral were obtained. When we used robust estimator, then we uses specific technique on a tail of the distribution of the rate of return. Presented chosen results (Tables 15.3, 15.4 and 15.5) confirm general rules, described in Sect. 15.2. We had to take into account robustness of applied quantiles risk measures (Table 15.6).

In the presented application of the quantile risk measures on the portfolios, we based on the selected sector. Portfolios from a selected sector were analyzed, and the variability of the distribution of the rate of return in the audited period was not so much significant. In the surveyed sector, all returns of the rate of return were

Table 15.5 RVaR measurement values for selected value values (α, β)

RVaR	ASTARTA	HELIO	IMCOMPANY	KSGAGRO	PEPEES	Portfolio
(0.95, 0)	0.0368	0.0599	0.0293	0.0652	0.0457	0.0384
(0.95, 0.01)	0.0399	0.0650	0.0304	0.0699	0.0504	0.0411
(0.95, 0.02)	0.0425	0.0693	0.0321	0.0744	0.0566	0.0441
(0.95, 0.03)	0.0454	0.0821	0.0354	0.0813	0.0704	0.0498
(0.95, 0.04)	0.0454	0.0821	0.0354	0.0813	0.0704	0.0498

Source Main calculation

Table 15.6 RVaR measurement values for selected value values (α, β) for portfolio

ES	Portfolio	RVaR	Portfolio	RVaR	Portfolio
0.95	0.0498	(0.95, 0)	0.0384	(0.95, 0)	0.0384
0.96	0.0531	(0.96, 0.01)	0.0433	(0.95, 0.01)	0.0411
0.97	0.0574	(0.97, 0.01)	0.0498	(0.95, 0.02)	0.0441
0.98	0.0628	(0.98, 0.01)	0.0628	(0.95, 0.03)	0.0498
0.99	0.0727	(0.99, 0.01)	0.0793	(0.95, 0.04)	0.0498

Source Main calculation

characterized by a significant asymmetry, which means volatility in the tail of the returns. These properties can have strong impact on the results.

15.5 Conclusion

In this paper, we present that the estimation properties as robustness and sensitivity are important and need to be accounted to the dataset, with the same attention as the coherence properties. An unstable or non-robust risk estimator can be useless in practice, never less it has to be related to a coherent measure of risk. Regulatory risk measures, as VaR and ES, in parametric estimation procedures for VaR and ES lead to non-robust estimators. On the other hand, weighted averages of historical VaR have robust empirical estimators. Historical VaR is a qualitatively robust estimation procedure. The family of RVaR was introduced in the context of robustness properties of risk measures. This family of two-parameter risk measures (RVaR) can be seen as a bridge connecting VaR and ES, which are the two most popular regulatory risk measures. Measures as VaR, ES, and RVaR can be represented as average quantiles of a random variable.

In the recent research, we obtain original results: We establish the level of RVaR as a measurement values for selected value values (α, β) for sector portfolio from

Warsaw Stock Exchange. We can claim that estimation RVaR level as the underlying risk measures in the real problem and connected with these procedures errors is still useful. Working with two-parameter quantile-based risk measures can have strong impact to manage expected levels of capital collateral. Additionally, by using two-parameter quantile-based risk measures, we received a tool for control a chosen part of the tail loss distribution of the portfolio in the estimating process. To conclude we would have to argue that the important impact form empirical results is that RVaR looks as an agile risk measures, which is also robust and coherent. That means RVaR should be an important part of the portfolio risk measurement procedure.

References

1. Acerbi, C.: Coherent measures of risk in everyday market practice. Quant. Finance **7**, 359–364 (2007)
2. Acerbi, C.: Spectral measures of risk: a coherent representation of subjective risk aversion. J. Bank. Finance **26**, 1505–1518 (2002)
3. Artzner, P., Delbaen, F., Eber, J., Heath, D.: Coherent measures of risk. Math. Finance **9**, 203–228 (1999)
4. Cont, R., Deguest, R., Scandolo, G.: Robustness and sensitivity analysis of risk measurement procedures. Quant. Finance **10**(6), 593–606 (2010)
5. Delbaen, F.: Monetary Utility Functions. Osaka University Press, Osaka (2012)
6. Embrechts, P., Liu, H., Wang, R.; Quantile-Based Risk Sharing. Working Paper, 24 Oct 2017
7. Embrechts, P., Wang, B., Wang, R.: Aggregation-robustness and model uncertainty of regulatory risk measures. Finan. Stochast. **19**(4), 763–790 (2015)
8. Föllmer, H., Schied, A.: Convex measures of risk and trading constraints. Finance Stochast. **6**, 429–447 (2002)
9. Gourieroux, C., Liu, W.: Sensitivity analysis of distortion risk measures. Working Paper (2006)
10. Gourieroux, C., Laurent, J., Scaillet, O.: Sensitivity analysis of values at risk. J. Empir. Finance **7**, 225–245 (2000)
11. Grigorova, M.: Stochastic dominance with respect to a capacity and risk measures. Statist. Risk Model. **31**(3–4), 259–295 (2014)
12. Huber, P.: Robust statistics. Wiley, New York (1981)
13. Kou, S., Peng, X., Heyde, C.C.: External risk measures and Basel accords. Math. Oper. Res. **38**(3), 393–417 (2013)
14. Krätschmer, V., Schied, A., Zähle, H.: Comparative and quantitative robustness for law-invariant risk measures. Finance Stochast **18**(2), 271–295 (2014)
15. Kusuoka, S.: On law invariant coherent risk measures. Adv. Math. Econ. **3**, 83–95 (2001)
16. Richter-Gebert, J., Sturmfels, B., Theobald, T.: First steps in tropical geometry. Contemp. Math. **377**, 289–318 (2005)
17. Song, Y., Yan, J.: Risk measures with comonotonic subadditivity or convexity and respecting stochastic orders. Insur. Math. Econ. **45**, 459–465 (2009)
18. Wang, R., Bignozzi, V., Tsakanas, A.: How superadditive can a risk measure be? SIAM J. Financ. Math. **6**, 776–803 (2015)

Chapter 16
Is the Three-Factor Better Than Single-Factor Capital Asset Pricing Model? Case of Polish Capital Market

Dorota Witkowska

Abstract The three-factor model was developed by Fama and French as a response to the poor performance of the single-factor capital asset pricing model (CAPM) in explaining realized returns. However, the evidence from different markets does not give clear conclusions regarding the appropriateness of this model, and CAPM is still most commonly used by practitioners. The study aims to find out which model better explains returns from portfolios containing selected companies listed on the Warsaw Stock Exchange in the years 2007–2017. In our investigation, four portfolios including: (1) big, (2) medium size, (3) small and (4) all considered companies are concerned. We also distinguish seven sub-periods which are characterized by different situation on the Polish capital market. The results show that the three-factor model better explains rates of returns from portfolios than CAPM, although the improvement is mostly visible for the portfolios of small and medium size companies. The risk factors concerning capitalization of companies and book-to-market value rates are statistically significant in about half of estimated models whereas risk premium significantly affects returns in all models.

Keywords Capital asset pricing model · Fama-French three-factor model · Polish capital market

16.1 Introduction

Capital asset pricing model (CAPM) was developed independently by William Sharpe [1], John Lintner [2] and Jan Mossin [3] twelve years after Harry Markowitz had laid down the foundation of modern portfolio management [4]. This model became a useful instrument to estimate the systematic risk of individual financial instruments or portfolio of securities, and its parameter—beta became one of the most frequently used risk measures. CAPM is also the capital cost model, which is

D. Witkowska (✉)
University of Lodz, ul. Matejki 22/26, 90-237 Łódź, Poland
e-mail: dorota.witkowska@uni.lodz.pl

W. Tarczyński and K. Nermend (eds.), *Effective Investments on Capital Markets*, Springer Proceedings in Business and Economics,
https://doi.org/10.1007/978-3-030-21274-2_16

most often used in practice, thanks to its simple form and easy application as well as clear interpretation (refer to [5–9]).

It should be noted that the classic capital asset pricing model has had both supporters and opponents since it was developed. Among the former, one should mention [10–12]. The latter have criticized CAPM mostly because of unrealistic assumptions that underlie the model and because it is a single-factor model. Roll's critique [13] refers to the model construction itself and concerns the lack of possibility of its empirical verification since it is impossible to create or observe a truly diversified market portfolio. While Fama and French in series of their works [14–16] prove that CAPM model fails to apply in capital estimation because beta coefficient does not provide a correct explanation for the expected return rates. At the same, they proved that good results are given by supplementing model with additional factors, i.e., price to book value ratio and measures of company size (see Fama and French [17]). In [18], it was found that most errors in cost of stock capital estimation using CAPM model are also caused by wrong assessment of risk premiums, while Pástor and Stambaugh in [19] presented that capital estimations may be corrected by Bayesian approach. However, Gibbson [20] who proposed a methodology to avoid errors in the measurement of variables and increase of appropriateness of estimates of model parameters proposes to reject CAPM. Whereas authors of [21] were not able to come to clear conclusions regarding appropriateness of CAPM and beta coefficient estimates. As they found by themselves, decades may pass by until additionally collected data allow for rejection of CAPM for a reasonable significance level.

Despite the criticism, the classic capital asset pricing model is still widely used amongst practitioners. According to a study on European firms (discussed in [22]), about 45% of chief financial officers (CFOs) rely on the CAPM and 73.5% of interviewed US CFOs "always or almost always" use the CAPM to estimate the cost of equity (see Graham and Harvey [5]).

Here, a question arises why Fama–French three-factor model, which seems to be the improved version of the capital asset pricing model, has not been used in practice and research as often as CAPM. In fact, the research on application three-factor model to the Polish capital market has been provided rather rarely. Therefore, the study aims to find out which model is more appropriate to explain rates of return of portfolios containing selected companies listed on the Warsaw Stock Exchange. Investigation is provided for the years 2007–2017.

16.2 Fama–French Three-Factor Model

The three-factor model was developed as a response to the poor performance of the CAPM in explaining realized returns. Its authors claim in [17] that anomalies relating to the CAPM are captured by the three-factor asset pricing model. These three risk factors defined in the Fama–French model are:

1. risk premium, i.e., excess market portfolio return;

2. the difference between the excess return on a portfolio of stocks with small capitalization and the excess return on a portfolio of stocks with big capitalization;
3. the difference between the excess return on a portfolio of stocks which is characterized by the high value of the book-to-market value (BV/MV) and the excess return on a portfolio of stocks which is characterized by low book-to-market value.

The three-factor model is formulated as following [15]:

$$R_i - R_f = \alpha + \beta_M \left(R_M - R_f \right) + \beta_{\text{SMB}} \text{SMB} + \beta_{\text{HML}} \text{HML} + \varepsilon \qquad (16.1)$$

where, R_i—rate of return from the portfolio, R_f—risk-free rate of return; R_M—rate of return from the market portfolio; $(R_M - R_f)$—risk premium; SMB—the difference between the excess return on a portfolio of small stocks and the excess return on a portfolio of big stocks (SMB, small minus big); HML—the difference between the excess return on a portfolio of high-book-to-market stocks and the excess return on a portfolio of low-book-to-market stocks (HML, high minus low); α—an intercept; β_M, β_{SMB}, β_{HML}—model parameters describing the effect of each risk factor; ε—residual.

One should note that the classical capital asset pricing model—CAPM, as a single-factor model, is a simplified version of the Fama–French model, i.e., it can be formulated as (16.1) for $\beta_{\text{SMB}} = \beta_{\text{HML}} = 0$.

Empirical tests of the Fama–French three-factor model have been provided for different markets and time spans. For instance, in the studies [15, 17, 23] Fama–French model is applied to the US market, in [24]—to seven developed markets (the US, Canadian, Australian, Japanese, German, British and French), in [25]—to Australian market. The author of [26] considers the Brazilian market and in [27] five Asian markets are considered. The authors of above-mentioned research confirm good performance of the Fama–French model. Although Blanco [23] and Lam [28] for the US market point out that the results depend on the portfolio construction. Also, the research provided for Australian in [29], British [30] and Turkish [31] markets shows that the three-factor model has limited abilities to explain rates of return, and it is hard to conclude that it performs better than CAPM.

There are also some studies on single-factor and three-factor capital asset pricing models dedicated for the Polish capital market, which were carried out for different stocks, periods and return intervals. Application of CAPM to evaluate returns from portfolios and companies listed on Warsaw Stock Exchange is described in [9, 32–37], to mention some of the research. One should notice that the Fama–French model is not used too often. Although, research presented in [38–42] confirm better performance of the Fama–French model in comparison to CAPM. However, [43] prove that the Fama–French model is adequate to describe bull market, but it is useless in explanation of returns in the bear market. Also [44] reports wrong valuation of stock returns.

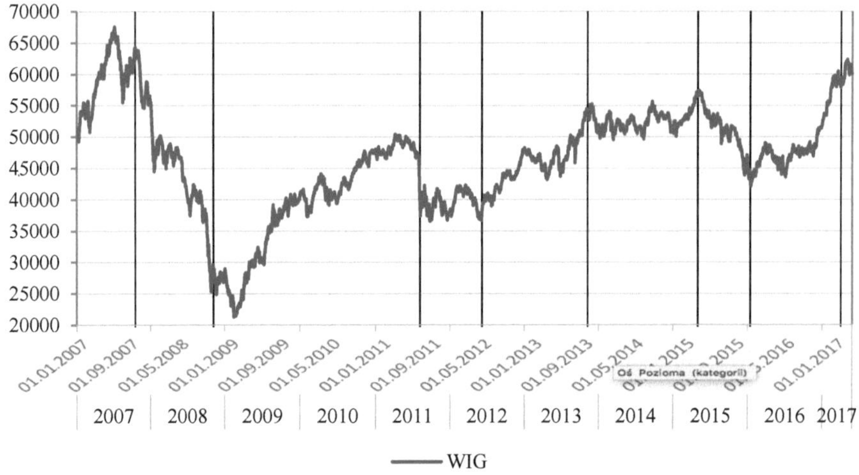

Fig. 16.1 Warsaw stock exchange index WIG quotations in the years 2007–2017. *Source* Own elaboration on the basis of [46, p. 49]

16.3 Assumptions and Data

Capital asset pricing model seems to be simple and elegant; however, there are some issues which must be determined before the model is estimated and applied. For instance, it is necessary to define [37, p. 45]: interval range for rates of return, market portfolio, risk-free instrument, estimation period and methods of model estimation.

In our study, the investigation is provided using daily logarithmic rates of return evaluated for closing prices. This approach is similar to [45] although in the above-mentioned literature monthly returns are usually used. The market portfolio is represented by WIG—the main index of Warsaw Stock Exchange and WIBOR 1Y—Warsaw Interbank Offered Rate (reference rate set for deposits for the 12 months maturities) is used as a proxy of the risk-free rate of return. All data concerning quotations, book values and capitalization of stocks are available on www.stooq.pl.

The time span of analysis is from October 15, 2007, to March 31, 2017. This period is characterized by the changing situation on the Polish capital market. Therefore, seven sub-periods of increasing, decreasing or stable tendency of the Warsaw Stock Exchange index are distinguished (see Fig. 16.1; Table 16.1). Selection of sub-periods results from the instability of beta which should be estimated for shorter periods, especially when less developed capital markets are concerned what is pointed out in [37 pp. 50–51, 81, 137–176, 45]. Also [43] prove different performance of the Fama–French model in bull and bear market.

In the study, two criteria of stocks selection are determined. Firstly, the company has been quoted incessantly in the whole horizon of investigation. Secondly, the company has been comprised in the portfolio of a one among three Warsaw Stock Exchange indexes: WIG20, mWIG40 or sWIG80. These indexes base on the value

Table 16.1 Selected periods of investigation

No.	Symbol	Dates		No. of observations
1	Bear1	15.10.2007	31.10.2008	262
2	Bull1	3.11.2008	5.08.2011	693
3	Stable1	8.08.2011	5.06.2012	207
4	Bull2	6.06.2012	31.10.2013	351
5	Stable2	4.11.2013	30.04.2015	367
6	Bear2	4.05.2015	15.01.2016	177
7	Bull3	18.01.2016	31.03.2017	306

of portfolios which are composed from shares of 20 big and most liquid companies, 40 medium size companies and 80 smaller companies listed at WSE Main List, respectively.

It is worth mentioning that in the years 2006–2017 only seven companies were incessantly comprised in the index WI20, six in mWIG40, and none in sWIG80. However, 35 companies belonged to the portfolio of any index during the period of analysis what is connected with periodical revisions of the index portfolio.[1]

Table 16.2 contains the list of companies selected for further investigation with information about the index portfolio which they belong to. These companies are used to construct four portfolios denoted as:

PB portfolio containing ten big companies belonging to the index WIG20,
PM portfolio containing ten medium size companies belonging to the index mWIG40,
PS portfolio containing ten small size companies belonging to the index sWIG80,
PT portfolio containing all (i.e. 30) selected companies.

The composition of these four portfolios is stable for the whole analyzed time span and all distinguished sub-periods.

Table 16.2 List of selected companies

Index WIG20		Index mWIG40		Index sWIG80	
KGHM	PKNORLEN	AMREST	ORBIS	DEBICA	COMP
MBANK	PKOBP	BUDIMEX	CIECH	JWCONSTR	DOMDEV
ORANGEPL	LOTOS	ECHO	EMPERIA	LENTEX	FAMUR
PEKAO	ASSECOPOL	INGBSK	KETY	RAFAKO	PELION
PGNIG	BZWBK	MILLENNIUM	NETIA	SNIEZKA	POLICE

[1]The WIG20, mWIG40, sWIG80 index participants are selected based on data following the last session in January (annual revision) and April, July and October (quarterly adjustments).

16.4 Analysis of Rates of Return and Risk from Portfolios

In our study, we consider rates of return evaluated for all portfolios constructed from selected shares of companies which are classified as big (PB), medium (PM) and small (PS), together with a portfolio comprised from all 30 distinguished equities (PT). Analysis consists of verification of following hypotheses concerning returns and risk.

$$H_0 : E(R_{\text{PB}}) = 0;\ H_0 : E(R_{\text{PM}}) = 0 \text{ and } H_0 : E(R_{\text{PS}}) = 0,\ E(R_{\text{PT}}) = 0 \quad (16.2)$$

using normally distributed test statistics:

$$u = \frac{R_k}{S_k}\sqrt{T_k} \quad (16.3)$$

$$\begin{aligned} &H_0 : E(R_{\text{PB}}) = E(R_{\text{PM}});\ H_0 : E(R_{\text{PM}}) = E(R_{\text{PS}}); \\ &H_0 : E(R_{\text{PS}}) = E(R_{\text{PB}}), \text{ and for each portfolio} \\ &H_0 : E(R_{t1}) = E(R_{t2}), \end{aligned} \quad (16.4)$$

applying Cochran-Cox test:

$$u = \frac{R_1 - R_2}{\sqrt{\frac{S_1^2}{T_1} + \frac{S_2^2}{T_2}}} \quad (16.5)$$

$$\begin{aligned} &H_0 : D^2(R_{\text{PB}}) = D^2(R_{\text{PM}});\ H_0 : D^2(R_{\text{PM}}) = D^2(R_{\text{PS}}); \\ &H_0 : D^2(R_{\text{PS}}) = D^2(R_{\text{PB}}), \text{ and for each portfolio} \\ &H_0 : D^2(R_{t1}) = D^2(R_{t2}) \end{aligned} \quad (16.6)$$

using Fisher statistics:

$$F = \frac{S_{\text{max}}^2}{S_{\text{min}}^2} \quad (16.7)$$

where $E(R)$—expected returns, $D^2(R)$—variance of returns, R_{PB}, R_{PM}, R_{PS} and R_{PT}—returns from the portfolio: PB, PM, PS and PT, respectively, R_k—the average rate of return observed in the k-th sample (i.e., the k-th period or portfolio), S_k^2—the variance of rates of return from the k-th sample, T_k—count of observations in the k-th sample, $S_{\text{max}}^2 = \max\{S_1^2, S_2^2\}$, $S_{\text{min}}^2 = \min\{S_1^2, S_2^2\}$, $t1$, $t2$—two neighboring periods of analysis.

The results of rates of return analysis are presented in Tables 16.3, 16.4, 16.5, 16.6 and 16.7. Null hypotheses (16.2), (16.4) and (16.6) are rejected for the significance level 0.05 what is marked in Tables by bold letters. In Tables 16.3, 16.4 and 16.6, values of test statistics (16.3) and (16.5) are positive for bigger values of returns

Table 16.3 Values of test statistics (16.3) and standard deviations of constructed portfolios

Period	H_0: E($R_{portfolio}$) = 0 for portfolios				Standard deviations of portfolios			
	PB	PM	PS	PT	PB (%)	PM (%)	PS (%)	PT (%)
Bear1	**−2.0460**	**−2.4947**	−1.5644	**−2.0313**	2.87	3.11	2.83	2.93
Bull1	0.5933	0.8331	0.7495	0.7304	2.35	2.54	2.49	2.46
Stable1	−0.0061	−0.5181	−0.3645	−0.3089	2.39	2.91	2.48	2.61
Bull2	1.5141	1.1520	0.9892	1.2239	1.98	2.50	1.91	2.13
Stable2	0.7656	−0.2584	0.2051	0.2171	1.75	2.10	1.66	1.84
Bear2	0.0555	−0.1903	−1.2281	−0.4335	1.83	2.11	2.08	2.00
Bull3	0.9483	0.8349	0.8827	0.8897	1.98	1.89	1.93	1.93

Table 16.4 Values of test statistics (16.5) comparing returns from constructed portfolios

Period	Null hypothesis (16.4) H_0		
	$E(R_{PB}) = E(R_{PM})$	$E(R_{PM}) = E(R_{PS})$	$E(R_{PS}) = E(R_{PB})$
Bear1	0.4446	−0.7896	0.3570
Bull1	−0.2077	0.0706	0.1367
Stable1	0.3966	−0.1585	−0.2581
Bull2	0.0371	0.3142	−0.4022
Stable2	0.6889	−0.3299	−0.4150
Bear2	0.1803	0.7274	−0.9604
Bull3	0.1067	−0.0465	−0.0601

Table 16.5 Values of test statistics (16.7) comparing the risk of portfolios

Period	Null hypothesis (16.6) H_0		
	$D^2(R_{PB}) = D^2(R_{PM})$	$D^2(R_{PM}) = D^2(R_{PS})$	$D^2(R_{PS}) = D^2(R_{PB})$
Bear1	*1.1725*	1.2032	*1.0262*
Bull1	***1.1643***	**1.0421**	1.1172
Stable1	***1.4838***	**1.3822**	1.0735
Bull2	***1.5938***	**1.7098**	*1.0728*
Stable2	*1.4357*	**1.6025**	*1.1161*
Bear2	*1.3370*	1.0262	**1.3029**
Bull3	1.0880	*1.0430*	*1.0432*

from the portfolio defined on the left-hand side of hypotheses (16.2) and (16.4). In Tables 16.5 and 16.7, cells containing statistics (16.7) are italicized when the bigger variance concerns portfolio from the right-hand side of hypotheses presented in (16.6).

Table 16.6 Values of test statistics (16.5) comparing returns from portfolios in distinguished periods

Comparing periods	Null hypothesis (16.4) H_0: $E(R_{t1}) = E(R_{t2})$			
	PB	PM	PS	PT
Bear1: Bull1	**−2.0939**	**−2.6031**	**−1.7326**	**−2.1398**
Bull1: Stable1	0.2906	0.8300	0.6840	0.6134
Stable1: Bull2	−0.8240	−1.0700	−0.8211	−0.9158
Bull2: Stable2	0.6542	1.0577	0.6268	0.7993
Stable2: Bear2	0.3629	0.0173	1.1826	0.4832
Bear2: Bull3	−0.5462	−0.6180	−1.5119	−0.8679

Table 16.7 Values of test statistics (16.7) comparing the risk of portfolios in distinguished periods

Comparing periods	Null hypothesis (16.4) H_0: $D^2(R_{t1}) = D^2(R_{t2})$			
	PB	PM	PS	PT
Bear1: Bull1	**1.4904**	**1.5009**	**1.3000**	**1.4194**
Bull1: Stable1	*1.0325*	*1.3159*	**1.0079**	*1.1214*
Stable1: Bull2	**1.4514**	**1.3513**	**1.6717**	**1.4955**
Bull2: Stable2	**1.2857**	**1.4272**	**1.3376**	**1.3390**
Stable2: Bear2	*1.0897*	*1.0148*	***1.5848***	*1.1851*
Bear2: Bull3	*1.1708*	1.2425	1.1609	1.0738

Table 16.3 contains information about rates of returns and risk generated by each portfolio in the distinguished sub-periods. It is visible that the performance of all portfolios in all periods is poor although significantly negative returns are observed only in the first bear market period for all portfolios except the one comprising small companies. Risk, measured by standard deviation, seems to be of the same range in all portfolios and time spans.

Comparing returns generated by pairs of portfolios in different sub-periods, no significant differences are observed (Table 16.4). Whereas the risk of the portfolio PM (Table 16.5) is significantly bigger than the risk of portfolios

- PB in all periods except the ones denoted as the first bear market and the last bull market periods and
- PS when the market was stable and during two first bull market periods.

Taking into consideration distinguished periods of analysis, one may notice that returns do not differ significantly except the first bear market period (Table 16.6). Although risk (Table 16.7) is significantly bigger in the first bear market period and the first stable period in comparison to the two first bull market periods for all portfolios. Also, the risk of each portfolio in the second bull market period is bigger than the one in the second stable market period. Whereas risk in the first stable market period (denoted by stable1) is significantly higher than the one in the first bear market period for the portfolio of medium size companies and significantly smaller for the portfolio of small size companies. The last-mentioned portfolio additionally generates a bigger risk in the second bear market period than in the second stable market period.

To sum up this stage of investigation, we notice that the performance of constructed portfolios does not differ significantly between each other and in distinguished periods (except the first bear market period when returns were significantly smaller) than in the neighbouring time span. However, significant differences are observed for risk generated by considered portfolios (when risk is measured by standard deviation).

16.5 Fama–French Three-Factor Model Construction

To construct the Fama–French model, it is necessary to distinguish (additionally in comparison to CAPM) risk factors SMB and HML. The former (small minus big) is calculated as the difference in returns from a portfolio of stocks characterized by small market value (MV) and from a portfolio of stocks with big MV.[2] The latter (high minus low) represents the difference in returns on a portfolio of high book-to-market value (BV/MV) stocks and on a portfolio of low BV/MV stocks. Therefore, companies are classified according to their capitalization, i.e., big or small value of MV and high, medium and low value of BV/MV rate. Split into small and big companies is made using a median of capitalization. Classification into three groups let us distinguish 30% of companies with the highest and the lowest book-to-market value ratios, and 40% of the rest companies belong to the group of medium BV/MV rate values.

In other words, six portfolios combining both risk factors are defined for each year of analysis. Table 16.8 contains information about composition of each portfolio, denoted as: SL (small and low), SM (small and medium), SH (small and high), BL (big and low), BM (big and medium) and BH (big and high), in every year of analysis.

Daily logarithmic rates of return are calculated for each portfolio assuming an equal share of each company in the portfolio. Then values of risk factors SMB and HML are evaluated, according to formulas:

$$\mathrm{SMB} = \frac{R_{\mathrm{SL}} + R_{\mathrm{SM}} + R_{\mathrm{SH}}}{3} - \frac{R_{\mathrm{BL}} + R_{\mathrm{BM}} + R_{\mathrm{BH}}}{3} \tag{16.8}$$

$$\mathrm{HML} = \frac{R_{\mathrm{SH}} + R_{\mathrm{BH}}}{2} - \frac{R_{\mathrm{SL}} + R_{\mathrm{BL}}}{2} \tag{16.9}$$

where $R_{\mathrm{SL}}, R_{\mathrm{SM}}, R_{\mathrm{SH}}, R_{\mathrm{BL}}, R_{\mathrm{BM}}, R_{\mathrm{BH}}$—rates of returns from the portfolios: SL, SM, SH, BL, BM, BH, respectively.

Arithmetic means of all three risk factors evaluated in each period of analysis are presented in Table 16.9. It is visible that HML average is always negative. It means that in average, returns from the companies, characterized by high values of

[2]Market value means capitalization and it is the multiplication of the share price and the number of shares.

Table 16.8 Number of companies which are comprised in each portfolio

Year	Type of portfolio					
	SL	SM	SH	BL	BM	BH
2007	5	4	5	5	8	3
2008	4	7	4	6	5	4
2009	4	6	5	5	6	4
2010	5	6	4	5	6	4
2011	3	6	5	6	6	4
2012	3	7	5	7	5	3
2013	4	6	5	6	6	3
2014	4	5	6	5	7	3
2015	4	6	5	6	6	3
2016	3	7	5	6	5	4
2017	3	6	6	6	6	3

Table 16.9 Table captions should be placed above the tables

Period	$R_M - R_f$	SMB	HML
Bear1	−0.3283%	−0.1328%	−0.1224%
Bull1	0.0437%	0.0057%	−0.0798%
Stable1	−0.0792%	−0.0478%	−0.0434%
Bull2	0.0976%	0.0626%	−0.1316%
Stable2	0.0076%	−0.0467%	−0.0414%
Bear2	−0.1488%	0.1381%	−0.1864%
Bull3	0.0869%	−0.0048%	−0.0827%
Whole	−0.0138%	−0.0063%	−0.0907%

BV/MV rate, are lower than returns generated by low book-to-market stocks. This conclusion is in line with Fama and French [15] findings. It is also visible that average risk premium in the bull market periods is positive, whereas excess market portfolio return in the bear market periods is negative.

16.6 Estimation Results

CAPM and Fama–French three-factor models are estimated using the OLS method. Parameter estimates and determination coefficients of the single-factor and three-factor capital asset pricing models obtained for four constructed portfolios and all distinguished sub-periods are presented in Tables 16.10 and 16.11.

It is worth mentioning that the risk premium is statistically significant in all estimated models. It is also visible that portfolio PB, containing the biggest and the most liquid companies, is an aggressive one in the majority of periods. While the reaction

Table 16.10 Results of Fama–French three-factor model estimation

Portfolio	Period	Parameter estimates			
		$(R_M - R_f)$	SMB	HML	R^2
PB	Bear1	1.0560	−0.2923	0.0649	0.5733
	Bull1	1.1220	−0.2667	0.0269	0.5474
	Stable1	0.9947	−0.1723	−0.0007	0.4779
	Bull2	1.0369	−0.1576	0.0265	0.3600
	Stable2	1.0005	−0.2520	0.1027	0.3673
	Bear2	0.9066	−0.3783	0.0553	0.3959
	Bull3	1.0219	−0.2178	0.0590	0.3710
PM	Bear1	0.8557	0.2758	−0.0384	0.3134
	Bull1	0.7749	0.2741	0.0232	0.2304
	Stable1	0.8452	0.2497	0.3046	0.3300
	Bull2	0.7695	0.2262	0.0543	0.1643
	Stable2	0.7995	0.1918	−0.0367	0.1901
	Bear2	0.7688	0.1680	−0.0018	0.2178
	Bull3	0.8079	0.1483	0.1124	0.1937
PS	Bear1	0.9917	0.8121	0.0613	0.3686
	Bull1	0.9584	0.8139	−0.0138	0.2326
	Stable1	0.9347	0.8570	0.1612	0.3183
	Bull2	0.8742	0.7422	−0.0312	0.1796
	Stable2	0.9666	0.8386	0.0849	0.1809
	Bear2	0.8884	0.7559	0.0703	0.1811
	Bull3	0.8546	0.1819	0.0412	0.2650
PT	Bear1	0.9678	0.2652	0.0293	0.4180
	Bull1	0.9518	0.2738	0.0121	0.3370
	Stable1	0.9249	0.3115	0.1550	0.3750
	Bull2	0.8935	0.2703	0.0165	0.2350
	Stable2	0.9222	0.2595	0.0503	0.2460
	Bear2	0.8258	0.6744	0.0525	0.1619
	Bull3	0.8852	0.2016	0.0746	0.2420

of returns to risk premium for portfolios PM and PS is similar, and the parameter estimates are below one. All risk factors present in Fama–French models are statistically significant in ten models (among 21)—in four models estimated for the portfolio PS and in three models estimated for big companies PB and medium size companies PM. The three-factor models explain returns better than the single-factor models although the differences in determination coefficients are not very big, except the models estimated for the portfolio PS in the last four sub-periods. In both types

Table 16.11 Results of CAPM estimation

Period	Portfolio PB		Portfolio PM		Portfolio PS		Portfolio PT	
	$(R_M - R_f)$	R^2	$(R_M - R_f)$	R^2	$(R_M - R_f)$	R^2	$(R_M - R_f)$	R^2
Bear1	1.1203	0.5237	0.7962	0.2655	0.8258	0.2308	0.9141	0.3400
Bull1	1.2261	0.5108	0.6637	0.1751	0.6351	0.1336	0.8416	0.2730
Stable1	1.0331	0.4565	0.8003	0.2734	0.7492	0.1738	0.8609	0.3010
Bull2	1.0946	0.3312	0.6899	0.1148	0.6055	0.0581	0.7967	0.1680
Stable2	1.0779	0.3157	0.7322	0.1353	0.6232	0.0716	0.8111	0.1740
Bear2	1.1152	0.3350	0.6814	0.1649	0.5131	0.0722	0.7699	0.1910
Bull3	1.1817	0.3427	0.6937	0.1342	0.3226	0.0403	0.7327	0.1720

of models, the best performance (measured by R^2) is observed for portfolio PB in two first sub-periods.

16.7 Conclusion

The results of the presented research let us formulate the following conclusions concerning the application of the Fama–French three-factor model to the constructed portfolios.

1. Risk premium is the most important factor affecting rates of return, and it is statistically significant in all estimated capital asset pricing models. Whereas two other risk factors (which appear in the three-factor models only) are significant in about half of models.
2. Presence of risk factors concerning capitalization and book-to-market value rate of companies improve the performance of the capital asset pricing models. However, this improvement is visible mostly for portfolios constructed from small and medium size companies.

Answering the question asked in introduction, why CAPM has been still in use much more often than Fama–French model, one should realize that the latter is much more complicated than the former. Evaluation of two additional (in three-factor in comparison to single-factor model) risk factors requires much more data and work connecting with data processing. Whereas the improvement of performance seems not to be essential. Therefore, results obtained from the three-factor model might not cover "the costs" of its construction and estimation.

References

1. Sharpe, W.F.: Capital asset prices: a theory of market equilibrium under conditions of risk. J. Finance **19**, 425–442 (1964)
2. Lintner, J.: The valuation of risk assets and the selection of risky investments in stock portfolios and capital budgets. Rev. Econ. Statist. **47**(1), 13–37 (1965)
3. Mossin, J.: Equilibrium in a capital asset market. Econometrica **34**(4), 768–783 (1966)
4. Markowitz, H.: Portfolio selection. J. Finance **7**(1), 77–91 (1952)
5. Graham, J.R., Harvey, C.R.: The Theory and practice of corporate finance: evidence from the field. J. Financ. Econ. **60**, 187–243 (2001)
6. Bartholdy, J., Peare, P.: Unbiased estimation of expected return using CAPM. Int. Rev. Financ. Anal. **12**(1), 69–81 (2003)
7. Da, Z., Guo, R. Jagannathan, R.: CAPM for estimating the cost of equity capital: interpreting the empirical evidence. NBER Working Papers 14889, National Bureau of Economic Research Inc (2009)
8. Tashfeen, H., Chakraborty, L.: Is the cost of capital an important determinant of market performance of private commercial banks in Bangladesh? Proc. ASBBS **17**(1), 389–399 (2010)
9. Cwynar, W.: Zmienność—dobra, czy zła? Analiza polskiego rynku kapitałowego. Finansowy Kwartalnik Internetowy e-Finanse **6**(2), 16–24 (2010)
10. Sharpe, W.F., Cooper, G.M.: Risk—return class of New York stock exchange common stocks 1931–1967. Financ. Anal. J. **28**(2), 46–56 (1972)
11. Black, F., Jensen, M.C., Scholes, M.S.: The capital asset pricing model: some empirical tests. In: Jensen, M.C. (ed.) Studies in the Theory of Capital Markets, pp. 79–121. Praeger Publishers, New York (1972)
12. Fama, E.F., MacBeath, J.D.: Risk, return and equilibrium: empirical tests. J. Polit. Econ. **81**, 607–636 (1973)
13. Roll, R.: A Critique of the asset pricing theory's tests: part I: on past and potential testability of the theory. J. Financ. Econ. **4**, 129–176 (1977)
14. Fama, E., French, K.: The cross-section of expected stock returns. J. Finance **47**, 427–465 (1992)
15. Fama, E., French, K.: Multifactor explanations of asset pricing anomalies. J. Finance **53**, 55–84 (1996)
16. Fama, E.F., French, K.R.: The capital asset pricing model: theory and evidence. J. Econ. Perspect. Am. Econ. Assoc. **18**(3), 25–46 (2004)
17. Fama, E., French, K.: Common risk factors in the returns on stocks and bonds. J. Financ. Econ. **3**, 3–56 (1993)
18. Ferson, W.E., Locke, D.H.: Estimating the cost of capital through time: an analysis of the sources of error. Manag. Sci. **44**, 485–500 (1998)
19. Pástor, L., Stambaugh, R.F.: Costs of equity capital and model mispricing. J. Finance, Am. Finance Assoc. **54**(1), 67–121 (1999)
20. Gibson, M.R.: Multivariate tests of financial models: a new approach. J. Financ. Econ. **10**, 3–27 (1982)
21. Chan, L.K., Lakonishok, J.: Are the reports of beta's death premature? J. Portfolio Manag. **19**(4), 51–62 (1993)
22. Brounen, D., De Jong, A., Koedijk, K.: Corporate finance in Europe confronting theory with practice. Financ. Manage. **33**, 71–101 (2004)
23. Blanco, B.: The use of CAPM and Fama and French three factor model: portfolios selection. Public Municipal Finance **1**(2), 61–70 (2012)
24. Maroney, N., Protopapadakis, A.: The book-to-market and size effects in a general asset pricing model: evidence from seven national markets. Eur. Finance Rev. **6**(2), 189–221 (2002)
25. Gaunt, C.: Size and book to market effects and the Fama French three factor asset pricing model: evidence from the Australian stock market. Acc. Finance **44**(1), 27–44 (2004)
26. Da Silva, A.C.: Modeling and estimating a higher systematic co-moment asset pricing model in the brazilian stock market. Latin Am. Bus. Rev. **6**(4), 85–101 (2006)

27. Chui, A.C.W., Wei, K.C.J.: Book-to-market, firm size, and the turn-of-the-year-effect: evidence from pacific—basin emerging markets. Pac.—Basin Finance J. **6**(3), 275–293 (1998)
28. Lam, K.: Is the Fama–French three factor model better than the CAPM?, In: M.A. Thesis, Simon Fraser University, Department of Economics, Burnaby (2005)
29. Kassimatis, K.: Size, book to market and momentum effects in the Australian stock market. Aust. J. Manag. **33**(1), 145–167 (2008)
30. Gregory, A., Michou, M.: Industry cost of equity capital: UK evidence. J. Bus. Finance Acc. **36**, 69–704 (2009)
31. Eraslan, V.: Fama and French three-factor model: evidence from istanbul stock exchange. Bus. Econ. Res. J. **4**(2), 11–22 (2013)
32. Wolski, R.: Badanie liniowego charakteru zależności opisanych klasycznym CAPM, technika Famy i MacBetha. In: Tarczyński (ed.) Rynek kapitałowy—skuteczne inwestowanie, Zeszyty Naukowe nr 389, Finanse. Rynki Finansowe. Ubezpieczenia nr 2, Uniwersytet Szczeciński, Szczecin, pp. 527–539 (2004)
33. Gajdka, J., Brzeszczyński, J.: Estymacja parametru β przy użyciu modeli klasy ARCH. In: Tarczyński (ed.) Rynek kapitałowy. Skuteczne inwestowanie. Część I, Wydawnictwo Naukowe Uniwersytetu Szczecińskiego, Szczecin, pp. 73–82 (2007)
34. Witkowska, D.: Badanie stabilności współczynnika beta oszacowanego na podstawie prób o różnej długości. In: Tarczyński (ed.) Rynek Kapitałowy. Skuteczne inwestowanie, Studia i prace Wydziału Nauk Ekonomicznych i Zarządzania, Uniwersytet Szczeciński, Nr 9, Szczecin, pp. 143–154, (2008)
35. Witkowska, D.: Badanie wrażliwości współczynnika beta na metodę estymacji. In: Barczak, A., Iskry, D. (eds.) Metody matematyczne, ekonometryczne i komputerowe w finansach i ubezpieczeniach 2010, Prace Naukowe UE w Katowicach, Katowice, pp. 395–419 (2012)
36. Byrka-Kita, K., Rozkrut, D.: Test CAPM w warunkach polskiego rynku kapitałowego wzorowany na technice Pettengilla, Sundarama oraz Mathura. In: Zarzecki, D. (ed.) Zarzadzanie finansami. Wycena przedsiębiorstw i zarządzanie wartością, Uniwersytet Szczeciński, Szczecin, pp. 685–697 (2009)
37. Tarczyński, W., Witkowska, D., Kompa, K.: Współczynnik beta. Teoria i praktyka, Pielaszek Research, Warszawa (2013)
38. Czapkiewicz, A., Skalna, I.: The CAPM and the Fama–French models in Warsaw stock exchange. Przegląd Statystyczny **57**(4), 128–141 (2010)
39. Kowerski, M.: The analysis of an investment risk within emerging capital markets. Case Warsaw Stock Exchange, e-Finance **6**(4), 1–23 (2010)
40. Zaremba, A.: Cross-sectional asset pricing models for the polish market, SSRN working paper http://dx.doi.org/10.2139/ssrn.2396884 (2014)
41. Urbański, S.: Comparison of a modified and classic Fama–French model for the polish market. Folia Oeconomica Stetinensia **17**, 80–96 (2017)
42. Redlicki, M., Borowski, K.: Wykorzystanie trzyczynnikowego modelu Famy–Frencha na GPW. Studia i Prace Kolegium Zarządzania i Finansów, Zeszyt Naukowy **153**, 81–102 (2017)
43. Czapkiewicz, A., Skalna, I.: Użyteczność stosowania modelu Famy i Frencha w okresach hossy i bessy na rynku akcji GPW w Warszawie. Bank i Kredyt **42**(3), 61–80 (2011)
44. Czapiewski, L.: Model CAPM i trójczynnikowy model Famy-Frencha w analizie zdarzeń na polskim rynku kapitałowym. Zeszyty Naukowe Uniwersytetu Szczecińskiego **854**, 609–620 (2015)
45. Bartholdy, J., Peare, P.: Estimation of expected return: CAPM versus Fama and French. Int. Rev. Financ. Anal. **14**(4), 407–427 (2005)
46. Rogowicz, T.: Model Famy-Frencha na Giełdzie Papierów Wartościowych w Warszawie, praca magisterska przygotowana pod kierunkiem K. Kompy, SGGW, Warszawa (2017)

Chapter 17
Beta Coefficient and Fundamental Strength in Companies Listed on the Warsaw Stock Exchange

Waldemar Tarczyński and Małgorzata Tarczyńska-Łuniewska

Abstract In the literature, the beta factor is regarded as a risk measure. It is calculated using the classic Sharpe model. The purpose of the paper is to examine the relationship between the beta coefficient and the fundamental strength index (FPI) for selected companies listed on the Warsaw Stock Exchange. The database of companies included in the survey consisted of companies included in the WIG20 stock exchange index at the end of 2006 and 2010. On that basis, it was established whether the beta coefficient affects the economic and financial standing of a company and should be used as a risk measure in stock exchange analyses. The study covered the years 2006–2010 on a quarterly basis and used economic and financial data published by *Notoria Service*.

Keywords Fundamental analysis · Stock exchange · Fundamental power indicator

17.1 Introduction

The issue of the use of the beta coefficient on the capital market is very important. This results from the fact of the broad area in which it is applied. In addition to problematic and ambiguous issues of how to determine the beta coefficient or what kind of rate of return should be used in the process of its estimation to the making investment decisions inclusive.

This is supported by a number of publications in this scope [1, 3–5, 8]. Besides, new areas of application of this coefficient in the practice of the capital market are

W. Tarczyński (✉)
Faculty of Economics and Management, Institute of Finance, University of Szczecin, Szczecin, Poland
e-mail: waldemar.tarczynski@usz.edu.pl

M. Tarczyńska-Łuniewska
Faculty of Economics and Management, Institute of Econometrics and Statistics, University of Szczecin, Szczecin, Poland
e-mail: malgorzata.tarczynska@usz.edu.pl

W. Tarczyński and K. Nermend (eds.), *Effective Investments on Capital Markets*, Springer Proceedings in Business and Economics,
https://doi.org/10.1007/978-3-030-21274-2_17

emerging. In the earlier work of authors: Tarczyński [9, pp. 275–300], [10], Tarczyński and Łuniewska [11], the use of the beta coefficient was suggested when constructing the taxonomic measure of attractiveness of investments (TMAI). It was one of the proposals for taking the beta coefficient into account in the process of constructing the measure. It should also be emphasized at the same time that this measure is treated in the subject literature as the first attempt to measure the fundamental strength of a company.

The development of the capital market, or more narrowly of the stock exchange market, initiated, among others, by the search for new investment opportunities and investment tools (new strategies, approaches) forces at the same time a broader perspective on issues related to the risk of activities undertaken within the market. Investors or market analysts while building investment tools and methods, try to look in a broader manner for information (factors) that could affect the effectiveness of taken investment decisions. Combining methods of analysis, and as a matter of fact of selected information which they provide, is nothing surprising at present. This approach is used, for example, in the context of horizontal and vertical diversification of risk, where during the construction of the securities portfolio, in the process of selection of companies for the portfolio, emphasis is placed on information derived from the fundamental analysis. The issue of fundamental strength of the operator gains broader significance. When undertaking the problem generally what follows is the linking of elements of the fundamental analysis with the portfolio analysis. It should also be noted that the development of capital markets or economies caused the role and importance of information derived from fundamental analysis to increase. This type of analysis in a broader context, in principle, can be used only in developed markets.

Continuing the issue of the link between the fundamental analysis and the portfolio one, it is interesting to consider the problem of whether the beta coefficient and the fundamental strength remain in a relationship with each other and what relationship it is.

The aim of the article is to examine the relationship between the sensitivity of rates of return on shares and their fundamental strength. The sensitivity was measured with the beta coefficient determined using the Sharpe model. The fundamental strength of companies was measured with the fundamental strength index. The study has allowed to answer the question whether the beta coefficient can be taken into consideration in the assessment of the fundamental strength of companies.

17.2 The Beta Coefficient

The beta coefficient in the analysis of securities is the result of a search of other concepts of constructing a portfolio of securities in relation to the Markowitz model. This coefficient as a measure of sensitivity of a share to market changes expresses the relationship between the market and the company. This approach was developed by Sharpe, who first described this relationship in the form of a regression function.

This function described the relationship between the level of the rate of return on a stock and the rate of return on the market (the stock index) (see Dębski et al. [2]). This approach greatly facilitated the analysis and calculations concerning the construction of the portfolio. Moreover, it allowed, in a simple and fast way, for the evaluation of the behavior of a share.

The formal record of the relationship between the rate of return on a share and the rate of return on the stock index is expressed by the following equation (see Sharpe [6, 7]):

$$R_i = \alpha_i + \beta_i \cdot R_m + U_i, \tag{17.1}$$

where

R_i—rate of return on ith share,
R_m—benchmark rate of return on market index,
α_i—intercept, a component of the rate of return on ith stock, independent from the market situation,
β_i—Share's beta coefficient constant in time, directional coefficient of the equation which measures expected volatility of R_i for a given change R_m,
U_i—an error term (unexplained return), random element.

Values of unknown parameters β_i and α_i are determined using the method of least squares:

$$\beta_i = \frac{\sum_{t=1}^{n}\left(R_{mt} - \bar{R}_m\right)\cdot\left(R_{it} - \bar{R}_i\right)}{\sum_{t=1}^{n}\left(R_{mt} - \bar{R}_m\right)^2}, \tag{17.2}$$

$$\alpha_i = \bar{R}_i - \beta_i \cdot \bar{R}_m. \tag{17.3}$$

where designation as above,

t—number of time series observations.

Application of the beta coefficient refers to a number of areas:

- It is a measure of sensitivity of a share price to move in the market price.
- This coefficient can be used also for measuring sensitivity of the described portfolio.
- It informs what the direction of correlation between movement rates of return on analyzed stocks and the benchmark is, i.e., market indices.

When using the beta coefficient, one should determine what market index will be taken into account in the analyses. In Poland, on the Warsaw Stock Exchange the beta coefficient is given into relation of WIG or WIG20 indices. Beta is also treated as a risk coefficient in the valuation of financial assets or cost of capital. Besides that, beta is a historical context which allows assessing past investment and the fundamental analysis. Usefulness of beta in the future is connected with treating it as a risk coefficient which allows assessment of the portfolio during its construction. An assumption should be made there that past data can be extrapolated in the future.

The Sharpe model, from a formal point of view, is an econometric model of a certain structure. It is a single-equation model, a model of relationships over time, a model with one explanatory variable. The estimation procedure, as previously mentioned, involves the use of the classical least squares method. As an econometric model, Sharpe's model, should therefore comply with the formal requirements of its construction, of estimation and of verification, which determines its practical application. More on the beta coefficient can be found in, e.g., Tarczyński et al. [12], Witkowska [17, 18], Weinraub and Kuhlman [16].

17.3 The Fundamental Power and the Fundamental Power Index—Essence: Definition, Construction, and Measurement

The application of the fundamental strength index in the analysis of investments on the stock exchange is an important element of the decision-making process. This is particularly important in long-term analyses based on the fundamental analysis. The first definition of the fundamental strength can be found in the work of Benjamin Graham, one of the founders of the fundamental analysis. In his works, he underlined the significance of the economic and financial standing of a company for the process of investing on the stock exchange.

The concept of fundamental strength has developed over time, especially in the area of long-term investment methods. Generally speaking, the fundamental strength makes it possible to describe the economic and financial health of a company in a synthetic way. Two issues need to be resolved: which factors should be taken into account when examining the fundamental strength and how to measure them. Thus, understood fundamental strength and the fundamental strength index (FPI) have found a very wide range of applications in stock market as well as in economic analyses.

For an analyst or an investor, key is not only the possibility to identify the factors responsible for the formation of the fundamental power of the operator, but also the question of its measurement. In this respect, the FPI—fundamental power index—finds its application.

FPI index is a multidimensional category directly immeasurable. FPI can be defined as a synthetic variable that captures the effect of the impact of various fundamental factors. Factors (quantitative and qualitative) determine the company's strength and relate to external and internal factors resulting from the functioning of companies on the market (see Tarczynska-Łuniewska [15]). In the FPI construction an important are (among others):

- Selection and incorporate the fundamental power factors.
- Data which is derived from the fundamental analysis.

FPI design:

$$
\begin{aligned}
\mathrm{FPI}_j &= w_{\mathrm{Q}} Q_{ij} + w_{\mathrm{FS}} \mathrm{FS}_{ij}, w_{(\mathrm{Q})} \\
&= \frac{n_Q}{N} \quad w_{(\mathrm{FS})} = \frac{n_{\mathrm{FS}}}{N}, \sum_{i=1}^{k} w_i \\
&= w_{(\mathrm{Q})} + w_{(\mathrm{FS})} = 1,
\end{aligned} \tag{17.4}
$$

where

FPI_i—the fundamental power index for the ith company,
$w_{(\mathrm{Q})}$—the weight for qualitative factors,
$w_{(\mathrm{FS})}$—the weight for the quantitative factors, measured as a fundamental power,
N—number of all variables included in the FPI,
n_{Q}—number of qualitative variables,
n_{FS}—number of quantitative variables,
Q_i—the indices of the fundamental power designated for qualitative factors,
FS_i—the indices of the fundamental power designated for quantitative factors,
i—refers to factors, j refers to objects (companies),
$i = 1, 2, \ldots, k;\ j = 1, 2, \ldots, l$ and $t = 1, 2, \ldots, n$.

Fundamental power is affected by two groups of factors:

1. Quantitative factors—taking into account internal factors, economic and financial variables (indicators of classical ratio analysis and/or levels of variables in their pure form), and market ratios.
2. Qualitative factors—primarily the selection of internal factors such as the position in the sector, on the market, product, quality and management structure, flexibility, recognizable brand, customers–suppliers diversity.

According to the provision of formula 17.4, these factors are also found in the fundamental power index. Several approaches may be applied in the concept of measuring the fundamental strength and the design of the index. One of them is to use the idea of a fundamentally stable database. This concept applies to building in the first step the base of companies stable in fundamental terms. Construction of the base entails implementing a certain procedure that allows identification of operators that feature stability over time and space of some specific fundamental factors. These factors, by way of a reminder, are responsible for creating the fundamental strength of the operator. In turn, applying the concept of the fundamental power index allows measuring the fundamental strength (a complex, multidimensional category) and expressing it in a synthetic manner by way of one value. Furthermore, given the fundamental strength indices that are taken into account in defining and measuring the fundamental power, it is possible to use only quantitative factors of the fundamental strength in this process, in particular economic–financial indicators illustrating the economic and financial situation of the economic operator. In this approach, an assertion is applicable that in order to be able to speak of good economic and financial standing, the company has to "function well" at all levels of its operation, which also includes the group of qualitative factors. Thus, through the prism of quantitative factors, the effect of the impact of qualitative factors is noticeable. The approach where the idea of fundamentally stable database is used:

$$\mathrm{FPI}_j = \mathrm{FS(ST)}_j,$$

where

FPI_j—fundamental power index for ith company, constructed on the base of fundamentally stable database, included only quantitative variables,
$\mathrm{FS(ST)}_j$—fundamental power (strength) quantitative indicator stable in time for jth company obtained by applying one synthetic measure of development or scoring methods included ith fundamental factors.

Measuring the fundamental power can also be done by employing various methods, for example, using the idea of the synthetic measure of development or the so-called scoring method. Since it was the point's method that was employed in the empirical example, only this method was briefly discussed in the paper. More on the approach employing the idea of synthetic measures of development can be found, e.g., in Tarczyński [10], Tarczyńska-Łuniewska [13, 14].

The scoring method involves assigning a relevant number of points to the fundamental factors in each of the analyzed periods. It should be emphasized that when determining the level of points, information on standards for factors (e.g., economic and financial indicators) is used.

In addition, in order to be able to speak of stability over time, this element must also be taken into account during the construction of the fundamental power index. Stability over time is defined through weights for successive periods of analysis, according to the principle: the lowest weight for the oldest period. Formal record of the procedures can thus be written as:

$$\mathrm{FPI}_j = \mathrm{FS}_j = \sum_{i=1}^{k}\sum_{t=1}^{n} w_t \cdot \mathrm{FS}_{ij},$$

$$w_t = \frac{nc_{it}}{N} \quad \sum_{t=1}^{n} w_t = 1 \quad w_t \geq 0,$$

where

$i = 1, 2, \ldots, k;\;\; j = 1, 2, \ldots, l$ and $t = 1, 2, \ldots, n$,
w_t—weight for t-period and ith factor,
nc_{it}—number (order) of ith quantitative factors in t-period,
N—sum of the order of ith factor in analyzed period ($t = 1, 2, \ldots, n$),
K—number of all fundamental factors used in index construction,
FS_{ij}—sum of point (scores) for all factors in a fundamental factors group.

17.4 Examples and Results

In our empirical studies, we focused on the correlation between the beta coefficient and the fundamental force measured by FPI. This has made it possible to answer the question whether the beta factor, being a measure of risk, should be used in the fundamental analysis to assess the economic and financial standing of a company. The research covered the years 2006–2010 and examined financial statements of the Warsaw Stock Exchange companies (annual data) published by *Notoria Serwis*. The analysis excluded companies for which data from the financial statements was incomplete. Finally, this gave a total of 203 companies listed on the main market on the WSE.

The Sharpe model and the beta coefficient were calculated by using a logarithmic rate of return for selected companies. As a benchmark WIG20 index, rates of return were used. The research was carried out in four steps:

1. A fundamentally stable database was built (203 companies). The base was divided into three groups: good companies (H), average companies (M), weak companies (W).
2. 10 companies were chosen as representation for each group.
3. The beta coefficient (in few variants) was calculated for companies which were selected in the second step. The variants of beta for companies and the FPI:
   - separately for each year in the period 2006–2010,
   - total for the period 2006–2010.
4. The Pearson correlation coefficient between beta and the FPI was calculated.

Tables 17.1, 17.2 and 17.3 contain values of the FPI and beta coefficients for the years 2006–2010 and average values of the FPI and the beta coefficient for these years for each company. The companies were divided into three groups (companies with a high level of the FPI—Table 17.1, an average level—Table 17.2 and a low level—Table 17.3). Subsequent Tables 17.4, 17.5, 17.6, 17.7, 17.8, 17.9, 17.10, 17.11, 17.12, 17.13, 17.14, 17.15, 17.16, 17.17 and 17.18 include values of beta coefficients for individual years and companies, broken down into three groups according to the level of the FPI. Analysis of the data in Tables 17.4, 17.5, 17.6, 17.7, 17.8, 17.9, 17.10, 17.11, 17.12, 17.13, 17.14, 17.15, 17.16, 17.17 and 17.18 indicates that statistically significant beta coefficients were not obtained in the investigated period. This means that their practical application should be done with great caution.

In Tables 17.4, 17.5, 17.6, 17.7, 17.8, 17.9, 17.10, 17.11, 17.12, 17.13, 17.14, 17.15, 17.16, 17.17 and 17.18 are included values of the beta coefficient for the 2006–2010 period according to division for 3 groups of companies in each year, high level of FPI—H, medium level of FPI—M, week level of FPI—W.

Tables 17.19, 17.20, 17.21 and 17.22 contain values of coefficients of the linear correlation between the FPI and the beta coefficient respectively for 2006–2010 and companies broken down into three groups, except for 2010, for companies with low and average FPI. This information indicates that the use of the beta coefficient in the

Table 17.1 Values of FPI and beta calculated for the best companies according to FPI (H)

Name	FPI					Beta					Average beta	FPI 2006–2010	Branch
H	2006	2007	2008	2009	2010	2006	2007	2008	2009	2010			
MENNICA	23	20	26	28	24	0.2389	0.3481	0.0905	0.2105	0.3108	0.2398	24.87	Metals
HYDROTOR	24	22	23	23	22	0.3768	0.7756	0.3679	0.5902	0.1603	0.4542	22.60	Electroengineering
KGHM	24	26	22	19	20	1.6582	1.4635	1.4407	0.9942	1.5726	1.4258	21.20	Metals
CCC	20	16	19	22	20	0.5781	1.4635	0.3060	0.2095	0.3738	0.5862	19.80	Retails
STALPROD	22	23	24	20	14	0.3234	1.4635	0.8529	0.5998	0.5785	0.7636	19.33	Metals
PROCHNIK	12	16	16	16	26	0.5712	1.4635	0.6898	0.3153	0.5327	0.7145	19.07	Light Industry
NOVITA	9	14	17	24	18	0.6797	1.4635	0.4565	0.1065	0.4006	0.6214	18.27	Light Industry
KRUSZWICA	8	12	17	22	20	0.3414	0.6265	0.5680	0.2604	0.2323	0.4057	18.07	Food
POLNA	13	22	14	21	17	1.0757	1.1177	0.5459	0.3116	0.6353	0.7372	17.87	Electroengineering
TIM	14	14	14	20	20	0.7562	0.9126	0.6386	0.6430	0.6764	0.7254	17.60	Wholesale

Source Own calculations

Table 17.2 Values of FPI and beta calculated for the average companies according to FPI (M)

Name	FPI					Beta					Average beta	FPI 2006–2010	Branch
M	2006	2007	2008	2009	2010	2006	2007	2008	2009	2010			
ŚNIEŻKA	14	15	15	15	13	0.0729	0.2847	0.4245	0.2367	−0.0068	0.2024	14.27	Building materials
BEDZIN	13	14	13	13	16	−0.2602	−0.1060	0.0411	−0.0325	0.3471	−0.0021	14.13	Energy
NOVITUS	16	14	14	14	14	0.3175	0.6733	0.4421	0.2813	0.2044	0.3837	14.13	IT
COGNOR	14	16	18	15	10	0.8283	1.7101	1.1171	0.6255	1.2015	1.0965	14.00	Wholesale
COMARCH	14	14	14	14	14	0.2605	0.9194	0.9334	0.8285	0.6710	0.7226	14.00	IT
ENERGOPL	17	16	10	14	15	0.9454	1.3558	0.6628	0.7208	0.4237	0.8217	14.00	Construction
VISTULA	14	16	6	19	14	0.3668	1.5197	0.7735	0.5428	0.5294	0.7464	14.00	Retails
AGORA	12	14	14	14	14	0.7955	0.5922	0.8523	0.9065	0.4483	0.7190	13.87	Media
POLICE	15	22	19	8	12	0.5569	0.4623	1.4133	0.6047	0.6923	0.7459	13.87	Chemicals
WILBO	14	14	14	16	12	0.7401	0.7478	0.6081	0.3387	0.5390	0.5947	13.87	Food

Source Own calculations

Table 17.3 Values of FPI and beta calculated for the weak companies according to FPI (W)

Name **W**	FPI					Beta					Average beta	FPI 2006–2010	Branch
	2006	2007	2008	2009	2010	2006	2007	2008	2009	2010			
AMICA	8	8	7	11	9	0.6612	0.5855	0.4871	1.1805	0.5372	0.6903	8.93	Electroengineering
HYGIENIK	6	10	9	6	8	1.7640	1.1875	1.5122	0.4142	0.6836	1.1123	7.80	Pharmaceutical
FON	10	6	9	6	8	0.5128	1.0130	2.1812	1.2607	0.2595	1.0454	7.53	Services—others
TORFAR	7	7	8	8	7	0.0369	0.1496	0.3988	0.3346	0.2592	0.2358	7.47	Wholesale
TRAVEL	9	8	4	6	8	0.6143	0.8309	0.6150	0.2335	0.4913	0.5570	6.73	Retails
BARLINEK	10	13	5	5	5	0.6849	0.9114	0.5854	0.9202	0.8090	0.7822	6.40	Building materials
SYGNITY	9	6	6	6	6	0.4550	1.2721	0.4011	0.5424	1.0161	0.7373	6.20	IT
AMPLI	7	7	3	7	7	1.2951	2.0806	1.0053	0.5415	0.8086	1.1462	6.20	Wholesale
CIECH	12	9	3	3	5	0.6534	0.6535	0.8343	0.6915	0.8890	0.7443	5.07	Chemicals
CERSANIT	1	1	7	1	7	0.6451	1.1877	0.8201	1.2230	0.6689	0.9090	4.20	Building materials

Source Own calculations

Table 17.4 Values of beta coefficients for 2006 year for companies with high level (H) of FPI

2006 H	Beta	R^2	*t* Stat
MENNICA	0.2389	0.0809	4.6354
HYDROTOR	0.3768	0.0836	4.7166
KGHM	1.6582	0.6588	21.7055
CCC	0.5781	0.2279	8.4888
STALPROD	0.3234	0.0305	2.7727
PROCHNIK	0.5712	0.0672	4.1925
NOVITA	0.6797	0.0728	4.3757
KRUSZWICA	0.3414	0.0400	3.1893
POLNA	1.0757	0.0599	3.9434
TIM	0.7562	0.2758	9.6387

Source Own calculations

Table 17.5 Values of beta coefficients for 2006 year for companies with medium level (M) of FPI

2006 M	Beta	R^2	*t* Stat
ŚNIEŻKA	0.0729	0.0081	1.4079
BEDZIN	−0.2602	0.0398	−3.1810
NOVITUS	0.3175	0.0549	3.7661
COGNOR	0.8283	0.0408	3.2226
COMARCH	0.2605	0.0318	2.8323
ENERGOPL	0.9454	0.0305	2.7698
VISTULA	0.3668	0.0575	3.8598
AGORA	0.7955	0.1957	7.7047
POLICE	0.5569	0.1422	6.3591
WILBO	0.7401	0.1736	7.1592

Source Own calculations

Table 17.6 Values of beta coefficients for 2006 year for companies with week level (W) of FPI

2006 W	Beta	R^2	*t* Stat
AMICA	0.6612	0.1637	6.9114
HYGIENIK	1.7640	0.2013	7.8416
FON	0.5128	0.0473	3.4813
TORFAR	0.0369	0.0007	0.4102
TRAVEL	0.6143	0.1049	5.3469
BARLINEK	0.6849	0.2725	9.5601
SYGNITY	0.4550	0.1407	6.3214
AMPLI	1.2951	0.1811	7.3452
CIECH	0.6534	0.1971	7.7401
CERSANIT	0.6451	0.1919	7.6114

Source Own calculations

Table 17.7 Values of beta coefficients for 2007 year for companies with high level (H) of FPI

2007 H	Beta	R^2	*t* Stat
MENNICA	0.3481	0.0532	3.6880
HYDROTOR	0.7756	0.1166	5.6524
KGHM	1.4635	0.5348	15.6800
CCC	1.0217	0.2326	8.5655
STALPROD	0.7951	0.1372	6.2030
PROCHNIK	1.2852	0.1646	6.9047
NOVITA	1.9447	0.2162	8.1695
KRUSZWICA	0.6265	0.1853	7.4187
POLNA	1.1177	0.0439	3.3371
TIM	0.9126	0.1191	5.7190

Source Own calculations

Table 17.8 Values of beta coefficients for 2007 year for companies with medium level (M) of FPI

2007 M	Beta	R^2	*t* Stat
ŚNIEŻKA	0.2847	0.0398	3.1696
BEDZIN	−0.1060	0.0067	−1.2804
NOVITUS	0.6733	0.1795	7.2752
COGNOR	1.7101	0.2043	7.8837
COMARCH	0.9194	0.2349	8.6190
ENERGOPL	1.3558	0.0472	3.4640
VISTULA	1.5197	0.0215	2.3059
AGORA	0.5922	0.1580	6.7399
POLICE	0.4623	0.0375	3.0718
WILBO	0.7478	0.1268	5.9295

Source Own calculations

Table 17.9 Values of beta coefficients for 2007 year for companies with week level (W) of FPI

2007 W	Beta	R^2	*t* Stat
AMICA	0.5855	0.1470	6.4585
HYGIENIK	1.1875	0.0592	3.9015
FON	1.0130	0.0126	1.7604
TORFAR	0.1496	0.0078	1.3749
TRAVEL	0.8309	0.0755	4.4468
BARLINEK	0.9114	0.2819	9.7473
SYGNITY	1.2721	0.1411	6.3046
AMPLI	2.0806	0.2788	9.6730
CIECH	0.6535	0.1104	5.4797
CERSANIT	1.1877	0.3569	11.5894

Source Own calculations

Table 17.10 Values of beta coefficients for 2008 year for companies with high level (H) of FPI

2008 H	Beta	R^2	*t* Stat
MENNICA	0.0905	0.0311	2.7987
HYDROTOR	0.3679	0.1534	6.6490
KGHM	1.4407	0.5442	17.0716
CCC	0.3060	0.0788	4.5681
STALPROD	0.8529	0.3605	11.7274
PROCHNIK	0.6898	0.1763	7.2257
NOVITA	0.4565	0.0867	4.8125
KRUSZWICA	0.5680	0.2184	8.2576
POLNA	0.5459	0.0908	4.9378
TIM	0.6386	0.2285	8.4998

Source Own calculations

Table 17.11 Values of beta coefficients for 2008 year for companies with medium level (M) of FPI

2008 M	Beta	R^2	*t* Stat
ŚNIEŻKA	0.4245	0.1763	7.2259
BEDZIN	0.0411	0.0061	1.2192
NOVITUS	0.4421	0.1887	7.5327
COGNOR	1.1171	0.4630	14.5033
COMARCH	0.9334	0.3961	12.6501
ENERGOPL	0.6628	0.1565	6.7279
VISTULA	0.7735	0.1860	7.4666
AGORA	0.8523	0.3597	11.7089
POLICE	1.4133	0.4745	14.8440
WILBO	0.6081	0.2306	8.5513

Source Own calculations

Table 17.12 Values of beta coefficients for 2008 year for companies with week level (W) of FPI

2008 W	Beta	R^2	*t* Stat
AMICA	0.4871	0.1261	5.9343
HYGIENIK	1.5122	0.5290	16.5471
FON	2.1812	0.0543	3.7446
TORFAR	0.3988	0.1544	6.6741
TRAVEL	0.6150	0.1620	6.8689
BARLINEK	0.5854	0.0923	4.9799
SYGNITY	0.4011	0.0503	3.5961
AMPLI	1.0053	0.2436	8.8647
CIECH	0.8343	0.2713	9.5309
CERSANIT	0.8201	0.2857	9.8785

Source Own calculations

Table 17.13 Values of beta coefficients for 2009 year for companies with high level (H) of FPI

2009 H	Beta	R^2	*t* Stat
MENNICA	0.2105	0.1085	5.4607
HYDROTOR	0.5902	0.2367	8.7163
KGHM	0.9942	0.4542	14.2787
CCC	0.2095	0.0428	3.3094
STALPROD	0.5998	0.1480	6.5241
PROCHNIK	0.3153	0.0394	3.1712
NOVITA	0.1065	0.0027	0.8127
KRUSZWICA	0.2604	0.0929	5.0116
POLNA	0.3116	0.0401	3.1977
TIM	0.6430	0.1804	7.3426

Source Own calculations

Table 17.14 Values of beta coefficients for 2009 year for companies with medium level (M) of FPI

2009 M	Beta	R^2	*t* Stat
ŚNIEŻKA	0.2367	0.0576	3.8680
BEDZIN	−0.0325	0.0021	−0.7162
NOVITUS	0.2813	0.0849	4.7668
COGNOR	0.6255	0.1035	5.3170
COMARCH	0.8285	0.4029	12.8567
ENERGOPL	0.7208	0.1639	6.9302
VISTULA	0.5428	0.0437	3.3453
AGORA	0.9065	0.3269	10.9089
POLICE	0.6047	0.1509	6.5975
WILBO	0.3387	0.0940	5.0423

Source Own calculations

Table 17.15 Values of beta coefficients for 2009 year for companies with week level (W) of FPI

2009 W	Beta	R^2	*t* Stat
AMICA	1.1805	0.2801	9.7636
HYGIENIK	0.4142	0.0801	4.6200
FON	1.2607	0.0100	1.5732
TORFAR	0.3346	0.0530	3.7035
TRAVEL	0.2335	0.0127	1.7748
BARLINEK	0.9202	0.3174	10.6735
SYGNITY	0.5424	0.1613	6.8632
AMPLI	0.5415	0.1305	6.0643
CIECH	0.6915	0.1865	7.4948
CERSANIT	1.2230	0.4307	13.6148

Source Own calculations

Table 17.16 Values of beta coefficients for 2010 year for companies with high level (H) of FPI

2010 H	Beta	R^2	*t* Stat
MENNICA	0.3108	0.1025	5.3014
HYDROTOR	0.1603	0.0176	2.0994
KGHM	1.5726	0.7472	26.9624
CCC	0.3738	0.1145	5.6393
STALPROD	0.5785	0.1348	6.1904
PROCHNIK	0.5327	0.0476	3.5052
NOVITA	0.4006	0.0570	3.8578
KRUSZWICA	0.2323	0.0389	3.1558
POLNA	0.6353	0.1254	5.9388
TIM	0.6764	0.1680	7.0467

Source Own calculations

Table 17.17 Values of beta coefficients for 2010 year for companies with medium level (M) of FPI

2010 M	Beta	R^2	*t* Stat
ŚNIEŻKA	−0.0068	0.0001	−0.1337
BEDZIN	0.3471	0.0366	3.0564
NOVITUS	0.2044	0.0428	3.3165
COGNOR	1.2015	0.1889	7.5710
COMARCH	0.6710	0.2340	8.6692
ENERGOPL	0.4237	0.0577	3.8800
VISTULA	0.5294	0.0846	4.7690
AGORA	0.4483	0.0853	4.7923
POLICE	0.6923	0.0985	5.1867
WILBO	0.5390	0.1884	7.5564

Source Own calculations

Table 17.18 Values of beta coefficients for 2010 year for companies with week level (W) of FPI

2010 W	Beta	R^2	*t* Stat
AMICA	0.5372	0.0371	3.0788
HYGIENIK	0.6836	0.1945	7.7070
FON	0.2595	0.0109	1.6491
TORFAR	0.2592	0.0753	4.4744
TRAVEL	0.4913	0.0595	3.9465
BARLINEK	0.8090	0.1794	7.3341
SYGNITY	1.0161	0.2460	8.9585
AMPLI	0.8086	0.0544	3.7623
CIECH	0.8890	0.1670	7.0176
CERSANIT	0.6689	0.0829	4.7145

Source Own calculations

Table 17.19 Values of the Pearson coefficient between FPI and the beta coefficient for the 2006–2010 period according to division into three groups of companies (H, M, W)

r_{ij}	2006	2007	2008	2009	2010
H	0.0713	−0.0518	−0.0383	−0.4409	−0.1603
M	0.2692	0.0724	0.4104	−0.0487	−0.6262
W	−0.2004	−0.1814	0.4269	−0.1354	−0.6218

Source Own calculations

Table 17.20 Values of the Pearson coefficient between FPI and the average beta coefficient for the 2006–2010 period according to division into four groups of companies (all, H, M, W)

2006/2010 Average	
Variant	r_{ij}
All	−0.24504
H	−0.23212
M	−0.65046
W	−0.13459

Source Own calculations

Table 17.21 Values of the Pearson coefficient between FPI and the median beta coefficient for the 2006–2010 period according to division into four groups of companies (all, H, M, W)

2006/2010 Median	
Variant	r_{ij}
All	−0.2566
H	−0.1060
M	−0.6173
W	−0.1346

construction of the FPI may be justified because it contains information on market risks that are not represented in the FPI. In the case of calculations for all companies without dividing them into groups and with the division for the entire 2006–2010 period, the total of conclusions as to the use of the beta coefficient in the construction of the FPI is analogous to the previous variant. Only in the group of companies with an average level of the FPI can one observe a significant correlation. In general, an increase in the value of the beta coefficient as a measure of risk reduces the value of the FPI. It is also indirectly confirmed by the correctness of the construction of the FPI. Average values, which were used in the calculation, are, respectively, the arithmetic mean (Table 17.20) and the median (Table 17.21). Calculations for the Pearson coefficient between the beta coefficient and FPI were only repeated for the year 2010 in the all-companies set-up and broken down into 3 groups depending on the level of FPI (H, M, W). The results are analogous to the preceding investigated variants.

Table 17.22 Values of the Pearson coefficient between FPI and the beta coefficient for the 2010 year according to division into four groups of companies (all, H, M, W)

Beta 2010	
Variant	r_{ij}
All	−0.16896
H	−0.06296
M	−0.57036
W	−0.50683

17.5 Conclusions

The aim of the paper was to examine whether there is a relationship between the beta coefficient and the fundamental strength measured by the FPI. For this purpose, beta coefficients and fundamental power indices were estimated for selected groups of companies in the period of 2006–2010. The findings of the carried out research indicate that there is a certain relationship between the analyzed coefficient and the fundamental power index. Beta coefficients have significantly different statistical significance. It is therefore important to check and eliminate those factors that are not statistically significant and are poorly matched with the low level of determination of the coefficient. No significant correlations were obtained (total and per group) between the beta coefficients and the FPI. This means that one can subject them to the selection procedure of the FPI, since they carry information about market risk which is missing in the traditional economic and financial factors used to determine the FPI.

The paper addressed the issue of relationships between elements of the fundamental analysis and the portfolio analysis. The approach presented in the empirical example points to the possibility of linking certain information derived from the fundamental analysis (which is represented by the level of the FPI) and the portfolio analysis (information on the sensitivity of a share to market changes—beta). The taking into account in the process of long term investment of information on the fundamental strength of the company as shown by numerous empirical studies conducted in this area, to a significant extent has an impact on reducing the risk of investing. In addition, the methodology of construction of the fundamental power index is so versatile that it allows for the consideration of various quantitative and qualitative factors that may affect the assessment of the fundamental strength of the investigated companies. The research that was carried out indicates the opportunity of taking into account in the measurement of the fundamental strength in a direct manner of the measure of the sensitivity of a share represented by the beta coefficient. The use of the beta coefficient in the process of construction of the FPI is possible from a theoretical point of view, and as shown in the empirical example—also reasonable.

References

1. Choueifaty, Y., Coignard, Y.: Towards maximum diversification. J. Portf. Manage. **35**(1), 40–51 (2008)
2. Dębski, W., Feder-Sempach, E.: Beta coefficients of polish blue chip companies in the period of 2005–2011. Folia Oeconomca Stetiniensa **12**(2), 90–102 (2012)
3. Hitaj, A., Zambruno, G.: Are Smart Beta strategies suitable for hedge fund portfolios? Rev. Financ. Econ. **29**, 37–51 (2016). https://doi.org/10.1016/j.rfe.2016.03.001
4. Liu, J., Stambaugh, R.F., Yuan, Y.: Absolving beta of volatility's effects. J. Financ. Econ. **128**(1), 1–15 (2018). https://doi.org/10.1016/j.jfineco.2018.01.003
5. Malamud, S., Vilkov, G.: Non-myopic betas. J. Financ. Econ. **129**(2), 357–381 (2018). https://doi.org/10.2016/j.jfineco.2018.05.004
6. Sharp, W.F.: A simplified model for portfolio analysis. Manage. Sci. **19** (1963)
7. Sharp, W.F.: Portfolio Theory and Capital Markets. McGraw-Hill, New York (1970)
8. Silva, A., Neves, R., Horta, N.: A hybrid approach to portfolio composition based on fundamental and technical indicators. Expert Syst. Appl. (2014). https://doi.org/10.1016/j.eswa.2014.09.050
9. Tarczyński, W.: Taksonomiczna miara atrakcyjności inwestycji w papiery wartościowe. Przegląd Statystyczny **3**, 275–300 (1994)
10. Tarczyński, W.: Fundamentalny portfel papierów wartościowych. PWE, Warszawa (2002)
11. Tarczyński, W., Łuniewska, M.: Dywersyfikacja ryzyka na polskim rynku kapitałowym. Placet, Warszawa (2004)
12. Tarczyński, W., Witkowska, D., Kompa, K.: Współczynnik beta teoria i praktyka. Pielaszek Research, Warszawa (2013)
13. Tarczyńska-Łuniewska, M.: Metodologia oceny siły fundamentalnej spółek (giełdowych i pozagiełdowych). ZAPOL, Szczecin (2013a)
14. Tarczyńska-Łuniewska, M.: Definition and nature of fundamental strengths. Actual Probl. Econ. **2**(1), 15–23 (2013b)
15. Tarczynski, W., Tarczynska-Łuniewska, M.: The procedure of building stable fundamental database with the use of Matlab software. Proc. Comput. Sci. **126**(2018), 2085–2096 (2018)
16. Weinraub, H.J., Kuhlman, B.R.: The effect of common stock beta variability on the variability of the portfolio beta. J. Financ. Strateg. Decis. **7**(2), 79–84 (1994)
17. Witkowska, D.: Badanie stabilności współczynnika beta oszacowanego na podstawie prób o różnej długości, Studia i Prace WNEIZ Uniwersytet Szczeciński Nr 9, Szczecin, pp. 143–154 (2008)
18. Witkowska, D.: Badanie wrażliwości współczynnika beta na metodę estymacji, Prace Naukowe UE w Katowicach, pp. 395–419 (2012)

Chapter 18
Comparison of the Results of Modelling Rates of Return Depending on the Financial Situation of Companies with the Use of Real and Transformed Values of Variables

Barbara Batóg and Katarzyna Wawrzyniak

Abstract The aim of the study is to find the relationship between rates of return on shares and indicators characterizing the financial situation of companies. Three approaches to modelling rates of return were used: classic econometric models, ordered logit models and discriminant analysis. In the first approach, the real quarterly rates of return were explained variable, and in the second and third approaches, the real rates of return were transformed into variants measured on an ordinal scale. In each approach for explanatory variables (financial indicators), time lags of up to two quarters were taken into account. Additionally, the explanatory variables were transformed—the nominants were transformed into stimulants or destimulants. The study used quarterly data from 2014 to 2017 on financial ratios for *Machinery* sector companies listed on the Warsaw Stock Exchange from the Notoria Serwis database and data on prices from Bank Ochrony Środowiska. As a result of research conducted with the use of particular models, the financial indicators which had the greatest impact on the level of return rates were identified. Knowledge of these indicators may help investors to make decisions on the selection of companies for the investment portfolio.

Keywords Rates of return on shares · Financial ratios · Econometric models · Ordered logit model · Discriminant analysis

---

B. Batóg (✉)
University of Szczecin, Szczecin, Poland
e-mail: barbara.batog@usz.edu.pl

K. Wawrzyniak
West Pomeranian University of Technology Szczecin, Szczecin, Poland
e-mail: katarzyna.wawrzyniak@zut.edu.pl

W. Tarczyński and K. Nermend (eds.), *Effective Investments on Capital Markets*,
Springer Proceedings in Business and Economics,
https://doi.org/10.1007/978-3-030-21274-2_18

18.1 Introduction

In order to carry out a fundamental analysis, information characterizing the environment (external factors) and the financial situation (internal factors) of a given company is required. The financial situation is reflected in the values of financial indicators, and the analysis of which in time and space is the basis for making decisions by investors, both current and long term. It can be expected that the better the financial condition of the company, the higher the value of its shares and the more attractive it is for the investor.

In the previous works, the authors modelled quarterly rates of return using models for qualitative variables to formulate diagnoses of the financial situation for companies listed on the Warsaw Stock Exchange. The modelling was based on data on rates of return and financial ratios on a quarterly basis [3, 4], and the ordered logit models were applied.

The aim of the current study is to identify the relationships between the rates of return and indicators characterizing the financial situation of companies. The research problem is to find a set of financial indicators that have the greatest impact on investors' decisions, which in turn determines the rate of return on shares. Moreover, an important aspect of the conducted research is to check whether the set of indicators varies depending on the modelling method applied.

Apart from the ordered logit models, an attempt has been made to use classic econometric models and discriminant analysis. The classic econometric models allow to determine which explanatory variables significantly influence the explained variable and what the direction of this influence is. The ordered logit models provide an answer to the question which financial ratios significantly increase the probability of belonging of a given company to a group of companies with higher rates of return. The discriminant analysis, on the other hand, allows to identify those indicators whose values differentiate in the best way between companies belonging to a different group on the basis of the rates of return. In the classical econometric models, real quarterly rates of return were the explained variable, and real values of financial ratios were explanatory variables. In ordered logit models and discriminant analysis, the explained variable and the grouping variable were transformations of real values of rates of return, and both the real values of financial ratios and their transformations were used as explanatory variables.

18.2 Literature Review

Logit models are widely used in practice. Their frequent application is forecasting bankruptcy of enterprises, where the explanatory variables are financial indicators [21, 25, 6, 2]. Piszczek [20] applied logit models to model bankruptcy on the basis of data on companies listed on the Warsaw Stock Exchange. The best model had two independent variables: debt service ratio three years before bankruptcy and the overall asset ratio one year before bankruptcy. Grochowina [8] applied a logit model to model bankruptcy with financial ratios as explanatory variables. The best set of explanatory variables was selected by means of the backward stepwise method.

Bieszk-Stolorz and Markowicz [5] used binomial models to analyse changes in stock prices depending on the sector of the industry. Prusak [22] studied the relationship between the rates of return on shares and the values of market indices of selected companies listed on the Warsaw Stock Exchange. A wide review of models where the rate of return on shares is an explained variable was presented by Gruszczyński [9]. Guris et al. [10] compared classic logit models with panel logit models where financial ratios were explanatory variables.

The review and verification of Polish discriminatory models for bankruptcy forecasting were carried out by Kisielińska and Waszkowski [14]. In their studies, samples were balanced, the grouping variable had two variants, and explanatory variables were both market and financial indicators. It turned out that all models with less than four variables gave poor classifications. This may mean that the information contained in two or three indicators is insufficient to make a correct assessment of the condition of the company. Łuniewska and Tarczyński [17] in their discriminant analysis defined a binary variable grouping on the basis of a synthetic measure, which took into account the total impact of financial ratios on the condition of companies. The set of explanatory variables consisted of seven indicators in the standard approach, and their number was limited by the application of the stepwise method.

Kisielińska and Skórnik-Pokarowska [13] carried out discriminant analysis where independent variables were financial indicators and the grouping variable was a binary variable determined on the basis of the median of rate of return—the first group was attractive according to the investor (rates of return above the median) and the second—unattractive (other companies). Interesting research on the use of discriminant analysis in the process of selecting companies for the investment portfolio was presented by Lach [16]. The grouping variable was determined using the k-average method on the basis of six financial indicators, and for each group the average rate of return was calculated which allowed to identify a group of attractive companies with an above-average rate of return. Okičić et al. [19] applied discriminant analysis to the selection of the best portfolio using beta coefficient, market capitalization and realized historical returns. Bal et al. [1] combined entropy measures derived from information theory with discriminant analysis in the prediction of construction business failure using financial ratios as explanatory variables. Wiśniewska [26] applied jointly discriminant analysis and selected technical analysis tools in order to forecast share prices in different periods.

The present study differs from the studies presented in the literature due to the use in modelling not only the original continuous values of explanatory variables (financial indicators) but also their transformation on an ordinal scale. The second novelty is the simultaneous use of three methods of modelling of rates of return (with different linkage functions), which allowed to identify three types of dependencies of rates of return and financial indicators.

18.3 Data and Methods

The examined group consisted of 24 companies from the *Machinery* sector listed on the Warsaw Stock Exchange. The research period was 2014–2017. The quarterly rates of return on shares published by Bank Ochrony Środowiska [28] were the explained (grouping) variable, and 26 financial indicators published by Notoria Serwis [18] were potential explanatory variables. The list of these indicators can be found in Table 18.1.

The first tool used in the study was a classical econometric model (Eq. 18.1). These models are well known and described in the literature (see for example [27, 12]).

Table 18.1 Potential explanatory variables (financial indicators)

Symbol of variable	Name
R_01	Gross profit margin on sales
R_02	Operating profit margin
R_03	Gross profit margin
R_04	Net profit margin
R_05	Return on equity (ROE)
R_06	Return on assets (ROA)
R_07	Working capital ratio
R_08	Current ratio
R_09	Quick ratio
R_10	Cash ratio
R_11	Receivables turnover
R_12	Inventory turnover
R_13	The operating cycle
R_14	Rotation commitments
R_15	Cash conversion cycle
R_16	Rotation assets
R_17	Rotation of assets
R_18	Assets ratio
R_19	Debt ratio
R_20	Debt service ratio
R_21	Rate debt security
R_22	Leverage
R_23	Asset utilization
R_24	Load gross profit
R_25	Load operating profit
R_26	EBITDA margin

$$Y = f(X_1, X_2, \ldots, X_k, U), \tag{18.1}$$

where

Y explained variable—the real values of quarterly rates of return on shares,
$X_1, \ldots, X_k$ set of explanatory variables (real values of financial indices),
k number of explanatory variables,
U random error.

The second method applied was an ordered logit model (Eq. 18.2). It is also a well-known model and many authors described its estimation and testing (e.g. [7, 15]). In ordinal models, the probability of an equal or smaller category (P_{ik}) is compared to the probability of a larger category ($1 - P_{ik}$) (see Eq. 18.2).

$$\ln \frac{P_{kj}}{1 - P_{kj}} = \beta_{0j} + \beta_1 x_{1kj} + \cdots + \beta_p x_{pkj}, \tag{18.2}$$

where

p number of independent variables,
n number of observations,
g number of categories,
P_{kj} the probability of category j or smaller for kth observation (cumulative probability),
$k = 1, \ldots, n$,
$j = 1, \ldots, g$,
x_{ikj} value of ith independent variable for observation k and group j,
$i = 1, \ldots, p$,
β_{0k}, β_i parameters of the ordered logit model.

The third method applied was a multiple discriminant analysis. The theory of this method could be found in Haerdle and Simar [11] or Tacq [24]. The aim of discriminant analysis is to classify observations into known (a priori) groups. The formula for a canonical discriminant function used for classification is given by Eq. 18.3.

$$D_{kj} = \beta_0 + \beta_1 x_{1kj} + \cdots + \beta_p x_{pkj}, \tag{18.3}$$

where

p number of discriminant variables,
n number of observations,
g number of groups,
D_{kj} the value of canonical discriminant function for observation k and group j,
$k = 1, \ldots, n$,
$j = 1, \ldots, g$,
x_{ikj} the value of the ith discriminant variable for observation k and group j,
$i = 1, \ldots, p$,

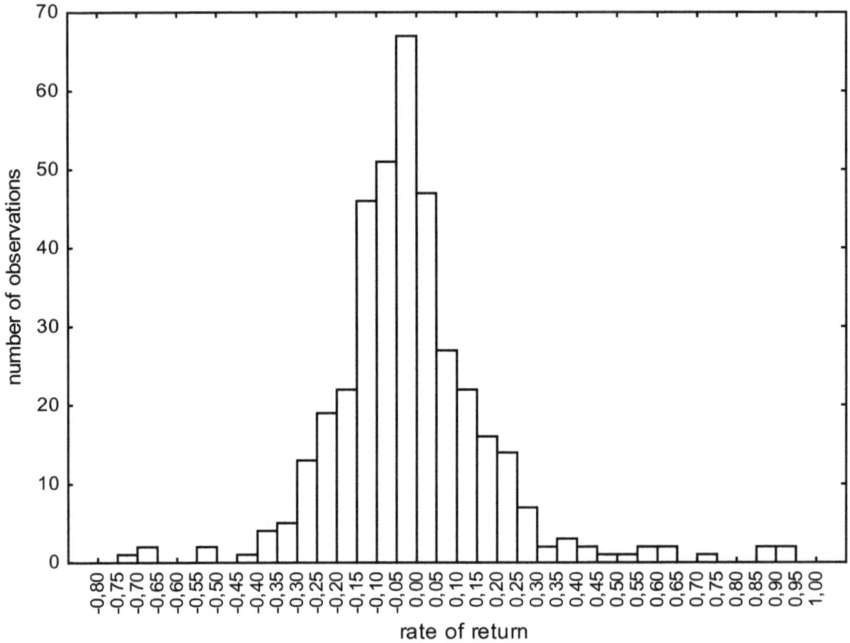

Fig. 18.1 Empirical distribution of the quarterly rate of return for *Machinery* companies in 2014–2017

β_i parameters of canonical discriminant function.

In the case of ordered logit models and discriminant analysis, the authors used a slightly different approach than in the works cited in the literature review. This applies to the way of defining the explained variable (grouping variable) in which the rate of return on shares was transformed into an ordinal variable by means of a quartile (Eq. 18.4). The distribution of the quarterly rate of return for all companies and years is shown in Fig. 18.1.

$$Y_i = \begin{cases} 1 \text{ for rate of return}_i \leq Q_1 \\ 2 \text{ for } Q_1 < \text{rate of return}_i \leq Q_2 \\ 3 \text{ for } Q_2 < \text{rate of return}_i \leq Q_3 \\ 4 \text{ for rate of return}_i > Q_3, \end{cases} \tag{18.4}$$

where Q_1, Q_2, Q_3—first quartile, median, third quartile.

Application of Eq. 18.4 results in a balanced sample which has a significant impact on the quality of the estimated models.

In the article in case of ordered logit models and discriminant analysis, the authors also propose to transform the explanatory variables by changing indicators—nominants to stimulants or destimulant with the use of the mean or median as an empirical

Table 18.2 The explanatory variables with significant parameters in econometric models

Period	Explanatory variables
2014	R_06, R_10, R_12, R_16, R_17, R_23
2015	R_01, R_03, R_04, R_06, R_19, R_24
2016	R_23, R_26
2017	R_01, R_11, R_12, R_16, R_17, R_23
2014–2017	R_03, R_04, R_05, R_14, R_19, R_24

normative value [23]. The mean was used in the transformation of indicators with symmetric distribution, and the median was used in the transformation of indicators with asymmetric distribution (Eq. 18.5).

$$X_{ij} = \begin{cases} x_{ij} & \text{for } x_{ij} \leq Q_j \\ 2Q_j - x_{ij} & \text{for } x_{ij} > Q_j \end{cases} \tag{18.5}$$

where Q_j—mean or median of explanatory variable X_j.

The following financial ratios had symmetric distribution: net profit margin, working capital ratio, inventory turnover, cash conversion cycle, debt ratio and asset utilization.

18.4 Empirical Results

In the process of estimation of classical econometric models of various analytical forms, ordered logit models and in discriminant analysis, the set of potential explanatory variables was reduced using the forward stepwise method. For all models, the estimation was carried out for the whole period (2014–2017) and for individual years. Moreover, it was also examined how the explained variable is affected by the values of indicators selected in the process of reduction, delayed by one and two quarters. In each case, it turned out that the best estimates were obtained when the explanatory variables were delayed by two quarters and the indicators—nominants were converted into stimulants or destimulants according to Eq. 18.5. The results of these estimations are presented in Tables 18.2, 18.3 and 18.4.

The linear models were the best among econometric models; however, their adjustment to empirical data was very weak (R^2 below 0.3). The explanatory variables listed in Table 18.2 corresponded to significant parameters ($p < 0.05$).

The explanatory variables with significant parameters in ordered logit models are presented in Table 18.3. As the measure of quality, the deviation D is presented and also the empirical level of significance p corresponding to it.

The value of the empirical level of significance is close to 1. It means that the hypothesis that the estimated model is as good as the saturated model cannot be rejected and indicates the good quality of an estimated model.

Table 18.3 The explanatory variables with significant parameters in ordered logit models

Period	Explanatory variables	Deviation D (p)
2014	R_18, R_22, R_23, R_25	194.16 (0.903)
2015	R_10	247.083 (0.886)
2016	R_16, R_23	113.216 (0.837)
2017	R_03, R_04, R_09, R_10, R_11, R_12, R_14, R_18, R_26	78.788 (0.998)
2014-2017	R_07	1033.19 (0.971)

Table 18.4 The explanatory variables with significant parameters in discriminant analysis

Period	Explanatory variables	Wilks' Lambda	χ^2 (p)
2014	R_02, R_03, R_05, R_06, R_10, R_11, R_16, R_17, R_18, R_23, R_25	0.045	100.97 (0.000)
2015	R_09, R_12, R_17, R_18. R_19, R_21	0.091	101.70 (0.000)
2016	R_08, R_09, R_11, R_12, R_16	0.284	52.82 (0.006)
2017	R_05, R_07, R_14, R_15, R_17, R_21	0.511	28.82 (0.050)

The explanatory variables with significant parameters in the discriminant analysis are presented in Table 18.4. As the measure of quality, the Wilks' Lambda is presented and the value of statistic χ^2 with the empirical level of significance p corresponding to it.

Additionally in Figs. 18.2, 18.3, 18.2 and 18.5, the results of discriminant analysis are presented in discriminant space.

The values of Wilks' Lambda are from the interval $\langle 0, 1 \rangle$. The closer to 0, the better is the discrimination. The Wilks' Lambdas are on a very good level in 2014, 2015, 2016 and on the moderate level in 2017. The empirical p is close to 0. It means that at least one discriminant function is statistically significant. One can observe very good discrimination in 2014 and 2015, good discrimination in 2016 and moderate discrimination in 2017.

18.5 Conclusions

On the basis of the research carried out, the following conclusions can be drawn concerning the research tools applied:

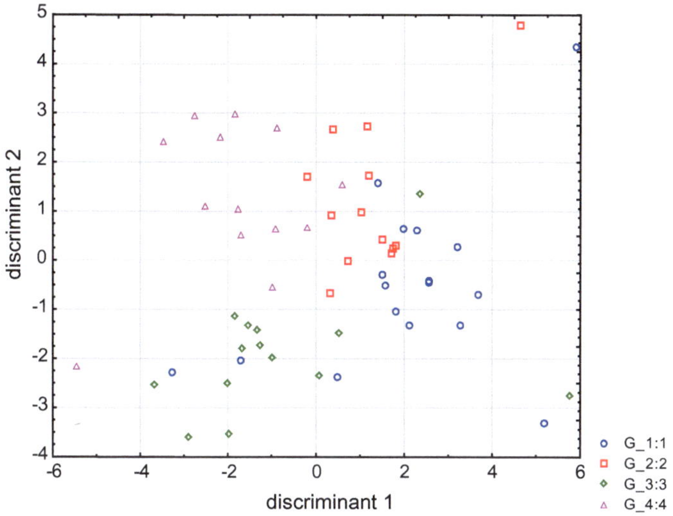

Fig. 18.2 Companies in quarters in 2014 in discriminant space

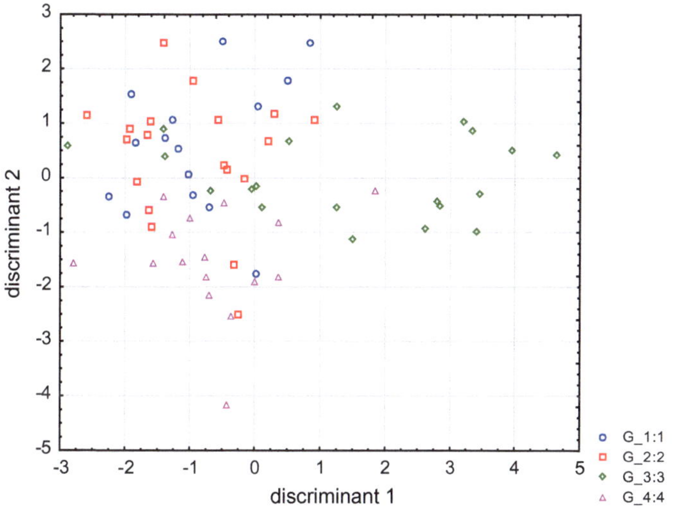

Fig. 18.3 Companies in quarters in 2015 in discriminant space

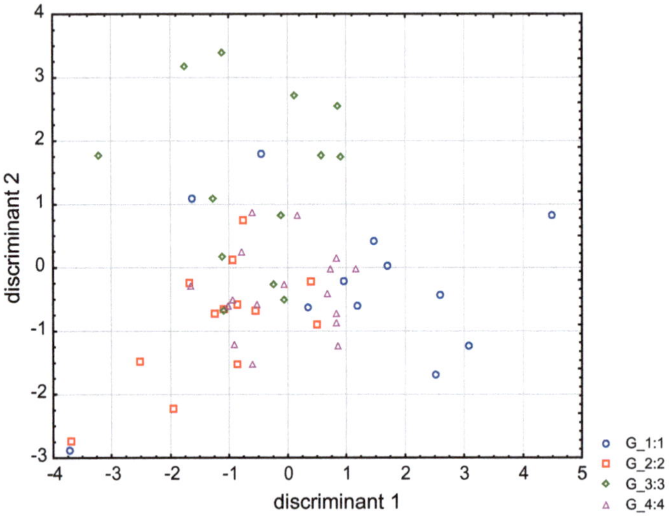

Fig. 18.4 Companies in quarters in 2016 in discriminant space

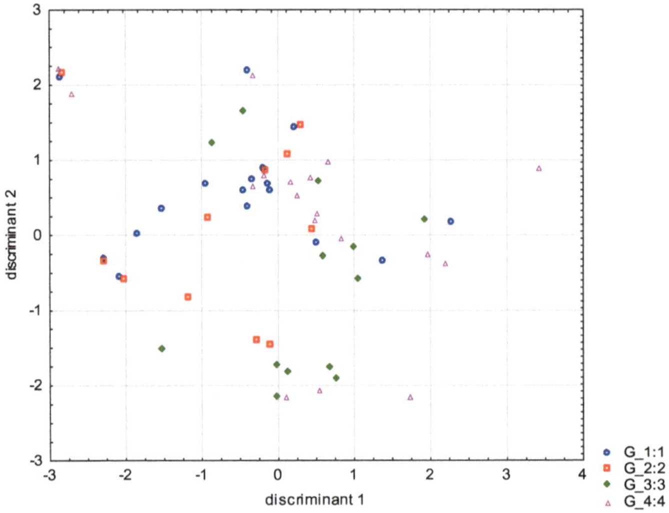

Fig. 18.5 Companies in quarters in 2017 in discriminant space

- linear econometric models were characterized by a weak adjustment to empirical data; however, it was possible to identify financial indicators with a significant impact on the quarterly rates of return on shares—sets of indicators were, however, different in the whole period and in individual years; most frequently there were indicators classified as profitability ratios (R_03, R_04, R_06) and activity indicators (R_12, R_16, R_17, R_23), twice the debt rate (R_19), and only once the ratio from the liquidity ratios group (R_10),
- the sets of financial ratios in the ordered logit models, increasing the probability of a given company belonging to a group of companies with higher rates of return were very different; only two ratios—cash ratio (R_10) and asset utilization (R_23)—repeated twice in the analysed years; it should also be noted that in 2015 and in 2014–2017, only one ratio (cash ratio R_10 and working capital ratio R_7, respectively) decided on increasing the probability of the company belonging to a group with a higher rate of return,
- the use of discriminant analysis allowed to find sets of indicators for the years 2014 and 2015 (different in different years), which very well differentiate the companies belonging to a given group on the basis of the rate of return on shares; this distinction was weaker in 2016 and 2017; however, it was not possible to identify a set of indicators with good discriminatory properties, when the research covered data from 2014 to 2017 (Wilks' Lambdas were above 0.8).

To sum up, the following could be stated:

- a proper selection of a set of financial indicators is essential in modelling the rates of return on shares (regardless of the research tool used), and it is impossible to find a single universal set of indicators (unchangeable in time and space),
- the results of the estimation improve significantly when the values of selected indicators are delayed by two quarters, i.e. investors' decision to buy or sell is influenced by information on the financial situation of the companies six months earlier,
- the improvement of the estimation results is also influenced by the inclusion in the set of indicators, indicators—nominants after the transformation into stimulants or destimulants, i.e. the indication of a single normative value instead of a range of normative values better differentiates companies on the basis of the value of a given indicator,
- poor adjustment of econometric models may be due to the fact that the set of explanatory variables included indicators of fundamental nature, and there were no indicators of technical analysis—the introduction of these indicators to the set of explanatory variables may be a direction of further research related to the modelling of quarterly rates of return on shares on the Warsaw Stock Exchange.

The applied research tools may be useful for investors on the capital market as an addition to the classical ratio analysis, especially when they want to make decisions about selling or buying shares on the basis of their knowledge of the relations between the financial situation of companies and the rates of return on shares.

References

Bal, J., Cheung, Y., Wu, H.-Ch.: Entropy for business failure prediction: an improved prediction model for the construction industry. Adv. Decis. Sci. 1–14 (2013). http://dx.doi.org/10.1155/2013/459751

Barnes, P.: The identification of U.K. takeover targets using published historical cost accounting data. Some empirical evidence comparing logit with linear discriminant analysis and raw financial ratios with industry-relative ratios. Int. Rev. Financ. Anal. **9**(2), 147–162 (2000)

Batóg, B., Wawrzyniak, K.: Funkcja diagnostyczno-prognostyczna porządkowych modeli logitowych kwartalnej stopy zwrotu dla spółek z sektora Budownictwo. Rynki kapitałowe. Skuteczne inwestowanie, Zeszyty Naukowe nr 768, Finanse, Rynki Finansowe, Ubezpieczenia, 63, 491–506 (2013)

Batóg, B., Wawrzyniak, K.: Sytuacja ekonomiczno-finansowa a poziom stóp zwrotu spółek giełdowych z wybranego sektora. Rynki kapitałowe. Skuteczne inwestowanie, Zeszyty Naukowe nr 862, Finanse, Rynki Finansowe, Ubezpieczenia, **75**, 55–66 (2015)

Bieszk-Stolorz, B., Markowicz, I.: Zastosowanie modelu logitowego i modelu regresji Coxa w analizie zmian cen akcji spółek giełdowych w wyniku kryzysu finansowego. Prace Naukowe Uniwersytetu Ekonomicznego we Wrocławiu, Inwestycje finansowe i ubezpieczenia – tendencje światowe a rynek polski, **254**, 33–41 (2012)

Chen, H.L.: Logit models for early warning of distressed capital projects. J. Bus. Econ. Manag. **14**(1), 145–167 (2012)

Cramer, J.S.: Logit Models from Economics and Other Fields. Cambridge University Press, Cambridge (2003)

Grochowina, D.: Wpływ metod imputacji danych na skuteczność klasyfikacyjną modelu logitowego zastosowanego do prognozowania upadłości przedsiębiorstw. Acta Universitatis Nicolai Copernici, Ekonomia **45**(2), 187–203 (2014)

Gruszczyński, M.: Empiryczne finanse przedsiębiorstw. Mikroekonometria finansowa. Difin, Warszawa (2012)

Guris, S., Metin, N.: Caglayan, E: Choosing the share bond by using qualitative dependent variable models in Turkey. Qual. Quant. **43**, 431–439 (2009)

Haerdle, W.K., Simar, L.: Applied Multivariate Statistical Analysis. Springer, Berlin (2012)

Hayashi, F.: Econometrics. Princeton University Press, Princeton (2000)

Kisielińska, J., Skornik-Pokarowska, U.: Wykorzystanie liniowej funkcji dyskryminacyjnej oraz metody głównych składowych w procesie doboru spółek do portfela inwestycyjnego. Zeszyty Naukowe Szkoły Głównej Gospodarstwa Wiejskiego. Ekonomika i Organizacja Gospodarki Żywnościowej, **60**, 159–167 (2006)

Kisielińska, J., Waszkowski, A.: Polskie modele do prognozowania bankructwa przedsiębiorstw i ich weryfikacja. Zeszyty Naukowe SGGW w Warszawie. Ekonomika i Organizacja Gospodarki Żywnościowej, **82**, 17–31 (2010)

Kleinbaum, D.G., Klein, M.: Logistic Regression. Springer, New York (2002)

Lach, B. Selekcja akcji z wykorzystaniem modeli dyskryminacyjnych oraz optymalizacji podziału zbioru obiektów. Studia Ekonomiczne 163, Modelowanie preferencji a ryzyko, 45–58 (2013)

Łuniewska, M., Tarczyński, W.: Metody wielowymiarowej analizy porównawczej na rynku kapitałowym. Wydawnictwo Naukowe PWN, Warszawa (2006)

Notoria Serwis: ir.notoria.pl. Accessed 15 April 2018

Okičić, J., Remetić-Horvath, S., Büyükdemir, B.: Stock selection based on discriminant analysis: case of capital market of Bosnia and Herzegovina. J. Econ. Soc. Stud. **4**(2), 5–30 (2014)

Piszczek, R.: Zastosowanie modelu logit w modelowaniu upadłości. Prace Naukowe Uniwersytetu Ekonomicznego we Wrocławiu, Ekonometria, Zastosowanie matematyki w ekonomii **26**, 133–148 (2009)

Pociecha, J., Pawełek, B., Baryła, M., Augustyn, S.: Statystyczne metody prognozowania bankructwa w zmieniającej się koniunkturze gospodarczej. Fundacja Uniwersytetu Ekonomicznego w Krakowie, Kraków (2014)

Prusak, B.: Stopy zwrotu z akcji a wskaźniki rynkowe. Ekonomika i Organizacja Przedsiębiorstwa **2**, 53–60 (2008)
Skoczylas, W., Batóg, B.: Wykorzystanie taksonomicznego miernika rozwoju w ocenie sytuacji finansowej przedsiębiorstw. Prace Naukowe Uniwersytetu Ekonomicznego we Wrocławiu, 472, Dylematy zarządzania kosztami i dokonaniami, 387–397 (2017)
Tacq, J.: Multivariate Analysis in Social Science Research. Sage, London (2007)
Waszkowski, A.: Wielomianowe modele zagrożenia finansowego przedsiębiorstw. Zarządzanie i Finanse, 11(1), 4, 569–579 (2013)
Wiśniewska, D.: Analiza dyskryminacyjna w prognozowaniu cen akcji. Uniwersytet Ekonomiczny w Poznaniu, Poznań (2012)
Wooldridge, J.M.: Introductory Econometrics: A Modern Approach. Mason, USA, South-Western, Cengage Learning (2013)
www.bossa.pl. Accessed 15 April 2018

Chapter 19
Diversification of the Equity Portfolio Using Precious Metals in Poland

Agnieszka Majewska and Urszula Gierałtowska

Abstract The asset allocation is a primary tactic according to theory practitioners. It allows investors to create portfolios to minimalize the overall risk of the portfolio for a given expected return or to get the strongest possible return without assuming a greater level of risk than they are comfortable with. This study presents the risk and the effectiveness of equity portfolios in Poland which are diversified using precious metals. The portfolios are built in according to the Markowitz model. We find that adding a gold or more metals reduces the overall risk of portfolio and improves portfolio performance substantially. Relative to silver, platinum and palladium, gold has better stand-alone performance and appears to provide a better hedge against the negative effects of prices changing. Overall, our evidence suggests that investors could improve portfolio performance considerably by adding precious metals.

Keywords Portfolio selection · Precious metals · Portfolio diversification · Risk spreading

19.1 Introduction

Equity risk has a component, much of which could be reduced through portfolio diversification. There are many ways to diversify the portfolio. Models of portfolio choice suggest that investors should have assets which are low correlated with one another. Choosing the pair that is less correlated or negatively correlated decreases the overall risk of the portfolio. Investors can use a wide variety of assets having different correlations with each other. But the risk of portfolio cannot be assessed without taking into account the rate of return. Modern portfolio theory allows to

A. Majewska (✉) · U. Gierałtowska
University of Szczecin, ul. Mickiewicza 64, 71-101 Szczecin, Poland
e-mail: agmieszka.majewska@usz.edu.pl

U. Gierałtowska
e-mail: urszula.gieraltowska@usz.edu.pl

W. Tarczyński and K. Nermend (eds.), *Effective Investments on Capital Markets*,
Springer Proceedings in Business and Economics,
https://doi.org/10.1007/978-3-030-21274-2_19

maximize the expected return for a given level of risk or to minimalize the overall risk of the portfolio for a given expected return.

In this paper, we examine the risk of equity portfolios which were diversified by using four major precious metals: gold, silver, platinum and palladium. The purpose of this paper is to investigate various combinations of portfolio assets and indicate which one should be taken by an investor who has a significant aversion to the risk. The first section of the paper presents the brief reviews of the portfolio theory and the diversification. The next one describes the methodology of the study and presents data which were used.

19.2 The Theory of Portfolio and Diversification

Modern portfolio theory dates back to the pioneering work of Markowitz [1]. But diversification of investments was a well-known practice before Markowitz published the paper on the equity portfolio selection in 1952. Investment trusts in Scotland and England already began to hold large numbers of securities to diversify the risk in the middle of the nineteenth century. Nonetheless, prior to 1952s some contribution to the theory of portfolio selection had scientific works of such researchers as Hicks [2–5]. The investigations of Roy [6] and Tobin [7] should also not be forgotten.

It should be noted that Markowitz model was the first theory of investment that covered the effects of diversification. Very important is that Markowitz distinguished between efficient and inefficient portfolios and analysed risk-return trade-offs on the portfolio as a whole. Noteworthy is the fact that the theory of portfolio selection falls within the domain of operations research [8]. Many selection models have advanced beyond its prototype [9–15] during the next four decades.

Many books and articles on investment refer to the desirability of diversification. Investors hold diversified portfolios to reduce or eliminate non-compensated risk. Diversification is desirable and makes sense as well as being common practice. The diversification choices depend on individual characteristics and behavioural patterns. The level of under-diversification is greater among younger, low-income, less-educated, and less sophisticated investors [16]. It is also correlated with investment choices that are consistent with over-confidence, trend-following behaviour, and local bias. The mentioned features determinate as well which assets will be taken by investors to their portfolios. The development of the financial market makes the possibility for choosing from a large different instrument. Recently, more investors besides financial instruments choose various investment tools, e.g. real estate, arts, precious metals, agricultural commodities. They anticipate that alternative instruments can reduce the risk and the total portfolio market value will not decrease substantially. It should also be said that when more investors start investing in alternatives, correlations between alternative assets and traditional assets can increase with time. The increasing correlations drive portfolio managers to search for fresh alternative assets that will provide the required diversification for their portfolios. Jacobs et al. [17] mention that diversification benefits tend to be especially prominent in times of unexpected inflation and declining stock markets. But diversification does not guarantee a profit or eliminate the risk of loss.

This paper gives an account of using precious metals in portfolio selection; therefore, several studies must be mentioned in this area. Sanibel [18] presents a unique advantage and numerous benefits for investors of using precious metals. Precious metals are another form of alternative investment which has gained popularity when the traditional financial instruments have failed. Usually, alternative investments find an increase in demand in the times of instability and markets collapses. The main features which make precious metals attractive for investors are the following:

- They are virtually indestructible and cannot be falsified.
- They offer protection from political and economic uncertainty.
- They hedge against inflation.
- They have a high liquidity (especially gold and silver which are demanded all over the world).
- They provide a good diversification tool to investors due to their correlation with the market.
- Inclusion them into the portfolio can protect the investor against the fluctuations of the markets.

The last two features indicate that with respect to protect the value of portfolio, they should be positively used. Draper et al. [19] investigated the investment role of three precious metals (gold, silver, platinum) in financial markets. The results of their study show that these three precious metals have low correlations with stock index returns. It suggests that these metals may provide diversification within broad investment portfolios. They also highlight the power of capability for playing the role of safe assets particularly during periods of abnormal stock market volatility.

Another evidence on the benefits of adding these three precious metals to equity portfolios is the study carried out by Conover et al. [20]. They investigated US equity portfolios over the 34-year period. The study shows that adding a 25% metals allocation to the equities of firms improves portfolio performance substantially. Furthermore, gold compared to silver and platinum has a better stand-alone performance and appears to provide a better hedge against the negative effects of inflationary pressures.

The study of Sari et al. [21] besides of four precious metals (gold, silver, platinum, and palladium) takes also oil price and the US dollar/euro exchange rate into account. There is evidence of existing a weak long-run equilibrium relationship, but strong feedbacks in the short-run. They conclude that investors may diversify a portion of the risk by investing in these assets.

Jensen et al. [22] find that using commodity futures substantially enhances portfolio performance for investors. Their findings indicate the benefits of adding commodity futures almost exclusively when the monetary policy is restrictive. It means that investors should gauge monetary conditions to determine the optimal allocation of commodity futures within a portfolio.

Out of four precious metals, most studies have been carried out in using gold as a good portfolio diversifier (e.g. [23–26]). More authors conclude that gold is a hedge against stocks and a safe asset in extreme stock market conditions. But the results of Ratner and Klein [23] indicate that investment in gold is inferior to a simple buy-and-hold strategy of US equities over the long term. A portfolio optimization technique using actual from 1975 to 2005 and simulated data indicates that the long-term portfolio benefits of holding gold are marginal at best. This interpretation contrasts with that of Dee et al. [26] who examined whether gold serves as a hedge for stock or/and inflation in China mainland market. Their empirical results show that gold always cannot hedge stock and inflation risk for short-term investors, but it is a good hedge for stock or inflation if you would hold gold for a long time. It must be remembered that it only involves the stock and inflation risk in China capital market. Erb and Harvey [27] also show that gold may be an effective hedge if the investment horizon is measured in centuries but over practical investment horizons, gold is an unreliable inflation hedge. Next two parts show the data and empirical results for portfolio selection using stocks and precious metals in Polish capital market. Modern portfolio theory in Polish bibliography is very rich. However, most of them are focused on finding alternative methods for portfolio selection [28, 29] and only several works concern treating precious metals as alternative assets to portfolio diversification.

19.3 Data Description

In our research, we used data from Warsaw Stock Exchange and London Metal Exchange for the period 1 January 2015 to 31 August 2018. We take into account stocks from WIG20 index (Fig. 19.1).

It is based on the value of portfolio with shares in 20 major and most liquid companies in the WSE main list. No more than five companies from a single sector can participate in the index. This structure enables to have stocks from different sectors in the portfolio. Prices of precious metals are measured in US dollars; so to determine the price of gold, silver, platinum, and palladium in the national currency, we have used average US dollar exchange rate from the National Bank of Poland. The figures below illustrate the prices of precious metals in the analysed time.

The degrees of variation of four major precious metals over time as measured by the standard deviation of logarithmic returns are shown in Fig. 19.2. All returns are modelled in natural logarithms.

Volatility shows that the seemingly close precious metals can be quite different. In all analysed period, palladium has the highest standard deviation, while gold has the lowest. The low volatility of the gold price is consistent with the fact that the annual demand and production of gold are less than 10% of its above-ground supply, and its stock is a supply buffer against fundamental shocks [30]. Gold as an important monetary component is not used frequently in exchange market interventions; therefore, we can observe a low degree of variation of a price over time. The highest volatility of palladium is the effect of its relatively small supply. Although gold and

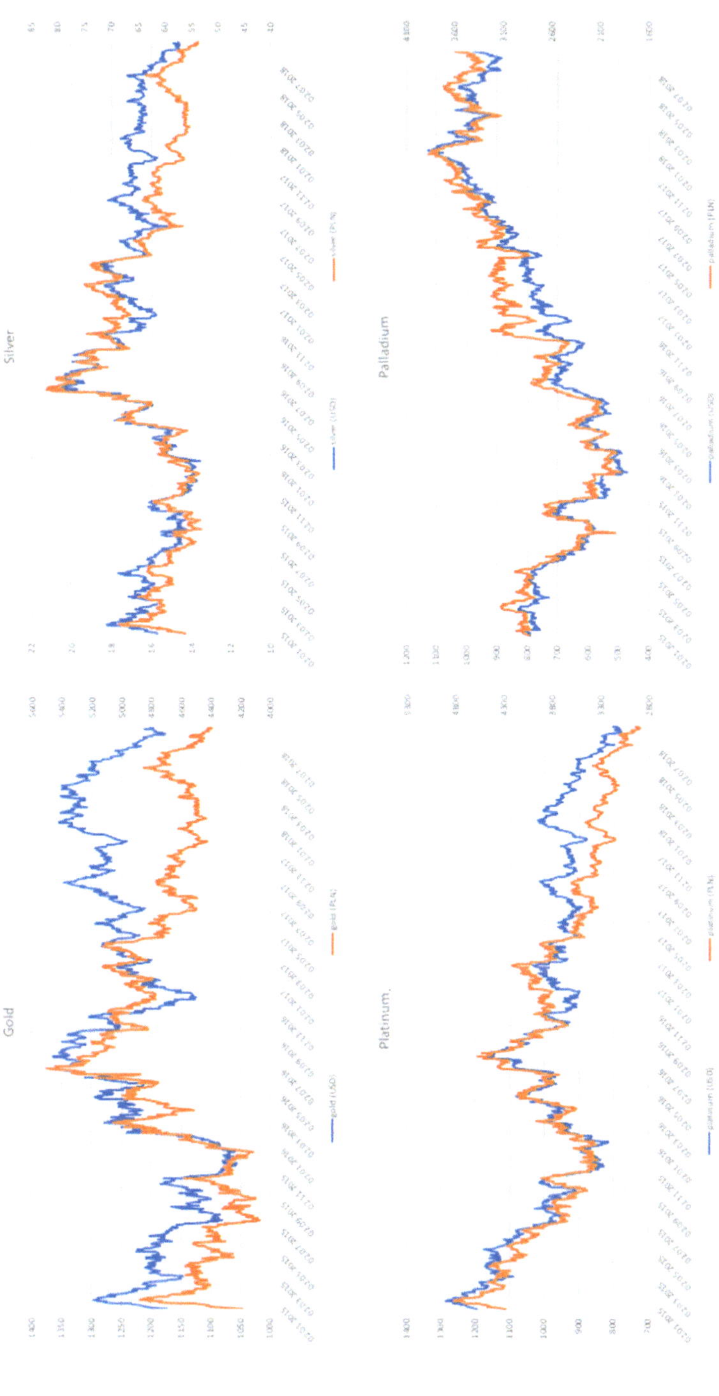

Fig. 19.1 Daily prices of precious metals. *Source* Own research

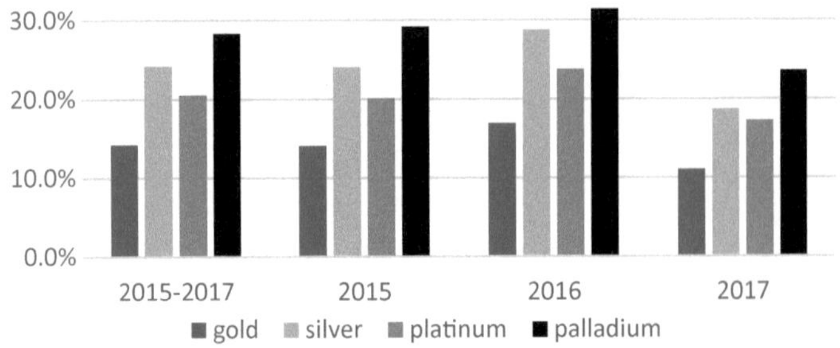

Fig. 19.2 Annual volatility for precious metals. *Source* Own research

Table 19.1 Number of assets with the normal distribution of returns

Year	*p*	Number of companies from WIG20 index	Precious metals		Metals which not have the normal distribution of returns
			Prices in USD	Prices in PLN	
2015	<0.01	9	2	3	USD—gold, platinum PLN—platinum
	<0.05	10	2	3	
	<0.1	13	2	3	
2016	<0.01	10	1	4	USD—gold, palladium
	<0.05	13	2	4	
	<0.1	14	2	4	
2017	<0.01	8	1	1	USD—platinum, palladium PLN—palladium
	<0.05	12	2	2	
	<0.1	14	2	3	
January 2015–August 2018	<0.01		4	4	

Source Own research

silver are closely related, silver is more commodity-driven and its monetary element has been gradually phased out.

In the next part of the paper, we will use these four precious metals for diversification of the equity portfolio. Assets are required to be normally distributed for consideration in the mean–variance model. Therefore, we have also tested a normal distribution of returns. Table 19.1 shows the results obtained from the Shapiro–Wilk test for each year separately and for the whole analysed period.

It is interesting to note that the normal distribution depends on the timescale over which returns are measured. The distributions are not normal for assets over short timescales. They have fatter tails and higher peaks than normal. Over longer periods, they start to have the normal distribution. Our study confirms that.

19.4 Results of Portfolio Selection

The portfolios in our research are constructed in accordance with the Markowitz model when the risk is minimalised. Harry Markowitz created theory of effective selection of assets to portfolio (*MV—mean–variance model*). We use the formula with the goal function:

$$S^2 = X' \cdot D \cdot X \to \min \tag{19.1}$$

where

X the vector of shares in portfolio
X' the transposed vector of X
D the matrix of variance and covariance of rates of return.

With conditions:

$$X_i \geq 0 \quad \text{for} \quad i = 1, 2, \ldots, n \tag{19.2}$$

$$\sum_{i=1}^{n} X_i = 1 \tag{19.3}$$

The analysed portfolio was constructed on the base of 20 shares, which have the greatest capitalization on the Warsaw Stock Exchange and four precious metals. Our research focuses on three years for which one we create 11 portfolios. In our empirical studies, we assume that investor has 100,000 PLN and buys assets from the diversified portfolio at the beginning of each year. The effectiveness of the investment is reviewed at the end of 2016, 2017 and August 2018. Results are presented in Tables 19.2, 19.3 and 19.4.

From the tables above, we can see that the portfolios with the gold and all metals have the lowest risk. Assuming that the risk of the WIG20 portfolio indicates the market risk, portfolios with gold and all metals have the risk lower than the market risk average about 26, 38 and 28% each analysed year. The risk of other portfolios with comparing to the market risk is lower at the order of 8, 12 and 9% on average annually. The evidence shows that using gold or all metals in portfolio selection, we can obtain the lowest risk of the investment. One quarter of the world's gold reserves are held by the government's central banks and other financial institutions as part of their international reserves; therefore, gold is considered to be the safe asset. This study confirms that. As an investment instrument, stocks are exposed to macroeconomic risks and global stock market risks. Gold is often believed to provide potential as a defensive asset, given its low correlation with equities. Relative to silver, platinum and palladium, gold has better stand-alone performance and appears to provide a better hedge against the negative effects of prices changing.

It is encouraging to compare the effectiveness of portfolios. Holding gold or more metals in the portfolio makes the higher profit or the less loss from the investment

Table 19.2 Characteristic of the portfolios of 2015

Assets	Rate of return (%)	Risk (%)	Share of the metals in the portfolio (%)	The effectiveness of portfolio		
				12.2016 (%)	12.2017 (%)	08.2018 (%)
WIG20	0.072	1.816	–	−2.424	−0.193	−2.450
WIG20 & gold (USD)	−0.049	1.328	49.05	7.221	14.423	−1.245
WIG20 & silver (USD)	−0.006	1.691	19.45	0.479	2.444	−2.434
WIG20 & platinum (USD)	−0.091	1.587	29.15	0.013	−0.101	−5.034
WIG20 & palladium (USD)	−0.056	1.734	14.50	1.150	13.970	9.380
WIG20 & all metals (USD)	−0.049	1.328	49.05[a]	7.217	14.377	−1.307
WIG20 & gold (PLN)	−0.017	1.361	46.18	10.662	14.298	2.175
WIG20 & silver (PLN)	0.003	1.682	20.97	3.462	3.442	−1.220
WIG20 & platinum (PLN)	−0.067	1.580	31.00	2.703	−2.030	−6.889
WIG20 & palladium (PLN)	−0.037	1.739	13.86	2.483	12.041	8.224
WIG20 & all metals (PLN)	−0.018	1.362	46.20[b]	10.595	14.166	2.081

Source Own research
[a]Only gold
[b]Only gold and platinum

Table 19.3 Characteristic of the portfolios of 2016

Assets	Rate of return (%)	Risk (%)	Share of the metals in the portfolio (%)	The effectiveness of portfolio	
				12.2017 (%)	08.2018 (%)
WIG20	0.148	1.830	–	1.900	2.283
WIG20 & gold (USD)	0.189	1.197	42.73	9.805	10.081
WIG20 & silver (USD)	0.23	1.644	21.10	4.633	3.120
WIG20 & platinum (USD)	0.180	1.617	20.56	5.262	8.988
WIG20 & palladium (USD)	0.252	1.708	10.51	14.362	20.275
WIG20 & all metals (USD)	0.186	1.206	45.02[a]	9.611	7.695
WIG20 & gold (PLN)	0.212	1.067	44.10	5.921	5.631
WIG20 & silver (PLN)	0.229	1.522	24.49	0.059	−1.145
WIG20 & platinum (PLN)	0.221	1.530	27.04	0.812	5.911
WIG20 & palladium (PLN)	0.267	1.666	13.16	11.797	17.436
WIG20 & all metals (PLN)	0.198	1.078	43.70[a]	3.298	1.943

Source Own research
[a]Only gold and palladium

money. The profit or the lost depends on market condition,[1] but it is known that in the uncertain environment, buying metals represents a safe-haven approach to diversification and a partial hedge against equities.

[1]Comparison of hedging using futures contracts when the prices of stock go down and grow has been made by Majewska [31].

Table 19.4 Characteristic of the portfolios of 2017

Assets	Rate of return (%)	Risk (%)	Share of the metals in the portfolio (%)	The effectiveness of portfolio
				08.2018 (%)
WIG20	0.253	1.484	–	−5.154
WIG20 & gold (USD)	0.256	1.105	53.68	−9.727
WIG20 & silver (USD)	0.196	1.340	24.16	−9.354
WIG20 & platinum (USD)	0.180	1.363	29.83	−10.252
WIG20 & palladium (USD)	0.453	1.419	22.92	−10.949
WIG20 & all metals (USD)	0.278	1.099	52.58[a]	−9.863
WIG20 & gold (PLN)	0.109	1.044	44.10	−6.194
WIG20 & silver (PLN)	0.103	1.299	28.21	−8.132
WIG20 & platinum (PLN)	0.058	1.327	33.81	−7.709
WIG20 & palladium (PLN)	0.302	1.332	20.14	−4.617
WIG20 & all metals (PLN)	0.082	1.029	52.62[b]	−6.383

Source Own research
[a]Only gold and palladium
[b]Only gold

19.5 Conclusion

This study presents the possibility of using precious metals in portfolio selection to minimalize the risk of whole portfolio. The final results obtained for portfolios show that adding gold or more metals can reduce the overall risk of the portfolio. Additionally, it is possible to obtain the higher profit from such diversified portfolios. It is because precious metals are not subjected to the same forces as stocks and other paper assets, therefore diversifying the portfolio with them can add an additional level of security for investors' wealth. It is important to have precious metals in portfolio to diversify the risk of different kinds of instruments.

It should be noted that precious metals should be used essentially in long-term investment. More likely is achieving a profitable rate of return when we have longer the investment period, because the risk of a price drop in short periods is partially eliminated. This also applies to direct investing in metals [32].

References

1. Markowitz, H.M.: Portfolio selection. The J. Financ. **7**(1), 77–91 (1952)
2. Hicks JR (1935) A suggestion for simplifying the theory of money. Economica (February), 1–19
3. Marschak, J.: Money and the theory of assets. Econometrica **6**, 311–325 (1938)
4. Williams, J.B.: The Theory of Investment Value. Harvard University Press, Cambridge, MA (1938)
5. Leavens, D.H.: Diversification of investments. Trust. Estates **80**(May), 469–473 (1945)
6. Roy, A.D.: Safety first and the holding of assets. Econometrica **20**, 431–449 (1952)
7. Tobin J (1958) Liquidity preference as behavior towards risk. Rev. Econ. Stud. **25**(1) (February), 65–86
8. Markowitz, H.M.: The optimization of a quadratic function subject to linear constraints. Nav. Res. Logist. Q. **3**, 111–133 (1956)
9. Sharpe WF (1963) A Simplified Model for Portfolio Analysis. Management Science vol. 9 No. 2 (January): 277–293
10. Sharpe WF (1964) Capital asset prices: a theory of market equilibrium under conditions of risk. J. Financ. **19**(3) (September), 425–442
11. Lintner J (1965) The valuation of risk assets and the selection of risky investments in stock portfolios and capital budgets. Rev. Econ. Stat. **47**(1) (February), 13–37
12. Mossin, J.: Equilibrium in a capital asset market. Econometrica **34**, 768–783 (1966)
13. Ross, S.A.: The arbitrage theory of capital asset pricing. J. Econ. Theory **13**(December), 341–360 (1976)
14. Markowitz, H.M., Perold, A.F.: Portfolio analysis with factors and scenarios. J. Financ. **36**(4), 871–877 (1981)
15. Markowitz, H.M.: Mean-Variance Analysis in Portfolio Choice and Capital Markets. Basil Blackwell, New York (1987)
16. Goetzmann, W.N., Kumar, A.: Equity portfolio diversification. Rev. Financ. **12**, 433–463 (2008)
17. Jacobs, H., Müller, S., Weber, M.: How should individual investors diversify? An empirical evaluation of alternative asset allocation policies. J. Financ. Mark. **19**, 62–85 (2014)
18. Sanibel, M.: Investing in precious metals, from forbes website (2010). http://www.forbes.com/2010/06/22/investingprecious-metals-personalfinancegold.html
19. Draper, P., Faff, R.W., Hillier, D.: Do precious metals shine? An investment perspective. Financ. Anal. J. **62**(2), 98–106 (2006)
20. Conover, C.M., Jensen, G.R., Johnson, R.R., Mercer J.M.: Can precious metals make your portfolio shine? J. Investing **18**(1), 75–86 (2009)
21. Sari, R., Hammoudeh, S., Soytas U.: Dynamics of oil price, precious metal prices, and exchange rate. Energy Econ. **32**(2), 351–362 (2010)
22. Jensen, G.R., Johnson, R.R., Mercer, J.M.: Tactical asset allocation and commodity futures. J. Portfolio Manage. **28**(4), 100–111 (2002)
23. Ratner, M., Klein, S.: The portfolio implications of gold investment. J. Invest. **17**(1), 77–87 (2008)
24. Baur, D.G., Lucey, M.B.: Is gold a hedge or a safe haven? An analysis of stocks, bonds and gold. The Financ. Rev. **45**, 217–229 (2010)
25. Mulyadi, M.S., Anwar, Y.: Gold versus stock investment: an econometric analysis. Int. J. Dev. Sustain. **1**, 1–7 (2012)
26. Dee, J., Li, L., Zheng, Z.: Is gold a hedge or a safe haven? Evidence from inflation and stock market. Int. J. Dev. Sustain. **2**(1), 12–27 (2013)
27. Erb, C.B., Harvey, C.R.: The golden dilemma. Financ. Anal. J. **69**(4), 10–42 (2013)

28. Tarczyński, M.: Different variants of fundamental portfolio. Folia Oeconomica Stetinensia **14**, 47–62 (2014)
29. Majewski S (2014) The Maslowian portfolio theory versus the pyramid portfolio. Folia Oeconomica Stetinensia **14** (22) No 1, 91–101
30. Hammoudeh, S.M., Yuan, Y., McAleer, M., Thompson, M.A.: Precious metals–exchange rate volatility transmissions and hedging strategies. Int. Rev. Econ. Financ. **19**, 633–647 (2010)
31. Majewska, A.: Porównanie strategii zabezpieczających portfel akcji z wykorzystaniem kontraktów futures na WIG20 w okresach spadków i wzrostów cen. Prace Naukowe Uniwersytetu Ekonomicznego we Wrocławiu nr **371**, 213–223 (2014)
32. Gierałtowska U (2016) Bezpośrednie i pośrednie inwestycje w metale szlachetne. Annales Universitatis Mariae Curie-Skłodowska Sectio H. Oeconomia. **50**(4), 125–137

Part III
Experimental Economies and Behavioral Finance on Capital Markets

Chapter 20
The Co-movement of the Czech Republic, Hungary and Poland Sovereign Credit Default Swaps Spreads

Paweł Miłobędzki and Sabina Nowak

Abstract We use a VEC DCC M-GARCH model to investigate the daily co-movement of the Czech Republic, Hungary and Poland one-, five- and ten-year sovereign credit default swap (CDS) spreads in the period Jan 2009–May 2018. To control for a systemic risk stemming from the EU and other international markets, we nest the analysis within a four-variate system including the Germany CDS spread and the CBOE VIX. The latter serves us as a proxy for the exogenous driver of spreads. The analysis shows that the long-run dependence among the logs of CDS spreads is rare. It is only the Czech Republic and Germany one-year CDS spreads that exhibit a common stochastic trend. The remaining spreads do not co-integrate. Each country maturity time t log change in the spread depends upon that of time $t-1$ and earlier. The dynamics of spreads are country specific. The Hungary CDS spreads Granger cause almost all their counterparts. The causality running other way round is incidental. The median of pairwise conditional correlation estimates among the countries of interest differs across the maturities in the way indicating that the Czech, Hungarian and Polish markets are better integrated among one another than any single with the German market.

Keywords CDS spreads · Price discovery · Granger causality · VEC DCC M-GARCH

P. Miłobędzki (✉) · S. Nowak
Department of Econometrics, Faculty of Management, University of Gdańsk, Armii Krajowej 101, 81-824 Sopot, Poland
e-mail: pawel.milobedzki@ug.edu.pl

S. Nowak
e-mail: sabina.nowak@ug.edu.pl

W. Tarczyński and K. Nermend (eds.), *Effective Investments on Capital Markets*, Springer Proceedings in Business and Economics,
https://doi.org/10.1007/978-3-030-21274-2_20

20.1 Introduction

A sovereign credit default swap (CDS) spread is the cost to be paid for protection against sovereign default. It is also widely regarded as a major indicator of the country's economic health [1].[1] The purpose of this paper is to analyse the co-movement of CDS spreads for the Czech Republic, Hungary and Poland in the aftermath of the global financial crisis (GFC). Severely hit by the crisis, these countries have responded with extensive reforms [4]. Our primary interest is in finding whether the market perception of their economic health in the post-crisis period exhibited in the spreads albeit time-varying is interrelated in the short and long run and revealing its nature. In doing so, we use the vector error correction dynamic conditional correlation multivariate GARCH (VEC DCC M-GARCH) model. The reason is that the spreads of both mature and emerging sovereigns are nonstationary, and their changes exhibit a high level of commonality [5]. However, little is known on that whether they closely co-move over time.[2] There is also no consent in the academia on whether the spreads are driven by global-or country-specific factors. Arguments for their global character are brought (to name few but the most recent) by Pan and Singleton [8], Longstaff et al. [9] and Ho [7] while those for their local conditioning or a mixed global and local nature by Fender et al. [10], Clark and Kassimatis [11], Fontana and Scheicher [12] and Kocsis and Monostori [13]. More interestingly, Ang and Longstaff [14] show that both the US and Eurozone systemic sovereign risk are strongly related to financial market variables including the CBOE VIX. Chen et al. [6] document that commonality and correlation in the spreads are due to the increasing integration of sovereign CDS markets which took place after the GFC. Taking these into account in what follows, we address the problem of whether nonstationary spreads are co-integrated and if they are so whether the spreads of spreads have a co-integrating property. In case they do not co-integrate, we conduct the analysis on their log changes within the DCC M-GARCH framework of Engle [15]. To control for risk stemming from the EU and other international markets, we extend our workhorse model to a four-variate system by including the Germany CDS spread and adding the VIX. The latter serves us as a proxy for the exogenous driver of spreads. We estimate it separately on the daily sampled data for one-, five- and ten-

[1] Butler and Fauver [2] show on the sample of 86 countries that the quality of a country's legal and political institutions are significant in determining sovereign CDS ratings. More recently [3] reveal that the U.S. expected growth and consumption volatility are closely related to the co-movement in sovereign spreads.

[2] We find only 2 papers that formally test for whether the spreads co-integrate. Chen et al. [6] applies the PANIC methodology to a panel of 8 credit indices from the Markit CDX family spanning October 2004 to June 2011 and show that co-integration is only achieved after the post-Lehman collapse period. They also find that either a higher perceived credit risk or generalized risk aversion are potentially driving forces of an increased CDS market integration in the post-crisis period. Ho [7] basing on the panel error correction model estimated on the quarterly data from 8 emerging countries (Brazil, Malaysia, South-Korea, Thailand, Turkey, South Africa, Indonesia and Mexico) from the period 2008Q4-2013Q2 documents that the government's liquidity and solvency as well as macroeconomic situation determine the long-run sovereign CDS spread.

year CDS spreads from the period 1 January 2009–21 May 2018 to reveal the long- and short-run dynamics of spreads, their correlation and causality structure. The data come from Thomson Reuters.[3] To the best of our knowledge, this is the first study embedded in a multivariate framework that enables to analyse the co-movement of CDS spreads from the trinity of Central European sovereigns at one time and on a longer period basis.[4]

Our analysis contributes to the field in several ways. We show that the long-run dependence among the logs of CDS spreads is very rare. It is only the Czech Republic and Germany one-year CDS spreads that exhibit common stochastic trend. The remaining spreads do not co-integrate. The short-run dependencies among the CDS spreads are manifold, however. First, each country maturity time t log change in the spread depends upon that of time $t-1$ and earlier but since the strength of such an impact differs from one country to another, the dynamics of spreads are country specific. Second, we reveal a special role of the Hungary CDS spreads. They Granger cause almost all their counterpart spreads. Surprisingly, the causality running other way round is incidental. Third, despite Germany sovereign credit risk exhibited in one-, five- and ten-year CDS spreads is the lowest among the country quartet within the whole period of interest; the volatility of Germany spreads is the largest for each maturity as measured by the median of conditional variance of their rates of return. Fourth, the median of pairwise conditional correlation estimates among the countries of interest differs across the maturities in the way indicating that the Czech, Hungarian and Polish markets are better integrated among one another than any single with the German market. We also find that all correlations are significantly raised for the upper centiles of VIX which may be interpreted in favour of the contagion.[5,6] Last but not least, for one- and five-year maturities, an increase in market fear as measured by the log change in VIX has a positive and almost equal in strength impact on all country spreads. Indeed, the VIX drives sovereign spreads.

The remainder of the paper proceeds as follows. In Sect. 20.2, we introduce a model to capture the long- and short-run dynamics of CDS spreads, their correlation and causality structure and sketch the way it is estimated and validated. In Sect. 20.3, we discuss the results we arrived to. Section 20.4 briefly concludes.

---

[3]The data are provided under a Partnership Agreement between the University of Gdańsk and the Thomson Reuters company.

[4]Kliber [16] investigates the dynamics of the Czech Republic, Hungary and Poland five Year CDS spreads using Yu and Meyer [17] multivariate stochastic volatility model with a dynamic conditional correlation but nests the analysis within the bivariate 'Czech Republic–Hungary' and 'Poland–Hungary' setting. She concludes on the daily sampled but of the shorter period data spanning March 10, 2008 through March 9, 2011.

[5]See Forbes and Rigobon [18] who identify the occurrence of contagion if the linkages between markets of interest significantly intensify during a crisis.

[6]Short-term periods in which the VIX takes the value from the 95th and 99th centile include inter alia those from the end of 2009 Eurozone sovereign debt crisis, the 2010 Greek crisis as well as the August 2015 Chinese stock market crash. The impact of the financial crises on the Eurozone sovereign CDS spreads is discussed inter alia in Gündüz and Kaya [1].

20.2 Model

We specify the four-variate VEC DCC M-GARCH model for Germany, the Czech Republic, Poland and Hungary CDS spreads on a pure empirical basis. We assume that the integrated of order one logs of country i k-year spreads, $x_{it}^{(k)}$ ($i = 1, \ldots, 4$ for Germany, the Czech Republic, Poland and Hungary, accordingly; $t = 1, 2, \ldots, T$) and the same kind log of the VIX, y_t, co-integrate, i.e. their $s \leq S$ linearly independent combinations $\sum_{i=1}^{4} \alpha_{is}^{(k)} x_{it}^{(k)} + \alpha_{5s}^{(k)} y_t = \theta_{st}^{(k)}$ are stationary. In such circumstance upon the Granger representation theorem, the VEC part of the model reads [19, 20]

$$\Delta x_{it}^{(k)} = \sum_{j=1}^{4} \sum_{l=1}^{L} \beta_{jl}^{(ik)} \Delta x_{jt-l}^{(k)} + \sum_{r=1}^{R} \gamma_{ir}^{(k)} \Delta y_{t-r} + \sum_{s=1}^{S'} \delta_{is}^{(k)} \theta_{st-1}^{(k)} + \epsilon_{it}^{(k)}, \tag{20.1}$$

where $\epsilon_{it}^{(k)}$ stands for an error term, with the number of error correction components $\theta_{st-1}^{(k)}$ be at most $S' = 3$. To control for the day of the week effect in the spreads, we append the right-hand side of Eq. (20.1) adding dummy variables d_{ht} which take value 1 for day h of the week and 0 otherwise ($h = 1, 2, \ldots, 5$ from Monday to Friday). $\delta_{is}^{(k)}$ exhibits the time t k-year spread of country i response to the time $(t-1)$ one per cent departure from long-run equilibrium of spreads s, $\beta_{jl}^{(ik)}$—the time t k-year spread of country i response to its own one per cent increase at time $t - l (i = j)$ or the time t k-year spread of country i response to the one per cent increase in k-year spread of country j at time $t - l$ $(i \neq j)$, $\gamma_{ir}^{(k)}$—the time t k-year spread of country i response to the one per cent increase in the VIX. Of a particular interest is the hypothesis stating that the k-year spread of country j does not Granger cause the k-year spread of country i, i.e. $\beta_{il}^{(ik)} = 0$ for all l.

An extension of Eq. (20.1) which complements the model specification is the DCC M-GARCH of Engle [15] exhibiting the dynamics of $\epsilon_{it}^{(k)}$ innovations:

$$\epsilon_t^{(k)} = \left[H_t^{(k)}\right]^{-0.5} \upsilon_t^{(k)}, \quad H_t^{(k)} = \left[D_t^{(k)}\right]^{-0.5} R_t^{(k)} \left[D_t^{(k)}\right]^{-0.5}, \tag{20.2}$$

$$R_t^{(k)} = \text{diag}\left[Q_t^{(k)}\right]^{-0.5} Q_t^{(k)} \text{diag}\left[Q_t^{(k)}\right]^{-0.5}, \tag{20.3}$$

$$Q_t^{(k)} = \left[1 - \lambda_1^{(k)} - \lambda_2^{(k)}\right] R + \lambda_1^{(k)} \tilde{\epsilon}_{t-1}^{(k)} \tilde{\epsilon}_{t-1}^{\prime (k)} + \lambda_2^{(k)} Q_{t-1}^{(k)}, \tag{20.4}$$

where $\epsilon_t^{(k)} = \left[\epsilon_{0t}^{(k)} \epsilon_{1t}^{(k)} \ldots \epsilon_{nt}^{(k)}\right]$, $\upsilon_t^{(k)}$ is a vector of i.i.d. innovations, $\left[H_t^{(k)}\right]^{-0.5}$ is the Cholesky factor of the time-varying conditional covariance matrix $H_t^{(k)}$, $D_t^{(k)}$ is a diagonal matrix of conditional variances in which each element evolves according to a univariate GARCH (p_f, q_f) process, $R_t^{(k)}$ is a matrix of conditional quasi correlations, $\tilde{\epsilon}_t^{(k)}$ is a vector of standardized residuals $\left[H_t^{(k)}\right]^{-0.5} \epsilon_t^{(k)}$, $\lambda_1^{(k)}$ and $\lambda_2^{(k)}$ are nonnegative parameters that govern the dynamics of conditional quasi correlations such that $0 \leq \lambda_1^{(k)} + \lambda_2^{(k)} < 1$.

We estimate Eqs. (20.1)–(20.4) in two steps. First, we test for the order of integration of sovereign CDS spreads logs using the unit root ADF-GLS test and stationarity KPSS test [21, 22]. Next, we fix order p of the VAR underlying short-term model (20.1) and test for the number of co-integrating vectors. To this end, we employ the Johansen procedure ([23], Chaps. 6–8). Since in case the logs of CDS spreads are highly persistent but hardly distinguishable from $I(1)$ variables and the properties of co-integration rank tests are severely distorted[7] for the robustness check of the number of co-integrating vectors, we apply the ADF and KPSS tests to residuals from the regressions of a given spread on the set of remaining spreads as in MacKinnon [25] and Shin [26]. Finally, in the second step, we use the residuals from co-integrating relations to estimate a full VEC DCC M-GARCH model by the maximum likelihood (ML).

20.3 Empirical Results

We begin the analysis by examining the nature of CDS spreads. We plot their log series on Fig. 20.1. As demonstrated, they rarely pass through their mean levels so that they may be nonstationary. The results of the ADF-GLS and KPSS tests support this conjecture. The same applies to the log of VIX. On the other hand, the first differences in variables of interest are stationary. Thus, both logs of CDS spreads and the VIX are $I(1)$ variables.[8]

Next, using the AIC information criterion, we set the lag order $p = 5$ (9, 9) of the VAR system for one- (five, ten) year CDS spreads including the VIX and the dummies exhibiting the day of the week effects in spreads. Then, based on the maximal eigenvalue and trace test statistics, we identify the existence of up to 3 (2, 2) co-integrating vectors, accordingly (see Table 20.1). Thus, we can provisionally conclude at this point that one- (five, ten) year CDS spread(s) follows a common (2, 2) stochastic trend(s). We also check these results for robustness applying the ADF and KPSS tests to residuals from the regressions of a given spread on the set of remaining spreads as in MacKinnon [25] and Shin [26]. The results of both testing procedures stacked in Table 20.2 indicate that there is only one co-integrating vector including Germany and the Czech Republic one-year CDS spreads. We also find on the ground of ADF-GLS and KPSS tests that they co-integrate with the co-integrating vector $[-1\ 1]$.[9]

Since the remaining spreads do not co-integrate, we estimated the VEC DCC M-GARCH given by Eqs. (20.1)–(20.4) using the residuals from the co-integrating vector only for the system of one-year spreads. For those of five and ten years, we

[7] See Hjalmarsson and Österholm [24].

[8] The results of both tests are available from the authors on a request.

[9] The estimates of the ADF-GLS (level) and KPSS (level) tests equal to −3.485 and 0.309.

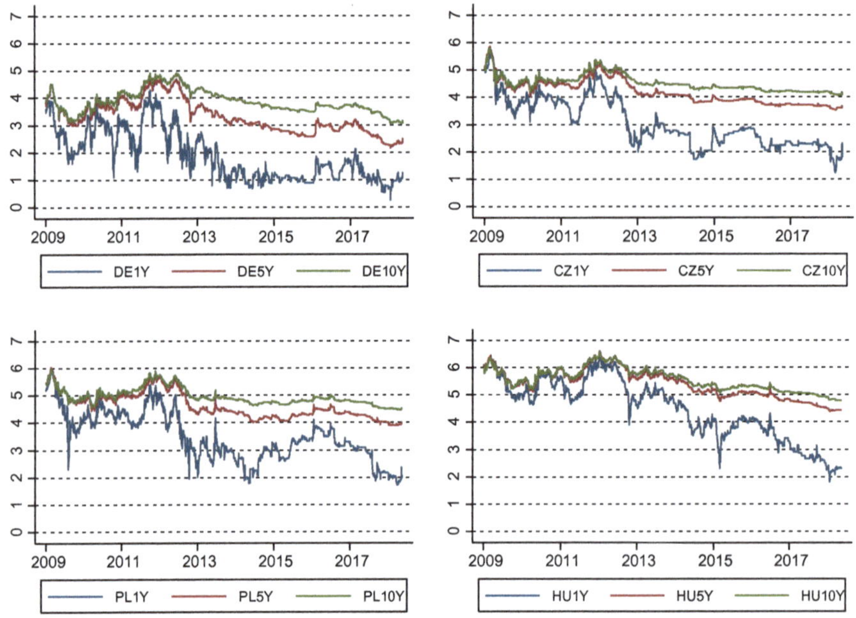

Fig. 20.1 Logs of Germany (DE), the Czech Republic (CZ), Poland (PL) and Hungary (HU) one-(1Y), five-(5Y) and ten-year (10Y) CDS spreads, 2 Jan 2009—21 May 2018

estimate a DCC M-GARCH alone. The results of utmost importance including those of validation and inference are reported in Table 20.3. They include:

1. The mean and variance equations of (VEC) DCC-M-GARCH model are properly specified as the Ljung-Box portmanteau test applied on standardized residuals from Eq. (20.1), and their squares shows that they are non-autocorrelated processes up to the 30th order (see the estimates of $Q(\cdot)$ test statistic).
2. In view of the data, a dynamic version of DCC M-GARCH is more likely than its constant correlation counterpart for the five- and ten-year maturities as the null hypothesis of $\lambda_1^{(k)} + \lambda_2^{(k)} = 1$ is rejected for its left-sided alternative.[10] We do not reject the hypothesis of integrated M-GARCH for one-, five- and ten-year spreads except that of Poland for ten-year maturity (see the estimates of W_{8i} test statistics).
3. We reject the hypothesis stating that each country maturity time t log change in the spread does not depend upon that of time $t-1$ and earlier (see the estimates of W_{ii} test statistic, $i = 1, \ldots, 4$).

   We find that Hungary one-, five- and ten-year CDS spreads Granger cause almost all their counterpart spreads. The causality running other way round is incidental (see the estimates of W_{ij} test statistic, $i = 1, \ldots, 4$ and $i \neq j$).

[10]The estimates of the Wald test statistics for 1, 5 and 10 year spreads distributed as $\chi^2(1)$ read 0.12, 6.61 and 6.36, respectively.

Table 20.1 Number of co-integrating vectors in the system including Germany, the Czech Republic, Poland and Hungary CDS spreads (co-integration with no intercepts or trends in the VAR, VIX and dummies exhibiting the day of the week effect included)

System													
		1Y	5Y	10Y					1Y	5Y	10Y		
Test													
Max. eigenvalue							Trace						
H_0	H_A	Est.	Est.	Est.	5% c.v.	10% c.v.	H_0	H_A	Est.	Est.	Est.	5% c.v.	10% c.v.
$r=0$	$r=1$	32.21	24.44	31.01	27.27	24.84	$r=0$	$r \geq 1$	74.81	57.16	65.50	49.56	45.95
$r \leq 1$	$r=2$	22.93	18.98	20.62	21.60	18.96	$r \leq 1$	$r \geq 2$	42.61	32.72	34.49	32.16	29.08
$r \leq 2$	$r=3$	13.93	8.78	10.68	14.79	12.83	$r \leq 2$	$r \geq 3$	19.68	13.74	13.87	17.79	15.83
$r \leq 3$	$r=4$	5.74	4.96	3.20	8.13	6.49	$r \leq 3$	$r=4$	5.74	4.96	3.20	8.13	6.49

Table 20.2 Results of unit root and stationarity tests in case parameters of the long-run relationship are not known

Variables incl. in the long-run relationship	Test																	
	ADF			Shin			ADF			Shin			ADF			Shin		
	ADF_c	Lag	5% c.v.	τ_c	k	5% c.v.	ADF_c	Lag	5% c.v.	τ_c	k	5% c.v.	ADF_c	Lag	5% c.v.	τ_c	k	5% c.v.
	1Y CDS						5Y CDS						10Y CDS					
DE,CZ,PL,HU	−5.330	2	−4.096	0.518	18	0.159	−3.880	17	−4.096	0.299	28	0.159	x	98[d]	−4.096	1.600	48	0.159
DE,CZ,PL	−5.590	1	−3.741	0.682	18	0.221	−2.860	20	−3.741	1.020	33	0.221	x	98[d]	−3.741	1.770	33	0.159
DE,CZ,HU	−5.280	1	−3.741	0.410	23	0.221	−3.600	17	−3.741	0.456	33	0.221	x	98[d]	−3.741	2.060	34	0.159
DE,PL,HU	−5.170	4	−3.741	0.625	41	0.221	−3.770	17	−3.741	0.464	28	0.221	−2.300	38	−3.741	2.300	0	0.159
CZ,PL,HU	−4.400	3	−3.741	x	49[c]	0.314	−2.980	24	−3.741	x	49[c]	0.221	x	98[d]	−3.741	0.918	0	0.159
DE,CZ	−5.360	1	−3.336	0.406[b]	43	0.314[b]	x	98[d]	−3.336	x	49[c]	0.314	x	98[d]	−3.336	1.760	45	0.314
DE,PL	−4.660	9	−3.336	1.520	38	0.314	−2.790	17	−3.336	1.300	30	0.314	x	98[d]	−3.336	1.660	33	0.314
DE,HU	−3.930	9	−3.336	x	49[c]	0.314	−3.620	17	−3.336	0.508	24	0.314	x	98[d]	−3.336	2.330	23	0.314
CZ,PL	−3.840	7	−3.336	x	49[c]	0.314	−2.170	98	−3.336	x	49[c]	0.314	x	98[d]	−3.336	x	49[c]	0.314
CZ,HU	−3.480	3	−3.336	x	49[c]	0.314	x	98[d]	−3.336	x	49[c]	0.314	x	98[d]	−3.336	x	49[c]	0.314
PL,HU	−3.190[a]	24	−3.336	x	49[c]	0.314	−2.400	6	−3.336	1.740	45	0.314	x	98[d]	−3.336	0.772	45	0.314

Critical values for the ADF test taken from MacKinnon [25]. x—n/a. [a]10% c.v. = −3.044. [b]1% c.v. = 0.533. [c]AIC at lag $k = x$ is not at its minimum. [d]Augmentation of order 98 does not remove autocorrelation

Table 20.3 Results of (VEC) DCC M-GARCH estimation and validation for Germany, the Czech Republic, Poland and Hungary 1Y, 5Y and 10Y CDS spreads

Test	Model																							
Stat.	VEC DCC M-GARCH, 1Y CDS spreads								DCC M-GARCH, 5Y CDS spreads								DCC M-GARCH, 10Y CDS spreads							
	Equation																							
	ΔDE_t		ΔCZ_t		ΔPL_t		ΔHU_t		ΔDE_t		ΔCZ_t		ΔPL_t		ΔHU_t		ΔDE_t		ΔCZ_t		ΔPL_t		ΔHU_t	
	Est.	p.v.	Est.	p.v.	Est.	p.v.	Est.	p.v.	Est.	p.v.	Est.	p.v.	Est.	p.v.	Est.	p.v.	Est.	p.v.	Est.	p.v.	Est.	p.v.	Est.	p.v.
W_{1i}	832.14	0.00	1.29	0.26	4.39	0.04	0.61	0.44	824.14	0.00	4.42	0.35	3.14	0.21	11.89	0.29	595.89	0.00	1.94	0.16	4.83	0.03	0.58	0.45
W_{2i}	1.71	0.19	529.33	0.00	1.21	0.27	0.02	0.89	5.04	0.08	392.14	0.00	1.95	0.38	13.22	0.21	2.50	0.11	552.27	0.00	3.07	0.08	0.63	0.43
W_{3i}	0.09	0.77	0.01	0.92	334.03	0.00	0.06	0.81	1.96	0.37	8.29	0.05	311.68	0.00	17.50	0.06	0.56	0.46	2.32	0.13	845.16	0.00	0.02	0.88
W_{4i}	8.90	0.00	4.25	0.04	3.12	0.08	610.86	0.00	6.61	0.04	16.61	0.00	14.57	0.00	271.18	0.00	2.04	0.15	6.54	0.01	5.23	0.02	611.62	0.00
W_{5i}	3.26	0.07	4.25	0.04	3.50	0.06	3.00	0.08	–	–	–	–	–	–	–	–	–	–	–	–	–	–	–	–
W_{6i}	10.85	0.00	7.53	0.01	7.91	0.00	11.72	0.00	6.30	0.01	5.92	0.01	12.03	0.00	6.98	0.01	3.80	0.05	3.49	0.06	1.92	0.17	5.03	0.02
W_{7i}	2.52	0.64	6.99	0.14	10.48	0.03	6.14	0.19	0.78	0.94	2.61	0.63	1.59	0.81	4.50	0.34	5.03	0.28	5.60	0.23	4.56	0.33	2.87	0.58
W_{8i}	1.21	0.27	0.55	0.46	0.44	0.51	2.34	0.13	1.48	0.22	0.64	0.42	0.67	0.41	0.16	0.69	0.67	0.42	1.23	0.27	4.91	0.03	0.43	0.51
Standardized residuals																								
$Q(1)$	0.37	0.54	0.47	0.49	0.53	0.47	0.10	0.75	1.03	0.31	0.17	0.68	3.05	0.08	0.01	0.91	0.82	0.37	0.97	0.32	0.07	0.79	1.41	0.23
$Q(5)$	1.46	0.92	2.12	0.83	3.68	0.60	4.73	0.45	5.72	0.33	5.71	0.34	4.33	0.50	6.73	0.24	5.26	0.29	8.85	0.12	1.07	0.96	7.51	0.19
$Q(10)$	2.82	0.99	7.20	0.71	6.14	0.80	16.39	0.09	11.10	0.35	10.50	0.40	6.80	0.74	9.85	0.45	8.14	0.62	15.73	0.11	3.45	0.97	14.14	0.13
$Q(20)$	11.36	0.94	10.56	0.96	10.30	0.96	27.74	0.12	18.57	0.55	20.52	0.43	13.47	0.86	23.78	0.25	12.60	0.89	24.25	0.23	9.70	0.97	29.23	0.08
$Q(30)$	27.04	0.62	21.33	0.88	16.51	0.98	37.30	0.17	31.34	0.40	31.15	0.41	19.12	0.94	31.54	0.39	21.28	0.88	30.08	0.46	13.65	1.00	35.82	0.21

(continued)

Table 20.3 (continued)

Test	Model																							
Stat.	VEC DCC M-GARCH, 1Y CDS spreads								DCC M-GARCH, 5Y CDS spreads								DCC M-GARCH, 10Y CDS spreads							
	Equation																							
	ΔDE_t		ΔCZ_t		ΔPL_t		ΔHU_t		ΔDE_t		ΔCZ_t		ΔPL_t		ΔHU_t		ΔDE_t		ΔCZ_t		ΔPL_t		ΔHU_t	
	Est.	p.v.	Est.	p.v.	Est.	p.v.	Est.	p.v.	Est.	p.v.	Est.	p.v.	Est.	p.v.	Est.	p.v.	Est.	p.v.	Est.	p.v.	Est.	p.v.	Est.	p.v.
Squares of standardized residuals																								
$Q(1)$	0.55	0.46	0.05	0.82	0.01	0.93	0.23	0.63	0.10	0.76	0.04	0.83	0.42	0.52	0.09	0.77	3.09	0.08	0.28	0.60	2.15	0.14	0.12	0.73
$Q(5)$	1.66	0.89	4.23	0.52	1.32	0.93	0.83	0.97	1.24	0.94	7.10	0.21	1.09	0.95	3.40	0.64	3.55	0.61	6.77	0.24	6.20	0.29	1.78	0.88
$Q(10)$	2.91	0.98	6.11	0.81	1.99	1.00	11.50	0.32	2.42	0.99	7.94	0.64	1.77	1.00	15.84	0.10	3.73	0.96	9.85	0.45	6.86	0.74	15.34	0.12
$Q(20)$	8.00	0.99	8.19	0.99	4.18	1.00	14.70	0.79	7.09	1.00	11.00	0.95	5.25	1.00	19.53	0.49	4.52	1.00	14.25	0.82	13.57	0.85	18.31	0.57
$Q(30)$	10.25	1.00	10.76	1.00	32.21	0.27	26.23	0.66	16.33	0.98	19.24	0.93	19.29	0.93	23.41	0.80	8.09	1.00	26.12	0.67	19.35	0.93	21.34	0.88

W_{ij}—the country j CDS spread does not Granger cause its country i counterpart (W_{ii}—the country i CDS spread at time t depends upon itself at time $t-1$), $i = 1, \ldots, 4$ for Germany, the Czech Republic, Poland and Hungary accordingly, under H_0 of no causality (dependence) distributed as $\chi^2(1)$ (1 and 10 Y model), $\chi^2(2)$ (Germany, Poland), $\chi^2(4)$ (the Czech Republic), $\chi^2(10)$ (Hungary) (5 Y model); W_{5i}—no CDS spread of country i departure from the long-run relationship of spreads, under H_0 of no departure distributed as $\chi^2(1)$; W_{6i}—VIX effect, under H_0 of no effect distributed as $\chi^2(1)$; W_{7i}—day of the week effect in mean for the CDS spread of country i, under H_0 of no effect distributed as $\chi^2(4)$; W_{8i}—GARCH versus IGARCH, under H_0 of IGARCH distributed as $\chi^2(1)$; $Q(k)$—Ljung-Box test statistic for autocorrelation, under H_0 of no autocorrelation of order up to k distributed as $\chi^2(k)$

Table 20.4 Characteristics of conditional variances and correlations for Germany, the Czech Republic, Poland and Hungary 1Y, 5Y and 10Y CDS spreads

Variable	Statistic															
	Centile									Min	Max	Mean	Std	CV[a]	Sk	Kurt
	*C*1	*C*5	*C*10	*C*25	*C*50	*C*75	*C*90	*C*95	*C*99							
	Conditional variance															
DE1	31.94	33.27	36.64	49.83	81.61	138.37	285.84	398.51	657.15	31.61	1207.64	126.10	129.35	108.49	2.88	14.10
CZ1	13.06	14.19	14.94	18.75	30.34	58.12	100.50	140.05	249.79	12.97	590.04	48.23	51.26	129.76	3.91	27.54
PL1	20.12	20.58	21.25	24.73	38.14	80.37	185.38	310.16	1062.89	19.91	5086.89	100.74	263.28	145.88	10.14	139.99
HU1	10.86	11.89	12.98	15.50	21.21	35.86	76.88	142.00	241.31	10.39	453.27	38.02	47.73	95.99	3.73	20.42
DE5	2.94	3.09	3.38	4.42	6.64	12.00	21.08	33.24	72.21	2.92	187.68	10.97	13.45	114.16	4.86	38.00
CZ5	0.52	0.54	0.56	0.72	1.92	6.64	20.24	33.64	139.41	0.51	1140.66	10.88	50.52	308.33	14.00	240.44
PL5	1.59	1.64	1.74	2.19	3.37	8.77	18.33	26.94	72.11	1.58	219.92	8.17	13.37	195.25	6.22	63.22
HU5	0.87	0.94	1.09	1.66	3.06	6.83	14.48	23.14	74.46	0.84	297.35	7.05	14.97	168.95	8.45	109.38
DE10	0.53	0.68	0.84	1.35	3.28	9.92	20.17	33.31	89.28	0.48	228.03	9.31	18.24	261.28	5.84	48.85
CZ1 0	0.22	0.23	0.25	0.40	1.42	5.85	19.33	33.38	119.46	0.22	411.81	8.39	26.58	383.80	8.82	103.15
PL10	0.29	0.34	0.40	0.61	1.79	7.16	16.39	25.89	62.64	0.28	183.72	6.47	12.45	365.92	5.06	41.84
HU10	0.38	0.43	0.52	0.96	2.29	5.99	12.72	20.73	55.47	0.18	154.63	5.71	11.02	219.65	6.04	55.47
	Conditional correlation															
DECZ1	0.03	0.11	0.14	0.18	0.20	0.23	0.27	0.29	0.37	−0.26	0.43	0.20	0.06	25.00	−0.77	10.02
DEPL1	0.05	0.15	0.17	0.20	0.22	0.25	0.29	0.32	0.37	−0.26	0.54	0.23	0.06	22.73	−0.84	12.44
DEHU1	0.11	0.16	0.18	0.19	0.21	0.24	0.29	0.32	0.39	0.02	0.55	0.22	0.05	23.81	1.20	7.31
CZPL1	0.13	0.22	0.24	0.28	0.30	0.33	0.37	0.39	0.46	0.05	0.57	0.30	0.06	16.67	−0.04	5.67
CZHU1	0.10	0.18	0.22	0.25	0.28	0.31	0.34	0.37	0.43	−0.08	0.56	0.28	0.06	21.43	−0.51	7.97

(continued)

Table 20.4 (continued)

Variable	Statistic															
	Centile									Min	Max	Mean	Std	CV[a]	Sk	Kurt
	$C1$	$C5$	$C10$	$C25$	$C50$	$C75$	$C90$	$C95$	$C99$							
PLHU1	0.14	0.24	0.28	0.32	0.34	0.38	0.42	0.45	0.45	−0.03	0.77	0.35	0.07	17.65	0.18	9.23
DECZ5	0.07	0.16	0.20	0.24	0.28	0.32	0.39	0.42	0.51	−0.23	0.66	0.28	0.08	28.57	−0.07	6.28
DEPL5	0.17	0.26	0.29	0.33	0.37	0.41	0.47	0.50	0.56	0.03	0.63	0.37	0.07	21.62	−0.03	4.42
DEHU5	0.17	0.22	0.25	0.29	0.33	0.37	0.42	0.46	0.52	0.03	0.64	0.33	0.07	24.24	0.30	4.29
CZPL5	0.23	0.37	0.42	0.48	0.51	0.56	0.60	0.64	0.70	0.00	0.90	0.51	0.08	15.69	−0.82	7.24
CZHU5	0.19	0.28	0.32	0.36	0.39	0.44	0.50	0.53	0.67	0.03	0.88	0.40	0.08	20.51	0.56	6.74
PLHU5	0.39	0.52	0.56	0.60	0.64	0.68	0.71	0.74	0.80	0.06	0.92	0.64	0.08	12.50	−1.63	12.74
DECZ10	−0.28	−0.05	0.05	0.16	0.26	0.36	0.44	0.51	0.56	−0.44	0.62	0.25	0.17	76.92	−0.73	4.21
DEPL10	0.06	0.14	0.16	0.22	0.30	0.42	0.51	0.57	0.66	0.00	0.69	0.32	0.14	66.67	0.44	2.62
DEHU10	−0.03	0.07	0.11	0.17	0.24	0.37	0.45	0.52	0.61	−0.11	0.65	0.27	0.14	83.33	0.30	2.85
CZPL10	−0.05	0.08	0.21	0.34	0.45	0.60	0.67	0.71	0.74	−0.22	0.76	0.45	0.19	57.78	−0.67	3.30
CZHU10	0.04	0.14	0.21	0.28	0.40	0.50	0.58	0.63	0.69	−0.02	0.80	0.39	0.15	55.00	−0.13	2.65
PLHU10	0.17	0.33	0.39	0.47	0.61	0.69	0.77	0.80	0.83	0.08	0.85	0.58	0.15	36.07	−0.53	2.84

[a] $\mathrm{CV} = 100(C75 - C25)/C5$

5. We reject the hypothesis for one- and five-year CDS spreads stating that an increase in market fear as measured by the log change in VIX has no impact on all country spreads (see the estimates of W_{6i} test statistic).
6. We find the existence of day of the week effect in Poland one-year CDS spreads (see the estimates of test statistic W_{71}).

We stack the main characteristics of conditional variance and conditional correlation distributions for Germany, the Czech Republic, Poland and Hungary one-, five- and ten-year CDS spreads obtained from model (20.1)–(20.4) in Table 20.4. Surprisingly despite, the German market is the most liquid, and the volatility of Germany one-, five- and ten-year CDS spreads is the largest as measured by the median of conditional variance of their rates of return. More interestingly, the median of pairwise conditional correlation estimates among the countries of interest differs across the maturities in the way indicating that the Czech, Hungarian and Polish markets are better integrated among one another than any single with the German market. We also find that all correlations are significantly raised for the upper centiles of VIX which may be interpreted in favour of the contagion.

20.4 Conclusion

This paper examines the co-movement of the Czech Republic, Hungary and Poland one-, five- and ten-year CDS spreads vis a vis their Germany counterparts in the aftermath of the global financial crisis in a novel four-dimensional VEC DCC M-GARCH setting which enables to control for risk stemming from international markets. Our main finding is that only the Czech Republic and Germany one-year CDS spreads are in the long-run equilibrium relation. Surprisingly, the Hungary CDS spreads play an important role within the spreads Granger causing almost all their counterpart spreads. The causality other way round is incidental. We also documented that the Czech, Hungarian and Polish CDS markets seem to be better integrated among one another than any single with the German market. Finally, we interpret the raised medians of pairwise conditional correlation coefficient estimates for all CDS spreads in the periods of market stress and turmoil as the evidence of contagion.

References

1. Gündüz, Y., Kaya, O.: Impacts of the financial crisis on eurozone sovereign CDS spreads. J. Int. Money Financ. **49**, 425–442 (2014)
2. Butler, A.W., Fauver, L.: Institutional environment and sovereign credit ratings. Financ. Manage. **35**(3), 53–79 (2006)
3. Augustin, P., Tédongap, R.: Real economic shocks and sovereign credit risk. J. Financ. Quant. Anal. **51**(2), 541–587 (2016)
4. Aslund, A.: Lessons from reforms in Central and Eastern Europe in the Wake of the Global Financial Crisis. Institute for International Economics Discussion Papers Series, No. WP 12-7 (2012)
5. Wang, P., Moore, T.: The integration of the credit default swap markets during the US subprime crisis: dynamic correlation analysis. J. Int. Financ. Mark., Inst & Money **22**, 1–15 (2012)
6. Chen, Y.-H.C., Härdle, W.K., Pham-Thu, H.: The integration of credit default swap markets in the pre and post-subprime crisis in common stochastic trends. SFB Discussion Paper No. 649 (2014)
7. Ho, S.E.: Long and short-runs determinants of the sovereign CDS spread in emerging countries. Res. Int. Bus. Financ. **36**, 579–590 (2016)
8. Pan, J., Singleton, K.J.: Default and recovery implicit in the term structure of sovereign CDS spreads. J. Financ. **63**(5), 2345–2384 (2008)
9. Longstaff, F.A., Pan, J., Pedersen, L.H., Singleton, K.J.: How sovereign is sovereign credit risk? Am. Econ. J.: Macroecon. **3**(2), 75–103 (2011)
10. Fender, I., Hayo, B., Neuenkirch, M.: Daily pricing of emerging market sovereign CDS before and during the global financial crisis. J. Bank. Finance **36**, 2786–2794 (2012)
11. Clark, E., Kassimatis, K.: Macroeconomic effects on emerging-markets sovereign credit spreads. J. Financ. Stab. **20**, 1–13 (2015)
12. Fontana, A., Scheicher, M.: An analysis of euro area sovereign CDS and their relation with government bonds. J. Bank. Finance **62**, 126–140 (2016)
13. Kocsis, Z., Monostori, Z.: The role of country-specific fundamentals in sovereign CDS spreads: Eastern European experiences. Emerg. Mark. Rev. **27**, 140–168 (2016)
14. Ang, A., Longstaff, F.A.: Systemic sovereign credit risk: lessons from the U.S. and Europe. J. Monet. Econ. **60**, 493–510 (2013)
15. Engle, R.F.: Dynamic conditional correlation: a simple class of multivariate generalized autoregressive conditional heteroskedasticity models. J. Bus. & Econ. Stat. **20**, 339–350 (2002)
16. Kliber, A.: The dynamics of sovereign credit default swaps and the evolution of the financial crisis in selected Central European Economies. Finance a úvěr-Czech J. Econ. Financ. **64**(4), 330–350 (2014)
17. Yu, J., Meyer, R.: Multivariate stochastic volatility models: Bayesian estimation and model comparison. Econ. Rev. **25**, 361–384 (2006)
18. Forbes, K.J., Rigobon, R.: No contagion, only interdependence: measuring stock market comovements. J. Financ. **57**(5), 2223–2261 (2002)
19. Engle, R.F., Granger, C.W.J.: Cointegration and error correction: representation, estimation, and testing. Econometrica **55**(2), 251–276 (1987)
20. Johansen, S.: Estimation and hypothesis testing of cointegration vectors in Gaussian vector autoregressive models. Econometrica **59**(6), 1551–1580 (1991)
21. Elliott, G., Rothenberg, T.J., Stock, J.H.: Efficient tests for auto-regressive unit root. Econometrica **64**(4), 813–836 (1996)
22. Kwiatkowski, D., Phillips, P.C.B., Schmidt, P., Shin, Y.: Testing the null hypothesis of stationarity against the alternative of a unit root. J. Econ. **54**, 159–178 (1992)
23. Lütkepohl, H.: New Introduction to Multiple Time Series Analysis. Springer, Berlin (2005)
24. Hjalmarsson E., Österholm P.: Testing for cointegration using the Johansen methodology when variables are near-integrated. IMF Working Paper No. WP/07/141 (2007)

25. MacKinnon, J.G.: Critical values for cointegration tests. Queen's Economics Department Working Paper No. 1227 (2010)
26. Shin, Y.: A residual-based test of the null of cointegration against the alternative of no cointegration. Econ. Theory **10**(1), 91–115 (1994)

Chapter 21
Characteristics of Dichotomous Variable Estimators

Jan Purczyński

Abstract The article covers the following probability models used in dichotomous variable analysis: logit, probit, and raybit—the last one proposed by the author. In the article, the following characteristics of estimators are derived: bias, variance, and mean squared error, which links them. The method of probability estimation which minimizes relative root mean squared error (RRMSE) is proposed. It is also shown that the goodness-of-fit measures of mean square error (MSE) and mean absolute error (MAE) models present in the field literature lead to the similar results.

Keywords Qualitative econometric models · Logit model · Probit model · Raybit model

21.1 Introduction

In the paper, the following probability models—used for the analysis of the dichotomous variable—are considered: logit, probit, and raybit (proposed by the author). The purpose of the publication is to indicate mean square error estimators of the probability of the aforementioned models. Three probability models and four estimation methods are considered, including maximum likelihood method (ML). The result of the mean square error analysis is the proposal of the method that minimizes relative root mean squared error. Computer simulations using a random number generator with a Bernoulli distribution are used as the main tool. In addition, the quality of models used in the literature is tested: mean absolute error (MAE), mean square error (MSE), and weighted mean squared error (WMSE). The ordinary least squares method (OLS) can be used for the binary estimation of the explained variable. However, the solution obtained by this method has a significant disadvantage: The theoretical probability may go beyond the range [0, 1]. The removal of this defect occurs when assuming that the probability corresponds to the cumulative distribution func-

J. Purczyński (✉)
Faculty of Electrical Engineering, West Pomeranian University of Technology, Szczecin, Poland
e-mail: jan.purczynski@zut.edu.pl

W. Tarczyński and K. Nermend (eds.), *Effective Investments on Capital Markets*, Springer Proceedings in Business and Economics,
https://doi.org/10.1007/978-3-030-21274-2_21

tion (CDF) of the random variable distribution. In the case of a logistic distribution, a logit model is obtained, whereas the adoption of a normal distribution leads to a probit model. An innovative model was proposed by Purczyński and Bednarz-Okrzyńska [1] in which the probability is expressed by the Rayleigh's distribution—hence, the model name: raybit.

The article consists of five parts: introduction, probability models for a binary variable, mean square error of dichotomous models estimators, model error estimation and summary.

Probability models for dichotomous variables are widely used in various researches, and an example of this is the literature review presented below.

Gruszczyński [2] draws attention to an increasing importance of qualitative models as they constitute a basic tool for describing microeconometric models used in empirical corporate finance. Barniv and McDonald [3] provide an extensive review of categorical techniques in the area of accounting and finance and compare the results of applying logit and probit models as opposed to other procedures. Ye and Lord [4] examine the impact of sample size on the three crash severity models: multinomial logit, ordered probit, and mixed logit. Cramer [5] explains the theory underlying logit transformation providing many empirical applications. Hoetker [6] identifies critical issues in the use of logit and probit models in strategic management research as well as provides implications for the conduct of such research with the models in question. Shi and Yin [7] have attempted to boost the conditional logit model. The method proposed by them is used in discrete choice modeling to predict the results. With this approach, they could get potential nonlinear effects of interdependence, make a small adjustment and make an automatic variable selection. In their simulations, they indicated that the presented method provides an accurate estimation of the true forms of covariate effects. The empirical studies on the convenient method of estimating the multinomial logit model with fixed effects by D'Haultfœuille and Iaria are somewhat different [8]. The authors note that the conditional maximum likelihood estimator in the logit model is limited by the size of fixed effects. They emphasize that the element in the denominator with constant effect grows exponentially. In their opinion, this barrier can be overcome by using a McFadden rule [34] and on this basis to estimate the logit model with fixed effects on random samples of permutations. An equally important procedure is the removal of heterogeneity bias from the logit model estimation, which was proposed by Jones and Landwehr [9]. They extended the evaluation procedure to the conditional evaluation developed by Chamberlain [10]. Using this method, they managed to remove the heterogeneity bias, which enhances the goodness of fit and increases the explanatory power of models. Also, Hausman and McFadden [11] conducted some research on discrete models. They found that the multinomial logit model is most commonly used. They offered two specifications' tests. One of them is the use of the Hausman [12] test procedure. The second is a classic approach to the nested logit model. Then, the classic test procedure is applied, including the Wald, likelihood ratio, and Lagrange multiplier tests. A slightly different approach is presented by Jones and Hensher [13]. They emphasize that the mixed logit model is better at explaining and predicting than the standard logit. In their opinion, the mixed logit model is a valuable tool in research on financial distress prediction. The research on the mixed logit was also carried out by Fox et al. [14].

A completely different approach to logit models was presented by Li and Wang [15]. They have embedded the concept of early financial warning models, extending forecasting with non-financial performance indicators.

Equally interesting are the observations of Brezigar-Masten and Masten about the predictions of financial distress (bankruptcies) with the use of the logit model [16]. They proposed a new procedure for selecting predictors based on nonparametric regression and the classification tree method (CART). Then, they checked it on the standard logit model. They noted that the standard logit model together with variables from the CART method is the most desirable and effectively take into account nonlinear effects.

Antunes et al. [17] also referred to the early warning models. They noted that banking crises are rare events, the effects of which are yet very negative. Therefore, they believe that the dynamics and characteristics of panel data should be studied using the (dynamic) probit models. They developed sensitivity indicators, which are early warning tools.

Also, the conclusions from Ng's research on the subject of "Forecasting US recessions with various risk factors and dynamic probit models" are important [18]. The author expanded probit recession forecasting models, while taking into account the different determinants of recession risk. He used advanced methods of dynamic probit modeling. He referred his research to predictions on the financial market, taking into account the problem of credit risk, liquidity in the general economy, and bursting of asset price bubbles. He presented specifications for three dynamic probit models and a standard static model.

Soyer and Sung [19] focused on the analysis of longitudinal data using Bayesian dynamic probit models. They used a dynamic probit model to track the first-order Markov process. The data augmentation method and forward filtering backward sampling algorithm for dynamic linear models were presented.

Proaño and Tarassow [20] examined the prognostic capacity of the probit using a three-regime dynamically ordered model of the economic system. This approach fits into the forecasting of recession, short increases and accelerations in the USA and Japan. They first used a nonparametric dating algorithm to identify three phases along the Proaño line [21].

Examples of similar papers on multidimensional plots about dichotomous variable models can be multiplied. Among the equally interesting are: Purczyński and Porada-Rochoń [22], Maddala [23], Han and Vytlacil [24], Mourifié and Méango [25], Papatla and Krishnamurthi [26], Amemiya [26–29], Hausman and Wise [30], Eichengreen et al. [31], Butler [32], Collett [33], McFadden [34], McFadden and Train [35].

In the next chapter, the author presents the probability models for binary variable.

21.2 Probability Models for Binary Variable

However, in Eq. (21.1) the author moves from a single decision problem to results of single decisions of group members, which are summarized as group ratios.

It is assumed that variable Y can take two values: one or zero, corresponding to the fact of making or not making a decision—an occurrence of event A.

If among n_i of decision-makers, y_i of them make a sensible decision, then quotient

$$p_i = \frac{y_i}{n_i} \quad (\mathrm{i} = 1, 2, \ldots, I) \tag{21.1}$$

represents an empirical frequency of making a decision in an ith group of the decision-makers.

The easiest model is a linear model of probability:

$$p = X\alpha + \varepsilon \tag{21.2}$$

where

- p I-dimensional vector of empirical probabilities,
- X $[I \times (k + 1)]$ dimensional matrix including k number of explanatory variables,
- α $(k + 1)$ vector of parameters,
- ε I-dimensional vector of random elements.

Based on Eq. (21.2), the following can be observed

$$p_i = P_i + \varepsilon_i \tag{21.3}$$

where

- p_i empirical probability of occurrence of event A for ith value of vector of explanatory variables,
- P_i probability of occurrence of event A for ith value of vector of explanatory variables,
- ε_i disturbance: $E(\varepsilon_i) = 0$ and $\mathrm{cov}(\varepsilon_i, \varepsilon_j) = 0$ for $i \neq j$.

Since variable y_i (Eq. 21.1) has binomial distribution, the variance of a disturbance is given by relation [36]:

$$V(\varepsilon_i) = \frac{P_i(1 - P_i)}{n_i} \tag{21.4}$$

which means that the random variable appearing in Eq. (21.4) is heteroskedastic.

For the linear probability model, the following relation is observed:

$$P_i = x_i^{\mathrm{T}}\alpha \tag{21.5}$$

where x_i^{T} is ith row of explanatory variable matrix.

It is assumed that probability P_i, with which a decision in question is made in an ith group of decision-makers, is function F of variable $x_i^{\mathrm{T}}\alpha$:

$$P_i = F\left(x_i^{\mathrm{T}}\alpha\right) \tag{21.6}$$

where F is the cumulative distribution function.

The most commonly applied are two models:

Logit model, hereafter referred to as LOG

$$P_i = L\left(x_i^{\mathrm{T}}\alpha\right) = \left[1 + \mathrm{e}^{-x_i^{\mathrm{T}}\alpha}\right]^{-1} \tag{21.7}$$

where L denotes the cumulative distribution function of a logistic distribution.

Probit model, hereafter referred to as PRO

$$P_i = \Phi\left(x_i^{\mathrm{T}}\alpha\right) = \frac{1}{\sqrt{2\pi}} \int\limits_{-\infty}^{x_i^{\mathrm{T}}\alpha} \mathrm{e}^{-\frac{t^2}{2}}\,\mathrm{d}t \tag{21.8}$$

where Φ denotes the cumulative distribution function of a standardized normal distribution.

In the paper by Purczyński and Bednarz-Okrzyńska [1], the probability model applying Rayleigh cumulative distribution function was proposed: raybit model, hereafter referred to as RAY

$$P_i = R\left(x_i^{\mathrm{T}}\alpha\right) = 1 - \exp\left[-\left(x_i^{\mathrm{T}}\alpha\right)^2\right] \tag{21.9}$$

where R denotes Rayleigh cumulative distribution function.

In the analysis of each model, the following three steps can be singled out [37]:

A. First step: estimation of vector $\alpha 0$ of parameters α

$$\alpha 0 = \left(X^{\mathrm{T}} W^{-1} X\right)^{-1} X^{\mathrm{T}} W^{-1} v \tag{21.10}$$

where W is a diagonal covariance matrix (of a size $I \times I$), where the elements on the main diagonal equal:

$$w_i = [n_i p_i (1 - p_i)]^{-1} \quad \text{LOG} \tag{21.11}$$

$$w_i = \frac{p_i (1 - p_i)}{n_i \left\{\varphi\left[\Phi^{-1}(p_i)\right]\right\}^2} \quad \text{PRO} \tag{21.12}$$

where $\varphi(t)$ denotes the density function of the standardized normal distribution, $\Phi^{-1}(p_i)$ is the inverse function to the cumulative distribution function of standardized normal distribution

$$w_i = \frac{p_i}{4n_i(1 - p_i)\ln\frac{1}{1-p_i}} \quad \text{RAY} \tag{21.13}$$

Depending on the model, vector v is given by the following formula:

$$v_i = \ln\left(\frac{p_i}{1 - p_i}\right) \quad \text{LOG} \tag{21.14}$$

$$v_i = \Phi^{-1}(p_i) \quad \text{PRO} \tag{21.15}$$

$$v_i = \sqrt{-\ln(1 - p_i)} \quad \text{RAY} \tag{21.16}$$

Estimation of the theoretical probability:

$$p0_i = L\left(x_i^{\mathrm{T}}\alpha 0\right) \quad \text{LOG} \tag{21.17}$$

$$p0_i = \Phi\left(x_i^{\mathrm{T}}\alpha 0\right) \quad \text{PRO} \tag{21.18}$$

$$p0_i = R\left(x_i^{\mathrm{T}}\alpha 0\right) \quad \text{RAY} \tag{21.19}$$

B. Second step

By applying the ordinary least squares (OLS), the following is obtained:

$$\alpha 1 = \left(X^{\mathrm{T}}X\right)^{-1}X^{\mathrm{T}}v$$

where v is defined by Formulas (21.14)–(21.16).

Estimation of theoretical probability $p1_i$ is derived from the formulas analogous to (21.17)–(21.19).

C. Third step

Estimation of vector $\alpha 2$ of parameters α

$$\alpha 2 = \left(X^{\mathrm{T}}W1^{-1}X\right)^{-1}X^{\mathrm{T}}W1^{-1}v \tag{21.20}$$

where v is defined by Eqs. (21.14)–(21.16).

$w1$ is a diagonal covariance matrix, where the elements on the main diagonal equal:

$$w1_i = [n_i p1_i(1 - p1_i)]^{-1} \quad \text{LOG} \tag{21.21}$$

$$w1_i = \frac{p1_i(1 - p1_i)}{n_i\{\varphi[\Phi^{-1}(p1_i)]\}^2} \quad \text{PRO} \tag{21.22}$$

$$w1_i = \frac{p1_i}{4n_i(1 - p1_i)\ln\frac{1}{1-p1_i}} \quad \text{RAY} \tag{21.23}$$

Estimation of theoretical probability:

$$p2_i = L\left(x_i^{\mathrm{T}}\alpha 2\right) \quad \text{LOG} \tag{21.24}$$

$$p2_i = \Phi\left(x_i^{\mathrm{T}}\alpha 2\right) \quad \text{PRO} \tag{21.25}$$

$$p2_i = R\left(x_i^{\mathrm{T}}\alpha 2\right) \quad \text{RAY} \tag{21.26}$$

The last method of theoretical probability estimation is the maximum likelihood method (MLM). The description of MLM in relation to logit and probit models can be found in the paper by Chow [38]. The application of MLM for the raybit model was described in the paper by Purczyński and Bednarz-Okrzyńska [1]. The theoretical probability obtained by means of MLM will be labeled as pM_i.

21.3 Mean Square Error of Dichotomous Model Estimators

The task is to estimate $\hat{\theta}$ of an unknown parameter θ.

One of the most important properties of the estimator $\hat{\theta}$ is its bias $b(\theta)$.

$$b(\theta) = E(\hat{\theta}) - \theta \tag{21.27}$$

The quality of the estimator determines also mean squared error (MSE)

$$\text{MSE} = E\left(\hat{\theta} - \theta\right)^2, \tag{21.28}$$

which fulfills the relation [38, 39]

$$\text{MSE} = V(\theta) + (b(\theta))^2 \tag{21.29}$$

where

$b(\theta)$ is an estimator bias (Formula 21.27);
$V(\theta)$ variance of the estimator.

In order to verify the properties of individual estimators, computer simulations were carried out using a random number generator with the Bernoulli distribution (21.3). Declared theoretical probability P_i was in the range (0.02–0.98). According

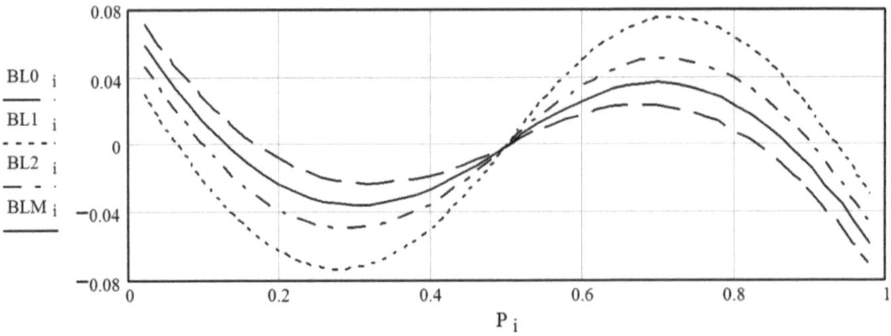

Fig. 21.1 Estimator bias for the logit model. The individual curves refer to the following estimates: the dashed line BL0–$p0$ (Formula 21.17), the dotted line BL1–$p1$, the dashed and dotted line BL2–$p2$ (Formula 21.24), the solid line BLM–pM (MLM)

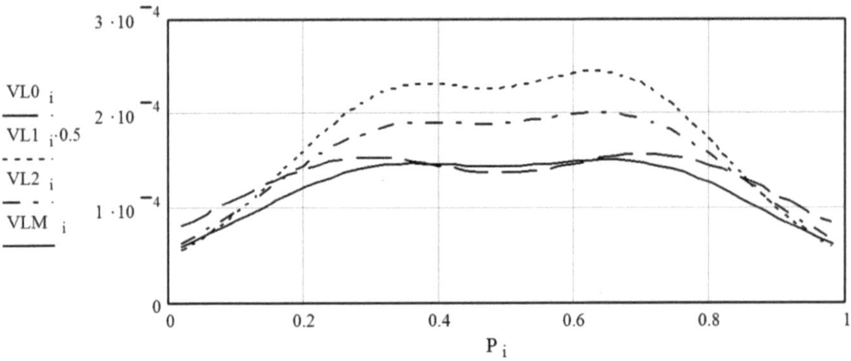

Fig. 21.2 Variance of the estimator for the logit model. Applied labeling: the same as in Fig. 21.1

to Formula (21.3), an empirical probability was obtained from the generator (p with an index i).

Figures 21.1, 21.2, 21.3 and 21.4 present simulation results for the logit model. Figure 21.1 shows estimator bias. It shows that the smallest fluctuation in the bias value is estimated by $p2$ (Formula 21.24) and the largest by $p1$.

Figure 21.2 presents the results of calculations for the variance of individual estimators. This time, the smallest fluctuations were recorded for the estimator $p0$ and the highest for $p1$. Figure 21.3 contains simulation results for mean squared error. The smallest MSE values are for estimator $p2$ and the largest for estimator $p0$.

The value of relative root mean squared error (Formula 21.29) is taken into account when estimating the quality of the estimator:

$$\text{RRSL} = \text{square root (SL) divided by P} \tag{21.30}$$

RRSL relative root mean squared error
SL mean squared error (Formula 21.29)

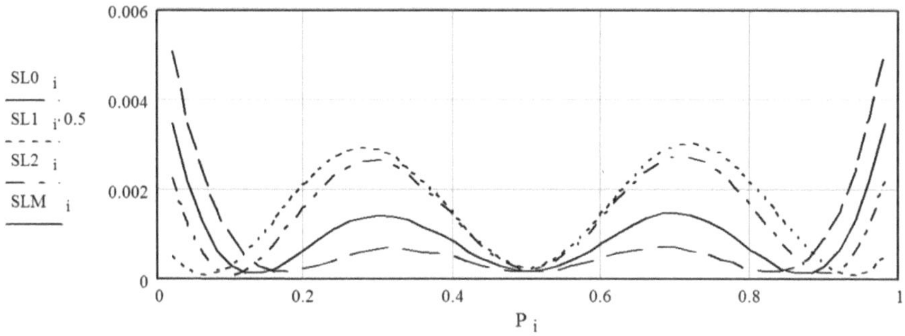

Fig. 21.3 Mean squared error of the estimator (Formula 21.29) for the logit model. Applied labeling: the same as in Fig. 21.1

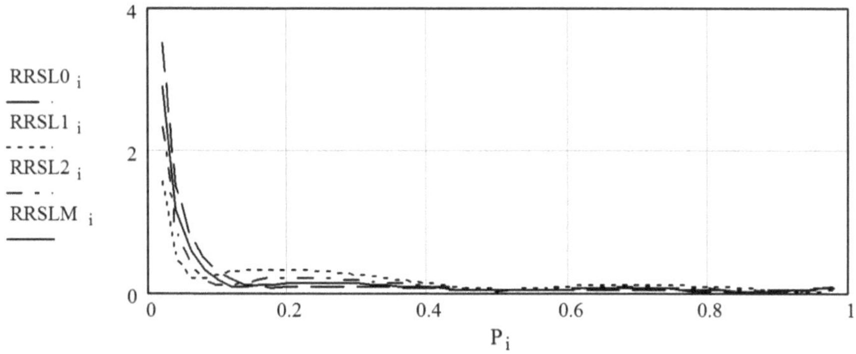

Fig. 21.4 Relative root mean squared error of the estimator (Formula 21.30) for the logit model. Applied labeling: the same as in Fig. 21.1

Figure 21.4 presents the results of calculations for individual estimators. Figure 21.4 shows very large (unacceptable) RRMSE values. The smallest value of RRSL1 = 1.566 is obtained for estimator $p1$, while the highest RRSL0 = 3.51 for the estimator $p0$.

The next four figures relate to the probit model. Based on Figs. 21.5, 21.6 and 21.7, the same conclusions can be drawn as for the logit model (Figs. 21.1, 21.2 and 21.3).

Figure 21.8 shows the results of RRMSE calculations for individual estimators. Similar to the logit model, RRMSE values are unacceptable (exceed 150%). The lowest value of RRSP1 = 1.540 is obtained for estimator $p1$, while the largest RRSP0 = 2.828 is for estimator $p0$.

Figures 21.9, 21.10, 21.11 and 21.12 were prepared on the basis of simulations made for the raybit model. Based on the results presented in Fig. 21.9, it is stated that the smallest fluctuation is shown by estimator $p2$ and the largest by estimator $p0$.

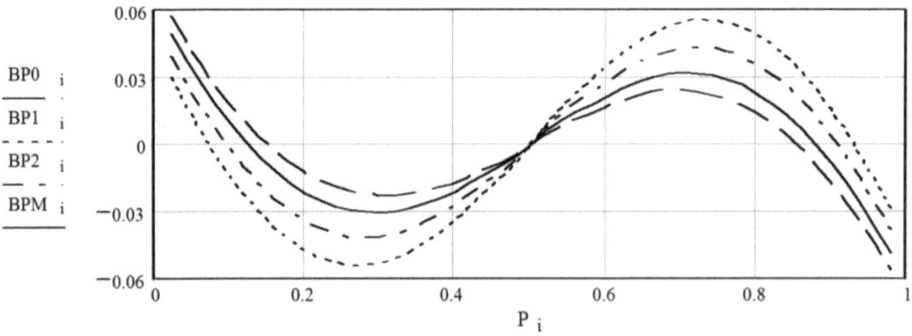

Fig. 21.5 Estimator bias for the probit model. The individual curves refer to the following estimates: dashed line BP0–$p0$ (Formula 21.18), dotted line BP1–$p1$, dashed and dotted line BP2–$p2$ (Formula 21.25), solid line BPM–pM (MLM)

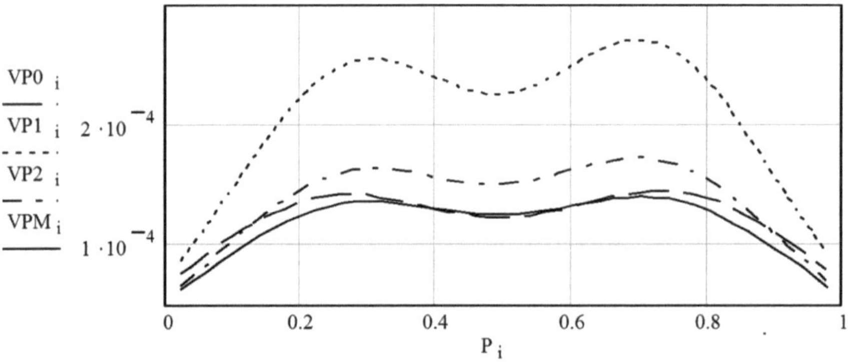

Fig. 21.6 Variance of the estimator for the probit model. Applied labeling: the same as in Fig. 21.5

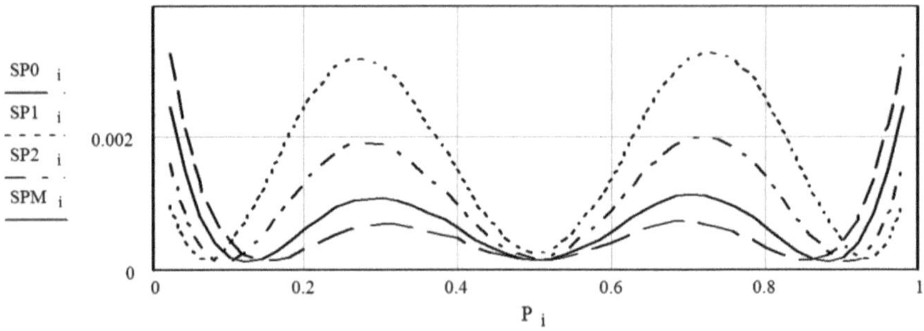

Fig. 21.7 Mean squared error of the estimator (Formula 21.29) for the probit model. Applied labeling: the same as in Fig. 21.5

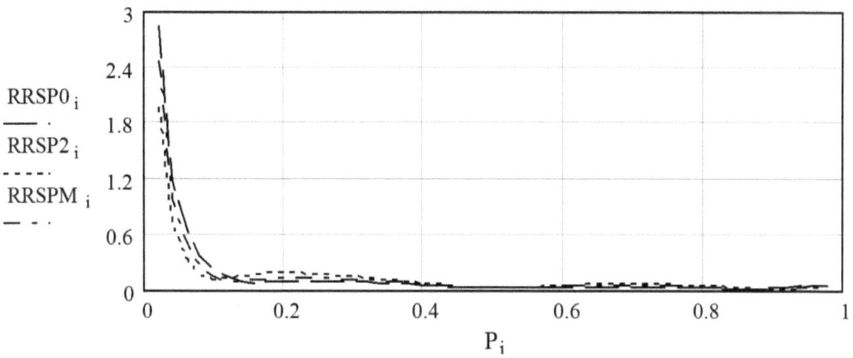

Fig. 21.8 Relative root mean squared error of the estimator (Formula 21.30) for the probit model. Applied labeling: the same as in Fig. 21.5

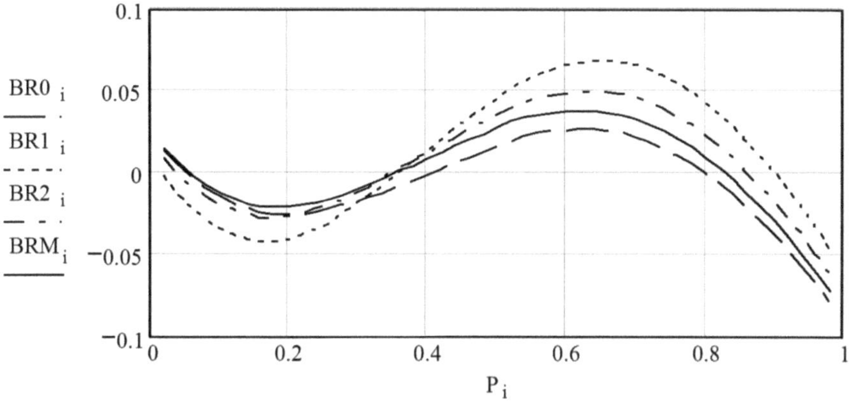

Fig. 21.9 Estimator bias for the raybit model. The individual curves refer to the following estimates: dashed line BR0–*p*0 (Formula 21.19), dotted line BR1–*p*1, dashed and dotted line BR2–*p*2 (Formula 21.26), solid line BR*M*–*pM* (MLM)

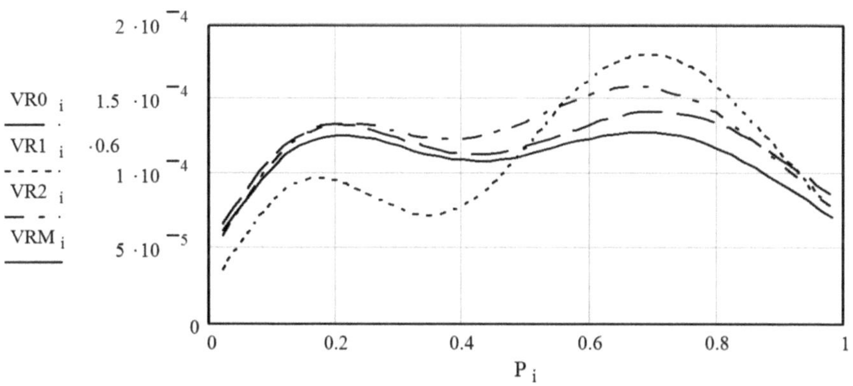

Fig. 21.10 Variance of the estimator for the raybit model. Applied labeling: the same as in Fig. 21.9

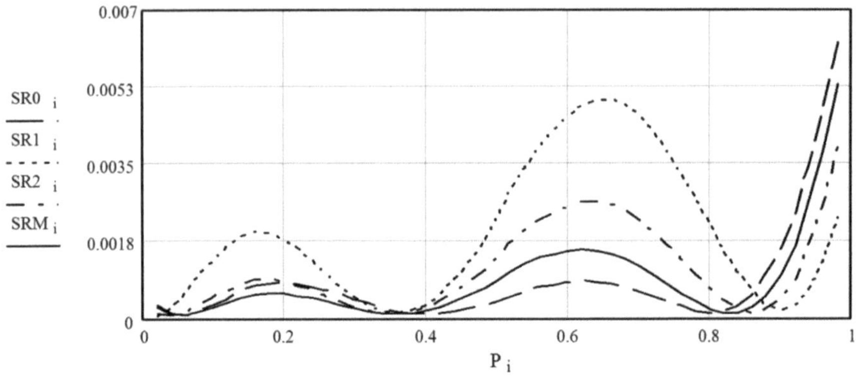

Fig. 21.11 Mean squared error of the estimator (Formula 21.28) for the raybit model. Applied labeling: the same as in Fig. 21.9

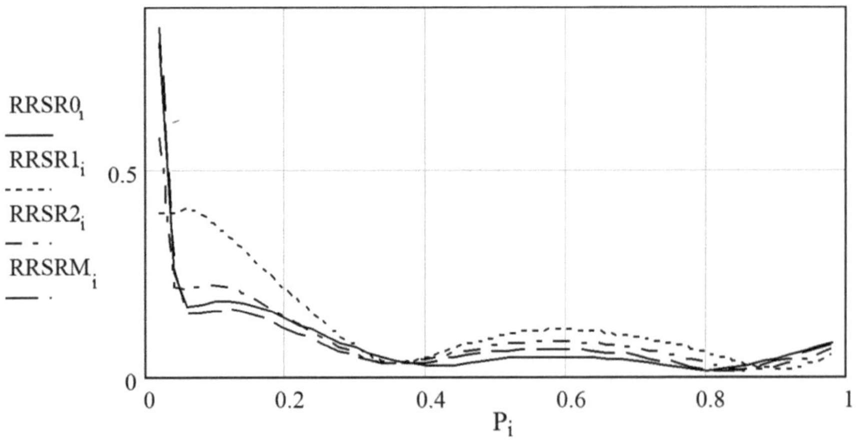

Fig. 21.12 Relative root mean squared error of the estimator (Formula 21.30) for the raybit model. Applied labeling: the same as in Fig. 21.9

Figure 21.10 shows that the smallest fluctuations in variance are recorded for estimation pM (MLM) and the highest for estimator $p1$. Figure 21.11 shows the mean squared error values for the raybit model. There is an increase in the value of MSE for increasing probability values P. This phenomenon has a beneficial effect on RRMSE. Namely, it leads to smaller error values for $P = 0.02$. Based on Fig. 21.12, it could be concluded that the smallest RRMSE error for $P = 0.02$ is burdened with estimator $p1$ RRSR1 $= 0.400$ and the largest estimator pM RRSRM $= 0.84$.

The task the author of this article set himself was to choose the right estimators to limit the RRMSE value. First 12 cases were examined including three models (L, P, R)—each including 4 formulas for estimating the empirical probability. Three cases proved useful: for probit model—formula $p0$ and raybit model—formulas $p1$ and $p2$.

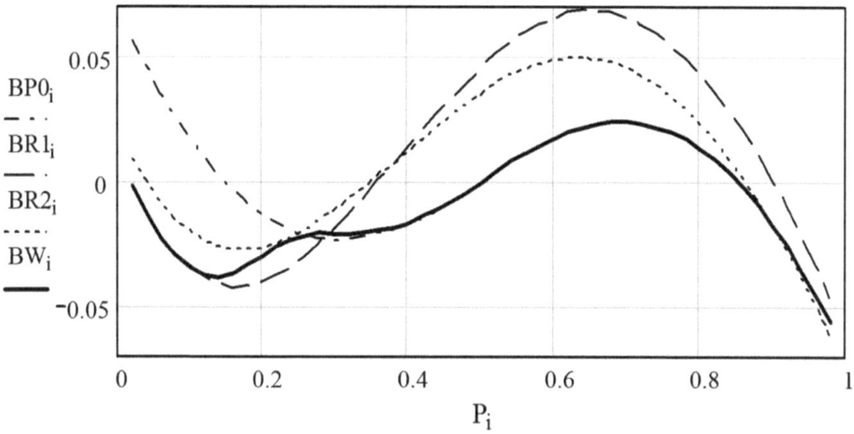

Fig. 21.13 Estimator bias which is used in the minimizing model of RRMSE. The individual curves refer to the following estimates: dashed and dotted line BP0–*p*0 (probit), dashed line BR1–*p*1 (raybit), dotted line BR2–*p*2 (raybit), solid line BW–optimum estimator

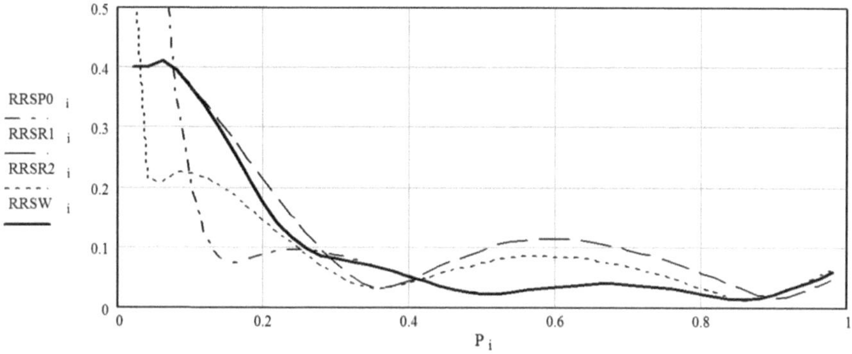

Fig. 21.14 Relative root mean squared error of the estimator which minimizes the value of RRMSE. Applied labeling: the same as in Fig. 21.13

Figure 21.13 presents the estimator bias used in the minimizing model of RRMSE. As the resultant estimator, the following are assumed: the values of $p1$ (raybit model) for $0 < P < 0.2$; $p2$ (raybit model) for $0.2 < P < 0.25$ and $p0$ (probit model) for $0.25 < P < 1$ are.

Figure 21.14 shows that for $P > 0.19$, RRSW < 0.2, and for $P > 0.26$, RRSW < 0.1.

21.4 Model Error Estimation

The most popular goodness-of-fit measure of a model is the mean squared error (MSE):

$$\text{MSE} = \frac{1}{I}\sum_{i=1}^{I}(p_i - pt_i)^2 \tag{21.31}$$

where

p_i the empirical probability (Formula 21.1);
pt_i the theoretical probability.

As pt_i in (21.31) results of four methods are assumed successively ($p0_i$, $p1_i$, $p2_i$, pM_i). Guzik et al. [40] recommend Formula (21.30) as a criterion for matching the theoretical model of probability.

Figure 21.15 shows the values of the goodness-of-fit measure of MSE for the probit model. This figure shows the disadvantage of this measure consisting in the dependence on the MSE from the empirical probability *P*. This relationship is measured by the ratio of the maximum to the minimum value. The smallest value was recorded for MSPO (estimator $p0$), where the ratio max/min = 2.599. The highest value of max/min = 7.507 occurs for MSP1 (estimator $p1$).

In the case of the logit model, the values of the error measures of MSE are characterized by similar dependence on probability *P* (as in Fig. 21.15). Figure 21.16 shows the values of MSE measure in the function of P for the raybit model.

The main difference is that for the logit and probit model, the dependence of MSE on the *P* value is symmetric with respect to the center, i.e., $P = 0.5$. However, for the raybit model, this dependence is asymmetrical and shows an upward trend for the growing *P*. Another measure is the mean absolute error (MAE):

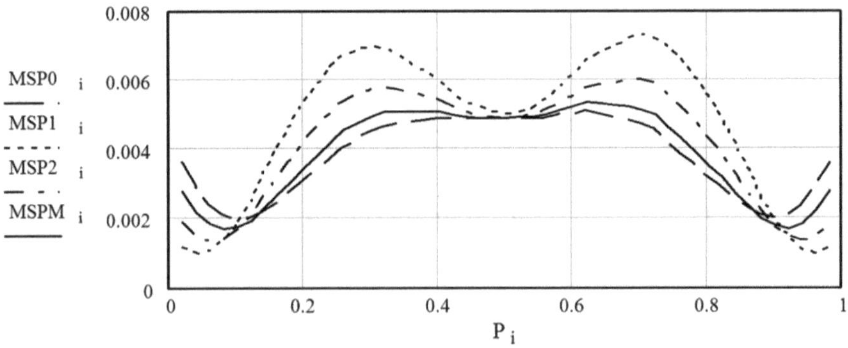

Fig. 21.15 Values of the error measure of MSE (Formula 21.30) for the probit model. Applied labeling: the same as in Fig. 21.5

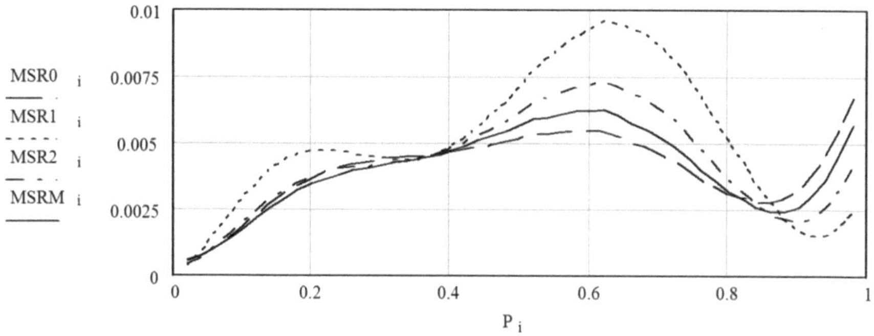

Fig. 21.16 Values of the error measure of MSE (Formula 21.30) for the raybit model. Applied labeling: the same as in Fig. 21.9

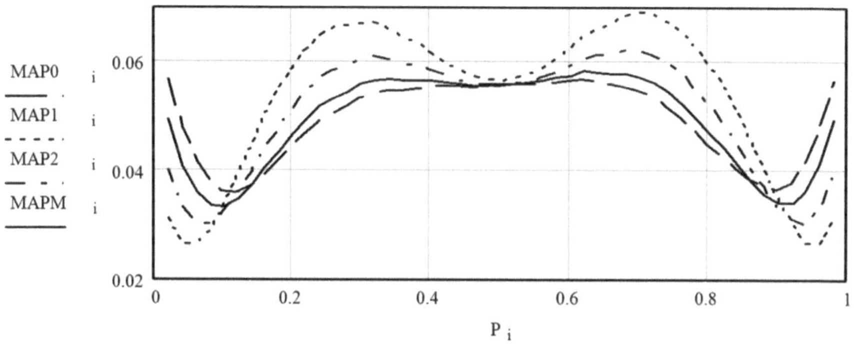

Fig. 21.17 Values of the error measure of MAE (Formula 21.32) for the probit model. Applied labeling: the same as in Fig. 21.5

$$\text{MAE} = \frac{1}{I}\sum_{i=1}^{I} |p_i - pt_i| \tag{21.32}$$

Figure 21.17 shows the values of the goodness-of-fit measure of MAE for the probit model. Similar to Fig. 21.15, the relationship between MAE values and empirical probability is observed. The ratio of the maximum to the minimum value is observed to be the smallest for MAPO (estimator $p0$), max/min = 1.582. The highest value of max/min = 2.592 occurs for MAP1 (estimator $p1$). In the case of the logit model, the values of the error measure of MAE are characterized by the similar dependence on probability P (as in Fig. 21.17). Figure 21.18 shows the values of MAE in the function of P for the raybit model.

Similar to the goodness-of-fit measure of MSE, in the case of MAE for the logit and probit models, the dependence of MAE on the P value is symmetric with respect to the center, i.e., $P = 0.5$. However, for the raybit model, the dependence of MAE on P is asymmetrical and shows an upward trend for the growing P.

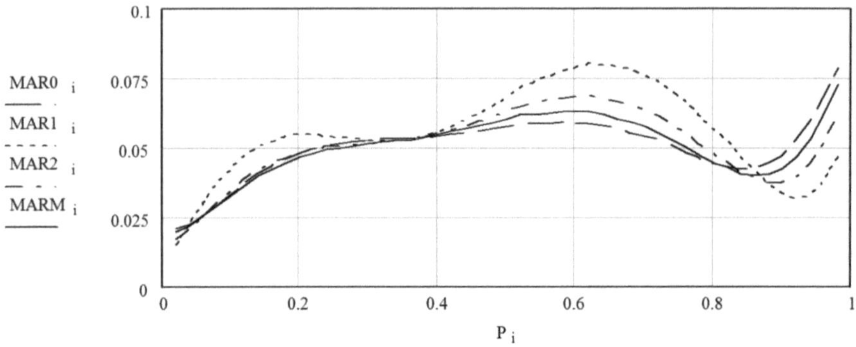

Fig. 21.18 Values of the error measure of MAE (Formula 21.32) for the raybit model. Applied labeling: the same as in Fig. 21.9

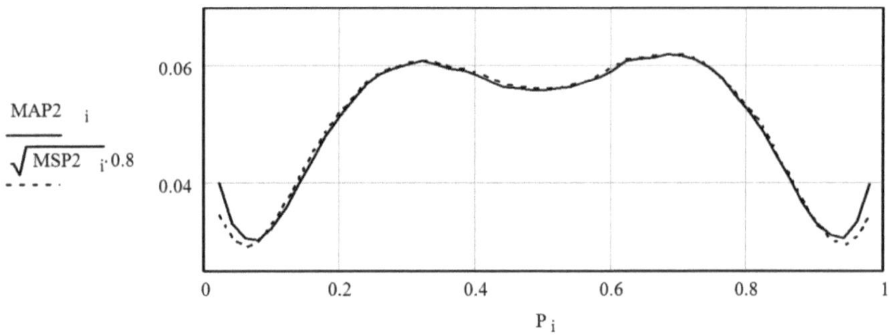

Fig. 21.19 Comparison of values of the MAE error measure (Formula (21.32)—solid line) and rescaled value of the root MSE (Formula (21.31)—dotted line) for the probit model and estimate $p2$

Based on Figs. 21.17 and 21.18, it could be noticed that the largest fluctuations in the MAE error values occur for estimator $p1$. Also on the basis of the results presented in Chap. 3 (Figs. 21.1, 21.2, 21.3, 21.5, 21.6, 21.7, 21.9, 21.10 and 21.11), it is can be noticed that estimator $p1$ shows the highest values of bias, variance, and mean squared error among the four considered estimators.

Figure 21.19 compares the value of the error measure of MAE (Formula 21.32)–solid line) and the rescaled value of the root of MSE (Formula (21.31)—dotted line) for the probit model and estimate $p2$.

Figure 21.19 shows that MAE values are equal (approximately) to $0.8\sqrt{\text{MSE}}$, which was positively verified for all 12 cases.

Due to the heteroskedasticity of the random component, many authors (see, e.g., Amemiya [41], Jajuga [37], Maddala [42]) propose a criterion called weighted mean squared error (WMSE) (Fig. 21.20):

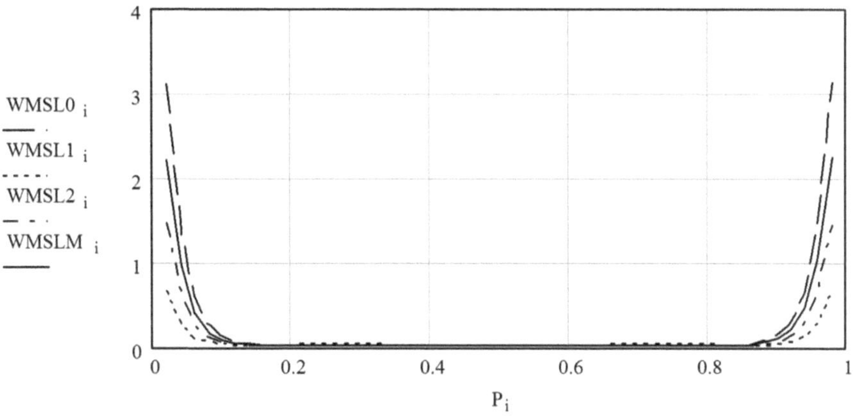

Fig. 21.20 Values of the error measure of WMSE (Formula 21.33) for the logit model. Applied labeling: the same as in Fig. 21.1

$$\mathrm{WMSE} = \sum_{i=1}^{I} \frac{n_i(p_i - pt_i)^2}{p_i(1 - p_i)} \tag{21.33}$$

As mentioned above, an important measure is the ratio of the maximum to the minimum value. In accordance with Fig. 21.20, it can be noticed that in the case of the logit model for the error measure of MSE, the smallest value was recorded for MSLO (estimator $p0$), where the ratio max/min = 2.35.The highest value of max/min = 10,811 occurred for MSL1 (estimator $p1$). The application of the weighted mean squared error (Formula 21.33) leads to the following results: for estimator, $p1$ max/min = 30.243, and for estimator, $p0$ max/min = 152.283. This means that the application of the error measure of WMSE (Formula 21.33) results in a 13-fold increase in the smallest value of the quotient of max/min and a 14-fold increase in the largest value of this quotient. Purczyński and Bednarz-Okrzyńska [43] proposed modification of the WMSE measure in the form of the following relation:

$$\mathrm{WMSE}' = \sum_{i=1}^{I} \frac{n_i(p_i - pt_i)^2}{(P0 + p_i)(P1 - p_i)} \tag{21.34}$$

where $P0 > 0$, $P1 > 1$.

In addition, in paper [22] a new measure (weighted mean absolute error) is proposed, described by the following formula:

$$\mathrm{WMAE}' = \sum_{i=1}^{I} \frac{n_i|p_i - pt_i|}{\sqrt{(P0 + p_i)(P1 - p_i)}} \tag{21.35}$$

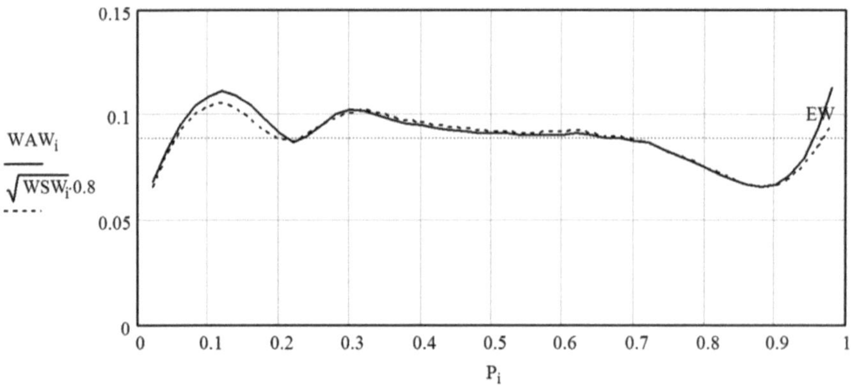

Fig. 21.21 Comparison of values of the error measure of WMAE (Formula (21.35)—solid line) and rescaled value of the root of WMSE (Formula (21.34)—dotted line) for the model implementing the minimum RRMSE—Fig. 21.14

Table 21.1 Ratio of the maximum value to the minimum of the error value of MAE and of WMAE for individual models (L, P, R) and estimators

Estimator	Logit		Probit		Raybit	
	MAE	WMAE	MAE	WMAE	MAE	WMAE
*p*0	1.823	2.447	1.582	2.040	3.999	2.120
*p*2	2.099	1.813	2.050	1.580	4.012	1.838
pM	1.712	2.129	1.750	1.845	3.498	2.024

Figure 21.21 compares the error measure of WMAE (Formula (21.35)—solid line) and the rescaled value of the root of WMSE (Formula (21.34)—dotted line) for the model implementing the minimum RRMSE—Fig. 21.14.

The figure was made for the parameters $P0 = 0.022$ and $P1 = 1.26$, which ensured the smallest deviation of the WAW measure from the average value $E(\text{WAW}) = 0.0896$. Taking into account the fact that MAE closely overlaps with the rescaled MSE (Figs. 21.19 and 21.21), the comparison of MAE (Formula 21.32) with the measure of WMAE (Formula 21.35) is made below.

Table 21.1 shows the ratio of the maximum value and the minimum value of MAE and WMAE for each model (logit, probit, raybit) and used estimators ($p0$, $p1$, $p2$, pM). In the case of the logit and probit models, the lowest WMAE (max/min) for estimator pM were obtained for $P0 = 0.1$ and $P1 = 1.1$. Minimizing WMAE (max/min) for estimator pM in the raybit model, identical results are obtained as for estimator pW ($P0 = 0.022$, $P1 = 1.26$). Taking into account the poor (not good) quality of estimator $p1$, there are no results for this estimator in Table 21.1.

In addition to Table 21.1, it should be added that for estimator pW when minimizing RRMSE (Figs. 21.13 and 21.14), the max/min ratio = 3.771 is obtained for MAE estimator, while for WMAE (Formula 21.35) max/min = 1.724. Based on the presented results, it can be concluded that the WMAE formula leads to a lower value of max/min compared to MAE for the raybit model and estimator pW. For logit and probit models only for estimator $p2$, WMAE leads to a smaller max/min ratio than MAE. Analyzing Figs. 21.1, 21.2, 21.3, 21.5, 21.6 and 21.7, it can be concluded that $p2$ has poorer properties than $p0$ and pM estimates. This means that in the case of the logit and probit models, it is recommended to use $p0$ and pM estimates.

21.5 Summary

Chapter 2 presents basic dependencies regarding the probability models used for the dichotomous variable analysis: logit, probit, and raybit. The properties of estimators are considered in Chap. 3: bias, variance, mean squared error, and relative root mean squared error. Subsequently, the method for estimating empirical probability is proposed, based on the probit and raybit models, which minimizes the relative root mean squared error (RRMSE). Chapter 4 deals with goodness-of-fit measures of binary models. It is found that the goodness-of-fit measure of MAE leads to similar results as the rescaled values of the root of MSE measure. Unfavorable properties of weighted mean squared error (Formula 21.32) are shown. To sum up, the following procedure can be recommended: In the case of logit and probit models, $p0$ and pM estimators as well as the MAE error measure should be used. In the case of the raybit model and estimator pW, the WMAE error measure is recommended.

References

1. Purczyński, J., Bednarz-Okrzyńska, K.: The raybit model and the assessment of its quality in comparison with the logit and probit models. Przegląd Statystyczny **3**, 305–322 (2017)
2. Gruszczyński, M.: Empiryczne finanse przedsiębiorstw. Mikroekonometria finansowa. Difin, Warszawa (2012)
3. Barniv, R., McDonald, J.B.: Review of categorical models for classification issues in accounting and finance. Rev. Quant. Financ. Account. **13**, 39–62 (1999)
4. Ye, F., Lord, D.: Comparing three commonly used crash severity models on sample size requirements: multinomial logit, ordered probit and mixed logit models. Anal. Methods Accid. Res. **1**, 72–85 (2014)
5. Cramer, J.S.: Logit Models from Economics and Other Fields. Cambridge University Press (2003)
6. Hoetker, G.: The use logit and probit models in strategic management research: critical use. Strateg. Manag. J. **28**, 331–343 (2007)
7. Shin, H., Yin, G.: Boosting conditional logit model. J. Choice Model. **26**, 48–63 (2018)
8. D'Haultfœuille, X., Iaria, A.: A convenient method for the estimation of the multinomial logit model with fixed effects. Econ. Lett. **141**, 77–79 (2016)
9. Jones, J.M., Landwehr, J.T.: Removing heterogeneity bias from logit model estimation. Mark. Sci. **7**, 41–59 (1988)
10. Chamberlain, G.: Asymptotic efficiency in estimation with conditional moment restrictions. J. Econom. **34**(3), (March 1987)
11. Hausman, J., McFadden, D.: Specification tests for the multinomial logit model. Econometrica **52**, 1219–1240 (1984)

12. Hausman, J.: Specification test in econometrics. Econometrica **46**, 1251–1272 (1978)
13. Jones, S., Hensher, D.A.: Predicting firm financial distress: a mixed logit model. Account. Rev. **79**, 1011–1038 (2004)
14. Fox, J.T., Kim, K., Ryan, S.P., Bajari, P.: The random coefficients logit model is identified. J. Econ. **166**, 204–212 (2012)
15. Li, S., Wang, S.: A financial early warning logit model and its efficiency verification approach. Knowl. Based Syst. **70**, 78–87 (2014)
16. Brezigar-Masten, A., Masten, I.: CART-based selection of bankruptcy predictors for the logit model. Expert Syst. Appl. **39**, 10153–10159 (2012)
17. Antunes, A., Bonfim, D., Monteiro, N., Rodrigues, P.M.M.: Forecasting banking crises with dynamic panel probit models. Int. J. Forecast. **34**, 249–275 (2018)
18. Ng, E.C.Y.: Forecasting US recessions with various risk factors and dynamic probit models. J. Macroecon. **34**, 112–125 (2012)
19. Soyer, R., Sung, M.: Bayesian dynamic probit models for the analysis of longitudinal data. Comput. Stat. Data Anal. **68**, 388–398 (2013)
20. Proaño, C.R., Tarassow, A.: Evaluating the predicting power of ordered probit models for multiple business cycle phases in the US and Japan. J. Japan. Int. Econ. (in press), 1–28 (2018)
21. Proaño, C.R.: Detecting and predicting economic accelerations, recessions, and normal growth periods in real-time. J. Forecast. **1**, 26–42 (2017)
22. Purczyński, J., Porada-Rochoń, M.: Ocena jakości modeli ze zmienną dychotomiczną. Logistyka **3**, 4064–4073 (2015)
23. Maddala, G.S.: Limited-Dependent and Qualitative Variables in Econometrics. Cambridge University Press (1983)
24. Han, S., Vytlacil, E.J.: Identification in a generalization of bivariate probit models with dummy endogenous regressors. J. Econ. **199**, 63–73 (2017)
25. Mourifié, M., Méango, R.: A note on the identification in two equations probit model with dummy endogenous regressor. Econ. Lett. **125**, 360–363 (2014)
26. Papatla, P., Krishnamurthi, L.: A probit model of choice dynamics. Mark. Sci. **11**, 189–206 (1992)
27. Amemiya, T.: The estimation of a simultaneous equation generalized probit model. Econometrica **46**, 1193–1205 (1978)
28. Amemiya, T.: The estimation of a simultaneous equation Tobit model. Int. Econ. Rev. **1**, 169–181 (1979)
29. Amemiya, T.: Advanced Econometrics. Harvard University Press (1985)
30. Hausman, J., Wise, D.A.: A conditional probit model for qualitative choice: discrete decisions recognizing interdependence and heterogeneous preferences. Econometrica **46**, 403–426 (1978)
31. Eichengreen, B., Watson, M.W., Grossman, R.S.: Bank rate policy under the interwar gold standard: a dynamic probit model. Econ. J. **95**, 725–745 (1985)
32. Butler, J.S.: Estimating the correlation in censored probit models. Rev. Econ. Stat. **78**, 356–358 (1966)
33. Collett, D.: Modelling binary data, 2nd edn. In: Text in Statistical Science. Chapman & Hall/CRC (2003)
34. McFadden, D.: Conditional logit analysis of qualitative choice behavior, chap. 4. In: Analysis of Qualitative Choice Behavior, pp. 105–142 (1973)
35. McFadden, D., Train, K.: Mixed MNL models for discrete response. J. Appl. Econ. **15**(5), 447–470 (2000)
36. Judge, G.G., Griffiths, W.E., Hill, R.C., Lee, T.C.: Theory and Practice of Econometrics. Wiley, New York (1980)
37. Jajuga, K.: Modele z dyskretną zmienną objaśnianą. In: Bartosiewicz, S. (ed.) Estymacja modeli ekonometrycznych. PWE, Warszawa (1989)
38. Chow, G.C.: Econometrics. Mc-Graw-Hill Inc., New York (1983)
39. Krzyśko, M.: Statystyka matematyczna (Part II). UAM, Poznań (1997)

40. Guzik, B., Appenzeller, D., Jurek, W.: Prognozowanie i symulacje. Wybrane zagadnienia. Wydawnictwo Akademii Ekonomicznej w Poznaniu, Poznań (2005)
41. Amemiya, T.: Qualitative response models: a survey. J. Econ. Lit., 1483–1536 (1981)
42. Maddala, G.S.: Ekonometria. Wydawnictwo Naukowe PWN, Warszawa (2006)
43. Purczyński, J., Bednarz-Okrzyńska, K.: Goodness of fit measures of models with binary dependent variable which take into account heteroscedasticity of a random element. Folia Oeconomica Stetinensia **18**, 182–194 (2018)

Chapter 22
Dynamics of the Financial Markets and the Wealth Concentration

Jerzy Marcinkowski

Abstract The concentration of investors' wealth is one of the most important factors shaping their investment strategies. It is reasonable to assume that it can impact the dynamics of financial markets, leading potentially to many undesirable phenomena such as lack of efficiency and collusions. Varying rates of return on investments and among investors over long periods of time favor wealth concentration. Inclusion of other factors such as skill and experience leading potentially to uniformization of behavior through learning cannot eliminate the phenomenon due to the stochastic nature of financial markets. We show that the dynamics of the market can significantly impact how quickly wealth concentration takes place. We present a simple model of wealth concentration among investors to assess the impact of randomness on the distribution of wealth in the function of time. We demonstrate that random fluctuations alone can lead to the accelerated, and under some conditions unlimited, concentration of wealth resulting in a lack of market efficiency.

Keywords Concentration of wealth · Financial markets · Randomness · Market efficiency · Prevention of excessive wealth concentration

JEL Classification G10 · G17

This research was partly supported by Subsidy for Quality Enhancement granted to the Faculty of Informatics and Electronic Economy, Poznan University of Economics and Business, course of study: Informatics and Econometrics by the Polish Ministry of Science and Higher Education (dotacja projakościowa przyznana przez Ministra Nauki i Szkolnictwa Wyższego dla Wydziału Informatyki i Gospodarki Elektronicznej, kierunek informatyka i ekonometria).

J. Marcinkowski (✉)
Department of Operations Research, Faculty of Informatics and Electronic Economy, Poznan University of Economics and Business, Al. Niepodległości 10, 61-875 Poznań, Poland
e-mail: jerzy.marcinkowski@ue.poznan.pl

W. Tarczyński and K. Nermend (eds.), *Effective Investments on Capital Markets*, Springer Proceedings in Business and Economics,
https://doi.org/10.1007/978-3-030-21274-2_22

22.1 Introduction

Wealth distribution is one of the most important factors that impact the dynamics of financial markets. It is of interest both to researchers and decision makers as the financial markets seem to favor wealth concentration, especially in times of expansive fiscal and monetary policy. The concentration itself has many economic, political, and social implications [1, 2, 6, 8, 10, 11, 13, 14].

Relatively low taxes on capital income and dividends combined with technological progress, availability of many financial instruments, free and practically unregulated movement of capital, and last but not least lack of alternative and attractive investments provide incentives to invest on the stock exchange despite high risks, thus potentially contributing to the increased productivity of the economy through supply of capital. However, large concentrations of wealth raise equity issues and may exert destructive influence on democracy itself, having in the long-run adverse effects on the market, contributing to its unpredictability, limited efficiency and increased volatility, which, in turn, may have destabilizing effects on the economy [2, 6, 13].

The problem of wealth distribution among financial speculators does not seem to attract interest from researchers, most probably due to lack of data allowing for validation of the proposed models. However, there is a question, whether it is possible to infer on the basis of the nature of return changes how quickly the concentration of wealth may take place. We will examine how the properties of the rate of return of financial instruments impact wealth concentration.

22.2 Problem Statement

In order to examine whether random fluctuations of returns can generate the highly concentrated wealth distribution observed among investors, we build a simple individual-based stochastic model that allows for compounding returns. First, we will examine whether the effects of chance alone can account for wealth concentration.[1] The effects of random fluctuations of returns on wealth distribution may be examined in models allowing for observing how randomly changing returns on investments impact the wealth of individual investors. The model differs from more commonly used general equilibrium models, such as CAPM, in that it allows for the differentiation effects among individuals [12]. To examine the role of chance in wealth concentration, we make assumptions that favor equality of wealth and exclude other factors than chance that could potentially lead to or accelerate wealth concentration. We assume that all individuals have equal knowledge of the stock market and begin with the same amount of capital. We also assume that success in one year does not exert any influence on future investment success. In other words, we do assume

[1] More detailed discussion can be found in [5]. The problem of wealth concentration is discussed in detail in the literature devoted to globalization, liberalization, rapid development of financial markets, etc., which are perceived as factors contributing to the increased rates of wealth concentration.

that experience does not play any role. It can be justified by the stochastic nature of the financial markets and the fact that even experienced fund managers do not seem to achieve systematically better results than "ordinary" investors. Having explored the implications of these assumptions, we test whether our conclusions are robust to variations in assumptions.

To examine how wealth distribution is changing over time, we make an assumption that initially wealth is evenly distributed among investors, which means that all investors begin with 1 unit of capital. In each time period ($k = 1, 2, \dots, t$), each investor $i = 1, 2, \dots, n$ invests his capital earning a return rate r_{ik}, that is randomly drawn from a normal distribution with mean μ and variance σ^2. As the goal of our model is to assess the impact of chance alone, we do not examine the sources of variance in return rate. It could be due to many factors such as market behavior, experience, the structure of portfolio and differ with investor.

We assume all investors have equal investment opportunities, and only chance is responsible for wealth differentiation. As returns are realizations of independent random variables for each individual for each period, we rule out (1) temporal autocorrelation, which means that a successful investment in one period does not translate into increased chance of getting a higher rate of return in subsequent periods, thus excluding correlations between returns and the existence of memory, (2) correlation across individuals in the same time period, which means a constant average rate of return over the years, and (3) differences among individuals in the chance of getting high or low returns, thus excluding role of experience skill, etc. Assumption (2) may be a bit unrealistic because returns are always correlated to some (though varying) degree and individual portfolios must in practice include the same financial instruments as number of financial instruments is less than number of investors. However, it is instructive to observe how quickly the concentration of wealth will take place under these assumptions and what will happen if we permit correlation. Thus, we have a tool enabling us to examine the impact of changing market dynamics on the concentration of wealth. The number of investors in this simplest version of the model is constant, nor is there any explicit treatment of investors entering or leaving the market, say, being the result of a series of negative returns discouraging from further investment (bad luck). The model describes the wealth changes of individual investors under the assumption that the number of speculators is constant over time and there are no "new" investments and no one withdraws money from the market.

22.3 Rate of Wealth Concentration

It is easy to demonstrate that with the passage of time the proportion of wealth held by an arbitrarily small fraction of investors asymptotically approaches 1. Given a rate of return r_{ik}, the factor by which investor i's capital increases in time period k is $\mathrm{e}^{r_{ik}}$. In period t, the total amount of capital accumulated by investor i is equal to $\mathrm{e}^{r_{i1}} * \cdots * \mathrm{e}^{r_{it}} = \mathrm{e}^{r_{i1}+\cdots+i_{it}} = \mathrm{e}^{x_i}$, where $x_i = \sum_{k=1}^{t} r_{ik}$.

If the rates r_{ik} are drawn from a normal distribution with mean μ and variance σ^2, the exponential portion of this number (i.e., the sum of the rates) will be normally distributed with mean μt and variance $\sigma^2 t$. The total wealth is the sum of accumulated wealth by the investors, e^{x_i}, integrated over the probability density function of the normal distribution and multiplied by the number of individuals. The share of wealth held by an arbitrarily small percentage of investors is equal to the ratio of two integrals: total wealth of the population of investors in the denominator and wealth of the top percentage in the numerator [5]:

$$\frac{\int_{\mu t+h\sigma\sqrt{t}}^{\infty} \frac{1}{\sigma\sqrt{2\pi t}} e^{-\frac{1}{2t}\left(\frac{x-\mu}{\sigma}\right)^2} e^x \mathrm{d}x}{\int_{-\infty}^{\infty} \frac{1}{\sigma\sqrt{2\pi t}} e^{-\frac{1}{2t}\left(\frac{x-\mu}{\sigma}\right)^2} e^x \mathrm{d}x} = \frac{1}{2}\left(1 + \mathrm{erf}\left(\frac{\sigma\sqrt{t} - h}{\sqrt{2}}\right)\right). \tag{22.1}$$

Total wealth of the whole population of investors is given by the denominator. The wealth accumulated by any segment of the investors is given by the integral in the numerator. Parameter h sets the lower limit of integration at a specific number of standard deviations above the mean. Because the integral extends to infinity, it captures the top portion of the wealth distribution, where h determines which top proportion is captured. To quantify the wealth accumulated by the top 1% of the investors' population that will do to substitute $h \approx 2.326$. The lower limit of the integral is then equal to 99%. The notation "erf" refers to the "error function" defined as follows [5]:

$$\mathrm{erf}(x) = \left(2/\sqrt{\pi}\right) \int_0^x e^{-z^2} \mathrm{d}z. \tag{22.2}$$

Since erf(x) approaches 1 as x approaches infinity, the right-hand side of (22.1) also approaches 1 as t approaches infinity, for any fixed value of h. In other words, the proportion of wealth held by an arbitrarily small proportion of investors approaches 1 through time. It means that all the wealth of the investors ultimately will be possessed by only an extreme fraction of individuals. Note that from the right-hand side of (22.1) follows that the rate at which wealth concentrates is positively related to the variance in individual rates of return σ^2, but independent of the mean rate μ. Thus, perhaps surprisingly, wealth will concentrate by this mechanism in growing, stagnant or shrinking markets depending only on their volatility.

In this simplest model, the concentration of wealth occurs merely because some investors are lucky by randomly receiving a series of high return rates, and once they are ahead with exponentially growing capital, they tend to stay ahead. Because the variance in the sum of return rates is additive, over time the individuals with interest rates at the right tail of the ever-widening normal distribution come to dominate the wealth. Recall that it is the exponents that are normally distributed, not the amount of wealth, so that individuals at the high end of the distribution achieve exponentially greater fortunes.

22.4 Simulation Results

The analytical results are illustrated by simulations of individual-based models (Fig. 22.1). To show how quickly wealth concentration can take place, we examine the process of accumulation of wealth in the top 1% of the population. The simulations results are in accordance with the theoretical results: the rate at which the top 1% accumulates wealth is dependent on the variance of returns; the higher the variance, the quicker wealth concentration. In other words, highly volatile markets when the returns can approximately be described by random walk processes, contrary to intuition, tend to favor wealth concentration.

These results, somewhat unanticipated, show that contrary to expectations, chance alone can lead to high concentrations of wealth. The mechanism of concentration is very simple. Lucky investors having a string of high returns and given enough time will accumulate the overwhelming majority of the wealth.

Looking for the analytical solution (22.1), we assumed that the population of investors is infinite, which guarantees the presence of some extremely lucky individuals. The larger the population, the greater the probability that such individuals exist. Nonetheless, simulations performed for populations of only 10,000 individuals produce approximately the same results. We even succeed in obtaining similar results for populations of only 1000 (not shown)—however, deviations from the analytical trajectories were a bit larger, (which could be expected) and concentration rates were

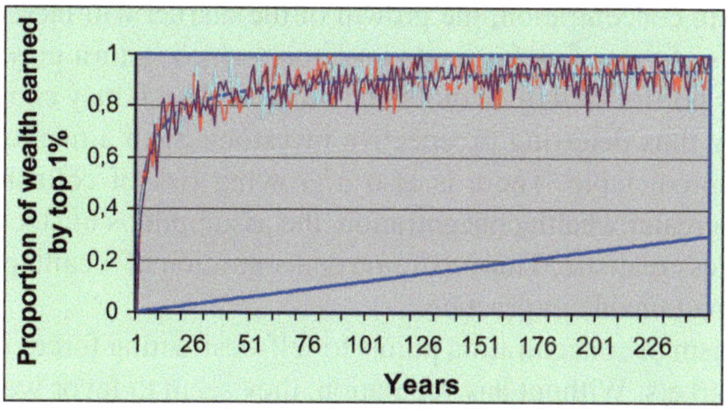

Fig. 22.1 Wealth concentration over time. Initially, the distribution of wealth is uniform. Performing simulations, we assume that the number of investors is 10,000 and a yearly average return on investment is 5%. Blue lines show (upper line for higher variance, line below for lesser variance) the analytically obtained trajectories; points show the results from individual-based simulations. Because of potentially greater deviations, simulations were replicated three times in the case of high variance ($\sigma = 0.5$). For $\sigma = 0.1$, only theoretical line is plotted as deviations are small. Higher variance among individual rates of return corresponds with increased rates of wealth concentration. Simulation results will deviate from theoretical values to a lesser degree if we restrict our attention to, say, top 5% wealthiest investors. (Compare to [5]. The results differ a bit because of a smaller population. The smaller the population, the greater the deviations. For the wealthiest 5% population, we can expect smaller deviations because of a broader sample). *Source* own study

a bit slower. Thus, the influence of random variation in individual returns manifests itself, though to a smaller degree, in finite, relatively small, populations.

22.5 Market Efficiency and Wealth Concentration

The concentration of wealth is reflected by the distribution of growth rate of capital hold by all investors. The average return for an individual is μ, with variance σ^2. The average of all investor' wealth in moment i is e^{x_i}, from which follows that the total wealth is equal to $e^{(\mu+\sigma^2/2)t}$. The greater the variance, the greater the accumulated wealth. Note, that the mode of the wealth distribution—the individual wealth which is most common—is $e^{(\mu-\sigma^2)t}$, not e^{μ}, from which follows that the greater the variance, the lower the mode. Initially, wealth is distributed evenly—so the mode, median, and mean wealth are all equal. However, the mean increases over time as $e^{(\mu+\sigma^2/2)t}$, much faster than the median, which increases only as $e^{\mu t}$, while the mode may actually decrease as $e^{(\mu-\sigma^2)\,t}$, if the exponent is negative. These counterintuitive results stem from the properties of the log-normal distribution: The uniform distribution tends to the log-normal distribution as t tends to infinity.

Thus, the wealth of the investors as a whole grows faster than the wealth of most investors making up the market. In sufficiently large populations with a diverse distribution of wealth, the most likely growth rate of the market will tend to the mean of $(\mu + \sigma^2/2)t$, the sum of many individual lines of capital growth. Gradually, as a result of wealth concentration, the growth of the market will increasingly depend upon the returns of those few fortunate investors, which in turn may destabilize the market as theirs portfolios will be more and more similar. It may contribute to lesser market liquidity thus deterring prospective investors. Such a market may be more volatile and unpredictable. There is also a growing risk of collusions. It may be argued that the greater wealth concentration, the assumptions of stochastic nature of the market are less realistic. Thus, extreme concentration of wealth predicted by the model seems unattainable in practice.

The mechanism of concentration points to self-destructing forces implemented in the financial markets. Without any regulation, they seem to favor wealth concentration which in turn contributes to gradually deteriorating market efficiency. Ironically, the benefits derived from free market forces and a lack of regulation can be counterbalanced or even destroyed in an extreme case by a property inherent in the market itself—the tendency to concentrate wealth by chance mechanisms, thus significantly reducing the diversity of investors and their strategies and eventually paralyzing the market. The greater the wealth concentration, the less role played by chance itself.

22.6 Model Robustness

The model suggests that concentration of wealth may arise naturally under the simplest conditions. As the model does not realistically describe all the features of financial markets, the stock exchange in particular, it is important to consider whether the tendency toward concentration of wealth generated by chance is likely to happen if additional features of real markets are incorporated into the model. Our conclusions seem to be robust to the incorporation of such modifications.

By the central limit theorem, our results are robust to some degree to violation of the assumption that returns on investment are drawn from a normal distribution. Annual returns drawn from any distribution that obey the central limit theorem (i.e., they are sufficiently centered around the mean; i.e., meet Lindeberg's condition and independent) will give exponents whose sum approaches the normal distribution [9]. Temporal correlations (long term memory) may be a problem, as the sum in question will tend to the normal distribution a bit slower or may not tend to this distribution at all. In the first case, the rate of concentration will be correctly described by the model after some years. The second case requires further investigation.

As periods of growth and decline are a characteristic feature of real markets, the average rate of return is changing from year to year. Because the results are not restricted to the case where the distribution of returns is normal, if deviations from this distribution are not significant, the model still may be used to explain the problem of wealth concentration. Detailed discussion is postponed to the next part of the paper.

22.7 Results

Our analysis leads to the conclusion that chance alone can potentially result in unlimited concentrations of wealth. Contrary to commonly accepted belief that in the long-run differences in returns among investors tend to zero and consequently prevent wealth concentration in reality different strategies applied by different investors, experiencing different rates of return on their investments, and reinvesting their capital income result in wealth concentration. The concentrations of wealth in the hands of a few investors slowly reduce the potential diversity of independent investment strategies as their portfolios become more and more correlated. It leads to loss of market efficiency, thus preventing further concentration of wealth. Our analysis suggests that random fluctuations may, at least to some degree, explain the high concentrations of wealth that are commonly observed empirically without resorting to collusion, conspiracy theories, etc. Our results are also consistent with the observations of Taleb [15], who argues that rather chance, not experience, plays a large role in determining success among professional stock traders. The performed analysis seems to support the view expressed by Taleb [15] that learning and expertise play less important role that is commonly believed.[2]

Disparities between modal and mean wealth are the signs of inequalities. They suggest that the distribution of wealth is more or less skewed. An increase in disparities translates into potential market instability. If our goal is to prevent the unlimited concentration of wealth to preserve market efficiency, our work suggests imposition of a tax, e.g., indexed to inflation, restricted to only the very wealthiest investors [4, 6, 7]. The tax must be imposed on yearly returns. If our aim is to preserve incentives to invest, the tax proposal reduces to the imposition of such a tax on the wealthiest investors only. An additional quality of such a tax is worth noting: because the concentration of wealth may reduce market efficiency and may, as a result, impact negatively the rate of economic growth and increase volatility on other markets, such a tax could contribute to maintaining growth across the economy as a whole ensuring relative market stability and preventing or limiting many undesirable phenomena such as collusions and decreased efficiency. From a more general perspective, some kind of intervention (such as taxes) is justified on pure mathematical grounds to prevent, or at least slowdown, self-destruction processes. It may be argued that it is objectively justified.

22.8 Conclusions

Our approach to the problem of wealth concentration is quite simplified. In practice, there exist a lot of factors preventing or at least slowing down wealth concentration and changing the limit the concentration tends to, which requires further study. One of them is correlation. If speculators have similar portfolios, irrespective of the fact that their components are correlated or not, the portfolios must be correlated to some degree as some financial instruments must belong to more than one portfolio. Of course, the more the returns are correlated, the more the portfolios are correlated. The greater the degree of portfolios' similarity, the slower concentration of wealth. In an extreme case, where the portfolios are perfectly correlated (e.g., they are identical), no wealth concentration takes place at all. It can be argued that bear and bull markets imply slower rates of wealth concentration, assuming that the group of investors is the same and no one invests "new" money and exits from an investment. In these circumstances, individual portfolios, irrespective of their similarity, must be (strongly) correlated. Herd behavior, contrary to expectation, contributes to slower rates of wealth concentration. In the short run, it destabilizes the market, contributing to its volatility; however in the long run, it seems to prevent negative effects being the consequence of wealth concentration. This is the mechanism by which financial mar-

[2]We focused on the role of chance in a very simple case without assuming any interactions among economic agents. Possible interactions can be taken into account. In [3], such an approach was presented. The paper includes an extensive survey of literature devoted to the role of chance in increasing wealth inequality.

kets seem to "defend" against excessive wealth concentration and self-destruction. It should be stressed here that the observed wealth concentration, not only in the case of financial markets, is a result of some mathematical properties of financial systems. It is a self-destructive mechanism for which chance alone is responsible.

This is why it is important to specify the properties responsible for such phenomena in order to limit their existence, if it desirable and possible. If for some reasons such a situation is hard to accept, then mathematical analysis, even simplified, can suggest solutions addressing the problems. The proposed approach may be a convenient tool to analyze the impact of herd behavior on wealth concentration. This may be achieved by simulating how correlation impacts the growth of wealth concentration.

Contrary to intuition, bear and bull markets slow down the rate of wealth concentration due to increased correlation. For acceleration of the rate in these circumstances, greed, panic, and herd behavior are responsible. Simply, investors enter the market too late and exit it at the worst possible moment. The impact of psychological factors is thus ambiguous: they may either contribute to increased or decreased rates of wealth concentration.

References

Atkinson, A.B.: Inequality: What Can be Done?. Harvard University Press, Cambridge (2015)

Berman, Y., Shapira, Y., Ben-Jacob, E.: Modeling the origin and possible control of the wealth inequality surge. PLOS ONE **10**, e0130181 (2015). https://doi.org/10.1371/journal.pone.0130181 [PMC free article] [PubMed]

Bouleau, N., Chorro, Ch.: The impact of randomness on the distribution of wealth: some economic aspects of the Wright–Fisher diffusion process. Phys. A **479**, 379–395 (2017)

Davies, J.B., Shorrocks, A.F.: The distribution of wealth. In: Atkinson, A.B., Bourguignon, F. (eds.) Handbook of Income Distribution, pp 605–675. Elsevier (2000)

Fargione, E.J., Lehman, C., Polasky, S.: Entrepreneurs, chance, and the deterministic concentration of wealth. Department of Applied Economics. University of Minnesota, St. Paul, Minnesota, United States of America & College of Biological Sciences, University of Minnesota, St. Paul, Minnesota, United States of America. PLOS ONE **6**, e20728 (2011). https://doi.org/10.1371/journal.pone.0154196. [PMC free article] [PubMed]

Hurst, C.E.: Social Inequality: Forms, Causes, and Consequences. Pearson Education, New York (2007)

Levine, R., Zervos, S.: Stock markets, banks, and economic growth. Am. Econ. Rev. **88**, 537–558 (2011)

Piketty, T., Saez, E.: Inequality in the long run. Science **344**, 838–843 (2011)

Lindeberg, J.W.: Eine neue Herleitung des Exponentialgesetzes. In der Wahrscheinlichkeitsrechnung, Mathematische Zeitschrift **15**(1), 211–225 (1922). https://doi.org/10.1007/bf01494395

Piketty, T., Saez, E.: Income inequality in the United States, 1913–1998. Q. J. Econ. **118**, 1–39 (2002). https://doi.org/10.1162/00335530360535135

Reich, R.B.: Beyond Outrage: What has Gone Wrong with Our Economy and Our Democracy and How to Fix It. Random House, New York (2012)

Sharpe, W.F.: Capital asset prices—a theory of market equilibrium under conditions of risk. J. Finan. **19**, 425–442 (1963)

Stiglitz, J.E.: The Price of Inequality: How Today's Divided Society Endangers Our Future. Norton, W. W. & Company, Inc, New York (2012)
Stiglitz, J.E.: The origins of inequality, and policies to contain it. Natl. Tax J. **68**, 425–444 (2015)
Taleb, N.N.: Fooled by Randomness: The Hidden Role of Chance in the Markets and in Life. W. W. Norton, New York City (2001)

Chapter 23
Examining Engagement and Emotions in Financial Simulation Games

Konrad Biercewicz, Jarosław Duda and Mariusz Borawski

Abstract The popularity of educational video games means that there is a need for methods to assess their content in terms of satisfaction and the educational element of the player right from the production stage. For this purpose, indices used in EEG studies and algorithms for detecting microexpression can be used. In the research work, the following devices, i.e. EEG, EyeTracker, were used for the engagement index and a film was shot to detect emotions at a later stage. The data were collected from five participants during the investment game created in MATLAB and online stock market simulator. Thanks to the use of the above-mentioned devices, it was found out whether the game connected only with investing evokes emotions and involvement.

Keywords Stock market simulators · Cognitive neuroscience · EEG · EyeTracker · Microexpression · Engagement index

23.1 Introduction

Scientists in finance and neuroscience decided to work together to understand how people make financial decisions. As a result, simulation games for financial management were created, thanks to which we learn how to make decisions. This is a

K. Biercewicz (✉) · M. Borawski
Department of Multimedia Systems, Faculty of Computer Science and Information Technology, West Pomeranian University of Technology Szczecin, Żołnierska 49, 71-210 Szczecin, Poland
e-mail: kbiercewicz@poczta.onet.pl

M. Borawski
e-mail: mborawski@wi.zut.edu.pl

J. Duda
Dean of Marine Engineering Faculty, Institute of Marine Electrical Engineering and Vessel Automation, Department of Automation and Robotics, Maritime University of Szczecin, Wały Chrobrego 1-2, 70-500 Szczecin, Poland
e-mail: j.duda@am.szczecin.pl

W. Tarczyński and K. Nermend (eds.), *Effective Investments on Capital Markets*, Springer Proceedings in Business and Economics,
https://doi.org/10.1007/978-3-030-21274-2_23

better approach than so-called cases or textbooks. In a fairly simple and controlled game environment, the user can apply previously learned techniques and develop new financial decision-making skills. This enables us to deepen our understanding of definitions and building communication skills in business. Specific analytical techniques used in finance can be used to make decisions related to each of the required elements of the decision.

Examples of such games include board games such as Cashflow 101, Monopoly, but also online games such as Wall Street Survior, How The Market Works and MarketWatch Fanatasy Earnings Trader Game. The common goal of these games is to teach the player the concept of investing and earning money.

If we want our game to be interesting and educational at the same time, tt is necessary to examine the emotions, the player's involvement in making decisions and the game itself. It is necessary to know which elements of the game make the researched person more involved, what emotions accompany him/her while making decisions, but also what he/she pays attention to during these decisions. For this purpose, EEG, GSR, Eyetracker and HR technology can be used. By obtaining data from these devices and combining conclusions, we will get what in the game can be improved so that the player makes better decisions and is more involved in the game. In addition, neuroscience can be used to examine how a person reacts to an advertisement [8], to examine the effectiveness of advertising [9], to see how neurnautics can contribute to increasing work efficiency and how analysts can support a multi-criteria decision-making process [7].

Examining emotions while making decisions in a financial game is not a new concept. Research on financial decision-making shows that investors with high regulatory capacity are performing better in trading. Hence, Jerčić et al. [4] conducted research aimed at creating an educational environment that can help decision-makers to improve their emotional regulation. Raggetti et al. [11] tried to detect how different areas of the brain are modulated by factors such as age, experience, psychological profile (seeking the speculative risk or reluctance), as well as the size and type (buy/sell) of stock market negotiations conducted through the direct access trading platform. Vieito et al. [13] using EEG examined brain mapping during the decision-making about the purchase, of sale in changing market conditions. Results showed that people could apply different strategies of reasoning in order to take financial decisions depending on experiencing them in the trade.

This article presents the results of a pilot study, which aimed to investigate the emotions of the player and the degree of his engagement in the game of educational value. Thanks to that, it was checked whether the game connected only with investing evokes any emotions and engagement.

23.2 Materials and Methods

EEG data were taken from five healthy participants aged 21 years on average. The respondents were informed about the course of the study. They then signed consent to participate in the study and were seated on a comfortable chair with keyboard and mouse access. The next step was to put on the cap and connect the electrodes to the skin of the participant's head and connect them to the device that recorded data from the brain. After completing the above steps, the examined person was informed what the game will be about and how to move in it. Immediately after the end of the game, each participant was interviewed about the experience with the stock exchange, as well as which elements of the game caused the participant to become more involved in the game, and at which less.

Each participant's game has been captured at 1920 × 1080 resolution by means of programmed in-game registration and Apowersoft Free Online Screen Recorder. Each screenshot generated a timestamp for EEG data to determine the position of the beginning and end of each section. Screenshots and the video were saved for later reference during the data analysis phase. In the study, apart from EEG, EyeTracker was used to track what the researcher was looking at and a camera to record the face in order to detect microexpression when making decisions to buy or sell.

Description of Game in MATLAB

The game was created especially in MATLAB for research. The game consisted in investing virtual cash in shares. The player had 10,000 PLN at his disposal and within 20 minutes he could invest money in 3 different companies. The player's task was to get a positive balance at the end of the game. The player made decisions on the basis of 60-day charts. In addition, there was information about the number of shares held by the player and what is the closing price, the opening price, the lowest and the highest price on a given day. The transaction was followed by another day. If the player claimed that he did not decide on a given day, he had the 'Next day' button at his disposal. During trading, screenshots (see Fig. 23.1) were recorded along with an excel file containing the screenshot number and the corresponding time. In addition, events were registered, i.e. purchase, sale or next day events, which were saved in a separate excel file.

Description of the Internet Game

The study used an online stock exchange simulator (available at the following address: http://www.gry.jeja.pl/33976,symulator-gieldy.html). As in the previous game, the test person's task was to achieve a positive balance after 20 min. The game differed from the previous one in that the player had only one company and the capital of 300 PLN at his disposal. The chart moved every 1 s, so the player had to make a quick decision. The red line talked about the buy price and the green line about the sell price. After the transaction, a dot was marked on the chart, which said at what point in time the transaction was concluded. During the game, a film

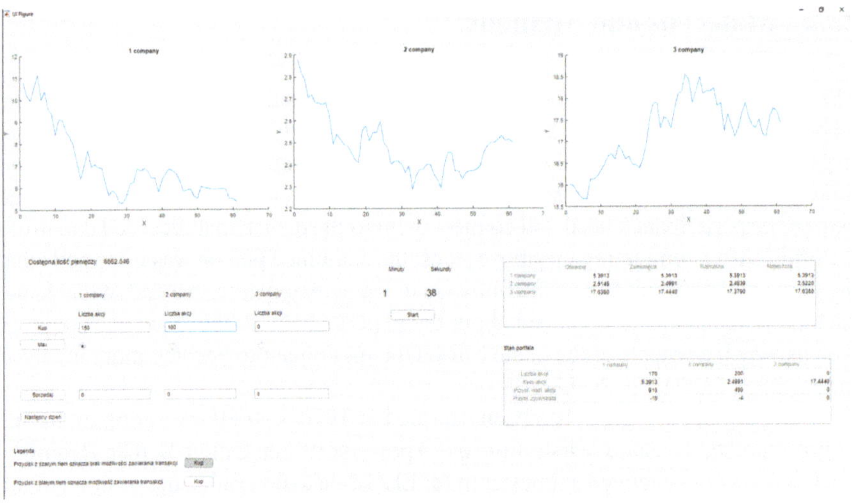

Fig. 23.1 Screenshot of the game during trading

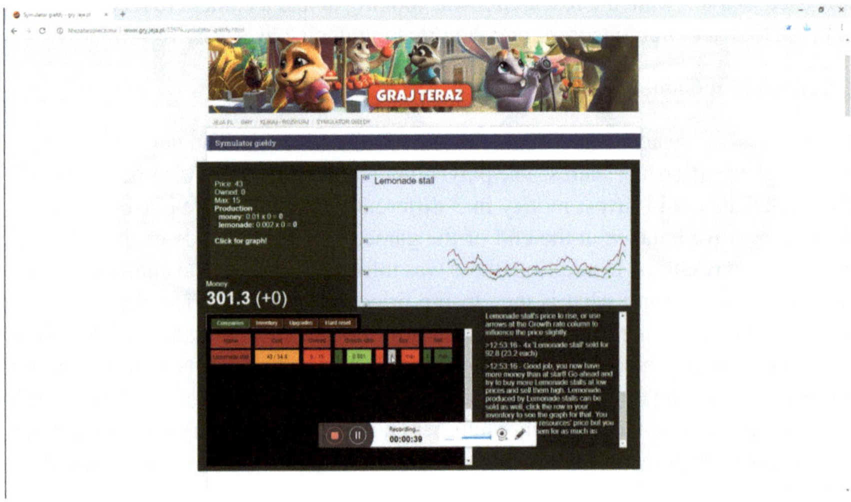

Fig. 23.2 Screenshot from an online stock market simulator

from the desktop was recorded (see Fig. 23.2), as well as buy and sell events and the corresponding time.

Electrodes Used in the Research

The cap was used with eight electrodes connected, distributed in F7, F8, F3, F4, Cz, Pz, P3 and P4. The channels were arranged according to the international 10–20 system. The electrodes required a moistened cap in order to improve conductivity. The sampling frequency was 500 Hz.

Questionnaire on the Game

The participants answered a series of questions assessing previous experience with the stock exchange. The participants were asked whether they had ever invested in the real stock market (among all the respondents no one invested in the stock market), whether they participated in classes/courses (also the answer was negative), and whether they knew the mechanism associated with the stock market earlier (the answer was positive among all the respondents).

The last questions were about the game itself, more specifically which elements of the game should be improved according to them, which game is 'better' according to them, as well as in which situations they think that their involvement has increased and in which it has been decreasing.

Analysis of Data

All data were analysed using MATLAB version R2017b.

Events such as blinking of eyes, head movements or body movements may cause undesired data in the EEG recording. Most EEG analyses require removal in order to identify medical problems. However, this is not a problem to analyse the game. Such events are common in the daily game [10].

The EEG spectral signal was analysed using a fast Fourier transform (FFT) and an overlapping 3-s time frame with a jump of 1 s for Delta (0.5–3.9 Hz), Theta (4–7.9 Hz), Alpha-1 (8–10.9 Hz), Alpha-2 (11–13.9 Hz), Beta-1 (14–19.9 Hz), Beta-2 (20–29.9 Hz) and Gamma (30–35 Hz).

Measuring the level of engagement is one part of determining the player's experience while playing a computer game. Hockey [3, 6] used the distribution of electrodes, which use the frontal lobe and temporal and parietal lobe connected in four places. Using the ratio of EEG bands [Beta/(Alpha + Theta)] (see Table 23.1).

In order to examine emotions accompanying the game, a facial expression of the face of persons participating in the games was recorded. The film had a 3840×2160 resolution (29 frames per second). For next cages of the film, 68 describing points were set key facial structures. The location of these points allows certain Facial Action Coding System (FACS) codes to be determined. It was originally created and published by the Swedish anatoma Carl-Herman Hjortsjö (Hjortsjö 1969), was subsequently adopted and corrected by Paul Ekman, Wallace V. Friesen and Joseph C. Hager [1, 2]. Their proposed codes which gives us way to easier detect emotions.

Table 23.1 Description of the indices used in the research

	Formula	Method of counting
Index 1 [5]	Beta-1/(Alpha-1 + Theta)	Average after all electrodes, i.e. F3, F4, F7, F8, Cz, P3, Pz, P4
Index 2 [5]	Beta-2/(Alpha-2 + Theta)	Average after all electrodes, i.e. F3, F4, F7, F8, Cz, P3, Pz, P4

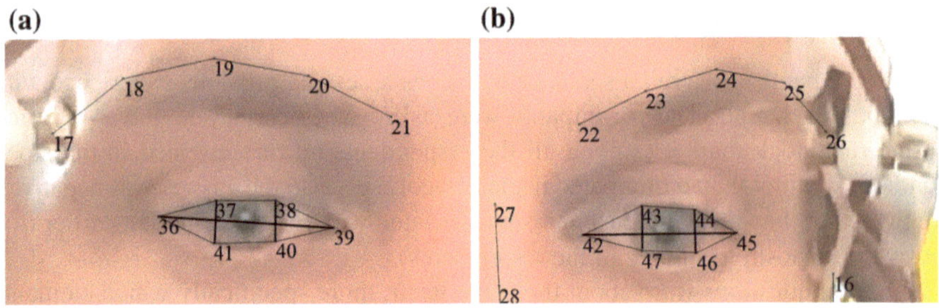

Fig. 23.3 Distances used to determine the EAR index for the eye: **a** left; **b** right

Eyelid closure (AU 7) can be detected on the basis of the index eye aspect ratio (EAR) [12] (Fig. 23.3):

$$\mathrm{EAR} = \frac{\|p_2 - p_6\| + \|p_3 - p_5\|}{2\|p_1 - p_4\|}, \tag{23.1}$$

where $p_1, p_2, \ldots p_6$ are the 2D landmark locations.

In the case of a 68-point system, the above formula for the left eye can be defined as follows:

$$\mathrm{EAR_L} = \frac{\left\|\vec{P}_{37} - \vec{P}_{41}\right\| + \left\|\vec{P}_{38} - \vec{P}_{40}\right\|}{2\left\|\vec{P}_{36} - \vec{P}_{39}\right\|}, \tag{23.2}$$

where $\vec{P}_{36}, \vec{P}_{37}, \ldots$ are vectors representing points, || ||—measure of distance.

Whereas, for the right eye, the formula is expressed as follows:

$$\mathrm{EAR_R} = \frac{\left\|\vec{P}_{43} - \vec{P}_{47}\right\| + \left\|\vec{P}_{44} - \vec{P}_{46}\right\|}{2\left\|\vec{P}_{42} - \vec{P}_{45}\right\|}. \tag{23.3}$$

The face in the picture may be of different sizes. When calculating any indices, a standardization factor is necessary. The majority of points is transferring under the influence of emotion. The only relatively invariable points are the points defining the corners of the eyes. On their base, it is possible to calculate the width of eyes, from which it is possible to appoint the standardizing factor (Fig. 23.4):

$$\mathrm{NORM} = \frac{\|p_{36} - p_{39}\| + \|p_{42} - p_{45}\|}{2} \tag{23.4}$$

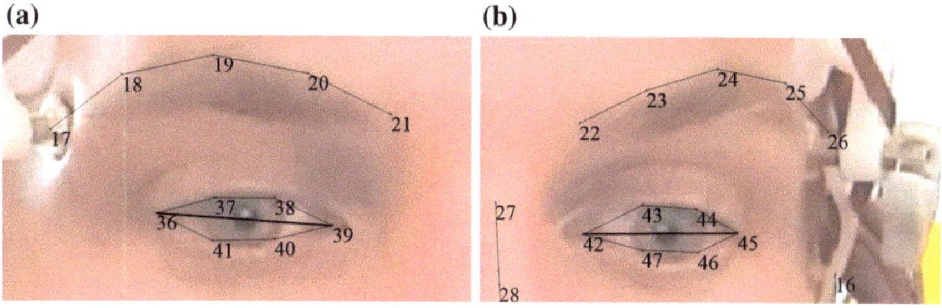

Fig. 23.4 Distances used for eye normalization: **a** left; **b** right

Raising the cheeks (AU 6) always involves raising the corners of the mouth upwards. The cheek lift index can be calculated from the points representing the corners of the eyes (points 36 and 45) and the corners of the mouth (points 48 and 54) (Fig. 23.5). Cheek lift always involves reducing the distance between the corners of the mouth and the corners of the eyes. Unfortunately, this distance is also affected by the dilatation and narrowing of the mouth. Therefore, the distance between the corners of the mouth and the corners of the eyes cannot be used to calculate the index. For this purpose, the displacement between these points along the *y*-axis in the local coordinate system of the face should be measured. The horizontal axis of such a system may be the vector $\vec{E} = \vec{P}_{45} - \vec{P}_{36}$, which is the difference between the points representing the corners of the eyes. The position of these points is relatively stable, and their up–down shifts are rare and small, but most often synchronized with each other. Determining the vertical axis is more problematic. The points of the outer envelope of the face are subject to considerable displacement when the face rotates. Points of the eyebrow, eyes and the mouth strongly are moving under the influence of the facial expression. The most stable seem to be the points marking the line of the nose. Unfortunately, these points are transferred towards themselves along the axis perpendicular to the camera. This causes them to move while moving their heads. As a result, the *y*-axis is a vector $\vec{E}'$, which is perpendicular to the vector $\vec{E}$.

For outlining the vector $\vec{E}'$, determined the vector $\vec{E}$ and $\vec{N} = \vec{P}_{33} - \vec{P}_{27}$.

The vector $\vec{N}$ is the difference between points 33 and 27, which are the extremes of the nasal line. The vector $\vec{E}$ was reduced to the form of a unit vector:

$$\vec{E}_N = \frac{\vec{E}}{\left\|\vec{E}\right\|}, \tag{23.5}$$

the vector was handled in a similar way $\vec{N}$:

$$\vec{N}_N = \frac{\vec{N}}{\left\|\vec{N}\right\|}. \tag{23.6}$$

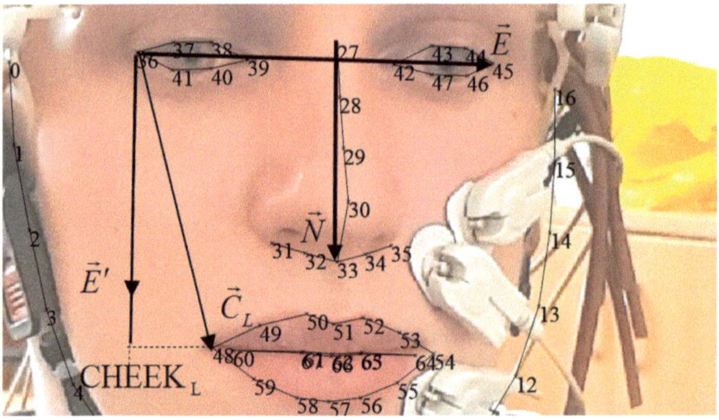

Fig. 23.5 Determination of the index $\mathrm{CHEEK_L}$

The vector $\vec{E}'$ perpendicular to $\vec{E}$ can be determined from the formula:

$$\vec{E}' = \vec{N}_N - \left(\vec{N}_N \circ \vec{E}_N\right)\vec{E}_N, \tag{23.7}$$

where $\circ$ is scalar product.

In order to be able to determine $\vec{E}'$, vectors $\vec{N}_N$ and $\vec{E}_N$ must not be parallel, which is never the case with a face. The vector $\vec{E}'$ is reduced to the form of a unitary vector:

$$\vec{E}'_N = \frac{\vec{E}}{\left\|\vec{E}\right\|}. \tag{23.8}$$

The left cheek lift index $\mathrm{CHEEK_L}$ requires the calculation of a vector $\vec{C}_L = \vec{P}_{48} - \vec{P}_{36}$, which is the difference between the vectors determining the position of the left corner of the mouth and the left corner of the left eye. The index $\mathrm{CHEEK_L}$ will take the following form:

$$\mathrm{CHEEK_L} = \frac{\vec{C}_L \circ \vec{E}'_N}{\mathrm{NORM}} = \frac{\left(\vec{P}_{48} - \vec{P}_{36}\right) \circ \vec{E}'_N}{\mathrm{NORM}}, \tag{23.9}$$

Similarly, you can calculate an index $\mathrm{CHEEK_R}$ for the right cheek:

$$\mathrm{CHEEK_L} = \frac{\left(\vec{P}_{54} - \vec{P}_{45}\right) \circ \vec{E}'_N}{\mathrm{NORM}}, \tag{23.10}$$

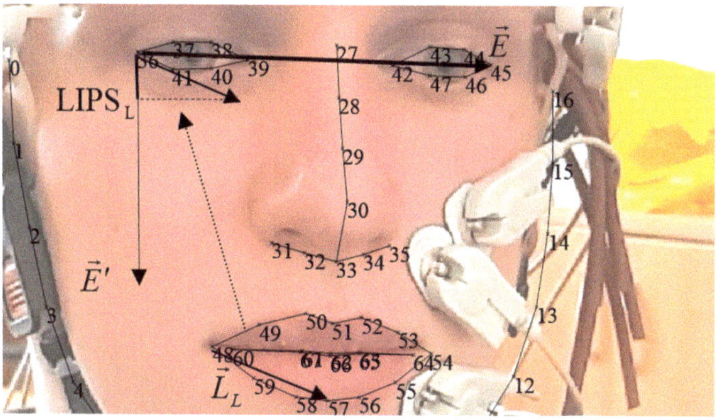

Fig. 23.6 Determination of the index

Elevation of the mouth angle (AU 11, AU 12) and lowering of the lower lip ends (AU 15) is connected with the movement of the mouth angles in relation to the lower lip. An index to help detect these codes can be determined from the vector $\vec{L}_L = \vec{P}_{57} - \vec{P}_{48}$, which is the difference between the vectors determining the centre of the lower lip and the left corner of the mouth (Fig. 23.6). For the left corner of the lip, this index ($\mathrm{LIPS_L}$) will have the following formula:

$$\mathrm{LIPS_L} = \frac{\vec{L}_L \circ \vec{E}'_N}{\mathrm{NORM}} = \frac{\left(\vec{P}_{57} - \vec{P}_{48}\right) \circ \vec{E}'_N}{\mathrm{NORM}}. \tag{23.10}$$

If for a given FACS code we assume the symmetry of the mouth system, it is enough to determine only the index $\mathrm{LIPS_L}$. Otherwise, the index $\mathrm{LIPS_R}$ or the right-hand corner of the mouth should be determined:

$$\mathrm{LIPS_R} = \frac{\left(\vec{P}_{57} - \vec{P}_{54}\right) \circ \vec{E}'_N}{NORM}. \tag{23.11}$$

Lowering the eyebrows (AU 4) is associated with the displacement of the middle part of the eyebrows in relation to the corner of the eye. The index for the detection of eyebrows lowering can be determined on the basis of the vector $\vec{B}_L = \vec{P}_{36} - \vec{P}_{19}$, which is the difference between the vectors determining the left eye corner and the centre of the left eyebrow (Fig. 23.7). For the left eyebrows, this ($\mathrm{BROW_L}$) index will have the following formula:

$$\mathrm{BROW_L} = \frac{\vec{B}_L \circ \vec{E}'_N}{\mathrm{NORM}} = \frac{\left(\vec{P}_{36} - \vec{P}_{19}\right) \circ \vec{E}'_N}{\mathrm{NORM}}. \tag{23.12}$$

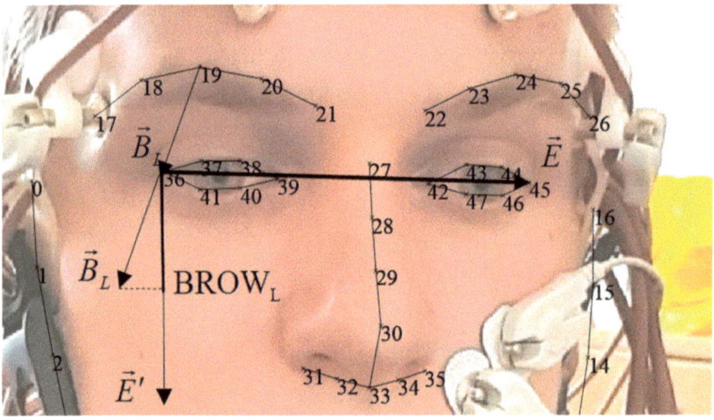

Fig. 23.7 Determination of the index BROW$_L$

For the right eyebrows, the index (BROW$_R$) will have the following formula:

$$\text{BROW}_R = \frac{\left(\vec{P}_{45} - \vec{P}_{24}\right) \circ \vec{E}'_N}{\text{NORM}}. \tag{23.13}$$

23.3 Discussion

The main objective of the pilot study was to assess the engagement and emotions in decision-making. As a result, it was determined whether a person without experience is active in the game and what emotions accompany him/her. The analysis was based on the MATLAB program and data from the relevant situation, i.e. purchase or sale. Among the most important results, we can mention:

(1) The first 5 min of gameplay among the respondents indicate that the involvement in the game is low due to the fact that they familiarize themselves with the whole game interface, how it all looks like. This is in line with the opinion of the respondents, which was expressed in the questionnaire. The study disagrees with one opinion, as the study found that at the beginning of the game his involvement was high. Figure 23.8 shows charts of the tested engagement indices from the initial phase of the game when buying shares, while the red dots in the screenshot indicate where the player is looking at a given moment. At this point in time, the indices have shown an increase, but it is not very significant.

(2) The biggest engagement was observed during the next 10 min. The player knows what to do, how the mechanism of the game works. He wants to achieve the best possible result. The last 5 min of the game might seem that the engagement in the game should be the biggest, because I want to improve my score, but on the contrary, the engagement is low.

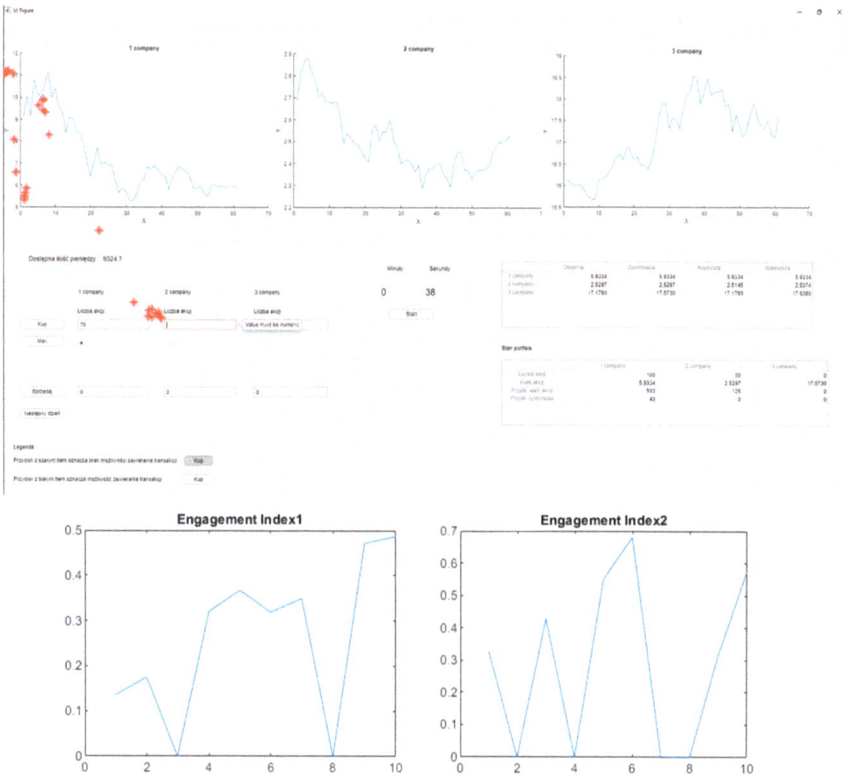

Fig. 23.8 Screenshot of the game while buying action

Figure 23.9 shows situations from about 12 min, where the researched person sells his or her shares and at the same time, you can see that, in this case, the engagement is growing. This is probably due to the fact that the player is excited about the profit achieved from one company. This can be seen from where he was looking at the moment.

(3) Usually, when the researched person clicked the next day and held shares in his/her portfolio, his/her engagement increased (Fig. 23.10). We can suppose, because after clicking she was looking at the state of the portfolio and whether the shares of a particular company bring her profit on that day.

(4) It is noteworthy to compare the average engagement during buying and selling throughout the game (Table 23.2). In the majority of respondents, the average engagement during the sale was higher than during the purchase. It can be assumed that this is due to the fact that by selling, they do not know exactly at what price the transaction will be executed, they hope that the transaction will be profitable. In most cases, when after the transaction the respondent saw that he or she had made a loss—the engagement fell, and when made a profit—the engagement grew.

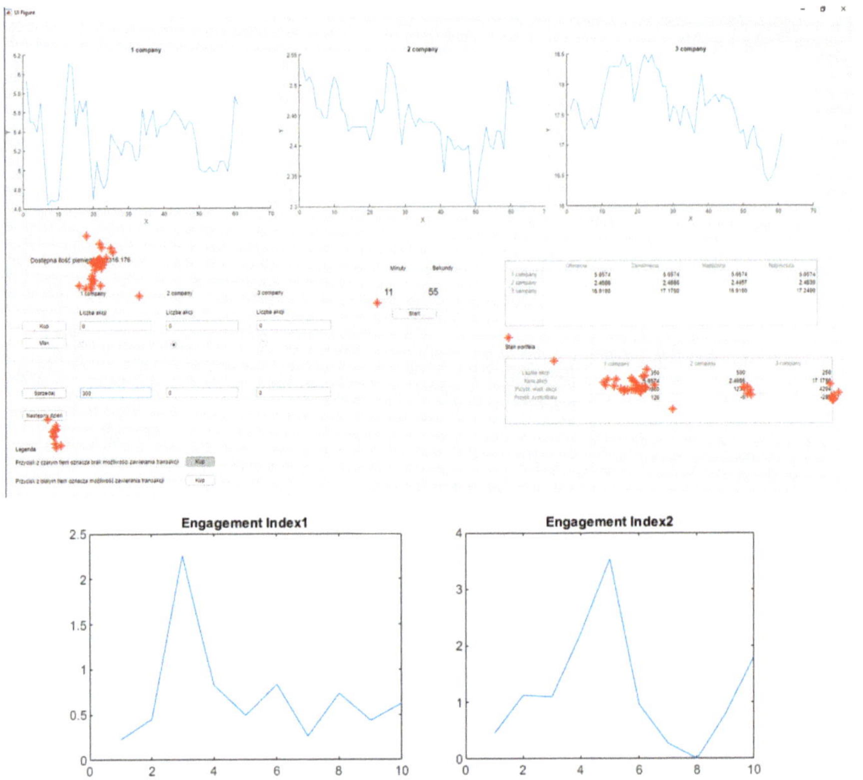

Fig. 23.9 Screenshot of the game while selling action

(5) Referring to the Internet game, the engagement of the respondents was higher at the time of sale (Fig. 23.11). Probably because, after buying the shares, they were waiting for the right moment to sell in order to make a profit from the transaction. If the course was going in the opposite direction than they thought, their engagement was falling.

(6) The majority of people while playing managed to detect the happiness, as evidenced by the combination of cheek raiser and lip corner puller. Figure 23.12 shows the situation just described, which can be seen in cheek and lips charts. In addition, there are graphs depicting eye and brow and a screenshot of the game at a given time. The blue line in the graph reflects the left part of the body, while the red line reflects the right part. Nevertheless, there were not many of these cases and in most people, it can be said that indifference was accompanied by indifference, but this cannot be clearly stated due to the fact that the number of people surveyed was too small.

(7) According to the opinions of the respondents, 4/5 of them stated that game in MATLAB was better than online game. The main argument in favour of this was the greater number of companies to invest in, and also the people

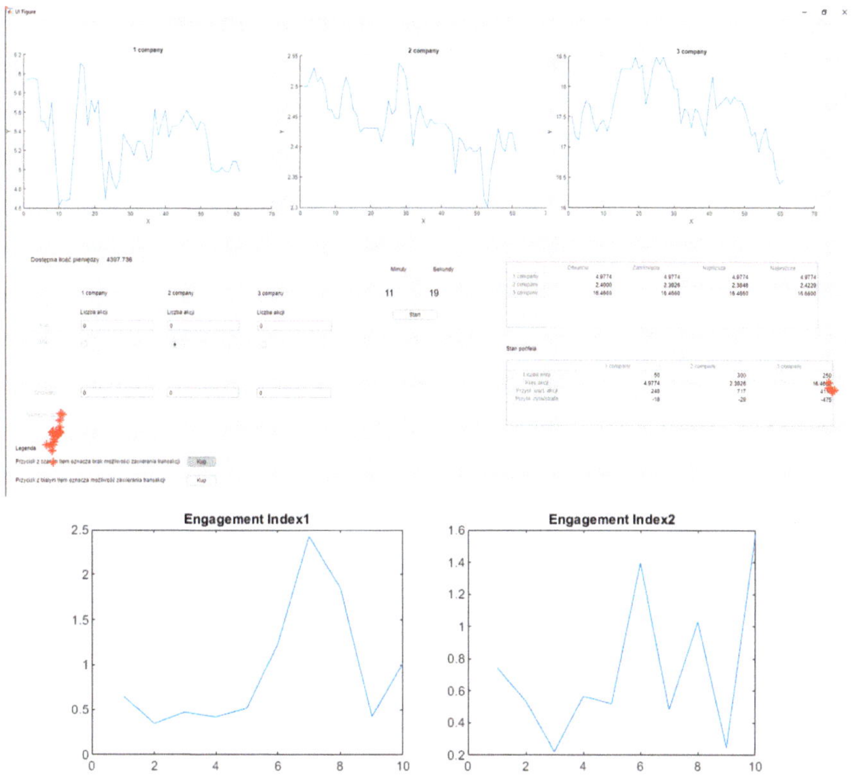

Fig. 23.10 Screenshot of the game while clicking on the button 'Next day'

surveyed believed that the game in MATLAB is more complicated, which in turn translated into the statement obtained. Despite the fact that the persons surveyed have no experience in investing, they stated that the game in MATLAB was more realistic.

Given the low involvement in the game (see Table 23.2), and that the game does not arouse much emotion. We should consider introducing elements from typical games, e.g. additional bonuses for good decisions and buying additional companies. It is possible to go in other direction, i.e. to create a real game with elements of the exchange, e.g. if you want to buy a better weapon and in order to do this you have to invest virtual money on the exchange first, if you get a positive result chosen by our item will be bought, otherwise the item will be lost. In this example way, we are able to arouse greater interest in the game, while retaining the mechanisms of the stock exchange.

These proposals should be understood in the context of certain limitations. The first is that the pilot study is a preparation for a larger study, hence the small sample for the moment. The next step will be to establish the reliability of the EEG by using a larger sample of participants to ensure that the current results are not an anomaly

Table 23.2 Average engagement in buying and selling for **a** Index 1 **b** Index 2

		Mean	Std. deviation	Min	Max
(a)					
Study 1	Buy	0.65	0.38	0.14	1.71
	Sell	0.58	0.46	0.00	2.12
Study 2	Buy	0.23	0.35	0.00	1.56
	Sell	0.33	0.29	0.00	1.02
Study 3	Buy	0.43	0.34	0.00	1.81
	Sell	0.48	0.31	0.00	1.31
Study 4	Buy	0.31	0.29	0.00	1.17
	Sell	0.32	0.28	0.00	0.98
Study 5	Buy	0.13	0.24	0.00	1.09
	Sell	0.10	0.20	0.00	0.74
(b)					
Study 1	Buy	0.65	0.38	0.14	1.71
	Sell	0.58	0.46	0.00	2.12
Study 2	Buy	0.23	0.35	0.00	1.56
	Sell	0.33	0.29	0.00	1.02
Study 3	Buy	0.43	0.34	0.00	1.81
	Sell	0.48	0.31	0.00	1.31
Study 4	Buy	0.31	0.29	0.00	1.17
	Sell	0.32	0.28	0.00	0.98
Study 5	Buy	0.13	0.24	0.00	1.09
	Sell	0.10	0.20	0.00	0.74

due to the small sample size. In addition, it is necessary to include changes in the research procedure, i.e. to add more companies to the investment, to improve the understanding of the profits made from the transaction, and to introduce elements that will make the game more playable and evoke greater emotions.

23.4 Conclusions

The results of research aimed at checking whether a game purely related to investing arouses any emotions and engagement. Therefore, it was decided to analyse situations in which the respondents bought or sold shares. On the basis of the players' opinions, it was obtained that the biggest engagement was in the so-called middle phase of the game, but still the engagement was low and during this period, the emotions accompanying them were negligible.

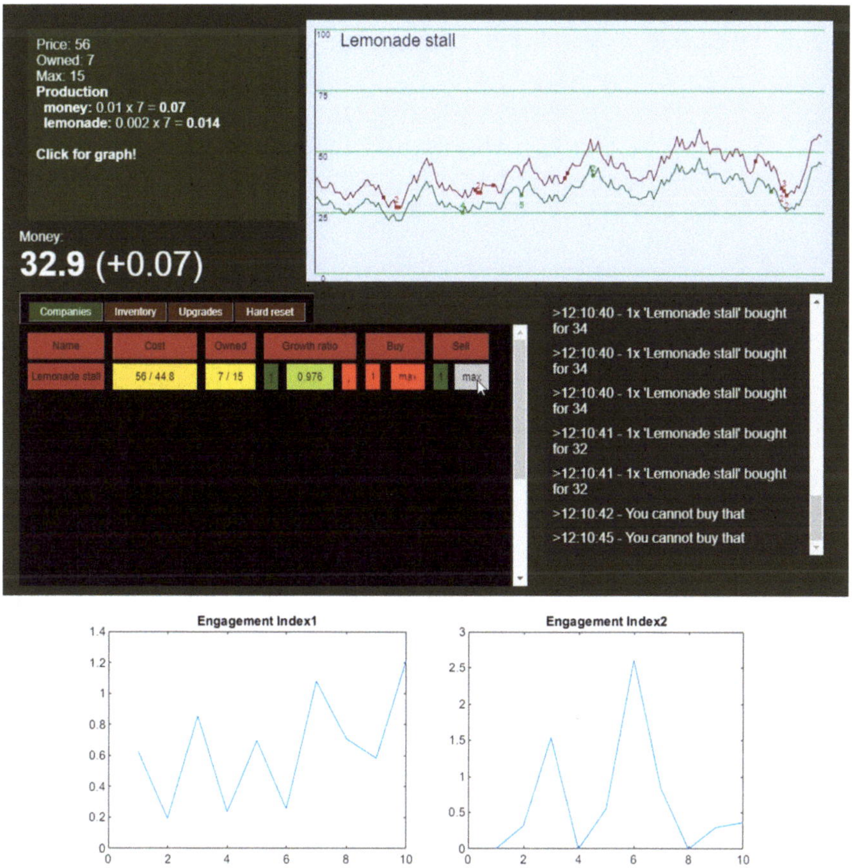

Fig. 23.11 Screenshot from the game while waiting for the right moment to sell

It should be taken into account that these findings are based on a relatively small sample size and future research will be needed in order to extend the results to a methodological approach to assessing the interest in the game after not only analysing engagement, emotions, but also adding further indices from other categories, such as concentration. Nevertheless, these results confirm the view that the purely investment game does not arouse emotions and involvement is relatively low. Therefore, the game should be extended to include elements that increase playability, while maintaining its educational value.

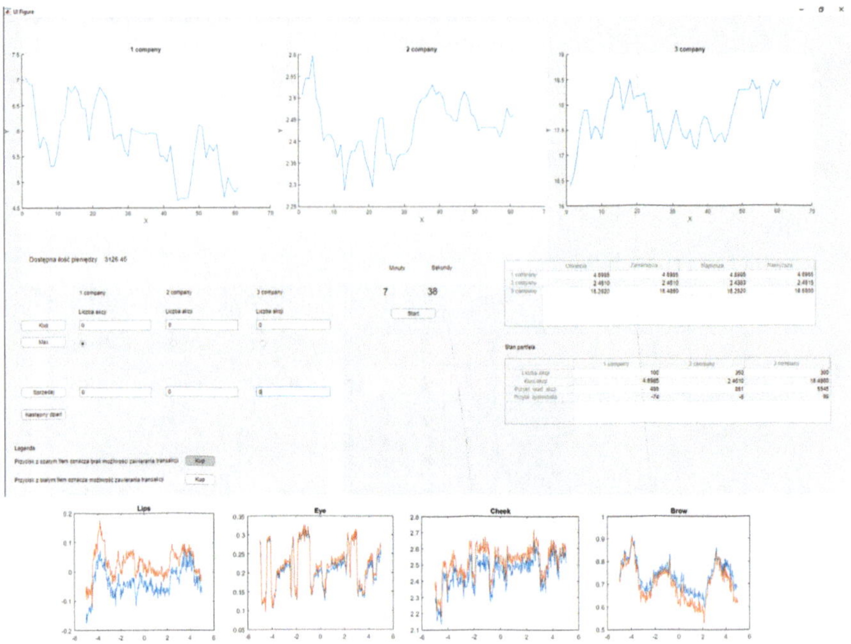

Fig. 23.12 Screenshot from the game showing emotions

References

1. Ekman, P., Friesen, W.V.: Facial Action Coding System: A Technique for the Measurement of Facial Movement. Consulting Psychologists Press, Palo Alto (1978)
2. Ekman, P., Friesen, W.V., Hager, J.C.: Facial Action Coding System. A Human Face. Salt Lake City (2002)
3. Hockey, G.R.J., Nickel, P., Roberts, A.C., Roberts, M.H.: Sensitivity of candidate markers of psychophysiological strain to cyclical changes in manual control load during simulated process control. Appl. Ergon. **40**, 1011–1018 (2009). https://doi.org/10.1016/j.apergo.2009.04.008
4. Jerčić, P.J., Astor, P., Adam, M., Hilborn, O.: A Serious Game Using Physiological Interfaces for Emotion Regulation Training in the Context of Financial Decision-Making (2012)
5. Kamzanova, A.T., Matthews, G., Kustubayeva, A.M., Jakupov, S.M.: EEG indices to time-on-task effects and to a workload manipulation (Cueing). World Acad. Sci. Eng. Technol. **80**, 19–22 (2011)
6. Nassef, A., Mahfouf, M., Linkens, D.A., Elsamahy, E., Roberts, A., Nickel, P., Hockey, G.R.J., Panoutsos, G.: The assessment of heart rate variability (HRV) and task load index (TLI) as physiological markers for physical stress. In: Dössel, O., Schlegel, W.C. (eds.) World Congress on Medical Physics and Biomedical Engineering, 7–12 Sept 2009, Munich, Germany, pp. 146–149. Springer, Berlin, Heidelberg (2010)
7. Nermend, K.: The implementation of cognitive neuroscience techniques for fatigue evaluation in participants of the decision-making process. In: Nermend, K., Latuszyńska, M. (eds.) Neuroeconomic and Behavioral Aspects of Decision Making, pp. 329–339. Springer International Publishing, Cham (2017)

8. Piwowarski, M.: Neuromarketing tools in studies on models of social issue advertising impact on recipients. In: Nermend, K., Latuszyńska, M. (eds.) Problems, Methods and Tools in Experimental and Behavioral Economics, pp. 99–111. Springer International Publishing, Cham (2018)
9. Piwowarski, M.: Cognitive neuroscience techniques in examining the effectiveness of social advertisements. In: Nermend, K., Latuszyńska, M. (eds.) Neuroeconomic and Behavioral Aspects of Decision Making, pp. 341–352. Springer International Publishing, Cham (2017)
10. Bos, D.P.O., Reuderink, B., van de Laar, B., Gürkök, H., Mühl, C., Poel, M., Nijholt, A., Heylen, D.: Brain-computer interfacing and games. In: Tan, D.S., Nijholt, A. (eds.) Brain-Computer Interfaces: Applying our Minds to Human-Computer Interaction, pp. 149–178. Springer, London (2010)
11. Raggetti, G., Ceravolo, M.G., Fattobene, L., Di Dio, C.: Neural correlates of direct access trading in a real stock market: an fMRI investigation. Front. Neurosci. **11**, 536 (2017). https://doi.org/10.3389/fnins.2017.00536
12. Soukupov, T., Cech, J.: Real-Time Eye Blink Detection Using Facial Landmarks. Rimske Toplice (2016)
13. Vieito, J.P., da Rocha, A.F., Rocha, F.T.: Brain activity of the investor's stock market financial decision. J. Behav. Finan. **16**, 220–230 (2015). https://doi.org/10.1080/15427560.2015.1064931

Chapter 24
Methods of Examining the Neuronal Bases of Financial Decisions

Mateusz Piwowarski, Konrad Biercewicz and Mariusz Borawski

Abstract Simulation games are often used to learn how to invest in the stock market. They allow you to get to know the tools and mechanisms of investing in financial markets. However, sometimes it is difficult to explain some investors' behaviour. Decisions are made under the influence of various emotional states. Using modern measurement methods, such as EEG or microexpression measurements, it is possible to study and analyse human behaviour resulting from various external stimuli.

Keywords Behavioural finances · Stock market simulators · Cognitive neuroscience · EEG · Microexpression

24.1 Introduction

Behavioural economics is a research trend which is taking achievements of psychology into account, of sociology, as well as other social science in economic studies. In this way, it gives the economy a more realistic basis for explaining many economic phenomena, while verifying the assumptions of the neoclassical economy [45]. A lot of various directions were educated in frames of behavioural economics (often not correlated closely with oneself), like experimental economics, behavioural macroeconomics, neuroeconomics or behavioural finances. Talking

M. Piwowarski (✉)
Department of Computational Methods in Experimental Economics, Faculty of Economics and Management, Institute of IT in Management, University of Szczecin, Mickiewicza 64, 71-101 Szczecin, Poland
e-mail: mateusz.piwowarski@usz.edu.pl

K. Biercewicz · M. Borawski
Department of Multimedia Systems, Faculty of Computer Science and Information Technology, West Pomeranian University of Technology Szczecin, Żołnierska 49, 71-210 Szczecin, Poland
e-mail: kbiercewicz@poczta.onet.pl

M. Borawski
e-mail: mborawski@wi.zut.edu.pl

W. Tarczyński and K. Nermend (eds.), *Effective Investments on Capital Markets*, Springer Proceedings in Business and Economics,
https://doi.org/10.1007/978-3-030-21274-2_24

about behavioural finances, one should emphasize that examinations in this area concern two assumptions well known for the theory of finances: founding markets about the effectiveness and establishing the decision of investors about the rationality [39]. Through a lot of past years, assuming the rationality of the market was a base of the decision-making theory about behaviours of investors on stock exchange markets. However, it has often turned out that without understanding human behaviours (of investors), it is hard to understand real functioning of financial markets.

Threads connecting the psychology among others to finances turned up at the literature on the subject much earlier, and then an area of behavioural finances was defined. It is possible here to summon even if well-known classical economist of Adam Smith, which in 1759, in one's book [42] kept an eye on the psychology department of the man in the context of financial decisions. Other example can be even if Keynes [28] which compared the investment activity to a beauty contest, in which investors are driven by choices of assets attractive from a point of view of other investors [27]. Along with the development of behavioural finances, as fields of finances, many different attempts for her to define appeared [2, 33, 39]. They show the relationship between human psychology and financial decision-making and its impact on financial markets. In some definitions, we will find calling to the imperfection the human in the context of behaviours of entities showing human restrictions [5]. Daniel Kahneman had a considerable contribution to the development of behavioural finances, Nobel Prize winner (in 2002) who received "for integrating psychological testing methods with economic studies". Behavioural finances, although more and more large crowds are finding supporters as well as are finding more and more big applications, are also being subjected to the criticism [5, 34]. Next, Richard Thaler claims that behavioural finances are finding application, have tools which some problems allow to explain, in some circumstances [44]. Thaler and Barberis are dividing subjects of which behavioural finances are taking care even [3].

Examinations conducted in frames of the field of behavioural finances include the issue of cognitive illusions, with which investors are surrendering at forecasting price courses on the stock market, as well as analysis of processes of the decision-making among others at the selection of assets to the investment portfolio and of them with sale. To describe this type of phenomena, various types of descriptive decision models and investment behaviours are formulated, in which the psychological singularities of the stock exchange are taken into account [51], e.g. behavioural portfolio theory [40]. Empirical checking models are not a simple task to do and is taking time. With the help, here two fields which developed in frames of economics are coming: behavioural game theory [47] and experimental economics [12]. First from them, it is connecting the game theory (rational behaviours of players) with behavioural psychology (examining real behaviours of people), in which observation of players, decisions made by them (strategies) are being made in laboratory conditions. Experimental economics is giving to the possibility of experimental testing models at different adjusting parameters what allows among others for better understanding manners of the decision-making, or also individual behaviours, e.g. of participants in the financial market. Many human mental processes are subconscious, therefore using of various methods, research models and explanations of economic (including financial) behaviour are even more complicated. Relying only and exclusively on declarations of the human concerning his states of mind can undermine the credibility of conducted examinations. People sometimes behave differently than are declaring, not always turning over just from it to the rightness [49]. Essential so, in the context of the credibility of examinations using measurement techniques with which they will provide us is happening information about reasons of the conduct of the human, his reaction to certain events, without the need to appeal to behaviours conscious of him, or interpretation. Techniques of the measurement and analyses of neurophysiological processes are giving us such a possibility [51]. A field of knowledge which is dealing with using techniques of inspecting neuronal economic bases of a decision is being called neuroeconomics [11, 22]. These techniques let the face the reading and analysis of impulses generated by brain, cardiac muscles, muscles (microexpressions), surface of the skin (electrical conduction) and the like.

The aim of this publication is to present the possibility of using selected methods of cognitive neuroscience (EEG, GSR, HR) and supporting methods (measurements of microexpression) to study the emotional states of financial market participants.

24.2 Exchange Market Simulators

The financial market is the place where financial instruments are bought and sold. We can buy or sell shares (equity securities), bonds, currencies, futures contracts, etc. We can also buy or sell shares (proprietary securities), bonds, currencies, futures contracts, etc. Behind this type of transactions, there are specific decisions which require appropriate theoretical knowledge, i.e. knowledge of terms related to the functioning of a given market (e.g. stock exchange), understanding market trends, acquaintances of tools functioning on the given market, etc. Moreover, one should possess a skill of analysing specific situations, not to say the entire markets and sensing good moments for making a decision. Investing own financial means, by trading in real cash, investors are succumbing to emotions, sometimes so considerable that they can obscure reasonable grounds for action. Appearing impatience, or desire for the maximization of profits (in varying conditions), can cause loss of invested funds or keeping profits. Exaggerated surrendering oneself for emotions is able to bring to ruin even experienced investors, acquainted with the financial market. Therefore, individual psychological predispositions are important which will let, e.g., reduce the unnecessary risk. Behavioural finance, which tries to explain the issues of cognitive illusions and analyses the processes of making financial decisions, is the subject of research in this area.

Simulation games help to keep the emotions on the rein, especially for beginner investors. They allow you to verify your ideas about investing in the financial market, such as the stock exchange, and also allow you to get to know the tools offered by the stock exchange. They are giving to the possibility of testing, e.g., of the most popular types of orders, such as Stop Loss, Buy Limit, Sell Limit, Sell Stop, Buy Stop, etc. They provide an empirical insight into the functioning of, e.g., financial leverage, short selling and many other mechanisms. Stock market simulations, as this will be particularly the case with the analysis, are an excellent training before the start of real investment activities. They enable decisions to be made using similar or the same tools that are available to real stock market investors. However, they forgive investment errors (which will certainly occur) and teach humility and patience. They also partly answer the question whether you are adequately prepared to enter the real world of financial investments.

There are many stock market simulators available on the market (stock market games). They partly differ in terms of functionality and purely technical solutions. Some of them are demo versions of existing trading platforms, others are tools that reflect the specificity of trading on the stock exchange, but do not reflect a specific environment. Some stock market simulators are implemented as web applications running in different environments (operating systems), and in order to use them, they have to be downloaded and installed. Other simulators are available through a web browser, and the basic requirement is to register on the website and open an account. To known simulators of stock exchange, global markets (not all of them) include: Wall Street Survivor (https://www.wallstreetsurvivor.com), Best Brokers: Stock Simulator (available on Google Play and App Store platforms), Investopedia Stock Simulator (https://www.investopedia.com/simulator), Stock Trainer: Virtual Trading (available on Google Play platform) and MarketWatch (available on website: https://www.marketwatch.com). There are also several simulators of this type on the Polish market, adapted to the Polish reality (in the Polish language version), for example, platform GPWtr@der (https://sigg.gpw.pl), GraGieldowa.pl (https://gragieldowa.pl) or Wirtualny Inwestor (https://www.pakietprzedsiebiorcy.pl/wirtualny-inwestor).

Wall Street Survivor is a browser game, so you do not have to download and install software. Uses counterfeit cash ($100,000 to start the game), but provides real action prices. The platform provides glossaries, courses, which are designed to help understand the functioning of stock markets. Players can join a so-called training league or create their own leagues in order to adjust the level of competition to experience. Access to the game is free of charge. An example of a simulator screen is shown in Fig. 24.1a.

Best Brokers: Stock Simulator is a simulation game available as an application for Android and iOS platforms. It provides a wide range of stock markets, including the ability to operate on assets such as Bitcoin and Ethereum cryptovalutes. It offers a number of investment options as well as many interesting order-related functions, such as the ability to place orders outside trading hours. In such situations, the application informs how long it will take to open a particular market, and at the same time plays an informative role with respect to the operating hours of individual exchanges. In addition, Best Brokers offers many training materials, such as videos. Access to the game is free of charge. An example of a simulator screen is shown in Fig. 24.1b.

Stock Trainer: Virtual Trading is an application available for the Android environment. It gives the possibility to choose from many regions and, as a result, makes available many related stock markets. The simulator is relatively easy to use; it pro-

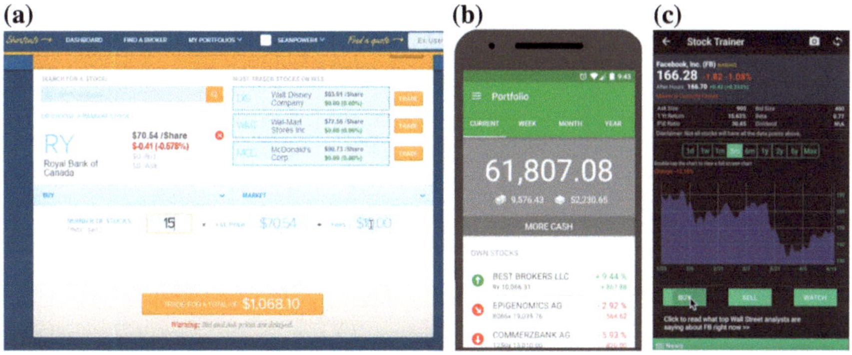

Fig. 24.1 Example screens of stock exchange simulators: **a** Wall Street Survivor, **b** Best Brokers: Stock Simulator, **c** Stock Trainer: Virtual Trading. *Source* Product owners' materials

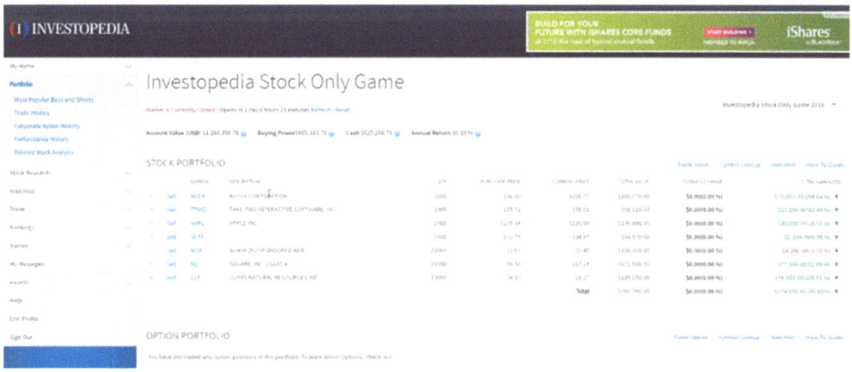

Fig. 24.2 Example screen of Investopedia Stock Simulator. *Source* Product owners' materials

vides a lot of information necessary in the investment process (it uses real markets and their data) although the graphical interface itself is not its strongest point. Examples of application functionalities include: management of own and observed portfolios, support for Stop Loss and limit orders, information about the highest profits and losses, or stock charts from 10 years ago. Access to the game is free of charge. An example of the simulator screen is shown in Fig. 24.1c.

Investopedia Stock Simulator is a simulation game available from the Investopedia website (www.investopedia.com). It is a comprehensive stock market simulator (with access to an advanced package) in which stock market news and information are integrated with the investment platform. This gives the impression of a real trading environment on the stock exchange. In addition, you can participate in competitions that allow you to individually assess your investment skills. The simulator is characterized by a high level of competition between market participants and gives the feeling of gamification. Access to the game is free of charge. An example of a simulator screen is shown in Fig. 24.2.

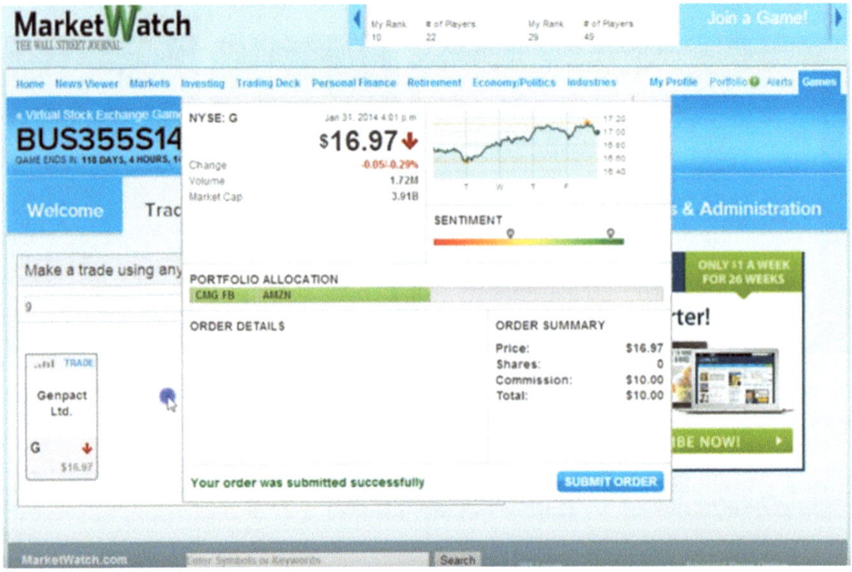

Fig. 24.3 Example screen of MarketWatch Simulator. *Source* Product owners' materials

MarketWatch, is a stock market simulator available through a web browser (responsive interface) from the MarketWatch financial service (https://www.marketwatch.com/game). Allows you to buy shares in real time using your virtual wallet. It allows you to set the size of your initial budget, set Stop Loss and limit orders, execute short selling, etc. You can create a private or public game within the platform and join an existing one. Rankings of users and games are made available as an additional mechanism of competition. An internal chat (social element) is used to interact with other market participants. Access to the game is free of charge. An example of the simulator screen is shown in Fig. 24.3.

Exchange games and simulators give beginner investors a chance to get to know the principles of financial markets. For more experienced traders, it is possible to compare their trading methods, strategies and techniques used by other players. Certainly, such games do not fully reflect the nature of investing real financial resources. The degree of emotion and engagement in decision-making are different in the real world and different in the virtual world. However, the users of exchange simulators perform the same actions as on the real market. They have to make decisions about buying, selling securities, cutting losses, making profits, developing investment strategies, etc. Properly motivated (competitiveness, possibility of getting awards) want to achieve the best possible results. Different emotional states appear in them, at different moments they react differently to the situation. As is well known, emotions do not go hand in hand with rational decisions. In addition, the impact of the environment, the behaviour of other market participants (players), the reaction to official announcements from companies and other incoming information can destroy even the best developed investment strategies. It is therefore worth examining and analysing the behaviour of investors, in particular the emotional states associated with the investment process. Traditional methods (interviews, surveys, etc.) do not obtain this type of information. Emotions and other feelings are born in the brain, and people are not always aware of them. There are, however, measurement methods that allow to record even the most subtle signals sent by the human body.

24.3 Measuring Methods in Examining an Emotional States

For examining emotional states of people, modern measurement techniques are more and more often exploited. The part from them allows for the registration of data which it is possible to recruit based on detailed observation of the examined object, e.g. facial expression of the face. It won't manage however to obtain some data without the specialist measuring equipment and the explored domain knowledge. Data is being ranked among this category (signals) coming from the inner life of the person, (so-called psychophysiological), in particular from the human brain. A cognitive neurolearning is dealing with these issues. Cognitive neuroscience is a part of different fields which examinations of the mind are exploiting, that is in particular neuroscience, mathematics, linguistics, physics, psychiatry [25]. Neuroscience focuses on the course and analysis of brain processes, but not on the biological structure of the brain. The development of neuroscience, that it was finding application in more and more new areas. Economics, but more precisely analysing economic behaviours are one of them, e.g. in the decision-making on the stock market [35]. Possibilities of the cognitive neurolearning result mainly from the development of techniques of the measurement of the activity of the brain and the connection with other technologies [10].

It is possible to divide methods of the cognitive neurolearning in four main categories [51]: brain neuroimaging methods, psychophysiological methods, single nerve cell examination and neuropsychological methods. In the context of the economic research, above all methods are being used of neuroimaging and psychophysiological.

Brain neuroimaging methods enable observation and analysis of changes in brain activity (or rather its fragments) depending on the activities performed. The most commonly used measuring techniques include: electroencephalogram (EEG), positron emission tomography (PET) and functional magnetic resonance (FMRI) [25, 51]. Due to the availability of devices and the complexity of research processes of these three techniques, EEG finds the greatest practical application in studying economic phenomena.

Psychophysiological methods enable to correlate different intellectual functions with physiological sensations, like the growth of the blood pressure, the increased pace of the action of the heart, increased skin conduction or also moves of muscles of the face. Used measuring methods most often from this group include measurements of the skin-galvanic reaction (GSR—galvanic response skinhead), measurement of the pulse (HR—Heart Rate), or e.g. evaluation of the function of muscles and nerve (EMG—electromyography). Moreover, measurement techniques which they are replacing are being exploited or are assisting psychophysiological methods, like in case of measurements of the microexpression (facial expressions of the face). Electrodes from EMG are being replaced with cameras about the high resolution which moves of muscles of the face are tracking.

24.3.1 Electroencephalography

Electroencephalography (EEG) is a non-invasive diagnostic method, in which with the electroencephalograph, the notation of the bioelectric activity of the brain is being read out (of neurons). An important part of it are electrodes placed on the head of the examined person, which are registering the electrical potential in a given place. Next he is strengthened, and signals are being recorded in the form of the electroencephalogram. This potential is a resultant of potentials of all sources of the electric field, that is apart from the electric activity of the brain, also of outside activity (e.g. of electromagnetic interference). The EEG signal has an individual course for every person, but is subject to peculiar changes depending on existing psychophysical factors [25]. In case of the healthy human, it is possible to distinguish certain rhythms, so-called EEG waves about the different frequency and the amplitude, which can however change along with age. The most frequently distinguished types of waves include [4, 25]:

- Alpha waves (frequency 8–13 Hz, amplitude approx. 30–100 μV) are, e.g., associated with low cognitive activity and relaxation,
- Beta waves (12–30 Hz, up to 30 μV) show how much the cerebral cortex is involved in cognitive activities, and their small amplitude is visible during attention concentration,
- Theta waves (4–8 Hz), are related to e.g. cognitive activity, and primarily concern memory processes,
- Delta waves (up to 4 Hz) are mainly noticeable in the sleep phase,
- Gamma waves (26–100 Hz) are related to consciousness, perception and mental activity.

The recording of the EEG signal should run in appropriate conditions, i.e. in the low-lighted room, and the examined person should sit down comfortably on the armchair or the chair. Electrodes are being put on the head, of which the location closely is determined. A process bequeathed to the recording of the EEG signal which is on a computer is taking place after the preliminary process of the calibration. After the test is completed, the signals are processed and the results are interpreted.

For the purposes of examinations, electrodes on the scalp are most often assembled according to guidelines of the system 10–20 [25]. In it, 21 electrodes are being used, where 19 electrodes are being put in appropriately designated places of the surface of the head and 2 referential electrodes located in regions of ears (Fig. 24.4).

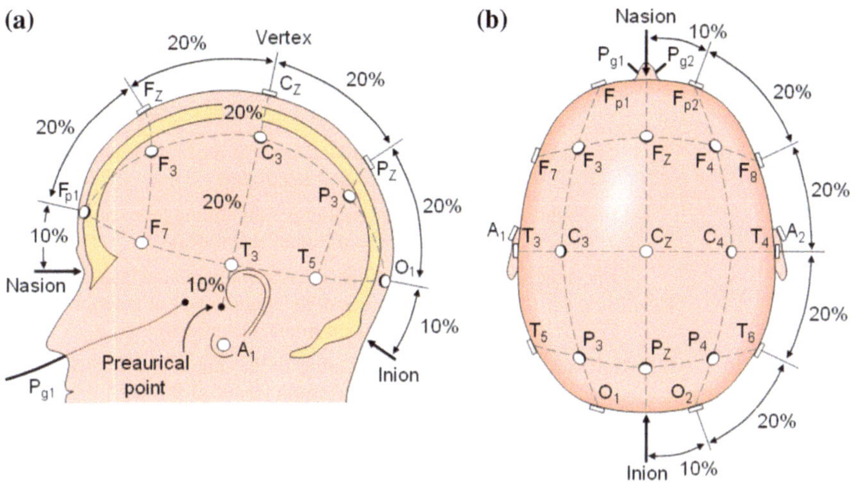

Fig. 24.4 System of 10–20 locations of electrodes; **a** left part of head and **b** top part of head [29]

Electrodes have their symbolism (letters and digits), where the letters denote the cerebral cortex on which they are placed, and the numbers the appropriate side: even right, odd left. The *F* letter means the frontal lobe (Lat. frontalis), *T*—the temporal lobe (temporalis), *P*—parietal lobe (parietalis), *O*—occipital (occipitalis), *C*—Rolando's fissure. Electrodes mounted along the line connecting the nasal cavity with occipital nodule are marked with a small letter *z*. Table 24.1 contains the symbolism of electrodes along with their location on the surface of the head.

While EEG examining apart from desired EEG signals, these undesirable, i.e., so-called artefacts, are also being registered. So the registered signal is a resultant of all potentials of the electric field, in it of disruptions coming from different technical devices (e.g. of power grid), or of physiological interferences (moves of eyeballs, muscle tensions, and the like). Various methods and devices are being used for the detection of artefacts. Frequency methods are often used to detect the dominant frequencies in the recorded signal. Removal of frequencies detected as deviating from the frequency of the EEG signal can be done in various ways, e.g. using classifiers, subtracting the interfering signal from the EEG signal, or using Blind Source Separation (BSS) technique, including Independent Component Analysis (ICA). In eliminating undesirable signals, a filtration is usually the first step (upper-capacity and low-pass filters), applied in order to cut the frequency out of range 1 up to 50 Hz (brainstorms are oscillating in this respect). The purified signal is undergoing further conversions in order to single out features which constitute the neurophysiological reply of the brain to the set stimulus from the signal (is regarding experimental studies). Frequency analysis allows for singling out from the full EEG signal his components (it is possible to make it e.g. with the transformation of Fourier), and next to make analysis of his features, e.g. amplitudes. Knowing ranges of wavelengths which are answering distinguished kinds (for rhythms) of waves: alpha, beta, gamma, and

Table 24.1 Symbolism of electrodes in the system 10–20 and areas of the brain, from which the recording of signals is taking place [29, 38]

Electrode symbolism	Surface of the head	Area of the brain, which the registration of the activity is taking place from
Fp1, Fp2	Left, right hemisphere	The frontal lobes of the brain (leading or prefrontal electrodes)
F3, F4	Left, right hemisphere	Surrounding of the frontal lobes of the brain (central frontal electrodes)
F7, F8	Left, right hemisphere	Orbital, anterior temporal and lateral frontal regions of the brain (lower or anterior temporal frontal electrodes)
Fz	Half-way line	Surrounding of the central and medial frontal region (central frontal electrode)
T3, T4	Left, right hemisphere	Anterior temporal and central temporal regions of the brain (central temporal electrodes)
T5, T6	Left, right hemisphere	Posterior temporal regions of the brain (posterior temporal electrodes)
C3, C4	Left, right hemisphere	Areas of Roland's fissure
Cz	Half-way line	Central and medial area (central–medial electrode)
P3, P4	Left, right hemisphere	Cerebral parietal area (parietal electrodes)
Pz	Half-way line	Central and medial parietal area (parietal electrode)
O1, O2	Left, right hemisphere	Occipital region of the brain (occipital electrodes)
A1, A2	Left, right hemisphere	Middle temporal area (ear electrodes, reference electrodes)

the like it is possible to examine specific intellectual phenomena [7, 25, 29]. For the purposes of examinations from changes including observation and analysis of the activity of the brain depending on performed activities, he was drawn up and implement author's system.

24.3.2 *Microexpression*

The face of the human is a medium showing emotions, and the transmission of emotion can partly be controlled. To a certain extent people can shape one's "emotional image". However, the part of shown emotions is apart from the deliberate control, and they are manifesting itself with small, short moves of muscles of the face (fractions of seconds). They are called the microexpression. They are pointing out to an emotional states truly gone through, which are becoming apparent even when they don't want to detect them [17]. They make it possible to determine what a person really feels, and even detect the moments when they lie. There are many examples of such analyses, such as analyses of the truthfulness of speeches made by politicians (published on the Internet). Microexpression studies can be carried out on the basis of EMG, whose aim is to evaluate the function of the muscular and peripheral nervous system. They can also be carried out with the use of high-resolution cameras, so-called face readers (Face Reader). In the following part of this publication, the technique of microexpression recognition with the use of a facial features reader will be briefly presented.

On the human face, it is possible to indicate sensitive points which a detailed analysis allows to read out microexpressions. Based on photographs or films, it is possible to a certain extent to automate the process of defining emotion. There are ready-made tools (programs), in which facial expression recognition algorithms have been implemented. They are also available specialize libraries containing functions which it is possible to exploit at creating author's solutions. They are usually these are multi-platform libraries of the general-purpose, containing the large range of special tools, e.g., of statistical machine learning. Thanks to such libraries programmers can create solutions more fitted to research needs.

For the purposes of research on the analysis of users' behaviour in the context of making financial decisions, an original system for recognizing emotions has been developed. This system is detecting and is analysing microexpressions, based on which it is possible to recognize emotions of investors in the moment of making decisions by them. This system uses a set of tools (library dlib) to detect and label key facial structures in the face region. For facial detection, the classic Histogram of Oriented Gradients (HOG) feature combined with a linear classifier, an image pyramid, and sliding window detection scheme was used. Detection of key facial structures in the face region is performed by pose estimator, implemented on the basis of the method described in the article [26]. Pose estimator was tested on iBUG 300-W face landmark data set [37]. This library for the indicated image provides the location and size of the area occupied by the face and 68 points describing the key facial structures (Fig. 24.5).

Points from 0 to 16 determine the outline of the face, 17–21—left eyebrow, 22–26—right eyebrow, 27–35—nose, 36–41—left eye, 42–47—right eye, 48–59—the external contour of the lip, 60–67—internal contour of the lip. These points are being used for the identification of emotion. Their identification is facilitated by the Facial Action Coding System (FACS), which introduces a taxonomy of human facial movements. It was originally created and published by the Swedish anatoma Carl-Herman Hjortsjö [24], which was subsequently adopted and corrected by Paul Ekman, Wallace V. Friesen and Joseph C. Hager [16, 18, 23]. Their proposed codes are shown in Table 24.2.

Intensities of FACS are annotated by appending letters *A–E* (for minimal–maximal intensity) to the action unit number: *A*—trace; *B*—slight; *C*—marked or pronounced; *D*—severe or extreme; *E*—maximum.

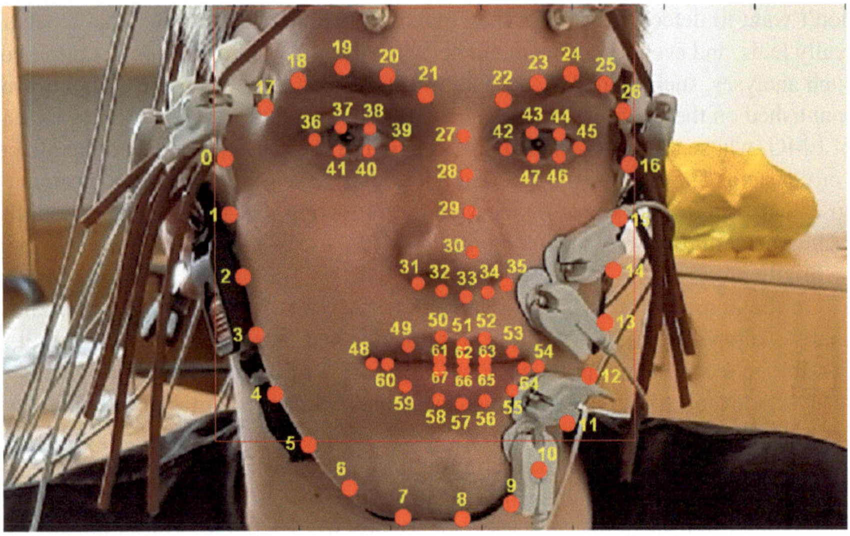

Fig. 24.5 Characteristic facial points describing key facial structures [18]

24.4 Determination of Behavioural Indicators

In order to determine behavioural indicators describing human behaviour in specific situations, data obtained on the basis of various measurement techniques are used. A discussed earlier electroencephalography (EEG) is one of such techniques which let the recording of electrical signals coming from various parts of the brain. Another technique that allows the recording of physiological changes is the measurement of skin-galvanic reaction (GSR). They are being carried out with the galvanometer measuring electrical conductivity of the skin, changing depending on general stimulating the sympathetic nervous system. Activation of the autonomic nervous system is associated with physiological stimulation, so changes in the skin's electrical resistance can mean experiencing feelings or spontaneous response to a stimulus [9, 14, 32]. Physiological data can also be obtained by heart rate measurements (HR). Such a measurement is usually being conducted on the wrist of the hand or on the chest, where is being registered frequencies of the heartbeats within the minute [15].

Based on the measurement data obtained in this way, various indices can be determined, which allow for the assessment of different affective states [46]. For example, using EEG, GSR and HR measurement data, it is possible to determine indices such as:

- Approach-Withdrawal Index,
- Memorization Index,
- Engagement Index,
- Emotional Index.

Table 24.2 FACS codes [18]

AU	FACS name	Facial muscle
0	Neutral face	
1	Inner brow raiser	Frontalis, pars medialis
2	Outer brow raiser	Frontalis, pars lateralis
4	Brow lowerer	Depressor glabellae, depressor supercilii, corrugator supercilii
5	Upper lid raiser	Levator palpebrae superioris, superior tarsal muscle
6	Cheek raiser	Orbicularis oculi (pars orbitalis)
7	Lid tightener	Orbicularis oculi (pars palpebralis)
8	Lips towards each other	Orbicularis oris
9	Nose wrinkler	Levator labii superioris alaeque nasi
10	Upper lip raiser	Levator labii superioris, caput infraorbitalis
11	Nasolabial deepener	Zygomaticus minor
12	Lip corner puller	Zygomaticus major
13	Sharp lip puller	Levator anguli oris (also known as caninus)
14	Dimpler	Buccinator
15	Lip corner depressor	Depressor anguli oris (also known as triangularis)
16	Lower lip depressor	Depressor labii inferioris
17	Chin raiser	Mentalis
18	Lip pucker	Incisivii labii superioris and incisivii labii inferioris
19	Tongue show	
20	Lip stretcher	Risorius w/platysma
21	Neck tightener	Platysma
22	Lip funneler	Orbicularis oris
23	Lip tightener	Orbicularis oris
24	Lip pressor	Orbicularis oris
25	Lips part	Depressor labii inferioris, or relaxation of mentalis or orbicularis oris
26	Jaw drop	Masseter; relaxed temporalis and internal pterygoid
27	Mouth stretch	Pterygoids, digastric
28	Lip suck	Orbicularis oris

Index of interests: **Approach-Withdrawal (AW) Index** is calculated on the basis of the formula:

$$\begin{aligned} \mathrm{AW} &= \frac{1}{N_P}\sum_{i\in P} x_{\alpha_i}^2(t) - \frac{1}{N_Q}\sum_{i\in Q} y_{\alpha_i}^2(t) \\ &= \text{Average Power}_{\alpha_{\text{right, frontal}}} - \text{Average Power}_{\alpha_{\text{left, frontal}}}, \end{aligned} \quad (24.1)$$

where x_{α_i} and y_{α_i} represent the ith EEG channel in the alpha band that have been recorded from the right and left frontal lobes, respectively, P and Q are the sets of right channels and left channels, and N_P and N_Q represent their cardinality. The value of the AW index is related to the increase of interest, its drop together with the decrease of interest [13].

Memorization Index (MI) is established in compliance with the formula:

$$\mathrm{MI} = \frac{1}{N_Q} \sum_{i \in Q} x_{\theta_i}^2(t) = \text{Average Power}_{\theta_{\text{left, frontal}}}, \tag{24.2}$$

where x_{θ_i} represents the ith EEG channel in the theta band that has been recorded from the left frontal lobe, Q is the set of left channels, N_Q represents its cardinality. The increase of the MI value is related to enhanced memorization [8, 43, 48].

Engagement Index (level), which is a measure related to information gathering, visual processing and the allocation of the attention can be appointed as a few ways [31]:

(a)

$$\mathrm{EnI(1)} = \frac{\text{Beta}}{(\text{Alpha} + \text{Theta})}, \tag{24.3}$$

averaged across all sensor locations [6, 19, 36],

(b)

$$\mathrm{EnI(2)} = \frac{\text{Theta}}{\text{Alpha}}, \tag{24.4}$$

average frontal midline theta and average parietal alpha [21, 41],

(c)

$$\mathrm{EnI(3)} = \text{Theta}, \tag{24.5}$$

averaged frontal theta [50].

Emotional Index (EI) is established according to the dependency:

$$\mathrm{EI} = 1 - \frac{\beta}{\pi}, \tag{24.6}$$

where

$$\beta = \begin{cases} \frac{\frac{3}{2}\pi + \pi - \vartheta}{\frac{\pi}{2} - \vartheta} & \text{if} \mathrm{GSR_Z} \geq 0, \mathrm{HR_Z} \leq 0, \\ & \text{otherwise.} \end{cases} \tag{24.7}$$

$\mathrm{GSR_Z}$, $\mathrm{HR_Z}$ represent the Z-score variables of GSR and HR, respectively; ϑ-arctan $g(\mathrm{GSR_Z}, \mathrm{HR_Z})$. The angle β is defined in order to obtain the EI varying between $[-1, 1]$.

Table 24.3 Example table of transition from FACS system (typical AU) to description of emotions

Emotion	Action units
Happiness	6 + 12
Sadness	1 +4 + 15
Surprise	1 + 2 + 5B + 26
Fear	1 + 2 + 4 + 5 + 7 + 20 + 26
Anger	4 + 5 + 7 + 23
Disgust	9 + 15 + 16
Contempt	R12A + R14A

According to [6] and [7], negative $HR_Z < 0$ and positive $HR_Z > 0$ values of the EI are related to negative and positive emotions [1, 30].

Using Face Reader data, microexpressions can also be recorded to assess emotional states. In order to classify human emotions, well-developed transition tables from the FACS system are used to assess emotions, e.g. Emotional Facial Action Coding System (EMFACS) [20], Facial Action Coding System Affect Interpretation Dictionary (FACSAID) (Hager). Such tables contain a list of selected emotional states and corresponding typical Action Units (AU) of the FACS system (Table 24.3).

In practical research, data are often recorded using several different devices; single indices are determined or combined.

24.5 Conclusions

The aim of this chapter was to present the possibility of using selected, modern measurement methods to study the emotional states of financial market participants. The links between human psychology and his financial decisions have been mentioned. The role of behavioural finance in explaining investors' behaviour was emphasized. The analysed stock exchange simulators confirm the thesis that virtual investment environments are functionally similar to real platforms. They allow you to learn how to invest, give you an opportunity to get to know the tools used on the market and reflect the specificity of investing on the stock market. However, they do not give direct information about the reasons for investors' behaviour or its reaction to the events. And it is emotions that often have a decisive influence on the decisions made and can obscure the rational basis for action. Examining and analysing an emotional states appearing during stock market investments, it is possible to identify key moments that influence specific behaviours. In order to obtain such information, it is possible to exploit measurement techniques enabling the registration of data coming from observation of the object (of face) and data (of signals) originating from the inside of a person, in particular from the brain.

This chapter presents methods of measuring psychophysiological data (in particular EEG) and microexpression. Basic behavioural indicators (emotions, involvement, interests, memories), on the basis of which we are able to determine the reactions of investors to various external stimuli, were also discussed.

Further research will consist in developing a simulation environment for investing in the stock exchange, and then, on the basis of the measurement methods discussed here, carrying out an experiment. The aim of this experiment will be to analyse the emotional states of investors during the process of making specific investment decisions.

References

1. Astolfi, L., De Vico, Fallani F., Cincotti, F., Mattia, D., Bianchi, L., Marciani, M.G., Salinari, S., Colosimo, A., Tocci, A., Soranzo, R., Babiloni, F.: Neural basis for brain responses to TV commercials: a high-resolution EEG study. IEEE Trans. Neural Syst. Rehabil. Eng. **16**, 522–531 (2008). https://doi.org/10.1109/TNSRE.2008.2009784
2. Barber, B.M., Odean, T.: The courage of misguided convictions. Finan. Anal. J. **55**, 41–55 (1999). https://doi.org/10.2469/faj.v55.n6.2313
3. Barberis, N., Thaler, R.: A Survey of Behavioral Finance. National Bureau of Economic Research, Cambridge, MA (2002)
4. Bear, M.F., Connors, B.W., Paradiso, M.A.: Neuroscience: Exploring the Brain, 3rd edn. Lippincott Williams & Wilkins, Baltimore, Md (2007)
5. Belsky, G., Gilovich, T.: Why Smart People Make Big Money Mistakes and How to Correct Them: Lessons from the New Science of Behavioral Economics. Simon & Schuster, New York, NY (1999)
6. Berka, C., Levendowski, D.J., Lumicao, M.N., Yau, A., Davis, G., Zivkovic, V.T., Olmstead, R.E., Tremoulet, P.D., Craven, P.L.: EEG correlates of task engagement and mental workload in vigilance, learning, and memory tasks. Aviat. Space Environ. Med. **78**, Supplement 1, B231–B244 (14) (2007)
7. Borawska, A., Alsakaa, A.: Prediction of decision outcome via observation of brain activity signals during decision-making process. In: Nermend, K., Łatuszyńska, M. (eds.) Neuroeconomic and Behavioral Aspects of Decision Making, pp. 255–269. Springer International Publishing, Cham (2017)
8. Borawski, M.: Use of computer game as an element of social campaign focusing attention on reliability of information in the internet. In: Nermend, K., Łatuszyńska, M. (eds.) Problems, Methods and Tools in Experimental and Behavioral Economics, pp. 127–139. Springer International Publishing, Cham (2018)
9. Boucsein, W., Fowles, D.C., Grimnes, S., Filion, D.L.: Publication recommendations for electrodermal measurements: publication standards for EDA. Psychophysiology **49**, 1017–1034 (2012). https://doi.org/10.1111/j.1469-8986.2012.01384.x
10. Camerer, C.F.: Neuroeconomics: using neuroscience to make economic predictions. Econ. J. **117**, C26–C42 (2007). https://doi.org/10.1111/j.1468-0297.2007.02033.x
11. Camerer, C., Loewenstein, G., Prelec, D.: Neuroeconomics: how neuroscience can inform economics. J. Econ. Lit. **43**, 9–64 (2005). https://doi.org/10.1257/0022051053737843
12. Chaudhuri, A.: Experiments in Economics: Playing Fair with Money. Routledge (2009)
13. Davidson, R.J.: What does the prefrontal cortex "do" in affect: perspectives on frontal EEG asymmetry research. Biol. Psychol. **67**, 219–234 (2004). https://doi.org/10.1016/j.biopsycho.2004.03.008
14. Dawson, M.E., Schell, A.M., Filion, D.L., Berntson, G.G.: The electrodermal system. In: Cacioppo, J.T., Tassinary, L.G., Berntson, G. (eds.) Handbook of Psychophysiology, 3rd edn, pp. 157–181. Cambridge University Press, Cambridge (2007)

15. Dulleck, U., Schaffner, M., Torgler, B.: Heartbeat and economic decisions: observing mental stress among proposers and responders in the ultimatum bargaining game. PLoS ONE **9**, e108218 (2014). https://doi.org/10.1371/journal.pone.0108218
16. Ekman, P., Friesen, W.: Facial Action Coding System: A Technique for the Measurement of Facial Movement. Consulting Psychologists Press, Palo Alto (1978)
17. Ekman, P., O'Sullivan, M.: Who can catch a liar? Am. Psychol. **46**, 913–920 (1991). https://doi.org/10.1037//0003-066X.46.9.913
18. Ekman, P., Hager, J.C., Friesen, W.V.: Facial Action Coding System: A Technique for the Measurement of Facial Movement (2002)
19. Freeman, F.G., Mikulka, P.J., Prinzel, L.J., Scerbo, M.W.: Evaluation of an adaptive automation system using three EEG indices with a visual tracking task. Biol. Psychol. **50**, 61–76 (1999). https://doi.org/10.1016/S0301-0511(99)00002-2
20. Friesen, W., Ekman, P.: EMFACS-7: emotional facial action coding system (1983)
21. Gevins, A.: High-resolution EEG mapping of cortical activation related to working memory: effects of task difficulty, type of processing, and practice. Cereb. Cortex **7**, 374–385 (1997). https://doi.org/10.1093/cercor/7.4.374
22. Glimcher, P.W., Fehr, E. (eds.): Neuroeconomics: Decision Making and The Brain, Second edn. Elsevier/AP, Academic Press is an imprint of Elsevier, Amsterdam, Boston (2014)
23. Hager, J.C.: FACSAID: Facial Action Coding System Affect Interpretation Dictionary
24. Hjortsjo, C.-H.: Man's Face and Mimic Language. Studentlitteratur, Lund, Sweden (1970)
25. Jaśkowski, P.: Neuronauka poznawcza: jak mózg tworzy umysł. Vizja Press & It, Warszawa (2009)
26. Kazemi, V., Sullivan, J.: One millisecond face alignment with an ensemble of regression trees. 2014 IEEE Conference on Computer Vision and Pattern Recognition, pp. 1867–1874. IEEE, Columbus, OH (2014)
27. Keynes, J.M.: The Collected Writings of John Maynard Keynes. Cambridge University Press for the Royal Economic Society, Cambridge [England]; New York (2013)
28. Keynes, J.M.: The general theory of employment, interest and money (1936). Kessinger Publishing, Whitefish, Mont. (2010)
29. Malmivuo, J., Plonsey, R.: Bioelectromagnetism: principles and applications of bioelectric and biomagnetic fields. Oxford University Press, New York, NY (1995)
30. Mauss, I.B., Robinson, M.D.: Measures of emotion: a review. Cogn. Emot. **23**, 209–237 (2009). https://doi.org/10.1080/02699930802204677
31. Mcmahan, T., Parberry, I., Parsons, T.: Evaluating Electroencephalography Engagement Indices During Video Game Play (2015)
32. Nermend, K., Duda, J.: Methodology for choosing the location for in-game advertising billboards. In: Nermend, K., Łatuszyńska, M. (eds.) Problems, Methods and Tools in Experimental and Behavioral Economics, pp. 89–97. Springer International Publishing, Cham (2018)
33. Nofsinger, J.R.: The Psychology of Investing, 5th edn. Pearson, Boston, Mass (2014)
34. Olsen, R.A.: Behavioral finance and its implications for stock-price volatility. Finan. Anal. J. **54**, 10–18 (1998). https://doi.org/10.2469/faj.v54.n2.2161
35. Peterson, R.L.: inside The Investor's Brain: The Power of Mind Over Money. Wiley, Hoboken, N.J. (2007)
36. Pope, A.T., Bogart, E.H., Bartolome, D.S.: Biocybernetic system evaluates indices of operator engagement in automated task. Biol. Psychol. **40**, 187–195 (1995). https://doi.org/10.1016/0301-0511(95)05116-3
37. Sagonas, C., Antonakos, E., Tzimiropoulos, G., Zafeiriou, S., Pantic, M.: 300 Faces In-The-Wild Challenge: database and results. Image Vis. Comput. **47**, 3–18 (2016). https://doi.org/10.1016/j.imavis.2016.01.002
38. Sharbrough, F., Chatrian, G.E., Lesser, R., Luders, H., Nuwer, M., Picton, T.: American Electroencephalographic Society Guidelines for Standard Electrode Position Nomenclature (1991)
39. Shefrin, H. (ed.): Behavioral finance. Elgar, Cheltenham (2001)
40. Shefrin, H., Statman, M.: Behavioral portfolio theory. J. Finan. Quantit. Anal. **35**, 127 (2000). https://doi.org/10.2307/2676187

41. Smith, M.E., Gevins, A.: Neurophysiologic monitoring of mental workload and fatigue during operation of a flight simulator. In: Caldwell, J.A., Wesensten, N.J. (eds.) Orlando, p. 116. Florida, USA (2005)
42. Smith, A.: The Theory of Moral Sentiments. Gutenberg Publishers, Kapaau (T.H.) (2011)
43. Summerfield, C., Mangels, J.A.: Coherent theta-band EEG activity predicts item-context binding during encoding. NeuroImage **24**, 692–703 (2005). https://doi.org/10.1016/j.neuroimage.2004.09.012
44. Thaler, R.H.: Advances in Behavioral Finance, vol. II. Princeton University Press, Princeton (2005)
45. Tomer, J.F.: What is behavioral economics? J. Socio-Econ. **36**, 463–479 (2007). https://doi.org/10.1016/j.socec.2006.12.007
46. Vecchiato, G., Maglione, A.G., Cherubino, P., Wasikowska, B., Wawrzyniak, A., Latuszynska, A., Latuszynska, M., Nermend, K., Graziani, I., Leucci, M., Trettel, A., Babiloni, F.: Neurophysiological tools to investigate consumer's gender differences during the observation of TV commercials. Comput. Math. Methods Med. **2014**, 12 (2014)
47. Von Neumann, J., Morgenstern, O.: Theory of Games and Economic Behavior, 60th anniversary ed. Princeton University Press, Princeton, N.J.; Woodstock (2007)
48. Werkle-Bergner, M., Müller, V., Li, S.-C., Lindenberger, U.: Cortical EEG correlates of successful memory encoding: implications for lifespan comparisons. Neurosci. Biobehav. Rev. **30**, 839–854 (2006). https://doi.org/10.1016/j.neubiorev.2006.06.009
49. Wilson, T.D.: Strangers to Ourselves: Discovering the Adaptive Unconscious. Belknap, Cambridge, Mass, London (2004)
50. Yamada, F.: Frontal midline theta rhythm and eyeblinking activity during a VDT task and a video game: useful tools for psychophysiology in ergonomics. Ergonomics **41**, 678–688 (1998). https://doi.org/10.1080/001401398186847
51. Zaleśkiewicz, T.: Psychologia ekonomiczna. Wydawnictwo Naukowe PWN, Warszawa (2013)

Chapter 25
Behavioural Finance Then and Now

Danuta Miłaszewicz

Abstract Behavioural finance, a relatively new field that is constantly developing, has grown up to criticize the assumptions and theories of standard finance. The aim of this article is to present the development of behavioural finance of the first and the second generation. The first generation of behavioural finance focused on the analysis of irrational decisions made by rational actors. The second generation of behavioural finance considers the decision-making processes of *normal people*. Its further development will be based on the achievements of neuroeconomics.

Keywords Generations of behavioural finance · Theory

25.1 Introduction

According to Claudini [3] "we are in a Golden Age of behavioural science". It is a science which "is making a significant difference to our everyday lives, from helping us make better choices in finance and health care, to guiding us to work more effectively, to influencing how we shop on the high street and online and nudging us to be more generous" [10].

The part of behavioural science is behavioural economics, which includes behavioural finance. And although behavioural economists still have to fight the rationality-versus-irrationality-of human-behaviour battle, as indicated by Rosalsky [21], today it is perceived as a well-established field providing knowledge on the real behaviour of entities (market participants in the economy) and the conditions of their economic decisions, which translates into the functioning of aggregated markets. According to Thaler [40], behavioural economists ask questions mostly about the way people make economic choices/judgments or the way particular financial systems (retirement plans, tax codes, etc.) affect those responses.

D. Miłaszewicz (✉)
Department of Economics, Faculty of Economics and Management, Institute of Economy, University of Szczecin, Mickiewicza 64, 71-101 Szczecin, Poland
e-mail: dmilaszi@wneiz.p

W. Tarczyński and K. Nermend (eds.), *Effective Investments on Capital Markets*, Springer Proceedings in Business and Economics,
https://doi.org/10.1007/978-3-030-21274-2_25

Various authors find the origin of the behavioural economics yet in *The theory of moral sentiments* by A. Smith, but primarily in the works of further authors who criticized the assumptions about the instrumental rationality of entities and effective market operation adopted in traditional (neoclassical) economics. However, great development of so-called new behavioural economics has started after Kahneman and Tverski [12] have published an article on their alternative descriptive model called prospect theory and criticized the expected utility model of decision under risk and uncertainty. Initially, this theory was referred to behaviour of investors on the capital market and finding made by W. F. M. De Bondt and R. Thalera that people systematically overreacting to unexpected and dramatic news events results in substantial weak-form inefficiencies in the stock market [4] that today, besides A. Tversky and D. Kahneman and also R. Thaler, is considered to be among the founding fathers of behavioural finance concept [9].

The article by Shiller [25], where he demonstrated that stock prices fluctuate too much to be justified by a rational theory of stock valuation [7, 26] is also considered to be a beginning of a discussion about behavioural finance.

Since then, more and more researchers in the fields of finance and psychology attempted to make a joint analysis of financial behaviours by stock exchange investors and this market anomaly, because initially, studies carried out since the early 1980s of the twentieth century focused mainly on these issues.[1] In this spirit, behavioural finance is defined as those which deals with the influence of psychology on the behaviour of financial practitioners and its subsequent impact on stock markets [22].

It considers how various psychological traits affect individual or group acts as investors, analysts and portfolio managers and tries to understand how emotions and cognitive errors influence behaviours of individual investors [13]. Behavioural finance also seeks to explain why and how investors can act beyond the boundary of rationality in ways that oppose to what they are supposed to do [1] and assume that, in some circumstances, financial markets are informationally inefficient [20].

Therefore, behavioural finance provides a means for understanding the financial market complex situations. But as indicated by Shefrin [23], behavioural finance is "the study of how psychological phenomena impact financial behaviour". This means that the importance of this relatively new, interdisciplinary approach might be crucial for the profound understanding of the other issues in the financial world.

Behavioural finance is developing constantly, and according to Forbes [6] it is now branched out far from its original founding fathers' intentions. Currently, in the scientific environment the behavioural approach is more and more applied also in other fields of finance, and as stressed out by Kuriakose [14] behavioural finance today is "a fledgling field of enquiry with a wide range of applications in not just financial behaviour, but in decision-making across areas like education, health and political choices".

---

[1] Short history of research and description of studies related to behavioural finances in the period 1896–2009 were presented by Sewell [22]. Presentation of newer research, the results of which were published by 2014, can be found in [7].

The objective of this article is to present the development of behavioural finance within the classification made by Statman [31] into behavioural finance of the first and the second generations. To reach this goal, the review of the reference literature was made and the study was divided into two main parts dedicated to a short description of both generations of behavioural finance.

25.2 Standard Behavioural Finance and the First Generation of Behavioural Finance

Standard finance theory is built upon the rational finance paradigms. According to Statman [28, 30, 32], standard finance fundamental assumptions include:

1. People are rational.
2. People should design portfolios by the rules of mean-variance portfolio theory where people's portfolio wants to include only high expected returns and low risk and do so.
3. Expected returns of investments are described by standard asset pricing theory, where differences in expected returns are determined only by differences in risk.
4. Markets are efficient, in the sense that prices equal values in them and in the sense that they are hard to beat.
5. People save and spend as described by standard life cycle theory, where people find it easy and follow the right way to save and spend.

Defined in such a way a paradigm of the standard (rational) finance is reflected in theories being basic elements on which financial decisions of entities are explained (Table 25.1). Theory of *homo oeconomicus*, i.e. fully rational individuals, properly using available public information, making decisions leading to maximize their own expected usefulness and emotions and other external factors do not have any impact on their choices, specified in the beginning of the table, formed the basis of each of the other theories of rational finances. Most of its creators received the Alfred Nobel awards granted by the Bank of Sweden in the field of economics for contribution to the development of the theory of finance. Initially, theoretical and empirical evidences suggested that rational finance theories aimed at prediction and explanation of some events, but over the time the scientists dealing with economy and finance began to find behaviours that could not be explained by theories available that time. Those theories could indeed explain some model "idealized" events; however, the real world turned out to be very complex.

The concept to be criticized first was *homo oeconomicus,* which in most cases does not reflect human behaviour in the real world, where people act irrationally [21]. Yet not only this assumption but also other theories were considered not realistic. In the classic form, those theories do not correspond to explain decisions and actions by not only individuals but also market reality which rational finance tried to explain using efficient market hypothesis. Besides the *homo oeconomicus*, the other principles of

Table 25.1 The main theories of rational (standard) finance [19, 28]

Year	Author	Theory
1776	Adam Smith	Economic man and *homo oeconomicus*
1844	John Stuart Mill	
1738	Daniel Bernoulli	Expected utility hypothesis
1944	John von Neumann Oscar Morgenstern	
1952	Harry Markowitz	Portfolio theory
1954	Franko Modigliani Richard Brumberg	Life cycle hypothesis
1957	Milton Friedman	Permanent income hypothesis
1958	Franko Modigliani Merton Miller	Capital structure theory
1962, 1964, 1965	Jack Treynor William Sharpe John Lintner	Capital asset pricing model
1966	Jan Mossin	
1972	Ficher Black	
1970	Eugene E. Fama	Efficient market hypothesis
1973	Fisher Black Myron Scholes Robert C. Merton	Option pricing theory

this theory admitted irrationality of a few individuals but indicated that they neutralize each other, act randomly and do not impact the prices of valuables and in case of occurrence of similar irrational activities of greater number of investors the rational participants of the market through arbitrage eliminate their impact on the price level ([5], p. 90). Although the standard finance admitted few irrational activities on the stock exchange, they attribute them to individual investors as individuals of less expertise than professional fund managers [41].

Efficient market hypothesis, one of the most important financial theories, states that at any given moment in time the price of any and all assets and securities being traded is correct and reflects all available public information. This hypothesis also includes the possibility of unlimited arbitrage, i.e. the law of one price, which means that there is only ever one price (regarded as an optimal estimate of true investment value) for an asset at any moment in time [24]. This rational price reflects only utilitarian characteristics (profit and risk), not value expressive characteristics (sentiments) [28].

For empirical finance, this theory turned out to be unrealistic. The conducted research indicated that the participants of the exchange market often behaved unpredictably, which led to occurrence of anomalies (deviations from the rationality of the market), which could not be explained by theories of rational finance.

Recognizing that people can be irrational, make errors when making investment decisions, and that irrationality also applies to the stock market, has led researchers to apply cognitive psychology and gave rise to behavioural finances. Rose under the critique of two assumptions of the standard finance: market effectiveness and rationality of its participants, behavioural finance aimed at explaining the real behaviour of individuals and stock market.

According to Statman [37], the first generation of behavioural finance was starting in the early 1980s. It tried to fill the failures in standard finance largely by accepting its notions of investors' wants as "rational" wants for utilitarian benefits (high returns and low risk), yet describing investors as "irrational", misled by cognitive and emotional errors on the way to realized their rational needs. In one of his works, Thaler [39] defined behavioural finance as an integration of classical economics and financial theories within studies investigating psychology and decision-making. Within these frames, attempts to explain the reasons for irrational behaviour of individuals and to show that they behave rational only within the set limits [8] were taken. According to Olsen [18], behavioural finance tried to understand the complexity of standard finance through psychological decision-making process of market; therefore, some stock market phenomenon can be better understood using such models in which some investors are not fully rational. Lintner [16], in turn, defined behavioural finance as "the study of how humans interpret and act on information to make informed investment decisions".

Shiller [24] pointed out that behavioural finance was taking into account the underlying behavioural principles from psychology and other social sciences. The underlying behavioural principles are: prospect theory, regret and cognitive dissonance, anchoring, mental compartments, overconfidence, over- and under-reaction, representativeness heuristic, the disjunction effect, gambling behaviour and speculation, perceived irrelevance of history, magical thinking, quasimagical thinking, attention anomalies, the availability heuristic, culture and social contagion, and global culture [24].

Behavioural finance initially sought to supplement standard finance theories by introducing psychology to the decision-making process. As noted by Ritter [20], behavioural finance, in its infancy, was not a separate discipline and ought to become increasingly part of mainstream finance. Behavioural finance had two building blocks: cognitive psychology (how people think) and the limits to arbitrage (when markets will be inefficient), and it used models in which some agents are not fully rational, either because of preferences (motivation sphere) or because of mistaken beliefs (cognitive sphere) [20].

25.3 Behavioural Finance Now

Like presented by Zielonka [42], behavioural finance, as the autonomous attempt to describe real behaviours of investors based on theory of perspective, supplemented by a long list of psychological inclinations (both in cognitive and in motivational areas), can in no way be treated as a competition or an alternative to the classical trend of finance. Each of these approaches represents totally different and non-comparable methodological assumptions.

This statement illustrates a tendency to narrow the research field of behavioural finance only to the analysis of the behaviour of stock market investors, as described by Statman [38], accurately reflecting the first generation of behavioural finance, which "attempted to fill the cracks in standard finance largely by accepting its notions of investors as rational, yet describing investors as irrational, and misled by cognitive and emotional errors".

Nowadays, many studies on the behavioural finance also refer to stock market investors and stock market itself, filling in the list of its cognitive errors, heuristics and anomalies.[2] However in these analyses, different assumptions for discussion, forming basic elements of behavioural finance, are made. According to Statman [37], behavioural finance is a work in ceaseless progress. Discussions on the behavioural finance 1.0 (of the first generation) resulted in foundations of many theories (Table 25.2) providing explanations for a wide spectrum of real financial decisions by behavioural finance 2.0 (the second generation).

According to Statman [38], nowadays the second generation of behavioural finance is a solid unified structure that incorporates parts of standard finance, replaces others and includes bridges between theory, evidence and practice. The author emphasizes that behavioural finance 2.0 offers an alternative foundation block for each of the five foundation blocks of standard finance incorporating knowledge about people's wants and their cognitive and emotional shortcuts and errors [37]. According to behavioural finance 2.0 [31, 37, 38]:

1. People are normal.
2. People design portfolios as described by behavioural portfolio theory, where people's portfolio wants extend beyond high expected returns and low risk, such as for social responsibility and social status.
3. People save and spend as described by behavioural life cycle theory, where impediments, such as weak self-control, make it difficult to find and follow the right way to save and spend.
4. Expected returns of investments are described and accounted for by behavioural asset pricing theory, where differences in expected returns are determined by more than difference in risk, such as by levels of social responsibility and social status.
5. Markets are not efficient in the sense that prices equal values in them, but they are efficient in the sense that they are hard to beat.

The second generation of behavioural finance describes people as normal, which means that [30, 31, 33, 37]:

[2] B. Benson divides 200 currently identified cognitive biases into groups, according to four problems they help to solve. These are biases that arise from too much information, not enough meaning, the need to act quickly and the limits of memory [2].

Table 25.2 Basic theories and concepts of behavioural finance [11, 19]: own elaboration)

Year	Author	Theory/concepts
1896	Gustave Le Bon	Cognitive bias theory
1955	Herbert Simon	Models of bounded rationality
1956	Leon Festinger	Theory of cognitive dissonance
1958	Fritz Heider	Self-attribution bias theory
1973, 1974	Daniel Kahneman Amos Tversky	Biases: availability, representativeness, anchoring adjustment
1979	Daniel Kahneman Amos Tversky	Prospect theory and loss aversion bias
1981	Amos Tversky Daniel Kahneman	Framing bias
1985, 1987	Werner F. M. De Bondt Richard Thaler	Stock market overreaction hypothesis
1985	Richard Thaler	Concept of mental accounting bias
1987, 2000	Hersh Shefrin Meir Statman	Behavioural portfolio theory
1988	Dersh Shefrin Richard Thaler	Behavioural life cycle theory
1994	Hersh Shefrin Meir Statman	Behavioural asset pricing model
1998	Nicholas Barberis Andrei Shleifer Robert Vishny	Investor sentiment model
1999	Meir Statman	Concept of three kinds of benefits
2000	Keyth E. Stanovich Richard F. West	Concept of two systems of mind
2011	David Kahneman	
2008	Cass R. Susttein Rihard H. Thaler	Concept of nudge

– Acknowledges that people are not irrational, they are mostly intelligent and usually "normal-smart", they do not go out of your way to be ignorant, and they do not go out of your way to commit cognitive and emotional errors. Instead, they do so on your way to seeking and getting the utilitarian, expressive and emotional benefits (from all products and services, including financial products and services) you want.
– Confers that sometimes, however, they are "normal-foolish", misled by cognitive errors (such as hindsight and overconfidence) and emotional errors (such as exaggerated fear and unrealistic hope).

- Takes into account the full range of people's normal wants (utilitarian, expressive and emotional benefits)[3]—hope for riches and freedom from the fear of poverty, nurturing children and families, staying true to values, gaining respect and high social status, promoting fairness, paying no taxes, playing games and winning and more—and the nature of these benefits and their sources varies from person to person.

Behavioural finance 2.0 distinguishes normal people's wants from errors and offers guidance on using shortcuts and avoiding errors on the way to satisfying normal wants. Exactly, people's normal wants, even more than their cognitive and emotional shortcuts and errors, underlie answers to important questions of finance, including saving and spending, portfolio construction, asset pricing and market efficiency [32].

Just as *homo oeconomicus* was the basis for all other theories of rational finance, the above described the first foundation block of the second generation of behavioural finance is the most important principle for all discussions on behavioural finance 2.0. This is argued by M. Statman in the book titled *Finance For Normal People: How Investors and Markets Behave* [31], dedicating one of two parts to describe *normal people*. He presents so in the articles promoting behavioural finance 2.0 and its main theories [33–36] in each case describing *normal people* in comparison with *homo oeconomicus*.

In his publications, M. Statman presents in a convincing manner how taking into account the characteristics of *normal people* (with their all psychologic inclinations, heuristics, cognitive and motivational errors and a whole range of preferences) can be helpful in making the right financial decisions. According to Statman, these decisions do not refer only to stocks, bonds and all other financial products and services, which differ from other goods and services providing benefits to people utilitarian, expressive and emotional. According to Statman, behavioural finance includes lessons:

- For consumers, savers, investors and managers [32].
- For all people who strive to transform themselves from ignorant to knowledgeable and increase the ratio of smart to foolish behaviour [31].
- For financial planners in understanding normal people and using the findings of the four main theories: behavioural portfolios, behavioural life cycle, behavioural asset pricing and behavioural efficient market theory [38].
- For public policy-makers and governments, who should: create policies protecting people from their own cognitive and emotional errors; nudge, shove and educate them to reconcile internal problems between saving and spending; and redistribute income from the well off to the poor [35].

[3]These kinds of benefits were described in [29, 30].

25.4 Conclusion

Behavioural finance is the part of the finance science dealing with effects of impact of factors (mainly psychological and sociological) that according to rational (standard) finance should not impact the decisions made. Determinants of financial decisions on the stock market and anomalies occurring there were the first area of studies taken by behavioural finance at the beginning of the 1980s of the twentieth century. The first generation of the behavioural finance has largely accepted the standard assumption about the rationality of people while making choices based on the assessment of utilitarian benefits and costs. At the same time, however it indicated that in the process of decision-making due to be a subject of cognitive and emotional errors, they behave irrational.

Thanks to such findings, just at the end of the 1990s of the twentieth century. It was recognized that not every human being (and not in every conditions) makes rational decisions (in the assessment of standard finance), and the theory of the effective markets can lead to drastically wrong interpretation of events [26]. It was also recognized that behavioural finance can explain irrationality of individual behaviours, market anomalies as well as ineffectiveness of the stock market [15]. Studies on behavioural finance 1.0 focused on irrationality of decisions explained by theory of cognitive deviations and prospect theory. Up to now, definitions which narrow issues of behavioural finance only to analysis of stock investors' behaviours—a problem where behavioural approach has already been applied and the results of studies are commonly known—are referred to in the literature on the subject. As indicated by Statman [30], behavioural finance 2.0 expands the domain of finance beyond portfolios, asset pricing and market efficiency and is set to continue that expansion while adhering to the scientific rigour. On the one hand, it does not define people as irrational, but on the other hand it analyses their cognitive errors, emotions and preferences, discovering more and more heuristics which *normal people* use when making broadly understood financial decisions. According to Mousavi [17], the research programme of heuristics and cognitive biases is one of the main sources of psychological insights provided by behavioural economics/finance nowadays.

Although so far studies focus mainly on behaviour of stock investors on the stock exchange, the importance of the obtained results and formulated conclusions makes that currently the behavioural approach is more and more applied in other areas of finance (e.g. issues in banking, corporate finance, private finance, financial crisis). Opportunities that bring interdisciplinary approach to issues of the world of finance are also used in the analysis of the other issues (e.g. various trade transactions, customers' sensitivity to price, consumers' decisions, in discussions about the consumer's bankruptcy, in establishing public policy prescriptions and the role of government which are evident in all decisions of people of investing, saving, spending, health).

As pointed out by Hammond [9] "today, behavioural finance researchers are questioning even the most basic of finance laws" and "behavioural finance has truly reached the level at which it is applicable to everyday professionals, which is a big step for any theory". While Frydman and Camerer [7], in making a perfect review of behavioural finance and associated fields as well as describing a decision-making process in four different areas: households, individual investors, markets and managers emphasize that cognitive science, especially neuroeconomics, in advancing our understanding of financial decision-making will be of great importance in the future.

References

1. Bakara, S., Ng Chui Yia, A.: The impact of psychological factors on investors' decision making in Malaysian stock market: a case of Klang Valley and Pahang. Procedia Econ. Finan. **35**, 319–328 (2016)
2. Benson, B.: Cognitive Bias Cheat Sheet, Simplified. Thinking is Hard Because of 4 Universal Conundrums. Available via https://medium.com/thinking-is-hard/4-conundrums-of-intelligence-2ab78d90740f (2017)
3. Cialdini, R.B.: Introduction. Why the world is turning to behavioral science. In: Samson, A. (ed.) The Behavioral Economics Guide 2018, pp. V–IV. Available via http://www.behavioraleconomics.com (2018)
4. De Bondt, W.F.M., Thaler, R.: Does the stock market overreact? J. Finan. **40**(3), 793–805 (1985)
5. Fama, E.: Efficient capital markets: a review of theory and empirical work. J. Finan. **25**(2), 383–417 (1970). https://doi.org/10.2307/2325486
6. Forbes, W.: Behavioral Finance. Wiley, Chichester, United Kingdom (2009)
7. Frydman, C., Camerer, C.F.: The psychology and neuroscience of financial decision making. Trends Cogn. Sci. **20**(9), 661–675 (2016)
8. Goldberg, J., Von Nitzsch, R.: Behavioural finance. Wiley (1999)
9. Hammond, R.C.: Behavioural Finance: Its History and its Future. Selected Honors Theses. Paper 30. Available via https://firescholars.seu.edu/cgi/viewcontent.cgi?article=1030&context=honors (2015)
10. Hollingworth, C., Barker, L.: How behavioural economics is shaping our lives. In: Samson, A. (ed.) The Behavioral Economics Guide 2017, pp. 19–46. Available via http://www.behavioraleconomics.com (2017)
11. Jurevičienė, D., Ivanova, O.: Behavioural finance: theory and survey. Business in XXI Century **5**(1), 53–58 (2013). https://doi.org/10.3846/Mla.2013.08
12. Kahneman, D., Tversky, A.: Prospect theory: an analysis of decision under risk. Econometrica: J. Econometric Soc. **47**(2), 263–291 (1979)
13. Kengatharan, L., Kengatharan, N.: The influence of behavioral factors in making investment decisions and performance: study on investors of colombo stock exchange, Sri Lanka. Asian J. Finan Account. **6**(1), 1–23 (2014)
14. Kuriakos, F.: Behavioural finance: beginnings and applications. SSRN Electron. J., 30. https://doi.org/10.2139/ssrn.2956364, https://ssrn.com/abstract=2956364 (2017)
15. Levy, H., Post, T.: Investment. Prentice Hall (2005)
16. Lintner, G.: Behavioral finance: why investors make bad decisions. The Planner **13**(1), 7–8 (1998)
17. Mousavi, S.: Gerd Gigerenzer and Vernon Smith: ecological rationality of heuristics in psychology and economics. In: Frantz, R., Chen, S.H., Dopfer, K., Heukelom, F., Mousavi, S. (eds.) Routledge Handbook of Behavioral Economics, pp. 88–100. Taylor & Francis, London (2016)
18. Olsen, R.: Behavioral finance and its implications for stock price volatility. Finan. Anal. J. **54**(2), 10–18 (1998)

19. Prosad, J.M., Kapoor, S., Sengupta, J.: Theory of behavioral finance. In: Copur, Z. (ed.) Handbook of Research on Behavioral Finance and Investment Journal Strategies: Decision Making in the Financial Industry, pp. 1–24, https://doi.org/10.4018/978-1-4666-7484-4.ch001 (2015)
20. Ritter, J.: Behavioral finance. Pac.-Basin Finan. J. **11**(4), 429–437 (2003)
21. Rosalsky, G.: Freeing Econ 101: Beyond the Grasp of the Invisible Hand. Available via http://behavioralscientist.org/freeing-econ-101-beyond-the-grasp-of-the-invisible-hand/ (2018)
22. Sewell, M.: Behavioral Finance. (Revised April). University of Cambridge. http://www.behaviouralfinance.net/behavioural-finance.pdf (2010)
23. Shefrin, H.: A Behavioral Approach to Asset Pricing. Academic Press, Burlington, MA (2005)
24. Shiller, R.J.: Human Behaviour and Efficiency of the Financial System. National Bureau of Economic Research, Working Paper W6375 (1998)
25. Shiller, R.J.: Do stock prices move too much to be justified by subsequent changes in dividends? Am. Econ. Rev. **71**, 421–436 (1981)
26. Shiller, R.J.: From efficient markets theory to behavioral finance. J. Econ. Perspect. **17**, 83–104 (2003). https://doi.org/10.2307/3216841
27. Simon, H.A.: Theories of bounded rationality. In: McGuire, C.B., Radner, R, (ed.) Decision and Organization, pp. 161–173. Nord Holand Publishing Company. Available via http://innovbfa.viabloga.com/files/Herbert_Simon___theories_of_bounded_rationality___1972pdf. Accessed 20 April 2017 (1972)
28. Statman, M.: Behavioral finance: past battles and future engagements. Finan. Anal. J. **55**(6), 18–27 (1999). https://doi.org/10.2469/faj.v55.n6.2311
29. Statman, M.: What Investors Really Want. McGraw Hill, New York (2011)
30. Statman, M.: Behavioral finance: finance with normal people. Borsa Istanbul Rev. **14**, 65–73 (2014)
31. Statman, M.: Finance for Normal People: How Investors and Markets Behave. Oxford University Press. Available at SSRN: https://ssrn.com/abstract=2963183 (2017a)
32. Statman, M: Behavioral Finance: Finance for Normal People. Investments & Wealth Monitor, pp. 15–19. Available via https://investmentsandwealth.org/getmedia/5f38f0ea-6129-4bc7-90bf-d1cb25424a58/IWM17MayJun-FinanceForNormalPeople.pdf (2017b)
33. Statman, M.: Financial advertising in the second generation of behavioral finance. J. Behav. Finan. **18**(4), 470–477 (2017c)
34. Statman, M.: Behavioral asset pricing: asset pricing for normal people. J. Portfolio Manag. **44**(1), 5–9 (2017d). https://doi.org/10.3905/jpm.2017.44.1.005
35. Statman, M.: Standard and behavioral life-cycle theories and public policy. J. Retirement **5**(2), 12–25 (2017e). https://doi.org/10.3905/jor.2017.5.2.012
36. Statman, M.: Behavioral Portfolios: Portfolios for Normal Peoples, pp. 43–47. Investments & Wealth Monitor (2017f)
37. Statman, M: Behavioral finance moves into its second generation. J. Finan. Planning, 30–32 (2018a)
38. Statman, M.: A unified behavioral finance. J. Portfolio Manag. **44**(7), 124–134 (2018b). https://doi.org/10.3905/jpm.2018.44.7.124
39. Thaler, R.H.: The end of behavioural finance. Finan. Anal. J. **55**(6), 12–17 (1999)
40. Thaler, R.H.: Behavioral Economics from Nuts to Nudges. Available via http://review.chicagobooth.edu/behavioral-science/2018/article/behavioral-economics-nuts-nudges (2018)
41. Zielińska, E., Ostrowska, E.: Uwarunkowania behawioralne decyzji inwestycyjnych. Zarządzanie i Finanse **11**(2/4), 489–499 (2013)
42. Zielonka, P.: Czym są finanse behawioralne, czyli krótkie wprowadzenie do psychologii rynków finansowych. Materiały i Studia NBP 158 (2003)

Part IV
Practical Issues-Case Studies

Chapter 26
Liquidity on the Capital Market with Asymmetric Information

Barbara Będowska-Sójka and Przemysław Garsztka

Abstract The effectiveness of the investment is strongly dependent on the liquidity of the shares and the degree of asymmetry of information between the market participants. There is a strong evidence in the literature that stock illiquidity should increase with information asymmetry. An important question is, if different approximations of information asymmetry are consistent in their indications. This study examines the various adverse selection measures including bid–ask spreads calculated on the basis of real transaction data and measures calculated from daily data. We consider stocks listed constantly from 2006 through 2016 on the Warsaw Stock Exchange and calculate the Pearson and the Spearman rank correlations for daily effective spread proxies across the sample. The capitalization and different periods of time are taken into account. We find that various adverse selection measures are characterized by different informational contents, resulting in relatively low coherence of the proxies used in the study.

Keywords High-frequency data · Emerging market · Market microstructure

26.1 Introduction

On the effective capital market, investors try to maximize their earnings or minimize the risk of the portfolio. The result of this activity depends on information. In the perfect capital market, information is delivered at no cost and at the same time for all market participants. In a real world, however, an asymmetry of information might occur: Some investors possess superior or more precise information than others [1]. In the literature, there exists the common division into informed and uninformed investors [5, 18]. Informed traders are said to possess private information. They buy when the prices are below the true and unknown value and sell when the prices are

B. Będowska-Sójka (✉) · P. Garsztka
Poznań University of Economics and Business, al. Niepodległości 10, 61-875 Poznań, Poland
e-mail: barbara.bedowska-sojka@ue.poznan.pl

W. Tarczyński and K. Nermend (eds.), *Effective Investments on Capital Markets*, Springer Proceedings in Business and Economics,
https://doi.org/10.1007/978-3-030-21274-2_26

above it. The other groups, uninformed investors or noise traders, are trading for liquidity reasons and have no informational advantages [14].

In the trading process, the asymmetry of information might occur: Institutional investors are believed to possess superior information over the individual investors [4]. The asymmetric information is less problematic in closed-end funds than for common stocks [19]. The majority of shareholders are said to have an access to wider information than the minority shareholders [9]. The existing asymmetry is one of the main reasons for taking different investment decisions by investors. It is reflected in the differences of portfolio contents [13, 17]. The asymmetry of information often leads to the adverse selection. An investor, who possesses better information, makes an order that is correlated with the expected change of a financial instrument's price, while an uninformed investor is faced with the risk of submitting orders on the already exhausted market. The uninformed investors are reluctant to trade with those who possess additional information, and expect privileges balancing additional risk. Therefore, a natural measure of the adverse selection, and thus the asymmetry of information, is a bid–ask spread [5, 6, 19]. The higher the spread is, the bigger these privileges are [2].

The models for spreads proposed in the literature are aimed to assess the risk of an adverse selection for a given asset [6, 19]. We examine asymmetric information within the transaction cost framework. Glosten and Harris [10] decompose the bid–ask spread into two components, one reflecting the asymmetry of information and the other representing inventory holding costs. They find that the adverse selection component of the bid–ask spread is significant and differs depending on the trade size. Glosten and Milgrom [11] show that a bid–ask spread is a pure informational phenomenon observed even in the absence of other trading costs and that the adverse selection is a main source of the observed bid–ask spreads. Thus, an adverse selection is one of the elements of trading cost that is measured by the price impact of trades and its informational content.

In this paper, we measure the risk of adverse selection with the bid–ask spreads obtained from the tick-by-tick transaction data, LOT [12, 16] and the high–low effective spread estimator [7]. Those measures are obtained for the data of different frequencies, and thus they measure different aspects of informational asymmetry. This asymmetry may differ depending on the stocks' size: Usually, higher asymmetry is found for the small stocks than for the big ones [3, 8]. The asymmetry of information may also change over time—as the market develops and informational requirements are extended, the area for adverse selection should narrow.

The aim of our paper is to examine if different measures (proxies) of spread proposed in the literature are coherent on the Warsaw Stock Exchange (WSE). We study to what extent there exist statistically significant correlations between adverse selection measures and if they differ depending on the size of the company. We also examine if the introduction of the new trading system on the WSE had an impact on correlations between different proxies. Last but not least, we propose two measures of adverse selection based on five best buy and sell offers from the order book.

The rest of the paper is the following: In Sect. 26.2, we present the methodology for the calculation of the spreads' proxies. In Sect. 26.3, the sample is presented. Section 26.4 shows the empirical results. The last section presents the conclusion.

26.2 Methodology

In order to study the coherence in the different spread measures, we examine the Pearson correlations and the Spearman rank correlations. As a proxy for the adverse selection measures, we use three measures of spreads obtained from tick-by-tick data (SPREAD) and two measures based on daily data: LOT measure [16] and high–low effective spread of Corwin and Schulz [7].

The bid–ask spreads are usually calculated as a difference between the best ask and the bid price before each transaction. We consider three different spreads: The formula for SPREAD1 is identical to the one used by the Warsaw Stock Exchange for daily spread measurement and is as follows:

$$\mathrm{SPREAD1}_j = \frac{\sum_{k=1}^{K} \mathrm{VOL}_k \cdot \left|\frac{P_k - P_k^{'}}{P_k^{'}}\right| \cdot c}{\mathrm{VOL}_j} \tag{26.1}$$

where P_k is a price of transaction k, $P_k^{'}$ is a mid-price $P_k^{'} = 0.5\left(P_{\mathrm{BID},k} + P_{\mathrm{ASK},k}\right)$, $P_{\mathrm{BID},k}$ and $P_{\mathrm{ASK},k}$ are bid and ask price respectively, c is a constant equal to 20,000, VOL_k is a number of shares traded in transaction k, K is a number of all transactions within a day j, and VOL_j is a daily volume, $\left(\mathrm{VOL}_j = \sum_{k=1}^{K} \mathrm{VOL}_k\right)$.

The second spread measure, SPREAD2, is the weighted average of the last five best offers, where the weights depend on the volumes of the transactions:

$$\mathrm{SPREAD2}_j = \sum_{k=1}^{K} \frac{S_k \cdot \mathrm{VOL}_k}{\mathrm{DVOL}} \tag{26.2}$$

where $S_k = \sum_{i=1}^{5} \left(P_{\mathrm{ASK}_{i,k}} \cdot \mathrm{VOL}_{\mathrm{ASK}_{i,k}} - P_{\mathrm{BID}_{i,k}} \cdot \mathrm{VOL}_{\mathrm{BID}_{i,k}}\right)$, i denotes the number of offer, and $\mathrm{VOL}_{\mathrm{ASK}_{i,k}}$ and $\mathrm{VOL}_{\mathrm{BID}_{i,k}}$ are volume of ask and bid offers, respectively.

SPREAD3 is a daily average of the temporary spreads based on last five offers:

$$\mathrm{SPREAD3}_j = \frac{1}{K} \sum_{k=1}^{K} S_k \tag{26.3}$$

SPREAD2 and SPREAD3 are our proposal to measure adverse selection risk by taking into account the additional information contained in the order book, namely the best buy and sell offer before the transaction.

There are other spread estimators in the literature. We choose two of them: LOT and effective high–low spread estimator. In LOT estimator [15, 16], it is assumed that stocks' returns follow the market model. Under this condition, the security returns are different from zero only if the latent true return exceeds the cost of trading. The higher are the transaction costs on the firm level, and thus the higher is the adverse selection, the more zero returns will be observed. The latent return R^*_{jt} of a stock j in the LOT estimator approach is given by:

$$R^*_{jt} = \beta_j R_{Mt} + \varepsilon_{jt} \tag{26.4}$$

where R_{Mt} is the market portfolio return in time t, and β_j is the sensitivity of stock j to R_{Mt}, while ε_{jt} is a public shock information on day t, $\varepsilon_{jt} \sim N\left(0, \sigma_j^2\right)$. Assume that $\alpha_{1\mathrm{j}} \leq 0$ is a transaction cost of selling stock j (in percentage), $\alpha_{2j} \geq 0$ is a transaction cost of buying stock j, and the observed return R_{jt} of stock j is expressed as:

$$\begin{aligned}
R_{jt} &= R^*_{jt} - \alpha_{1j} \text{ if } R^*_{jt} < \alpha_{1j} < 0\\
R_{jt} &= 0 \text{ if } \alpha_{1j} < R^*_{jt} < \alpha_{2j}\\
R_{jt} &= R^*_{jt} - \alpha_{2j} \text{ if } R^*_{jt} > \alpha_{2j} > 0
\end{aligned}$$

The difference $\alpha_{2j} - \alpha_{1j}$ is a liquidity threshold for informed investor and as such it constitutes the effective spread estimator LOT [7, 15]. With the above conditions $\alpha_{1j} \leq 0$ and $\alpha_{2\mathrm{j}} \geq 0$, it is always positive. In order to calculate $\alpha_{2j} - \alpha_{1j}$, the following log-likelihood function is maximized:

$$\begin{aligned}
\ln L = &\sum_1 \ln \frac{1}{\sqrt{2\pi\sigma_j^2}} - \sum_1 \frac{1}{2\sigma_j^2}\left(R_{jt} + \alpha_{1j} - \beta_j R_{Mt}\right)^2\\
&+ \sum_2 \ln \frac{1}{\sqrt{2\pi\sigma_j^2}} - \sum_2 \frac{1}{2\sigma_j^2}\left(R_{jt} + \alpha_{2j} - \beta_j R_{Mt}\right)^2 +\\
&+ \sum_0 \ln\left(\Phi_{2j} - \Phi_{1j}\right)
\end{aligned} \tag{26.5}$$

where $\Phi_{\mathrm{i}j}$ is the cumulative normal distribution of $\left(\alpha_{\mathrm{i}j} - \beta_j R_{Mt}\right)/\sigma_j$. Σ_1 represents a region 1, where stock returns are nonzero, whereas market returns are negative, Σ_2 represents the region 2 where nonzero returns are accompanied by positive market portfolio returns, and Σ_0 represents region 0 with zero stock returns [12, 16]. For the calculation of LOT, daily stock and market returns are used.

As a proxy for bid–ask spread, we use also the effective high–low spread estimator of Corwin and Schultz [7], in which calculation is based on the daily high and low prices only. High–low spread estimator (CS) reflects the observation that daily high prices are usually buyer-initiated trades, whereas daily low prices are usually seller-initiated trades. This spread estimator encompasses volatility of a stock (dispersion of prices) as well as the transaction costs of trades, because it shows the cost of reverting position. This spread is calculated using the following formulas:

$$\mathrm{CS}_t = \frac{2(\mathrm{e}^{\alpha} - 1)}{1 + \mathrm{e}^{\alpha}}, \tag{26.6}$$

where H_t is the high price in day t, L_t is the low price in day t,

$$\alpha_t = \frac{\sqrt{2\beta_t} - \sqrt{\beta_t}}{3 - 2\sqrt{2}} - \sqrt{\frac{\gamma_t}{3 - 2\sqrt{2}}}, \quad \beta_t = \left[\ln\left(\frac{H_t}{L_t}\right)\right]^2 + \left[\ln\left(\frac{H_{t+1}}{L_{t+1}}\right)\right]^2,$$

and $\gamma_t = \ln\left[(\max\{H_t, H_{t+1}\})/(\min\{L_t, L_{t+1}\})\right]$.

To calculate effective spread, one requires the high and the low daily prices.

26.3 Sample

Our sample consists of 52 stocks quoted constantly on the Warsaw Stock Exchange since 2000. The relatively long history of listings guarantees that the investors are "familiar" with these stocks and the potential asymmetry between investors is not caused by the fact that the stock is new on the market. The different measures of the adverse selection are obtained from the transaction and daily data starting on 2006-01-02 and ending on 2016-12-30.

The LOT model for adverse selection risk is estimated on the basis of 100 daily observations within the moving windows. The main index on the WSE, WIG, is used as a proxy for the market portfolio. The high–low spread estimator is obtained on the basis of daily data for each day separately. The measures of spreads, SPREAD1, SPREAD2 and SPREAD3, are calculated from the tick-by-tick data collected for each day separately. Thus, we obtain time series of different adverse selection proxies of the length of 2653 observations. The daily data are obtained from database www.stooq.pl, whereas tick-by-tick data are from CAIT, the firm that provides data for brokers (www.ftp1.cait.com.pl/).

We also divide our sample of stocks into three categories depending on the capitalization at the end of 2016: There are big stocks with capitalization over 500 mln euro, medium size with capitalization between 50 and 500 mln euro and small stocks that have capitalization lower than 50 mln euro. Altogether in the sample, we have 15 big, 22 medium and 15 small stocks.

Figure 26.1 shows the range of mean values for adverse selection proxies for all stocks (ALL) and for stocks divided into three size groups (BIG, MEDIUM, SMALL). The lower is the stocks' size measured by capitalization, the higher is the adverse selection risk, and the higher is the range of average proxy values. However, as the ranges of a given measure for different size categories are overlapping, no distinct boundaries between the averages are found. This may be the reason for often

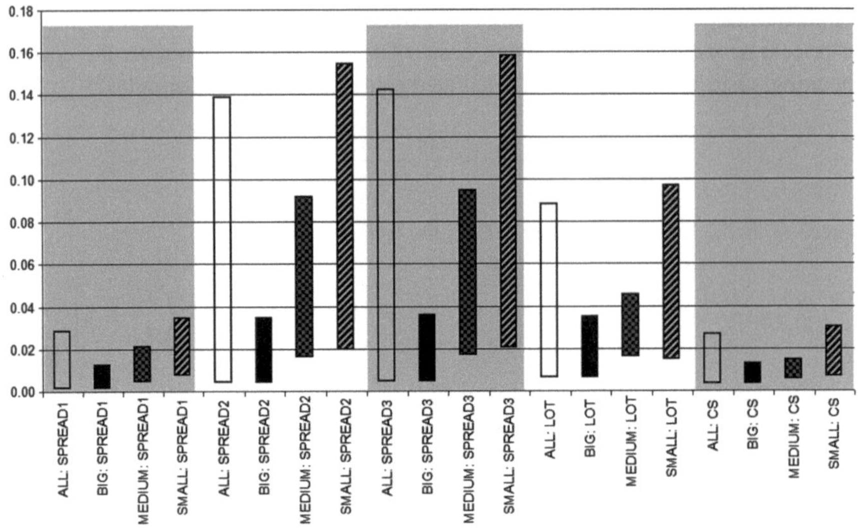

Fig. 26.1 Mean value of measures of illiquidity: value range

ambiguous conclusions from empirical analyses conducted on companies with a different capitalization.

Note: Each column represents the range of values obtained for a given risk measure of negative selection, namely SPREAD1, SPREAD2, SPREAD3, LOT and CS, across three size groups, BIG, MEDIUM and SMALL. The bottom edge corresponds to the smallest value of the measure, and the upper one corresponds to the highest value.

26.4 Empirical Results

In order to examine the interdependencies between the various adverse selection proxies, we calculate Pearson correlation and Spearman rank for all stocks. Table 26.1 presents the descriptive statistics of correlation coefficients.

The highest correlation with the remaining adverse selection measures is observed for SPREAD3. It is very highly correlated with SPREAD2, as the formulas of both proxies are similar, and strongly positively correlated with SPREAD1. The lowest correlations are obtained for the high–low spread of Corwin and Schultz (CS) [7]. It might come from the fact that this proxy encompasses not only liquidity, but also volatility. When LOT and CS are compared, the former obtains significantly higher correlations than the latter. CS seems to show no coherence with the real spreads calculated on the basis of transaction data.

Table 26.1 Mean and standard deviation (in brackets) of Pearson correlation (down-left) and Spearman correlation (upper right): full period, all companies

	SPREAD1	SPREAD2	SPREAD3	LOT	CS
SPREAD1	1	0.68 (0.11)	0.66 (0.12)	0.24 (0.21)	0.08 (0.07)
SPREAD2	0.58 (0.20)	1	0.95 (0.04)	0.39 (0.21)	0.03 (0.10)
SPREAD3	0.59 (0.20)	0.95 (0.04)	1	0.42 (0.20)	0.03 (0.09)
LOT	0.26 (0.19)	0.34 (0.21)	0.35 (0.21)	1	0.01 (0.10)
CS	0.13 (0.10)	0.08 (0.11)	0.09 (0.11)	0.07 (0.11)	1

Note In all tables, we show the average of all coefficients across the sample together with the standard deviation of correlation coefficients (in brackets)

Table 26.2 Percentage of statistically significant Pearson correlation coefficients (down-left) and Spearman correlation (upper right): full period

All stocks	SPREAD1	SPREAD2	SPREAD3	LOT	CS
SPREAD1		100%	100%	92%	75%
SPREAD2	100%		100%	96%	75%
SPREAD3	100%	100%		100%	75%
LOT	96%	98%	100%		54%
CS	90%	67%	71%	73%	

Table 26.2 presents the fraction of statistically significant correlation coefficients for each spread proxy across the sample. In most cases, the correlation coefficients are statistically significant; however, the smallest fraction of significant values is observed for the correlations in which effective spread of Corwin and Schultz (CS) is included. Adverse selection measures based on bid–ask spreads from transaction data as well as LOT estimated on the basis of daily data are statistically significant in almost all instances.

We also calculate correlation coefficients for group of companies divided on the size basis. Table 26.3 presents the coefficients for big stocks, whereas Tables 26.4 and 26.5 present the coefficients for medium and small stocks, respectively. The correlations for stocks divided into size groups are neither statistically significantly different from those obtained for all stocks, nor different from those obtained for other groups. Thus, we conclude that the correlation is not dependent on the stock size.

On April 15, 2013, the Warsaw Stock Exchange introduced a new trading system, Universal Trading Platform (UTP). One of the reasons for launching UTP was to accelerate its transaction system and increase the amount of trading messages. That potentially may have an effect on liquidity of listed stocks and an impact on the asymmetry of information.

In Table 26.6, we present the correlation coefficients across the sample in two subperiods, before and after introducing the new system. We find no significant differences between the correlations in subperiods, reflecting the old system and the new one, and the whole sample. The introduction of the new system could have

Table 26.3 Mean and standard deviation (in brackets) of Pearson correlation (down-left) and Spearman's rank correlation (upper right): full period, big companies

	SPREAD1	SPREAD2	SPREAD3	LOT	CS
SPREAD1	1	0.69 (0.10)	0.64 (0.12)	0.21 (0.24)	0.07 (0.06)
SPREAD2	0.66 (0.18)	1	0.91 (0.05)	0.34 (0.21)	0.04 (0.07)
SPREAD3	0.68 (0.18)	0.94 (0.05)	1	0.40 (0.20)	0.05 (0.06)
LOT	0.29 (0.16)	0.34 (0.17)	0.37 (0.17)	1	0.03 (0.05)
CS	0.13 (0.07)	0.09 (0.07)	0.10 (0.07)	0.05 (0.06)	1

Table 26.4 Mean and standard deviation (in brackets) of Pearson correlation (down-left) and Spearman's rank correlation (upper right): full period, medium companies

	SPREAD1	SPREAD2	SPREAD3	LOT	CS
SPREAD1	1	0.67 (0.09)	0.67 (0.09)	0.22 (0.16)	0.08 (0.05)
SPREAD2	0.54 (0.20)	1	0.95 (0.03)	0.39 (0.18)	0.01 (0.08)
SPREAD3	0.55 (0.20)	0.94 (0.04)	1	0.42 (0.18)	0.02 (0.08)
LOT	0.23 (0.17)	0.31 (0.16)	0.32 (0.17)	1	−0.01 (0.08)
CS	0.12 (0.07)	0.08 (0.08)	0.09 (0.08)	0.07 (0.08)	1

Table 26.5 Mean and standard deviation (in brackets) of Pearson correlation (down-left) and Spearman's rank correlation (upper right): full period, small companies

	SPREAD1	SPREAD2	SPREAD3	LOT	CS
SPREAD1	1	0.72 (0.14)	0.72 (0.14)	0.34 (0.24)	0.08 (0.11)
SPREAD2	0.57 (0.23)	1	0.98 (0.02)	0.48 (0.25)	0.02 (0.15)
SPREAD3	0.58 (0.23)	0.97 (0.03)	1	0.48 (0.25)	0.03 (0.14)
LOT	0.29 (0.25)	0.40 (0.28)	0.40 (0.28)	1	0.01 (0.16)
CS	0.13 (0.16)	0.09 (0.18)	0.10 (0.18)	0.10 (0.18)	1

enhanced liquidity on the market, but it had no impact on the interdependencies between various adverse selection measures.

26.5 Conclusions

We examine the coherence of different spread measures as the proxies for the adverse selection risk calculated on the basis of intraday and daily data. We find that these measures are coherent with each other only partially. The correlations between daily spreads calculated on the basis of the transaction data are high, but become weaker when these spreads are paired with spread estimators calculated on the basis of daily data. The high–low spread of Corwin and Schultz [7] differs from the other measures significantly, showing low correlations not only with bid–ask spreads obtained from

Table 26.6 Mean and standard deviation (in brackets) of Pearson correlation (down-left) and Spearman correlation (upper right): period 2006.01.02–2013.04.15, all companies

2006.01.02–2013.04.15					
	SPREAD1	SPREAD2	SPREAD3	LOT	CS
SPREAD1	1	0.68 (0.11)	0.66 (0.12)	0.22 (0.17)	0.08 (0.06)
SPREAD2	0.59 (0.21)	1	0.94 (0.05)	0.32 (0.20)	0.02 (0.09)
SPREAD3	0.61 (0.21)	0.94 (0.05)	1	0.33 (0.20)	0.03 (0.09)
LOT	0.22 (0.19)	0.28 (0.23)	0.29 (0.23)	1	0.01 (0.09)
CS	0.13 (0.08)	0.07 (0.10)	0.08 (0.10)	0.06 (0.09)	1
2013.04.15–2016.12.30					
SPREAD1	1	0.67 (0.11)	0.68 (0.11)	0.15 (0.23)	0.11 (0.10)
SPREAD2	0.62 (0.19)	1	0.94 (0.04)	0.23 (0.25)	0.05 (0.12)
SPREAD3	0.63 (0.20)	0.95 (0.04)	1	0.24 (0.26)	0.05 (0.12)
LOT	0.17 (0.25)	0.26 (0.28)	0.27 (0.28)	1	0.01 (0.12)
CS	0.14 (0.13)	0.11 (0.14)	0.12 (0.14)	0.04 (0.15)	1

the transaction data, but also with LOT measure derived from daily data. This is a rather surprising result, taking into account that the same measure appeared to be highly correlated with spreads based on tick-by-tick data on the US market [7].

The proposed new measures based on bid–ask spread and calculated on the basis of tick-by-tick data are strongly correlated with the spread used as a standard measure on the WSE. In addition, they have a slightly higher correlation with the other adverse selection proxies.

We do not find the evidence of any change in the dependencies between the spread proxies under two different transaction systems. When one considers two subperiods, reflecting the old trading system and the new one, the coherence of measures remains similar. We find that the dependencies between adverse selection measures do not change significantly in different size groups.

The results suggest that either the market is still in the emerging phase and the proxies used in the study cannot adequately assess the risk under asymmetric information or, less likely, sources of information asymmetry change over time, resulting in rather slow adaptations of the applied measures.

Acknowledgements This work was supported by the National Science Centre in Poland under the Grant No. UMO-2017/25/B/HS4/01546. We are thankful to two anonymous referees, the participants of the 9th *International Conference Economic Challenges in Enlarged Europe*, Tallinn University of Technology, in Tallinn, 2017, and participants of 9th Conference *Rynek Kapitałowy. Skuteczne Inwestowanie* in Międzyzdroje, 2018, for suggestions and comments on the earlier version of the paper. All remaining errors are ours.

References

1. Acharya, V.V., Johnson, T.C.: Insider trading in credit derivatives. J. Financ. Econ. **84**, 110–141 (2007)
2. Acker, D., Stalker, M., Tonks, I.: Bid-ask spreads around earnings announcements. J. Bus. Finan. Account. **29**, 1149–1180 (2002)
3. Amihud, Y.: Illiquidity and stock returns: cross-section and time-series effects. J. Financ. Markets **5**(1), 31–56 (2002)
4. Amihud, Y., Mendelson, H., Pedersen, L.H.: Liquidity and asset pricing. Found. Trends Finan. **1**(4), 269–364 (2005)
5. Bagehot, W.: The only game in town. Financ. Anal. J., 12–22 (1971)
6. Chen, J.-H., Jiang, C.X., Kim, J.-C., McInnish, T.S.: Bid-ask spreads, information asymmetry, and abnormal investor sentiment: evidence from closed-end funds. Rev. Quant. Financ. Acc. **21**, 303–321 (2003)
7. Corwin, S.A., Schultz, P.: A simple way to estimate bid-ask spreads from daily high and low prices. J. Finan. **67**, 719–759 (2012). https://doi.org/10.1111/j.1540-6261.2012.01729.x
8. Degryse, H., de Jong, F., Lefebvre, J.J.G.: Legal insider trading and stock market liquidity. De Economist **164**(1), 83–104 (2016). https://doi.org/10.1007/s10645-015-9261-0
9. Glosten, L.R.: Components of bid-ask spread and the statistical properties of transaction prices. J. Finan. **42**(6), 1293–1307 (1987)
10. Glosten, L.R., Harris, L.E.: Estimating the components of the bid/ask spread. J. Financ. Econ. **21**, 123–142 (1988)
11. Glosten, L.R., Milgrom, P.R.: Bid, ask and transaction prices in a specialist market with heterogeneously informed traders. J. Financ. Econ. **14**, 71–100 (1985)
12. Goyenko, R.Y., Holden, C.W., Trzcinka, C.A.: Do liquidity measures measure liquidity? J. Financ. Econ. **92**, 153–181 (2009). https://doi.org/10.1016/j.jfineco.2008.06.002
13. Kaniel, R., Liu, H.: So what orders do informed traders use? J. Bus. **79**, 1867–1913 (2006)
14. Kyle, A.S.: Continuous auctions and insider trading. Econometrica **53**, 1315–1335 (1985). https://doi.org/10.2307/1913210
15. Lesmond, D.A.: Liquidity of emerging markets. J. Financ. Econ. **77**, 411–452 (2005). https://doi.org/10.1016/j.jfineco.2004.01.005
16. Lesmond, D.A., Ogden, J.P., Trzcinka, C.A.: A new estimate of transaction costs. Rev. Financ. Stud. **12**, 1113–1141 (1999). https://doi.org/10.1093/rfs/12.5.1113
17. Llorente, G., Michaely, R., Saar, G., Wang, J.: Dynamic volume-return relation of individual stocks. Rev. Financ. Stud. **15**(4), 1005–1047 (2002)
18. Madhavan, A.: Market microstructure: a survey. J. Financ. Markets **3**, 205–258 (2000)
19. Neal, R., Wheatley, S.M.: Adverse selection and bid-ask spreads: evidence from closed-end funds. J. Financ. Markets **1**, 121–149 (1998)

Chapter 27
Stock Market Reactions to Dividend Announcements: Evidence from Poland

Bogna Kaźmierska-Jóźwiak

Abstract The paper investigates the market reaction to announcements of dividend changes on the Warsaw Stock Exchange. The research was conducted on a population of non-financial companies paying regular dividends over the period 2014–2016. The sample of dividend announcements (in total 186 observations: 106 dividend increases, 43 dividend decreases and 37 no changes in dividend value) was divided into three subsamples: dividend increases, decreases, and no change. According to the dividend signalling theory, we hypothesize that the market reacts positively to announcements of dividend increases, negatively to dividend decreases, while there is no market reaction to the announcements of stable dividends. Using daily data from the Warsaw Stock Exchange, we implement the event study methodology. As expected, we can observe that the dividend increases are associated with positive abnormal returns and dividend decreases with negative abnormal returns. However, the results are statistically insignificant. Thus, there is no statistically significant relationship between the changes in dividend value and abnormal rates of return on event day and the subsequent days. Therefore, the results of the study do not support the signalling power of dividend changes on the Polish capital market.

Keywords Dividend · Abnormal returns · Signalling theory · Event study

27.1 Introduction

Dividend policy has attracted the interest of researchers all over the world. They have attempted to formulate and testify theories to explain dividend behaviour. One of the key issues of dividend decisions is the dividend signalling effect.

According to the dividend signalling theory, firms can use dividends as a signalling tool to send information to the market in order to close the information gap and signal

B. Kaźmierska-Jóźwiak (✉)
Department of Finance and Corporate Strategy, Faculty of Management, University of Lodz, Łódź, Poland
e-mail: bogna.kazmierska@uni.lodz.pl

W. Tarczyński and K. Nermend (eds.), *Effective Investments on Capital Markets*, Springer Proceedings in Business and Economics,
https://doi.org/10.1007/978-3-030-21274-2_27

future prospects of the firm. The announcement of a dividend increase (decrease) will be taken as good news and the market will increase (decrease) share prices accordingly. Consequently, a dividend increase (decrease) should be followed by an improvement (reduction) in a firm's profitability and earnings.

There is an abundance of empirical evidence [1, 6, 11, 23, 30] which indicates that there is a positive relationship between dividend changes and subsequent share price reaction. This evidence indicates that the announcements of dividend increases (decreases) are associated with positive (negative) abnormal returns, while announcements of stable dividend policy with only normal returns for the shareholders of announcing firms.

The aim of the study is to examine the stock price reaction to dividend changes announced by companies paying regular dividends and listed on the Warsaw Stock Exchange (WSE). According to the dividend signalling theory, we hypothesize that the market reacts positively to the announcements of dividend increases, negatively to dividend decreases, while there is no market reaction to the announcements of stable dividend.

The paper is organized as follows. Section 27.2 reviews the literature. In Sect. 27.3 the data and methodology are described, while Sect. 27.4 presents the results of the research and the discussion. The conclusions and implications for further research are presented in the last section.

27.2 Literature Review

Miller and Modigliani [26] sustained that, in a perfect capital market, dividend policy is irrelevant to either the price of a firm's stock or its cost of capital. Therefore, a firm's value is independent of the dividend policy. Since then, many theories have been developed to explain dividend behaviour when various market imperfections are present. In the late 1970s and early 1980s, signalling theories were developed. These models are based on several assumptions. The most important is the existence of information asymmetry between the firm's top managers (insiders) and outside investors (minority shareholders). Dividends contain information about the future prospects of the firm.

According to the theory, a firm can use dividends as a signalling tool to send information to the market in order to close the information gap. The announcement of a dividend increase will be taken as good news and the market will bid up share prices accordingly. Consequently, a dividend increase (decrease) should be followed by an improvement (reduction) in a firm's profitability, earnings and growth. Moreover, there should be a positive relationship between dividend changes and subsequent share price reaction.

As Al-Malkawi et al. [2] noticed that the empirical studies on dividend signalling have examined two main issues. Firstly, whether share prices move in the same direction with dividend change announcements. Secondly, whether dividend changes could predict a firm's future earnings.

Share price reactions to dividend announcements have been examined in numerous studies during the past decades. Researchers from the USA were the first who empirically tested market reactions to dividend announcements. Pettit [30] who examined 625 companies listed on the NYSE in the period of 1964–1968. He divided the research sample into some categories, depending on the dividend policy changes (e.g. dividend omissions, dividend reductions, no change, initial payment of dividend, etc.). The findings of his study confirmed that dividend increases (decreases) resulted in positive (negative) abnormal returns.

Aharony and Swary [1] investigated a sample of 149 US companies listed on the NYSE, dividing the sample into three subsets: increases in dividends, no change and decreases in dividends. The researchers found statistically significant abnormal reaction on dividend increases and dividend decreases. They noticed that abnormal returns for the decreased dividend groups were of much greater magnitude (in absolute terms) than those of the increased dividend groups. Almost all of the price adjustment occurred within the day of the announcement and the day before. However, the announcements of no changes in dividend policy gave not clear results.

Asquith and Mullins [5] analysed 168 firms initiating dividend payments, either for the first time in the history or after 10-years of break. Their results show positive abnormal returns larger than in any previous research on dividend initiations. It should be noted that the results do not depend on any other events (such as company's earnings announcement). Moreover, the study results confirm that the abnormal return is positively related to the size of the dividend payment. There were also subsequent dividend increases for the same sample of firms examined. The findings imply that subsequent dividend increases may cause a larger positive influence on shareholders' value. The authors suggest that other studies may have underestimated the market's reaction to dividend increases. Asquith and Mullins [5] argue that the results are in line with the view that both dividends initiations and dividend increases do matter as valuable information. Further studies conducted by i.e. Healy and Palepu [19] indicate that firms initiating dividend payments are characterized by the increase in earnings not only before, but also after dividend initiation. On the other hand, firms omitting dividend payments are characterized by a decrease in earnings. Therefore, the authors argue that investors interpret the dividend initiation and omission announcements as the adequate firms' forecasts of the changes in earnings.

Michaely et al. [25] have examined the impact of both initiations and omissions of dividend payments on share prices reaction. They analysed 887 dividend omissions events and 561 cash dividend initiation events announced by NYSE and AMEX companies from 1964 to 1988. They documented that the announcements of dividend omissions are associated with a mean price decrease of about 7%, and the announcements of dividend initiations with a mean price increase of over 3%. The results are in line with prior research on dividend omissions [19] and initiations [5, 19]. The findings of Officer [28] show that firms with high cash flow and low value of Tobin's Q ratio have significantly higher dividend initiation announcement abnormal returns than the other firms initiating dividends. Officer interpreted this evidence as consistent with the agency cost hypothesis. Firms that initiate dividend payments reduce the probability of agency costs occurrence by paying cash out by. This reduction in agency costs is reflected in the dividend initiation announcement returns. Lee and Mauck [22] focused on divided initiations and dividend increases over the period 1963–2013. The results of their study confirmed statistically significant cumulative abnormal return for dividend initiations (dividend increases) of 2.66% (1.82%).

The impact of dividend announcements on the stock markets has also attracted researchers from Europe and other parts of the world, since the signalling power of dividends, however, may not be the same in markets other than USA.

The UK market, one of the most important European capital markets, was evaluated for the first time by Lonie et al. [24]. Their sample consisted of dividend announcements of 620 London Stock Exchange listed companies over the period January to June 1991. The findings confirmed statistically significant cumulative abnormal returns for a two-day period-CAR (−1; 0) of 2.03% for dividend increases and −2.15% for dividend cuts. The UK stock market as well as the French and Portuguese were examined by Vieira and Raposo [35]. The research sample was drawn from dividend announcements of firms listed on the London Stock Exchange (LSE), Euronext Paris (EP) and Euronext Lisbon (EL). For the French and the UK markets, they consider the dividend announcements over the period 1994–2002, and for the Portugal 1988–2002. The results are rather unclear and only partially support the dividend signalling hypothesis. The authors observed a statistically significant positive stock market reaction only to stable and decreasing dividend announcements on the French stock market. There were no price reactions on the UK and Portuguese markets observed.

Gunasekarage and Power [13, 14] and Bozos et al. [7] also carried out research in on the UK stock market. Their results are in line with the findings of Lonie et al. [24].

Amihud and Murgia [3] investigated 255 events of dividend increases and 51 events of dividend decreases announced by companies listed on the German stock market during the period 1988–1992. They found that the stock price reaction to dividend news in Germany is similar to that found in the USA. The results of the study confirmed a statistically significant abnormal cumulative return for the announcement day and the previous day of 0.96% for dividend increases, and −1.73% for dividend decreases. The authors underlined that due to the German accounting rules, which are considered less informative than in the USA, dividends are important in providing information about companies' current earnings.

Further studies conducted by Andres et al. [4] confirmed significant share price reactions after dividend announcements on the German market. The author also found that the price reaction to dividend surprises is related to the ownership structure of the firm.

Gurgul et al. [17] investigated the Austrian stock market reaction to dividend changes in terms of prices and trading volume. The findings show that dividend increases induce a significant positive reaction in stock prices (0.72% for the announcement day), whereas announced dividend decreases lead to a significant fall in stock prices (−1.26%). In the case of constant dividends, the average abnormal returns are not statistically different from zero on any day of the event window.

Capstaff et al. [9] examined the role of dividends in Norway, where the motivation to use dividends as a signalling mechanism appears to be stronger due to the different corporate ownership structure from the USA and the UK. They used data from the period 1993–1998. The results indicate significant abnormal stock returns are associated with announcements of dividend changes. Statistically significant abnormal returns are observed on the announcement day for both the positive (0.76%) and negative (−0.95%) dividend changes announcements. Stable dividend announcements are associated with insignificant negative abnormal returns. The authors conclude that the findings provide minor support for the dividend signalling hypothesis in Norway; however, it does not support the proposition that corporate ownership plays an important role on the use of dividends as a signalling mechanism.

Similar studies which tested the dividend signalling hypothesis were also carried out for other markets, i.e. Travlos et al. [34] analysed the Cyprus market, Harada and Nguyen [18] examined the Japanese market, while Yilmaz and Gulay [36] the Turkish market.

The market reaction of dividend announcements on the Polish stock market have been examined by i.e. Gurgul and Majdosz [16], Gurgul [15], Czerwonka [10], Pieloch-Babiarz [31], Perepeczo [29], Frasyniuk-Pietrzyk and Walczak [12] and Kaźmierska-Jóźwiak [20], Mrzygłód and Nowak [27], Kubiak and Czapiewski [21], Słoński and Zawadzki [32, 33].

Gurgul and Majdosz [16] examined 45 dividend announcements over the period 2000–2004. The results of the study confirmed a positive reaction of the market (+0.79%, p-value of 0.02) on the day following the announcement ($t + 1$). Additionally, the researchers examined the stock price reaction of the company's rivals coming from the same sector of the economy and reveal that industry rivals also experience positive stock price movements on the second day after announcement ($t + 2$).

Perepeczo [29] focused on companies which paid a dividend at least once during the period 1992–2011. The results of the study show that investors react positively to dividend announcements (113 cases).

Słoński and Zawadzki [32] conducted research on the Polish companies listed on the WSE during 2005–2009, which paid out dividends in at least two subsequent years. Changes in the dividend policy were defined in three different ways: change in the dividend per share, change in the dividend yield and change in the dividend payout ratio. The study results indicate that there is no statistically significant relationship between the changes in dividend payouts and the abnormal returns neither in the day of the announcement nor the following day. The authors conclude that the changes in the dividend policy do not secure abnormal rates of return.

Słoński and Zawadzki [33] examined the market reaction to a surprise dividend increase within the period 2006–2010. The findings of the study show that a surprise dividend increase is connected with a positive average abnormal return (2.24%, $p < 0.001$). The shareholders of the firms announcing relatively high increases in a dividend payout earned a 3.2% abnormal return on average.

Frasyniuk-Pietrzyk and Walczak [12] examined the market reaction of dividends announced by companies which paid dividends regularly over the years 2005–2013

(13 firms). The authors observed, contrary to the assumption, that the dividend increase (decrease) announcements produced negative (positive) abnormal returns. The shareholders of firms announcing a dividend decrease earned a statistically significant abnormal return of about 1% ($p < 0.05$), in case of dividend increases −0.4% ($p < 0.1$). The abnormal returns were statistically significant only on the event day.

Kaźmierska-Jóźwiak [20] investigated the market reaction to announcements of dividend initiations. The research was conducted on a population of non-financial companies initiating dividends payments in 2011–2015 (either for the first time or at least after three years break) and listed on the Warsaw Stock Exchange. Using daily data, the researcher investigated the reaction of stock prices of the 67 announcing firms. The shareholders of the firms announcing an initial dividend payment intention earned a statistically significant abnormal return of 0.79% ($p < 0.05$) on the day prior to the announcement ($t - 1$).

Mrzygłów and Nowak [27] examined market reactions to 56 dividend announcements among companies listed on the WSE in the year 2013. The findings are mixed. The market reaction turns out to be statistically significant and positive only on the announcement day and one day after. The average cross abnormal returns are found to be insignificantly different from zero for all ten days around the dividend payment day. Therefore, the researchers concluded that the effect of a dividend announcement is immediately reflected in stock prices. Moreover, the results of the study confirm that the effect of dividend announcements is in line with the informational content of the dividend hypothesis as well as with dividend signalling models [27].

Kubiak and Czapiewski [21] analysed the stock market reaction on the dividend changes of non-financial companies listed on the WSE over the period 1996–2014. In the event study methodology, there were three models used as a benchmark: index model, market model and CAPM model. The findings of the study are not clear. However, in the case of companies which increased the dividend rate, a positive market reaction was observed.

27.3 Data and Methodology

The study focuses on non-financial companies listed on the WSE which were paying dividends regularly within the period 2014–2016. The research sample contains dividend announcements released by above-described 66 firms.

The first step in the event study methodology is to define the event date. In this study, the event date—the dividend information announcement date—is defined as the day of the General Shareholders' Meeting.

All the dividend announcements were divided into subsequent subsets:

- dividend increase,
- no change in dividends
- and dividend decrease.

While we defined dividend increases (decreases) as positive (negative) dividend per cent changes:

$$\frac{\mathrm{Div}_t - \mathrm{Div}_{t-1}}{\mathrm{Div}_{t-1}} \tag{27.1}$$

The research covers 66 companies and 198 dividend announcement (50 dividend decreases, 38 observations of no change in dividends and 117 dividend increases). Table 27.1 presents the number of observations per year.

The results of the study presented in Table 27.1 show that companies regularly paying dividends over the period 2014–2016 have announced 117 dividend increases, 50 dividend decreases and only 38 times no change in dividends.

An important problem at this stage was the companies characterized by low liquidity of quotations. If the shares of the company were not listed for several days, the missing values were supplemented by calculating the proportional increases or decreases in share prices. In a situation where deficiencies concerned 20% of data and included day '0' and 'around-incident' days, a given case was removed from the sample (finally 19 cases were removed). Then, the research sample was checked for possible errors.

The aim of the paper is to analyse the market reaction to dividend changes announcements. One of the most popular methods of calculating abnormal returns is the methodology for calculating abnormal returns based on the work of Brown and Warner [8]:

$$AR_{it} = R_{it} - R_{mt} \tag{27.2}$$

where

AR_{it} abnormal market adjusted returns on stock i at time t,
R_{it} denotes the stock return of company i for day t,
R_{mt} denotes the market return for day t.

Furthermore $i = 1, \ldots, n$; $t = 1, \ldots, T$.

To check the null hypothesis about zero average abnormal returns against the alternative that average abnormal returns are statistically different from zero, a test based on the t-statistic was used:

$$t = \frac{\overline{AR_t}}{\overline{\sigma}}\sqrt{N} \tag{27.3}$$

Table 27.1 Number of dividend announcements (dividend increases, decreases, no changes) per year

	2014	2015	2016	Total
Dividend increases	36	39	42	117
No change	14	15	9	38
Dividend decreases	18	15	17	50

where

$$\hat{\sigma}(AR_t) = \sqrt{\frac{1}{N-1}\sum\nolimits_{i=1}^{N}\left(AR_{it} - \overline{AR_t}\right)^2} \tag{27.4}$$

To run such a test, it is assumed that the rate of returns is independent and the form of their parametric distribution is known. We checked the null hypothesis for all the days within the event window.

The cumulative abnormal returns on *i*-stock in (t_1, t_2) time window were calculated using the following equation:

$$\mathrm{CAR}_i(t_1, t_2) = \sum_{t=t_1}^{t_2} AR_{it} \tag{27.5}$$

After calculating the cumulative abnormal returns over a given time, the average cumulative abnormal returns (ACAR) were calculated as:

$$\mathrm{ACAR}(t_1, t_2) = \frac{1}{N}\sum_{i=1}^{N} \mathrm{CAR}_i(t_1, t_2) \tag{27.6}$$

where
$\mathrm{ACAR}(t_1, t_2)$—cumulative abnormal returns for all the stocks in (t_1, t_2) time window.

The dates of General Shareholders' Meetings are derived from Yearbooks published by the Warsaw Stock Exchange. Daily closing prices are derived from Thomson Reuters and the WSE.

Figure 27.1 presents the average AR's movement around the announcement date for dividend increases, decreases and no changes. On the event day, the average AR's fall can be observed in all three subsamples.

Parametric tests results for the average daily abnormal returns around the dividend announcement day in three subsamples (dividend increases, decreases and no changes) are presented in Table 27.2.

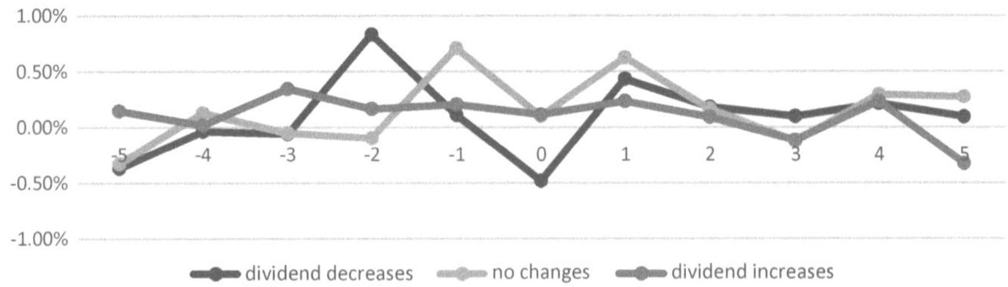

Fig. 27.1 The average daily abnormal returns movement around the announcement date

Table 27.2 Parametric tests results for the average daily abnormal returns around the dividend announcement day in three subsamples

	Dividend increases		No changes in dividend		Dividend decreases	
Event period day	$\overline{AR_t}$ (%)	t_{stat}	$\overline{AR_t}$ (%)	t_{stat}	$\overline{AR_t}$ (%)	t_{stat}
−5	0.10	0.797	−0.33	−1.051	−0.37	−1.396
−4	0.01	0.116	0.13	0.378	−0.03	−0.168
−3	0.30	1.421	−0.05	−0.136	−0.06	−0.241
−2	0.20	0.894	−0.10	−0.539	**0.83***	**2.655**
−1	0.20	1.056	**0.71***	**2.681**	0.11	0.474
0	0.10	0.581	0.10	0.255	−0.48	−1.353
+1	0.20	1.258	0.63	1.580	0.43	1.547
+2	0.10	0.503	0.17	0.528	0.18	0.674
+3	−0.10	−0.705	−0.13	−0.401	0.10	0.460
+4	0.20	1.145	0.29	1.112	0.21	0.798
+5	−0.30	−1.257	0.27	0.934	0.09	0.274
Sample size	106		37		43	

Significance at level: *0.10

As expected, dividend increases are associated with positive abnormal returns and dividends decreases with negative abnormal returns. However, the results are statistically insignificant. The findings of the study show that there is no statistically significant relationship between the changes in dividend value and abnormal rates of return on the subsequent days.

The study finds positive abnormal returns on the day prior to the dividend announcement of 'no change in dividend' (0.71%, $p < 0.1$) and on the second day before the announcement of 'dividend decreases' (0.83%, $p < 0.1$). These results are only statistically significant for the event period (−5; +5) (Table 27.3).

The results of the study confirm that the average cumulative abnormal returns around the 'dividend increase' and 'no change' announcements are statistically significant at the standard level of confidence in most of the (−5; +5) time windows. In the 3-day window, the ACAR (−1; +1) = 0.55% ($p < 0.1$) for increases, 1.4% (p < 0.001)—for no changes.

Widening the event window, the ACAR's increase and reach the statistically significant level, i.e. ACAR (−5; +5) = 1.12% ($p < 0.1$) for increases and ACAR (−5; +5) = 1.7% ($p < 0.05$) for no changes. The ACAR around the "dividend decreases" announcements is statistically significant only in 41-day window, ACAR (−20; + 20) = 3.19% ($p < 0.1$).

Table 27.3 Parametric test results for the cumulative average daily abnormal returns around the dividend announcement day in three subsamples

	Dividend increases		No changes in dividend		Dividend decreases	
Event period day	$ACAR_t$ (%)	t_{stat}	$ACAR_t$ (%)	t_{stat}	$ACAR_t$ (%)	t_{stat}
ACAR (−1; 0)	0.32	1.203	0.8	1.613	−0.37	−0.815
ACAR (0; 1)	0.35	1.355	0.7	1.598	−0.05	−0.104
ACAR (−1; +1)	**0.55***	**1.707**	**1.4*****	**2.803**	0.06	0.111
ACAR (−2; +2)	**0.81****	**2.001**	**1.5****	**2.424**	1.07	1.590
ACAR (−3; +3)	**1.04****	**2.510**	**1.3****	**2.166**	1.11	1.488
ACAR (−4; +4)	**1.29****	**2.497**	**1.8****	**2.309**	1.29	1.569
ACAR (−5; +5)	**1.12***	**1.910**	**1.7****	**2.684**	1.02	1.232
ACAR (−10; +10)	0.14	0.196	0.5	0.469	1.89	1.613
ACAR (−20; +20)	−01.38	−0.892	0.5	0.355	**3.19***	**2.037**
Sample size	106		37		43	

Significance at level: *0.10, **0.05, ***0.01

27.4 Conclusions

The aim of the study was to investigate the market reaction to dividend changes on the Warsaw Stock Exchange. The analysis uses a sample of dividend announcements, divided into three subsamples: dividend increases, decreases and no changes, of firms paying regular dividends over the period 2014–2016.

As expected, we can observe that the dividend increases are associated with positive abnormal returns, dividends decreases with negative abnormal returns. However, the results are statistically insignificant. Therefore, there is no statistically significant relationship between the changes in dividend value and abnormal rates of return on event day and the subsequent days. The results of the previous studies conducted on the Polish market are also not clear [12, 21, 32].

There might be many reasons for such results. Firstly, the way of defining the event day. In this study, the event day is defined as the day of the General Shareholders' Meeting. Taking into consideration the fact that earlier declarations of the management are often imprecise, maybe another event day should be defined. Secondly, the change in dividend policy could be investigated in different ways. Thirdly, the resolutions of the GSM can contain a lot of information. Some of them may cause contradictory reactions. Therefore, the potentiality of the dividend's effect could be abolished. Maybe in the next phase of the research, the sample should be revised to remove the above-described observations.

References

1. Aharony, J., Swary, I.: Quarterly dividend and earnings announcements and stockholders' returns: an empirical analysis. J. Financ. **35**(1), 1–12 (1980)
2. Al-Malkawi, H.A.N., Rafferty, M., Pillai, R.: Dividend policy: a review of theories and empirical evidence. Int. Bull. Bus. Adm. **9**(1), 171–200 (2010)
3. Amihud, Y., Murgia, M.: Dividends, taxes, and signaling: evidence from Germany. J. Financ. **52**(1), 397–408 (1997)
4. Andres, C., Betzer, A., Van den Bongard, I., Haesner, C., Theissen, E.: The information content of dividend surprises: evidence from Germany. J. Bus. Financ. Account. **40**(5–6), 620–645 (2013)
5. Asquith, P., Mullins Jr., D.W.: The impact of initiating dividend payments on shareholders' wealth. J. Bus. **56**(1), 77–96 (1983)
6. Benesh, G.A., Keown, A.J., Pinkerton, J.M.: An examination of market reaction to substantial shifts in dividend policy. J. Financ. Res. **7**(2), 131–142 (1984)
7. Bozos, K., Nikolopoulos, K., Ramgandhi, G.: Dividend signaling under economic adversity: evidence from the London Stock Exchange. Int. Rev. Financ. Anal. **20**(5), 364–374 (2011)
8. Brown, S.J., Warner, J.B.: Using daily stock returns—the case of event studies. J. Financ. Econ. **14**(1), 3–31 (1985)
9. Capstaff, J., Klaeboe, A., Marshall, A.P.: Share price reaction to dividend announcements: empirical evidence on the signaling model from the Oslo stock exchange. Multinatl. Financ. J. **8**(1), 115–139 (2004)
10. Czerwonka, L.: Wpływ zainicjowania wypłaty dywidendy na cenę akcji spółki. Zeszyty Naukowe Uniwersytetu Szczecińskiego. Finanse. Rynki finansowe. Ubezpieczenia **34**, 67–85 (2010)
11. Dhillon, U.S., Johnson, H.: The effect of dividend changes on stock and bond prices. J. Financ. **49**(1), 281–289 (1994)
12. Frasyniuk-Pietrzyk, M., Walczak, M.: Wpływ informacji o wypłacie dywidendy na notowania spółek na GPW w Warszawie w latach 2006–2013. Zeszyty Naukowe Wyższej Szkoły Bankowej we Wrocławiu **7**(45), 119–128 (2014)
13. Gunasekarage, A., Power, D. M.: The post–announcement performance of dividend–changing companies: The dividend–signalling hypothesis revisited. Accounting & Finance. 42(2), 131-151 (2002)
14. Gunasekarage, A., Power, D.M.: Anomalous evidence in dividend announcement effect. Manag. Financ. **32**(3), 209–226 (2006)
15. Gurgul, H.: Analiza zdarzeń na rynkach akcji. Wpływ informacji na ceny papierów wartościowych. Oficyna a Wolters Kluwer business, Warszawa (2012)
16. Gurgul, H., Majdosz, P.: Effect of dividend and repurchase announcements on the Polish Stock Market. Oper. Res. Decis. **1**, 25–39 (2005)
17. Gurgul, H., Mestel, R., Schleicher, C.: Stock market reactions to dividend announcements: empirical evidence from the Austrian stock market. Financ. Mark. Portf. Manag. **17**(3), 332–350 (2003)
18. Harada, K., Nguyen, P.: Dividend change context and signaling efficiency in Japan. Pac.-Basin Financ. J. **13**(5), 504–522 (2005)
19. Healy, P.M., Palepu, K.G.: Earnings information conveyed by dividend initiations and omissions. J. Financ. Econ. **21**(2), 149–175 (1988)

20. Kaźmierska-Jóźwiak, B.: Reakcja rynku kapitałowego na inicjowanie dywidend na rynku polskim. Ekonomika i Organizacja Przedsiębiorstwa **6**, 109–118 (2017)
21. Kubiak, J., Czapiewski, L.: Reakcja inwestorów na zapowiedzi wysokości dywidend spółek notowanych na GPW w Warszawie. Finanse, Rynki Finansowe, Ubezpieczenia **86**, 47–58 (2017)
22. Lee, B.S., Mauck, N.: Dividend initiations, increases and idiosyncratic volatility. J. Corp. Financ. **40**, 47–60 (2016)
23. Lippert, R.L., Nixon, T.D., Pilotte, E.A.: Incentive compensation and the stock price response to dividend increase announcements. Financ. Rev. **35**(4), 69–94 (2000)
24. Lonie, A.A., Abeyratna, G., Power, D.M., Sinclair, C.D.: The stock market reaction to dividend announcements: a UK study of complex market signals. J. Econ. Stud. **23**(1), 32–52 (1996)
25. Michaely, R., Thaler, R.H., Womack, K.L.: Price reaction to dividend initiations and omissions overreaction of drift? J. Financ. **50**(2), 573–608 (1995)
26. Miller, M.H., Modigliani, F.: Dividend policy, growth, and the valuation of shares. J. Bus. **34**(4), 411–433 (1961)
27. Mrzygłód, U., Nowak, S.: Market reactions to dividends announcements and payouts. Empirical evidence from the Warsaw Stock Exchange. Contemp. Econ. **11**(2), 187–204 (2017). https://ssrn.com/abstract=3176998
28. Officer, M.S.: Overinvestment, corporate governance, and dividend initiations. J. Corp. Financ. **17**(3), 710–724 (2011)
29. Perepeczo, A.: Reakcja akcjonariuszy na decyzje o wypłacie dywidendy w spółkach publicznych–wyniki badań empirycznych. Prace Naukowe Uniwersytetu Ekonomicznego we Wrocławiu **323**, 253–264 (2013)
30. Pettit, R.R.: Dividend announcements, security performance, and capital market efficiency. J. Financ. **27**(5), 993–1007 (1972)
31. Pieloch-Babiarz, A.: Reakcja rynku kapitałowego na wypłatę dywidendy inicjalnej w świetle cateringowej teorii dywidendy. Studia Ekonomiczne **263**, 88–102 (2016)
32. Słoński, T., Zawadzki, B.: Analiza reakcji inwestorów na zmianę wielkości wypłacanej dywidendy przez spółki notowane na GPW w Warszawie. Annales Universitatis Mariae Curie-Skłodowska. Sectio H. Oeconomia **46**(1), 125–135 (2012)
33. Słoński, T., Zawadzki, B.: The impact of a surprise dividend increase on a stocks' performance. The analysis of companies listed on the Warsaw Stock Exchange. Oper. Res. Decis. **22**(2), 45–54 (2012)
34. Travlos, N.G., Trigeorgis, L., Vafeas, N.: Shareholder wealth effects of dividend policy changes in an emerging stock market: the case of cyprus. Multinatl. Financ. J. **5**(2), 87–112 (2015). https://ssrn.com/abstract=2627623
35. Vieira, E.S., Raposo, C.C.: Signalling with dividends? The signalling effects of dividend change announcements: new evidence from Europe (2007). Available at http://dx.doi.org/10.2139/ssrn.955768
36. Yilmaz, A.K., Gulay, G.: Dividend policies and price-volume reactions to cash dividends on the stock market: evidence from the Istanbul Stock Exchange. Emerg. Mark. Financ. Trade **42**(4), 19–49 (2006). https://doi.org/10.2753/REE1540-496X420402

Chapter 28
Gold Market and Selected Stock Markets–Granger Causality Analysis

Katarzyna Mamcarz

Abstract The aim of the paper was to examine the bidirectional linkages between gold returns and stock indices returns. Four indices were considered (S&P500, NIKKEI, DAX, WIG). To achieve this goal, the augmented Dickey–Fuller test (ADF), Engle–Granger, and Johansen cointegration tests were applied. On the basis of the vector autoregressive (VAR) model, the Granger causality test was carried out to investigate causality between the analyzed time series. In this context, the following study hypothesis was formulated: Rates of return on stock markets were the Granger cause of the rates of return on the gold market. The research covered the period between January 1, 1997, and March 31, 2018, and two subperiods (bull and bear markets). The comparison of results for alternative VAR models estimated by employing daily and monthly data was presented. Studies for daily data have shown that feedback Granger causality appeared in four cases and the unidirectional causality was identified in eight cases. Referring to monthly data, no evidence of feedback causality was found. The unidirectional causality was present in five cases.

Keywords Stock market · Gold price · Granger causality · VAR models

28.1 Introduction

Investments in gold and stock markets can be considered as two alternative forms of capital investment. Gold is one of the assets displaying low or negative correlation with the stock market and represents an interesting alternative for investments [14]. Especially, breakdowns on stock markets compel investors to return to gold as a safe investment, while an increase in stock prices is reflected in reduced interest in gold among investors. Gold serves as a hedge and safe haven on stock markets [7, 9]. The direction and type of the Granger causality exhibit the relationship between stock and gold markets.

K. Mamcarz (✉)
Maria Curie-Sklodowska University, Plac Marii Curie-Skłodowskiej 5, 20-031 Lublin, Poland
e-mail: katarzyna.mamcarz@poczta.umcs.lublin.pl

W. Tarczyński and K. Nermend (eds.), *Effective Investments on Capital Markets*, Springer Proceedings in Business and Economics,
https://doi.org/10.1007/978-3-030-21274-2_28

The aim of the paper was to examine the bidirectional linkages between gold returns and stock indices returns. Four stock market indices were considered: Standard & Poor's 500 Index (S&P500), Nikkei Stock Average 225 Index (NIKKEI), Deutsche Boerse DAX Index (DAX), Warszawski Indeks Giełdowy (WIG). These are the most popular indices, which are key to investors. The vector autoregressive (VAR) model was used to achieve the said objective. It served as a basis for applying the linear Granger non-causality test [28]. In this context, the following study hypothesis was formulated: Rates of return on stock markets were the Granger cause of the rates of return on the gold market. The study used basic descriptive statistics and descriptive analysis. It covered the period from 1997 (January) to 2018 (March), additionally distinguishing two subperiods on the gold market (bull and bear market). The empirical data were derived from the Web portals, Yahoo Finance [34], WGC [33], and NBP [23].

28.2 Literature Review

An analysis of the dependences between gold and other asset classes initially involved studies of correlation strength and direction. In this respect, three functions were indicated in the literature (Table 28.1).

In the first case, the price of such assets (gold) is not correlated or is negatively correlated; in the second case, it is positively correlated (though it is not a perfect positive correlation); and in the third case, it is not correlated or negatively correlated in the periods of disruptions on markets or oil shocks with other assets [6].

Then, the study focused on an analysis of the causal relations between the variables using vector autoregressive (VAR) models and Granger test. This concerned the relations between various asset classes.

Bayraci et al. [8] applied vector autoregressive (VAR) model of the Turkish financial markets to forecasts ISE100 index, TRY/USD exchange rate, and short-term interest rates. Their research covered the period of June 15, 2006—June 15, 2010. They conducted the linear Granger causality tests to investigate the causal relationship between analyzed variables. The research has shown the existence of bivariate causal relationship between interest rates and foreign exchange rates, one-way causal relationships between interest rates and stock index, and between foreign exchange rates and stock index. No causality was observed from changes in interest rates and foreign exchange rates to changes in the stock index. Le and Chang [21] studied the impact of oil price fluctuations on returns on gold in the period from 1994 (May) to 2011 (April). They observed that in the periods of oil shocks, the oil price displayed a statistically significant correlation with the real rates of return on gold. It is a symmetrical, but nonlinear correlation. Anand and Madhogaria [1] studied the correlation and causality between the stock markets of six countries (the USA, the UK, Germany, Japan, and India) and gold prices in the period from 2002 (January) and 2011 (December). They used the Granger causality test and the vector error correction model (VECM). In developing countries, stocks are a Granger cause of gold

Table 28.1 Functions of gold as a financial asset

Function	Results' review
Hedge	• Gold is a hedge against fluctuations in the foreign exchange value of the dollar (sterling–dollar; yen–dollar). However, the extent to which it played this role was dependent on unpredictable political issues [10] • Gold serves as a full hedge against inflation expressed by headline, expected, and core CPI in the USA and the UK. The ability of gold to do so was on average higher in the USA than in the UK [4] • Gold price expressed in a domestic currency was not a good hedge against inflation in Malaysia for the period from July 2001 to February 2013. Gold did not keep value in relatively short run and was not able to remain the level of its purchasing power throughout the time [16] • Investment in gold was not a hedge against inflation in Poland in a long run [18]
Diversifier	• Investors could consider bullion gold as a crucial component of a diversified portfolio in a short and long run [13] • Gold served as an instrument of portfolio risk reduction due to its negative market beta [29] • Gold gave specific diversification opportunities as its price reacted opposite to stock and bond prices' movements [14] • Gold served as an important portfolio diversifier when combined with stocks but not with bonds [30]
Safe haven	• Gold was considered both as a hedge and a safe haven for main stock markets of European countries (emerging and developing) and USA. This was not the case of Australia, Canada and Japan or BRIC countries [6] • Gold could act as a hedge or a safe haven for stock market, yet its role differed between countries [9] • During some periods of time, gold did not act as a safe haven in comparison with silver, platinum and palladium in USA. Even if gold fulfilled this role, other metals were stronger havens than gold [22] • Gold acted as a safe haven in Chinese stock market during the global financial crisis [2]

Source own elaboration

prices, and in developed countries, the direction of causality is reverse. The analysis covered the period from January 2002 to December 2011.

Krawiec [19] analyzed the relation between changes in the rate of return on global resources' markets (11 resources) and stock markets (2 indices) and the rates of return on eight specialized investment funds in Poland. In most causes, Granger causality was observed in the direction from the rates of return on resources to the rates of return on resources' funds, while it covered only a few cases of the impact of stock indices. Chang et al. [11] analyzed the correlations between changes in gold prices on five global gold markets (London, New York, Japan, Hongkong, and Taiwan) in 2007–2010. They used the augmented VAR model in order to study the correlations between investment strategies on the gold market in Taiwan and other markets. They found a bidirectional causality between the gold market in London and New York and a unidirectional causality between the gold market in New York and other markets. Wang and Chueh [31] studied the short- and long-term relations between interest rates, oil prices, gold prices, and the US dollar exchange rate. They used the threshold cointegration model and the threshold error correction model (TECM). The analysis covered the period between January 2, 1998, and December 20, 2007. They demonstrated that gold and oil prices were positively correlated in a short period. In addition, they found that while interest rates have a negative impact on gold futures quotes, oil prices impact positively on those futures. They also observed the influence of changing interest rates on gold prices. Baur and Tran [5], in studying the relation between the prices of gold and silver in the period 1970–2011 using the error correction model (ECM) and Granger causality test, clearly indicate the impact of gold prices on silver prices and the existence of a long-term correlation. Syczewska [28] studied the causal relations between the USD/PLN exchange rate and two stock indices: WIG20 and S&P500 during the time of the financial crisis (2008–2009) and in a later period, considering the possible shifts in direction and strength of the analyzed correlations in those subperiods. She found stronger causal relations in the period of the financial crisis than in other periods. Zhou and Zhang [35] analyzed casual relations between the following macroeconomic variables: exchange rate, HIBOR, money supply and T-bill rate, and Hong Kong stock market index (HSI) to estimate the likelihood of financial crisis by using vector autoregressive (VAR) and vector error correction models (VCEMs) and Granger causality test. The research covered period from 1987 to 2013. Referring to VAR results, none of the independent variables can Grange cause Hong Kong stock market index (HSI). In case of VECM, changes of HIBOR can Granger cause changes of HIS. Shaique et al. [26] assessed the impact of gold prices on the stock market in Pakistan in the period from October 1993 to May 2014, using the VAR model. They did not find a long-term correlation between Karachi Stock Exchange 100 index and the gold price. For this reason, investors should not treat KSE 100 index and the gold price as alternative markets. Eryiğit [15] analyzed the correlations between the gold price and the variables included in two asset groups, i.e., precious metals (palladium, silver, and platinum) and energy resources (oil and gasoline). In the first case, he used the VAR model to study the short-term relations; in the second, he used the VECM model. He demonstrated that there was a short-term unidirectional relation from gold prices to silver prices and from platinum to gold and silver. A bidirectional relation was found between silver and palladium, while gasoline and oil did not show a long-term relation with gold, but both gold and oil prices showed a long-term relation with gasoline prices. Widz [32] was analyzing Granger causality between return rates/return rates volatility and trading volume of the main Warsaw Stock Exchange (WSE) indices (WIG, WIG20, mWIG40, sWIG80) in the period from 3 October 2001 to 20 January 2016. She indicated the poor correlation between considered variables. The existence of the Granger causality was only observed in direction from stock rates/return rates volatility to trading volume of WIG and mWIG40 indices. Studies by Schweikert [25] conducted for the period 1971–2017 show an asymmetrical relation between silver and gold prices. A stronger reaction of silver prices to changes in gold prices was observed when silver prices were on a relatively high level and a stronger reaction of gold prices to changes in silver prices when gold prices were on a relatively high level. Therefore, long-term relations between the prices of gold and silver depend on the situation in those markets. Aydin and Caliskan Cavdar [3] investigated the causal relationship between different Turkish macroeconomic variables such as gold prices, the exchange rate of USD/TRY, and the Borsa Istanbul (BIST) 100 index by means of two different methods of artificial neural networks (ANNs) and the vector autoregressive (VAR) method. The analysis covered the period of January 2000 and September 2014. According to Authors' findings of the ANN method, there is a possibility of significant fluctuations for the USD/TRY exchange rate and the BIST 100 index except for gold prices. The results which were obtained with the method of VAR are consistent with the results of ANN method. Moreover, their results show that the ANN approach has more superior prediction power than the VAR method.

28.3 Empirical Data and Research Method

The empirical studies involved data on the stock and gold markets for the period from January 1, 1997, to March 31, 2018. The data were collected on the Web portals, Yahoo Finance [34], WGC [33], and NBP [23]. The analysis used daily and monthly prices of indices characteristic of the stock markets in selected countries, i.e., S&P500 (the USA), DAX (Germany), NIKKEI 225 (Japan), WIG (Poland), and gold prices in respective currencies (USD, EUR, JPY, PLN). These data were used to determine the daily and monthly logarithmic rates of return. The number of observations included in the study was 4874, as days with missing data for any of the variables were removed from the sample, and 256 respectively. A study of Granger causal relations was conducted based on the vector autoregressive (VAR) model. An analysis of the correlation coefficient was also included. All calculations were carried out using the GRETL software package.

The first stage of the analysis involved determining the basic descriptive statistics for time series. After that, the variables were expressed as logarithms and their degree of integration was studied using the augmented Dickey–Fuller (ADF) test. Due to the non-stationary nature of variables, differentiation was performed on them (variable increments) to reach a stationary time series. However, estimating a model based on variables in the form of increments would not allow the differentiation of a long-term relation, but would only provide information about how individual variables affect the dependent variable in a short term. In the next step, it was studied whether the model estimated based on first-differenced variables can be supplemented with the error correction model (ECM) to express the long-term relation between the non-stationary variables. Such a model would allow the separation of long- and short-term impacts for cointegrated variables. Cointegration testing was carried out using the Engle–Granger procedure (ADF test for residues) and Johansen's test involving the testing of the null hypothesis assuming that there are no cointegrating vectors (H0: $r = 0$) in the VAR model in relation to the alternative hypothesis, H1: $r \leq 1$. Eventually, the correct VAR model was assumed to be the standard model based on first differences of variables (logarithmic returns, as no cointegration was found [20, 12].

The general VAR model is as follows [24]:

$$Z_t = \sum_{i=1}^{p} A_i Z_{t-i} + \varepsilon_t \tag{28.1}$$

where $Z_t = [Y_t, X_t]$—observation vector of the current process values: Y_t, X_t; A_i—autoregressive operator matrices for individual processes, ε_t—vector of residual processes, p—VAR process rank.

Such a model, in accordance with the adopted assumptions, relates to two processes, i.e., Y_t, defined as a process effect and X_t, defined as a process cause, which cover all of the available information. It is assumed that these processes are stationary in the broader sense, usually non-deterministic. A linear relation between the processes is also indicated and the criterion used for comparing models is the mean square error of residues [24].

The VAR model was the basis for conducting the so-called Granger non-causality test. To this end, the parameters of a two-dimensional VAR(p) model describing the correlations between the analyzed variables, i.e., pairs of returns (index—gold price). The model consisted of two equations:

$$Y_{t=} \sum_{i=1}^{p} \alpha_i X_{t-i} + \sum_{j=1}^{p} \beta_j Y_{t-j} + \varepsilon_{1t} \tag{28.2}$$

$$X_{t=} \sum_{i=1}^{p} \gamma_i X_{t-i} + \sum_{j=1}^{p} \delta_j Y_{t-j} + \varepsilon_{2t} \tag{28.3}$$

where Y_t—logarithmic return on the ith index; X_t—logarithmic return on investments in gold; $\alpha, \beta, \gamma, \delta$—the structural parameters of the model; ε_{it}—random component. The number of lags (p) for the estimated model was selected using the following information criteria: Akaike (AIC), Schwarz (BIC), Hannan-Quinn (HQC).

The Granger test allows to determine whether variable X is a Granger cause Y ($X \to Y$) (Eq. 28.2). Therefore, it was studied whether the current Y values can be predicted with a higher precision on the basis of the future values of the X variable in comparison with the situation where it was not included in the model, unless the remaining information remains unchanged. The opposite relation ($Y \to X$) was also considered (Eq. 28.3) [12].

In the case of Eq. (28.2), the following null hypothesis (H0) was verified: X is not a Granger cause of Y, i.e., $\sum \alpha_i = 0$, in relation to the alternative hypothesis (H1): There is a linear causality from X to Y, i.e., $\sum \alpha_i \neq 0$. A similar procedure was carried out for causality occurring in the opposite direction (from Y to X), testing the significance of parameters next to variable Y_t in Eq. (28.3). Testing the significance of parameters made it possible to determine whether this relation is uni- or bidirectional, or whether it does not occur [17].

For Eq. (28.2), an F-test was performed as follows [17]:

$$F = \frac{(\mathrm{RSS}_R - \mathrm{RSS}_{\mathrm{UR}})/m}{\mathrm{RSS}_{\mathrm{UR}}/(n-k)} \tag{28.4}$$

where: $\mathrm{RSS}_{\mathrm{R}}$—the residual sum of squares for the limited model, i.e., not taking into account the lagged values of variable X_t, but only the lagged values of variable Y_t, potentially other variables in the model, if they are present; $\mathrm{RSS}_{\mathrm{UR}}$—the residual sum of squares of the unlimited model (Eq. 28.2); m—the number of lags of value X_t determined on the basis of the Akaike information criterion (AIC) or Schwarz information criterion (SIC); k—the number of parameters estimated in the unlimited model.

Statistics has F-distribution with m and $(n - k)$ degrees of freedom. The same procedure may be applied to Eq. (28.3) correspondingly. In each case, it is assumed that the variables are stationary.

28.4 Results

28.4.1 Specification of the Study Sample

The analysis of causal relations involved eight time series: four stock market indices (S&P500, NIKKEI, DAX, WIG) and four time series of gold prices expressed in the currencies corresponding to those indices. Table 28.2 shows the properties of the analyzed time series.

Of the analyzed indices, the highest variability was shown by the WIG index and the lowest by NIKKEI. A similar situation occurred for gold prices expressed in the currencies corresponding to the stock markets. All variables were characterized by positive-skew distributions. The largest skew was in the case of the S&P500 index and the lowest in the case of WIG. The highest asymmetry concerned gold prices in EUR and the lowest in JPY. Only the S&P500 index had a leptokurtic distribution, while other variables (indices and gold prices in respective currencies) were characterized by a weak concentration around the mean in comparison to normal distribution (platykurtic distributions).

Logarithmic values were used in further analysis, as logarithms allow the transformation of nonlinear relations into linear and the calculated continuous returns are characterized by a more normal distribution than discrete returns. This satisfies the premise of capital market models [27].

Augmented Dickey–Fuller (ADF) unit root test was used to test the integration of the analyzed data. The AIC was used for determining the lag. Table 28.3 presents the results for daily (Panel A) and monthly (Panel B) data, respectively.

On the basis of the presented unit root test results, it can be assumed that all the analyzed series were non-stationary, as the null hypothesis on the non-stationary nature of the series at a significance level $\alpha = 0.01$ cannot be rejected, while their first differences were already stationary, so the series were characterized by the first

Table 28.2 Descriptive statistics of time series in the period from January 1, 1997, to March 31, 2018

Variable	Mean	Median	Min	Max
S&P500	1402.10	1288.70	676.53	2872.90
NIKKEI	13964.00	14091.00	7055.00	24124.00
DAX	6666.30	6135.40	2203.00	13560.00
WIG	35112.00	38859.00	10474.00	67569.00
PUSD	813.33	687.75	252.85	1895.00
PJPY	83301.00	79705.00	26811.00	156720.00
PEUR	657.84	512.39	236.96	1384.70
PPLN	249.69	243.32	56.32	653.36
Variable	Standard deviation	Coefficient of variation	Skewness	Kurtosis
S&P500	443.15	0.3161	1.0890	0.5432
NIKKEI	3839.80	0.2750	0.1897	−1.0589
DAX	2554.00	0.3831	0.7742	−0.1466
WIG	16248.00	0.4627	0.0509	−1.3741
PUSD	480.59	0.5909	0.3229	−1.3428
PJPY	43096.00	0.5174	0.1541	−1.6176
PEUR	363.49	0.5525	0.3958	−1.4470
PPLN	158.23	0.6337	0.3356	−1.1994

Source Own calculations based on [23, 33, 34]

degree of integration, $I(1)$. This means that the basic condition necessary for the application of the VAR model estimated on the basis of the logarithmic series in the causality analysis, i.e., the stationary nature of variables, is not fulfilled. In further analysis, the application of the first differenced variables was considered and it was determined whether the model should be supplemented by an error correction model.

28.4.2 Analysis of Variable Cointegration

The results of the cointegration analysis according to the Engle–Granger procedure and the Johansen cointegration test for a series of logarithms (index, gold price) in the first degree of integration I(1) are presented in Table 28.4 for daily (Panel A) and monthly (Panel B) data, respectively.

Referring to the Engle–Granger cointegration test, the results of the ADF test ($\alpha = 0.01$) indicate that there is no basis for rejecting the null hypothesis on the non-stationary nature of the residues obtained for the models being linear combinations of specific indices and gold prices estimated on the basis of daily data (Panel A). This means that there is no long-term relation between stock market indices' characteristic

Table 28.3 ADF test results for a series of logarithms in the period from January 1, 1997, to March 31, 2018

Index/price	Variable	First difference
	Tau statistic [*p*-value]	Tau statistic [*p*-value]
Panel A (daily data)		
S&P500	−0.885633 [0.7934]	−31.5609 [1.44×10^{-45}]
NIKKEI	−1.60438 [0.4803]	−51.9119 [0.0001]
DAX	−1.48835 [0.5398]	−33.5047 [4.80×10^{-41}]
WIG	−2.28548 [0.4414]	−15.8756 [1.05×10^{-37}]
PUSD	−0.485179 [0.8918]	−15.9226 [7.71×10^{-38}]
PJPY	−0.55843 [0.8772]	−16.7666 [3.80×10^{-40}]
PEUR	−0.541237 [0.8808]	−14.7891 [1.57×10^{-34}]
PPLN	−1.60268 [0.7924]	−15.536 [9.78×10^{-37}]
Panel B (monthly data)		
S&P500	−0.935012 [0.776]	−14.7082 [3.987×10^{-26}]
NIKKEI	−1.62431 [0.4701]	−14.0586 [3.97×10^{-25}]
DAX	−2.28643 [0.4408]	−14.782 [3.121×10^{-26}]
WIG	−2.46661 [0.345]	−15.2216 [7.939×10^{-27}]
PUSD	−0.3674 [0.9123]	−12.9078 [1.191×10^{-28}]
PJPY	−2.20741 [0.4849]	−19.5516 [3.117×10^{-29}]
PEUR	−1.94176 [0.6323]	−23.5926 [1.402×10^{-25}]
PPLN	−0.832702 [0.8077]	−21.6161 [4.784×10^{-28}]

Source Own calculations based on [23, 33, 34]

of selected stock markets and the gold prices in their corresponding currencies (lack of cointegration). Referring to calculation carried out on monthly basis (Panel B), all residuals were not cointegrated except for model reflecting linear combination between WIG and gold price in PLN (Engle–Granger test). However, it was not confirmed by the Johansen test. Generally, in the case of the Johansen test, both the results of the matrix trace test and the test of the maximum eigenvalue show that there was no basis for rejecting the null hypothesis assuming that there were no cointegrating vectors in the VAR model (H0: $r = 0$).

Due to the determined non-stationary nature of the variables and the zero rank of matrix Π ($r = 0$), the model based on variable increments without the error correction model was assumed as the correct form of the VAR model in the causality analysis.

Table 28.4 Engle–Granger's cointegration test and Johansen cointegration test

Model (stocks' index; gold price)	Engle–Granger test	Johansen test			
	ADF [*p*-value]	Rank *r*	Eigenvalue	Trace Statistic [*p*-value]	Max-Eigen Statistic [*p*-value]
Panel A (daily data)					
S&P500; USD	−1.46006 [0.7783]	0	0.001585	8.6451 [0.7688]	7.7279 [0.5895]
		1	0.000188	0.91719 [0.9465]	0.9172 [0.9459]
NIKKEI; JPY	−1.63269 [0.7086]	0	0.001012	7.7866 [0.8378]	4.9293 [0.8843]
		1	0.000586	2.8573 [0.6151]	2.8573 [0.6139]
DAX; EUR	−2.24828 [0.3989]	0	0.001604	10.827 [0.5663]	7.8159 [0.5792]
		1	0.000618	3.0109 [0.5873]	3.0109 [0.5862]
WIG; PLN	−2.6306 [0.2254]	0	0.002225	13.613 [0.3243]	10.852 [0.2724]
		1	0.000567	2.7610 [0.6327]	2.7610 [0.6315]
Panel B (monthly data)					
S&P500; USD	−1.45266 [0.781]	0	0.037871	11.433 [0.5092]	9.4201 [0.4023]
		1	0.0082151	2.0128 [0.7720]	2.0128 [0.7708]
NIKKEI; JPY	−1.66561 [0.6939]	0	0.028757	10.263 [0.6200]	7.1195 [0.6604]
		1	0.012801	3.1436 [0.5637]	3.1436 [0.5626]
DAX; EUR	−2.29694 [0.3745]	0	0.027163	9.2463 [0.7155]	6.7195 [0.7063]
		1	0.010302	2.5268 [0.6761]	2.5268 [0.6749]
WIG; PLN	−4.18701 [0.004542]	0	0.032262	11.466 [0.5061]	8.0017 [0.5577]
		1	0.014096	3.4640 [0.5088]	3.4640 [0.5078]

Source Own calculations based on [23, 33, 34]

28.4.3 An Analysis of the Causal Relations

The first differences of the output values expressed as logarithms are the logarithmic returns on investment on the stock market (R index) and physical gold (R price). Those variables, as previously demonstrated, are stationary, so there is no spurious correlation present. Table 28.5 shows correlation coefficients between the rates of returns (indices, gold prices), which were the basis for estimating the VAR models based on daily and monthly data.

Table 28.5 demonstrates that there was a weak linear correlation between the rates of return on investments in gold and the rates of return on the WIG and NIKKEI indices and virtually no correlation in the case of gold and other indices: S&P500 and DAX as well as for daily and monthly data. The obtained results were always statistically significant for the former but not for the latter.

Table 28.6 compares Akaike (AIC), Schwarz (BIC), and Hannan-Quinn (HQC) information criteria, which served as a basis for selecting the number of lags for the estimated models based on daily and monthly data, Panel A and Panel B, respectively. The level according to the AIC was selected as the most optimal. Three lags were assumed for three models (1, 2, and 4), and model 3 was an exception with four lags. In the case of models based on monthly data, the number of lags was more discrepant and varied from 1 to 3.

Table 28.7 shows the result of tests of the overall significance of the parameters and the test of the normality of distribution of residues in the whole sample in case of daily and monthly data, Panel A and Panel B, respectively.

Referring to daily data, Granger causality test in the direction from the rates of return on investments in gold to the rates of return on stock indices demonstrated causality only in the case of the NIKKEI index with the standard confidence level $\alpha = 0.01$ and WIG index at the confidence level $\alpha = 0.1$. In the case of monthly data, causality was confirmed for NIKKEI, and additionally, it was identified for DAX.

Granger causality test (daily) in the direction from the rates of return on stock markets to the rates of return on gold indicates that the returns on S&P500 and WIG indices with the confidence level $\alpha = 0.01$; NIKKEI with the confidence level $\alpha = 0.05$ and DAX with the confidence level $\alpha = 0.1$ were the cause of changes on the

Table 28.5 Pearson's correlation coefficients between the analyzed rates of returns

Stock index return	Gold return	Daily data		Monthly data	
		Correlation coefficient	*p*-value	Correlation coefficient	*p*-value
RS&P500	RUSD	−0.03019443	0.0351	0.02064450	0.7428
RNIKKEI	RJPY	0.14050899	0.0000	0.17705986	0.0046
RDAX	REUR	0.05609096	0.0001	−0.00169006	0.9786
RWIG	RPLN	0.18767994	0.0000	0.20717777	0.0009

Source Own calculations based on [23, 33, 34]

Table 28.6 Optimal number of lags for VAR models by information criterion

Model	Number of lags [Information criterion value]		
	AIC	BIC	HQC
Panel A (daily data)			
Model 1 (RS&P, RUSD)	3 [−12.034665*]	1 [−12.021228*]	2 [−12.029768*]
Model 2 (RNIKKEI, RJPY)	3 [−11.516867*]	1 [−11.503104*]	2 [−11.511094*]
Model 3 (RDAX, REUR)	4 [−11.645796*]	1 [−11.635639*]	2 [−11.640869*]
Model 4 (RWIG, RPLN)	3 [−11.112218*]	2 [−11.097423*]	2 [−11.106082*]
Panel B (monthly data)			
Model 1 (RS&P, RUSD)	2 [−6.598228*]	1 [−6.511582*]	1 [6.561942*]
Model 2 (RNIKKEI, RJPY)	2 [−6.147027*]	1 [−6.031910*]	2 [−6.087111*]
Model 3 (RDAX, REUR)	3 [−5.977791*]	1 [−5.884414*]	1 [−5.937604*]
Model 4 (RWIG, RPLN)	1 [−5.242144*]	1 [−5.153005*]	1 [−5.206195*]

Source own elaboration
*optimal number of lags

Table 28.7 Results of the F-test for the overall significance of VAR model parameters and the Doornik-Hansen residual normality test

Model	Null hypothesis	F-test statistics [*p*-value]	Normality test statistics [*p*-value]
Panel A (daily data)			
1	RUSD ↛ RS&P	0.53665 [0.6572]	2888.24 [0.0000]
	RS&P ↛ RUSD	**4.6846 [0.0029]***	2293.61 [0.0000]
2	RJPY ↛ RNIKKEI	**8.5371 [0.0000]***	1878.88 [0.0000]
	RNIKKEI ↛ RJPY	**2.9821 [0.0301]****	1862.32 [0.0000]
3	REUR ↛ RDAX	1.4760 [0.2066]	1814.47 [0.0000]
	RDAX ↛ REUR	**2.1332 [0.0741]*****	2881.46 [0.0000]
4	RPLN ↛ RWIG	**2.5184 [0.0563]*****	2293.61 [0.0000]
	RWIG ↛ RPLN	**6.5327 [0.0002]***	1891.26 [0.0000]
Panel B (monthly data)			
1	RUSD ↛ RS&P	1.9642 [0.1424]	19.931 [4.69932×10^{-5}]
	RS&P ↛ RUSD	0.57304 [0.5646]	21.1062 [2.61124×10^{-5}]
2	RJPY ↛ RNIKKEI	**2.5558 [0.0797]*****	11.5078 [0.00317045]
	RNIKKEI ↛ RJPY	0.034605 [0.9660]	49.6143 [1.68418×10^{-11}]
3	REUR ↛ RDAX	**3.0125 [0.0308]****	27.2301 [1.22198×10^{-6}]
	RDAX ↛ REUR	0,58560 [0,6250]	11.1437 [0.00380352]
4	RPLN ↛ RWIG	1,2914 [0,2569]	45.6703 [1.21012×10^{-10}]
	RWIG ↛ RPLN	0,086535 [0,7689]	37.5419 [7.04495×10^{-9}]

H0 **is rejected for the significance level: *$\alpha = 0.01$; **$\alpha = 0.05$; ***$\alpha = 0.1$**
Source Own calculations based on [23, 33, 34]

gold market. These results were not confirmed by analysis on monthly basis. The distributions of residues are not normal.

To summarize analysis conducted on the daily basis, bidirectional Granger causality throughout the whole analyzed period was found for gold and two indices: NIKKEI and WIG but with various confidence levels. No such bilateral relations were found for indices S&P500 and DAX. However, the causality was unidirectional from the rates of return on investment in gold to these indices at $a = 0.01$ (S&P500) and $a = 0.1$ (DAX). Changes on stock markets influenced the gold market in four cases, while a reverse relation was also found for the NIKKEI and WIG indices. Unidirectional causality from gold to stock indices returns for monthly data was identified only in two cases (Japan, Germany). In other cases, the independence between variables was observed.

The detailed analysis also involved two subperiods determined on the basis of the trend in gold prices expressed in the US dollar. Tables 28.8 and 28.9 present the results of tests of the overall significance of parameters and residual normality test as divided into the bull and bear markets for VAR models estimated on daily and monthly basis, Panel A and Panel B, respectively.

Referring to Panel A during the bull market, Granger causality test in the direction from the rates of return on investments in gold to the rates of return on stock indices demonstrated causality only in the case of the NIKKEI index with the standard confidence level $\alpha = 0.01$ and DAX index at the confidence level $\alpha = 0.05$. The increase in gold prices did not affect the stock market represented by the S&P500 and WIG indices. In the case of Panel B, the Granger causality was not identified for standard levels of significance. However, after extending the level of significance, say up to 0.2, the gold market could affect the Japanese and German stock market.

Granger causality test in the direction from the rates of return on stock markets to the rates of return on gold indicated that the returns on NIKKEI indices with the confidence level $\alpha = 0.01$ and S&P500 and WIG with the confidence level $\alpha = 0.05$ were the cause of changes on the gold market. As for the changes in rates of return on stock markets represented by the DAX index, they did not affect the gold market. In comparison if we consider results presented in Panel B, changes in the stock market (DAX) were only the Granger cause for gold market in Germany at standard significance level $\alpha = 0.1$. In other cases, the results were not confirmed.

During the bull market, bidirectional causality only occurred for the NIKKEI index and gold price. Changes on stock markets influenced the gold market in three cases for daily data (S&P500, NIKKEI, WIG) while a reverse relation was also found

Table 28.8 Results of the F-test for the overall significance of VAR model parameters during the bull markets in gold and the Doornik-Hansen residual normality test

Model	Null hypothesis	F-test statistics [p-value]	Normality test statistics [p-value]
Panel A (daily data)			
1	RUSD ↛ RS&P	1.0698 [0.3606]	1723.68 [0.0000]
	RS&P ↛ RUSD	**2.9830 [0.0301]****	1328.93 [2.67061 × 10^{-289}]
2	RJPY ↛ RNIKKEI	**8.4999 [0.0000]***	1378.29 [5.10507 × 10^{-300}]
	RNIKKEI ↛ RJPY	**4.5527 [0.0035]***	829.805 [6.45692 × 10^{-181}]
3	REUR ↛ RDAX	**2.8320 [0.0233]****	1179 [9.62298 × 10^{-257}]
	RDAX ↛ REUR	1.3975 [0.2322]	1651.54 [0.0000]
4	RPLN ↛ RWIG	1.5358 [0.2031]	1025.93 [1.668 × 10^{-223}]
	RWIG ↛ RPLN	**3.1117 [0.0253]****	800.207 [1.7265 × 10^{-174}]
Panel B (monthly data)			
1	RUSD ↛ RS&P	0.38779 [0.6792]	11.8009 [0.00273817]
	RS&P ↛ RUSD	0.33121 [0.7185]	18.9505 [7.67275 × 10^{-5}]
2	RJPY ↛ RNIKKEI	1.8722 [0.1570]	9.06329 [0.0107629]
	RNIKKEI ↛ RJPY	0.95975 [0.3851]	37.556 [6.99539 × 10^{-9}]
3	REUR ↛ RDAX	1.6627 [0.1770]	13.6856 [0.00106709]
	RDAX ↛ REUR	**2.2320 [0.0864]*****	6.02834 [0.0490866]
4	RPLN ↛ RWIG	0.53303 [0.4663]	23.8534 [6.61137 × 10^{-6}]
	RWIG ↛ RPLN	0.12533 [0.7238]	37.6426 [6.69913 × 10^{-9}]

I(1); **H0 is rejected for the significance level: *α = 0.01; **α = 0.05; ***α = 0.1**
Source Own calculations based on [23, 33, 34]

for the NIKKEI and DAX indices. The impact of DAX on gold returns was observed in case of monthly data. The distributions of residues are not normal.

While analyzing Table 28.9, Panel A during the bear market, Granger causality test in the direction from the rates of return on investments in gold to the rates of return on stock indices demonstrated causality only in the case of the WIG index with the standard confidence level $\alpha = 0.05$. It was also confirmed for monthly data after extending the level of significance to 0.2. This type of relationship was not observed for S&P500 and DAX indices. A decrease in gold prices did not affect the stock market represented by the said two indices. On the contrary, if we take a glance at Panel B results, the unidirectional causality was observed for S&P500 and DAX.

Granger causality test in the direction from the rates of return on stock markets to the rates of return on gold indicates that the returns on WIG with the confidence level $\alpha = 0.01$ and S&P500 with the confidence level $\alpha = 0.05$ were the cause of changes

Table 28.9 Results of the F-test for the overall significance of VAR model parameters during bear markets in gold and the Doornik-Hansen residual normality test

Model	Null hypothesis	F-test statistics [p-value]	Normality test statistics [p-value]
Panel A (daily data)			
1	RUSD $\nrightarrow$ RS&P	1.2001 [0.3084]	272.248 [7.62379 × 10^{-60}]
	RS&P $\nrightarrow$ RUSD	**3.1840 [0.0231]****	853.995 [3.60918 × 10^{-186}]
2	RJPY $\nrightarrow$ RNIKKEI	x	x
	RNIKKEI $\nrightarrow$ RJPY	x	x
3	REUR $\nrightarrow$ RDAX	1.7842 [0.1294]	191.245 [2.96222 × 10^{-42}]
	RDAX $\nrightarrow$ REUR	1.3362 [0.2542]	1240.14 [5.10021 × 10^{-270}]
4	RPLN $\nrightarrow$ RWIG	**2.7087 [0.0439]****	264.338 [3.97849 × 10^{-58}]
	RWIG $\nrightarrow$ RPLN	**7.3018 [0.0001]***	396.371 [8.49361 × 10^{-87}]
Panel B (monthly data)			
1	RUSD $\nrightarrow$ RS&P	**3.1900 [0.0469]****	6.38213 [0.0411279]
	RS&P $\nrightarrow$ RUSD	2.3494 [0.1025]	6.80637 [0.0332671]
2	RJPY $\nrightarrow$ RNIKKEI	x	x
	RNIKKEI $\nrightarrow$ RJPY	x	x
3	REUR $\nrightarrow$ RDAX	**3.3062 [0.0249]****	1.03068 [0.597299]
	RDAX $\nrightarrow$ REUR	1.4658 [0.2311]	15.439 [0.000444079]
4	RPLN $\nrightarrow$ RWIG	2.1505 [0.1466]	3.578 [0.167127]
	RWIG $\nrightarrow$ RPLN	0.010445 [0.9189]	4.84496 [0.0887014]

Legend: x logarithmic series were at various degrees of integration, i.e., JPY I(0), NIKKEI I(1); **H0 is rejected for the significance level: *$\alpha = 0.01$; **$\alpha = 0.05$; ***$\alpha = 0.1$**
Source Own calculations based on [23, 33, 34]

on the gold market for models estimated on daily basis, but it was not supported by the results obtained for monthly data. Referring to daily data for Germany, no causality was observed for gold and the DAX index in any direction yet gold returns influenced DAX if we consider monthly data.

During the bear market, analysis carried out on daily data has shown that bidirectional causality only occurred for the WIG index and gold price. Changes on stock markets influenced the gold market in two cases (S&P500 and WIG), while a reverse relation was found for the WIG index. Unidirectional causality relations from gold to stocks were observed for monthly data only in two cases (USA, Germany). The distributions of residues are not normal with two exceptions indicated for monthly intervals.

The summary of result is presented in Table 28.10.

In most cases, results obtained for daily data were not supported by monthly data analysis.

Table 28.10 Types of causality relations between the analyzed variables

Model	Causality	Whole period (daily/monthly)	The bull market (daily/monthly	The bear market (daily/monthly
1	RUSD → RS&*P*	Not existing/Not existing	Not existing/Not existing	Not existing/Unidirectional
	RS&P → RUSD	Unidirectional/Not existing	Unidirectional/Not existing	Unidirectional/Not existing
2	RJPY → RNIKKEI	Bidirectional/Unidirectional	Bidirectional/Not existing	Not specified/Not specified
	RNIKKEI → RJPY	Bidirectional/Not existing	Bidirectional/Not existing	Not specified/Not specified
3	REUR → RDAX	Not existing/Unidirectional	Unidirectional/Not existing	Not existing/Unidirectional
	RDAX → REUR	Unidirectional/Not existing	Not existing/Unidirectional	Not existing/Not existing
4	RPLN → RWIG	Bidirectional/Not existing	Not existing/Not existing	Bidirectional/Not existing
	RWIG → RPLN	Bidirectional/Not existing	Unidirectional/Not existing	Bidirectional/Not existing

Source Own elaborations based on Tables 28.7, 28.8, 28.9

28.5 Conclusion

Different cases of the Granger causality regarding analyzed variables were observed. They exhibit the relationship between the stock and gold markets. Both uni- and bidirectional causalities were found. For models estimated on daily basis, bidirectional relations were found in four cases: 2 whole period (NIKKEI ↔ gold, WIG ↔ gold), 1 bull market (NIKKEI ↔ gold), 1 bear market (WIG ↔ gold). Unidirectional relation from the index to gold occurred in five cases: 2 whole period (S&P500 → gold, DAX → gold), 2 bull market (S&P500 → gold, WIG → gold), 1 bear market (S&P500 → gold). The study hypothesis on the Granger causality from the rates of return on stock markets to the rates of return on the gold market was confirmed in this scope. Unidirectional relation from gold to the index was found once during the bear market (gold → DAX) and was not found in any of the directions in one case for the bear market (REUR↛RDAX; RDAX↛REUR). For one model, it was impossible to verify the hypothesis due to the variable degree of integration of series of returns in one case during the bear market. Identified directions of causality presented above were not supported by results obtained for monthly data in nine cases. However, we can observe the impact of gold returns on stock returns in four other cases (RS&P—the bull market; RNIKKEI—the whole period; RDAX—the whole period and the bear market) and one in the opposite direction (REUR—the bull market). In the last case, the research hypothesis was positively verified.

References

1. Anand, R., Madhogari, S.: Is gold a 'Safe-Haven'?—an econometric analysis. In: International Conference on Applied Economics (ICOAE) 2012. Procedia Economics and Finance 1, pp 24–33 (2012). https://doi.org/10.1016/S2212-5671(12)00005-6
2. Arouri, M., Lahian, A., Nguyen, D.K.: World gold prices and stock returns in China: insights for hedging and diversification strategies. Econ. Model. **44**, 273–282 (2015). https://doi.org/10.1016/j.econmod.2014.10.030
3. Aydin, A.D., Caliskan Cavdar, S.: Two different points of view through artificial intelligence and vector autoregressive models for ex post and ex ante forecasting. Comput. Intell. Neurosci. 2015 (2015), https://doi.org/10.1155/2015/409361
4. Bampinas, G., Panagiotidis, T.: Are gold and silver a hedge against inflation? A two century perspective. Int. Rev. Finan. Anal. **41**, 267–276 (2015). https://doi.org/10.1016/j.irfa.2015.02.007
5. Baur, D.G., Tran, D.T.: The long-run relationship of gold and silver and the influence of bubbles and financial crises. Empirical Econ. **47**(4), 1525–1541 (2014). https://doi.org/10.1007/s00181-013-0787-1
6. Baur, D.G., Lucey, B.M.: Is gold a hedge or a safe haven? An analysis of stocks, bonds and gold. Financ. Rev. **45**, 217–229 (2010)
7. Baur, D.G., McDermott, T.K.: Is gold a safe haven? International evidence. J. Bank. Financ. **34**(8), 1886–1898 (2010). https://doi.org/10.1016/j.jbankfin.2009.12.008
8. Bayraci S, Ari Y, Yildirim Y (2011): A Vector Auto-Regressive (VAR) Model for the Turkish Financial Markets. https://mpra.ub.uni-muenchen.de/id/eprint/30475 (last accessed 26.10.2018)
9. Beckmann, J., Berger, T., Czudaj, R.: Does Gold Act as a Hedge or a Safe Haven for Stocks? A Smooth Transition Approach. Economic Modelling **48**(8), 16–24 (2015). https://doi.org/10.1016/j.econmod.2014.10.044
10. Capie, F., Mills, T.C., Wood, G.: Gold as a hedge against the dollar. Journal of International Financial Markets, Institutions and Money **15**(4), 343–352 (2005). https://doi.org/10.1016/j.intfin.2004.07.002
11. Changa, C.-L., Della Chang, J.-C., Huang, Y.-W.: Dynamic price integration in the global gold market. North Am. J. Econ. Financ **26**, 227–235 (2013). https://doi.org/10.1016/j.najef.2013.02.002
12. Charemza, W.W., Deadman, D.F.: Nowa ekonometria. PWE, Warszawa (1997)
13. Chua, J., Stick, G., Woodward, R.: Diversifying with gold stocks. Financ. Anal. J. **46**(4), 76–79 (1990)
14. Demidova-Menzel, N., Heidorn, T.: Gold in the investment portfolio. Frankfurt School—Working Paper Series **87**, 3–45 (2007)
15. Eryiğit, M.: Short-term and long-term relationships between gold prices and precious metal (Palladium, Silver and Platinum) and energy (Crude Oil and Gasoline) prices. Econ. Research-Ekonomska Istraživanja **30**(1), 499–510 (2017). https://doi.org/10.1080/1331677X.2017.1305778
16. Ghazali, M.F., Lean, H.H., Bahari, Z.: Is gold a good hedge against inflation? Empirical evidence in Malaysia, Kajian Malaysia 33, Supp. 1, 69–84
17. Gujarati, D.N.: Basic econometrics, 4th edn. McGraw Hill, Boston (2003)
18. Kasprzak-Czelej, A.B.: Inwestycje w złoto jako zabezpieczenie przed inflacją w Polsce. Annales Universitatis Maria Curie - Skłodowska Lublin Polonia, Sectio H (Oeconomia), XLIX (4), 205–2014 (2015), http://dx.doi.org/10.17951/h.2015.49.4.205
19. Krawiec, M.: Testing the granger causality for commodity mutual funds in Poland and commodity prices. Metody Ilościowe w Badaniach Ekonomicznych/Quant. Methods Econ. XIII **2**, 84–95 (2012)
20. Kusideł, E.: Modele wektorowo-autoregresyjne VAR. Metodologia i zastosowanie, Absolwent, Lodz (2000)

21. Le, T.-H., Chang, Y.: Oil price shocks and gold returns. Int. Econ. **131**, 71–104 (2012). https://doi.org/10.1016/S2110-7017(13)60055-4
22. Lucey, B.M., Li, S.: What precious metals act as safe havens and when? Some US evidence. Appl. Econ. Lett. **22**(1), 35–45 (2015). https://doi.org/10.1080/13504851.2014.920471
23. National Bank of Poland (NBP). https://www.nbp.pl/
24. Osińska, M.: Ekonometryczna analiza zależności przyczynowych. Wydawnictwo Naukowe Uniwersytetu Mikołaja Kopernika, Torun (2008)
25. Schweikert, K.: Are gold and silver cointegrated? New evidence from quantile cointegrating regressions. J. Bank. Finance **88**, 44–51 (2018). https://doi.org/10.1016/j.jbankfin.2017.11.010
26. Shaique, M., Aziz, A., Herani, G.M.: Impact of gold prices on stock exchange market: a case of Karachi stock exchange market of Pakistan. Int. J. Acc. Econ. Stud. **4**(1), 60–63 (2016). https://doi.org/10.14419/ijaes.v4i1.5899
27. Steiner, M., Bruns, C.: Wertpapiermanagement. Schäffer Poeschel Verlag, Stuttgart (1996)
28. Syczewska, E.M.: Przyczynowość w sensie Grangera - wybrane metody. Metody Ilościowe w Badaniach Ekonomicznych/Quant. Methods Econ. XV **4**, 169–180 (2014)
29. Tully, E., Lucey, B.M.: A power GARCH examination of the gold market. Res. Int. Bus. Financ **21**(2), 316–325 (2007). https://doi.org/10.1016/j.ribaf.2006.07.001
30. Van Hoang, T.H., Lean, H.H., Wong, W.K.: Is gold good for portfolio diversification? A stochastic dominance analysis of the Paris stock exchange. Int. Rev. Financ. Anal. **42**, 98–108 (2015). https://doi.org/10.1016/j.irfa.2014.11.020
31. Wang, Y.S., Chueh, Y.L.: Dynamic transmission effects between the interest rate, the US dollar, and gold and crude oil prices. Econ. Model. **30**, 792–798 (2013). https://doi.org/10.1016/j.econmod.2012.09.052
32. Widz, E.: Stopy zwrotu indeksów giełdowych na Giełdzie Papierów wartościowych w Warszawie i ich zmienność a wolumen obrotu akcjami – analiza zależności. Finanse, Rynki finansowe, Ubezpieczenia 2/2017 (86), 401–412 (2017)
33. World Gold Council (WGC). https://www.gold.org/
34. Yahoo Finance. https://finance.yahoo.com/
35. Zhou, Y, Zhang, K.: Warning signals of stock market crash during financial crisis: using Hong Kong as an empirical study. Int. J. Bus. Soc. Sci. **5**(9), 134–149 (2014)

Chapter 29
Investment Decision Support on Precious Metal Market with Use of Binary Representation

Krzysztof Piasecki, Michał Dominik Stasiak and Żaneta Staszak

Abstract In this paper, a detailed analysis of HFT systems' properties is performed with use of binary exchange rate representation for precious metals: gold and silver. The binary representation is based on transforming tick data into a binary string. In order to assess the probabilities of changes on the researched exchange market, authors use mentioned binary representation. This paper contains an analysis of the following assessment criteria: expected annual number of transaction, systemic probability of success, expected single unitary payment, expected annual unitary payment, transaction risk assessment, single unitary risk bonus, annual unitary risk bonus, expected return rate, expected interest rate, return risk premium and interest risk premium. The research was performed on five-year historical data for precious metals to dollar exchange rates (XAU/USD and XAG/USD), with use of dedicated Mql4 and C++ software created by the authors.

Keywords Metal market · High-frequency econometric · Technical analysis · Investment decision support

29.1 Introduction

High-frequency trading (HFT) systems are becoming more and more popular due to the development in the information technologies. The exchange rates of nowadays' precious metals became an important financial instrument on the global financial market.

K. Piasecki (✉) · M. D. Stasiak
Poznan University of Economics, Poznań, Poland
e-mail: krzysztof.piasecki@ue.poznan.pl

M. D. Stasiak
e-mail: michal.stasiak@ue.poznan.pl

Ż. Staszak
Poznan University of Technology, Poznań, Poland
e-mail: zaneta.staszak@put.poznan.pl

W. Tarczyński and K. Nermend (eds.), *Effective Investments on Capital Markets*, Springer Proceedings in Business and Economics,
https://doi.org/10.1007/978-3-030-21274-2_29

The main purpose of the following paper is the possibility of using HFT systems on the precious metal market. In order to achieve that, a binary representation was applied in the research [1], to DPT-dedicated transaction systems described in [2] as probabilistic decision models. DPT systems are a special case of HFT systems.

The prediction tables for HFT systems were obtained by the use of the binary representation. Next, we present a description, criteria and evaluation and comparison methods for DPT systems. These formal financial tools were, among others, applied to a DPT system financial effectiveness optimization.

In the research, authors used the quotations of gold and silver expressed in dollar (XAU/USD and XAG/USD), from a five-year time period (from 31 December 2012 to 01 January 2018), obtained from the Dukascopy broker. The analysis of older data is ineffective due to general technological changes applied to the markets and stemming from technological advancement of used tools and equipment.

The paper is organized as follows. Section 29.1 contains an introduction and justification of choosing the topic. Section 29.2 presents the concept of binary course representation, while Sect. 29.3 describes the prediction table. Section 29.4 includes a description of the precious metal market. Section 29.5 presents the DPT transaction system. In Sect. 29.6, we introduce and apply the tools of evaluating DPT systems applied on mentioned metal market. Section 29.7 includes formal financial tools allowing for a comparison of DPT systems used on different markets. Section 29.8 summarizes the obtained results and indicates the direction of future research.

29.2 Binary Representation

The main focus of the following paper will be the precious metal market, represented by exchange pair XPM/QCR and observed in $[0, T]$ time period. XPM denotes the base precious metal, and QCR denotes the quoted currency. In this paper, we will consider the gold market represented by exchange pair XAU/USD and the silver market represented by exchange pair XAG/USD.

In each moment, $t \in [0, T]$, we can note the price Ask $Q_{\text{Ask}}(t)$, which is a price of 1 troy ounce (1 oz) of base precious metal XPM in the quoted currency QCR. Here, the price Ask is shortly called 'course'. This way we can determine a trend $Q_{\text{Ask}} : [0, T] \rightarrow \mathbb{R}$, which describes the dynamics of the exchange pair XPM/QCR.

The usual unit for measuring the change in an exchange rate value is 1 pip $= 0.01$ for the pair XAU/USD and 1 pip $= 0.001$ for the XAG/USD pair.

The changes on the market are characterized by an unitary return, defined as a quotient of a return expressed in QCR by the amount of the base precious metal. The unitary return $\mathcal{ur}(t', t'')$of a BUY transaction opened at t' and closed at $t'' > t'$ equals:

$$\mathcal{ur}(t', t'') = Q_{Ask}(t'') - Q_{Ask}(t'). \tag{29.1}$$

The Ask price of the gold or silver changes, on average, every 1–2 s. Most of these changes result from the white noise of few pips [3–5]. Such a high change frequency causes a need to use a proper HFT system rate trajectory representation.

In the trading system presented further in the paper, each operation opened at $t' \in [0, T]$ will be closed as soon as possible at $t'' > t'$, which fulfils the following condition:

$$|\mathcal{ur}(t', t'')| = \delta > 0, \tag{29.2}$$

where $\delta > 0$ is a given magnitude of unitary return. Therefore, we can encounter only one out of the two following cases:

$$\min\{\tau > t' : \mathcal{ur}(t', \tau) = \delta\} < \min\{\tau > t' : \mathcal{ur}(t', \tau) = -\delta\}, \tag{29.3}$$

$$\min\{\tau > t' : \mathcal{ur}(t', \tau) = -\delta\} > \min\{\tau > t' : \mathcal{ur}(t', \tau) = \delta\}. \tag{29.4}$$

Closing the transaction in case (29.3) means the realization of 'take profit' strategy (TP), as there was an increase of exchange rate by δ. Such course change is a random event denoted by $\mathcal{I}_\delta$. Closing the transaction in the case (29.4) means the implementation of 'stop loss' strategy (SL), as there was a decrease in exchange rate. Such course change is an opposite event to s and it is denoted as $\mathcal{I}_\delta^C$.

Such trading system is compatible with a binary representation of exchange rate quotations [1]. The binary representation of a course trend observed in time period $\mathcal{T}$ consists of transforming these observations into a binary sequence $\mathcal{E}(\delta, \mathcal{T}) = (\varepsilon_i)_{i=1}^n$, in which the ensuing values represent the occurring decreases and increases of the size of a discretization unit equal to assumed magnitude δ of unitary return. The binary representation $\mathcal{E}(\delta, \mathcal{T}) = (\varepsilon_i)_{i=1}^n$ is determined in the following way:

- if the ith change is an increase of the course $\mathcal{I}_\delta$, then $\varepsilon_i = 1$;
- if the ith change is a decrease of the course $\mathcal{I}_\delta^C$, then $\varepsilon_i = 0$.

If the binary representation $\mathcal{E}(\delta, \mathcal{T})$ is assigned to the exchange pair XPM/QCR, then it can be denoted as $\mathcal{E}(\text{XPM/QCR}, \delta, \mathcal{T})$.

This kind of binary representations will be used to describe the trajectory of exchange rate between XAU/USD and XAG/USD from the time period of five years ($\mathcal{T} = 5Y$), (from 31 December 2012 to 01 January 2018), obtained from the Dukascopy broker. An analysis of older data is aimless due to the changes in technology, accessibility to market, etc., which occurred before the stated period and caused major changes in the character of quotations.

29.3 Prediction Tables

The For set time scope m, a given binary representation $\mathcal{E}(\text{XPM/QCR}, \delta, \mathcal{T})$ can be applied for describing XPM/QCR market by means of its states:

$$s_j = (e_1, e_2, \ldots, e_m), \tag{29.5}$$

here:

$$j = \sum_{k=1}^{m} 2^{m-k} e_k + 1. \tag{29.6}$$

is a m-element permutation with repetition from the set $\{0, 1\}$. In this situation, all possible states of XPM/QCR market are given as a state space:

$$\mathbb{E}_m = \{s_j : j = 1, 2, \ldots, k;\ k = 2^m\} \tag{29.7}$$

of all possible historical observations. In this paper, we will use the state space:

$$\mathbb{E}_4 = \left\{ \begin{array}{c} s_1 = (0,0,0,0), s_2 = (0,0,0,1), s_3 = (0,0,1,0), \\ s_4 = (0,0,1,1), s_5 = (0,1,0,0), s_6 = (0,1,0,1), \\ s_7 = (0,1,1,0), s_8 = (0,1,1,1), s_9 = (1,0,0,0), \\ s_{10} = (1,0,0,1), s_{11} = (1,0,1,0), s_{12} = (1,0,1,1), \\ s_{13} = (1,1,0,0), s_{14} = (1,1,0,1), s_{15} = (0,1,1,0), \\ s_{16} = (0,1,1,1) \end{array} \right\}. \tag{29.8}$$

Each moment of opening a transaction is attributed an observed state of metal market. This way we can create a sequence [1]:

$$(\tilde{s}_i)_{i=1}^{n-m+1} = \left((\varepsilon_k)_{k=i}^{i+m-1}\right)_{i=1}^{n-m+1} \tag{29.9}$$

of following observations of market states. Each state s_j is observed exactly $n_j > 0$ times. Thanks to this, for each state s_j we can establish a probability:

$$p(s_j) = \frac{n_j}{n - m + 1} \tag{29.10}$$

of reaching that state by the exchange pair XPM/QCR. After each state s_j, the course increase $\mathcal{I}_\delta$ is observed exactly $n_j^* > 0$ times. In the next step, each state s_j is assigned a conditional probability:

$$p(\mathcal{I}_\delta | s_j) = \frac{n_j^*}{n_j} \tag{29.11}$$

Table 29.1 Prediction table for XAU/USD

State s_j	Number of observations n_j	Probability of the occurrence of state $p(s_j)$	Probability of the increase of a rate $p(\mathcal{I}_\delta \vert s_j)$
s_1	981	0.0521	0.5586
s_2	1171	0.0622	0.5047
s_3	1264	0.0672	0.4968
s_4	1225	0.0651	0.4914
s_5	1284	0.0682	0.5467
s_6	1118	0.0594	0.4991
s_7	1207	0.0641	0.4996
s_8	1162	0.0617	0.4923
s_9	1171	0.0622	0.5320
s_{10}	1318	0.0700	0.4810
s_{11}	1138	0.0605	0.4306
s_{12}	1144	0.0608	0.4895
s_{13}	1205	0.0640	0.5112
s_{14}	1163	0.0618	0.5030
s_{15}	1161	0.0617	0.4823
s_{16}	1106	0.0588	0.4837

Source Own calculations

of course increase $\mathcal{I}_\delta$, due to market pair XPM/QCR reaching the state s_j.

The set of triples $\{(n_j, p(s_j), p(\mathcal{I}_\delta|s_j)) : j = 1, 2, \ldots, k\}$ forms a prediction table allowing to foresee the changes in exchange rate of XPM/QCR pair. Each state s_j is a prediction premise. Total probability $p(\mathcal{I}_\delta)$ of a rate increase can be denoted as

$$p(\mathcal{I}_\delta) = \sum_{j=1}^{m} p(s_j) \cdot p(\mathcal{I}_\delta|s_j). \tag{29.12}$$

Table 29.1 presents a prediction table obtained for the given state space $\mathbb{E}_4$ with use of the binary representation $\mathcal{E}(\text{XAU/USD}, 300, 5Y)$. This table can be further used in order to manage the speculations on XAU/USD market. The method of appointing the discretization unit $\delta = 300$ is described in Sect. 29.5.

Table 29.2 presents a prediction table obtained for the given state space $\mathbb{E}_4$ with use of the binary representation $\mathcal{E}(\text{XAG/USD}, 280, 5Y)$. This table can be further used in order to manage the speculations on XAG/USD market. The method of appointing the discretization unit $\delta = 280$ is described in Sect. 29.5.

Table 29.2 Prediction table of XAUG/USD

State s_j	Number of observations n_j	Probability of the occurrence of state $p(s_j)$	Probability of the increase of a rate $p(\mathcal{I}_\delta \vert s_j)$
s_1	96	0.0648	0.4688
s_2	88	0.0594	0.4205
s_3	101	0.0682	0.5941
s_4	78	0.0527	0.4487
s_5	89	0.0601	0.5730
s_6	117	0.0790	0.5897
s_7	92	0.0621	0.5000
s_8	82	0.0554	0.4146
s_9	88	0.0594	0.4886
s_{10}	91	0.0614	0.4505
s_{11}	117	0.0790	0.5897
s_{12}	95	0.0641	0.4947
s_{13}	90	0.0608	0.4444
s_{14}	84	0.0567	0.4167
s_{15}	82	0.0554	0.4634
s_{16}	80	0.0588	0.5750

Source Own calculations

29.4 A Description of the Metal Market

A metal market is a place where the exchange rate of XPM/QCR is traded. The current value of the exchange rate is noted in two prices: Bid price (further denoted as Q_{Bid}) and Ask price (Q_{Ask}). Ask price is a price of the precious metal XPM equivalent of QCR. Bid price is a selling price that reflects how much of the quoted currency QCR will be obtained by selling one unit of the precious metal XPM. Ask price is not lower than Bid price, which can be showed as:

$$Q_{\text{Ask}} \geq Q_{\text{Bid}}. \tag{29.13}$$

The transactions on the metal market are made by brokers of exchange market and investors. Metal market brokers set their fees based on commission equal to the spread that is to the difference between current Ask and Bid prices. On the metal market of the XPM/QCR pair, an investor can order the broker to BUY or SELL. BUY is executed with the Ask price Q_{Ask} and means buying XPM with QCR. SELL is executed with the Bid price Q_{Bid} and means selling XPM with QCR. Each of the SELL and BUY orders can simultaneously be an 'open' or 'close' order. The amount of the orders is defined by the investor and expressed in standard lot size. On the gold market XAG/USD, the unit of trade is 1 lot = 100 oz AU. On the silver market XAG/USD, it is 1 lot = 1000 oz Ag.

An investor operating on the metal market of XPM/QCR pair wants to achieve a profit caused by an accurate prediction of a change of chosen exchange rate. On the metal market, each transaction is defined by its opening and closing. The only opening or closing orders can be BUY or SELL orders. A broker accepting an opening order is obliged to undertake the closing order. At the moment t' of opening a transaction, the levels of Ask and Bid prices are represented by a pair $\left(Q'_{\mathrm{Ask}}, Q'_{\mathrm{Bid}}\right)$. Opening order is accompanied by determining the value of the spread

$$\overline{\mathrm{spr}} = Q'_{\mathrm{Ask}} - Q'_{\mathrm{Bid}} \geq 0. \tag{29.14}$$

The value of spread $\overline{spr}$ depends on the offer given by the broker. At the moment t'' of closing a transaction, the levels of Ask and Bid prices are represented by a pair of $\left(Q''_{Ask}, Q''_{Bid}\right)$. The transactions concluded on metal market are settled in QCR. Metal market allows two positions: long and short.

If at the opening moment t' investors expect an increase in the value of XPM/QCR pair, then they give a BUY order in Ask price Q'_{Ask} of $\boldsymbol{v}$ value and they go long. Going long means that in a determined time the investors place a SELL order with a Bid Q''_{Bid} price.

If at the opening moment t' the investors expect a decline in XPM/QCR pair, then they place a SELL order with a Bid price Q'_{Bid} of a $\boldsymbol{v}$ value and go short. Taking a short position means that in a determined closing time t'', the investor places a closing BUY transaction with the Ask Q''_{Ask} price.

29.5 Proposed Trading System

Since the market operates 24 h, 5 days a week, placing the orders manually is tiresome and, regarding the short-term transactions, just impossible. In such case, HFT systems are very helpful. HFT is a trading platform program that uses powerful computers to transact a large number of orders at very fast speed and operates with investment strategies.

In most HFT systems, the signals to open or close a particular position are created via the analysis of ratios. A popular trading system places orders when two average lines intersect: short- and long-term average of quotations. The system bases on two decision-making rules:

- If the short-term average of quotations intersects with a higher long-term average, then place a BUY order;
- If the long-term average of quotations intersects with a higher short-term average, then place a SELL order.

Investment decisions made in the most of above-mentioned HFT systems are characterized by a lack of explicitly determined potential payments. This lack makes the investment strategy analysis way more difficult.

Regulated transactional systems which have the prior stated payments are devoid of that disadvantage. For each single transaction conducted by a regulated transactional system, one needs to state in advance what follows:

- The Q_{TP} price which closes the transaction with a profit (TP rule);
- The Q_{SL} price which closes the transaction with a loss (SL rule).

A proposal of a regulated transactional DPT[1], which satisfies the (29.2) condition, is proposed and considered in [2]. For DPT system, the decision-making premise is a prediction table presented in Sect. 29.2.

According to that condition and the profitability criterion $\delta > \overline{\mathrm{spr}}$, the DPT system also satisfies the following condition:

$$\left|Q''_{\mathrm{Ask}} - Q'_{\mathrm{Ask}}\right| = \delta > \overline{\mathrm{spr}} \geq 0. \tag{29.15}$$

Then the decision-making premise is a prediction table presented in Sect. 29.2.

In a general case, the proposed transactional system is dependent on a given threshold $\overline{\mathrm{Thr}} \geq 0.5$ and consists of three following decision rules, used only if the state s_j occurs:

(A) if the following condition is satisfied

$$p\left(\mathcal{I}_\delta | s_j\right) > \overline{\mathrm{Thr}}, \tag{29.16}$$

place a BUY order and go long.

(B) if the following condition is satisfied

$$1 - p\left(\mathcal{I}_\delta | s_j\right) > \overline{\mathrm{Thr}}, \tag{29.17}$$

place a SELL order and go short.

(C) if the transaction was opened with the Ask price C'_{Ask} and a current Ask price C''_{Ask} satisfies condition (29.15), close the opened transaction.

The results of decision rules (A) and (B) are called recommendations.

A DPT system which depends on a multiple use of the above-mentioned set of decision-making rules is a particular case of HFT [6]. In [2], it is shown that the individual payments gained thanks to DPT system for precious metal XPM, depend only on the spread value $\overline{\mathrm{spr}}$ and the assumed magnitude of unitary return δ.

Additionally, opening order depends on exceeding the decision-making threshold $\overline{\mathrm{Thr}}$. To illustrate those facts, a DPT system which initiates—after exceeding the decision-making threshold $\overline{\mathrm{Thr}}$—the transaction with a magnitude of unitary return

[1]From a Discrete Probabilistic Transactional.

Table 29.3 Recommendations given by a trading system DPT(0.525, 300, 15) for the pair XAU/USD

State s_j	Recommendation	Probability of success $\pi(\mathcal{I}_\delta \mid s_j)$
s_1	BUY	0.5586
s_2	–	0.5047
s_3	–	0.5032
s_4	–	0.5086
s_5	BUY	0.5467
s_6	–	0.5009
s_8	–	0.5004
s_8	–	0.5077
s_9	BUY	0.5320
s_{10}	–	0.5190
s_{11}	SELL	0.5694
s_{12}	–	0.5105
s_{13}	–	0.5112
s_{14}	–	0.5030
s_{15}	–	0.5177
s_{16}	–	0.5163

Source Own calculations

δ and bearing the spread $\overline{\text{spr}}$ will be denoted as DPT(Thr, δ, $\overline{\text{spr}}$), where the values δ and $\overline{\text{spr}}$ are given in pips.

Closing order with a positive payment is considered a success. In [2], it is shown that the probability $\pi\left(\mathcal{I}_\delta \mid s_j\right)$ of a successful finish of a transaction, appointed based on observation of a current premise s_j, equals

$$\pi\left(\mathcal{I}_\delta \mid s_j\right) = \max\left\{p\left(\mathcal{I}_\delta \mid s_j\right), 1 - p\left(\mathcal{I}_\delta \mid s_j\right)\right\}. \tag{29.18}$$

The probability $\pi\left(\mathcal{I}_\delta \mid s_j\right)$ is called a 'probability of success'. It enables to assess an expected payment on the entered transaction based on information stated in a given prediction table. For the pair XAU/USD, the distribution of probability of success is given in Table 29.3. For the pair XAG/USD, it is given in Table 29.4.

A positive expected payment is identified with an expected profit. Among other things, any DPT system is characterized by lower probability of success π_{up}, which guarantees that evaluated DPT system will ensure an expected profit. In [2], it is proved that for any DPT$\left(\overline{\text{Thr}}, \delta, \overline{\text{spr}}\right)$, we have:

$$\pi_{\text{up}} = \frac{\delta + \overline{\text{spr}}}{2 \cdot \delta}, \tag{29.19}$$

Obviously, any decision-making threshold $\overline{\text{Thr}}$ should satisfy the following condition

$$\overline{\text{Thr}} \geq \pi_{\text{up}}. \tag{29.20}$$

Table 29.4 Recommendations given by a trading system DPT(0.5179, 280, 10) for the pair XAG/USD

State s_j	Recommendation	Probability of success $\pi(\mathcal{I}_\delta \vert s_j)$
s_1	SELL	0.5312
s_2	SELL	0.5795
s_3	SELL	0.5941
s_4	SELL	0.5513
s_5	BUY	0.5730
s_6	BUY	0.5897
s_7	–	0.5000
s_8	SELL	0.5854
s_9	–	0.5114
s_{10}	SELL	0.5495
s_{11}	BUY	0.5897
s_{12}	–	0.5053
s_{13}	SELL	0.5556
s_{14}	SELL	0.5833
s_{15}	SELL	0.5366
s_{16}	BUY	0.5750

Source Own calculations

For a given decision-making threshold $\overline{\text{Thr}} > 0.5$, a set

$$\mathbb{D}\left(\overline{\text{Thr}}\right) = \left\{s_j : \pi\left(\mathcal{I}_\delta | s_j\right) > \overline{\text{Thr}}\right\} \subset \mathbb{S} \tag{29.21}$$

constitutes a set of all decision-making acceptable premises.

In the further analysis, we will use the value of spreads similar to those offered by one of the most popular IC Markets brokers.

For the pair XAU/USD, the spread is equal to $\overline{\text{spr}} = 15$ pips. Then, for any DPT system $\text{DPT}\left(\overline{\text{Thr}}, 300, 150\right)$, we have a lower success probability $\pi_{\text{up}} = 0.525$. The maximal set $\mathbb{D}(0.525)$ of all accepted premises is distinguished in Table 29.3 (for the pair XAU/USD).

For the pair XAG/USD, the spread is $\overline{\text{spr}} = 10$ pips. Then, for any DPT system $\text{DPT}\left(\overline{\text{Thr}}, 280, 10\right)$, we have a lower probability of success $\pi_{\text{up}} = 0.5179$. The maximal set $\mathbb{D}(0.5179)$ of all accepted premises is distinguished in Table 29.4 (for the pair XAG/USD).

29.6 Evaluation of DPT

An important element of each decision-making process on any market is the proper choice of a trading system. The realization of that choice should be accompanied by a set of criteria selected in advance. In [2], the following criteria are proposed for evaluation of any single DPT system $\text{DPT}\left(\overline{\text{Thr}}, \delta, \overline{\text{spr}}\right)$:

- the expected annual number of transactions

$$\mathcal{N}\left(\overline{\mathrm{Thr}}\right) = \sum_{s_j \in \mathbb{D}\left(\overline{\mathrm{Thr}}\right)} \tilde{n}_j, \tag{29.22}$$

where $\tilde{n}_j$ is a n_j number of annually calculated observations of the state s_j collected during the construction of the prediction table;

- the systemic probability of success

$$\pi\left(\mathcal{I}_\delta|\mathbb{D}\left(\overline{\mathrm{Thr}}\right)\right) = \frac{\sum_{s_j \in \mathbb{D}\left(\overline{\mathrm{Thr}}\right)} p\left(s_j\right) \cdot \pi\left(\mathcal{I}_\delta|s_j\right)}{\sum_{s_j \in \mathbb{D}\left(\overline{\mathrm{Thr}}\right)} p\left(s_j\right)}, \tag{29.23}$$

- the expected single unitary payment

$$\mathcal{y}\left(\overline{Thr}, \delta, \overline{spr}\right) = 2 \cdot \pi\left(\mathcal{J}_\delta \middle| \mathbb{D}\left(\overline{Thr}\right)\right) \cdot \delta - \delta - \overline{spr}, \tag{29.24}$$

- the expected annual unitary payment

$$\mathcal{Y}\left(\overline{Thr}, \delta, \overline{spr}\right) = \mathcal{N}\left(\overline{Trh}\right) \cdot \mathcal{y}\left(\overline{Thr}, \delta, \overline{spr}\right), \tag{29.25}$$

- the assessment of transactional risk:

$$\mathcal{E}\left(\overline{\mathrm{Thr}}, \delta, \overline{\mathrm{spr}}\right) = \frac{-\sum_{s_j \in \mathbb{D}\left(\overline{\mathrm{Thr}}\right)} p\left(s_j\right) \cdot \left(\pi\left(\mathcal{J}_\delta|s_j\right) \cdot \ln \pi\left(\mathcal{J}_\delta|s_j\right) + \left(1 - \pi\left(\mathcal{J}_\delta|s_j\right)\right) \cdot \ln\left(1 - \pi\left(\mathcal{J}_\delta|s_j\right)\right)\right)}{\ln 2 \cdot \sum_{s_j \in \mathbb{D}\left(\overline{\mathrm{Thr}}\right)} p\left(s_j\right)}, \tag{29.26}$$

- the single unitary risk bonus:

$$\mathcal{b}\left(\overline{Thr}, \delta, \overline{spr}\right) = \frac{\mathcal{y}\left(\overline{Thr}, \delta, \overline{spr}\right)}{\mathcal{E}\left(\overline{Thr}, \delta, \overline{spr}\right)}, \tag{29.27}$$

- the annual unitary risk bonus:

$$\mathcal{B}\left(\overline{\mathrm{Thr}}, \delta, \overline{\mathrm{spr}}\right) = \frac{\mathcal{Y}\left(\overline{\mathrm{Thr}}, \delta, \overline{\mathrm{spr}}\right)}{\mathcal{E}\left(\overline{\mathrm{Thr}}, \delta, \overline{\mathrm{spr}}\right)}. \tag{29.28}$$

Table 29.5 Juxtaposition of characteristics of DPT systems applied for XAU/USD market

Characteristics	DPT(0.525, 300, 15)	DPT(0.550, 300, 15)
Acceptable decision-making premises	$\{s_1, s_5, s_9, s_{11}\}$	$\{s_1, s_{11}\}$
Expected annual number of transactions	914.8	423.8
Systemic probability of success	0.5512	0.5645
Expected single unitary payment	15.70 $	23.65 $
Expected annual unitary payment	14,358 $	10,023 $
Assessment of a transactional risk	0.9919	0.9879
Single unitary risk bonus	15.82 $	23.93 $
Annual unitary risk bonus	14,475.70 $	10,145.70 $

Source Own calculations

The above-listed criteria refer to the proposal presented in [7] and [6]. Indicators (29.24), (29.25), (29.27) and (29.28) are appointed for an investment in 1 lot of precious metal XPM. The criteria (29.24) and (29.25) can be used by the investors to maximize their benefits. The efficiency of $\mathrm{DPT}\left(\overline{\mathrm{Thr}}, \delta, \overline{\mathrm{spr}}\right)$ trading system increases along with the decrease of (29.26) criterion. Summing up, the efficiency of each $\mathrm{DPT}\left(\overline{\mathrm{Thr}}, \delta, \overline{\mathrm{spr}}\right)$ trading system should be evaluated by a pair

$$\left(\mathcal{Y}\left(\overline{Thr}, \delta, \overline{spr}\right), \mathcal{E}\left(\overline{Thr}, \delta, \overline{spr}\right)\right) \tag{29.29}$$

or a pair

$$\left(\mathcal{Y}\left(\overline{\mathrm{Thr}}, \delta, \overline{\mathrm{spr}}\right), \mathcal{E}\left(\overline{\mathrm{Thr}}, \delta, \overline{\mathrm{spr}}\right)\right). \tag{29.30}$$

The pair (29.29) enables to evaluate the efficiency of a single use of a $\mathrm{DPT}\left(\overline{\mathrm{Thr}}, \delta, \overline{\mathrm{spr}}\right)$ trading system, while the pair (29.30) should be used to evaluate a multiple use of the same trading system. For this reason, for any given pair XPM/QCR, we evaluate any DPT system by means of (29.30). A supporting criterion of choosing an effective DPT system will be the maximization of the annual unitary risk bonus (29.28).

For XAU/USD pair market, complete evaluations of DPT systems DPT(0.525, 300, 15) and DPT(0.550, 300, 15) are given in Table 29.5. The values of decision-making threshold $\overline{\mathrm{Thr}}$ and unitary return magnitude δ parameters were chosen based on a search for the highest value of the indicator (29.25). In order to perform such kind of analysis, a dedicated software written in C++ language was created, allowing for the analysis of all possible parameter combinations.

The results presented in the table above illustrate the fact that with the increase of the decision-making threshold $\overline{\mathrm{Thr}}$, we observe an increase in the systemic probability of success and a simultaneous decrease in the number of transactions. All this leads to the fact that in the observed cases, the increase of the $\overline{\mathrm{Thr}}$ causes a simultaneous

Table 29.6 Juxtaposition of characteristics of DPT systems applied for XAG/USD market

Characteristics	DPT(0.5179, 280, 10)	DPT(0.5500, 280, 10)
Acceptable decision-making premises	$\left\{\begin{matrix} s_1, s_2, s_3, s_4, s_5, s_6, s_8, \\ s_{10}, s_{11}, s_{13}, s_{14}, s_{15}, s_{16} \end{matrix}\right\}$	$\left\{\begin{matrix} s_2, s_3, s_4, s_5, s_8, s_{11}, \\ s_{13}, s_{14}, s_{15}, s_{16} \end{matrix}\right\}$
Expected annual number of transactions	241.2	161.8
Systemic probability of success	0.5638	0.5772
Expected single unitary payment	25.75 $	33.26 $
Expected annual unitary payment	6212 $	5382 $
Assessment of a transactional risk	0.9867	0.9822
Single unitary risk bonus	26.10 $	33.87 $
Annual unitary risk bonus	6295.68 $	5479.80 $

Source Own calculations

decrease in the expected annual unitary payment and the transactional risk. It means that, in considered case, both DPT(0.525, 300, 15) and DPT(0.550, 300, 15) systems are effective. We recommend the DPT system DPT(0.525, 300, 15) because of its being characterized by higher annual unitary risk premium.

For XAG/USD pair, complete evaluations of DPT(0.5179, 280, 10) and DPT(0.5500, 280, 10) systems are given in Table 29.6. The values of decision-making threshold $\overline{\text{Thr}}$ and unitary return magnitude δ parameters were chosen based on a search for the highest value of the indicator (29.25). In order to perform such kind of analysis, a dedicated software written in C++ language was created, allowing for the analysis of all possible parameter combinations.

The results collected in the table above illustrate the fact that the increase in the decision-making threshold $\overline{\text{Thr}}$ causes an increase in the systemic probability of success and a simultaneous decrease in the expected number of transactions. All this leads to the conclusion that in observed cases, the increase in $\overline{\text{Thr}}$ causes a simultaneous decrease in the expected annual unitary payment and the transactional risk. It means that, in considered case, both systems DPT(0.5179, 280, 10) and DPT(0.5500, 280, 10) are effective. We recommend the DPT system DPT(0.5179, 280, 10) due to its higher annual unitary risk premium.

29.7 Comparison of DPT Systems Applied on Different Markets

In this chapter, we will compare the DPT systems used on the markets of different precious metals. We can suppose that on each of these markets, the value of 1 lot of a metal expressed in QCR is different. Indeed, in the time when the research was performed:

- average value of 1 lot of gold was equal to $v_{\mathrm{AU}} = 126{,}142\$$;
- average value of 1 lot of silver was equal to $v_{\mathrm{AG}} = 19{,}197\$$.

Because of this, unitary payments (29.24) and (29.25) cannot be applied for comparison of DPT systems applied on different markets. Then, for the DPT system $\mathrm{DPT}\left(\overline{\mathrm{Thr}}, \delta, \overline{\mathrm{spr}}\right)$ applied on XPM/QCR market with the value expressed in QCR, price v_{PM} of 1 lot of PM, the coefficients (29.24), (29.25), (29.27) and (29.28) should be replaced by following characteristics:

- the expected return rate

$$\mathcal{r}\left(\overline{Thr}, \delta, \overline{spr}\right) = \frac{\mathcal{y}\left(\overline{Thr}, \delta, \overline{spr}\right)}{v_{PM}}, \tag{29.31}$$

- the expected interest rate

$$\mathcal{i}\left(\overline{Thr}, \delta, \overline{spr}\right) = \frac{\mathcal{Y}\left(\overline{Thr}, \delta, \overline{spr}\right)}{v_{PM}}, \tag{29.32}$$

- the return risk premium

$$\mathcal{p}\left(\overline{Thr}, \delta, \overline{spr}\right) = \frac{\mathcal{b}\left(\overline{Thr}, \delta, \overline{spr}\right)}{v_{PM}}, \tag{29.33}$$

- the interest risk premium

$$\mathcal{P}\left(\overline{\mathrm{Thr}}, \delta, \overline{\mathrm{spr}}\right) = \frac{\mathcal{B}\left(\overline{\mathrm{Thr}}, \delta, \overline{\mathrm{spr}}\right)}{v_{\mathrm{PM}}}. \tag{29.34}$$

The criteria (29.31) and (29.32) can be used by investors to maximize their benefits. The efficiency of $\mathrm{DPT}\left(\overline{\mathrm{Thr}}, \delta, \overline{\mathrm{spr}}\right)$ trading system increases along with the decrease of (29.26) criterion. Summing up, the efficiency of each $\mathrm{DPT}\left(\overline{\mathrm{Thr}}, \delta, \overline{\mathrm{spr}}\right)$ trading system should be evaluated by the pair

$$\left(\mathcal{r}\left(\overline{Thr}, \delta, \overline{spr}\right), \mathcal{E}\left(\overline{Thr}, \delta, \overline{spr}\right)\right) \tag{29.35}$$

or

$$\left(\mathcal{i}\left(\overline{Thr}, \delta, \overline{spr}\right), \mathcal{E}\left(\overline{Thr}, \delta, \overline{spr}\right)\right). \tag{29.36}$$

Table 29.7 Juxtaposition of characteristics of DPT systems applied for XAU/USD market

Characteristics	DPT(0.525, 300, 15)	DPT(0.550, 300, 15)
Expected return rate	0.0001245	0.0001875
Expected interest rate	0.1138	0.0794
Assessment of a transactional risk	0.9919	0.9879
Return risk premium	0.00012541	0.0001897
Interest risk premium	0.1148	0.0804

Source Own calculations

Table 29.8 Juxtaposition of characteristics of DPT systems applied for XAG/USD market

Characteristics	DPT(0.518, 280, 10)	DPT(0.5500, 280, 10)
Expected return rate	0.001341	0,001,732
Expected interest rate	0.3235	0.2803
Assessment of a transactional risk	0.9867	0.9822
Return risk premium	0,001,359	0,001,764
Interest risk premium	0.3280	0.2855

Source Own calculations

The pair (29.35) enables evaluation of the efficiency of a single use of a $\text{DPT}(\overline{\text{Thr}}, \delta, \overline{\text{spr}})$ trading system, while (29.34) should be used to evaluate a multiple use of the same trading system. For this reason, for any given pair XPM/QCR, DPT systems will be evaluated by the means of (29.34). A supporting criterion will be the maximization of the interest premium due to risk (29.32).

For XAU/USD pair, complete evaluations of DPT(0.525, 300, 15) and DPT(0.550, 300, 15) systems are given in Table 29.7.

For XAG/USD pair, complete evaluations of DPT(0.5179, 280, 10) and DPT(0.5500, 280, 10) systems are given in Table 29.8.

The comparison of results summarized in Tables 29.7 and 29.8 allow for a conclusion that when comparing the DPT systems on XAU/USD and XAG/USD markets:

- DPT systems obtained visibly higher expected return rates on the XAG/USD market,
- DPT systems obtained visibly higher expected interest rates on the XAG/USD market,
- Using DPT system on the XAG/USD market is burdened with a lower risk,
- DPT systems obtained visibly higher return risk premium on the XAG/USD market,
- DPT systems obtained visibly higher interest risk premium on the XAG/USD market.

All of the partial comparisons allow for formulating the following conclusion: speculations made on XAG/USD market with use of researched DPT systems are more effective than the speculations made on the XAU/USD market, also with use of researched DPT systems. Because of this, only the recommendation holds for DPT system DPT(0.5179, 280, 10) applied for the XAG/USD market.

29.8 Summary

In the paper, we have proved that if the dynamics of XAG/USD and XAU/USD markets are described by a binary representation, then using chosen DPT systems allows for obtaining positive expected return rates. This conclusion was obtained by a diligent and multi-variant statistical analysis of financial outcomes achieved using the mentioned DPT systems.

By performing the above-mentioned analysis, we have proved that the applied DPT systems evaluation tools allow for a total management of profit and risk connected with the DPT systems' application. This conclusion implies a possibility of appointing a hyperspace of all financially effective DPT systems. Assessment of this kind of hyperspace would allow for optimal choice of applied DT systems.

In case of only one XPM/QCR market, the hyperspace of all financially effective DPT systems can be appointed as the Pareto optimum in a two-criteria comparison of pair (29.30).

In case of speculation possibilities on different exchange markets, the hyperspace of all financially effective DPT systems can be obtained as a Pareto optimum in a two-criteria comparison of pair (29.36).

References

1. Stasiak, M.D.: Modelling of currency exchange rates using a binary representation. In: Proceedings of 37th International Conference on Information Systems Architecture and Technology—ISAT 2016, Springer (2016). https://doi.org/10.1007/978-3-319-46592-0_13
2. Piasecki, K., Stasiak, M.D.: The currency trading system with constant magnitude of unitary return In: Szkutnik W., Sączewska-Piotrowska A., Hadaś-Dyduch M., Acedański J. (eds.) 10th International Scientific Conference "Analysis of International Relations 2018. Methods and Models of Regional Development. Summer Edition", pp. 40–49 (2018)
3. Logue, D.E., Sweeney, R.J.: White noise in imperfect markets: the case of the franc/dollar exchange rates. The J. Financ., **32**(3), 761–768 (1977). https://doi.org/10.1111/j.1540-6261.1977.tb01986.x
4. Neely, C.J., Weller, P.A.: Technical analysis in the foreign exchange market. Federal Reserve Bank of St. Louis Working Paper No. (2011), https://doi.org/10.1002/9781118445785.ch12
5. Lo, A.W., Mamaysky, H., Wang, J.: Foundations of technical analysis: computational algorithms, statistical inference, and empirical implementation. The J. Financ. **55**(4), 1705–1770 (2000). https://doi.org/10.1111/0022-1082.00265
6. Li, W., Wong, M.C., Cenev, J.: High frequency analysis of macro news releases on the foreign exchange market: a survey of literature. Big Data Res. **2**(1), 33–48 (2015)
7. García, B.Q., Gaytán, J.C.T., Wolfskill, L.A.: The role of technical analysis in the foreign exchange market. Glob. J. Bus. Res. **6**(3), 17–22 (2012)

Chapter 30
Underdevelopment of the Financial Market in China as a Barrier to the Internationalization of the Renminbi

Katarzyna Twarowska

Abstract Purpose: The Chinese economy is one of the largest and the fastest growing economy in the modern world. The importance of the renminbi as an international currency is not relevant to China's economic potential and role in the global economy. This fact encouraged the author to explore barriers limiting the position of the renminbi as an international currency. The aim of the paper is to assess the development of the Chinese financial market and its liquidity conditions from the perspective of their impact on currency internationalization. Methods: The study includes theoretical and empirical research. A descriptive comparative analysis has been used to assess the development of the financial market in China in comparison with other economies (contemporaneously and historically) and to evaluate the renminbi's role in the main functions of international currency using the Cohen matrix. Results and conclusions: The author confirmed the research hypothesis that one of the important constraints for the renminbi internationalization is the relatively shallow and underdeveloped financial market in China.

Keywords International currency · Liberalization of capital flows · Financial depth and liquidity · Emerging economy · SDR

30.1 Introduction

China is the world's second largest economy behind the USA, whose share in global GDP in 2017 amounted to 18.2% in PPP and 15% in current prices (the shares of the USA amounted to 15.3% in PPP and 24.3% in current prices, respectively) [25]. China's share in merchandise exports in 2017 amounted to 12.8% of global exports (8.7% for the USA) [37], and China's foreign exchange reserves in 2017 constituted 26.9% of global official currency reserves [5].

K. Twarowska (✉)
Maria Curie-Skłodowska University, Lublin, Poland
e-mail: k.twarowska@umcs.pl

W. Tarczyński and K. Nermend (eds.), *Effective Investments on Capital Markets*, Springer Proceedings in Business and Economics,
https://doi.org/10.1007/978-3-030-21274-2_30

China's economic power is confirmed by its dominant role in foreign trade in the Asian region, as well as in trade, production and financial relations beyond the countries of the region [27]. It is not surprising, therefore, that China is making efforts to promote its own currency, the status of which would reflect the role of China's economy not only on a regional but also on a global level. For several years, the Chinese authorities have been critical of the international monetary system based on the single currency, which is the US dollar and the global financial and economic crisis of 2008–2009 intensified the efforts of the Chinese authorities to internationalize the renminbi.

These circumstances encouraged the author to explore barriers limiting the position of the renminbi as an international currency, especially connected with the financial market. The aim of the paper is to access the development of Chinese financial market and its liquidity conditions, and to compare it with those in other economies, historically and contemporaneously from the perspective of their impact on currency internationalization. Furthermore, the author explores the main obstacles to further deepening and development of China's financial market for renminbi internationalization. The author attempts to find an answer to the research question whether the Chinese financial market is deep and liquid enough for the renminbi internationalization. The following research hypothesis was formulated, which is verified in the paper: one of the important constraints for the renminbi internationalization is the relatively shallow and underdeveloped financial market in China.

30.2 Financial Market Development as a Determinant of the International Currency Status—Theoretical Framework and Literature Review

Many scientific studies indicate that domestic financial market development is a crucial determinant of a currency's international status [4, 7, 8, 11, 20, 33]. Eichengreen [8] emphasizes that the size and liquidity of the financial market increase the probability that other countries will choose the currency issued by that country as their intervention and reserve currency. Moreover, the effectiveness, competitiveness and security of the financial market are very important. Currency internationalization is also supported by the independence of the central bank. Chinn and Frankel [4] have selected four main groups of factors that are crucial to achieving key international currency status. They argued that an important factor is a financial market, which should be open, liquid and well developed. The other three factors are: the country's (currency issuer) share in the world economy, in particular, in world production and trade; reliability and predictability of the value of the currency; network externalities—a process similar to spillover, i.e. the use of currency in international transactions has a strengthening effect, which increases the possibilities for its further use.

Likewise, Galati and Wooldridge [12] pointed out the factors determining the use of money as a reserve currency, which on the one hand derives from the fact that the currency performs other functions of international money, and on the other hand it becomes a premise for choosing a given currency both in functions of the official sector (anchor currency and intervention currency) and the private sector (e.g. currency used in invoicing and financing merchandise trade). Among the factors indicated, they took into account the development of the financial market. Other factors are the following: the magnitude of the currency issuer's economy and its position in the world economy (share in international trade), macroeconomic stability and network externalities.

In the case of China, which is one of the leaders in terms of GDP and shares in international trade, the barriers to the internationalization of the renminbi are the development of the financial market, macroeconomic stability, lack of confidence in the currency and weak network externalities. Cruz et al. [7] argued that the pace of the renminbi internationalization will be closely linked to the Chinese financial market development. To extend the use of currency abroad (e.g. for the settlement of foreign trade and financial transactions), international traders and investors must have access to a wide range of financial assets denominated in that currency. Chinn and Frankel [4] explained that in order to achieve reserve currency status, the renminbi must be easily accessible with necessary abundance. Also, a reserve currency must be a credible store of value and assets denominated in the currency must be held both by the private sector as a medium of exchange and investment asset and by the public sector as a store of value.

Cruz et al. [7] drew attention to three aspects of financial market development from the perspective of the currency internationalization: breadth—availability of financial instruments and markets for various transaction purpose, depth—the volume of financial instruments in the markets, liquidity—ease of carrying out transactions for market participants. Similarly, Eichengreen [9] found that three essential attributes for an international currency to be used in private, commercial and financial transactions and held as official reserves are scale, stability and liquidity. Scale refers to international transactions between the country issuing the currency and the rest of the world, which is essentially linked to the breadth and depth of domestic financial markets. A currency with stable value helps build users' confidence, which contributes to a wider use of the currency in the functions of international money. Liquidity may be considered as funding liquidity, the availability of credit or the ease with which institutions can borrow or take on leverage. The second dimension is market liquidity, which means the ability of markets to absorb large transactions without much impact on prices.

30.3 Evaluation of the Breadth, Depth and Liquidity of China's Financial Market Compared to Other Economies with Key Currencies

The financial sector has developed rapidly since the mid-1990s, which was reflected in an increase in market turnover and in the value of financial instruments. The increase in the size of the capital market, measured as the sum of equities, bonds and bank assets, is shown in Fig. 30.1.

Table 30.1 presents data for the size of the capital market in the largest economies, including China. As the data show, the greatest capital market is still in the USA, despite the fact that its share in the global capital market has decreased. In 2013, it amounted to 72.7 trillion dollars and it was above 25% of the global capital market, but in 2001 the US share was 36.3% (Fig. 30.2). The euro area has the second largest capital market (about 23% in 2013). Japan is still an important market, although its share in the global capital market decreased significantly, and in 2013 the Japanese capital market only slightly outperformed the Chinese market (Fig. 30.2).

Furthermore, Cruz et al. [7] assessed that absolute size of China's financial sector is the fourth largest in the world, only after the USA, the combined euro financial systems and Japan. Therefore, China's domestic financial system seems big enough to support an international currency.

The assessment of countries looks slightly different when analysing relative quantities (size of the capital market in relation to GDP) (Table 30.1). The highest level of the indicator (sum of equities, bonds and bank assets in relation to GDP) in 2013 was in Japan (576.5% of GDP), in the euro area (504.2%) and then in the USA (433.5%), but in all analysed years the indicator was the highest in the euro area in 2001. (625.4%). In China, the value of this indicator is much lower (291.7%) than in developed countries.

Since establishment in the early 1990s, China's stock market has grown substantially in terms of turnover, liquidity, issuances and number of participants [7]. Although stock market capitalization in China remains rather modest as a ratio to

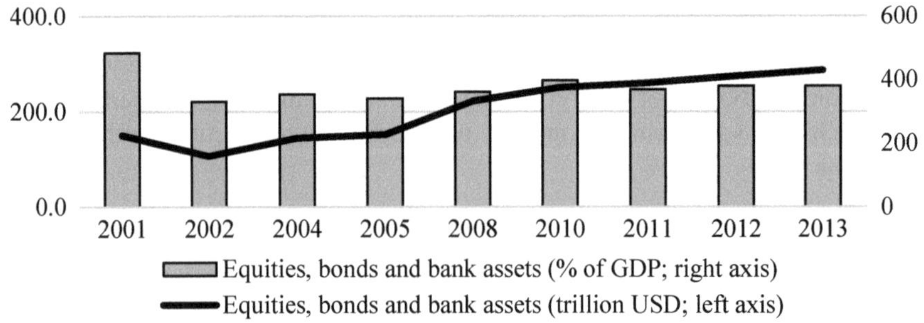

Fig. 30.1 World's capital market size in 2001–2013 (trillion USD and % of GDP) *Source* Own calculations based on: [14–19, 21–23]

Table 30.1 Selected indicators of the capital market size in 2001 and 2013

Selected indicators		World		Euro area		United States		Japan		China
		2001	2013	2001	2013	2001	2013	2001	2013	2013
1. GDP	Billions of US dollars	30,995	75,471	6113.0	13,110	10,082	16,768	4165	4920	**9469**
	Percent of world total (%)	100	100	19.7	17.4	32.5	22.2	13.4	6.5	**12.5**
2. Total reserves minute gold	Billions of US dollars	2136	12,128	198	331	58	134	395	1237	**3840**
	Percent of world total (%)	100	100	9.3	2.7	2.7	1.1	18.5	10.2	**31.7**
3. Stock market capitalization	Billions of US dollars	28,875	62,552	4277	7539	13,827	22,281	2294	4599	**3361**
	Percent of world total (%)	100	100	14.8	12.1	47.9	35.6	7.9	7.4	**5.4**
4. Total debt securities	Billions of US dollars	41,792	97,289	9492	22,461	18,504	34,494	6925	12,261	**4094**
	Percent of world total (%)	100	100	22.7	23.1	44.3	35.5	16.6	12.6	**4.2**
5. Bank Assets	Billions of US dollars	79,402	126,744	24,464	36,100	22,157	15,921	12,409	11,500	**20,167**
	Percent of world total (%)	100	100	30.8	28.5	27.9	12.6	15.6	9.1	**15.9**
6. Equities, bonds and bank assets (3 + 4 + 5)	Billions of US dollars	150,069	286,585	38,233	66,101	54,488	72,696	21,628	28,360	**27,621**
	Percent of world total (%)	100	100	25.5	23.1	36.3	25.4	14.4	9.9	**9.6**
	Percent of GDP	484	380	625.4	504	540.4	434	519.3	577	**292**

Source [14, 23]

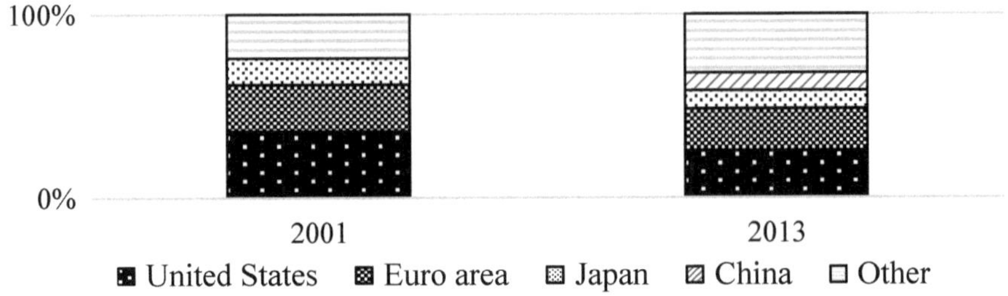

Fig. 30.2 Countries' shares in the world capital market (sum of bonds, equities and bank assets) in 2001 and 2013. *Source* Own calculations based on: [14, 23]

GDP (Table 30.2), China's stock market in absolute size is in the group of largest in the world (Table 30.1). Such a huge market and supply of assets could be attractive for foreign investors if they were allowed access. However, the stock market is highly regulated and foreign participation is restricted, which hinders its development as well as its supporting role in the internationalization of the renminbi.

Development of the bond market development may have a greater impact on currency internationalization than the stock market [7], as equities are more risky than bonds as a result of unsecure future earnings and the risk of bankruptcy of the issuer. Moreover, the participation of the public sector in the bond market stabilizes that market by providing lower risk assets. It also provides additional liquidity to facilitate trading on the market. Public sector participation in the equity market is much more limited or not at all.

Since the 1990s, China's bond market has developed from a small isolated domestic market to one of the greatest in the world. As China encourages the internationalization of renminbi while limiting capital flows, an offshore renminbi denominated bond market has also emerged. China has evolved a broad and increasingly diversified bond market with instruments issued by public and private entities. In 2017, the amount of China's bond turnover reached RMB 265.3 million (Fig. 30.3). As a

Table 30.2 Market capitalization (% of GDP)

	Last (2017)	Min	Max	Range
China	**71.2**	**17.6 (2005)**	**126.1 (2007)**	**2003–2017**
United States	165.7	39.4 (1981)	165.7 (2017)	1980–2017
European Union	77.9	7.6 (1981)	84.2 (2000)	1975–2017
France	100.1	5.1 (1982)	106.2 (2000)	1975–2017
Germany	57.9	7.6 (1980)	67.3 (1999)	1975–2017
Japan	128.3	48.0 (2002)	128.3 (2017)	1994–2017
United Kingdom	109.4 (2016)	81.5 (2008)	131.8 (2006)	1999–2016

Source [3]

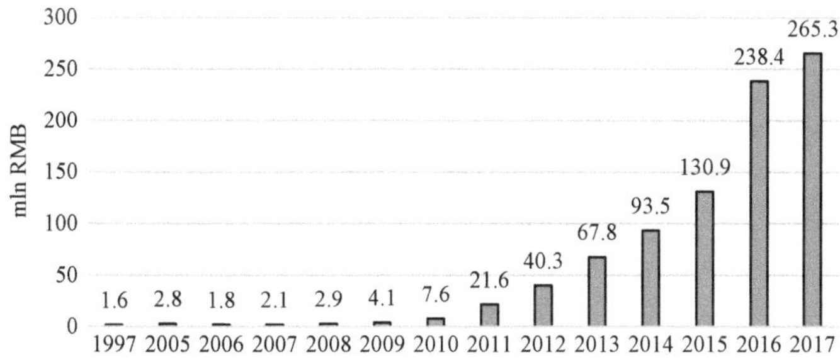

Fig. 30.3 China's bond turnover (million RMB). *Source* Own work based on: [3]

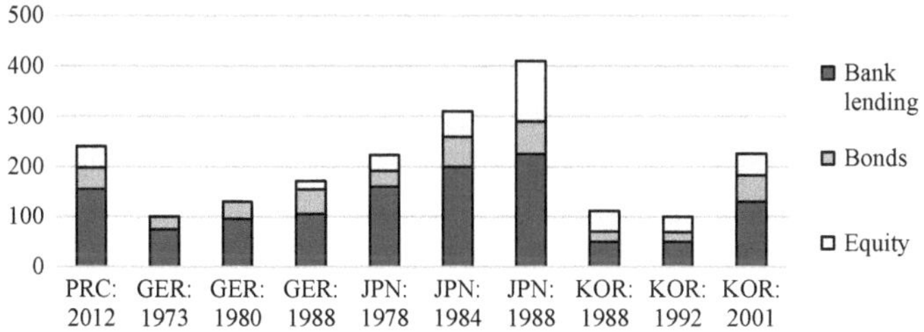

Fig. 30.4 Financial depth—historical comparison (% of GDP). *Source* [7]

percentage of GDP and in absolute size, China's bond market is modest compared to countries with international currencies.

It is worth mentioning that China's financial sector is captured by major state-owned commercial banks. The business activity is mainly financed by bank lending as the bond and equity markets are not well developed [7]. China's money market is less developed than in other economies with key currencies but is developing rapidly and undergoing substantial changes. It is also noted that it has become much more active in recent years. It is important because liquid and efficient money market is necessary for an international currency.

It is also interesting to compare the development of the financial sector in China nowadays with some developed economies in the past, when they were at a comparable level of development to China today and whose currencies are international now (Fig. 30.4). The group of countries selected for comparison includes: Germany, Japan and the Republic of Korea [7]. Germany and Japan are chosen because they expanded their financial market efficiently and internationalized their currencies. Then, the Republic of Korea is considered as a historical benchmark because it is a developing economy, but its currency is being internationalized. The time period of historical analysis is based at the time when selected countries "internationalized" their currencies.

Compared with countries at a similar stage of development (GDP per capita), China's financial sector in 2012 was deeper than in Germany in the late 1980s and in the Republic of Korea in the early 1990s and was on par with Japan's financial sector

Table 30.3 Geographical distribution of foreign exchange turnover (daily averages in April, shares in %)

Country	2001	2004	2007	2010	2013	2016
United Kingdom	31.8	32.0	34.6	36.8	40.8	37.1
United States	16.0	19.1	17.4	17.9	18.9	19.4
Euro area	14.1	12.9	12.2	11.6	9.1	8.4
Singapore	6.1	5.1	5.6	5.3	5.7	7.9
Hong Kong	4.0	4.1	4.2	4.7	4.1	6.7
Japan	9.0	8.0	5.8	6.2	5.6	6.1
China	0.0	0.0	0.2	0.4	0.7	1.1

Source Author's elaboration based on: [2]

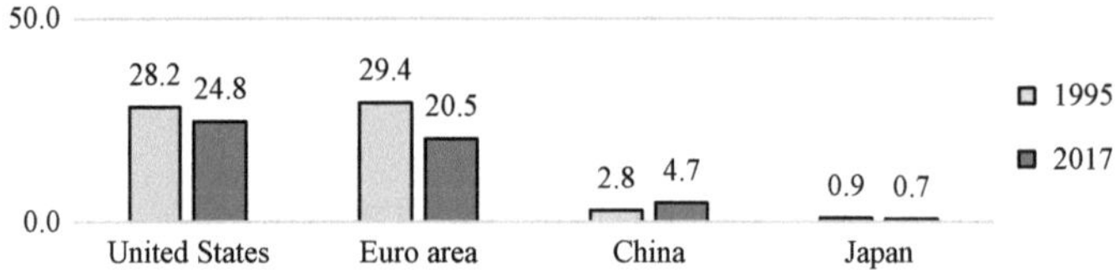

Fig. 30.5 Shares in world foreign direct investment (inward, stock, percentage of the total world). *Source* Author's elaboration based on: [37]

in the early 1980s [7]. Using the "currency internationalization" year as a baseline, the Chinese financial sector was deeper compared to Germany in 1973, on par with the Republic of Korea in 2001 but lags behind Japan in 1984 [7].

It can be stated that not only market size matters, but reliability, convenience, facility and costs may be more crucial for a currency to be approved internationally. China's financial sector is deeper than in other emerging economies (size of the financial sector in relation to GDP), but it is shallower than developed economies like the USA, Japan, the UK, France or the European Union average (Table 30.2).

In addition, considering another sector of the financial market, which is the foreign exchange market, it can be noted that China's involvement in this market was relatively low. The UK had the largest share in foreign exchange turnover (above 37% in 2016), which was a result of the historically rooted financial centre in London. The USA had the second largest share in market turnover in 2016, next the euro area (8.4%) and then three Asian countries: Singapore (7.9%), Hong Kong (6.7%) and Japan (6.1%). China's share was only 1.1% (Table 30.3).

Moreover, market openness can be measured by a share in world capital flows. Figure 30.5 shows the shares in the world foreign direct investment (FDI) in the mid-1990s and in 2017. The highest share of the cumulative FDI in 1995 flowed to the euro area (29.4%) and the USA (28.2%). In 2017, the euro area's share fell to 20.5%, the USA had 24.8%. Whereas, China had 4.7% share in 2017, which is significantly higher than in Japan (Fig. 30.5).

China has been consistently implementing the strategy of liberalizing capital flows for years. China's involvement in the internationalization of its currency concerns solutions aimed directly at the promotion of the renminbi, starting from facilitation of settlements in the renminbi, through the establishment of clearing banks, to bilateral swap agreements with foreign central banks. Indirectly, the internationalization of the Chinese currency is to be facilitated by the concept of the New Silk Road [27] and the launch of the Asian Infrastructure Investment Bank in 2016.

Despite the opening of the Chinese financial market to foreign investors, numerous restrictions remain. Foreign investors are keen to engage in the largest Chinese financial companies, especially commercial banks, but foreign capital usually remains limited to 25% of the company's total shares. In addition, in most cases, foreign entities do not have a management role function [13]. Furthermore, China's financial sector is captured by banks. The share of bank loans in domestic sources of business financing is the highest of all major economies and even higher than other emerging economies at a comparable stage of development [7]. State-owned entities as well as central and local government agencies still have significant shareholdings in most commercial banks [28].

30.4 Evaluation of Renminbi Internationalization

The use of renminbi as an international currency can be evaluated by using the Cohen matrix (Table 30.4), a concept that is based on the money function matrix. The international version of the matrix was invented by Cohen [6] and developed by Kenen [26]. It is often used as a basis for the analysis of the use of international currencies.

Assessing the position of international currencies in the private sector, several areas of analysis can be identified:

- use of currencies in transactions on the international financial market (evaluation of the currency position as a store of value—investment and financing currency, the medium of exchange—vehicle currency on the currency market),
- use of currencies for invoicing trade transactions and for payments (evaluation of the currency position as a unit of account—invoicing currency and medium of exchange—vehicle currency).

As a store of value, the international currency is used in the private sector for investment. Both in the debt market and in terms of international loans and deposits,

Table 30.4 Matrix of the international currency use

	Private use	Official use
Medium of exchange	Vehicle currency	Intervention currency
Unit of account	Quotation currency	Anchor currency
Store of value	Investment and financing currency	FX reserves currency

Source [6, 26]

the USD continues to prevail [35]. The role of the renminbi is rather small, but growing, particularly as a currency used by the countries of the Asian region. If renminbi is to become a truly international currency—as one of the most popular currencies—then capital market development is important, especially for fix income securities. Nowadays, China is the sixth largest bond market (broadly defined). It is about 10% of the US market size and about the average size of the main euro area member states [30].

In case of the renminbi, using it as an investment and financing currency is possible mainly due to the development of offshore markets and the progressive liberalization of portfolio flows. Recently, mainly the fixed income asset market has become a segment of the financial market which is subject to far-reaching changes. In general, the Chinese bond market is becoming increasingly accessible thanks to the changes introduced in 2015–2016 in the China Interbank Bond Market (CIBM).

Thanks to the introduced reforms, foreign institutional investors with (RQFII) status Renminbi Qualified Foreign Institutional Investors were granted access to the Chinese bond market only after registering with the People's Bank of China. The other two programmes—(QFII) Qualified Foreign Institutional Investors and (QDII) Qualified Domestic Institutional Investors, under which rights to invest in the Chinese bond market are acquired and are still in operation. The current system of granted amounts is less and less restrictive and the rules of taxation of income from the capital have been liberalized, but they are still unstable. The development of the stock market is to be facilitated by cross-border platforms (Stock Connect) connecting Chinese stock exchanges with foreign exchanges. Institutional solutions to promote the renminbi as an international investment currency are summarized in Table 30.5.

The presented solutions, in particular swap agreements with the Chinese central bank, clearing banks and investment programs are initiatives designed to promote the

Table 30.5 Institutional solutions to promote the renminbi as an international investment currency

Instruments	Purpose
QFII	Access for domestic and foreign institutional investors to the Chinese bond and equity market, as well as for domestic institutional investors to the bond and offshore equity market
RQFII	
QDII	
Stock Connect:	Mutual access to stock markets in China and to foreign exchanges
– Shanghai–Hongkong	
– Shenzhen–Hongkong	
– Shanghai–London (in progress)	
CIBM	Access of foreign institutional investors to the Chinese bond market
Bond Connect (in progress)	Mutual access to China's bond and offshore markets (Hong Kong)

Source Own elaboration based on [31, 34]

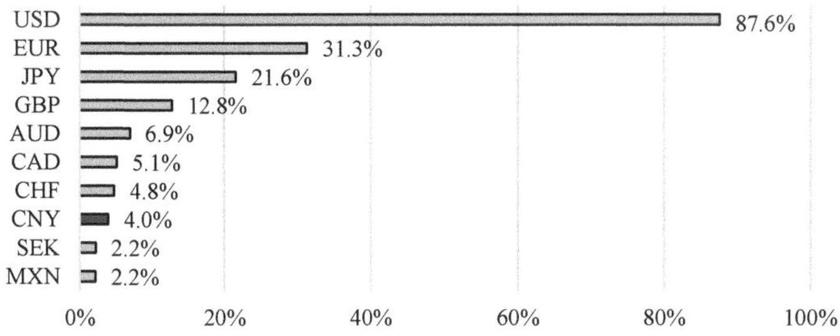

Fig. 30.6 Currency distribution of OTC foreign exchange turnover in April 2016 (in %). *Note* Because two currencies are involved in each transaction, the sum of the percentage shares of individual currencies totals 200% instead of 100%. *Source* Author's elaboration based on: [2]

use of renminbi in the international market. At the same time, all three include state interference, albeit to a different extent. They require negotiations and the consent of the Chinese authorities. Although procedures in this area are being gradually simplified, the final decision belongs to the administrative authorities. This is why they can still be treated as "three gifts" from the state [10].

The internationalization of the currency is also confirmed by its use on the foreign exchange market. In 2001, the share of the Chinese currency was insignificant, and it was ranked 35th among the currencies used on the currency market. In 2016, the renminbi was already ranked eighth with a share of 4%. However, the dollar is still the first currency and has a significant advantage over other currencies (Fig. 30.6 and Table 30.6). As the presented data show, the position of the renminbi on the currency market has significantly improved over the last several years; however, it is not significant yet.

China's high share in world trade, and in particular its position as the leading exporter, is contributing to the growing position of the renminbi among other currencies used for invoicing international trade and for payments [29, 36]. According to SWIFT data in December 2017, the renminbi was the fifth international payment currency with a share of 1.61% when looking at domestic and cross-border payments (in December 2015 it was even 2.31%, Fig. 30.7). Moreover, the US dollar is still the dominant currency in international and domestic payments, although its share dropped from almost 44% in 2015 to 39.85% in 2017 while the share of the euro increased from 29.39 to 35.66% over the same period [32]. The share of renminbi activity share is lower (0.98%) if only cross-border payments are taken into account and payments intra-euro area is excluded. On the contrary, the share for the euro and the US dollar is higher (respectively 39.45% and 41.27%).

The new (CIPS) Cross-border Interbank Payment System, established in 2015, with the strong involvement of the People's Bank of China, has made an exceptionally significant contribution to the current dynamic development of the Chinese foreign trade settlement process in the renminbi [34]. The People's Bank of China is actively involved in promoting the use of renminbi for invoicing and settlement of transactions, opening new clearing banks. Furthermore, the use of the renminbi as a

Table 30.6 Currency distribution of OTC foreign exchange turnover (in %)

Currency	2001		2004		2007		2010		2013		2016	
	Share (%)	Rank	Share (%)	Rank	Share (%)	Rank	Share (%)	Rank	Share (%)	Rank	Share (%)	Rank
USD	89.9	1	88.0	1	85.6	1	84.9	1	87.0	1	87.6	1
EUR	37.9	2	37.4	2	37.0	2	39.1	2	33.4	2	31.3	2
JPY	23.5	3	20.8	3	17.2	3	19.0	3	23.1	3	21.6	3
GBP	13.0	4	16.5	4	14.9	4	12.9	4	11.8	4	12.8	4
AUD	4.3	7	6.0	6	6.6	6	7.6	5	8.6	5	6.9	5
CAD	4.5	6	4.2	7	4.3	7	5.3	7	4.6	7	5.1	6
CHF	6.0	5	6.0	5	6.8	5	6.3	6	5.2	6	4.8	7
CNY	**0.0**	**35**	**0.1**	**29**	**0.5**	**20**	**0.9**	**17**	**2.2**	**9**	**4.0**	**8**
SEK	2.5	8	2.2	8	2.7	9	2.2	9	1.8	11	2.2	9
MXN	0.8	14	1.1	12	1.3	12	1.3	14	2.5	8	2.2	10

Source Author's calculations based on: [2]

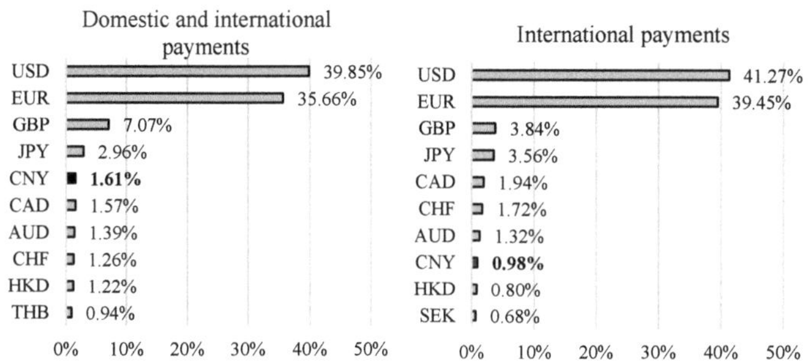

Fig. 30.7 Currency activity share for payments (customer initiated and institutional payments) in December 2017. *Source* [32]

means of payment by central banks means the provision of liquidity in the renminbi through bilateral swap agreements between the People's Bank of China and central banks of other countries [10].

High availability of assets denominated in an international currency and ease of trading in these instruments, as well as low costs may encourage foreign authorities to choose that currency as a reserve and intervention currency. As a reserve currency, the dollar has been dominant for years, which has all the attributes of a store of value and confidence among foreign investors. The second currency in terms of shares in official foreign exchange reserves is the euro (Table 30.7). Among the currencies of developing countries, the most important is the currency of China, which in 2016 accounted for 1.08% of global foreign exchange reserves and 1.39% at the end of the first quarter of 2018.

Another area in which the internationalization of renminbi can be assessed is its use as an anchor currency. After the adoption of a more flexible exchange rate policy by China in July 2005 and with an acceleration in the liberalization of the capital account as well as a strong push for the renminbi cross-border use since the onset of the global financial crisis, the role of the renminbi as an international currency has grown in strength. The renminbi has become an anchor currency for a few major currencies in the Asian region (especially ASEAN), along with the US dollar, which was the traditional anchor [36].

Advances in the liberalization of the financial sector in China and the growing role of the renminbi are confirmed by its inclusion in the SDR basket. In 2016, the Chinese renminbi was included in the SDR basket as the fifth currency. SDR basket expansion reflects the ongoing evolution of the global economy and is a significant change for the IMF. The weights of the five currencies in the SDR basket since 2016 are presented on Fig. 30.8.

Projections of Bénassy-Quéré and Capelle [1] indicate that the share of renminbi in SDR will grow steadily and, depending on the adopted scenario, it is expected to range from 21.3 to 27.6% in 2030, and from 29.9 to 43.5% in 2050. The authors agree that renminbi could be the main currency of the basket in 2050.

Table 30.7 Currency composition of official foreign reserves (in %)

Shares of	1995	1998	1999	2005	2008	2012	2014	2016	2017	2018Q1
US dollars	58.96	69.28	71.01	66.51	63.77	61.47	65.14	65.34	62.72	62.48
Euros	–	–	17.90	23.89	26.21	24.05	21.20	19.13	20.15	20.39
Japanese yen	6.77	6.24	6.37	3.96	3.47	4.09	3.54	3.95	4.89	4.81
Pounds sterling	2.11	2.66	2.89	3.75	4.22	4.04	3.70	4.34	4.54	4.68
Canadian dollars	–	–	–	–	–	1.42	1.75	1.94	2.02	1.86
Australian dollars	–	–	–	–	–	1.46	1.59	1.69	1.80	1.70
Chinese renminbi	–	–	–	–	–	–	–	**1.08**	**1.22**	**1.39**
Swiss francs	0.33	0.33	0.23	0.15	0.14	0.21	0.24	0.16	0.18	0.17
Deutsche mark	15.75	13.79	–	–	–	–	–	–	–	–
ECUs	8.53	1.30	–	–	–	–	–	–	–	–
French francs	2.35	1.62	–	–	–	–	–	–	–	–
Netherlands guilders	0.32	0.27	–	–	–	–	–	–	–	–
Other currencies	4.87	4.50	1.60	1.74	2.20	3.26	2.83	2.37	2.49	2.50

Source Author's calculations based on: [5]

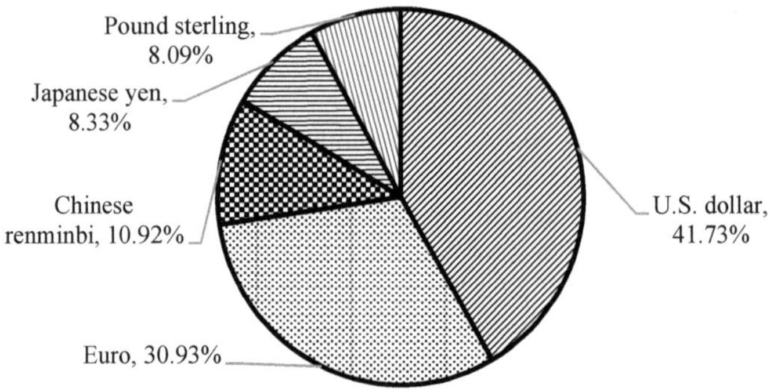

Fig. 30.8 Structure of the SDR basket. *Source* Author's elaboration based on: [24]

30.5 Conclusions

The review of the literature on the breadth, depth and liquidity of the Chinese financial market from the perspective of currency internationalization indicates that there is wide agreement that the Chinese financial market is relatively shallow and underdeveloped and need to expand further to support renminbi internationalization.

Empirical analyses indicate that the financial market in China is underdeveloped compared to the financial markets of countries with key currencies, which confirm the research hypothesis that one of the important constraints for the renminbi internationalization is the relatively shallow and underdeveloped financial market in China.

The problem is in particular access to the market for foreign investors and transaction costs, which limit the efficiency of the market. The size of the financial market in China is large, and this feature should not limit the internationalization of the renminbi. The main barriers to renminbi internationalization related to China's financial market identified in the study are as follows:

- financial depth and liquidity: China's financial markets are shallow and much less liquid compared to the economies with international currencies,
- restricted access to the capital market,
- lack of transparency for foreign investors,
- involvement of the government in the financial market,
- the dominance of state-owned banks and state-owned enterprises in the financial sector,
- regulated interest rates,
- the degree of competition in China's financial sector is low and does not support market development, domestic institutions are protected from foreign competition,
- high transaction costs.

The analyses carried out in the study make it possible to formulate recommendations that China's authorities need to further deregulate the financial sector and ensure financial stability to promote the renminbi internationalization.

References

1. Bénassy-Quéré, A., Capelle, D.: On the Inclusion of the Chinese Renminbi in the SDR Basket, CESIFO Working Paper, No. 3989, Novembers 18 (2012)
2. BIS: Triennial Central Bank Survey. Global foreign exchange market turnover in 2016, Monetary and Economic Department, 11 December. https://www.bis.org/publ/rpfx16fx.pdf (2016)
3. CEIC: CEIC Data. https://www.ceicdata.com/en/indicators (2018)
4. Chinn, M., Frankel, J.A.: Will the euro eventually surpass the dollar as leading international reserve currency? In: Clarida, R.H. (ed.) Current Account Imbalances: Sustainability and Adjustment. University of Chicago Press, Chicago, US (2007)
5. COFER: Currency Composition of Official Foreign Exchange Reserves, International Monetary Fund. http://data.imf.org (2018)
6. Cohen, B.J.: The Future of Sterling as an International Currency. Macmillan, London (1971)

7. Cruz, P.C., Gao, Y., Song, L.L.: The People Republic of China's Financial Markets: Are They Deep and Liquid Enough for Renminbi Internationalization? ADBI Working Paper 477. Asian Development Bank Institute, Tokyo. http://www.adbi.org/working-paper/2014/04/30/6239.prc.financial.markets/ (2014)
8. Eichengreen, B.: The euro as a reserve currency. J. Jpn. Int. Econ. **12** (1998)
9. Eichengreen, B: ADB distinguished lecture: renminbi internationalization: tempest in a teapot? Asian Dev. Rev. **30**(1) (2013)
10. Eichengreen, B., Lombardi, D.: RMBI or RMBR: IS the Renminbi Destined to Become a Global or Regional Currency? NBER Working Paper, No. 21716 (2015)
11. Forbes, K.: Financial deepening and global currency usage. In: Pisani-Ferry, J., Posen, S.A. (eds.) The Euro at Ten: The Next Global Currency?. Peterson Institute of International Economics, Washington, DC (2009)
12. Galati, G.G., Wooldridge, P.: The Euro as the Reserve Currency: A Challenge to the Preeminence of the US Dollar? BIS Working Papers, no 218, October (2006)
13. Herd, R., Pigott, C., Hill, S.: China's Financial Sector Reforms. OECD Economics Department Working Papers No. 747. OECD Publishing, Paris (2010)
14. IMF: Global Financial Stability Report. Statistical Appendix, April (2003)
15. IMF: Global Financial Stability Report. Statistical Appendix, April (2004)
16. IMF: Global Financial Stability Report. Statistical Appendix, April (2005)
17. IMF: Global Financial Stability Report. Statistical Appendix, April (2006)
18. IMF: Global Financial Stability Report. Statistical Appendix, April (2010)
19. IMF: Global Financial Stability Report. Statistical Appendix, September (2011)
20. IMF: Internationalization of Emerging Market Currencies: A Balance Between Risks and Rewards. IMF Staff Discussion Note SDN 11/17, 19 October (2011)
21. IMF: Global Financial Stability Report. Statistical Appendix, April (2013)
22. IMF: Global Financial Stability Report. Statistical Appendix, April (2014)
23. IMF: Global Financial Stability Report. Statistical Appendix, April (2015)
24. IMF: Review of the Special Drawing Right (SDR) Currency Basket, October 13, 2017. https://www.imf.org/en/About/Factsheets/Sheets/2016/08/02/19/35/Review-of-the-Special-Drawing-Right-SDR-Currency-Basket (2017)
25. IMF: World Economic Outlook Database April 2018. [Online]. Retrieved 5 Sept 2018, https://www.imf.org/external/pubs/ft/weo/2018/01/weodata/index.aspx (2018)
26. Kenen, P.B.: The Role of the Dollar as an International Currency, Group of Thirty, Occasional Paper, no 13 (1983)
27. Kołodko, G.W.: Czy Chiny zbawią świat?. Prószyński i S-ka, Warszawa (2018)
28. Martin, M.F.: China's Banking System: Issues for Congress. Congressional Research Services, Washington, DC (2012)
29. Mucha-Leszko, B., Kąkol, M.: Globalizacja i zmiany w układzie sił gospodarczych a międzynarodowy system walutowy. In: Molendowski, E. (ed.) Globalizacja i regionalizacja we współczesnym świecie. Wydawnictwo Uniwersytetu Ekonomicznego w Krakowie, Kraków (2012)
30. Overholt, W.H., Ma, G., Law, Ch.K.: Renminbi Rising. A New Global Monetary System Emerges, Wiley, United Kingdom (2016)
31. Standard Chartered: RMB Internationalization: Change, Alignment and Maturity. RMB Investors Forum. White Paper (2017)
32. SWIFT: RMB Internationalization: Where We Are and What We Can Expect in 2018, RMB Tracker, January 2018. https://www.swift.com/.../rmb-tracker-january-2018-special-report (2018)
33. Tavlas, G.: On the International Use of Currencies: The Case of the Deutsche Mark. Essays in International Finance No. 181 (1991)
34. Thiele, C.L.: Internationalization of the Renminbi—Prospects and Challenges. BIS Central Banker's Speeches (2016)
35. Twarowska, K.: The configuration of the world's economic powers and its influence on currency stability in global dimension in 2000–2016. J. Int. Sci. Publ. Econ. Bus. **11** (2017)

36. Twarowska, K.: Analysis of the use of the Chinese renminbi as an international currency. In: Soliman, K.S. (eds.) Proceedings of the 31st International Business Information Management Association Conference IBIMA, Italy (2018)
37. UNCTAD: UNCTADstat Data Center. http://unctadstat.unctad.org (2018)

Chapter 31
The Mechanisms of Changes in the Infrastructure of the Payment Card Market—A Comparative Analysis of Poland and China

Wiśniewski Jerzy Witold, Sokołowska Ewelina and Wu Jinghua

Abstract The Chinese payment card market differs significantly from the Polish one. The strategies for and the levels of its development vary in both countries. The subject of this work constitutes an attempt to compare the development of the infrastructure servicing the payment card markets in Poland and in China. The study was carried out based on the quarterly time series from the years 2008 to 2017. The subject of consideration is the infrastructure networks used to service payment cards. Two most important components of the payment card infrastructure were considered: the number of the point of sale terminals handling payment cards (POS) and the number of the automated teller machines (ATMs). The similarities and the differences in the construction of this infrastructure, resulting from various internal and external conditions, have been presented. The radical size differences between Poland and China result in the need to apply solutions that use quantitative market characteristics, expressed per capita, and to use measures of intensity, which are characterized by comparability of the results. The study used statistical and econometric tools for analysis of the characteristics of the payment card market infrastructure. A hypothesis was formulated about the existence of a feedback between the number of POSs and the number of ATMs, per 1 million payment cards, both in Poland and in China. This hypothesis was verified using an econometric model. The empirical econometric model allows a description of the mechanisms of the payment card market infrastructure and can be used to construct short-term forecasts.

W. J. Witold (✉)
Faculty of Economic Sciences and Management, Department of Econometrics & Statistics, Nicholas Copernicus University, ul. Gagarina 13 A, 87-100 Toruń, Poland
e-mail: Jerzy.Wisniewski@umk.pl

S. Ewelina
Faculty of Management, Department of Corporate Finance, University of Gdansk, ul. Armii Krajowej 101, 81-824 Sopot, Poland
e-mail: ewelina.sokolowska@ug.edu.pl

W. Jinghua
Sichuan Agricultural University, 611130 Sichuan Chengdu, China
e-mail: hhhjjjww@163.com

W. Tarczyński and K. Nermend (eds.), *Effective Investments on Capital Markets*, Springer Proceedings in Business and Economics,
https://doi.org/10.1007/978-3-030-21274-2_31

Keywords Payment card market · E-commerce · Comparative analysis · China

31.1 Introduction

The global trend in payments is characterized by a dynamic increase in non-cash transactions. In most countries worldwide, non-cash trading has been displacing cash. One of the instruments used in non-cash payments is payment cards. Their usage requires the development of an infrastructure servicing the cards. The most important components of this infrastructure are ATMs and the terminals handling payment card transactions (POS).

Research on payment cards had appeared in the economic literature at the end of the twentieth century. Examples include works such as: Humphrey et al. [6], Hancock et al. [4] and many other. More advanced research results were published at the beginning of the twenty-first century. Examples include works such as: Hauswald and Marquez [5], Amromin and Chakravorti [1], Rysman [7], Sokołowska [8], Sokołowska and Wiśniewski [10], Wiśniewski et al. [13], which contain various results of empirical studies on the payment card market.

Payment cards belong to the category of innovative financial instruments, which has been tackled in works such as: Tufano [11] and Sokołowska [9]. The need to substitute cash payments with electronic cash and its consequences has been addressed in the work of a team of the authors: Evans et al. [2]. The impact of the development of payment card infrastructure on the increase in the number of transactions in Poland has been discussed in the work by Sokołowska and Wiśniewski [8]. The work by Wiśniewski [14] is devoted to the process of substituting cash payments with non-cash payments through payment cards.

The aim of this work is to analyse the process of the changes in the payment card market infrastructure in Poland and China as well as to study the mechanisms governing those changes. It is necessary to answer the question of whether the level and the changes in the payment card market infrastructure in Poland and China are similar or do they differ significantly.

The tool used for analysis of the payment card market infrastructure mechanisms was econometric models. As a result, the explanation is expected regarding what degree and why the Polish and the Chinese payment card market infrastructure systems differ.

31.2 Methodology and Data

In the initial period of the payment card usage by bank customers, the cards were primarily used to withdraw cash from the ATMs. It reduced the costs of the banking system as well as facilitated and accelerated the money holders' access to cash. Along with the development of the infrastructure intended for handling non-cash transactions through payment cards, a rapid increase in the number and in the value of non-cash payments occurred.

In modern countries, cash transactions have been perishing. Cash is being replaced by electronic money. The subject of this study constitutes an analysis of the development of the infrastructure servicing payment cards, both in Poland and in China. Withdrawing cash from ATMs and payments by the means of payment cards require a network of ATMs and POSs, at which it is possible to make payments and transactions through payment cards. These networks have been developing differently in Poland and in China. The state of equipping people with payment cards is different in both countries as well.

In the empirical econometric equations presented in this work, the following variables characterizing the payment card market infrastructure occur:

(a) In Poland:

CARTPPLPL	the number of payment cards per 1000 inhabitants in Poland;
APAYPL	the average monthly remuneration in Poland;
POSCDPL	the number of POSs per 1 million payment cards in Poland (expressed in thousands);
ATMCDPL	the number of ATMs per 1 million payment cards in Poland (expressed in thousands);

(b) In China:

CARDPPLCH	the number of payment cards per 1000 inhabitants in China;
APAYCH	the average quarterly remuneration of the urban population in China;
ATMCDCH	the number of ATMs per 1 million payment cards in China (expressed in thousands);
POSCDCH	the number of POSs per 1 million payment cards in China (expressed in thousands).

The following linear econometric equations were used in the study:

$$y_t = \sum_{j=0}^{k} \alpha_j x_{tj} + \sum_{i=1}^{4} \beta_i y_{t-i} + \sum_{l=1}^{4} \sum_{j=1}^{k} \lambda_{lj} x_{t-l,j} + \alpha_{k+1} t + \sum_{h=1}^{3} \gamma_h \mathrm{d}q_h + \eta_t, \quad (1)$$

where:

y_t—observations on the explanatory variable (t = 1, …, n);
x_{tj}—observations of exogenous variables;
t—the time variable;
$\mathrm{d}q_1, \mathrm{d}q_2, \mathrm{d}q_3$—the dummy variables, taking the value of 1 in the distinguished quarter and the value of 0 in the remaining quarters;
η_t—the random component of the equation;
α_j, β_i, λ_{lj}, …, γ_h (j = 0,1, …, k, i = 1, …,4, l = 1, …, 4, h = 1, 2, 3)—structural parameters of the equation.

Using appropriate regression equations, the impact of the remuneration on the development of the infrastructure servicing payment cards and the interaction between its components were examined. The impact of the remuneration changes on the number of payment cards per 1000 inhabitants, both in Poland and in China, was examined as well. Payment cards had appeared in Poland sooner than in China. Therefore, at the end of 2017, there were 1018 payment cards per 1000 inhabitants in Poland, while in China only 481, respectively. It can be assumed that the tendency to own payment cards has been increasing, along with the increase of the citizens' wealth. As such, the impact of the remuneration on the state of people being equipped with payment cards was examined. The impact of the average monthly remuneration (APAYPL) on the number of payment cards per 1000 inhabitants (CARDPLPL) was considered for Poland. The impact of the autoregression as well as the impact of the delays of the variable APAYPL, the trend and seasonal fluctuations were examined as well. After elimination of the statistically insignificant variables, the results presented in Table 31.1 and in Fig. 31.1 were obtained.

The Polish payment card market can be regarded as developed. In 2017, the number of payment cards exceeded the number of inhabitants in Poland. A stable mechanism of the impact of the citizens' wealth on the number of cards, measured

Table 31.1 Dependent variable (Y): CARTPPLPL

Variable	Coefficient	Std. error	t-statistic	Prob. p	
Const.	126.576	49.5707	2.5534	0.0156	**
APAYPL	0.0545076	0.0162247	3.3595	0.0020	***
CARDPPLPL_1	0.829975	0.104508	7.9417	<0.0001	***
CARDPPLPL_4	−0.209222	0.0814304	−2.5693	0.0151	**
Mean dependent var.	891.3295		S.D. dependent var.	55.44564	
Sum squared resid.	4632.454		S.E. of regression	12.03180	
R-squared	0.956947		Adjusted R-squared	0.952910	
F(3. 31)	237.0872		Prob (F-statistic)	6.30e-22	
Log-likelihood	−138.5136		Akaike info criterion	285.0272	
Schwarz criterion	291.3613		Hannan–Quinn criterion	287.2380	
Autocorrel. coeff. (rho1)	0.021145		Durbin h-statistic	0.162867	

Source Own calculations using the GRETL package
**significance level until 0.05
***significance level until 0.01

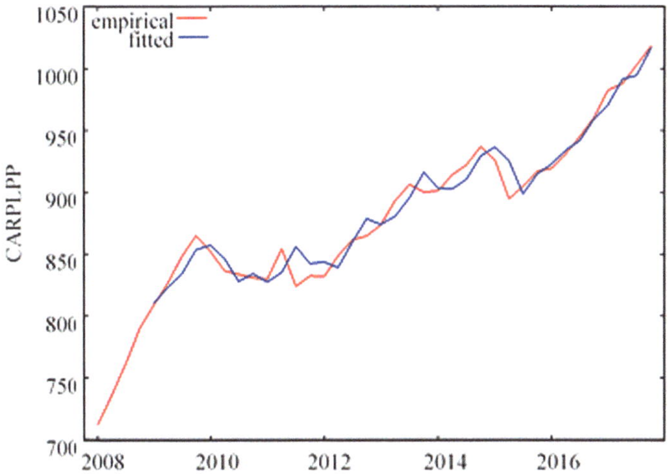

Fig. 31.1 Empirical and fitted values of the variable CARDPPLPL (*source* own calculations using the GRETL package, Table 31.1)

by the average monthly remuneration, has formed. The increase in the average remuneration (APAYPL) has been significantly rising the number of payment cards per one inhabitant. What is more, the first-order autoregression signals a positive inertia of the system. At the same time, the fourth-order autoregression reveals the alternating fluctuations of the number of cards (CARDPLPL), substituting the seasonal fluctuations, which do not occur directly.

Table 31.2 and Fig. 31.2 show the mechanism of the volatility in the number of payment cards in China, calculated per one inhabitant.[1] The Chinese payment card market is at a lower level of the development, in terms of the number of cards per one inhabitant, in comparison with the Polish market. The volatility mechanism of the variable CARDPLCH is also different, compared with the market in Poland.

The number of payment cards per 1000 inhabitants in China is dependent on the average quarterly remuneration of the urban population, with a delay of 3 quarters. A first-order autoregression occurs as well, with an intensity similar to that in Poland. In addition, seasonal fluctuations in each quarter of the year are significant.

[1]The study on the Chinese market involved the average quarterly remuneration of the urban population. The wages of the rural population, which are significantly lower compared to the wages in the cities, were omitted. It can also be assumed that in the current state of market advancement payment cardholders mainly originate from the cities, especially from the large ones.

Table 31.2 Dependent variable (Y): CARDPPLCH

Variable	Coefficient	Std. error	t-statistic	Prob. p	
const	−30.3888	7.65617	−3.9692	0.0004	***
APAYCH_3	0.019701	0.00416584	4.7292	<0.0001	***
dq1	16.8542	3.68052	4.5793	<0.0001	***
dq2	11.8502	2.98578	3.9689	0.0004	***
dq3	14.0902	2.83216	4.9750	<0.0001	***
CARDPPLCH-1	0.838167	0.0374113	22.4041	<0.0001	***
Mean dependent var.	292.5705		S.D. dependent var.		110.4158
Sum squared resid.	258.2930		S.E. of regression		2.886526
R-squared	0.999411		Adjusted R-squared		0.999317
F(3. 31)	10529.04		Prob (F-statistic)		4.40e-49
Log-likelihood	−88.44949		Akaike info criterion		188.8990
Schwarz criterion	198.5645		Hannan–Quinn criterion		192.3065
Autocorrel. coeff. (rho1)	0.097009		Durbin h-statistic		0.605979

Source Own calculations using the GRETL package
***significance level until 0.01

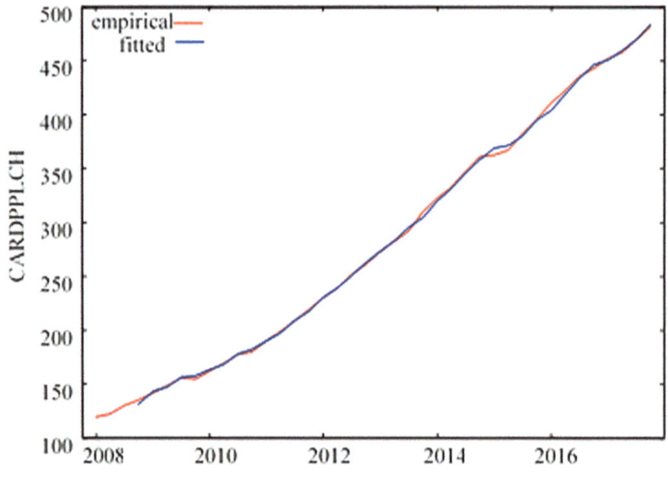

Fig. 31.2 Empirical and fitted values of the variable CARDPPLCH (*source* own calculations using the GRETL package, Table 31.2)

31.3 Results and Discussion

The Polish and the Chinese markets definitely differ, in terms of the development of the infrastructure servicing payment cards. Poland's entry into the European Union has made travelling through Europe easier. Travellers—to facilitate payments during their travel—eagerly equipped themselves with payment cards. Development of the infrastructure in Poland took place with some delay, initially mainly of ATMs, later on of the terminals servicing non-cash payments. On the Chinese market, the infrastructure was built (ATMs and POSs) in the first place, which was intended to encourage the citizens to own payment cards. The Chinese do not use the payment cards issued by large global companies; they use Chinese cards.

A Chinese payment cardholder has easier access—in a statistical sense—to ATMs and to the terminals handling non-cash payments. In China, there were nearly 1436 ATMs per one million payment cards, while in Poland only 594 ATMs, respectively. The number of the terminals handling non-cash transactions in this period in China was 46,622 per 1 million cards, while the analogous number in Poland in this period was 11,380. This reveals that a Chinese cardholder had much easier access to ATMs and POSs, compared to a Polish citizen.

The construction of a payment card market infrastructure begins with the installation of ATMs, which substitute the tellers at bank branches. Next, terminal posts are created, whose task is to service non-cash payments through payment cards. A hypothesis can be made about the existence—on a developed market—of a feedback between the number of ATMs (ATMCDPL) and the number of the POSs servicing non-cash payments through payment cards (POSCDPL), calculated per 1 million cards, that is:

$$\text{ATMCDPL} \rightleftarrows \text{POSCDPL}$$

The system of equations is identifiable ambiguously. For estimation of the parameters of such an equation, the economic literature recommends the double least squares method (2LS). Meanwhile, the structural parameters of the equations presented in Tables 31.3 and 31.4 were estimated using the ordinary least squares method. The results of the parameter estimation of the equation describing the variable POSCDPL, carried out using the OLS and the 2 LS, proved to be identical. However, as a result of using the 2OLS, the feedback was "broken". In the equation describing the variable ATMCDPL, the explanatory variable POSCDPL turned out to be statistically insignificant. This is a result of the loss of precision (efficiency) by the 2LS estimator ([3, pp. 455–456] and Wiśniewski [12], subchapter 5.5). Application of the OLS to estimate the parameters of this equation eliminates this defect of the 2LS estimator. All the equations are characterized by a high degree of the theoretical hyperplanes fitting to the empirical data. In most empirical equations, the R^2 values exceed the level of 0.99.

The empirical equations describing the mechanism of the interdependence between the variables ATMCDPL and POSCDPL are presented in Tables 31.3 and

Table 31.3 Dependent variable (Y): ATMCDPL

Variable	Coefficient	Std. error	t-statistic	Prob. p	
const	297.619	74.5763	3.9908	0.0004	***
APAYPL_3	−0.0515471	0.0216186	−2.3844	0.0236	**
POSCDPL	0.0244325	0.00680846	3.5886	0.0012	***
POSCDPL_3	−0.0304291	0.00618531	−4.9196	<0.0001	***
Time	3.32661	0.933529	3.5635	0.0012	***
dq2	−9.19183	3.07305	−2.9911	0.0055	***
ATMCDPL_1	0.743574	0.0960311	7.7431	<0.0001	***
Mean dependent var.	554.4412		S.D. dependent var.		54.80691
Sum squared resid.	1589.550		S.E. of regression		7.279080
R-squared	0.985301		Adjusted R-squared		0.982361
F(3. 31)	335.1488		Prob (F-statistic)		4.28e–26
Log-likelihood	−122.0661		Akaike info criterion		258.1321
Schwarz criterion	269.4085		Hannan–Quinn criterion		262.1076
Autocorrel. coeff. (rho1)	−0.096191		Durbin h-statistic		−0.720879

Source Own calculations using the GRETL package
**significance level until 0.05
***significance level until 0.01

31.4 as well as in Figs. 31.3 and 31.4. These equations also examined the impact of the increase in the citizens' wealth on the development of the components of the payment card market infrastructure, as well as investigated the autoregression, the linear trend and the seasonal fluctuations. The simultaneous increase in the value of the variable POSCDPL causes an increase in the value of the variable ATMCDPL. However, the increase in the level of the variable POSCDPL_3, delayed by 3 quarters, results in a decrease in the size of the variable ATMCDPL, whereas the negative impact of the delayed variable is clearly greater (in terms of the module) and is clearly stronger from the simultaneous impact of the variable POSCDPL. This may signify a tendency to displace ATMs by the terminal posts servicing non-cash payments (POSs).

In the equation describing ATMCDPL, there is a first-order positive autoregression, a linear trend and negative seasonal deviations in the second quarter of the year. The average monthly remuneration significantly impacts the number of ATMs, calculated per 1 million cards, with a delay by 2 quarters (APAYPL_3); however, it is a negative impact. It follows that along with an increase in the Polish citizens' wealth, the need to equip the payment card infrastructure with ATMs decreases.

Table 31.4 shows the empirical equation describing the volatility mechanism of the variable POSCDPL. An illustration of the real and the theoretical values representing the number of the terminal posts per 1 million payment cards is presented in Fig. 31.4. In the considered empirical equation, there is no trend, no seasonal fluctuations nor any impact of the average monthly remuneration. There are, however, a first-order

Table 31.4 Dependent variable (Y): POSCDPL

Variable	Coefficient	Std. error	t-statistic	Prob. p	
Const.	−576,745	339.6	−1.6983	0.0992	*
ATMCDPL	6.68975	0.923083	7.2472	<0.0001	***
ATMCDPL_3	−5.90609	1.24959	−4.7264	<0.0001	***
POSCDPL_1	0.568573	0.133415	4.2617	0.0002	***
POSCDPL_2	0.473522	0.13748	3.4443	0.0016	***
Mean dependent var.	7719.826		S.D. dependent var.	1997.485	
Sum squared resid.	0.237435		S.E. of regression	0.086139	
R-squared	0.998347		Adjusted R-squared	0.998140	
F(3. 31)	4831.654		Prob (F-statistic)	5.27e–44	
Log-likelihood	40,90167		Akaike info criterion	−71,80334	
Schwarz criterion	−63,74875		Hannan–Quinn criterion	−68,96372	
Autocorrel. coeff. (rho1)	−0,249497		Durbin h-statistic	−2,597291	

Source Own calculations using the GRETL package
*significance level until 0.1
***significance level until 0.01

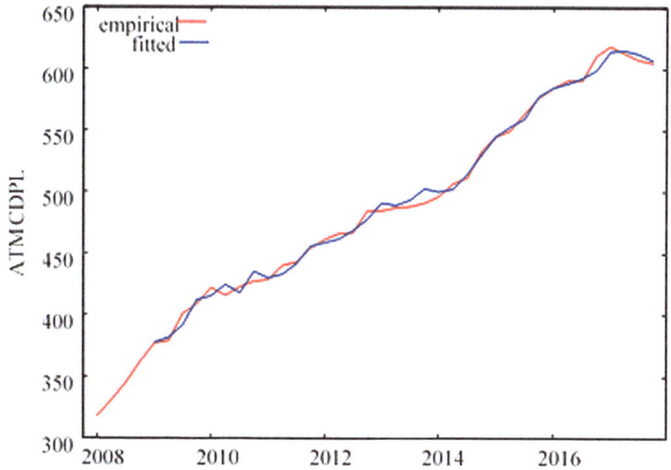

Fig. 31.3 Empirical and fitted values of the variable ATMCDPL (*source* own calculations using the GRETL package, Table 31.3)

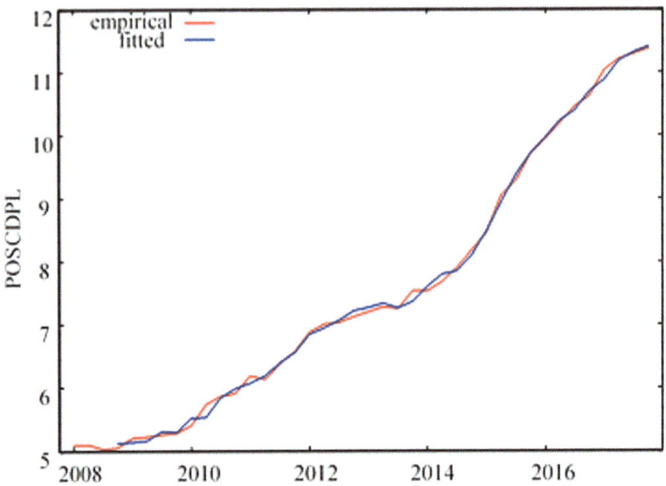

Fig. 31.4 Empirical and fitted values of the variable POSCDPL (*source* own calculations using the GRETL package, Table 31.4)

and a second-order autoregression with the total value of the coefficients exceeding 1. This signifies a strong inertia and a dynamic increase of the number in POSs calculated per 1 million payment cards. The feedback hypothesis is confirmed, since the variable POSCDPL is significantly affected by the variable ATMCDPL. The impact of the number of ATMs per 1 million payment cards is negative, with a delay of 3 quarters (ATMCDPL_3). This signifies an increase in the payment cardholders' propensity for non-cash payments realized at the posts equipped payment terminals, against the need to withdraw cash from ATMs. Since 2017, the number of ATMs in Poland has been decreasing. Along with a simultaneous increase in the number of the payment cards used by the citizens, there has been a decrease in the value of the variable ATMCDPL. Consequently, it can be expected that over the next several quarters, in Poland, the direction of the simultaneous impact of the variable ATMCDPL on the number of terminal posts per 1 million payment cards will change.

Table 31.4 shows the empirical equation describing the volatility mechanism of the variable POSCDPL. An illustration of the real and the theoretical values representing the number of the terminal posts per 1 million payment cards is presented on Fig. 31.4. In the considered empirical equation, there is no trend, no seasonal fluctuations nor any impact of the average monthly remuneration. There are, however, a first-order and a second-order autoregressions with the total value of the coefficients exceeding 1. This signifies a strong inertia and a dynamic increase of the number of POSs calculated per 1 million payment cards. The feedback hypothesis is confirmed, since the variable POSCDPL is significantly affected by the variable ATMCDPL. The impact of the number of ATMs per 1 million payment cards is negative, with a delay of 3 quarters (ATMCDPL_3). This signifies an increase in the payment card holders' propensity for non-cash payments realized at the posts equipped payment

Table 31.5 Dependent variable (Y): ATMCDCH

Variable	Coefficient	Std. error	t-statistic	Prob. p	
Const.	145.431	47.0651	3.0900	0.0041	***
APAYCH	0.0548343	0.0201929	2.7155	0.0106	**
dq1	−53.8339	23.2368	−2.3168	0.0271	**
dq3	−38.7219	16.4356	−2.3560	0.0248	**
ATMCDCH_1	1.29625	0.14535	8.9181	<0.0001	***
ATMCDCH_2	−0.571748	0.157888	−3.6212	0.0010	***
Mean dependent var.	1239.435		S.D. dependent var.	218.5017	
Sum squared resid.	55047.43		S.E. of regression	41.47568	
R-squared	0.968838		Adjusted R-squared	0.963969	
F(3. 31)	198.9781		Prob (F-statistic)	4.07e-23	
Log-likelihood	−192.2086		Akaike info criterion	396.4172	
Schwarz criterion	406.2427		Hannan–Quinn criterion	399.9130	
Autocorrel. coeff. (rho1)	0.062727		Durbin h-statistic	0.870777	

Source Own calculations using the GRETL package
**significance level until 0.05
***significance level until 0.01

terminals, against the need to withdraw cash from ATMs. Since 2017, the number of ATMs in Poland has been decreasing. Along with a simultaneous increase in the number of the payment cards used by the citizens, there has been a decrease in the value of the variable ATMCDPL. Consequently, it can be expected that over the next several quarters, in Poland, the direction of the simultaneous impact of the variable ATMCDPL on the number of terminal posts per 1 million payment cards will change.

Table 31.5 and Fig. 31.5 present the equation describing the volatility mechanism of the number of ATMs per 1 million payment cards in China. There is no simultaneous nor delayed impact of the variable POSCDCH on the variable ATMCDCH. Thus, the number of ATMs in China increases, regardless the changes in the number of the terminal posts servicing non-cash payments calculated per 1 million payment cards.

The number of ATMs per 1 million payment cards in China had been increasing dynamically until 2015, followed by a decrease in the value of the variable ATMCDCH, mainly due to a rapid increase in the number of payment cards on this market (Fig. 31.5). The value increments of the variable ATMCDCH are caused mainly by the increase in wealth, expressed by an increase in the average quarterly remuneration of the urban population (APAYCH). The positive autoregression of the first order

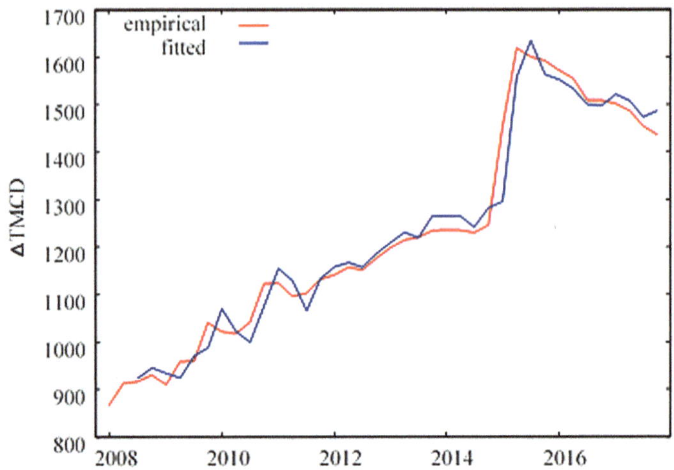

Fig. 31.5 Empirical and fitted values of the variable ATMCDCH (*source* own calculations using the GRETL package, Table 31.5)

and the negative autoregression of the second order are also strong. The changes in the value of the variable ATMCDCH are characterized by significant seasonal fluctuations. In the first and the fourth quarters of the year, the value of the variable ATMCDCH was higher than the so-called systematic component of the equation, on average by over 23 ATMs per 1 million cards. This could be due to the specificity of the fluctuations of the average remuneration, the highest values of which were recorded in the first quarter of the year. In the second and the third quarter of the year, the value of the variable ATMCDCH was visibly lower than the systematic component of the equation, respectively, by nearly 31 and over 23 ATMs per 1 million payment cards. In the considered equation, there is no linear trend, as eliminated by the first-order and the second-order autoregressions.

The empirical equation describing the volatility mechanism of the variable POSCDCH is presented in Table 31.6. Figure 31.6 illustrates the description accuracy of the number of POSs per 1 million payment cards in China. The value of the variable POSCDCH increases rapidly and systematically. A linear trend, seasonal fluctuations and simultaneous values of the variables APAYCH and ATMCDCH were eliminated from the equation—as statistically insignificant. This means that the system of the equations describing the basic components of the Chinese payment card market infrastructure is not a system of interdependent equations nor a recursive model. A simple model with two equations was created. The impact of the variable representing the number of ATMs per 1 million payment cards, delayed by 4 quarters (ATMCDCH_4), signals that the system will be moving towards recursiveness, when this market develops significantly. The increase in the value of the variable ATMCDCH_4 resulted in a decrease in the number of POSs calculated per 1 million cards. The decrease in the value of the variable ATMCDCH, observed in subsequent

Table 31.6 Dependent variable (Y): POSCDCH

Variable	Coefficient	Std. error	t-statistic	Prob. p	
Const.	126.172	2141.92	0.0589	0.9534	
APAYCH_1	1.69374	0.441284	3.8382	0.0006	***
APAYCH_2	1.24556	0.452181	2.7546	0.0097	***
ATMCDCH_4	−7.35638	2.61006	−2.8185	0.0083	***
POSCDCH_1	0.918956	0.0588588	15.6129	<0.0001	***
Mean dependent var.	26058.29		S.D. dependent var.	12490.61	
Sum squared resid.	34788662		S.E. of regression	1059.346	
R-squared	0.993629		Adjusted R-squared	0.992807	
F(3. 31)	1208.715		Prob (F-statistic)	1.51e-33	
Log-likelihood	−299.1449		Akaike info criterion	608.2898	
Schwarz criterion	616.2074		Hannan–Quinn criterion	611.0532	
Autocorrel. coeff. (rho1)	−0.081960		Durbin h-statistic	−0.525629	

Source Own calculations using the GRETL package
***significance level until 0.01

quarters since [8], therefore causes an increase in the number of non-cash payment terminal posts per 1 million cards, in the last two years.

The increase in the wealth of the Chinese citizens, expressed by an increase in the average quarterly remuneration, results in an increase in the number of the non-cash payment terminal posts servicing payment cards, as calculated per 1 million payment cards. The effects of the average remuneration on the increase in the value of the variable POSCDCH are, however, revealed with delays of 1 or 2 quarters. The positive impact of the first-order autoregression is strong as well.

31.4 Conclusions

The payment card market infrastructures in Poland and China arose under different circumstances. Poland's accession to the structures of the European Union has resulted in the demand for payment cards on the part of the poles travelling across Europe. Offers emerged from the banks recommending debit cards and credit cards. The citizens' possession of cards encouraged the financial sector to create a network of ATMs, replacing the teller windows at banks. In the next stage, a network of terminal posts servicing non-cash payments for goods and services was built. Exces-

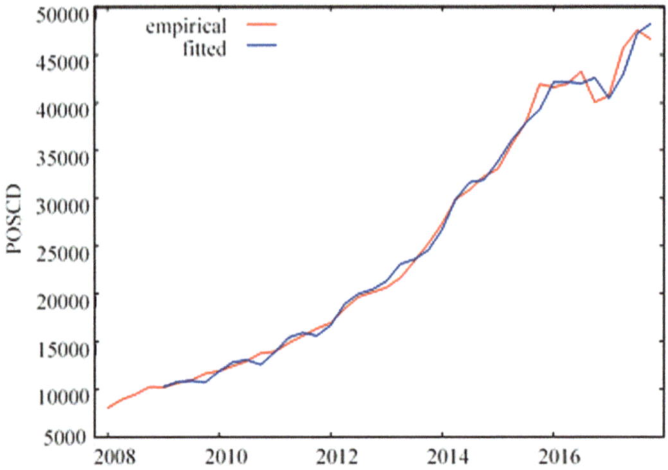

Fig. 31.6 Empirical and fitted values of the variable POSCDCH (*source* own calculations using the GRETL package, Table 31.6)

sively high fees for non-cash payments through payment cards limited their use for transactions. Only the statutory reduction of the fees and emergence of contactless cards caused a dynamic increase in non-cash payment transactions. As a result, in 2018, the values of non-cash payments per 1 payment card approached the values of ATM withdrawals calculated per 1 card. This means that non-cash payments in Poland have been replacing cash.

The Chinese payment card market, in the initial phase, was developing differently than the Polish one. First, a network of ATMs was created, in order to facilitate access to cash for payment cardholders. Then, the construction of a network of terminal posts servicing non-cash payments through payment cards was started. As a result, payment cardholders have easier access to ATMs and POSs, in comparison with Poland, at a comparable level of the market development.

It can be assumed that on the payment card markets at a similar development level, as in China, there are no links between the number of ATMs and the number of the terminal posts servicing non-cash payments through cards, calculated per 1 million cards. The fact that this market has achieved such a high level results in a substitution of cash payments with non-cash transactions through payment cards. As a result, there is a feedback between the variables ATMCDPL and POSCDPL, indicating that the terminal posts servicing non-cash transactions through payment cards have been replacing ATMs, reducing the demand for cash. It can be expected that as early as in the first half of the twenty-first century, such a feedback will appear in China between the variables ATMCDCH and POSCDPL. In this way, traditional money will gradually be displaced by electronic money. The only difficulty is to establish the limit, at which payments with the use of traditional money will stop all together.

References

1. Amromin, G., Chakravorti, S.: Debit card and cash usage: A cross-country analysis (2007)
2. Evans D.S., Webster K., Colgan G.K., Murray S.R.: Payments innovation and the use of cash, social science research network working paper series (5 June 2013) (2013)
3. Goldberger A.S.: Teoria ekonometrii (Econometrics Theory), PWE Warsaw (1972)
4. Hancock, D., Humphrey, D.B., Wilcox, J.: Cost reductions in electronic payments: the roles of consolidation, economies of scale, and technical change. J. Banking & Finan. **23**, 391–421 (1999)
5. Hauswald, R., Marquez, R.: Information technology and financial services. Competition Rev. Financ. Stud. **16**(3), 921–948 (CrossRef) (2003)
6. Humphrey, D.B., Pulley, L.B., Vesala, J.M.: Cash, paper, and electronic payments: a cross-country analysis. J. Money, Credit and Banking 914–939
7. Rysman, M.: An empirical analysis of payment card usage. J Ind Econ **55**(1), 1–36 (2007). https://doi.org/10.1111/j.1467-6451.2007.00301.x
8. Sokołowska, E.: Innovations in the payment card market: the case of Poland. Electron. Commer. Res. Appl. **14**(5), 292–304 (2015)
9. Sokołowska, E.: The Principles of alternative investments management: a study of the global market. Springer International Publishing Switzerland, Cham (2015)
10. Sokołowska, E., Wiśniewski J.W.: Forecasts of payment card payments against the changes in the infrastructure of the payment system in Poland, 10th International Scientific Conference, Financial Management of Firms and Financial Institutions, 7th–8th September 2015, Ostrava, Czech Republic VŠB—Technical University of Ostrava Faculty of Economics, Department of Finance, part IV, pp. 1174–1182 (2015)
11. Tufano, P.: Financial innovation. Handb. Econ. Financ. **1**, 307–335 (2003)
12. Wiśniewski, J.W.: Microeconometrics in business management. Wiley, Chichester (2016)
13. Wiśniewski, J.W., Sokołowska, E., Jinghua, W.: The dynamics of the payment card market. A comparative analysis of Poland and China. In: Szkutnik, W., Sączewska-Piotrowska, A., Hadaś-Dyduch, M., Acedański, J. (eds.) 8th International Scientific Conference "Analysis of International Relations 2017. Methods and Models of Regional Development". Conference Proceedings, Publishing House of the University of Economics in Katowice, pp. 132–141 (2017)
14. Wiśniewski J.W.: Substitution of payments on the payment cards market in Poland, X International Scientific Conference Analysis of International Relations 2018. Methods and Models of Regional Development, Summer Edition, Katowice, 19–20 June 2018 (2018)

Chapter 32
The Econometric Analysis of the Food Sector Performance on the Background of the Main Market at Warsaw Stock Exchange

Dorota Żebrowska-Suchodolska and Andrzej Karpio

Abstract The presented work attempts an econometric analysis of the quotations of companies from the food sector against the background of the main market of the Warsaw Stock Exchange. The entire sector was examined, not individual entities, treating the WIG-food index as a portfolio of shares. The aim of the research is to identify the relationship between the agri-food sector and stock market segments. Determining the correlation strength of the WIG index—foodstuffs with the WIG, WIG20, mWIG40 and sWIG80 indices will allow linking this sector with individual markets. The formulated goal is implemented using linear regression models with one explanatory variable. The studies were limited to 2008–2017 years taking into account the monthly rates of change. The results indicate that the agri-food sector can be included in the stock market segment described by the sWIG80 index.

Keywords Linear regression · Stock indices · Agri-food industry

JEL codes C01 · C13 · Q10 · Q19

32.1 Introduction

The pioneering research of the securities market in the USA conducted at the end of the nineteenth by Charles Dow showed that the quotations of companies reflect not only the expectations of investors regarding individual assets but most of all the entire sectors of the economy. The consequence of the research was the calculation of the average stock market, in the first account only railway companies were considered, believing that this is a key industry for the whole American economy.

D. Żebrowska-Suchodolska
Warsaw University of Life Sciences—SGGW, Zawady 120, 15-697 Bialystok, Poland
e-mail: dorota_zebrowska_suchodolska@sggw.pl

A. Karpio (✉)
Warsaw University of Life Sciences—SGGW, Gajowa 92, 15-794 Bialystok, Poland
e-mail: andrzej_karpio@sggw.pl

W. Tarczyński and K. Nermend (eds.), *Effective Investments on Capital Markets*, Springer Proceedings in Business and Economics,
https://doi.org/10.1007/978-3-030-21274-2_32

A few years later, Ch. Dow introduced the second average in which other industries were represented. This was dictated by the proposed measurement of the stock market situation by observing the behaviour of both averages—the continuation of the trend or its change must be confirmed by both indicators. From the first half of the twentieth century to the present, the calculation of stock market indices has become a standard. Each stock exchange calculates many of them, ranging from the indices of the entire market to industry ones. Dow's hypothesis about the relationship between the economic situation and the behaviour of the stock market indices has been repeatedly confirmed. For these reasons, the authors of this study decided to examine the behaviour of companies in the agri-food sector listed on the Warsaw Stock Exchange against the background of the markets described by the basic stock indices WIG, WIG20, mWIG40, sWIG80. The capitalization of the Polish stock exchange in relation to GDP has been close to 30% for many years. Therefore, the connection between the stock exchange and the economy is not very large, but it is undoubtedly impossible to ignore. Instead of focusing on particular values, the WIG-food index, which is the portfolio of all companies in the industry listed on WSE, was subjected to research. The research was carried out using standard econometric models. In the summary, the results of the model with many variables were mentioned, which were not presented due to the lack of space. In this case, the results confirm the conclusions resulting from the presented models.

32.2 Review of the Literature

Many statistical and econometric tools can be used to study the dependencies of financial markets. It can indicate here the correlation analysis, linear regression model, cointegration analysis, vector autoregression models (VaR) or GARCH type models. Such research is carried out in the literature both within a given market, for sectoral indices as well as for individual companies, as well as between markets of different countries.

Correlations between market sectors were investigated, among others, Nagendra et al. [13] or Kurisetti et al. [10]. The Nagendra studies [13] concerned the Indian market for which the NSE NIFTY index was surveyed, including the 50 largest and most liquid companies, with seven industry indices of the NSE market. The research was carried out for monthly rates of return in 2006–2010 using Pearson's correlation coefficient. The results indicate that the monthly rates of return of the NSE NIFTY index are correlated with the majority of industry indices. This means that the NSE NIFTY index strongly affects sectoral indices. Short-term and long-term dependencies between selected sectoral indices of the NSE market were observed by Kurisetti et al. [10]. For the data from 2010 to 2016, the ADF test, the Granger test for cointegration and the error correction model (ECM) were used.

Research on correlations between sectors of various countries was carried out, among others Fasnacht and Loeberge [7]. They showed that the inter-sector relationships of different countries are more stable over time than the inter-sectoral dependencies within individual countries. Similar results were observed by Meric et al. [12] who analysed the US, the UK, German, French and Japanese markets. Sectors listed on London Stock Exchange were investigated by Amin et al. [1]. The lack of dependence between the Chinese market branches and international markets was indicated by Cao et al. [4], while noticing an upward trend. Using the Pearson correlation coefficient for research, they pointed to the existence of a correlation between sectoral indices, i.e. finance, industry and energy with the CSI 300 index, covering 300 shares listed on the Shanghai and Shenzhen Stock Exchange.

In recent years, the fundamental analysis methods were applied to the investigation of the sector and share performance listed on the stock exchange [14]. The validity of the capital asset pricing model was examined on the Pakistan Stock Exchange [16]. It seems that these researches can be treated as the extensions of the econometric methods applied to the analysis of sectors listed on the stock exchanges.

Research for the Polish market focuses on the analysis of the relationship between the Polish market and the markets of other countries. A strong dependence of the Polish market on the American market [6] and European markets [2] has been demonstrated here. Augustynski [2] used a correlation coefficient and a single equation linear model for his research. Using the same research methods, Gluzicka [8] confirmed the existence of dependence, indicating mainly dependencies on the European markets. Due to the fact that the authors did find just one research on the dependence of food index on the Polish market [15] but from the risk aspect, it is reasonable to conduct such research for the Polish market.

32.3 Theoretical Basics

Linear regression models are the standard methods of studying interdependencies between variables that have a large application in economics and finance. Obviously, the linearity is a significant simplification. However, it can be treated as the first step in the search for more complex dependencies or as the first approximation. From the interpretative point of view, the explanation of the variable by another one is justified by the occurrence of correlation. In this work, the agri-food sector is represented by the WIG-food index which is a portfolio of 25 companies. In turn, the explanatory variables are also portfolios but the shares that make up the WIG, WIG20, mWIG40 and sWIG80 indices. They represent the majority of companies listed on the WSE (WIG), the respective 20 largest (WIG20), then medium and small (mWIG40 and sWIG80, respectively). The basis for the aforementioned correlation is a quite obvious observation that the situation on stock exchanges concerns the majority of the quoted shares. If one talks about the bullish market, on the one hand, the WIG or WIG20 growth is meant, but investors are willing to buy companies from outside of these indices. Often, they do not even know which ones are included in the indices. A similar situation takes place in the case of a bearish market. This behaviour of the stock exchange markets indicates the correlation between various market indexes.

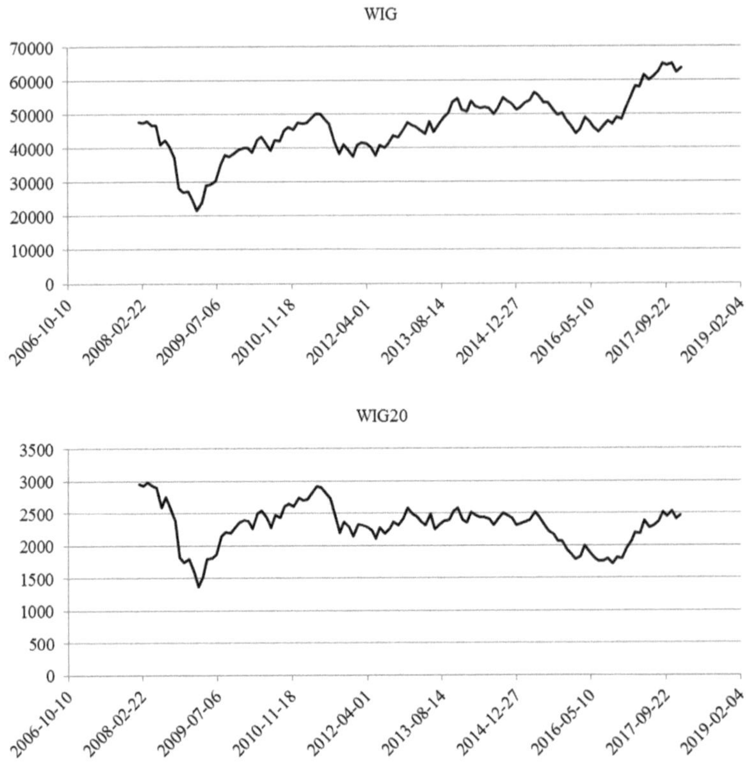

Fig. 32.1 Quotations of WIG and WIG20 indices during the research period (*Source* own study)

From the point of view of this work, this can be considered as a justification for choosing the explanatory variable (WIG-food) and explained variables.

The following charts show the quotations of the stock exchange indices used in the research. WIG and WIG20 were compared to the first one (Fig. 32.1).

It can be seen that the waveforms are very close to each other, but remember that index values differ significantly from each other. The WIG value is more than ten times higher than WIG20. Thus, both describe a similar economic situation but expressed entirely by other numbers and quotations of other companies. So, the similarity of mileage does not mean that they contain identical information about the stock market situation. A similar situation takes place in the case of medium and small company indices (Fig. 32.2).

This time, the mWIG40 quotes are three times higher than the sWIG80 index. Against the background of the chart graphs shown, the WIG-food index is shown in Fig. 32.3. It should be noted, however, that the subject of the research will be the percentage changes in index quotations, and WIG-food will be the explained variable.

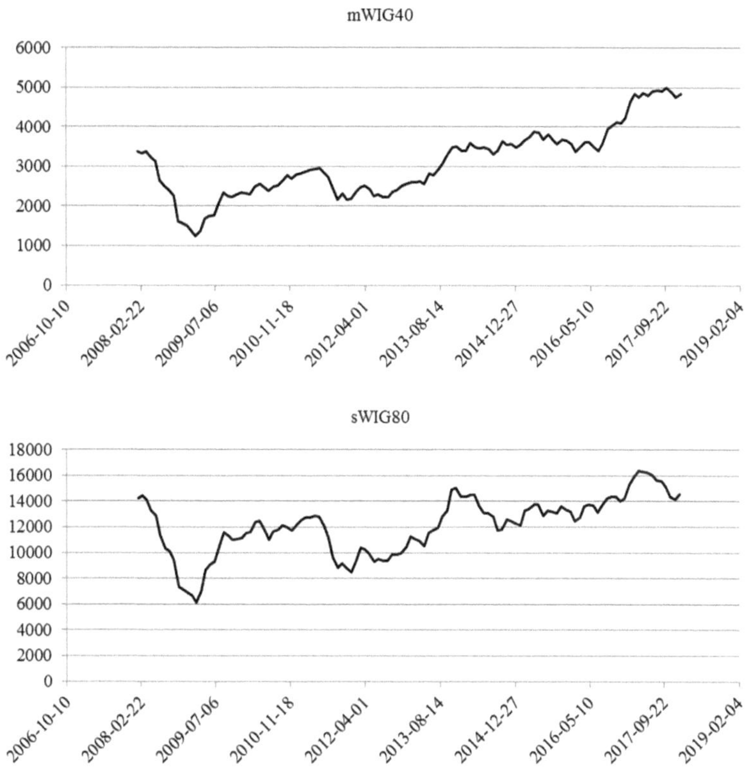

Fig. 32.2 Listing of mWIG40 and sWIG80 indices during the research period (*Source* own study)

Fig. 32.3 The course of quotations of the WIG-food index (*Source* own study)

Built models will help to determine the strength of the dependence between the agri-food sector and the broad market situation, divided into large, medium and small companies. The structural parameters of the models being built are estimated using the linear least square method. In the case of financial variables, and such are the percentage changes of the prices, this method often fails. However, the authors decided on LLSQ mainly because it is the first step towards further research. It is necessary to identify the causes of possible imperfections of the method in order to be able to change it into a more adequate one. There are two factors behind LLSQ. First of all, it is particularly simple. Secondly, the volatility of portfolios is smaller than individual values, and it is the nature of the volatility of financial variables that makes the classical method cannot check. Nevertheless, the inadequacy of the least squares method allows us to draw conclusions about the direction of further research.

32.4 Linear Regression Models for the WIG-Food Index

The basis of the research are the Warsaw Stock Exchange indices WIG, WIG20, sWIG60, mWIG80 treated as explanatory variables for the portfolio of the companies' shares in the agri-food sector represented by WIG-food. It consists of 25 companies, both Polish and foreign, Ukrainian first of all. From the conducted surveys point of view, the presence of non-Polish companies in indices is irrelevant, as they have an impact on the stock exchange situation on a par with Polish ones. In addition, foreign companies appear in all the stock market indices. It can be assumed that the vast majority of investors, when choosing an investment, are guided mainly by expectations regarding future prices, and not by national criteria.

In the first step, linear regression models are built with one explanatory variable (WIG-food index), and then models for selected indexes, in which the explanatory variable is WIG-food. In the first case, the following equations are used:

$$r_{\text{WIG-food}} = \alpha + \beta \cdot r_{\text{Index}} + \varepsilon \tag{1}$$

where the "index" refers to the used indices: WIG, WIG20, mWIG40 and sWIG80, respectively. In the second case, the equation is analogous, but the variables are changed places.

The basis for the estimation of structural parameters is the monthly percentage changes of indices in the period from January 2008, until the end of 2017, calculated "traditionally" not logarithmically, i.e. as the ratio of the change in the value of the index to its value at the beginning of the month. The choice of the beginning of the research period is dictated by the end of the financial crisis. The authors assume that the disturbances of the economic processes taking place in crisis situations cannot be treated on a par with the more or less "quiet" periods. Therefore, times of crisis should be the subject of a separate analysis. The model parameters are estimated using the linear least squares method. Then, the classic tests are performed to verify model estimation by examining [9]. Luszniewicz and Slaby [11]: homoscedasticity (White's test), first-order autocorrelation (Ljung-Box), residual normality (Doornik-Hansen test) and randomness (series test). The data used in the work were obtained from the portal www.stooq.pl. The measures of matching the models to the empirical data are the coefficients of determination. In the case of beta coefficients, their significance at 5% level was tested.

32.5 Results and Discussion

The results of the estimation of structural parameters of the four linear regression models with the WIG, WIG20, mWIG40 and sWIG80 indices as explanatory variables have been collected in Table 32.1.

The bold font indicates beta is statistically significant at 5% level. In the first place, it should be noted that the WIG-food index is not correlated with the WIG broad market index; the beta coefficient is zero from a statistical point of view. The WIG at the end of December 2017 consisted of 391 companies. Therefore, it can be concluded that its impact on changes in companies from the agri-food sector was negligible. The confirmation of this conclusion is the very low coefficient of determination (2.2%) which proves that WIG changes cannot be treated as the variable explaining the changes of the quotations of the food sector companies.

The situation looks a bit different for the other market indicators. The beta coefficients are statistically significant, but only in the case of sWIG80 it assumes a value that can be considered as large. However, the coefficient of determination equal to 46% indicates that the impact of this index on the agri-food sector is not significant, and other factors explaining WIG-food changes should be sought. As a consequence, the measures of matching linear models indicate the existence of other variables having a greater impact on this sector than the indexes used. This may be due to the fact that the capitalization of the Polish stock exchange accounts for approximately 30% of GDP; therefore, its interdependence with the economy of the country is rather small.

Similar conclusions can be drawn by examining single-indicator models, in which the explained variables are the percentage changes of four indexes, and the explanatory variable is WIG-food changes. The results are summarized in Table 32.2.

It can be seen that most of the conclusions formulated above remain valid. Changes in the WIG-food index have a slight impact on the changes on the four indexes under review. It means that the stock market trend measured by these indices is to a small extent dictated by the behaviour of agri-food companies.

It should be added that the verification of the constructed models leads to not very optimistic conclusions regarding the applied method. In both cases, the lack of homoscedasticity prevails. It means that the estimation of structural parameters is not reliable because as the sample size increases, they do not aim at their actual values. A similar situation occurs in the case of the normality of residues, with one exception they do not have a normal distribution. However, this property only forces

Table 32.1 Linear regression models with WIG, WIG20, mWIG40, sWIG80 indices as explanatory variables

Index	Alpha coefficient	Standard error of alpha coefficient	Beta coefficient	Standard error of beta coefficient	Coefficient of determination	Heteroscedasticity	First-order autocorrelation	Randomness	Normality
WIG	0.3483	0.6511	0.0385	0.0235	0.0224	Lack	Lack	Yes	No
WIG20	0.4201	0.5694	**0.6025**	0.0971	0.2477	Yes	Yes	Yes	No
mWIG40	0.1369	0.5579	**0.5027**	0.0741	0.2823	Yes	Lack	Yes	No
sWIG80	0.2746	0.4822	**0.8336**	0.0833	0.4611	Yes	Lack	Yes	No

Source own study

Table 32.2 Linear regression models with WIG, WIG20, mWIG40, sWIG80 indices as explained variables

Index	Alpha coefficient	Standard error of alpha coefficient	Beta coefficient	Standard error of beta coefficient	Coefficient of determination	Heteroscedasticity	First-order autocorrelation	Randomness	Normality
WIG	1.9530	2.5260	0.5816	0.3551	0.0224	Lack	Yes	Yes	No
WIG20	−0.1562	0.4712	**0.4111**	0.0662	0.2477	Yes	Lack	Yes	Yes
mWIG40	0.3462	0.5889	**0.5615**	0.0828	0.2823	Lack	Lack	Yes	No
sWIG80	−0.0493	0.3933	**0.5531**	0.0553	0.4611	Yes	Lack	Yes	No

Source own study

the use of statistical tests that do not require the assumption of normality. Therefore, it is technical and not interpretative.

Some optimism is aroused by the fact that apart from two cases, there is no autocorrelation of random components except the case with WIG index. The occurrence of autocorrelation has an impact on the efficiency of the estimators, i.e. the error with which they are determined. It can therefore be concluded that the considered models dominate the lack of autocorrelation. This conclusion does not apply to models with WIG because in these cases all structural variables are not significant. At the end, there was a problem of the randomness of the rests. The situation is now unambiguous, the rests of all models show randomness. It means that the functional form of all models has been chosen correctly. Therefore, it can be assumed that one should look for additional variables affecting WIG-food. This is proved by relatively small values of determination coefficients. In addition, further research should be based on other methods of estimating structural parameters than LLSQ [3].

32.6 Summary

Summarizing the results of the research, it should be stated that from the point of view of the Warsaw Stock Exchange market, the agri-food sector has a relatively small share in shaping the market situation. The results suggest that investors base their decisions on off-exchange factors when they opt for transactions in this sector. The proof is small values of beta coefficients, both when WIG-food is an explanatory and explained variable. In addition, the coefficients of determination suggest the selection of explanatory variables other than the indices used. In the case of the broad market index WIG, in all cases the beta coefficients are equal to zero. Only the correlation of the surveyed sector with the market represented by small companies seems to be significant. In models with WIG-food as an explanatory variable and sWIG80 being a dependent variable, the beta factor is definitely more valuable than the others. This thesis is confirmed by the result obtained in the multiple regression model with all four indices as explanatory ones. The results are not presented here, but they were obtained by authors and they are preparing to be published. Then the beta coefficient at sWIG80 is the only one significantly different from zero. As a consequence, it can be concluded that the agri-food sector plays an important role on the Warsaw Stock Exchange but mainly in the small-sized sector represented by the sWIG80 index. The situation can be explained by the size of the food sector. Its capitalization is not significant with the comparison to other sectors. The market value of the food sector is equal to 1.29% of the whole stock exchange capitalization (the end of 2017). Financial institutions especially banks have market value about 62% and dominate between all sectors. That is why their impact for the indices is much greater than other ones. It must be noticed that some financial institutions come into all used market indices. The share of financials in turnover of WSE is almost 37%, but food sector is less than 1%. It seems that the described situation of the food sector is the main explanation of the obtained results.

Literature

1. Amin, S., Aslam, S.: Intellectual capital, innovation and firm performance of pharmaceuticals: a study of the London stock exchange. J. Inf. Knowl. Manage. **16**(02) (2017), https://doi.org/10.1142/s0219649217500174
2. Augustynski, I.: The impact of foreign stock exchanges on the main stock exchange indexes in Poland E-Fnanse **7**(1), 1–12 (2011)
3. Borkowski, B., Dudek, H., Szczesny, W.: Ekonometria. Wybrane zagadnienia. Wydawnictwo Naukowe PWN, Warszawa (2003)
4. Cao, D., Long, W., Yang, W.: Sector indices correlation analysis in China's stock market. Procedia Comput. Sci (17), 1241–1249 (2013)
5. Chow, G.: Ekonometria. Wydawnictwo Naukowe PWN, Warszawa (1995)
6. Dudek, A.: Wpływ sytuacji na amerykanskiej gieldzie papierow wartosciowych na zachowania inwestorow w Polsce – analiza ekonometryczna, Ekonomiczne Problemy Funkcjonowania Wspolczesnego Swiata, (red.) Kopycinska D., Szczecin (2009)
7. Fasnacht, P., Loeberge, H.: International stock market correlations: a sectorial approach, Finance International Meeting AFFI-EURO FIDAI, Paris, December 2007, Paper
8. Gluzicka, A.: Wpływ swiatowych rynkow finansowych na Gielde Papierow Wartosciowych w Warszawie. Studia Ekonomiczne, Uniwersytet Ekonomiczny w Katowicach **162**, 144–157 (2013)
9. Kufel, T.: Ekonometria. Rozwiazywanie problemow z wykorzystaniem programu GRETL. Wydawnictwo Naukowe PWN, Warszawa (2007)
10. Kurisetti, P., Yeldandi, S., Perumandla, S.: Test of co-integration and equilibrium relationship among the selected sectoral indices: empirical evidence from NSE India. Pac. Bus. Rev. Int. **10**(11), 114–123 (2018)
11. Luszniewicz, A., Slaby, T.: Statystyka z pakietem komputerowym STATISTICA PL. Teoria i zastosowania, C.H. Beck, Warszawa (2003)
12. Meric, I., Ratner, M., Meric, G.: The co-movements of sector index returns in the world's major stock markets during bull and bear markets: Portfolio diversification implications. Int. Rev. Fin. Anal. **17**(1), 156–177 (2008)
13. Nagendra, M., Haritha, M., Ravi, V.: NSE NIFTY and its correlation with sectorial indexes. Int. J. Conceptions Manage. Soc. Sci **2**(1) (2014)
14. Ozturk, H., Karabulut, T.A.: The relationship between earnings-to-price, current ratio, profit margin and return: an empirical analysis on Istanbul stock exchange. Account. Finance Res. **7**(1), 109–115 (2018), https://doi.org/10.5430/afr.v7n1p109
15. Pera, J.: Linear and non-linear relationships between shares of the agri-food industries of the Warsaw Stock exchange. Risk Aspect, Prob. World Agric. Sci. J., Warsaw Univ. Life Sci.—SGGW **17**(4), 249–262 (2017), https://doi.org/10.22630/prs.2017.17.4.101
16. Wu, M., Imran, M., Feng, Y., Zhang, L., Abbas, M.: Review and validity of capital asset pricing model: evidence from Pakistan stock exchange. Int. Res. Econ. Finance **1**(1), 21–31 (2017). https://doi.org/10.20849/iref.v1i1.267

Chapter 33
Fuzzy AHP and VIKOR to Select Best Location for Bank Investment: Case Study in Kurdistan Region of Iraq

Ahmet Demir, Sarkhel Shawkat, Bzhar Nasradeen Majeed and Taylan Budur

Abstract Location selection is one of the most important decisions of the operations manager. One of the effectiveness criteria of the organizations is the correct location. And the appropriate location for the banking sector means better network to the customers and a competitive advantage in the market. The present paper investigates the best location as using the fuzzy AHP and VIKOR analysis in the Kurdistan Region of Iraq. The research revealed that "security in the region" and "willingness to work with the bank" have been the most important criterions in location strategy. These results show contrast with the developed countries.

Keywords Fuzzy AHP · Location strategy · VIKOR · MCDMA · Bank location strategy

33.1 Introduction

As long as world market keeps on expanding, global nature of every business also gains speed. From this point of view, operations manager job is harder than ever in this global acceleration. As one of the ten strategic decisions of operations managers is location strategy, it is significantly important to select initially where to locate a firm.

A. Demir (✉) · T. Budur
Department of Business and Management, Faculty of Economics and Administrative Sciences, Ishik University, Qirga, Sulaimani, Iraq
e-mail: ahmet.demir@ishik.edu.iq

T. Budur
e-mail: taylan.budur@ishik.edu.iq

S. Shawkat · B. N. Majeed
Faculty of Economics and Administrative Sciences, Charmo University, Chamchamal, Sulaimani, Iraq
e-mail: sarkhel.mohammed@charmouniversity.org

B. N. Majeed
e-mail: bzhar.majeed@charmouniversity.org

W. Tarczyński and K. Nermend (eds.), *Effective Investments on Capital Markets*, Springer Proceedings in Business and Economics,
https://doi.org/10.1007/978-3-030-21274-2_33

A poor location strategy may increase transportation cost, cause losing competitive advantage, and consequently impact the overall success of the business [19, 50]. Beside this, good location strategy may affect overall costs of a firm up to 50% [25].

Although there are many location selection strategies and methods such as integer programming [35], multiple regression analysis [38], and branch and bound methods [16], multi-dimensional decision-making analysis is a method that calculates all complex criterions and provides a solution for decision-maker. However, there is a general flow of location selection process such as determining the main and subcriterions for location strategy, specifying the alternatives to be selected among, and using a specific model to calculate all criterions with the values of alternatives in a rank so that one of the alternatives can be chosen. Multi-criteria decision-making analysis can be proposed for all decision types as well as banking business location strategy.

Over decades, there are many changes have been in banking business market. As the acceleration in all over the global market pressures banks as well as many other sectors, it became vitally important to decide strategically at every operations' issue. Due to the location strategic decision is important for the quality of network, competitive advantage in the market, and being closer to the customers, managers must select best location for a bank. This importance brought the issue interesting for the researchers.

There are many researches which have been studied in location strategy. Those researchers have proposed various techniques of multi-criteria decision-making analysis such as analytic hierarchy process (AHP) [53], analytic network process (ANP) [17], DEMATEL [51], SWARA, WASPAS [56], TOPSIS, ELECTRE, Grey Theory [41], and fuzzy models [18]. Beside this, there are only a few or no researches have studied VIKOR method in integration with the fuzzy analytic hierarchy process in banking business location strategy. Secondly, we believe that due to Kurdistan Region of Iraq is newly being adopted with the banking system, there are special criterions such as "security" and "willingness of society to work with banks" in the region. This might not be the case in developed countries. Third, the location selection via multi-criteria decision-making analysis is a new approach in Kurdistan Region of Iraq, and the investors are not very familiar with the method while selecting the best location for their business. From these aspects, this research is important to show a methodology of location selection to the practitioners in the region.

The current study is intended to analyze main and subcriterions for bank location strategy in Kurdistan Region of Iraq. To do this, we have determined the main and subcriterions for bank location selection from the literature [12, 36, 37, 43, 54] and banking experts. Beside what we have found from the literature, experts have determined that "willingness of customers" and "security" are also important aspects which determine the best location in the region. Therefore, we have added two new criterions to the bank location decision. Secondly, we have arranged a meeting with three bank experts to evaluate the importance of each criterion comparing to each other. After the results of discussions, we have investigated the national–international reports to obtain real values for each criterion. Further, we have proposed fuzzy AHP with VIKOR method to calculate the best alternative. The results show that Erbil is the best alternative as initial location for bank investors.

33.2 Literature Review

33.2.1 Location Strategy

Any organization that wants to expand to a new site is faced with the challenge of selecting an appropriate location. Out of all of the criteria necessary for the success and survival of a firm, location seems to be the most important criterion [8, 15, 18, 22, 23]. Therefore, a great deal of thought should be given to the decision-making process for selecting a spot, because unlike other criteria, location cannot be easily changed [15, 22]. Pointing out the importance of location in the retailing industry, Jain and Mahajat [27] stated "in the development of competitive strategies, prices can be matched, services can be extended and improved, but a retailer's location advantages are difficult to assail or neutralize." Location is a particularly important contributor to the profitability and success in the banking industry [23]. Further emphasizing this importance, Fung [21] noted that 39% of customers choose their banks primarily due to the convenience of their locations.

Selecting a location for a new bank branch is not without its challenges. What makes selecting a new branch location so challenging is the multi-criteria nature of the problem and the fuzziness of some of its main determinants [15, 18]. Adding to the complexity of the problem is the fact that, depending on their strategies, different banks will consider different criteria in their decision to select a location for a new branch [9, 10, 54]. Perhaps this is the reason for why there is no consensus in the literature as to the exact number of factors that affect the performance of bank branches.

Vafadarnikjoo et al. [51] consider competition, access to public facilities, demographic attributes, cost and flexibility, and transportation as some of the most important criteria when selecting location for a new branch. Allahi et al. [4] utilize cost, access to public facilities, transportation, demographic attributes, flexibility, and competition in their model for selecting the optimal bank branch location. Cinar and Ahiska [18] use demographic, sectoral employment, socio-economic, trade potential, and banking criteria in their model for selecting a location for a new bank branch, whereas Gorener et al. [23] used demographic, economic, and investment and banking criteria in their model for selecting a bank branch location. Abbasi [1] divides the factors that affect the bank location selection into three main categories, namely general factors, business-related factors, and population-related factors, while Başar et al. [9] proposed a methodology for identifying the most important criteria and their properties for the location problem, namely number of potential customers, social potential, competition, easement of access, socio-economic situation, commercial potential, financial situation, and growth potential. But for Brealey and Kaplanis

[13], size of trade or foreign direct investment (FDI) is one of the reasons for favoring a location over another when a bank wants to open a branch in a foreign country.

Although there is no fixed set of determinants or criteria for selecting a new location, it can be drawn from the literature that demographic, economic, and competition are some of the most considered factors in the location selection problem. So, it would be a mistake from our side not to consider these factors in our study.

The problem of site selection for new branches in the banking industry has received considerable attention in the literature (see [1, 4, 9, 10, 12, 13, 15, 18, 23, 24, 33, 51]). Consequently, a variety of models and/or strategies have been developed to deal with the issue.

In their paper, Lord and Wright [33] outlined three unique strategies when it comes to selecting a location for opening a new branch in the banking industry, namely defensive, offensive, and follow-the-leader. Defensive is when the bank branch joins a cluster of other bank branches not because they want to capture new customers, but because they fear losing their existing customers. Offensive is when a firm selects a location where there are no competitors. This strategy is suitable for market leaders rather than small firms, due to the risky nature of such strategy. Finally, follow-the-leader strategy is used by smaller firms who follow a market leader to a location in hopes of capturing the attention of some of the market leader's customers.

Boufounou [12] developed a model for identifying the best location for a new bank branch using regression analysis. They found out that criteria like average household size, domestic per capita income, position of competitors, total population, and population growth rate are critical determinant of success for bank branches. Therefore, they can be used as factors affecting the location selection problem. Abbasi [1] built a decision support system (DSS) to aid the banking industry decision-makers in their struggle to find the optimal location for new branches. After defining the five most important factors in selecting a location for a new bank branch, Cinar and Ahiska [18] used fuzzy analytical hierarchy process (AHP) to establish a decision support model (DSM) that could help the banking industry firms in deciding where to place their new branches. Similarly, after consulting with experts in the banking industry, Vafadarnikjoo et al. [51] identified the most important determinants in selecting bank branch location and then used intuitionistic fuzzy set theory in combination with decision-making trial and evaluation laboratory (DEMATEL) model to prioritize the criteria that affect the decision for choosing a new bank branch. Having not found a "one-size-fits-all" procedure for selecting a new bank branch location, Cabello [15] attempted to produce a model that would suit the maximum number of situation when dealing with the location problem.

Having studied relative literature on the location selection problem in the banking industry, it was seen that location selection problem is a multi-criteria problem, as such multiple criteria decision model (MCDM) and fuzzy set theory are among the very commonly used models for solving the location problem in the banking industry [9]. Secondly, depending on the banking strategy, different banks will consider different criteria to solve their location problem. Finally, there is no one model that will be suitable for every location problem scenario. Consequently, different banking firms should consider different criteria when dealing with the location problem.

33.2.2 Fuzzy AHP Model

33.2.2.1 Fuzzy Set Theory

According to Zimmerman [55], fuzzy set theory helps to understand complex phenomena through rigid mathematical guidelines. Similarly, Wu et al. [52] noted vague expressions of people like "not very clear, probably so, and very likely" could be analyzed by fuzzy set model. Fuzzy set theory is a crucial method to measure the uncertain events related to the human beings [47].

For instance, Kwong and Bai [32] have used AHP and fuzzy AHP model to define the importance of degrees of customer requirements for product planning. Kahraman et al. [28] have used fuzzy AHP model to select the best supplier firm according to service importance weights. Similarly, Ly et al. [34] have used the same model to predict the effective impact indicators on Internet of things (IoT) system for related companies. In addition, Sanayei et al. [46] have used VIKOR analysis to determine the eligible supplier in the supply chain of a company. Further, newly Abdel-Basset and his associates have used VIKOR model to analyze the government Web sites according to quality, security, and accessibility [2].

33.2.2.2 Fuzzy Number Set

Fuzzy numbers, which defined as triangular and trapezoidal, are the subset of real numbers. The widely used one is the triangular numbers. In this study, the triangular numbers are produced through linguistic assessments of the bank managers and construct the pairwise comparison for the model [6, 20].

A triangular fuzzy number can be shown as $M = (l, m, u)$. Its membership function $\mu_M(x)$: R $\rightarrow$ [0, 1] is equal to

$$\mu_M(x) = \begin{pmatrix} \left(\frac{x}{m-l} - \frac{l}{m-l}, & x \in [\boldsymbol{l}, \mathbf{m}] \\ \frac{x}{m-u} - \frac{u}{m-u}, & x \in [\boldsymbol{l}, \mathbf{u}] \\ 0, & \text{otherweise} \end{pmatrix}$$

where $l \leq m \leq u$, the triangular numbers are: l is lower, m is mid, and u is the upper values for the support of M. When $l = m = u$, it is a non-fuzzy number by convention. The main operational laws for two triangular fuzzy numbers $M1$ and $M2$ are as follows [29]:

$$\begin{aligned} &M_1 + M_2 = (l_1 + l_2, m_1 + m_2, u_1 + u_2) \\ &M_1 \otimes M_2 \approx (l_1 l_2, m_1 m_2, u_1 u_2) \\ &\lambda \otimes M_1 = (\lambda l_1, \lambda m_1, \lambda u_1), \quad \lambda > 0, \quad \lambda \in \mathrm{R} \\ &M_1^{-1} \approx (1/u_1, 1/m_1, 1/l_1) \end{aligned}$$

Fig. 33.1 Triangular fuzzy number

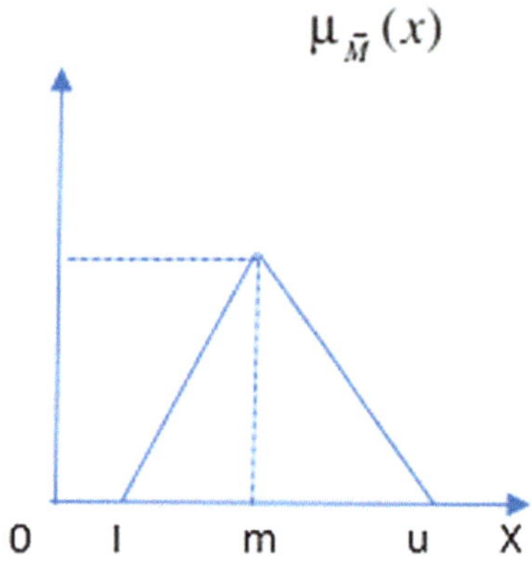

A triangular membership function is illustrated in Fig. 33.1.

33.2.2.3 Fuzzy AHP

Analytic hierarchy process (AHP) is one of the broadly used decision-making method, which was improved by Saaty in 1980 [45, 47]. According to the method, there are three categories to make the decision, which are the creation of hierarchies, determination of superiority, and providing logical and numerical consistency [30]. Criterions are hierarchically structured for the calculation and divided into importance levels, and finally, according to importance weights' best results reached through analysis. But because of the imprecise behaviors of the person, different kinds of multi-criteria calculation methods, such as fuzzy AHP and VIKOR, might be used as an integrated model with AHP [5, 47]. Steps of fuzzy AHP can be sequenced as:

Determining the fuzzy weights of each variable. To do this, the following formula has been used;

$$FW_i = \sum_{j=1}^{m} M_{gi}^{j} * \left[\sum_{j=1}^{n} \sum_{j=1}^{m} M_{gi}^{j} \right]^{-1} \tag{33.1}$$

in order to obtain $\sum_{j=1}^{m} M_{gi}^{j}$, the fuzzy summation of m extent values for a specific matrix can be calculated as;

$$\sum_{j=1}^{m} M_{gi}^{j} = \left(\sum_{j=1}^{m} l_j, \sum_{j=1}^{m} m_j, \sum_{j=1}^{m} u_j \right) \tag{33.2}$$

Further,

$$\left[\sum_{j=1}^{n}\sum_{j=1}^{m} M_{gi}^{j}\right]^{-1}$$

can be obtained via summation of M_{gi}^{j} ($j = 1, 2, 3 \ldots m$) numeric values proposed such as

$$\sum_{j=1}^{n}\sum_{j=1}^{m} M_{gi}^{j} = \left(\sum_{j=1}^{m} l_j, \sum_{j=1}^{m} m_j, \sum_{j=1}^{m} u_j\right) \tag{33.3}$$

And then, the inverse of the vector can be computed such as dividing each summation by one.

33.2.3 VIKOR

VIKOR method is one of the multi-criteria decision-making analysis that determines the compromise ranking list of alternatives, compromise solutions for complex problems, and the weight stability intervals for choice stability of the compromise solution obtained with the initial given weights [40]. The model gives best alternative as solution that is closest to the ideal [39]. Steps for the VIKOR calculation are as follows [40, 48]:

1. Determine the best (f_i^*) and the worst (f_i^-) values among all alternatives ($j = 1, 2, 3, \ldots m$) and by each criterion ($i = 1, 2, 3, \ldots n$).
   a. If it is a benefit criterion that is to be maximized: $f_i^* = \mathrm{Max}_j f_{ij}$
   b. If it is a benefit criterion that is to be minimized: $f_i^- = \mathrm{Min}_j f_{ij}$.
2. Compute S_j (Eq. 33.1) and R_j (Eq. 33.2) for $j = 1, 2, 3 \ldots m$. S_j and R_j, respectively, represent utility and regret measures for alternative.

$$S_i = \sum_{j=1}^{n}\left[w_i\left(\frac{f_i^* - f_{ij}}{f_i^* - f_i^-}\right)\right] \tag{33.4}$$

$$R_j = \sum_{j=1}^{n}\max_j\left[w_i\left(\frac{f_i^* - f_{ij}}{f_i^* - f_i^-}\right)\right] \tag{33.5}$$

   where W_i is the weight of the criterion.
3. Compute Q_j (Eq. 33.3) for $j = 1, 2, 3 \ldots, m$
   where $S^* = \min S_j$, $S^- = \max S_j$, $R^* = \min R_j$, $R^- = \max R_j$, v is the weight for the decision-making strategy of the maximum group utility, and $(1-v)$ is the

weight of the individual regret; generally, v is assumed equal 0.5 corresponding to the consensus.

$$Q_i = \sum_{j=1}^{n} \left[v \left(\frac{S_i - S_i^-}{S_i^* - S_i^-} \right) + (1 - v) \left(\frac{R_i - R^-}{R^* - R^-} \right) \right] \tag{33.6}$$

4. Rank the alternatives by the values S, R, and Q in ascending order by forming three ranking lists such that the lower the value, the better the alternative.
5. Propose the alternative a' as a compromise solution which is ranked the best by the minimum value of Q if the following two conditions are satisfied:

   Condition 1. Acceptable advantage: $Q(a'') - Q(a') \geq DQ$ where a'' is the alternative which is ranked second by Q and $DQ = 1/(m - 1)$.
   Condition 2. Acceptable stability in decision making: Alternative a' must also be the best ranked by S or/and R.

6. If one of the conditions in Step 5 is not satisfied, propose a set of compromise solutions which include:

   - Alternatives a' and a'' if only Condition 2 is not satisfied, or
   - Alternatives a', a'', ..., $a(n)$ if only Condition 1 is not satisfied; the closeness of the alternative $a(n)$ ranked nth by Q is determined by $Q(a(n)) - Q(a') < DQ$.

33.3 Materials and Methods

This study aims to propose multi-dimensional decision-making analysis to understand the best location for bank investment. To do this, we have initially prepared a questionnaire that contains criterions for bank location selection. The criterions have been abstracted from the current literature studied by various researchers. The criterions have been mainly demographic, socio-economic, sectoral employment, banking, trade potential, willingness to work with banks, and security in the region. Consequently, the subcriterions of the main ones also have been determined.

The structured criterions have been discussed with the experts in the banking sector. We have met three banking experts separately and asked them the importance of each criterions comparing to one another. The answers of each expert have been discussed with four academics from the finance, economics, and operations management fields. The answers of each expert have been entered in the "expert choice" analytic hierarchy process software in order to calculate the inconsistency levels. As it has been seen that all inconsistency levels were below 0.10, it was concluded that all answers have been consistent.

Initially, global weights of each main criterions (demographic, socio-economic, sectoral employment, banking, trade potential, willingness to work with banks, and security in the region) have been calculated. Secondly, weights of subcriterions have been calculated comparing to each other. As the last step of analytic hierarchy process, we have multiplied the weight score of each subcriterion with global weight of the concerning main criterion. By this way, we have obtained the real weights of each subcriterions via analytic hierarchy process.

After calculating the importance weights of each subcriterions, we have proposed VIKOR method to calculate the minimum utility regret for each city and find the best location for start banking business. Doing this, we have initially determined the values of each subcriterions. For example, the first criterion under demographic was total population.

We have determined the demographic information from the Kurdistan Region Statistical Office and International Organization for Immigration [26]. Values for socio-economic criterion have been obtained from BBC News, facts [7], Kurdistan Region Statistical Office [31], Socio-economic monitoring system report [49]. Sectoral employment and trade potential values have been received from Boi [11]. Finally, banking criterion's real values have been determined by Abdullah [3]. The values of all subcriterions have been obtained from various national and international reports. Beside this, willingness to work with banks and security in the region criterions unfortunately did not have any value. Instead, we have asked those criterions to experts in the region to rate from one to ten for Erbil, Sulaimani, and Dohuk. The nominal values for those two main criterions have been used in the current study.

Calculating VIKOR method, obtained values have been used. First of all, best value (f_i^*) and the worst value (f_i^-) for each subcriterions, starting from the total population of each city, have been selected. Secondly, relative S_j and R_j values have been calculated for each criterions. Finally, global S_j, R_j, and Q_j values have been calculated consequently in order to select the best decision among three cities of Kurdistan Region of Iraq.

33.3.1 Findings

33.3.1.1 Fuzzy AHP

While conducting multi-criteria decision-making analysis, it is very important to structure decision criteria in a hierarchical form (Fig. 33.2). By this way, importance of each subcriteria comparing to another is calculated. Moreover, success of a decision analysis initially and strongly depends on this process [44]. By this way, overall view of very complex relations between each subcriterion can be determined. On the other hand, there is no consensus among researchers about how to structure the hierarchy of criterions among each other (Kannan). Therefore, as many authors did in their past studies [42], we have constructed the hierarchy discussing with the three experts in the banking field and four academics in finance, economics, and operations management fields.

Table 33.1 shows the fuzzy pairwise comparison weights of main criterions. Initially, three banking experts have discussed together to compare each main criterion with another by using Saaty's 1–9 scale. Later, fuzzy theory has been conducted

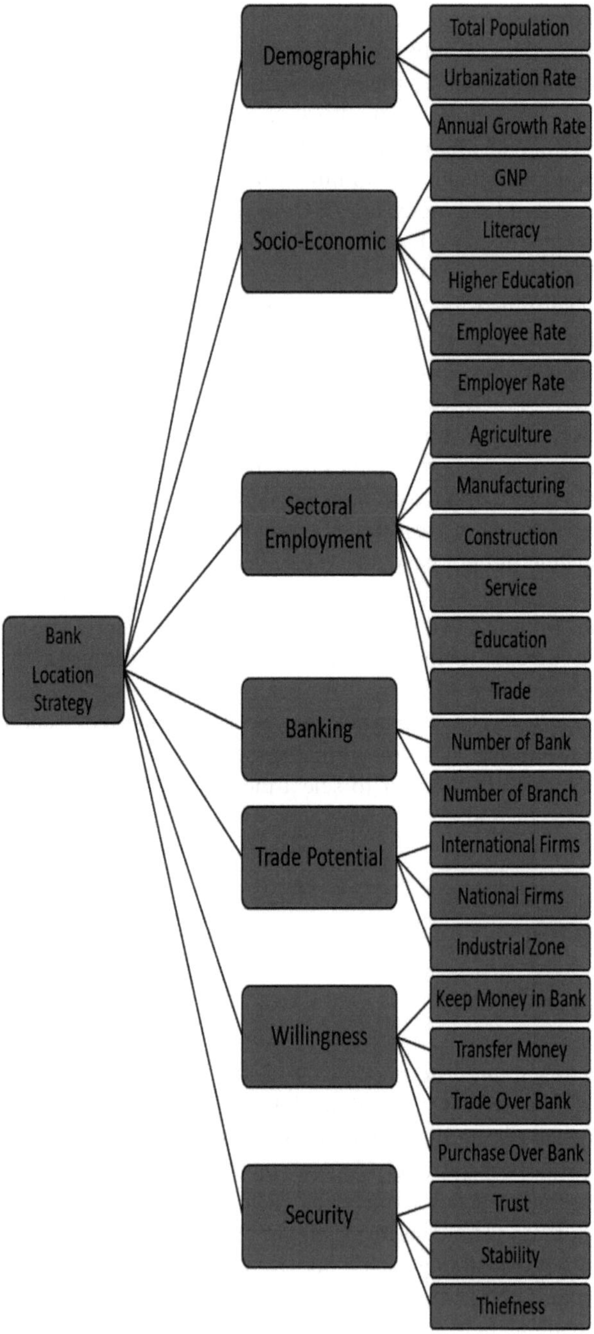

Fig. 33.2 The model of multi-criteria decision-making analysis

to create fuzzy pairwise comparison matrix. By this way, we have converted basic comparison values of the criterions into triangular fuzzy numbers in Table 33.1.

1. **Step**: From Table 33.1, fuzzy geometric mean of each variable with respect to main goal is calculated by using formula [14]:

Fuzzy geometric mean $(S_i) = (l_1, m_1, u_1,)^{1/n} * (l_2, m_2, u_2,)^{1/n} * (l_3, m_3, u_3,)^{1/n}$ where n is number of criterions.

$$
\begin{aligned}
S_D &= (1 * 1/2 * 1/2 * 1/4 * 1/4 * 1/4 * 1/6)^{1/7},\\
&\quad (1 * 1/3 * 1/3 * 1/5 * 1/5 * 1/5 * 1/7)^{1/7},\\
&\quad (1 * 1/4 * 1/4 * 1/6 * 1/6 * 1/6 * 1/8)^{1/7} = (0.42, 0.28, 0.23)\\
S_{SE} &= (2 * 1 * 1 * 1/2 * 1/2 * 1/2 * 1/2)^{1/7},\\
&\quad (3 * 1 * 1/2 * 1/3 * 1/3 * 1/3 * 1/3)^{1/7},\\
&\quad (4 * 1 * 1/3 * 1/4 * 1/4 * 1/4 * 1/4) = (0.74, 0.57, 0.47)\\
S_{SEM} &= (2 * 1 * 1 * 1/2 * 1 * 1 * 1/2)^{1/7}, (3 * 2 * 1 * 1/3 * 1/2 * 1 * 1/3)^{1/7},\\
&\quad (4 * 3 * 1 * 1/4 * 1/3 * 1 * 1/4)^{1/7} = (0.91, 0.85, 0.82)\\
S_B &= (4 * 2 * 1 * 1/2 * 1 * 2 * 1)^{1/7}, (5 * 3 * 2 * 1/3 * 1 * 3 * 1/2)^{1/7},\\
&\quad (6 * 4 * 3 * 1/4 * 1 * 4 * 1/3)^{1/7} = (1.35, 1.47, 1.64)\\
S_{TP} &= (4 * 2 * 1 * 1/2 * 1/2 * 1 * 1/2)^{1/7}, (5 * 3 * 1 * 1/3 * 1/3 * 1 * 1/3)^{1/7},\\
&\quad (6 * 4 * 1 * 1/4 * 1/4 * 1 * 1/4)^{1/7} = (1, 0.92, 0.87)\\
S_W &= (4 * 2 * 2 * 1/2 * 1 * 2 * 1)^{1/7}, (5 * 3 * 3 * 1/3 * 2 * 3 * 1)^{1/7},
\end{aligned}
$$

Table 33.1 Fuzzy pairwise comparison matrix

	D	SE	SEM	SEC	B	TP	WILL
D	1, 1, 1	1/2, 1/3, 1/4	1/2, 1/3, 1/4	1/6,1/7, 1/8	1/4, 1/5, 1/6	1/4, 1/5, 1/6	1/4, 1/5, 1/6
SE	2, 3, 4	1, 1, 1	1, 1/2, 1/3	1/2, 1/3, 1/4	1/2, 1/3, 1/4	1/2, 1/3, 1/4	1/2, 1/3, 1/4
SEM	2, 3, 4	1, 2, 3	1, 1, 1	1/2, 1/3, 1/4	1, 1/2, 1/3	1, 1, 1	1/2, 1/3, 1/4
B	4, 5, 6	2, 3, 4	1, 2, 3	1/2, 1/3, 1/4	1, 1, 1	2, 3, 4	1, 1/2, 1/3
TP	4, 5, 6	2, 3, 4	1, 1, 1	1/2, 1/3, 1/4	1/2, 1/3, 1/4	1, 1, 1	1/2,1/3,1/4
W	4, 5, 6	2, 3, 4	2, 3, 4	1/2, 1/3, 1/4	1, 2, 3	2, 3, 4	1, 1, 1
SEC	6, 7, 8	2, 3, 4	2, 3, 4	1, 1, 1	2, 3, 4	2, 3, 4	2, 3, 4

Note: *D* demographic distributions; *SE* socio-economic situation; *SEM* sectoral employment; *B* banking; *TP* trade potential; *W* willingness to work with banks; *SEC* security in the region

$$(6 * 4 * 4 * 1/4 * 3 * 4 * 1) = (1.49, 1.90, 2.25)$$

$$S_{\text{SEC}} = (6 * 2 * 2 * 1 * 2 * 2 * 2)^{1/7}, (7 * 3 * 3 * 1 * 3 * 3 * 3)^{1/7},$$
$$(8 * 4 * 4 * 1 * 4 * 4 * 4) = (2.13, 2.89, 3.62)$$

After those calculations, the fuzzy geometric means have been represented on Table 33.2.

2. **Step**: Determining the fuzzy weights of each variable. To do this, the following formula has been used;

$$FW_i = \sum_{j=1}^{m} M_{gi}^{j} * \left[\sum_{j=1}^{n}\sum_{j=1}^{m} M_{gi}^{j}\right]^{-1} \tag{33.7}$$

in order to obtain $\sum_{j=1}^{m} M_{gi}^{j}$, the fuzzy summation of m extent values for a specific matrix can be calculated as;

$$\sum_{j=1}^{m} M_{gi}^{j} = \left(\sum_{j=1}^{m} l_j, \sum_{j=1}^{m} m_j, \sum_{j=1}^{m} u_j\right) \tag{33.8}$$

Further,

$$\left[\sum_{j=1}^{n}\sum_{j=1}^{m} M_{gi}^{j}\right]^{-1}$$

can be obtained via summation of M_{gi}^{j} $(j = 1, 2, 3 \ldots m)$ numeric values proposed such as

$$\sum_{j=1}^{n}\sum_{j=1}^{m} M_{gi}^{j} = \left(\sum_{j=1}^{m} l_j, \sum_{j=1}^{m} m_j, \sum_{j=1}^{m} u_j\right) \tag{33.9}$$

Table 33.2 Fuzzy geometric means

Demographic	0.42	0.28	0.23
Socio-economic	0.74	0.57	0.47
Sectoral employment	0.91	0.85	0.82
Banking	1.35	1.47	1.64
Trade potential	1.00	0.92	0.87
Willingness	1.49	1.90	2.25
Security	2.12	2.89	3.62

And then the inverse of the vector can be computed such as dividing each summation by one. After all calculations, fuzzy weights and the defuzzied weights are shown in Table 33.3;

3. **Step**: Center of gravity. Fuzzy weights have been calculated by the formulas which have been introduced above. Further, in order to calculate the final weights of the fuzzy analytic hierarchy process, we need to propose center of gravity function which is

$$W_i = \frac{l + m + u}{3} \tag{33.10}$$

where lower, medium, and upper values are summed up and divided by three. The results show that the most important parameter among bank location selection criterions is security. The importance percentage of the criterion is 32% as the biggest value comparing to others. This result shows that the most secure city has competitive advantage among others. Secondly, willingness to work with a bank (21%), banking (17%), trade potential of the city (11%), and sectoral employment (10%) are other important criterions, respectively, while selecting the best location for a banking business. Finally, it has been observed that socio-economic situation of the city (7%) and demographic (4%) are the least important criterions.

Based on the importance weights of each criterion, the importance of the subcriterions has been also calculated in the same methodology. For example, demographic has three subcriterions in total. Further, the subcriterions also have already been evaluated by the same expert group. The results are shown in Table 33.4.

Table 33.4 shows the normalized important weights of each subcriterion. Beside this, those weights are still need to be processed and calculated to distribute the importance weights of main criterions conveniently to the subcriterions.

There are mainly three subcriterions under demographic criterion. The normalized weights of those subcriterions (total population, urbanization rate, and annual population growth rate) are 0.28, 0.64, and 0.07, respectively. On the other hand, these are the values which have been calculated before taking main criterions into account. By

Table 33.3 Importance weights matrix

	Fuzzy weights			Defuzzied weights
Demographic	0.05	0.03	0.02	0.04
Socio-economic	0.09	0.06	0.05	0.07
Sectoral employment	0.11	0.10	0.08	0.10
Banking	0.17	0.17	0.17	0.17
Trade potential	0.13	0.10	0.09	0.11
Willingness	0.19	0.21	0.23	0.21
Security	0.27	0.33	0.37	0.32
Inconsistency: 0.05				

Table 33.4 Importance weights matrix of subcriterions

Variables		Fuzzy weights			Defuzzied weights
Demographic	Total population	0.32	0.28	0.25	0.28
	Urbanization rate	0.59	0.65	0.69	0.64
	Annual population growth	0.09	0.07	0.06	0.07
Socio-economic	GNP	0.44	0.49	0.52	0.48
	Literacy rate	0.08	0.07	0.06	0.07
	Higher education	0.07	0.05	0.04	0.06
	Employee rate	0.27	0.26	0.26	0.27
	Employer rate	0.14	0.13	0.12	0.13
Sectoral employment	Agriculture	0.08	0.06	0.05	0.06
	Manufacturing	0.12	0.12	0.12	0.12
	Construction	0.28	0.28	0.27	0.28
	Service	0.04	0.03	0.02	0.03
	Education	0.09	0.08	0.07	0.08
	Trade	0.39	0.43	0.46	0.43
Banking	Number of bank	0.50	0.67	0.75	0.64
	Number of branch	0.22	0.14	0.10	0.15
Trade potential	International firms	0.71	0.74	0.76	0.74
	National firms	0.15	0.17	0.17	0.16
	Industrial zone	0.14	0.09	0.07	0.10
Willingness	Keep money in bank	0.26	0.18	0.15	0.20
	Transfer money	0.34	0.46	0.52	0.44
	Trade over bank	0.31	0.30	0.28	0.30
	Purchase over bank	0.08	0.06	0.05	0.06
Security	Trust	0.61	0.67	0.71	0.66
	Stability	0.27	0.24	0.22	0.24
	Robbery	0.12	0.09	0.07	0.09

another meaning, those values are relative importance weights of each subcriterion only comparing to each other. Further, by multiplying the normalized weights of main criterions with each subcriterions, we will obtain the final importance weight of each subcriterion comparing to the all subcriterions (Table 33.5).

The other relative weights of subcriterions have been calculated by the same methodology. The table below shows the results of all subcriterions (Table 33.6).

Table 33.6 shows the relative priority within the concerning criterion. To expand the explanation, there are mainly three criterions for security. Perceived trust of the society to the banks, security in the region, and the robbery rate in the region have been discussed by the three banking experts and have been evaluated. Further, they have

Table 33.5 Relative weights of subcriterions under demographic

Variable name	Subcriterion weight	Operation	Weight of demographic	Relative weights of subcriterions
Total population	0.28	×	0.04	0.009
Urbanization rate	0.64	×	0.04	0.021
Annual population growth	0.07	×	0.04	0.002

rated the comparative importance of each criterion to one another. Secondly, using the fuzzy AHP methodology, we have calculated the weights of each subcriterion. After that, we have multiplied the normalized weight of security criterion (0.319) by each subcriterion (0.664, 0.245, and 0.092), and the relative weights have been 0.21, 0.08, and 0.03, respectively. The other relative weights have been calculated with the same methodology.

33.3.1.2 VIKOR

In order to select the best place for banking business investment, we have explained the methodology how the weights have been calculated by using fuzzy analytic hierarchy process. However, in this section, we have proposed VIKOR method in

Table 33.6 Relative weights of AHP

Criterion	Subcriterion	Global weights	Weights of subcriterion	Relative weights of subcriterion
Demographic (*D*)	Total population (*D*1)	0.033	0.284	0.009
	Urbanization rate (*D*2)	0.033	0.643	0.021
	Annual population growth rate (*D*3)	0.033	0.074	0.002
	Inconsistency: 0.06			
Socio-economic (SE)	Gross national product per capita (SE1)	0.068	0.484	0.033
	Literacy rate (SE2)	0.068	0.068	0.005
	Rate of population with higher education (SE3)	0.068	0.057	0.004

(continued)

Table 33.6 (continued)

Criterion	Subcriterion	Global weights	Weights of subcriterion	Relative weights of subcriterion
	Employee rate (SE4)	0.068	0.265	0.018
	Employer rate (SE5)	0.068	0.126	0.009
	Inconsistency: 0.04			
Sectoral employment (SEM)	Agricultural employment rate (SEM1)	0.098	0.063	0.006
	Manufacturing employment rate (SEM2)	0.098	0.121	0.012
	Construction employment rate (SEM3)	0.098	0.276	0.027
	Services employment rate (SEM4)	0.098	0.033	0.003
	Education sector employment rate (SEM5)	0.098	0.080	0.008
	Trade sector employment rate (SEM6)	0.098	0.426	0.042
	Inconsistency: 0.05			
Banking (*B*)	Number of bank (*B*1)	0.167	0.639	0.107
	Number of branch (*B*2)	0.167	0.155	0.026
	Inconsistency: 0.00			
Trade potential (TP)	Number of international firms (TP1)	0.106	0.737	0.078
	Number of national firms (TP2)	0.106	0.163	0.017
	Number of industrial zones (TP3)	0.106	0.101	0.011
	Inconsistency: 0.01			

(continued)

Table 33.6 (continued)

Criterion	Subcriterion	Global weights	Weights of subcriterion	Relative weights of subcriterion
Willingness (W)	Willingness to keep money in banks ($W1$)	0.209	0.198	0.041
	Willingness to transfer money over banks ($W2$)	0.209	0.441	0.092
	Willingness to trade over banks ($W3$)	0.209	0.296	0.062
	Willingness to purchase over banks ($W4$)	0.209	0.065	0.014
Inconsistency: 0.02				
Security (SEC)	Perceived trust of society to the banks (SEC1)	0.319	0.664	0.212
	Security in the region (SEC2)	0.319	0.245	0.078
	Robbery rate in the region (SEC3)	0.319	0.092	0.029
Inconsistency: 0.01				

order to find the minimum utility regret and the opportunity cost. To do this, in order to use the values in the concerning VIKOR formulas, we have investigated the national and international reports to find the required values for demographic, socio-economic, sectoral employment, trade potential, and banking criterions. Further, due to there is no information about willingness of society to work with the banks and security in the region, we have used nominal values which have been evaluated by the three banking experts. They have rated the values of three subcriterions of security and four subcriterions of willingness for each region from one up to ten. The values for each city have been used like a data in the concerning formulas of VIKOR method.

VIKOR is a multi-criteria decision-making analysis method which has been found by Serafim Opricovic in order to solve highly complex conflicts by selecting the choice which is closest to the ideal. In order to propose VIKOR, the best (f_i^*) and the worst (f_i^-) values for each criterion have been determined. S_j and R_j values for each alternative have been calculated by proposing the Eqs. (33.4) and (33.5), respectively (Table 33.7).

As a result of these calculations, relative utility regret (RS_j) has been obtained. The relative utility regret shows how much the users would be regretful for the concerning alternative in case they select. For example, perceived trust of society to

Table 33.7 S_j and R_j values of service providers at each subcriterion

CR	SC	City	Value	GWC	GWSC	RWSC	f_i^*	f_i^-	RS_j
Demographic (*D*)	*D*1	E	2,190,738	0.03	0.28	0.009	2,190,738	1527,413	0.00
		S	2,157,832	0.03	0.28	0.009	2,190,738	1,527,413	0.00
		D	1,527,413	0.03	0.28	0.009	2,190,738	1,527,413	0.01
	*D*2	E	1,789,395	0.03	0.64	0.021	1,789,395	1,247,591	0.00
		S	1,762,517	0.03	0.64	0.021	1,789,395	1,247,591	0.00
		D	1,247,591	0.03	0.64	0.021	1,789,395	1,247,591	0.02
	*D*3	E	2.48	0.03	0.07	0.002	4.17	2.48	0.00
		S	3.46	0.03	0.07	0.002	4.17	2.48	0.00
		D	4.17	0.03	0.07	0.002	4.17	2.48	0.00
Socio-economic (SE)	SE1	E	9,858,322	0.07	0.48	0.033	9,858,322	6,873,357	0.00
		S	9,710,245	0.07	0.48	0.033	9,858,322	6,873,357	0.00
		D	6,873,357	0.07	0.48	0.033	9,858,322	6,873,357	0.03
	SE2	E	78.65	0.07	0.07	0.005	80.4	76.6	0.00
		S	80.4	0.07	0.07	0.005	80.4	76.6	0.00
		D	76.6	0.07	0.07	0.005	80.4	76.6	0.00
	SE3	E	1.4	0.07	0.06	0.004	1.7	1.075	0.00
		S	1.7	0.07	0.06	0.004	1.7	1.075	0.00
		D	1.075	0.07	0.06	0.004	1.7	1.075	0.00
	SE4	E	50.2	0.07	0.27	0.018	55	50.2	0.02
		S	55	0.07	0.27	0.018	55	50.2	0.00

(continued)

Table 33.7 (continued)

CR	SC	City	Value	GWC	GWSC	RWSC	f_i^*	f_i^-	RS_j
		D	51	0.07	0.27	0.018	55	50.2	0.02
	SE5	E	2.4	0.07	0.13	0.009	4.7	2.4	0.01
		S	4.7	0.07	0.13	0.009	4.7	2.4	0.00
		D	4.5	0.07	0.13	0.009	4.7	2.4	0.00
Sectoral employment (SEM)	SEM1	E	5	0.10	0.06	0.006	16	5	0.01
		S	16	0.10	0.06	0.006	16	5	0.00
		D	9	0.10	0.06	0.006	16	5	0.00
	SEM2	E	54	0.10	0.12	0.012	87	54	0.01
		S	87	0.10	0.12	0.012	87	54	0.00
		D	60	0.10	0.12	0.012	87	54	0.01
	SEM3	E	50	0.10	0.28	0.027	81	36	0.02
		S	81	0.10	0.28	0.027	81	36	0.00
		D	36	0.10	0.28	0.027	81	36	0.03
	SEM4	E	4	0.10	0.03	0.003	4	0	0.00
		S	3	0.10	0.03	0.003	4	0	0.00
		D	0	0.10	0.03	0.003	4	0	0.00
	SEM5	E	6	0.10	0.08	0.008	11	6	0.01
		S	8	0.10	0.08	0.008	11	6	0.00
		D	11	0.10	0.08	0.008	11	6	0.00
	SEM6	E	59	0.10	0.43	0.042	59	35	0.00
		S	39	0.10	0.43	0.042	59	35	0.03

(continued)

Table 33.7 (continued)

CR	SC	City	Value	GWC	GWSC	RWSC	f_i^*	f_i^-	RS_j
		D	35	0.10	0.43	0.042	59	35	0.04
Banking (*B*)	B1	E	11	0.17	0.64	0.107	20	6	0.07
		S	10	0.17	0.64	0.107	20	6	0.08
		D	4	0.17	0.64	0.107	20	6	0.12
	B2	E	6	0.17	0.15	0.026	10	2	0.01
		S	10	0.17	0.15	0.026	10	2	0.00
		D	2	0.17	0.15	0.026	10	2	0.03
Trade potential (TP)	TP1	E	11	0.11	0.74	0.078	47	11	0.08
		S	47	0.11	0.74	0.078	47	11	0.00
		D	19	0.11	0.74	0.078	47	11	0.06
	TP2	E	203	0.11	0.16	0.017	298	203	0.02
		S	298	0.11	0.16	0.017	298	203	0.00
		D	211	0.11	0.16	0.017	298	203	0.02
	TP3	E	1530	0.11	0.10	0.011	3100	1530	0.01
		S	3100	0.11	0.10	0.011	3100	1530	0.00
		D	420	0.11	0.10	0.011	3100	1530	0.02
Willingness (*W*)	W1	E	8	0.21	0.20	0.041	8	6	0.00
		S	6	0.21	0.20	0.041	8	6	0.04
		D	7	0.21	0.20	0.041	8	6	0.02
	W2	E	9	0.21	0.44	0.092	9	7	0.00
		S	8	0.21	0.44	0.092	9	7	0.05

(continued)

Table 33.7 (continued)

CR	SC	City	Value	GWC	GWSC	RWSC	f_i^*	f_i^-	RS_j
		D	7	0.21	0.44	0.092	9	7	0.09
	W3	E	8	0.21	0.30	0.062	8	6	0.00
		S	6	0.21	0.30	0.062	8	6	0.06
		D	6	0.21	0.30	0.062	8	6	0.06
	W4	E	7	0.21	0.06	0.014	7	5	0.00
		S	5	0.21	0.06	0.014	7	5	0.01
		D	6	0.21	0.06	0.014	7	5	0.01
Security (SEC)	SEC1	E	8	0.32	0.66	0.212	8	7	0.00
		S	7	0.32	0.66	0.212	8	7	0.21
		D	7	0.32	0.66	0.212	8	7	0.21
	SEC2	E	9	0.32	0.24	0.078	9	8	0.00
		S	8	0.32	0.24	0.078	9	8	0.08
		D	8	0.32	0.24	0.078	9	8	0.08
	SEC3	E	8	0.32	0.09	0.029	8	7	0.00
		S	7	0.32	0.09	0.029	8	7	0.03
		D	7	0.32	0.09	0.029	8	7	0.03

Note: *E* Erbil, *S* Sulaimani, *D* Dohuk, *CR* criterion, *SC* subcriterion, *GWC* global weight of criterion, *GWSC* global weight of subcriterion, *RWSC* relative weight of subcriterion, f_i^* best value among alternatives, f_i^- worst value among alternatives, *RSj* relative weights for utility regret

Table 33.8 Final values of alternatives for location strategy

	S_j	R_j	s_j^*	s_j^-	R_j^*	R_j^-	Q_j
Erbil	0.283	0.078	0.283	0.917	0.078	0.212	0.000
Sulaimani	0.603	0.212					0.752
Dohuk	0.917	0.212					1.000

the banks (SEC1) is a criterion which relatively important for customers. Considering alternatives, Erbil, Sulaimani, and Dohuk, it was observed that utility regret values were 0.00, 0.21, 0.21, respectively. It shows that the investor, who selects Erbil, would have the least utility regret about trust of society to the banks. The result shows that Erbil promises the least utility regret about trust with the value 0.00 regret which is lower than Sulaimani (0.21) and Dohuk (0.21). All utility regret values have been calculated and evaluated the same methodology. The details are in Table 33.7.

Secondly, global S_j and global R_j values have been calculated by adding up all S_j values for each alternative at each subcriterion and R_j values for each alternative at each subcriterion. For example, in order to calculate S_j value for Erbil alternative, we have added up all S_j values of Erbil under each subcriterion in the table above. Further, for the R_j values, we have selected maximum values among all S_j values of the alternatives from the same table. Other S_j and R_j values for each alternative have been calculated by the same methodology. Finally, Q_j values for each alternative have been calculated by using Eq. (33.6). For this calculation, we have used "V" vector value as 0.5 like other authors [40, 48]. The results of the calculations can be observed in Table 33.8.

The results of global utility regret (S_j) and (R_j) values show consistency with the maximum utility (Q_j) that Erbil is the best location for investment on banking business rather than Sulaimani and Dohuk based on the evaluation of all locations. However, $C1$ ($Q_{\text{Erbil}} - Q_{\text{Sulaimani}} \geq 1/3 - 1$) and the $C2$ (that Erbil is best alternative based on S_j and R_j values) criteria have been satisfied.

33.4 Practical Implications

There are several implications of the current research for the practitioners and theorists. First, by using the current study, public and private business investors in Kurdistan Region of Iraq may understand a method of decision making about location selection at the beginning of their investments. Such a methodology in location strategy is a new concept for the region, and the study plays an important role from this point of view.

Secondly, the study added two more important criterions (willingness and security) to the location selection problem in banking sector. It shows that for some geographies, such as Kurdistan Region of Iraq, some particular variables may play more important role rather than they do in developed countries. From this point of view, the study contributes both theoretically and practically to the literature from some specific aspects of the location problem. On the one hand, investors may use those two new criterions for the further decision analysis in order to increase the precision in location selection. On the other hand, theoretically new criterions have been added to the problem.

Third implication of the study is that the current bank investors and managers may evaluate their location performances using the current study in the region. For example, any investment started in different city than Erbil can evaluate what are the advantages and disadvantages for their location decisions. This may help them evaluate the future strategies on location selection.

Location strategy is important for businesses as it is a structural decision area which is long term and costly to change. From this point of view, investors must evaluate location analysis critically in order to increase the business performance and decrease the total costs.

This research has studied some special criterions of bank location strategies; beside, it has reused the existing criterions in the literature. The results show that the most important criterion for location selection is security in Kurdistan Region of Iraq. Secondly, willingness of the society to work with the banks plays an important role in location problems' solutions. It has been seen that rather than any other developed countries, there are some particular aspects that determine where to locate the investment. Moreover, other criterions, such as socio-economic, sectoral employment, trade potential, banking, and demography, play less importance than the security and willingness. The reason might be the society is newly getting integrated with the banks and interact in their businesses.

Results show that Erbil is the best location currently to start investment in banking business comparing to Sulaimani and Dohuk. The results show that from the willingness of the society to work with the banks and security in the city, Erbil is the best location. Further, Sulaimani is the second, and the Dohuk is the last option for the bank investment.

As all researches, this study also has some limitations. Initially, it would be beneficial to discuss the limitations of data in the region. For example, Cinar and Ahiska [18] have studied "banking deposit per branch, credits per branch, credit per capita, and bank deposit per capita" in their researches. On the other hand, we have excluded the concerning parts as we are unable to obtain the concerning data in the region. This might be the first limitation of the study. Secondly, we have used the nominal values which have been evaluated by the banking experts in order to compare security and willingness of societies in three cities of the region. Beside this, we could propose a survey questionnaire among three cities' societies in order to contribute more realistic values for the willingness and security perception of populations in the concerning regions.

In the current study, we have focused on different cities to select the best of them. Further, the future studies may focus on the inside city location strategies to select best location in a city. By this way, the further researches may increase the number of detailed researches in the current literature.

33.5 Conclusions, Limitations, and Directions for the Future Studies

This research have studied some special criterions of bank location strategies beside it has reused the existing criterions in the literature. The results shows that the most important criterion for location selection is security in the region were society trust banks. Secondly, willingness of the society to work with the banks play an important role in location problems' solutions. It has been seen that rather than any other developed countries, there are some particular aspects that determines where to locate the investment. Moreover, other criterions such as socio-economic, sectoral employment, trade potential, banking, and demography plays less importance than the security and willingness. The reason might be the society is newly getting integrated with the banks and interact in their businesses.

Results show that Erbil is the best location currently to start investment in banking business comparing to Sulaimani and Dohuk. The results show that from the willingness of the society to work with the banks and security in the city, Erbil is the best location. Further, Sulaimani is the second and the Dohuk is the last option for the bank investment.

As all researches, this study also has some limitations. Initially, it would be beneficial to discuss about the limitations of data in the region. For example, Cinar and Ahiska [18] have studied "banking deposit per branch, credits per branch, credit per capita and bank deposit per capita" in their researches. On the other hand, we have excluded the concerning parts due to we have been unable to obtain the concerning data in the region. This might be the first limitation of the study. Secondly, we have used the nominal values which have been evaluated by the banking experts in order to compare security and willingness of societies in three cities of the region. Beside this, we could propose a survey questionnaire among three cities' societies in order to contribute more realistic values for the willingness and security perception of populations in the concerning regions.

In the current study, we have focused on different cities to select the best of them. Further, the future studies may focus on the inside city location strategies to select best location in a city. By this way, the further researches may increase the number of detailed researches in the current literature.

References

1. Abbasi, G.Y.: A decision support system for bank location selection. Int. J. Comput. Appl. Technol. **16**(4), 202–210 (2003)
2. Abdel-Basset, M., Zhou, Y., Mohamed, M., Chang, V.: A group decision making framework based on neutrosophic VIKOR approach for e-government website evaluation. J. Intell. Fuzzy Syst. **34**(6), 4213–4224 (2018)
3. Abdullah, D.F.: The role of organizational strength resources and strategic implementation requirements in the possibility of switching to smart organizational. Ph.D. Thesis applied to College of Administrative and Economic—Sulaimani University (2018)

4. Allahi, S., Mobin, M., Vafadarnikjoo, A., & Salmon, C.: An integrated AHP-GIS-MCLP method to locate bank branches. In: Proceeding of the 2015 ISERC Conference, May 2015
5. Ayağ, Z.: A combined fuzzy AHP-simulation approach to CAD software selection. Int. J. Gen Syst **39**(7), 731–756 (2010)
6. Ayağ, Z., Özdemir, R.G.: A fuzzy AHP approach to evaluating machine tool alternatives. J. Intell. Manuf. **17**(2), 179–190 (2006)
7. BBC News: Iraqi Kurdistan Profile—Facts (2014). https://www.bbc.com/news/world-middle-east-28147264
8. Baron, O., Milner, J., Naseraldin, H.: Facility location: a robust optimization approach. Prod. Oper. Manag. **20**(5), 772–785 (2011)
9. Başar, A., Kabak, Ö., Topçu, Y.İ.: Identifying the criteria and their priorities for locating bank branches in Turkey (2014)
10. Başar, A., Kabak, Ö., Topçu, Y.İ., Bozkaya, B.: Location analysis in banking: a new methodology and application for a Turkish bank. In: Applications of Location Analysis, pp. 25–54. Springer, Cham (2015)
11. BOI: Licenced Projects (2018). http://boi.gov.krd/docs/licensed_projects.pdf
12. Boufounou, P.V.: Evaluating bank branch location and performance: a case study. Eur. J. Oper. Res. **87**(2), 389–402 (1995)
13. Brealey, R.A., Kaplanis, E.C.: The determination of foreign banking location. J. Int. Money Finance **15**(4), 577–597 (1996)
14. Buckley, J.J.: Fuzzy hierarchical analysis. Fuzzy Sets Syst. **17**(3), 233–247 (1985)
15. Cabello, J.G.: A decision model for bank branch site selection: define branch success and do not deviate. Socio-Econ. Plann. Sci. (2017)
16. Canel, C., Khumawala, B.M., Law, J., Loh, A.: Algorithm for the capacitated, multi-commodity multi-period facility location problem. Comput. Oper. Res. **28**(5), 411–427 (2001)
17. Cheng, E.W., Li, H., Yu, L.: The analytic network process (ANP) approach to location selection: a shopping mall illustration. Constr. Innov. **5**(2), 83–97 (2005)
18. Cinar, N., Ahiska, S.S.: A decision support model for bank branch location selection. Int. J. Hum. Soc. Sci. **5**(13), 846–851 (2010)
19. Cinar, N.: A decision support model for bank branch location selection. World Acad. Sci. Eng. Technol. **60**(1), 126–131 (2009)
20. Dağdeviren, M.: Bulanik analitik hiyerarşi prosesi ile personel seçimi ve bir uygulama. Gazi Üniversitesi Mühendislik-Mimarlık Fakültesi Dergisi **22**(4) (2007)
21. Fung, A.: Half of consumers still prefer branches, poll finds. American Banker **17** (2001)
22. Ghosh, A., Craig, C.S.: Formulating retail location strategy in a changing environment. J. Mark. 56–68 (1983)
23. Gorener, A., Dincer, H., & Hacioglu, U.: Application of multi-objective optimization on the basis of ratio analysis (MOORA) method for bank branch location selection (2013)
24. Gulamhussen, M.A.: A theoretical perspective on the location of banking FDI. Manag. Int. Rev. **49**(2), 163–178 (2009)
25. Heizer, J., Render, B., Munson, C., Sachan, A.: Operations Management: Sustainability and Supply Chain Management, 12th edn. (2017)
26. International Organization for Migration: Demographic Survey: Kurdistan Region of Iraq (2018). http://iomiraq.net/reports/demographic-survey-kurdistan-region-iraq
27. Jain, A.K., Mahajan, V.: Evaluating the competitive environment in retailing using multiplicative competitive interactive models. Res. Mark. **2**, 217–235 (1979)
28. Kahraman, C., Cebeci, U., Ulukan, Z.: Multi-criteria supplier selection using fuzzy AHP. Log. Inf. Manag. **16**(6), 382–394 (2003)
29. Kauffman, A., Gupta, M.M.: Introduction to fuzzy arithmetic: theory and application (1991)
30. Kuo, R.J., Chi, S.C., Kao, S.S.: A decision support system for locating convenience store through fuzzy AHP. Comput. Ind. Eng. **37**(1–2), 323–326 (1999)
31. Kurdistan Region Statistical Office, Ministry of Planning (2018). http://www.krso.net/Default.aspx?page=list&c=latestpublication

32. Kwong, C.K., Bai, H.: Determining the importance weights for the customer requirements in QFD using a fuzzy AHP with an extent analysis approach. IIE Trans. **35**(7), 619–626 (2003)
33. Lord, J.D., Wright, D.B.: Competition and location strategy in branch banking: spatial avoidance or clustering. Urban Geogr. **2**(3), 189–200 (1981)
34. Ly, P.T.M., Lai, W.H., Hsu, C.W., Shih, F.Y.: Fuzzy AHP analysis of Internet of Things (IoT) in enterprises. Technol. Forecast. Soc. Chang. **136**, 1–13 (2018)
35. Melkote, S., Daskin, M.S.: Capacitated facility location/network design problems. Eur. J. Oper. Res. **129**(3), 481–495 (2001)
36. Miliotis, P.M. Dimopoulou, M., Giannikos, I.: A hierarchical location model for locating bank branches in a competitive environment. Int. Trans. Oper. Res. **9**(5), 549–565 (2002)
37. Min, H.: A model based decision support system for locating banks. Inf. Manag. **17–4**, 207–215 (1989)
38. Nobuaki, S., Akira, U., Atsushi, D., Akira, O., Seiji, S., Satoshi, H.: Commercial facility location model using multiple regression analysis. Comput. Environ. Urban Syst. **22**(3), 219–240 (1998)
39. Opricovic, S.: Multicriteria optimization of civil engineering systems. Faculty Civil Eng. Belgrade **2**(1), 5–21 (1998)
40. Opricovic, S., Tzeng, G.H.: Compromise solution by MCDM methods: a comparative analysis of VIKOR and TOPSIS. Eur. J. Oper. Res. **156**(2), 445–455 (2004)
41. Özcan, T., Çelebi, N., Esnaf, Ş.: Comparative analysis of multi-criteria decision making methodologies and implementation of a warehouse location selection problem. Expert Syst. Appl. **38**(8), 9773–9779 (2011)
42. Özmen, Ö., Demir, A., Celepli, M.: An analysis of Iraq's pre-import inspection, testing and certification program: A'WOT Analysis. Procedia-Soc. Behav. Sci. **99**, 85–93 (2013)
43. Ravallion, M., Wodon, Q.: Banking on the poor? Branch location and nonfarm rural development in Bangladesh. Rev. Dev. Econ. **4**(2), 121–139 (2000)
44. Saaty, T.L.: How to make a decision: the analytic hierarchy process. Interfaces **24**(6), 19–43 (1994)
45. Saaty, T.: The Analytical Hierarchical Process. New York (1980)
46. Sanayei, A., Mousavi, S.F., Yazdankhah, A.: Group decision making process for supplier selection with VIKOR under fuzzy environment. Expert Syst. Appl. **37**(1), 24–30 (2010)
47. Seçme, N.Y., Bayrakdaroğlu, A., Kahraman, C.: Fuzzy performance evaluation in Turkish banking sector using analytic hierarchy process and TOPSIS. Expert Syst. Appl. **36**(9), 11699–11709 (2009)
48. Sennaroglu, B., Celebi, G.V.: A military airport location selection by AHP integrated PROMETHEE and VIKOR methods. Transp. Res. Part D: Transp. Environ. **59**, 160–173 (2018)
49. Socio-Economic Monitoring System Report: Ministry of planning—Kurdistan regional government. Rand Corporation (2013)
50. Stevenson, W.J.: Production/ operations management, 4th edn. Richard D.I., Homewood (1993)
51. Vafadarnikjoo, A., Mobin, M., Allahi, S., Rastegari, A.: A hybrid approach of intuitionistic fuzzy set theory and DEMATEL method to prioritize selection criteria of bank branches locations. In: Proceedings of the International Annual Conference of the American Society for Engineering Management, p. 1. American Society for Engineering Management (ASEM) Jan 2015
52. Wu, H.Y., Tzeng, G.H., Chen, Y.H.: A fuzzy MCDM approach for evaluating banking performance based on Balanced Scorecard. Expert Syst. Appl. **36**(6), 10135–10147 (2009)
53. Yang, J., Lee, H.: An AHP decision model for facility location selection. Facilities **15**(9/10), 241–254 (1997)
54. Zhao, L., Garner, B., Parolin, B.: Branch bank closures in Sydney: a geographical perspective and analysis. In: 12th International Conference on Geoformatics, Sweden, (2004)
55. Zimmermann, H.J.: Fuzzy Set Theory and Its Applications, 2nd edn. Kluwer Academic Publishers, Boston (1991)
56. Zolfani, S. H., Aghdaie, M. H., Derakhti, A., Zavadskas, E. K., Varzandeh, M. H. M.: Decision making on business issues with foresight perspective; an application of new hybrid MCDM model in shopping mall locating. Expert Sys. Appl. **40**(17), 7111–7121 (2013)

MIX
Papier aus verantwortungsvollen Quellen
Paper from responsible sources
FSC® C105338

If you have any concerns about our products,
you can contact us on
ProductSafety@springernature.com

In case Publisher is established outside the EU,
the EU authorized representative is:
Springer Nature Customer Service Center GmbH
Europaplatz 3, 69115 Heidelberg, Germany

Printed by Libri Plureos GmbH
in Hamburg, Germany